The Geography
of Perversion

*Male-to-male Sexual Behaviour outside the West
and the Ethnographic Imagination, 1750–1918*

Rudi C. Bleys

NEW YORK UNIVERSITY PRESS
Washington Square, New York

First published in the U.S.A. in 1995 by
NEW YORK UNIVERSITY PRESS
Washington Square
New York, N.Y. 10003

Library of Congress Cataloging-in-Publication Data
Bleys, Rudi.
    The geography of perversion : male-to-male sexual behaviour outside
the West and the ethnographic imagination, 1750–1918 / Rudi C.
Bleys.
        p.   cm.
    Includes bibliographical references and index.
    ISBN 0–8147–1262–2 (hardback)
    1. Homosexuality, Male—History. 2. Ethnology—History.
I. title.
HQ76.B56   1995
306.76'6—dc20   95–30161
                                                                      CIP

Printed in Great Britain

Contents

Acknowledgements

Throughout the years preceding the completion of this book, I have received support, encouragement and guidance from many and I express my gratitude to them.

As its foundation was laid at the History Department of Boston University in 1983–4, I want to thank Professor T. Glick, whose influence has been most crucial to the initial definition of the project.

I would also like to thank the Belgian National Fund for Scientific Research, which granted me four years of loyal support. I am also grateful to the academic staff of the History Department of the Katholieke Universiteit Leuven, Belgium, for offering me hospitality for more than six years. Stimulating were my advisor, Professor R. De Schryver, whose knowledge of intellectual history from the eighteenth century onwards has provided feedback during those years, and Professor R. Devisch of the Center for Cultural Anthropology, whose critical recommendations were instrumental to the interdisciplinary character of my work. I am also grateful to Professor E. Stols, whose veritable cosmopolitanism has safeguarded me, I hope, from the pitfalls of academic provincialism and theoretical dogmatism.

Gratitude must be expressed towards the staff of the various libraries of the Katholieke Universiteit at Leuven, of the Royal Library Albert I in Brussels, of the library at the Central-African Museum in Tervuren, Brussels, of the libraries of the Free University of Amsterdam, the Bibliothèque Nationale in Paris, the Staatsbibliothek Preussischer Kulturbezitz in Berlin, the Biblioteca Braidense in Milan, the Biblioteca Municipale in Venice, the British Library in London, the Bodleian Library in Oxford, the New York Public Library, the Mugar Library at Boston University, Boston, the Beinecke Library at Yale University, New Haven, the Van Pelt Library and the Library of the Anthropological Museum in Philadelphia, the Kinsey Institute for Research on Sex, Gender and Reproduction in Bloomington, the Huntington Library in San Marino, the Homodokumentatiecentrum in Amsterdam, and the Canadian Gay Archives in Toronto.

Many colleagues have been essential to my upholding the ideal. In Belgium I would like to thank Petra Rebmann and Daniel Christaens. Abroad, I owe gratitude to Robert Aldrich, Giovanni Dall'Orto, John DeCecco, Wayne Dynes, Stephen Forster, Gert Hekma, Michel Maffesoli, Robert Martin, Rommel Mendes-Leite, Carlos Messeder Pereira, Klaus Müller, Stephen Murray, Emmanuel Nelson, Guy Poirier, George Rousseau, Maarten Schild, Arno Schmitt, and Randolph Trumbach.

Completion of the project would have been unthinkable, however, if there had not been the moral support and friendship, during the years that went by, of Rita Bleys and Leo De Nocker, Victor Bloise, Michael Conyers, Kristof Degrauwe and Jos Smets, Lieve Dehasque, Ivanilson de Souza Silva, Jerry Goodman, Marcel Malor, John Mitzel, Fernando Jorge Monteiro, Ricardo Francelino Nazareth, Maria Ines Guimarães Portugal, Guy Rasandifera, Mark Sergeant and Hans Soetaert. During the revision of the manuscript while in San Francisco, I enjoyed the support of Scott Bravmann and the inspiring presence of Gregory 'Bansuri' Bell.

I owe most, however, to my best friends Joshua Enker, Jurandir Crescêncio, Zachary Christian Hester, and to my parents, to whom I dedicate this work.

Rudi Bleys
Ciudad de México, May 1995

List of Abbreviations

Aac	*Archives d'anthropologie criminelle*
Aae	*Archivio per l'antropologia e l'etnologia*
AfR	*Archiv für Religionswissenschaft*
Ahmc	*Archives d'hygiène et de médecine coloniale*
AHR	*American Historical Review*
An	*Archives de neurologie*
APN	*Archiv für Psychiatrie und Nervenkrankheiten*
ARGB	*Archiv für Rassen- und Gesellschaftsbiologie*
BHMed	*Bulletin for the History of Medicine*
BTLV	*Bijdragen tot de Taal-, Land- en Volkenkunde van Nederlandsch-Indië*
CSSH	*Comparative Studies in Society and History*
Geschlecht	*Geschlecht und Gesellschaft*
GLQ	*Gay and Lesbian Quarterly*
GPH	*Gai Pied Hebdo*
JCH	*Journal of Contemporary History*
JfsZ	*Jahrbuch für sexuelle Zwischenstufen*
JHom	*Journal of Homosexuality*
JHS	*Journal of the History of Sexuality*
JMH	*Journal of Modern History*
JRAI	*Journal of the Royal Anthropological Institute of Great Britain and Ireland*
ZdmG	*Zeitschrift der deutschen morgenländischen Gesellschaft*
ZfE	*Zeitschrift für Ethnologie*
ZfvR	*Zeitschrift für vergleichende Rechtswissenschaft*

Note: Where reference is made to a source in a language other than English, the quotation has been translated by the present author and the original text either follows in parentheses, if short, or is given in the relevant note at the end of the chapter.

Voor mijn ouders

In memory of
C. U., J. B., F. D., P. de D.

Introduction

Historically, the European construction of sexuality coincides with the epoch of imperialism and the two inter-connect.

– Kobena Mercer[1]

Une orgie de différences

– Jean Baudrillard[2]

This study aims at deconstructing what I describe, metaphorically, as the *geography of perversion and desire,* that is, the representations of sexual behaviour, more particularly male-to-male sexual behaviour, in Latin America, Africa, Asia and Oceania, as this was formulated more or less explicitly in European texts between approximately 1750 and 1918. I address the history of the changing ethnographic narrative describing and interpreting male-to-male sexual behaviour among non-western populations, as presented, embraced or criticized by travellers, ethnographers, anthropologists, physicians, sexologists, publicists, and *littérateurs* alike. Though repeatedly addressing issues of ethnicity, emphasis will be placed upon the historical significance of the ethnographic imagination within the wider context of the European construction of homosexual identity as we know it today. In due course, this book may contribute to a better historical understanding of the so-called 'modernization' of sex since the Enlightenment, and to its deconstruction in the wake of postmodern and postcolonial politics.

The awkward phrase 'male-to-male sexual behaviour' in the subtitle calls for some clarification. I deliberately omit the word 'homosexuality', invented in 1869, which was meant to refer specifically to sexual behaviour among males who are identified by others and identify themselves as such according to the sex of their partner and independently from the role taken during sexual intercourse.[3] Static notions of (male) 'homosexual identity', largely a western creation, do not correspond to the cross-cultural realities of 'bisexual' practices and role-defined sexual identities during the era surveyed in this study. Often only the passive partner would be labelled and, eventually, stigmatized.[4] Others expressed their sexuality in various ways, sometimes exclusively heterosexually, sometimes with boys[5] or with men and women alike.[6] Thus the terms 'same-sex behaviour' and 'male-to-male sexual behaviour', though hardly elegant, seem to safeguard the historian from the trappings of western sexual taxonomy as well as the deadly sin of ana-chronism.

The debate on sexual variance focused not only on sexual behaviour. As the Enlightenment tightened the ropes between gender[7] and sexuality, spec-ulations about one person's sexual identity became closely related to observations about anatomy, vestimentary codes, social roles, processes of socialization and family 'nurturing'. An attempt to deconstruct ethnographic discourse therefore ought to include a critical reading of the descriptions of cross-gender behaviour and cross-gender roles, that were – and are – more or less prominent in most cultures.[8] As European constructions of a 'third sex', combining male and female characteristics, became popular from the 1870s onward, this seems all the more important, even when its cultural ontology was different at times from a non-western one. 'Sexual orientation and identity', says Herdt, 'are not the keys to conceptualising a third sex and gender across time and space',[9] yet they were increasingly represented as such in European narratives. To unravel the complexities of such distorted repre-sentations will be central to the argument of this book.

A note on chronology must be made here, for whereas the *scientia sexualis* has been seen as a particularly 'Victorian' creation, it seems rather to be embedded deeply in the intellectual innovations of the eighteenth century. Historians, withdrawing their attention from the infamous model of nineteenth-century sexual repression, are now focusing increasingly on what they call the 'gender revolution' of the Enlightenment. It is believed that this embraced an altogether new *cognitive* definition and classification of sexual desire, based on biological assumptions concerning the normative authority of human nature, and connecting sex and gender to one another in a way that was far more coercive than before. The growing impact of science has often been seen as liberating, not least because it opened perspectives for a more secularized vision of the world. Yet it also implied far-reaching reification of sexual desire in fixed identities, just as it crystallized cultural difference in racial identities. Along with the increasingly systematic classifications of 'races', the gender revolution led to a new kind of moral orthodoxy, even when it was no longer based exclusively on religious doctrine.[10]

The absence of a cultural consensus after World War I and the polarization within Europe, call for an independent investigation. Perhaps it will reveal how 'progressive' ideas may have contained germs of conservatism, as revealed by the persistent Eurocentrism, sexism and heterosexism of psycho-analysis. Fascism in its turn remained ambiguous on sexual matters, and despite an official ideology of heterosexual reproduction within the family, nurtured peculiar forms of homosocial bonding. The ethnographic data in each of these discursive traditions will no doubt reflect some of these ambiguities, yet it would lead too far afield to extend this study beyond the approximate date of 1918.

Historiography and context

Only very recently have 'ethnographic narratives' been interpreted as sources for a historical study of non-western sexuality. But there is a growing awareness of their often biased character, not only morally but also on the level of conceptualization and theory.

Before, sex was seen as an unproblematic 'natural' category, and sexual discourse as a result was perceived as trivial. Intellectual historians, for example, focused too much on the moral aspects of sexual debate, too little on the problematic, historical dimension of sexual categories and culture. To them, sexual matters were mostly a 'no man's land between the scandalous and the frivolous' (' "no man's land" entre l'honteux et le frivole').[11] Philologists and archaeologists also tended to maintain an idealist rhetoric, despite the omnipresence, on a more basic level, of sexual wonder and bewilderment. Said's *Orientalism* exceptionally acknowledges the 'vital' dimension of western fascination for the East:

Just as the various colonial possessions – quite apart from their economic benefit to metropolitan Europe – were useful as places to send wayward sons, superfluous populations of delinquents, poor people, and other undesirables, so the Orient was a place where one could look for sexual experience unobtainable in Europe.[12]

Such colonial praxis, Said rightly remarks, implied static perceptions of 'Oriental' sexuality that are to be explained by the cultural historian. Yet he too refrains from clarifying the relationship between European theories about sexuality and the construction of a static, sexual Orient. His book does constitute a major break, however, with the academic stuffiness of traditional philological research.[13]

The scarcity, and for a long time unintelligibility, of pre-Columbian codices prevented sound conclusions about the sexual behaviour of the Native American populations. This allowed for more or less speculative narratives on ritualized sexuality and the role therein of various forms of sodomy. Their deciphering in the course of the twentieth century has weakened such fantastic reconstructions, yet offers only limited conclusive evidence for the historian of pre-Columbian sexuality. The Americanist's silence on sex seems justified, therefore, as he is limited to archaeology, to western reports postdating Columbus' letters or even to oral history.[14]

Academic indifference was challenged by early postcolonial criticism pointing out the moral connotations of Eurocentrism in particular. But it too was dependent on European values and failed to grasp some of the underlying dimensions of the Old World's discourse of sexual 'otherness'. It subscribed to the emphasis of mainstream social science upon the presumably 'essential' differences and incompatibilities between people of different skin colour. The Algerian psychiatrist Frantz Fanon thus embraced the representation of colonial relations as the nurturing ground of white expectations about the sexuality of blacks, while using it to denounce black homosexuality as the exclusive result of the white man's abuse of power or of the unbalanced sex ratio on the plantations at early times. It certainly did not belong to the black people's natural disposition in the French Antilles: 'We could not witness any manifest presence in Martinique. One must see this as the result of an absent Oedipal complex in the Antilles (. . . il ne nous a pas été donné de constater la présence manifeste en Martinique. Il faut y voir la conséquence de l'absence de l'Oedipe aux Antilles).' He did mention some transvestites, but rather than questioning their sexuality, he simply described their behaviour as normal, if extravagant. The homosexual praxis of some Antillian expatriates in Paris was merely called 'pragmatic': 'In Europe, we have found some friends who became consistently passive pederasts. But this had little to do with neurotic homosexuality. For them, it was a way out just as was being a pimp for others (En Europe, nous avons trouvé quelques camarades qui sont devenus pédérastes, toujours passifs. Mais ce n'était point là homosexualité névrotique, c'était pour eux un expédient comme pour d'autres celui de souteneur).'[15]

Fanon's rationalization was no doubt due to psychoanalysis's rigid view of homosexuality as a neurosis. His critique of both people who *hated* and people who *loved* blacks because of them being black was inspired by psychoanalysis and challenged Europeans to question the racialist assumptions of their exoticist rhetoric. But it also provoked changes in 'ethnic' politics of affirmation, and diversified postcolonial narratives of national identity. In due course, it consolidated a common strategy among black writers to denounce homosexuality as alien to their culture, at the most as an emergency solution to problems of another kind.

In fact Fanon's works reflected ambiguity between a desire to uphold a genuine difference, which he borrowed from Césaire's movement of *négritude*, and a strong determination to eradicate difference altogether, as it seemed doomed by racism. The wave of newly declared independence by nations in Africa and Asia lent particular momentum to Fanon's work, but the dilemma that would soon divide his readers, had in fact dominated ethnic minority ideology for many years. Usually homosexuality was only briefly addressed, but these passages were not without interest as they reflected how the negotiation of one's own identity remained closely intertwined with European standards of morality. The 'ethnic' writers' dismantling of the perennial association between racial inferiority and sexual lasciviousness, that was common in the North as well as among the local elites, was of course justified. Yet it gave birth to an unconvincing and artificial picture of sexual 'normality'. For the sake of virtue, minority writers became all too eager to deny any 'vice'.[16]

Sexual Liberation in the 1970s did not rise above a mere recommendation of permissiveness either, nor did it lead to a more critical assessment of the

European cognitive discourse about sexuality as such. Much of its rationale was tributary to Freudian and post-Freudian insights about the 'unconscious'. It entailed a conviction that, previously, sexuality had been erroneously explained as a biological matter. Individuals, according to psychoanalysis, are

> not determined products of biological imperatives, ... nor are they the effects simply of social relations: psychoanalysis proposes that there is a psychic realm with its own rules and history where the biological possibilities of the body acquire meaning.[17]

Such an approach evidently offered new, more dynamic perspectives, as sex was not a mere given fact. Indeed, 'sexuality [was] more', Jeffrey Weeks summarizes, 'than the irrepressible instincts which wrack the body; it is a force that is actually constructed in the process of the entry into the domain of culture, language and meaning'.[18] The emphasis on a person's sexual development from an original blank page to adult sexual identity evidently stimulated historical research of the societal factors that promoted the individual's growth to sexual adulthood or, for that matter, obstructed it.

Within a Freudian-inspired history of sexuality, male and female homosexuality could theoretically be interpreted as a healthy and unproblematic outcome of the individual's personal sexual development. In such perspective, the increasingly intolerant attitude towards same-sex behaviour among men or women could be seen as a source of neurosis and mental illness.

But homosexuality was seen mostly as a neurosis in itself,[19] which also directed the reading of ethnographic data on same-sex behaviour in non-western societies. In fact, its virtual absence was postulated through the application of Oedipal theory to cross-cultural research. Thus anthropologists, not fully aware of their own primitivist bias, stressed the presumably 'healthy' sexual economy of tribal societies and explained the absence of homosexuality as a proof of balanced personal development.[20] When same-sex behaviour could not be denied, as was the case in many Melanesian ethnic groups for example, it was 'explained' as part of a *rite de passage* that implied symbolic reversal, yet consolidated the tribal society's sense of sexual normality once the initiation ceremony was over.[21]

Gay Liberation in its turn triggered new, politicized readings of old and new ethnographic data on same-sex practices in Africa, Asia, the Southern Pacific and Latin America. Its initially omnivorous rhetoric, embracing the traditional 'effeminate queen' as well as his overly virile alternative the macho clone, led to a relatively uncritical usurpation of cultural models from so-called 'primitive' societies. Gender-crossing roles were often taken for 'homosexual' ones without further questioning. Similarly, ritualized forms of homosexuality among some indigenous societies were seen as a *pars pro toto* of daily life tolerance.[22] Some used cross-cultural data merely to document a rather unconvincing plea for humanity to recognize one's 'bisexual' or, even more radically, 'homosexual nature'.

But ethnic and sexual politics embraced new challenges to historical, sociological and anthropological research, that in the end became critical of some of the minority politics' premises. More emphasis was laid on the historicity of cognition than on the relativity of moral values and, along with a critique upon 'modern' concepts of racial, ethnic, sexual and gender identities, a deconstruction has shown how early minority politics were subject to the classificatory schemes of the past.

The new perspective has shifted from a narrowly confined history of ideas to a study of past discursive praxis. Within such a framework, sex was no longer a purely biological matter, about which theologians and clerics, statesmen and politicians, scientists and administrators, elites and common men *felt* this or that way. It is now believed that sexuality is thoroughly defined by culture, that is: by people's symbolic structuring of desire. Opposing 'essentialist' views of sexuality,[23] Michel Foucault claimed that these were tributaries of the *scientia sexualis* developed in the nineteenth century that had brought sex into the realm of public discourse. The speaking of 'truth' about sex manifested itself as a kind of

imprisonment, especially since the nineteenth century, guaranteed and reproduced by the countless economic advantages that sprang both from this analytical demultiplication of pleasure and this increase of power controlling it thanks to the intermediary role of medicine, psychiatry, prostitution and pornography.[24]

Some historians have criticized Foucault for 'mystifying' power and thus for failing to offer an operational model for research. The description, however, of sexual history as the outcome of a *discours de vérité* enabled others to break away from the essentialist bias of medical and psychoanalytical theory and to reconstruct our own 'knowledge' of the sexual self. Historians inspired also by MacIntosh, Gagnon and Simon, Plummer, Deleuze and Guattari, accordingly reject the thesis that there exists a homosexual role across the world and throughout time. They are equally influenced by symbolic anthropology, more particularly by Mary Douglas' hypothesis that 'nothing is more essentially transmitted by a social process of learning than sexual behaviour'.[25] The emphasis upon the weight of society's attribution of meaning to sexual practices did not mean that the range of meaningful possibilities would go beyond its biological constraints. 'Biological sexuality', said Padgug, 'is the necessary precondition for human sexuality. But biological sexuality is only a precondition, a set of potentialities, which is never unmediated by human reality, and which becomes transformed in qualitatively new ways in human society.'[26]

Initially, social constructionists stressed the historicity of homosexual identity as a product of social and cultural changes during the nineteenth century, when medical writings lifted matters of sexuality from the realm of religion and morality. Medical theory, so they stated, was picked up by members of the rising homosexual subcultures in the cities as a vehicle of self-affirmation and self-defence.[27]

The emphasis on the nineteenth century as a turning point would soon be modified, as the transition from an Early Modern pattern of 'sodomy' to 'modern homosexuality' proved to have been much slower as well as more complex. Studies by Bray, Rey, Trumbach, and others depicted the emergence of sodomite subcultures in the urban centres of Early Modern Europe as a sign of increasing self-awareness among homosexually active men as a separate group.[28] The long-term change from an act-orientated definition to an 'identity'-orientated definition is now generally known as 'the construction of modern homosexuality'.

The divide between essentialist and constructionist approaches to gay and lesbian history is less immense than is often presented in apologetic literature from either side. John Boswell rightly indicated how the opposition between both reiterates an old, familiar opposition between a 'realist' and a 'nominalist' epistemology. Within gay and lesbian history, the degree of incommensurability between both is largely dependent on the historians' willingness to accept a substratum – a kind of minimalist description – of 'homosexuality', that can be traced through time as well as in different cultures.[29]

Meanwhile, new voices are rising against the 'universalist' pretentions of Gay Liberation. The parameters of historical research are changing once again as 'gay identity' is deconstructed and emphasis is placed upon the study of non-western sexual cultures. The new focus on diversity in so-called 'queer' politics aims to provide an alternative – I prefer a 'widening' – for the category 'gay and lesbian', that is inflated by media simplification and reduces the complexity of homosexual subculture to an all too homogeneous, white, male, middle-class and middle-aged image. Too much compromised by both mainstream gay subculture and public discourse, 'gay identity' no longer seems flexible enough to fit today's new cultural politics of difference, which incorporate various models of 'queer' identity, each corresponding to the rich reality of multiple age groups and ethnic backgrounds.[30] Queer theory counters not only the negative rhetoric of classical, biological sexology but also the monolithic alternative of liberationist gay politics. It intends to avoid reductionism by focusing on 'the respective and/or common grounding of current discourses and practices of homo-sexualities in relation to gender and to race, with their attendant differences of class or ethnic culture, generational, geographical, and sociopolitical location'.[31]

The current debate on 'multiculturalism' as an alternative to assimilationist ethnic politics is sharply felt in the recent formation of groups of people of colour within the gay community, first in the United States but now also in Europe, Latin America, Asia and the Southern Pacific. These groups address the needs of gay and lesbian people of colour, who find themselves between a predominantly white, middle-class gay population on the one hand and their own ethnic background on the other.[32] Queer politics thus lends new urgency to the project of historical understanding. 'The fact of the matter', says de Lauretis, 'is that most of us, lesbians and gay men, do not know much about one another's sexual history, experience, phantasies, desire, or modes of theorising'.[33] Too little research is done on class, ethnic, generational, geographical and socio-political differences within the gay and lesbian community. A study of ethnographic discourse may contribute to a better understanding of an ethnic or national minority's homosexual history. Travel narratives and ethnological studies alike, though biased, contain valuable evidence indeed about sexual praxis, that is excluded from 'emic' mythology, due either to inherent taboos or western influence, each making sexual matters unspeakable.

A critical reading of 'white' discourse/mythology is needed, both *as a tool* for deconstructing racist marginalization/exoticization of ethnic minorities within the white gay community, and *because* it provokes reactions from the minorities, ranging from blunt adoption and interiorization of the current stereotypes to their fierce denial in political rhetoric.[34]

An earlier generation of 'postcolonial' writers more or less deliberately obfuscated the presence of homosexual praxis in order to gain respectability. Today, Homi Bhabha, bell hooks, Kobena Mercer, Trin Minh-ha, Edward Said, Gayatri Spivak, Cornel West, and others argue that the alternative, presented by Fanon, is itself subject to criticism as he upheld a self-repressive and western-defined code of identity. Rhonda Cobham points to how in African literature 'the figure of the Western homosexual preying on the defenseless African [often] emerges as a way of externalising disorder or of registering alienation from a more "natural" definition of self'.[35] She then stresses the close relationship between colonial and postcolonial rhetoric, especially when addressing the 'issue' of homosexuality:

The African novelists' use of homosexuality as a marker for a social relationship between coloniser and colonised rather than as an aspect of sexual identity may ... be read as an internalisation of the process within orientalist discourse by which the subaltern 'other' was constructed as feminine or effeminate as a way of representing the power imbalance in the relationship between Europe and its colonies.[36]

Homosexuality, often perceived as a 'foreign import' from either Europe or the Arab world,[37] thus assumes a signifying position within early post-colonial rhetoric. Its idealism accordingly is rightly understood as a reaction against the perennial 'perversification' of the colonial subject.

But Homi Bhabha denounces the replacement of the presumably 'genuinely perverse' African, Indian or Asian man and woman by a presumably 'genuinely normal' one. While trading terms, the early generation has adopted the very same rhetoric upon which colonial discourse itself was based.[38] A deconstruction is needed, instead, of the cognitive strategies, that were based upon a 'tension between the synchronic panoptical vision of domination – the demand for identity, stasis – and the counterpressure of the diachrony of history – change, difference'.[39] A 'decolonization' of gender and sexuality will thus show how race and sexuality were enacted as 'modes of differentiation, realized as multiple, cross-cutting determinations, polymorphous and perverse'.[40]

A new academic and political context has thus arisen, that has been instrumental to the writing of this study. If homosexuality was redefined substantially from the eighteenth century onward, then such cognitive changes ought to be reflected in European ethnographic discourse about male-to-male sexual behaviour outside the West as well. Recent postcolonial criticism has pointed out how a historical deconstruction of this discourse may in its turn contribute to a better understanding of the European 'making' of racial, ethnic or cultural 'otherness'. This study, deconstructing the string of discursive fragments that, collectively, I call a *geography of perversion and desire*, will I hope contribute to the project outlined by both queer theory and postcolonial criticism.

Discourse about male-to-male sexuality is pervaded by judgements that are either positive or negative, seldom neutral. Those men who fancied or pursued sexual relations with members of their own sex, not surprisingly perceived these relations differently from mainstream society, which was less embracing, if not homophobic. This incompatibility is reflected in the metaphoric juxtaposition of 'perversion' with 'desire'. The word 'geography', in this context, must be interpreted equally as a metaphor for the strategies and discourses of, respectively, *stigmatization* and *legitimation* of same-sex relations, that were respectively hidden within either party's ethnographic argumentation.

The project is not to outline a map of 'homosexual variance' across the world. This can be found in the cross-cultural studies on homosexuality by Baumann, Bleibtreu-Ehrenberg, Cory, Ford and Beach, Herdt, and Opler, who evaluate the available literature on homosexuality in view of actual anthropological research.[41] A similar *status quaestionis* approach can be found in the chapters on Mexico and the Amazon basin in *Male Homosexuality in Central and South America* and *Cultural Diversity and Homosexualities* (both ed. Murray), as well as in João Trevisan's *Perverts in Paradise*. David Greenberg provides an extensive survey of the old ethnographic literature on same-sex behaviour outside the western world, yet selects and analyses it exclusively in view of a reconstruction of the actual sexual practices in other cultural contexts.[42] And, finally, a collection of classical texts, *Ethnographic Studies of Homosexuality*, should be mentioned, if only for its merit of making some classical texts readily accessible.[43]

Envisaged here, rather, is a historical reconstruction of how cross-cultural records were collected, created, structured, manipulated, excerpted, reformulated and/or omitted in interaction with the changing theoretical debate on male-to-male sexuality between 1750 and 1918. A study of this kind, reviewing the ethnographic literature on male-to-male sexual relations as a single body of texts, has not as yet been made. A few authors have drawn some outlines for such a project, but provided a limited anthology only of passages from the best-known texts. Hekma referred only briefly to Burton, Karsch-Haack, Carpenter, and Westermarck in order to continue with a critical analysis of more recent anthropological studies on homosexuality. His main goal was to stress the qualitative difference between today's anthropological research and the surveys of preceding pioneers, yet he abstained from analysing its historical significance any further.[44] An essay, written by myself at an earlier stage, also raises a limited number of random questions about how to interpret ethnographic discourse on same-sex behaviour outside the West.[45] Cardín's publication is perhaps the most profound analysis of western discourse about same-sex behaviour outside the western world. The author points to the often highly arbitrary character of ethnology's classifications. In fact, a particular culture's own classification usually turns out to be incompatible with western sexual taxonomy, which 'calls for accuracy when talking about "homosexuality" in general terms when discussing sexual contacts among men observed amidst exotic people'.[46] Yet this book too provides cross-cultural evidence, rather than a deconstruction of ethnographic discourse itself.

A brief note on methodology

The historical deconstruction of discourse on homosexuality fails when such discourse is isolated from discursive constructions of other minorities and when historical research is confined to its mere province alone. It will become clear, indeed, that each of these discourses' discriminatory weight sprang from their links with one another. Stuart Hall points out the ideological strength of the 'inter-discursive space of several discourses working together: of race, and colour, and sexuality, and [national identity] itself'.[47] By focusing on the so-called 'intersecting rhetorics' of the discourses at play one can make visible, says Ludmilla Jordanova, how 'apparently distinct areas of life are linked through sets of symbols and metaphors'.[48] Kobena Mercer's claim, accordingly, that the construction of modern sexuality coincided with western colonialism is not merely rhetorical, as it emphasizes how sexual and ethnographic discourse, more specifically sexology and colonial anthropology, were mutually intertwined.[49]

Ideally, the reconstruction of a 'geography of perversion and desire' transcends the provincial domains of gay and lesbian history, cultural history, and the history of science alike as it becomes an exercise in 'multiple contextualisation' (E. P. Thompson) and investigates how the intersecting rhetorics of racialist and sexual discourse were embedded in European civilization, ideology and scientific innovation at the same time.

The linguistic dimension is very important, as language and speech are pivotal tools for distinction and identification. But a historical interpretation of discourse stretches beyond the merely semantic and lexicological. It also aims at describing the vocabularies' shifting positions within the wider framework of what is known as the tropes of narration.[50] Such a strategy is inevitable, as the historical meaning of words and concepts is co-defined by their applications in wider contexts, by their position, as says White, within the 'plot',[51] and cannot be fully retrieved by a semantic analysis of those words and concepts alone. It focuses equally on the *poetics* and *politics* of discourse in order to de-code the so-called 'content of the form'. 'The things to look at', according to Said, 'are style, figures of speech, setting, narrative devices, historical and social circumstances, not the correctness of the representation nor its fidelity to some great original.'[52]

An extra problem facing the historian is the 'unspoken' character of homosexual discourse. Yet, between the candour of some and the taciturnity of others, a subcultural discourse exists, that allowed many to express a homosexual sensibility in a more or less coded way. Stockinger, while developing a research strategy to understand such codified *discursivité* , first called this, quite adequately, 'homotextuality'.[53] Since then, other concepts have been proposed, which all envisage a de-codification of the homosexual dimension in literature and art.[54]

Codification of a homosexual sensibility also took on different forms in travel/ethnographic narratives. When describing foreign societies, writers may choose to focus on particular themes. Thus, the extensive treatment of primitive warfare, male initiation rites, phallic cult, body decoration and even circumcision allowed the author to focus on a world of virility and masculinity without revealing an erotic fascination. Slavery, seraglios and eunuchism provided plots that corresponded to a *fin-de-siècle* sense of urban decadence, deliberately shared by some homosexuals in the West. Exoticism in paintings, sculpture or photography facilitated the depiction of Arab, African, Indian or Asian male nudes, whereas the white male had been set aside by a disproportionate preference for its female counterpart at home. Evidently, the 'ethnographic gaze' provided an opportunity to produce works of male homoerotic tenor without becoming suspect.[55]

Homotextuality manifests itself more often in rhetorical style than in content. A document becomes 'of homosexual interest' by its use of carefully chosen adjectives, by the adoption of particular 'signifying' images, names or terms, or by its connection to an Orientalist or Primitivist trope. Of course, not all problems of interpretation of homotextuality can be solved. But one would discard an important body of information if one were to uphold unreasonably severe standards of epistemological orthodoxy. As subcultural expression by means of a coded *semiosis* through homotextuality constitutes an unmistakable part of European discourse on same-sex behaviour outside the West, it will be studied accordingly.

Notes

1. K. Mercer and I. Julien, 'Race, sexual politics and black masculinity: A dossier', in R. Chapman and J. Rutherford (eds), *Male Order. Unwrapping Masculinity* (London, 1988), p. 106.
2. J. Baudrillard, *La transparence du mal. Essai sur les phénomènes extrêmes* (Paris, 1990), p. 129.
3. J.-C. Féray, 'Une histoire critique du mot "homosexualité" ', *Arcadie*, 28 (January 1981), 11. For a long time, female-to-female sexual behaviour remained outside the reach of cultural and scientific reification, as it was conceived an impossibility altogether because women could not penetrate another body. Its history is in many ways very different from that of male homosexuality, and will as a result be excluded, unless inevitable, from this study. For an overview of lesbian history in Europe, see L. Faderman, *Surpassing the Love of Men* (London, 1981), pp. 23–9, and M.-J. Bonnet, *Un choix sans équivoque* (Paris, 1981).
4. This remains true today in most parts of the Arab world and among the lower classes in Latin America. On the level of speech, and to a lesser extent of sexual praxis, this pattern also remains discernible in rural Mediterranean Europe. See A. Boudhiba, *La sexualité en Islam* (Paris, 1984 (1975)), pp. 43–57; M. Chebel, *L'esprit de sérail. Perversions et marginalités sexuelles au Maghreb* (Paris, 1988), pp. 13–52; S. O. Murray (ed.), *Male Homosexuality in Central and South America* (San Francisco, 1987), *passim*; D. D. Gilmore (ed.), *Honour and Shame and the Unity of the Mediterranean* (Washington, 1987); M. D. Murphy, 'Masculinity and selective homophobia: A case from Spain', *ARGOH Newsletter*, 5, 3 (Summer/Fall 1984), 6–12; D. Rünzler, *Machismo. Die Grenzen der Männlichkeit* (Vienna, Cologne, Graz, 1988).
5. For a cross-cultural survey of pedophilia, see, among others, E. Brongersma, *Jongensliefde. Seks en erotiek tussen jongens en mannen*, vol. 1: *Partners* (Amsterdam, 1987), pp. 96–112; and R. Bauserman, 'Man-boy sexual relationships in a cross-cultural perspective', *Paidika*, 2, 1 (Summer 1989), 28–40.
6. For surveys of male and female same-sex sexual behaviour, see C. S. Ford and F. A. Beach, *Patterns of Sexual Behavior* (New York, 1953), chapter 7; M. K. Opler, 'Anthropological and cross-cultural aspects of homosexuality', in J. Marmor (ed.), *Sexual Inversion. The Multiple Roots of Homosexuality* (New York and London, 1965), pp. 108–23; and D. L. Davis and R. G. Whitten, 'The cross-cultural study of human sexuality', *Annual Reviews in Anthropology*, 16 (1987), 69–98. Less comprehensive is E. Gregersen, *Sexual Practices* (New York, 1983).
7. 'Gender' refers to the social roles, ascribed to the male and female biological sex. As opposed to the latter, gender roles are socially and culturally constructed and change through history. See S. Garrett, *Gender* (London, 1987).
8. 'Cross-gender behaviour' and 'cross-gender roles' – one may also use 'transgender behaviour/roles' – trespass the boundaries of one's biological sex, mostly at work, socially (dressing code) and/or sexually. While 'roles' are more or less permanent, 'behaviour' may occur only occasionally. 'Transgression' depends on how gender roles themselves are defined and may take different forms.

9. See G. Herdt, 'Introduction: Third sexes and third genders', in G. Herdt (ed.), *Third Sex, Third Gender. Beyond Sexual Dimorphism in Culture and History* (New York and Cambridge, MA, 1994), p. 47.

10. M. Foucault, *Histoire de la sexualité, 1: La volonté de savoir* (Paris, 1976), was the first to stress the cognitive dimension of our sexual past, even when he still held on to the model of an 'epistemic change', that took place in the nineteenth century. More empirical research led to a gradual shift towards the eighteenth century. See P.-G. Boucé (ed.), *Sexuality in Eighteenth-Century Britain* (New York and Manchester, 1982); G. S. Rousseau and R. Porter, 'Introduction', in G. S. Rousseau and R. Porter (eds), *Sexual Underworlds of the Enlightenment* (Chapel Hill, 1988), pp. 2–4. See also M. Bloch and J. H. Bloch, 'Women and the dialectics of nature in eighteenth century French thought', in C. P. MacCormack and M. Strathern (eds), *Nature, Culture and Gender* (Cambridge, 1980), pp. 25–41; R. Trumbach, 'Sodomitical subcultures, sodomitical roles, and the gender revolution of the eighteenth century: The recent historiography', in R. P. Maccubbin (ed.), *Unauthorised Sexual Behavior during the Enlightenment* (Williamsburg, 1985), pp. 109–21; L. Jordanova, *Sexual Visions. Images of Gender and Medicine between the Eighteenth and Twentieth Centuries* (New York, 1989), ch. 2, pp. 19–42; G. S. Rousseau, *Perilous Enlightenment: Pre- and Postmodern Discourses. Sexual, Historical* (Manchester, 1991); and L. Stone, *The Past and the Present Revisited* (London and New York, n.d.), pp. 378–82.

11. J.-P. Aron, 'La problématique de l'histoire du corps', lecture at the Department of History, Katholieke Universiteit Leuven, Belgium, 5 November 1981. See, among these studies, H. Baudet, *Paradise on Earth* (New Haven, 1965); U. Bitterli, *Die 'Wilden' und die 'Zivilisierten'* (Munich, 1976); W. Brandon, *New Worlds for Old* (Athens, OH and London, 1986); L. de Albuequerque, A. L. Ferronha, J. da Silva Horta and R. Loureiro, *O confronto de olhar* (Lisbon, 1991); M. Duchet, *Anthropologie et histoire au siècle des Lumières* (Paris, 1971); H. P. Duerr, *Traumzeit. Ueber die Grenze zwischen Wildnis und Zivilisation* (Frankfurt/Main, 1978); J. Ehrard, *L'idée de nature en France dans la première moitié du XVIIIe siècle* (Paris, 1963); J. H. Elliott, *The Old World and the New* (Cambridge, 1970); H. N. Fairchild, *The Noble Savage. A Study in Romantic Naturalism* (New York, 1928); A. Gerbi, *La disputa del Nuevo Mundo* (México, 1982 (1960, original edition in Italian, 1955)); F. Gewecke, *Wie die neue Welt in die alte kam* (Stuttgart, 1986); M. T. Hodgen, *Early Anthropology in the Sixteenth and Seventeenth Centuries* (Philadelphia, 1971 (1964)); H. Honour, *The New Golden Land* (New York, 1975); V. G. Kiernan, *The Lords of Human Kind* (Boston, 1969); D. F. Lasch, *Asia in the Making of Europe*, 2 vols (Chicago and London, 1965–70); A. Pagden, *The Fall of Natural Man* (Cambridge and New York, 1982); and A. Pagden, *European Encounters with the New World* (New Haven, 1993).

12. E. Said, *Orientalism* (New York, 1971), p. 190.

13. E. Said, *Orientalism*, p. 240.

14. Within the field of American Studies, focusing on pre-Columbian heritage, sexuality does remain a rather marginal issue – a fact that is sadly reflected, for example, in the separate exhibition of Peruvian ceramics 'with sexual content' in the Museo Rafael Larco Herrera in Lima, Peru. The 'erotic' ceramics of mostly Mochica culture were often interpreted as signs of decadence – a theory more revealing of moral bias than of detachment. See R. L. Hoyle, *Checan. Essay on Erotic Elements in Peruvian Art* (Geneva, 1965). Equally biased is F. Guerra, *The Pre-Columbian Mind* (London, 1971). A more descriptive work is F. Kauffmann Doig, *El Comportamiento Sexual en el Antigua Perú* (Lima, 1979), also translated in German as *Sexualverhalten im Alten Peru* (Lima, 1979). For a critical review see E. Vergara, 'De rol van de sexualiteit in het Oude Peru', in *Inca-Perú. 3000 jaar geschiedenis* (Brussels, 1990), pp. 400–11.

15. F. Fanon, *Peau noire, masques blancs* (Paris, 1952), p. 146.

16.   C. I. Nero, 'Toward a black gay aesthetic. Signifying in contemporary black gay literature', in E. Hemphill (ed.), *Brother to Brother. New Writings by Black Gay Men* (Boston, 1991), pp. 231–2. Nero also points at a hidden homophobic rhetoric in the fiction of Toni Morrison and wonders if this, 'as that of so many other black intellectuals, is perhaps more closely related to Judaeo-Christian beliefs than to the beliefs of her ancestors. Male homosexuality is associated with biblical ideas of weakness as effeminacy. Many of these intellectuals would also argue that the Judaeo-Christian tradition is a major tool of the western eurocentric view of reality that furthers the oppression of blacks. Paradoxically, by their condemnation of homosexuality and lesbianism, these intellectuals contribute to upholding an oppressive eurocentric view of reality' (p. 235).

17.   J. Weeks, *Sexuality and Its Discontents*, pp. 127–8.

18.   *Ibid.*, p. 128.

19.   *Ibid.*, 144. For a more extensive analysis, see K. Lewes, *The Psychoanalytic Theory of Male Homosexuality* (New York, 1988).

20.   See D. L. Davis and R. G. Whitten, 'The cross-cultural study of human sexuality', *American Reviews in Anthropology*, 16 (1987), 69–98, esp. 79–88. See also E. Blackwood, 'Breaking the mirror: The construction of lesbianism and the anthropological discourse on homosexuality', *JHom*, 11, 3/4 (Summer 1985), 1–4; T. K. Fitzgerald, 'A critique of anthropological research on homosexuality', *JHom*, 2, 4 (Summer 1977), 385–97; S. O. Murray, 'The history of anthropology's lavender fringe', *ARGOH Newsletter*, 6, 1 (January 1985), 8–10.

21.   For critical commentary see D. L. Davis and R. G. Whitten, *Annual Reviews in Anthropology*, 16 (1987), 80–3; S. O. Murray, *Social Theory, Homosexual Realities*, Gai Saber Monographs, 3 (New York, 1984), pp. 5–15; and G. H. Herdt (ed.), *Ritualised Homosexuality in Melanesia* (Berkeley, 1984), pp. 1–9.

22.   See, e.g., A. Evans, *Witchcraft and the Gay Counterculture* (Boston, 1978).

23.   For a historiographical essay on the essentialism/constructivism debate in lesbian and gay studies, see J. Escoffier, 'Inside the ivory closet: The challenges facing lesbian and gay studies', *Out/Look*, 10 (Fall 1990), 40–8.

24.   'enchaînement, depuis le XIXe siècle surtout, [qui] est assuré et relayé par les innombrables profits économiques qui grâce à l'intermédiaire de la médecine, de la psychiatrie, de la prostitution, de la pornographie, se sont branchés à la fois sur cette démultiplication analytique du plaisir et cette majoration du pouvoir qui le contrôle'. M. Foucault, *Histoire de la Sexualité, I: La volonté de savoir*, p. 66.

25.   M. Douglas, *Natural Symbols* (New York, 1973), p. 93.

26.   R. Padgug, 'Sexual matters: on conceptualizing sexuality in history', *Radical History Review*, 20 (1979), 9.

27.   See J. Weeks, 'Movements of affirmation: Sexual meanings and homosexual identities', *Radical History Review*, 20 (Spring/Summer 1979), 164–79.

28.   See A. Bray, *Homosexuality in Renaissance England* (London, 1982); M. Rey, 'Police et sodomie à Paris au XVIIIe siècle: du péché au désordre', *Revue d'histoire moderne et contemporaine*, 39 (January–March 1982), 113–24; M. Rey, 'L' art de "raccrocher" au XVIIIe siècle', *Masques*, 24 (Winter 1984/85), 92–9; M. Rey, 'Parisian homosexuals create a lifestyle, 1700–1750. The police archives', *Eighteenth-Century Life*, 9 (1985), 179–91; G. Ruggiero, *The Boundaries of Eros* (Oxford, 1985); M. J. Rocke, 'Policing homosexuality in 15th century Florence: the Ufficiali di Notte', *Quaderni Storici*, 22, 3 (December 1987), 701–24; R. Carrasco, *Inquisición y represión sexual en Valencia* (Barcelona, 1985); M. E. Perry, *Gender and Disorder in Early Modern Seville* (Princeton, 1991); L. Mott, 'Inquisição e homossexualidade', in M. H. Carvalho dos Santos (ed.), *Inquisição. Comunicações apresentadas ao 1° Congresso Luso-brasileiro sobre Inquisição, Lisboa, 1987* (Lisbon, 1990), vol. 2, pp. 473–508; R. Trumbach,

'London's sodomites: Homosexual behaviour and western culture in the eighteenth century', *Journal of Social History*, 11 (1977), 1–33; T. Van der Meer, *De wesentlijke sonde van sodomie en ander vuyligheeden* (Amsterdam, 1984).

29. J. Boswell, *Christianity, Social Tolerance, and Homosexuality. Gay People in Western Europe from the Beginning of the Christian Era to the Fourteenth Century* (Chicago and London, 1980), pp. 91 ff. See also M. Dannecker, 'Towards a theory of homosexuality: Socio-historical perspectives', *JHom*, 9, 4 (1984), 1–8; and G. Herdt, 'Representations of homosexuality: An essay on cultural ontology and historical comparison, Part I' and 'Part II', *JHS*, 1, 3 (January 1991), 481–504 and 1, 4 (April 1991), 603–22.

30. See 'Queer theory. Lesbian and gay sexualities', *Differences*, 3, 2 (Summer 1991); and C. Smyth, *Queer Notions* (London, 1992). The phrase 'new cultural politics of difference' is taken from Cornel West's identically titled article in *October*, 53 (Summer 1990), 93–109.

31. T. de Lauretis, 'An Introduction', 'Queer theory. Lesbian and gay sexualities', *Differences. A Journal of Feminist Cultural Studies*, 3, 2 (Summer 1991), iii–iv.

32. See C. Clarke, 'The failure to transform: Homophobia in the black community', in B. Smith (ed.), *Home Girls: A Black Feminist Perspective* (New York, 1983), pp. 197–208; D. Garrett, 'Other countries: the importance of difference', in C. A. Johnson *et al.* (eds), *Other Countries. Black Gay Voices* (New York, 1988), pp. 17–28.

33. T. de Lauretis, 'An Introduction', *Differences*, viii.

34. For a brilliant analysis of the problem, see D. Scott, 'Jungle fever? Black gay identity politics, white dick, and the utopian bedroom', *GLQ*, 1, 3 (1994), 299–321.

35. R. Cobham, 'Misgendering the nation: African nationalist fictions and Nurrudin Farah's *Maps*', in A. Parker *et al.* (eds), *Nationalisms and Sexualities* (New York and London, 1992), p. 46.

36. *Ibid.*, p. 47.

37. *Ibid.*, p. 46.

38. H. K. Bhabha (ed.), *Nation and Narration* (New York and London, 1990), p. 7.

39. H. K. Bhabha, 'Of mimicry and man: The ambivalence of colonial discourse', *October*, 28 (Spring 1984), 126.

40. H. K. Bhabha, 'The other question: Difference, discrimination and the discourse of colonialism', in Ferguson, R., *et al.* (eds), *Out There. Marginalization and Contemporary Cultures* (New York and Cambridge, MA, 1990), p. 72.

41. H. Baumann, *Das doppelte Geschlecht* (Berlin, 1986 (1955)); G. Bleibtreu-Ehrenberg, *Mannbarkeitsriten* (Berlin, 1980); D. W. Cory (ed.), *Homosexuality: A Cross-cultural Approach* (New York, 1956); C. S. Ford and F. A. Beach, *Patterns of Sexual Behavior* (New York, 1953), pp. 125–43; G. Herdt, *Ritualised Homosexuality in Melanesia*, pp. 1–81; M. K. Opler, 'Anthropological and cross-cultural aspects of homosexuality', in J. Marmor (ed.), *Sexual Inversion* (New York, 1965), pp. 108–23.

42. D. F. Greenberg, *The Construction of Homosexuality* (Chicago and London, 1988), pp. 25–123.

43. W. R. Dynes and S. Donaldson (eds), *Studies in Homosexuality*, vol. 2: *Ethnographic Studies of Homosexuality* (New York, 1992–3).

44. G. Hekma, 'De verre einders van de homoseksuele verlangens. Homoseksualiteit en culturele antropologie', *Homologie*, 8, 6 (November–December 1986), 37–9.

45. R. Bleys, 'Perversie in het paradijs. Over kolonisatie en homoseksualiteit', *Homologie*, 10 (1988), 4–7.

46. 'obliga a una canta actitud a la hora de hablar de "homosexualidad" en términos genéricos, al referirse a los equivocos contactos entre varones observables en los pueblos exóticos'; A. Cardín, *Guerreros, chamanes y travestís. Indicios de homosexualidad entre los exóticos* (Barcelona, 1984), p. 48.

47.   S. Hall, 'Reconstruction work', *Ten.8*, 16 (1984), 9.
48.   L. Jordanova, 'Natural facts: A historical perspective on science and sexuality', in C. P. MacCormack and M. Strathern (eds), *Nature, Culture and Gender*, p. 67. See also N. L. Stepan, 'Race and gender: The role of analogy in science', *Isis*, 77 (1986), 261–77.
49.   K. Mercer and I. Julien, 'Race, sexual politics and black masculinity: A dossier', in R. Chapman and J. Rutherford (eds), *Male Order. Unwrapping Masculinity* (London, 1988), p. 106.
50.   The term 'trope', borrowed from language theory and literary criticism, has now become current in cultural and intellectual history. It denominates the content that is hidden within the structure of textual narration rather than in the semantics of the words. See H. V. White, The *Content of the Form: Narrative Discourse and Historical Representation* (Cambridge, 1987). See also E. W. Said's concept of the *forma informans* in *Beginnings: Intention and Method* (New York, 1975), p. 319.
51.   H. V. White, *Metahistory* (Baltimore and London, 1973), p. 53.
52.   E. Said, *Beginnings*, p. 21.
53.   J. Stockinger, 'Homotextuality: a proposal', in Louie Crew (ed.), *The Gay Academic* (Palm Springs, 1978), pp. 135–51.
54.   E. Kosofsky Sedgwick describes the deconstruction of hidden homosexual discourse as an 'epistemology of the closet', in *Epistemology of the Closet* (Berkeley, 1990). L. Edelman uses the term 'homographesis', in *Homographesis. Essays in Gay Literary and Cultural Theory* (London, 1994).
55.   See E. Cooper, *The Sexual Perspective. Homosexuality and Art in the Last 100 Years in the West* (London, 1986), pp. 24 ff.

Chapter one

The Pre-Enlightenment Legacy

*Among the Illinois one can find numerous hermaphrodites; they
wear women's clothes but behave like both men and women. These
Illinois have an unfortunate inclination towards Sodomy, just like
other Savages living near the Mississippi river.*

– Baron de Lahontan, *Nouveaux voyages dans l'Amérique
Septentrionale (1703)*[1]

*I expected at every moment that my master would accuse the
yahoos of those unnatural appetites in both sexes, so common
among us. But Nature, it seems, hath not been so expert a
schoolmistress, and these politer pleasures are entirely the
production of art and reason on our side of the globe.*

– Swift, *Gulliver's Travels*, (1726)[2]

To understand the novelty of Enlightenment discourse about same-sex
behaviour outside the West, one ought to look into the legacy of the
Medieval and Early Modern eras. Some narrative tropes, at once describing
and evaluating such behaviour, had already been disseminated among a
cultivated European audience at the dawn of the Enlightenment when
discourse on cultural 'otherness' became instrumental to the construction of
a new view of the world. The innovative character of the philosophers'
système du monde did not trespass some of the crucial structures of mentality, outlined since the early days of European discovery and expansion in the
sixteenth and seventeenth centuries.

The Medieval Crusaders' portrayals of Muslim and Mameluke sodomy
were juxtaposed to reports of similarly 'pagan' practices in the newly
explored territories of both India Orientalis and India Occidentalis as well as
the African coast. Stories about eunuchs that spiced up travel narratives since
late antiquity and were often told in the same breath with descriptions of
sodomy, were enriched with new, unfamiliar narratives about men dressed
and behaving like women, commonly called *effeminati* or *hermaphrodites*.

One may ask if the Europeans' exploration of new horizons significantly altered traditional perceptions of sodomy as a sin against nature. Was the example of *les Indes merveilleuses* powerful enough to suppress Christian intolerance in favour of a less strenuous sense of relativity? Or did the requirements of proto-capitalist exploitation of the new, marvellous possessions overseas[3] invoke an equally deprecatory and oppressive policy despite the then nascent anthropological rhetoric of human diversity? How was sodomy explained? To what extent did it become a token in the new debate on human nature? Which of the Early Modern explanations already envisaged Enlightenment ethnography?

The quotations above, taken from two almost contemporary sources, reveal that a consensus on the nature of male-to-male sexual behaviour was absent at the very dawn of the Enlightenment. The first reiterated the by then secular belief that sodomy was a trait of barbarism, of nature in its crudest form. On the other hand the second, fictitious, narrative of Gulliver's journey into the land of the Houyhnhnms – American Indians? – seemed to uphold an idyll of primitive purity and opposed this to the moral baseness of the 'civilized' West. In both cases, as in almost every other, sodomy was excluded from blueprints of a Utopian state just as it had been banned by Christians from the Garden of Eden centuries before. Only a few reserved a place for it within the realm of sexual Arcadia and set the tone for a subcultural discourse of resistance and, at times, for an incipient exile of men, who felt inclined to engage in what Joseph-François Lafitau delightfully described in 1728 as *amitiés particulières*.

At first, the perennial and ubiquitous mentality structure is one of moral condemnation, that will remain visible throughout this study as a persistent reflection of homophobia. Underneath it, however, a complementary descriptive pattern crystallized, that connected discourse on sexuality to representations of cultural and ethnic difference. The cognitive changes that were brought about by this process will prove to be far more important and I will describe, accordingly, how reports on sodomy – among other practices – were increasingly read as a parameter of 'civilization'. By the mid-eighteenth century, a predisposition to define sodomy's *locus originis* had already become deeply rooted in European consciousness. Gradually disconnected from other non-procreative sexual acts, and seen less as an act that anyone was potentially able to commit,[4] it was increasingly perceived as a characteristic of someone else, as something alien to oneself, in sum, as a sign of difference within the boundaries of Europe. How both processes of cognitive change coincided chronologically will be described accordingly as a *formal* characteristic, instrumental to the innovation of discourse at the eve of the Enlightenment.

But was there more to it than the fact that both discourses coincided in time? It would be wrong to describe the logic of Early Modern anthropological narrative rather dogmatically as a coherent, 'semi-conspirational design' – the term is Edward Said's – that aimed at the marginalization of both ethnic and sexual minorities from an early stage. Such an interpretation, though fashionable, remains as yet purely hypothetical and calls for verification. How, actually, were discourses on *cultural* and sexual difference mutually intertwined? Did the early texts already contain the germs of *geographically* differentiated ethnographic tropes, that would contribute later on to a forthcoming racialist discursivity? How did discourse on sexuality and discourse on *gender* relate to one another in pre-Enlightenment travel narratives? Did new reports on hermaphrodites, that unleashed speculation about the cross-gender nature of sodomites, influence it and, if so, how? Or did stories about active, 'priapic' sodomitical acts stand in the way?

Sodomy and the shock of the new

Sodomy, of course, had already figured prominently in European discourse on cultural otherness for centuries. Herodotos had already distinguished between βαρβαροι, who presumably indulged in sodomitical practices, and ἑλληνικοι, who did not. The point here is not the veracity of his claim, but the fact that sodomy thus entered Western discourse about the 'other' at an early stage.

The condemnation of sodomy within both Judaic[5] and Christian tradition,[6] as well as by the Christian Church in the following centuries was instrumental to the definition of paganism and heresy. Yet no single 'Judaeo-Christian' attitude towards male-to-male sexual praxis persisted through time. The history of canonic law and church policies from Early Christianity to today instead reveals a continuous process of redefinition.[7] The differences within the Christian tradition itself as well as between Judaic and Christian thought about sexuality, however, have not weakened the ever recurrent narrative of the destruction of Sodom that underlies the condemnation of homosexuality. The city of Sodom and Gomorrah actually provided a powerful metaphor for Christian and non-Christian observers of sexual mores alike. Eventually the story of Sodom's destruction was used for anti-Semitic purposes as Jews were identified with the People of Lot. Such association of sexual 'sin' and 'otherness' became a pervasive element in Western thought centuries before it was given pseudo-scientific status by racialist theory. It was applied similarly to heretic groups, *marranes* and *moriscos* within the Catholic world itself, and to the outside world of Islam.

Initially, the French word *bougrerie* was a name for religious heresy, that was believed to be of Eastern European origin, specifically Bulgarian, and became commonly used from the twelfth century onward. The word *bougre*, as such, is derived from *Bulgare*. Originally, no sexual connotation was attached to the word, but gradually it was used as a term for bestiality and anal intercourse with a woman. Only in the fourteenth century did it mean male-to-male sexuality, as is revealed in a trial in Reims dating from 1372.[8] By then, however, the word's initial geographic meaning had evaporated.[9] This was different from accusations made against newly converted Christians (*cristianos nuevos, cristãos-novos*) who were Muslims or Jews previously, and who were regarded with suspicion by the Catholic church as Spain regained territory from the Moors on the Iberian peninsula.[10]

As for the *marranes* or converted Jews, the Inquisition called upon the biblical narrative of the destruction of Sodom as it accused them disproportionately of committing the crime against nature. A conviction grew that sexual immorality was inherent to Jewish identity. The accusation that *moriscos* committed sodomy was no more than a perpetuated suspicion towards Islam. The sin of sodomy indeed was most tenaciously ascribed to Europe's most dreaded enemy. The Crusaders' fear, once captured, of being used to satify Arab sexual demands deeply penetrated into the mind of Europeans and intensified as the Mamelukes, a military caste made up of men of Georgian and Caucasian origin, dominated Egypt from 1249. These displayed an outspoken preference for boys rather than women, did not marry but enslaved people instead, both for the purpose of pederasty[11] and to guarantee their survival as a military caste.[12] At home, both Jews and Christians were believed to have 'learned' the practice of sodomy in Egypt or Arab Spain.[13]

European references to sodomy in the Arab and Persian world mostly meant male-to-male sexuality, and more particularly anal intercourse, and did indeed correspond to social reality. Same-sex sexuality, especially trans-generational or age-structured, that is, between men and boys or adolescents, surely was more common than in Europe itself and the official Muslim condemnation of homosexual behaviour hardly reflected its widespread reality in daily life.[14] A vast and rich literature, describing the beauty of boys and techniques for seducing them, was written by authors such as Abu Nuwas, Ibn al-'Abbar, Ibn Khafaja, Ibn Quzman, Ibn Arabi, Sa'di, Al-Hariri, and, of course, Al-Nefzawi. Islamic theologians themselves, such as Al-Ghazali, disapproved of it, yet wrote delirious poetry about young boys. And Ibn Khaldun somewhat anticipated later European theories about homosexuality as a source of a civilization's decline, yet included numerous homoerotic passages in his major work, The Muqaddimah.

Thus male-to-male sexuality remained current despite the opposition of Islamic religious law. But contemporary European observers, caught within the rhetoric of religious animosity, failed to capture the ongoing ambiguity within the Arab and Persian world as they simply associated sodomy with Islam. John Boswell describes how this did not spring directly from a homophobic intent *per se*, though it did, in the end, stimulate people's contempt for Islam and sodomy alike:

Significantly, the earliest examples used homosexual rape – not consensual homosexual acts – as instances of Muslim immorality. But the regular association of minority sexual preferences with the most dreaded of Europe's enemies inevitably increased popular antipathy toward the minority as well as the Muslims.[15]

This association between constructions of cultural and sexual identity, though *ad hoc* and inspired by the factual reality of same-sex praxis in the Arab world, remained persistent throughout the *ancien régime*. Meanwhile the changing political reality was reflected in sexual discourse as sodomy, until then depicted by Europeans as a 'Muslim' vice, was increasingly declared a 'Turkish' one in the wake of the Ottoman expansion in the Middle-East.

Nicolas de Nicolay described how men slept naked on the floor 'while mutually committing the abominable and damnable luxury of sodomy in ways that are more beastly and unnatural than those of wild and savage animals'.[16] In one of his letters, Ogier Ghiselin de Busbecq wrote about the 'strange passion' of a passing woman, that is: a woman, disguised as a man and assuming a male role, whom he had seen while a diplomat in Turkey. He also reported various social arrangements that encouraged diverse sexual practices, including sodomy. George Rousseau rightly wonders to what extent the letters of de Busbecq 'fed into preexisting ... myths about Turkish sodomy'[17] yet they did not in any way present an image that was merely sensational. In contrast to de Nicolay, de Busbecq pretended that Turks remain rather cautious about their 'secret vices'.[18] Other significant references can be found in the writings of William Lithgow, Henry Blount, Pietro della Valle, and Jean de Thévenot.[19] The eunuchs of the Turkish seraglio, as well as the *hammans* or Turkish baths, titillated the imagination of the Westerner and have been inventoried by historians as favourite *topoi* of the Orientalist imagination, and as accomplices and hotbeds of 'Turkish vice'.[20]

The construction of Turkish vice did not, however, make redundant an ongoing association of sodomy with Islam in general. Travellers observing sodomy in Egypt did not feel compelled to explain it as 'of Turkish origin' despite the country's incorporation into the Ottoman empire since 1517. Vincent Stochove, for example, clearly outlined the indigenous nature of both male and female same-sex practices in his *Voyage du Levant* (1643; 1650):

The inhabitants of this country are generally devoted to lasciviousness and, more awfully, Sodomy reigns in such a degree that men despise women, ... [women] also despise men and sleep with one another, committing these horrible and bastard acts of love more frequently than natural, honourable and legitimate ones.[21]

Other descriptions that include the realm of Turkish sodomy can be found in texts about Persia – among many, Thomas Herbert's *Some Yeares Travaile*, published in London in 1634, Olfert Dapper's *Naukeurige beschryving van Asie* (1680), and Jean Chardin's *Voyage en Perse* of 1686.

Geographic and geopolitical qualifications thus remained secondary to the emphasis placed upon the world of Islam in general, where it 'is common for men there to fall in love with boys as 'tis in England to be in love with women'.[22] It was a haven for sodomites, that revealed its religious heresy in its disregard of the Bible's prescriptions on sex.

The mobilization of sexuality in European discourse about paganism deeply influenced the Old World's representations of the newly discovered people across the Atlantic and Pacific Ocean as well. But the fifteenth- to seventeenth-century rhetoric of discovery and conquest mixed religious motives with considerations of a more profane tenor and crystallized into a comprehensive ideology of exploration and colonization that was different from the representations accompanying Europe's conflict-ridden relationship with the world of Islam.

Constructing the New World's sexuality

Europe was altogether more successful at converting the indigenous populations of the New Worlds than at eradicating the religion of Islam. Shortly after its instalment in Europe itself, the Inquisition also spread its tentacles to the far outreaches of the colonies overseas in order to guarantee obedience to the moral prescriptions of the Catholic church. Protestant settlers, in their turn, ensured moral policing in a different, yet equally pervasive manner.

Surely, the effect of Christianization was not always equally impressive, as shown by its annals in China and Japan, nor was it total, as is revealed by religious syncretism, especially in Latin America. But it hardly left indigenous morality unchanged. Sex became a major target of Christianity's policing intervention and was disciplined according to the principles that were valid in Europe as well. Thus sodomy, comprising everything 'against nature', was condemned along with other practices such as nudity, cannibalism and animist rituals.[23]

Also echoed in Early Modern discourse on sodomy outside the West were other narratives, that were inherited from Late Antiquity and the Middle Ages yet remained influential sources of imagination about the New World. Among these the stories of Saint Brendan, John Mandeville, and Marco Polo were perhaps most influential.[24] Other narrative elements were taken from popular imagination, such as the Wild Man – the Wild Woman was less common[25] – who was seen as an almost naked man in a bearskin with a big club in his hand. His rude behaviour and sexual proneness was often recognized in the new narratives of exploration of the sixteenth and seventeenth centuries.[26]

Of more literary origin was the image of the 'Plinian races'. Pliny the Elder's legendary taxonomy not only influenced Early and High Medieval descriptions of the world, but imprinted its stamp on Late Medieval cosmographies as well. Pierre d'Ailly's *Tractatus de imagine mundi*, for example, deliberately omitted thirteenth- and fourteenth-century travel narratives in favour of the old taxonomy of mankind. The Plinian races persisted in the Early Modern *imaginaire* as well, though the vagueness of their classification allowed for recognition at various points in time as well as at different places in the world. Ethiopia and India were frequently presented as the places of origin of the monstrous races, but their naming remained imprecise – which explains why the tradition on the existence of the Plinian races, though 'not impervious to influences from the Orient [allowed for] situating them in the New World too after the discovery.'[27] But as worldwide exploration, cartography and a nascent ethnography developed from the sixteenth century onwards, both the Wild Man and the Plinian races became increasingly obsolete and gradually disappeared from the traveller's narrative.[28]

Early Modern relativism soon dissipated as the increasing pressures of colonial exploitation put an end to initial ethnographic speculation. Early tales of discovery, such as Staden's or de Léry's, already exchanged an original tenor of idyllism for a rhetoric of primitive barbarism, focusing on the 'other's' monstrosity, cannibalism and sexual lechery. Sexuality thus became a vehicle of propaganda not only against the paganism of indigenous populations, but also against their presumed cultural inferiority. Sodomy, though common only in very particular circumstances and pursued by only a small group of the entire population, would be represented accordingly as ubiquitous, thus justifying its suppression through military and political violence.

India occidentalis

Some of the more generalizing descriptions, by emphasizing the Indians' indulgence in sodomy, tempted historians to claim that the *conquista* was partially justified.[29] Hernán Cortés's claim that 'all [were] sodomites and engaged in this abominable sin' was probably the most extreme and the most conducive to such an interpretation.[30] A similar accusation can be found in the report of the so-called Anonymous Conquistador, first published in an Italian translation in the third volume of Giovanni Battista Ramusio's *Navigationi e Viaggi* (1556): 'most of them are sodomites ... and they all drink an awful lot (sono come si è detto, per la maggior parte sodomiti, e bevono smisuratamente)'.[31] Various authors mentioned sodomy in one breath with anthropophagy and human sacrifice so as to stress the horrific state of pre-Columbian society and to rationalize the colonizer's policy against such practices. Thus a plainly disapproving Bernal Diaz del Castillo (1605), whose comment on sodomy figured neatly between descriptions of human sacrifices and cannibalism: 'Most of them moreover were sodomites, especially those who lived in the coastal and warm areas. Boys walked about dressed like women and engaging in this diabolic and abominable activity (Y además desto, eran los más dellos sométicos, en especial los que vivían en las costas y tierra caliente, en tanta manera, que andaban vestidos en hábito de mujeres muchachos a ganar en aquel diabólico y abominable oficio).'[32]

Although serving the purpose of justification, this occurred *ex post facto* only, when the chronicles were published in Europe itself. Many texts, as a matter of fact, were less reductive in their descriptions of indigenous sexuality and emphasized how sexual mores diverged widely among the various Indian ethnicities.

Among the most reliable was Pedro Cieza de León's *Crónica del Perú* (1553). It described how sodomy was common, 'despite the presence of beautiful women', in the province of Santiago de Puerto Viejo, the territory of the precedent culture of Mochica-Chimú: 'As they were bad and vicious, and despite the fact that there were plenty of women around, some even beautiful, I was assured that many among them engaged publicly and openly in the nefarious sin of sodomy, and they were even proud of it (Pues, como éstos fueron malos y viciosos, no embargante que entre ellos había mujeres muchas, y algunas hermosas, los más dellos usaban (a lo que a mí certificaron) pública y descubiertamente el pecado nefando de sodomía, en lo cual dicen que se gloriaban demasiadamente)' and continued by describing how the Spanish authorities intervened to put an end to the sinful practice of sodomy.[33] Yet, the author's contrast of Chimú sodomy to his own description of the mountain people or *serranos* (i.e. the Colla of the Aymara family, and the Tarma), where he believed such practice to be nonexistent, at least modifies the traditional role of sodomy in narrative as a rationale for military submission. It was not, as Cieza de León's detailed ethnic description reveals, an indispensable and unconditional trope of the conquerors' rhetoric.

Research, that cannot be pursued here, may indicate if the descriptions of sodomy or their absence in the sixteenth-century chronicles reflected changing political realities, that is: if new alliances may have inspired an author to adjust his description of indigenous sexuality. That such an 'anthropology of war'[34] was real is revealed in another story by Cieza de León. It is a most remarkable one as it offers a justification of almost mythological significance for the Spanish repression of sodomy, yet puts it in the mouth of an indigenous tribe, that was said to have been ruled by giants. These, tyrannizing the local people and engaging in sodomy, were punished by an all-consuming fire from heaven from which an angel appeared, who killed them all and left only a few of their bones to commemorate them.[35] Agustín de Zárate also included this story in his *Historia del Descubrimiento y Conquista del Perú* (1555),[36] yet claimed to have taken it from an indigenous oral tradition that did not by any means relate the giants' destruction to their presumed sodomy. It merely provided an explanation to the Spanish captain, Juan de Olmos, who had found bones of a considerable size in a valley in 1543.[37]

How, then, should Cieza de León's version be interpreted? And how should we interpret the similar adaptation of indigenous myth to an anti-sodomy crusade in the often fantastic *Commentários reales*, written by Garcilaso de la Vega between 1586 and 1612?[38] It seems that sexuality was emphasized when military and political circumstances required it, while it was played down when alliances were made to combat a joint enemy, such as the Incas. In the latter case, Spanish chroniclers would rather stress how the allied ethnic group did not tolerate sodomy among its members even before Spanish intervention.

Early reports of Indian customs in the territories of Brazil were not significantly different from Spanish sources, and reveal, in their turn, how the authors were at once astounded and horrified by the degree of sexual 'freedom' among the Tupinambà. Some of the best known texts – Jean de Léry and Michel de Montaigne's essay on *Les cannibales* – are based on information provided by European men who had 'gone native' for many years, and sometimes show rather amusing descriptions of sodomy among the Indians.[39]

But the overall tenor was very negative as Europeans observed how sodomy figured among so many other sinful practices including polygamy, polyandry, incest, endogamy, prostitution and wives offering women to their own husband. Meanwhile, the adage that below the equator there is no sin – *infra equinoxialem nihil peccari* – spread across the European continent and added to the dismay of some at the corrupting impact of indigenous sexual practices. Pêro de Magalhães Gandavo observed in 1576 that Indian men indulged in sodomy 'as if they did not have the reason of men'.[40] The Portuguese Jesuit José de Anchieta was upset to see the apparent libertinism of the Indians of Brazil, and his colleague Manuel da Nóbrega complained how 'if one were to count all the households of this land, they would all be found ridden with deadly sins, including adultery, fornication, incest, and abominations, this to an extent that I went to bed wondering if Christ has anything pure in this land (se contarem todas as casas d'esta terra, todas acharão cheias de pecados mortais, cheias de adultérios, fornicações, inces-tos, e abominações, em tanto que me deito a cuidar se tem Cristo algum limpo nesta terra)'.[41] Gabriel Soares de Souza wrote, probably in 1587, how 'the Tupinambas are so luxurious that there is not one luxurious sin, that they do not commit (são os tupinambàs tão luxuriosos que não há pecado de luxúria que não cometam)'. After dwelling on the adolescents' sexual preco-ciousness, incest and endogamy, Soares described how young men engage in sodomy merely to boast about it and to confirm their virility.[42] Father Pêro Correia wrote a letter from São Vicente in 1551, relating that female homosexuality, 'as in Africa, is most common'. These women, he continued, carry weapons like men and marry other women. Being called 'women' was perceived as a major insult.[43] Ambrósio Brandão, for his part, commented on women who prefer chastity to sexual communion with men and turn away their help.[44]

The exaggeration of the virility of Indian woman together with a reduction of the masculinity of Indian men is said to have been a common trait of Early Modern descriptions, both literary and pictorial, of the American.[45] Such 'unbalanced' relations between the sexes was, in this view, postulated by a European rhetoric of conquest, where the 'lack of a clearly marked masculinity invited the thrust of European penetration'.[46] Such a far-reaching interpretation, however tempting, remains problematic as the few existing texts are too sparse. One must not forget, also, that European observers were rather predisposed by both mythology – about the Amazons, for example[47], or the *androgini* of Plinius – and narratives about eunuchs and sodomy in the Middle East. This certainly must have provoked a moment of 'recognition' among the early observers of the New World. It is obvious, at the same time, that these very same travellers and chroniclers felt compelled to dwell upon precisely those aspects of indigenous societies that were most extraordinary and, indeed, sensational. Alfredo Jiménez rightly emphasizes that the prominence of stories about sodomy were the outcome of their authors' bewilderment at how openly it was pursued by some of the indigenous tribes, rather than by the mere frequency of such practices.[48]

Despite such flaws, Early Modern discourse on the sexuality of American Indians *was* indeed verifiable to a certain degree and cannot be reduced to a preconceived rhetoric of conquest and penetration. To read a well-defined sexual politics into only a handful of reports thus seems deficient in the light of historical circumstance.

This criticism does not, however, affect a 'deconstructionist' claim that the early literature about the New World did in fact contribute to the formation of a particular discourse of 'otherness'. Careful description indeed converged with the desire or need to define the Other as a single, monolithic category. Sodomy, along with cannibalism, in fact became a major vehicle for defining another tribes' identity and was extrapolated from one ethnic group to another. Its juxtaposition with anthropophagy, moreover, lent rhetorical power to both.[49]

The very prominence given to stories about sodomy within the authors' narratives, easily turned it into a metonymical representation of American Indian identity, partly because they neglected to specify the circumstances of same-sex behaviour among the Indians, partly because readers at home failed to realize how such an omission made descriptions of same-sex practices into a *pars pro toto* as a result.

Early Modern discourse about the Indian-American also included descriptions and interpretations that were of a very different tenor. Just as some exaggerated the weight of same-sex sexual practices within a particular tribe either to coerce the Indians into political obedience or to emphasize their 'otherness', so others, mostly missionaries, often minimized them in order to uphold an image of indigenous innocence and, secondly, to denounce the cruelty of worldly power.

Among the missionaries the *mestizo* father Diego Muñoz Camargo stressed that homosexuality led to a penalty of death among the indigenous people of Tlaxcala and thus refuted the conquerors' assertion that the Indians simply indulged in sodomy.[50] Muñoz Camargo's position is of course understandable as he was himself of mixed ethnic origin. Similarly the Maya informant and collaborator of the Franciscans in Yucatán, Gaspar Antonio Chi, assured that sodomy did not occur among his folk after the instalment of severe punishment by his ancestor, Tutul Xiu.[51] But both authors' insistence on the moral purity of the Indians surely is more revealing of their European patrons' attitude than of sexual reality both in New Spain and elsewhere.

As early as 1613, Bartolomé de Las Casas objected to the overall accusation by the Spanish colonizers that the Indians were sodomites, and stated that it was invented by them as an excuse for ruthless treatment. His assurance that sodomy did not exist on the islands of Jamaica, Cuba, Hispaniola and San Juan significantly paralleled a denial of cannibalism, thus confirming the thesis that both 'vices' were often invoked simultaneously as symbols of inferiority or, for de Las Casas, as a refutation of such. When evidence about indigenous same-sex practices was indisputable, de Las Casas ascribed it to the intervention of a devil, disguised in the figure of Cu, and exempted the Indians from guilt.[52]

It is probable that such obstinate 'corrections' of the official discourse of military and political rulers were inspired by the then rising debate within the Catholic church on the humanity of the Indians. The 'abominable sin' was presented by Juan Ginés de Sepulveda as an argument *a fortiori* to justify the war against the Indians. Father Bernardo de Sahagún, too, fiercely condemned the practice of sodomy, so ubiquitous among the Indians: 'The passive sodomite is abominable, nefarious and despicable, worthy to be ridiculed and laughed at by the people. The stench and ugliness of his nefarious sin are unacceptable and disgust mankind. He shows himself womanlike or effeminate, both in his way of walking and talking, all for which he deserves to be burnt at the stake.'[53] Such opinions faced criticism by many missionaries, who believed the Indians capable of redemption. They felt compelled to accentuate the positive side of indigenous people and were prepared to remain silent on sodomy, when it occurred, or to take ethnic groups where sodomy did not carry approval, as exemplary for all Indians.

It may well be that the picture, drawn from both sympathetic and inimical reports, is a complex one. But that the reports reflected contemporary political and social controversies is obvious, and the nuances made did not always correspond with ethnographic reality. It is impossible, as a result, to extract a reliable picture of sexual reality in pre-Columbian America from these reports. Meso-America alone, emphasizes Olivier, was – and is – a cultural and social mosaic, and sexual experience varied widely from one ethnic or cultural group to another. It also changed through time. The ethnic maps of North America, the Caribbean, the Andes, Brazil and the Rio de la Plata basin were no less complex and contrasted sharply with the altogether rather simplistic image of Indian sexuality that Early Modern writers were offering.[54]

Generally, same-sex practices of some individuals were easily 'read' as representative for the sexual customs of all members of a tribe. Frequently, same-sex praxis was detached from its context of ritual and initiation and made a daily occupation. Observations about sodomy among men of a single tribe eventually were extrapolated to Early Modern constructions of *the* American Indian. Such textual effects were the combined result of military conquest, of Christianization, and of the already existing representations of the sexuality of the Other, particularly Muslims, Jews and New Christians.

The latter especially must not be underestimated as it explains how the insistence of some authors on the Indian's sexual innocence may very well have been contrary to the chroniclers of conquest, yet hardly questioned the symbolic dimension of sexuality itself in the European construction of cultural 'otherness'. The way both parties were tangled up in an evaluation of Indian sexuality very well illustrates how the act of defining Indian cultural identity remained subservient to existing tropes of Arab and Jewish difference.

India orientalis

Whereas in America the clergy mitigated the *conquistadores*' rhetoric of indigenous sodomy, it did little to deny similar allegations against the indigenous populations in the Far East. Francis Xavier set the trend from the mid-sixteenth century onward as he complained about the ephebophile practices of the Buddhist *bonzes* of Japan, 'who are inclined to sins, abhorred by nature. They even confess it and don't deny it. It is visible and public to all, including men and women, young and old, none of whom think much of it nor despise it as it seems to be a common habit indeed (los cuales son inclinados a pecados que natura aborrece, y ellos lo confiesan y no lo niegan; y es tan público y manifiesto a todos, así hombres como mujeres, pequeños y grandes, que, por estar en mucha costumbre, no lo extrañan ni lo tienen en aborrecimiento)'.[55] It is known that Francis Xavier's initiatives to suppress same-sex practices were hardly welcomed in Japan. He was in fact ridiculed for trying to ban sodomy, and seemed well aware of this when describing how people in the streets laughed at him.[56]

The Jesuits' frustration was also expressed by Alessandro Valignano, who faced Japanese students engaging deliberately in sodomy. Gaspar Vilela directed his *odium theologicum* at the founder of the Shingon convent of Koyasan, whom he alleged of having introduced the unspeakable sin.[57] Father Cabral, in his turn, ascribed the failure of Christianization to the Japanese elite's habit of sending their sons to the *bonzes* of Buddhist convents, where they would 'serve their lust'.[58] Eventually European missionaries had to give up their attempts to eradicate pederasty along with their hope to Christianize the Japanese people. At the dawn of Tokugawa Japan, they were either murdered or expelled from the country. Pederasty, from then on called *shudô*, remained an integral part of Japanese life.[59]

In China, the Jesuits were hardly more successful. They were impressed by the widespread and public presence of sodomy, first revealed by writers such as Galeote Pereira and Gaspar da Cruz in the third quarter of the sixteenth century,[60] and showed great determination to suppress it since. Matteo Ricci, arriving in Macao in 1582 and settling subsequently in Zhaoqing, Shaozhou, Nanjing, Nanchang and Peking, went so far as to change 'Thou shalt not commit adultery' into 'Thou shalt not do depraved, unnatural, or filthy things' in his translation into Chinese of the Ten Commandments. He condemned pederasty in other writings on religious doctrine and called the city of Peking a 'true Babylon of confusion', where *gente effeminata* abounded.[61]

The comparison, says Spence, of Peking with Babylon was 'astonishingly like the kind of charges that Reformation priests had launched against Rome and its corrupt popes as the "whores of Babylon" '.[62] Such a fact may suggest that the Jesuits' descriptions were to a high degree rhetorical and therefore exaggerated. One may conclude that similarly dramatic narratives about Japanese sodomy served the purpose of propaganda rather than of veritable description.

Yet, whereas no American written records survive that allow for concluding unmistakably that sodomy did occur, both China and Japan produced plentiful, unmistakable evidence. From this it becomes clear that same-sex praxis among males was indeed common for centuries, even though it did not take place indiscriminately and was bound to specific rules.

Same-sex relations remained a privileged practice within the compounds of Buddhist convents of China and Japan as among the military caste of the *samurai* in Japan.[63] At the imperial court of China, eunuchs were employed for sexual purposes while playing a rather active role in imperial politics.[64] Theatre also provided a platform for same-sex socializing, as the female roles were commonly performed by boys, who worked as male prostitutes outside the theatre at the same time. The relations were most often age- and gender-structured, even outside the context of prostitution, and quite similar in both

China (*xiaochang* or 'little singer') and Japan (*wakashu* in Kabuki theatre).[65] Like other sexual practices, they were openly visualized in erotic drawings and so-called 'pillow books'.[66]

The missionaries' descriptions were very much in tune, moreover, with reports by European merchants, travellers and compilers, who described Japan and China as part of a geographical sphere, where sodomy flourished. Less preoccupied with converting the indigenous people to Christendom, they were nevertheless equally impressed by the apparent ubiquity of same-sex practices in the various countries of the Far East. In 1547 the Portuguese captain Alvares was astounded at the ubiquity of sodomy in Japan,[67] and so was the Dutch admiral Van Noort.[68] Other reports about sodomy in Japan by Varenius[69] and Montanus[70] supported François Caron's statement that neither the priests nor many of the gentry of Japan abstained from 'unnatural passion' nor did they perceive it as a sin.[71] As early as 1595, Antonio de Morga felt that the Chinese especially were responsible for spreading sodomitical vice among the Philippine population.[72] A century later, Robert Knox relates stories about the bloodthirsty king Radja Siga of Ceylon, who surrounded himself with beautiful young men. The casually performed decapitation after services certainly must have challenged the imagination of European readers. The author, alas, remains utterly silent on what these services meant. The king's apparently misogynous neglect of women, including his catholically baptized wife Dona Catharina, may well be an indication, however, of a rather sadistic predilection for adolescent boys.[73] Such an eccentric individual case does not say much, on the other hand, about more general popular attitudes, nor was Knox's account of it prototypical. De Argensola, Navarrete (Philippines), Dapper, Fryer (East India), Hamilton (Johore), and Psalmanazar, presumably a local Christian convert of Formosa (Taiwan), are only a few among others who offered sometimes shocked, sometimes amused descriptions of pederasty in other regions of the Far East, but these too are quite hard to evaluate.[74]

Often, the climate was believed to cause extreme lasciviousness and it was said that the heat seduced men into committing sodomy. As for the world of Islam, such conviction had already been prepared by Jacques de Vitry, who distinguished a morality of the Iberian peninsula and Sicily on the one hand, and a Middle Eastern one on the other, where 'bestial and wanton people ... easily embark on the path which leads to death'.[75] So, when confronted with Islam in Central Asia and the Indian subcontinent, Europeans were prone to recognize a 'Middle-Eastern' morality – or lack of it.

The climate, however, crossed the boundaries of the Muslim world and seemed to trigger a loose morality all across the Eastern hemisphere. Just as 'below the equator, no sin existed', so too was the Far East seen by many a traveller as a hotbed of sexual lasciviousness. The French merchant Pyrard de Laval described the – in his eyes – relaxed sexual mores on the Maldives.[76]

The Italian Francesco Carletti was 'transfixed with admiration at the result-ing sensuality, the men in wide-sleeved, dangling, loose, white clothes'.[77]

The image of an Oriental tendency to sodomy in particular became central to a new, independent discourse about Asian identity. Just as Islam had been associated with sodomy for many centuries, the Orient in its turn became almost synonymous with 'sodomitical'. To some extent, such a vision merely paralleled the expansion of Islam into Central Asia (Safavids) and the Indian subcontinent (Moghul India). But as Europeans perceived that same-sex practices proliferated in other non-Muslim societies as well, the image of an Oriental sexual morality became more and more appealing.

Both Lach and Spence have demonstrated that the widespread practice of sodomy in the Far East was soon taken for granted and that some authors felt compelled rather to explain why it was *not* so overwhelmingly present in some places.[78] Among them, Cesare Fedrici, a merchant of Venice, believed that the women's wear in Burma was designed so as to seduce men from choosing male partners instead.[79] John Huyghen van Linschoten similarly explained the Burma women's near-nudity and suggested that female infibu-lation was to make women more attractive to the rather reluctant men.[80] Frederick Coyett, representative of the Dutch East Indian Company in Formosa from 1656 till 1662, warned the Dutch against the then-current prejudice that the 'effeminate Chinese' could hardly represent a military threat.[81]

Such rationalizations parallelled the ones of missionaries, who assumed same-sex practices to be ubiquitous in the Far East and went to extremes when explaining why they were less prominent occasionally. One explana-tion by Nicolò de Conti, who pretended that sodomy had disappeared in Burma when all the men were forced by the king to pierce a tiny bell through their penis's prepuce, actually became famous for centuries afterwards.[82]

Sexuality – and sodomy in particular – thus became a major vehicle for European constructions of Asian identity from an early stage. It was shared from the beginning by worldly and religious observers alike and sharpened as attempts at Christianization were only partially successful. As with Amer-ican Indians, same-sex praxis, that occurred within a context of either religious or military education, was represented as 'endemic'. Minority behaviour was represented as everyone's vice. Evidence about one ethnic group was extrapolated to others.

The generalizing constructions of an Oriental sexual morality, regardless of religious creed, social circumstance or cultural context, may lead us to believe that here were laid the germs of a racialist theory of human sexuality. Yet, the Europeans' ever recurrent ascription of sodomy to almost all people of the New Worlds calls for scepticism towards such an interpretation of the evidence. How important was the weight of race identity, when sodomy was common currency among Muslims, Indian Americans, and Asians at once?

And in the coastal regions of Africa as well same-sex practices were said to be commonly visible.

Subsaharan Africans and African Americans

At first sight, Early Modern discourse on same-sex behaviour among Sub-saharan Africans, both in their homeland and in the American colonies, is less extensive than that on Muslims, Indians, or Asians. Perhaps this sprang from a Medieval belief in the virtue of the Ethiopian race, even though at that time Ethiopia was located eastward from the actual African continent.[83] Such an explanation is not entirely convincing, however, as biblical tradition imposed an ominous fate upon the sons of Ham that was comparable to its stigmatization of the people of Sodom. Ham, or Cham, was cursed by his father Noah for not having covered his body when he had seen him lying asleep naked and drunk. Instead he had told his brothers, Shem and Japheth, who then 'took a garment, and laid it upon the nakedness of their father; and their faces were backward, and they saw not their father's nakedness'.[84] The biblical representation of Ham, traditionally understood as the progenitor of the 'black' race, would soon trigger conscious or unconscious associations of the latter's identity with forbidden sexuality along with his presumed destiny to a slave's existence.[85] The presumed link between 'blackness' and sexual concupiscence became a pervasive trope of European literature and paved the way for later, racialist representations of the black man's presumed polymorphous perversity.

Sander Gilman speculated that such a fate was provoked by the 'homo-sexual' nature of Ham's unfortunate confrontation with his father's nakedness: 'For blacks, the sons of Ham, all sexual license is permitted because their nature was revealed (or formed) in the most heinous of all sexual acts, the same-sex gaze.'[86] Such schematic conclusions seem spec-ulative and at least premature, as too few studies have been made as yet of western representations of black male sexuality.[87] In fact, most studies focus rather one-dimensionally on the black man's presumed phallic power and his potential threat to white male dominance, while neglecting the more latent discursive theme of sexual ambiguity.[88] Equally compelling, though also hypothetical, are claims that the fate of both Lot's and Ham's children became more intertwined as European definitions of the 'other' grew more pregnantly racialist. In this context, Maurice Dorès described how each one's marginal status was nevertheless phrased in different terms: 'Si le Noir terrible, sanguinaire et fort, brutalise, le Juif, quant à lui, séduit, corrompt et souille.'[89]

If justified, then this hypothesis calls for an alternative explanation of the relatively marginal share of Africa in Early Modern discourse on sodomy. Probably this was due largely to the fact that Europeans had explored only the coastal regions of Africa. Contacts, moreover, were superficial initially and became more intense only as the transatlantic slave trade grew into a full-blown enterprise. Yet, by then, observations of Africans in their original setting had been replaced by the physical and social context of a plantation economy.[90]

Some observers and compilers surely did report same-sex practices among males in Subsaharan Africa. João dos Santos, later quoted by Samuel Purchas,[91] reported about passive men or *chibudi* in Bacongo.[92] Petrus Jarric quoted from oral reports by two priests, who saw *chibados*, men who dressed like women and married other men, in Angola.[93] Etienne de Flacourt first described the *tsecats*, young men, assuming a female role, in his *Histoire de la grande isle Madagascar*, yet remains vague about their sexual praxis.[94] Olfert Dapper's *Naukeurige beschrijvinge der Afrikaensche Gewesten*, published in 1668 and later translated in German, also reported about *chibados*: 'There are among them many shamans, called Chibados, who walk dressed like women (Daar zijn bij hen ook veel wichelaers, Chibados genaemd, die gekleet gaen gelijk vrouwen).'[95] The *Beschrijvinge* also contains a description of cross-gender roles among the Dongo in Angola. Yet it is hard to derive from Dapper's account to what extent these were common outside the eccentric realm of queen Anna Xinga's royal court:

[She] also maintains fifty to sixty concubines, whom she dresses like women, even though they are young men, just in order not to be named a woman herself. Even though they know it, she dresses these fifty to sixty strong and beautiful young men in female garment, according to her habit, and dresses herself as a man. She calls these men women and herself a man. The cross-dressed young men are said to be her concubines.[96]

Antonio Oliveira de Cardonega included the following picture of the cross-gender role of *quimbanda* in his *Historia Geral das Guerras Angolanas* of 1681:

Among the people of Angola, there is much sodomy among men, who pursue their dirty practices dressed like women. In the country's own language, those who have relations among one another in this district are called 'quimbandas'. Some among them are wizzards, who control everything, and are esteemed by most of the people …[97]

Peter Kolb's *Caput Bonae Spei Hodiernum* offers yet another report of same-sex praxis among the Khoi-Khoin or Hottentots and contains a description of *koetsire*, that is, men or boys who assume a passive role during sexual intercourse.[98]

In his *Relation historique de l'Ethiopie occidentale*, father Jean-Baptiste Labat included a description of what probably must have been a male initiation rite among the *Nquiti* (Congo),[99] but which the author himself interpreted as mere lasciviousness.[100] Descriptions of dances, such as the *npambuatari*, the *quitombé* or the *mampombo*, seem to suggest that the author recognized signs of incidental, disguised homoeroticism.[101]

The *mampombo*, claimed Labat, was continued in Martinique as *calenda*. But Labat's portrayal of the Caribbean isles remains silent on male-to-male sexual praxis itself.[102] And explicit descriptions of male-to-male sexual practices are altogether hard to find in Early Modern European discourse about African slave life in the Americas. They were not entirely uncommon, however, as can be seen from local archival evidence. Jonathan Katz retrieved the history of Jan Creoli, identified as a 'negro', who had committed sodomy with a ten-year-old African boy, Manuel Congo, and was burnt at the pillory in New Amsterdam in 1646. The boy, for his part, was flogged.[103]

Gilberto Freyre provided some evidence about male black slaves, who deliberately engaged in sexual relations either among themselves or with men of Indian or European origin in colonial Brazil. Eager to dismantle an age-old prejudice about the sexually debilitating effect of the African presence in Brazil, however, he insisted that such initiatives remained marginal to male-to-male sexual relations, that were enforced upon the Africans.[104] Recent studies nevertheless reveal that there were African males in both Portugal[105] and Brazil,[106], who upheld the behavioural pattern of a *jimbanda*. This was a cross-dressing role, comparable to the *quimbanda*, observed by Cardonega in Angola, that most probably went along with a passive role in sexual intercourse.

A well-known, if more recent document remains the autobiographical report of Esteban Montejo, a nineteenth-century Cuban runaway slave, whose testimony may be valid retrospectively. Montejo claimed that male sodomy did occur among African slaves on the plantations. He accounted for this partly as the outcome of a shortage of women, yet he also said that some men 'did not want to know anything of women'. Some actually set up house, where one effeminate man 'washed the clothes, and did the cooking too'.[107] Montejo's description of the hatred of older slaves towards such effeminate men is proof to Mary Karash of how 'homosexual relations . . . were contrary to African values which favored large families'.[108] However, family values did not exclude homosexual praxis in itself. Nero suggested that the elderly's disapproval of effeminacy may in fact have been marginal to a more general acceptance of same-sex relations, especially as no pejorative term was used for these until after the abolition of slavery in 1886.[109]

It remains hazardous, however, to put forward any even tentatively conclusive statement about same-sex relations in particular. As yet, most attention has been paid to the historical study of Afro-American heterosexual practices, and research on their male-to-male counterpart is only taking off today.[110] The occurrence of same-sex praxis may indeed have been an outcome of a demographic surplus of men to women, compelling men to have sexual intercourse with a male, most often a younger partner to a degree that was unusual in Africa itself.[111] And the plantation system surely was conducive to sexual violence, inflicted not only upon female but also upon male slaves by the owners, the overseers and their sons.[112]

Nevertheless the evidence of same-sex behaviour among Subsaharan Africans indicates that its occurrence among Afro-Americans cannot be explained exclusively as the outcome of a mere shortage of women or a 'side-effect' of unequal power relations within the context of a plantation economy. The task is doomed to remain extremely difficult, however, because retrieving more precise information about the ethnic background of the slaves, who were said to have engaged in same-sex relations with other men, is virtually impossible. Ethnographic detail, already sparse in the texts about Africa, disappeared almost entirely after transport and migration overseas. Once arrived in the West Indies and the Americas, individuals of divergent ethnic origin were easily mingled with one another – a fact that was consolidated by the marriage patterns of the slave population afterwards as much as by the more or less widespread miscegenation with people of European, Indian or mixed descent.

That male-to-male sexuality was unknown among black Africans and Afro-Americans is altogether contradicted by the narratives reviewed above by dos Santos, de Flacourt, Dapper, Cardonega, Kolb and Labat. Yet whereas their descriptions were fairly similar to those of American Indian and Asian sodomy, they remained in the end less quintessential to European constructions of African identity. One wonders, in fact, if the demand for a black labour force in the Americas did not somehow promote a discourse about black 'masculinity' that deliberately discarded evidence about same-sex practices among black men and made these invisible to a European audience?[113]

The few portrayals of male-to-male sexuality nevertheless reveal how descriptions of same-sex behaviour were attached to a definition of African 'otherness'. The incidental evidence of ritualized homosexuality was presented as mere sodomy and the male-to-male relations of some were represented as a reflection of an entire tribe's immorality. As such, Africanist discourse hardly diverged from constructions of American and Asian identity, as it equally turned indigenous sexuality into a metaphor of cultural difference.

The European association of sodomy with 'otherness', that originally crossed the continent's boundaries in the wake of the war against Islam, was repeated as the West explored the world from the fifteenth century onwards. Within the narratives of discovery and conquest, same-sex behaviour was employed as a *signifier* of the cultural difference of the people of both *India Orientalis* and *India Occidentalis*, and Africa too was submitted to a similar, if perhaps less visible, symbolizing discourse.

Yet the link between otherness and sexuality, as described above, was not a deterministic one. The occurrence, in other words, of sodomitical practices among people of the New Worlds was seen only as a sign of failing morality.

It presented same-sex praxis as the reflection of a socially constructed behavioural code, rather than as a characteristic that originated from the physical constitution of these people or of a minority within. It was racialist only in so far as it interpreted this social code as a sign of inferiority.

The essentially moralistic tenor of Early Modern discourse was upheld by the Catholic church's rhetoric of sin and redemption when the Inquisition spread its tentacles across the Atlantic and Pacific oceans. Sodomy trials, within the realm of Puritan colonial America, were hardly different as they also defined male-to-male praxis as a sinful act.

The tropicalization of 'abominable sin'[114]

The historiography of the Inquisition in the overseas colonies reveals that it upheld the perception of sodomy as an act that everyone was potentially capable of performing. It included all forms of non-procreative sexual behaviour that were condemned by the Catholic church because they did not encompass the expression of matrimonial love and procreation.[115]

In America, relatively few Indians, blacks, or people of mixed blood were tried for having committed sodomy. This is remarkable, when compared with the initial insistence by Europeans on the ubiquity of same-sex practices among indigenous people. The statistical record indeed shows no disproportionate figures for any of the ethnic groups, who were put to trial for sodomy. Due to a lack of evidence about the population's ethnic composition in the cities of Mexico and Puebla, it is impossible, says Gruzinski, to see if an individual's ethnic origin did influence his risk of being tried by the Inquisition for the nefarious sin of sodomy.[116]

If quantitative data leave us guessing at the historical effect of a people's ethnic background on the colonizer's perception of their sexuality, qualitative evidence seems to suggest that this was hardly substantial. The Inquisitorial records did not adopt a different rhetoric when identifying, describing and evaluating sodomitical acts performed by any of the non-white males. Confession manuals even reflected a reluctance by the authorities to address the issue of sodomy in front of the Indians, if only to prevent them from considering it as an option.[117] Mott and Vainfas present a relatively low number of trials, involving Indians, blacks, *mestiços*, *mulatos*, or *mamelucos* in colonial Brazil, yet interpret this as the outcome of an only minor interest of the authorities in the sexual life of Indians and slaves.[118] In general, the verdict was in no significant way more severe than it was for men of European origin. In fact, it remained fairly mild.[119]

It would be erroneous, however, to assume that ethnic difference remained insignificant at all times. The accusation of *tivira* – a Tupinambà term for the passive role in same-sex encounters between men – of an Indian in Bahia in 1591 clearly indicates that the Inquisition was by no means unaware of the presence of sodomy among the Indians. A similar 'ethnic' explanation was given, also in Bahia, to the behaviour of a black slave and cobbler's apprentice, Francisco Manicongo, who refused to wear men's clothes and was accused of passive sodomy. The accuser described how, in Angola and the Congo, men wore a loincloth with the ends in front and leaving an opening behind. He then continued by emphasizing that such a role was actually known among the African people – 'These passives are called *jimbandaa* in the language of Angola and the Congo, which means passive sodomite' – and considered the black slave's wearing of such a loincloth sufficient evidence for accusing him.[120]

Other cases too reveal an ongoing awareness of the presumed ethnic signature of sexual mores, yet it remained marginal in the light of the church's universalist rhetoric of sin and redemption. Occasionally the ethnic dimension of deviant sexuality was stressed more emphatically, especially when it accompanied a more far-reaching threat to religious and social order. Obviously this was the case in 1633 in Tolu, near Cartagena de Indias, where a large group of Afro-American women had engaged in witchcraft 'embracing Lucifer in the shape of a goat, drawing a cross on the ground with their left foot and then dragging their behinds across it, and then with demons as their "companions and godparents", having anal intercourse'.[121] Stuart Schwartz emphasizes how the Inquisition of Cartagena stressed the women's black identity despite the clearly European script of their heretic rituals. Yet he also points at how such apparently ethnic rhetoric was inspired by the Spanish fear of Portuguese domination in the port city of Cartagena, where a large African presence coincided with a climate of political dissidence and religious deviance.[122]

The incidental evidence of an ethnic explanation of same-sex behaviour in the Inquisitorial records of America clearly contrasted with the ongoing rhetoric of sodomy's affinity with religious heresy. The ethnic background of an individual was thought relevant only incidentally or was to camouflage motives of a political or religious kind. The discontinuity with earlier discourse on American Indian and Afro-American sexual morality, where same-sex praxis was believed to abound, should be explained rather as the outcome of successful Christianization and of the regulation of indigenous sexuality that accompanied it.

An apparently very different picture can be drawn from European experience in Asia. Mid-sixteenth-century documents from the Inquisition in both Goa and Manila reveal a sharp awareness of an apparently widespread practice of sodomy and a strong determination to wipe it out.[123]

Jonathan Spence explains the Inquisition's harsh intervention in the Far East as, in the eyes of Catholics, a just reaction to the widespread and public presence of same-sex practices in a climate that inspired men to extreme lasciviousness. Yet the contrast with the Catholic church's apparent reluctance to punish indigenous sodomitical behaviour in America calls for clarification. Not only was same-sex behaviour current among both Indians and Afro-Americans, but climatological circumstances in the tropical and subtropical regions, if relevant, ought to have called for an equally severe policy of repression by the Inquisition if Spence is right.

One may argue that the greater influence in Asia of Jesuits like Francis Xavier, Matteo Ricci and Alessandro Valignano, as opposed to Franciscans and Dominicans in America, accounts for a harsher oppression of sodomy. Surely, this may sound plausible as the Jesuits indeed made themselves the watchdogs of sexuality to an extent that it became suspicious in the eyes of the Enlightenment's *Philosophes*. They were said to have been involved in the very behaviour that they so fiercely condemned, 'homosexual scandals' *avant-la-lettre*,[124] and became far more reticent, as a result, about Chinese sodomy. In order to prevent further incriminations, states Donald Guy, they simply eliminated descriptions of male-to-male sexuality from their subsequent editions of the *Lettres édifiantes*: 'The Society already had to sustain enough criticism and charges against this tendency [i.e. to dwell on indigenous sexuality] and was wary, lest Voltaire, or another like him, seize on such incidents as would prove more conducive to laughter and ridicule than to good works.'[125]

The publications by Trigault, Lecomte, Du Halde and Grosier, all Jesuits,[126] offered an altogether very virtuous image of China, that resembled contemporary descriptions by Catholics of the American Indian. The Jesuits' self-imposed censorship was pragmatic, of course, and did not change their intolerance of sodomy. But this was shared with Dominicans and Franciscans alike, not only in South-East Asia, but also in the *reducciones* of America.[127]

Therefore other motives must have nurtured the unusual fervour of the Inquisition in the Far East. Up to now, far too little research has been done on the history of sexual praxis and discourse in Early Modern Asia to even formulate an adequate hypothesis. Yet it seems that, if the Inquisition's policy in this region was indeed disproportionately severe, it was not merely congruous with the widespread and open practice of sodomy itself.

Perhaps the Inquisition's outspoken intolerance towards sodomy in the Far East can best be explained as the outcome of an only partially successful campaign against competing religions, Islam, Hinduism and Buddhism. Especially in the inaccessible lands of China and Japan, it was a frustrating experience, when compared to the achievements of Christianization in Latin America. The very presence of same-sex practices within the core of imperial courts and Buddhist convents as much as their public visibility in the streets gave them a particularly polemic aura within the European struggle for cultural and religious hegemony. The regulation of indigenous sexuality thus remained an urgent matter in Asia, where the West managed insufficiently to impose its own religion.

Puritanism, sodomy and ethnicity[128]

The enforcement of sodomy laws in colonial America was similar to the situation in Britain. Anal penetration had to be proved for a defendant to be convicted. The precariousness of family life in the small, rural settlements of the colonies did not substantially change this, not even within circles of a more extremist Puritanical creed.[129]

The physical segregation of the Native American population from the European settlements evidently accounts for the absence of sodomy trials involving Indians. 'Rather', says Williams, 'than ruling Indian populations in an empire, as the Spanish did in Latin America, the English pushed the natives out of the way.'[130] The conviction of African slaves for having committed sodomy was no more severe initially than for whites. I have mentioned earlier the one known case of Jan Creoli and his ten-year-old mate, Manuel Congo, who were tried in the New Netherlands. Both Higgin-botham and Katz have demonstrated how, by the beginning of the eighteenth century, Quaker legislation in Pennsylvania proscribed divergent penalties for blacks, who had engaged in sodomy. The laws of 1700 and 1706 were the first ones in America that abolished the death penalty, yet they provided life imprisonment for whites, and reinstalled the death sentence for blacks.[131] 'It is ... a matter of some irony', Katz comments, 'that the most lenient colonial sodomy laws ... should also be the first to formalize the inferior status of blacks guilty of sodomy.' In 1712, Mingo alias Cocke Negro was executed for 'forcible Buggery'.[132]

On a more general level, these legal changes revealed an increasingly racist rhetoric about blacks, whose sexuality was seen as threatening, perhaps not so much for sodomy[133] as for the presumed insecurity of the white plantation owners' wives in the presence of the black male slaves.[134] The relative paucity of sodomy trials of blacks suggests that no extraordinary propensity existed to depict them as sodomitical, which conforms with the relative indifference both in Latin America and the Caribbean that I have described earlier. Again it is not clear if this was the outcome of an obstinately upheld image of black masculinity for the purpose of slave labour, or of a factual improbability of same-sex relations either among blacks or, less probable still in a North American context of segregation, between blacks and whites. No source evidence allows for a conclusive statement, alas, and interpretations are doomed to remain speculative. The legal discrimination of blacks, however, indicates that the black man's act of sodomy was considered more offensive than the white man's, which corroborated the contemporary rhetoric about the cultural difference of blacks.

The preceding evidence again illustrates how western religious discourse on same-sex practices in the New Worlds was intimately related to matters of morality. The dominant influence, despite the ongoing antagonism between Catholics and Protestants, of Christianity overseas kept the debate on sodomy largely within the realm of sinful acts. In the Americas (and the coastal regions of Africa), the native population's 'difference' was somewhat annulled as it allowed itself to be converted to Christianity and gave up sodomy in exchange for redemption. But the fight against indigenous sodomy remained a most vivid cornerstone of European religious policy in territories that, like the world of Islam, opposed it more or less successfully. The factual history of the European clergy's unequal successes thus may have nurtured the belief that people were indeed of different kind. The simultaneous awareness of the failure to eradicate sexual sin may have tightened the knot between constructions of cultural identity and a discourse of sexual difference. The imperatives of slavery, finally, contained the germs of a similar entanglement, within European discourse, of race and sexuality.

But other developments too pushed European discourse about non-western culture towards matters of sexuality. A nascent trope of cultural relativism emphasized rather than obliterated the initial evidence of ethnic difference and cultural diversity. It stressed the different attitudes of the people of the New World towards the body and sexuality, as revealed in nudity, courting habits, marriage patterns, and gender roles. At first a deliberating alternative to the hegemonizing rhetoric of Christianity, it soon proved to contain the germs of a new mode of hierarchical thinking. Guided by the newly rising ideas about human nature, it would drastically reduce the scope of a social and sexual Utopia at the costs either of entire indigenous populations or of minorities within them. Same-sex behaviour, still called 'sodomy', was banned from *felicitas paradisii* yet again.

Europe's quest for paradise

As man gradually made himself the master of creation, he also set sail in search for the human race in an unspoilt state. The original reports, dating from the days of discovery and exploration of the New World yet absorbed by Christian ideology, were reinterpreted, along with new, differently inspired narratives of newly discovered territories. Sexuality, previously seen as pagan, would now be included in the new definition of humanity. Yet, little consensus existed on whether sexual variety across the world ought to reinforce cultural relativism or lead to more precise definitions of sexuality's natural boundaries instead. Especially when assessing new information on unfamiliar or marginal forms of sexual behaviour, Europe was in fact confronted with the Janusface of sex.

The impulse to initiate discourse originated not solely from a need to oppose religious doctrine, nor did proto-Enlightenment writers, who countered both Reformatory and Counter-Reformatory ideology, monopolize the virtues of comparison and relativity. It was the New World itself as well that compelled European observers to adjust their representations of human sexuality, as they 'recognized' phenomena that had until then remained somewhat mythological.

The widespread evidence of cross-gender roles in particular proved most challenging. Men, dressing and behaving like women, and assuming female roles, both socially and – but not always – sexually, were virtually unknown in Europe. Surely, travesty had remained a pastime within the frivolous confines of the aristocracy.[135] And in most European countries, there were *castrati*, whose 'unmanly' status in no ways prevented them from becoming the most worshipped protagonists of musical theatre until the late eighteenth century.[136] But apart from this small minority, eunuchs were known in Europe as part of ancient civilizations.

Like eunuchs and *castrati* in ancient times, those adopting a cross-gender roles in the New World occasionally enjoyed great social prestige. Yet they were not emasculated, which made their profile different from familiar categories in the Old World. And, while this cross-gender behaviour did not necessarily embrace (passive) sexual relations with men, it was often claimed that such was the case among many an indigenous population of the New World.

Cross-gender roles in American Indian societies were commonly called 'berdaches', the English variant of the French word *bardache*.[137] This, in turn, had developed from the Italian words *bardassa* and *bardascia*, both derivatives from the Persian *bardag*, a young slave. In Early Modern France, a *bardache* was identical to the passive, male partner, termed 'catamite' in Renaissance English or *pathicus* in Latin. The word was first used in an American context by French missionaries and explorers in the Gulf of Saint Lawrence to describe Indian men, who dressed and behaved as if they were women. Other writers too had seen similar individuals in other regions of the American continent and had associated their female behaviour with the abominable sin of sodomy.[138]

De Las Casas, ready to defend the Indian's moral integrity, believed that such allegations were wrongly inspired by their observations of cross-dressing men and tried to detach sexual praxis from a vestimentary role. To him, cross-dressing did not immediately imply sodomitical acts.[139] In principle he was right, even when he referred to the single well-known story, described by López de Gomara in 1552, of Vasco Nuñez de Balboa's assassination, by mastiffs, of some presumed sodomites in the Panamá region. But his interpretation remained marginal to the overwhelming majority of authors, who assumed a relation between sexual passivity and effeminacy, and claimed that the cross-gender behaviour of some Indians did indeed go together with sodomitical sin.

More problematic, however, were observations of berdaches who combined male and female characteristics in one. Cabeza de Vaca, for example, witnessed a 'marriage' between two men, one of whom dressed like a woman, in the Gulf of Mexico. Such *hombres amarionados, impotentes* seem to be commonly accepted, he claimed, surprised only at how they were nevertheless physically strong: 'they are bowmen and carry great weights ... Their limbs are longer than those of other men and they are taller also; they support great cargos (tiran arco y llevan muy gran carga ... y son más membrudos que los otros hombres y más altos; sufren muy grandes cargas)'.[140] The coincidence of masculine and feminine traits can also be found in a description of a berdache by Jacques Lemoyne de Morgues: 'There are many hermaphrodites, who are both man and woman, and who are hated by the Indians as well; because they are robust and strong, they are used to carry loads in the place of oxes (Frequentes istic sunt Hermaphroditi utriusque naturae participes, ipsis etiam Indis exosi; eorum tamen opera, quod robusti et validi sint, ad onera ferenda utuntur jumentorum loco).' This text was first published in the *Grands Voyages* of Théodore de Bry,[141] who also included an engraving, made after a watercolour by Lemoyne de Morgues himself, representing two hermaphrodites, who carry a wounded man away from the battlefield. The bodies of both look virile, yet their facial features and hair suggest an outspoken femininity.

Another remarkable document, in this context, was left to us by the missionary Louis Hennepin:

There are numerous hermaphrodites among them. They usually have more women ... [and] shamelessly commit the sin against nature. They have boys, whom they dress like girls, because they use them for this abominable sin. These boys only do women's work and abstain from hunting as well as warfare. They are very superstitious ... [142]

The description of cross-gender roles – 'des garçons à l'équipage des filles' – immediately follows Hennepin's claim that many hermaphrodites exist in American Indian society. But the use of a capital 'H' may well indicate that a classical reference was implied, which allowed for 'locating' the newly discovered ethnographic reality within the cognitive framework of an Early Modern European mind.

How original were the numerous other descriptions of American Indian cross-gender roles?[143] Did these narratives spring from the authors' independent observation, or did they reflect their need, as with Hennepin, to identify gender-crossing behaviour within the mould of already existing constructions of 'hermaphrodites' in Europe itself? Again, the question cannot be answered straightforwardly. But certainly, some authors felt compelled to fit the ethnographic evidence into the mould of the mythological hermaphrodite.

In Europe, positive and negative images of hermaphroditism had proliferated one beside the other since classical antiquity. The former, mythological, represented a spiritual and moral ideal, uniting the good characteristics of both the male and the female sex.[144] The latter figured within teratology and reduced the essence of hermaphroditism to an apparently simultaneous and thus anomalous presence of male and female genitalia. Their significance grew as hermaphroditism became an urgent legal problem in the seventeenth century.[145]

The mixture of fascination and horror in Early Modern texts seemingly reflected an uncertainty about how to interpret the berdache's ambiguous outlook. Their outstanding role in ritual surely indicated their proximity to a higher, metaphysical ideal, yet this was easily annulled by the simultaneous observations of their sodomitical practices. And they were men and, in the anatomical sense of the word, not hermaphrodites. They were 'androgynous' in so far as they assumed female social and, frequently, sexual roles, notwithstanding their masculine body and genitalia.

Earlier I reviewed European reports on cross-gender roles, such as *quimbanda*, *chibados* and *tsecats*, in parts of Subsaharan Africa. In Asia too, such roles were not absent, if less prominent within the more dominant narrative trope on Asian 'effeminacy'.[146] In the Philippines, the Spanish father Juan de Plascencia had already pointed out men who were dressed like women in 1589. Other references to these *bayoguin* can be found, next, in a document of 1738 by the friar Juan Francisco de San Antonio: 'effeminate men ... inclined to being women and to all the matters of this feminine sex'.[147] The Flemish merchant and adventurer Jacques de Coutre, when visiting the court of the Great Indian Moghul Jahanghir (1605–27) in Agra, saw people who were neither men nor women. These *yzaras* received money from elder colleagues 'of the same kind' and lived together in groups. He continued by describing how men were recruited and castrated when they proved 'impotent'. They then were abducted to the Moghul's court, where they would serve as *badarnos*: 'When they know if a man is impotent ... they oblige him to dress like a woman so that he will join his group (of equals). If, by accident, he refuses, they bring him to a prostitute and order him to have sex with her in their presence in order to see if he is impotent or not. If he is, then he is caught and fully castrated after which he is taken away, no matter if he is a lord or great man of the empire. All those men serve [the moghul] as *Badarnos*' (my italics).[148] The word *badarnos* is wrongly presented by the editors as a local, 'emic' term, equivalent of 'hermaphrodites'. Very probably, de Coutre meant *bardaje*, a term current in Europe by then, as I indicated above, for a man who engages in passive anal intercourse.[149]

Along with the demythification of hermaphrodites that sprang from narratives of cross-gender sexuality, an increased awareness grew of the relativity of European sexual theory. In the mind of many writers, the berdache and its equivalents in Asia and Africa not only challenged one's sense of moral orthodoxy, but also competed with the traditional belief that sodomy was an act that virtually everyone was capable of committing.

Observations of cross-gender roles did not, of course, replace stories about a presumably ubiquitous sodomitical praxis among many a people of the New World, but they challenged it by defining sodomy within the confines of a minority. New to Europeans also was the social phenomenon of men who adopted a passive sexual role and were both recognized and recognizable as such. Whereas in Europe, men who engaged in sodomy had hardly been visible, the American berdache was clearly visible within the social landscape of his tribe as a member of a well-defined minority.

It is important here to stress that the ethnographic framing of sodomy within the image of a minority went hand in hand with an emphasis upon femininity and sexual passivity, while the age-structured character of many male-to-male sexual relations was often marginalized if not omitted entirely. It thus paved the way not only for a discursive shift from 'sodomy' to 'sodomites', but also for a definition, often expressed in the word 'hermaphrodites', of the latter as feminine and sexually passive. Sodomy, briefly, was increasingly claimed to be only the passive partner's vice, and became tributary to a discourse about gender identity. The representation of sodomy as closely tied to an effeminate, sexually passive minority also constituted a major shift away from traditional, Christian discourse about an ubiquitous, ever luring sodomitical sin. It underlined the relativity of Christianity's sexual categories when applied to an unfamiliar world and made simple ascriptions of abominable sin to the culturally 'other' less direct.

In Europe itself, the social reality of sodomitical praxis was also changing gradually.[150] A new rhetoric about 'sodomites' arose, replacing the secular narrative of the act of 'sodomy', and taking on its shape as subcultures of 'sodomites' grew more visible in the urban centres of Early Modern Europe. Similar with ethnographic discourse was not only the gradual shift of attention from 'sodomitical acts' to 'sodomites', but also the incipient prominence of gender-structured sodomitical relations. If the cognitive transition in narratives on non-western sodomy facilitated the institution of discourse about same-sex praxis at home cannot be confirmed, neither can it be excluded. It may well be that knowledge about cross-gender roles in the Americas, Africa and Asia was conducive to identifications of sodomy with femininity on a social level, and with passivity on a sexual level. Cross-cultural evidence may actually have played a role, albeit limited, in the cognitive emphasis, becoming visible at the dawn of the Enlightenment, upon the gender-crossing and passive partner in same-sex relations, while the active, masculine partner was gradually less focused upon.

Before studying how this developed through time, it is necessary to portray yet another dimension, for, whereas ethnographic evidence from the New

World altered European conceptualization of sexuality, it was sexuality that in its turn helped to reshape the Old World's new map of mankind.

Sodomy, hermaphrodites and the mapping of mankind

Sexual variety – and notably the indigenous peoples' attitudes towards it – challenged the Christian notion of a single human race. Soon it became a vehicle for classification for authors who, in contrast, emphasized human diversity. Such intellectual departures were still very far removed from any comprehensive taxonomy, yet they clearly anticipated this by focusing on a people's physical identity rather than on its culture. Nor was the explanatory role of gender as yet clearly defined. But two major significant tropes can be distinguished at an early stage. The first consisted of an assessment of an entire people's position on a gradual scale of masculinity, lending metaphorical status to gender in the mapping of mankind. The other, not seldom intertwined with the first yet different, weighed the relative share of deviant personalities within a population and represented it as indicative, metonymically, of the latter's cultural or, gradually, racial status.

Whereas earlier the non-western people's behaviour had offered a criterion to Europeans for defining and evaluating its moral *alterité*, it was gradually seen also as an indicator of physical status. A new 'scientific' rigour, given to definitions of male and female gender by the new anatomical physiology of the genitalia, nourished initial speculation about the presumably 'unmasculine' nature of non-western people alongside other paradigmatic schemes, such as the doctrine of human temperaments, that would become instrumental to later theories of race.[151]

Asian people were depicted most frequently as feminine, and this from an early stage. Such allegations went hand in hand with a rhetoric about an almost ubiquitous practice of sodomy, as I described briefly above. It was often explained as the outcome of a debilitating climate that had made the entire population weak and effeminate.

Gradually, the American Indian too was described by some as 'feminine'. Gabriel Sagard claimed that 'one can hardly distinguish the face of a man from that of a woman (on ne peut presque discerner le visage d'un homme avec celui d'une femme)' and described the lack of facial hair (beard, moustache) among American men as a sign of feeble masculinity, equally applicable to Oriental men.[152] Father García equally read the lack of facial hair as a physical shortcoming of Indian men, and explained it as resulting from climatological circumstance. As with others, the logic behind his conjecture was very much *ad hoc* as he neglected to specify which aspects of climate conduced to an effeminization of the Indian race. It leaves today's historian wondering if he believed the impact of the climate in the high Andes to be different from the one of the subtropical coastal regions on both the Atlantic and Pacific side of the continent.[153]

Martin de Murúa pointed out the 'limp and meagre limbs' of the Indians.[154] Bernabé Cobo confirmed the debilitating effect of the climate on the American Indian race: 'As the weather weakens and dampens the body's limbs, their flesh is very soft and delicate (Como la flema hace blanda y húmeda la sustancia de los miembros del cuerpo tienen muy blandas y delicadas carnes).' Still, as his work, written in 1653, remained unpublished until 1891–93, it can hardly have had any influence on writers to come.[155]

Initially, the image of 'unmanly' Indians fitted within a more general discourse of America's degeneracy, even before it was given an evolutionary dimension by Buffon.[156] The population's physical debility thus reflected a flora and fauna that was said to be inferior and infertile. Yet, as people of mixed-blood (*mestizo, criollo*) came to represent a higher percentage of the total population through time, miscegenation itself was claimed to be debilitating and a 'feminine' physique was projected upon its offspring as well.[157]

Apparently, the African people were not so easily depicted as 'feminine', yet it remains unclear why European observers felt less tempted to do so. Perhaps the robust physical appearance of many African ethnic populations precluded this. But, as I pointed out earlier, a study should be made of the impact of the slave trade and slavery upon the Early Modern construction of black sexuality, as an image of black male effeminacy was probably incompatible with the requirements of a slave labour force. Similarly, one ought to study how constructions of black femininity were affected by the slave economy's need both for new offspring (fertility) and for strong physical power (productivity).

Parallel with attempts to situate non-western populations on a masculinity/femininity scale, speculation arose on the symptomatic character of sexually deviant individuals for the entire population's physical health. Such a theory was a substantial departure from earlier times, when sodomy and eunuchism were seen as proof of a people's immorality and barbarism. Hermaphrodites, now given a visible profile, potentially became representative of the foreign people's natural or, for that matter, 'unnatural' status and were represented as a metonymy of a foreign people's identity.

I have described how the social and vestimentary ambiguity of so-called 'hermaphrodites' of the New World were presented as the pendant of sexual disorder. Far removed from the mythological image of a human being, that combined both male and female qualities into a spiritual union, they were now the exponent of confusion and regression among the people of the New World.[158] Jean-Pierre Guicciardi has commented that this discursive development, opposing the hermaphrodite's anomalous identity to the normal one of man and woman, corresponded to a deeply rooted division, in the

European mind, between masculinity and femininity.[159] Though no doubt true, it is clear also that the European debate about the New World's hermaphrodites may have intensified the need for clear definitions of the male and female sex in their turn. Historiography, at the present, seems to underestimate the impact of ethnographic data on European discourse about human sexuality, in particular on the biological construction of male and female identity, that was current in the mid-eighteenth century. The problem of hermaphrodites, then, was not brought about by ambiguous genital constitution – a rarity then as it is today – but by their social and sexual behaviour. Their trespassing of one's biological sex, more than anything else, threatened Europeans, who felt increasingly compelled to pin sexual and social roles down to biological constitution.

The intellectual confusion between anatomical aberration and deviant behaviour, before hermaphroditism was refuted in 1741 in James Parsons' *Mechanical and critical enquiry into the nature of hermaphrodites*,[160] actually allowed hermaphroditism to represent the cultural 'otherness' of people in the New World, along with other phenomena, that were also read as signifiers of alterity. Eunuchism for centuries had symbolized a different kind of morality, and clitoridectomy was made a vector of difference since European authors such as Ambroise Paré[161] and John Bulwer[162] had read about it in the writings of the Arab geographer Leo Africanus. The actual practices of emasculation and female circumcision were seen as more revealing of cultural difference than their objects, the eunuch and the circumcised woman, and together with the cross-gender behaviour of hermaphrodites were presented as *metaphorical* instances of the 'otherness' of people either in America or in Africa and the Middle East. In Europe, both practices were widely known, 'but only in the context of what other people did'.[163]

From the early eighteenth century onwards, however, a shifting emphasis 're-located' the immorality from the act of emasculation and circumcision upon the emasculated and circumcised. In 1707 the eunuch himself became the object of scientific scrutiny in Charles Ancillon's *Traité des eunuques*.[164] Seen until then as a monstrous curiosity, he was now described as the 'witness of a sexual ambiguity, independent of any surgical manipulation', as a looking-glass, really, for new speculations on the biological roots of sexual identity.[165] Similarly, clitoridectomy was explained as a measure against the excessive lust and lewdness of women, who suffered from clitoral hypertrophy especially in the hot climate of Africa and the Middle East. Often, so it was presumed, these women also engaged in sexual relations with one another, which indirectly tightened the knot between discourse on the sexual lasciviousness of non-western women and discourse on female-to-female sex.[166]

Hermaphrodites, eunuchs and hypertrophic women were thus presented as the personified *indices* of the 'otherness' of the people amidst whom they lived. Here it is crucial to understand how moral responsibility is transferred from the surrounding society to a minority within it, allowing for the latter's representation as a *metonymy* rather than a mere metaphor of difference.

Not all of Europe's Early Modern narrative about cultural difference was of a negative tenor, as is known. As the mirror image of the mobilization through metonymy of sexuality in discourse on cultural inferiority, a counter-rhetoric arose that instead presented indigenous sexuality as a sign of cultural superiority. To some, the New World's vice became the New World's virtue.

The publication in 1728 of the *Moeurs des sauvages Américains comparées aux moeurs des premiers temps* by Joseph-François Lafitau illustrated the ambiguity that had arisen about the widespread evidence of same-sex practices across the world. The author included an apology for the male friendships – *amitiés particulières*[167] – current in most regions of the American continent: 'The *athenrofera* or "particular friendships" among youngsters, that are more or less equally spread from one end of America to the other, are one of the most interesting aspects of their morality because they are related to one of the most curious products of Antiquity ... (*L'athenrofera*, ou les *amitiés particulières* entre les jeunes gens, qui se trouvent établies à peu près de la même manière d'un bout de l'Amérique à l'autre, sont un des points les plus intéressants de leurs moeurs, parce qu'elles renferment un article des plus curieux de l'Antiquité ...).' But he hastily emphasized that it was, in the end, very different from vice: 'These bonds of friendship among the Savages of North America are exempt from any suspicion either about the actual existence or about the mere possibility of real vice (Ces liaisons d'amitié, parmi les Sauvages de l'Amérique septentrionale, ne laissent aucun soupçon de vice apparent, quoiqu'il y ait, ou qu'il puisse y avoir beaucoup de vice réel).'[168]

On the one hand, Lafitau was a late exponent of a cultural relativism *à la* Montaigne, and he highly esteemed male-to-male friendships and compared them to the classical homoerotic bonds known from mythology and literature, between Zeus and Iolaus, Theseus and Pylades, Achilles and Patrocles. At the same time, he stressed how such friendships were, not infrequently, part of an initiation rite, which made them, in his eyes, more acceptable.[169]

Whereas the author's willingness to acknowledge male-to-male bonding, when not sexual, departed significantly from a Christian tradition, it simultaneously embraced new ideas about orthodox sexuality. Lafitau thus described the cross-gender role of the Native American berdache at first in neutral terms:

Wouldn't these be the same people as the Asians, worshippers of Cybele, or the Orientals about whom Julius Firmicus spoke and who knew priests of either the goddess of Phrygia or Venus Urania, who dressed like women, tried to look female, perfumed themselves and disguised their real sex underneath clothes of those whom they tried to imitate?[170]

Yet, while linking evidence from the New World with classical tradition, Lafitau speculated on the degenerative effect of sexual anomaly:

Although the spirit of religion that makes them embrace such a state makes them look like extraordinary men, they are nevertheless fallen men in the eyes of the Savages, just like the priests of Venus Urania and Cybele in ancient times; and despite the fact that they actually provoked the disdain by delivering themselves to scandalous passions, or that the ignorance of Europeans about the causes of their condition instilled ominous suspicions against them, the fact is that suspicions arose concerning the bad nature of such impulses.[171]

Lafitau's analysis of the changed attitudes towards the berdache among American Indians was highly ambiguous, as it ascribed these to both the spontaneous reactions from within their communities and the intervention of the European colonizers. By doing so, Lafitau indirectly justified the infamous repression of 'sodomites' by Vasco Nuñez de Balboa, first related in 1552 by Lopez de Gomara[172] and reiterated in narratives of the New World since. His message, however, was indisputable: if any place at all was to be reserved for cross-gender roles, by no means can it be accompanied by a homosexual praxis either within or outside the context of ritual.

Lafitau's *Moeurs* illustrates how sexuality had become a cornerstone of European constructions of a social utopia. It already embraced some elements of the Enlightenment theory of human sexuality. But it was in many ways a synopsis of the difficulties arising with the definition of the *bon sauvage* in former years. Sodomy was gradually incorporated within the realm of the primitive, that is: of what is 'no longer' acceptable to mankind. It reflected well how sexual variety, as perceived worldwide, at first challenged European attitudes, but in the end was absorbed by the new rhetoric of sexual normality.

To a large majority in Europe, the relatively widespread presence of sodomy, along with other 'vices' among the people of the New World, contributed to the fall from grace of the American *bon sauvage*. 'The counter-image . . . of barbarism', says Duviols, 'will partially bury the angelic vision that preceded (La contre-image . . . de la barbarie va partiellement recouvrir la vision angélique précédente).'[173] A new paradise was called for as a result. Tahiti would be its name, and same-sex practices, though common in Polynesian society, were silenced in the euphoric texts about the newly discovered *Nouvelle Cythère*.

To a small minority, on the other hand, the reality of same-sex praxis in the New World seemed far less offensive since they perceived it as an antidote to mainstream society's condemnation of sodomy.[174] I will describe in the following chapter how the distinction, initiated by Lafitau, between male bonding and plain sodomy would soon dominate the subcultural discourse of sodomites that became visible during the Enlightenment. It embraced an idealization, a desexualization of Greek παιδερασθεια, while reducing the symbolic and cultural dimension of same-sex practices in the New World to a mere game of sexual gratification.

Inevitably, this chapter has addressed the issue of morality, as it describes how the apparent innocence of same-sex sexual relations among many populations of the New Worlds challenged the colonizers' preconceived ideas about sexual sin. Along with nudity, polygamy and other sexual practices, sodomy was soon suppressed, however, in an all-encompassing strategy of sexual regulation by the colonizing authorities. Soon, indigenous sexuality was regulated with an Inquisitorial zeal, that was comparable to both Catholic and Protestant policies at home.

Yet, whereas the outcome of moral debate remained undecided at the dawn of the Enlightenment, there had been intellectual developments that significantly altered Europe's representation of same-sex behaviour overseas. Cognitive shifts had taken place. The traditional, Christian doctrine against the sinful 'act' of sodomy was juxtaposed to new, proto-ethnological constructions of 'different' sexualities. With the shift from a Medieval 'universalist' rhetoric of sin and redemption to an Early Modern model of multiple sexual roles, there was an incipient tendency to tighten the rope between sexual praxis and gender identity. A newly defined essence of gender ambiguity was attached to 'sodomite' identity as well, while age-structured homosexual relations were deemed to be less relevant.

Along with these changes, springing from the physical circumstances of exploration, observation and cultural policy overseas and from intellectual innovation at home, another discursive fact came into being, that consolidated sexuality as a parameter of civilization and, eventually, as a criterion within the nascent racialist theory of humanity. The role of same-sex praxis within this new, hierarchical thinking differed significantly from before as it not only offered an indirect guideline for positioning people on a scale of masculinity, but it also operated as a textual *metonymy* of a people's physical and civilizational status. Thus began an incipient 'geography of perversion' and, parallel to it, a 'geography of desire'.

Notes

1.   'L'on trouve parmi les Illinois quantité d'hermaphrodites; ils portent l'habit de femme, mais ils font indifferemment usage des deux Sexes. Ces Illinois ont un malheureux penchant pour la Sodomie, aussi bien que les autres Sauvages qui habitent aux environs du Fleuve de Mississipi.' B. de Lahontan, *Nouveaux voyages dans l'Amérique Septentrionale* (The Hague, 1703), p. 142.
2.   J. Swift, 'A voyage to the Houyhnhnms' *Gulliver's Travels*, ed. H. Davis (Oxford, 1965 (1726)), IV, 7, p. 264.
3.   S. Greenblatt, *Marvellous Possessions. The Wonder of the New World* (Chicago and London, 1991).
4.   This was in fact inherent to a Medieval notion of 'unnatural sin', of which everyone was thought to be capable. It was not considered substantially different from other non-

procreative forms of sexual behaviour. See D. F. Greenberg, *The Construction of Homosexuality* (Chicago and London, 1988), p. 263: 'Like all men, he was a sinner, but he was to be forgiven if he repented. He was not a "homosexual" – a distinct type of person – but someone who had engaged in a homosexual act.'

5. On the destruction of Sodom and Gomorrah, often interpreted 'as a demonstration of God's wrath towards homosexuality' (D.F. Greenberg, *Construction of Homosexuality*, p. 136), see the Hebrew Bible, Deut. 29: 23, 32. Also, see other relevant passages in Isa. 1: 9–10, 3: 9, 13: 19; Jer. 23: 14, 49: 18, 50: 40; Lam. 4: 6; Ezek. 16: 46–56; Amos 4: 11; Zeph. 2: 9.

6. See New Testament, Matt. 5: 22, 19: 3–12; 1 Cor. 6: 9–10, 7: 1–7; 1 Tim. 1: 9–10; Old Testament, Leviticus 18: 22 and 20: 13.

7. For a description of changing Christian doctrine, see, among others, D. Bailey, *Homosexuality and the Western Christian Tradition* (London, 1955); J. Boswell, *Christianity, Social Tolerance and Homosexuality* (Chicago and London, 1980); V. L. Bullough, *Sexual Variation in Society and History* (New York, 1976), pp. 74–86, 159–96; M. Goodich, *The Unmentionable Vice* (Santa Barbara, 1979); and D. F. Greenberg, *Construction of Homosexuality*, pp. 218–34, 250–5, 261–8, 269–72, 280–92, 302–46.

8. See C. Courouve, *Vocabulaire de l'homosexualité masculine* (Paris, 1985), p. 70.

9. On this complex history, see J. Boswell, *Christianity, Social Tolerance, and Homosexuality*, pp. 283–4.

10. See B. Bennassar, *L'inquisition espagnole (XV°–XIX° siècles)* (Paris, 1979), pp. 339 ff., and A. Redondo, 'Le discours d'exclusion des "déviants" ', in A. Redondo (ed.), *Le problème de l'exclusion en Espagne (XVI°–XVII° siècles)* (Paris, 1983), p. 43. See also R. Carrasco, *Inquisición y represión sexual en Valencia* (Barcelona, 1985) and M. B. Perry, *Crime and Society in Early Modern Seville* (Hanover, NH, 1980).

11. By 'pederasty' I mean transgenerational sexual relations, either between a man and a prepubescent boy (paedophilia) or between a man and an adolescent (ephebophilia). Historical sources often do not reveal which of these was meant, as the distinction is in fact fairly recent. On the word's complex lexicography in different languages, see C. Courouve, *Vocabulaire de l'homosexualité masculine*, pp. 169–78, and W. R. Dynes, *Homolexis* (New York, 1985), pp. 109–10.

12. S. O. Murray, 'The Mamelukes', in S. O. Murray (ed.), *Cultural Diversity and Homosexualities* (New York, 1987), pp. 213–19.

13. See J. Schirmann, 'The ephebe in Medieval Hebrew poetry', *Sefarad*, 15 (1955), 55–68; S. D. Goitein, 'The sexual mores of the common people', in A. L. Al-Sayyid-Marsot (ed.), *Society and the Sexes in Medieval Islam* (Malibu, 1979), pp. 43–62; N. Roth, ' "Deal gently with the young man": Love of boys in Medieval Hebrew poetry of Spain', *Speculum*, 57 (1982), 20–51; H. Leneman, 'Reclaiming Jewish history: Homo-erotic poetry of the Middle Ages', *Changing Men* (Summer/Fall 1987), 22–3.

14. On Arab ambiguity towards same-sex behaviour in the past, see A. Boudhiba, *La sexualité en Islam* (Paris, 1975); M. Chebel, *Le corps dans la tradition au Maghreb* (Paris, 1984); M. Chebel, *L'esprit de sérail* (Paris, 1988); M. Daniel, 'Arab civilisation and male love', in W. Leyland (ed.), *Gay Roots* (San Francisco, 1991), pp. 33–76; B. W. Dunne, 'Homosexuality in the Middle East: an agenda for historical research', *Arab Studies Quarterly*, 12, 3/4 (Summer/Fall 1990), 55–82; A. Schmitt and J. Sofer (eds), *Homosexuality in Islam* (Binghamton, 1991); M. Schild, 'De citadel van integriteit. Een studie van homoseksueel gedrag in het Midden Oosten', unpubl. thesis (R. U. Utrecht, 1985); A. Schmitt, 'Vorlesung zur mann-männlicher Sexualität: Erotik in der islamischen Gesellschaft', in G. De Martino and A. Schmitt (eds), *Kleine Schriften zur zwischenmännlicher Sexualität und Erotik in der muslimischen Gesellschaft* (Berlin, 1985), pp. 1–22; G. Turbet-Delof, *L'Afrique barbaresque dans la littérature française*

aux XVI° et XVII° siècles (Genève, 1973), pp. 97–8; and A. Wormhoudt, 'Classic Arabic poetry', *Gay Books Bulletin*, 4 (Fall 1980), 23–5.

15. J. Boswell, *Christianity, Social Tolerance, and Homosexuality*, p. 279.

16. 'en usance de leur abominable et damnable luxure sodomitique les uns avec les autres plus bestiallement et desnaturallement, que ne feroyent les bestes brutes et sauvages.' N. de Nicolay, *Les Navigatiens peregrinatiens et voyages, faicts en la Turquie* (Antwerp, 1576), p. 191.

17. G. S. Rousseau, 'The pursuit of homosexuality in the eighteenth century: "Utterly confused category" and/or rich repository?', in R. P. Maccubbin (ed.), *Unauthorised Sexual Behaviour during the Enlightenment* (Williamsburg, 1985), p. 153.

18. A. G. Busbequius, *The Life and Letters of Ogier Ghiselin de Busbecq, seigneur of Bousbecque, Knight, Imperial Ambassador*, ed. C. T. Forster and F. H. B. Daniell (Geneva, 1971 (1881)), vol. 1, p. 232.

19. W. Lithgow, *The Totall Discourse of the Rare Adventures and Painful Peregrinations* (Glasgow, 1906) (travels in Italy and Ottoman empire from 1609 till 1622); H. Blount, *A Voyage into the Levant* (London, 1636); P. della Valle, *Viaggi cioè la Turchia, la Persia, e l'Inde* (Rome, 1650); J. de Thévenot, *Relation d'un Voyage fait au Levant* (Paris, 1664).

20. R. Kabbani, *Europe's Myths of Orient. Devise and Rule* (Houndsmills, 1986).

21. 'Les habitans de ce païs sont généralement adonnez à la lubricité, et ce qui est horrible, la Sodomie y regne tellement, que les hommes ont les femmes en horreur, ... [les femmes] abhorent aussi les hommes, et s'acouplent femmes à femmes et font plus de cas de ces amours horribles et bastards, que des naturels, honnestes, et des legitimes.' The first, limited edition, *Voyage du Sieur De Stochove Faict es années 1630. 1631. 1632. 1633* (Brussels, 1634) was followed by a second, revised one in 1650: *Voyage Du Levant Du Sr. De Stochove Esc. Seig. de Ste. Catherine.* I have quoted from a recent edition, covering the author's journey in Egypt only: V. Stochove, *Voyage en Egypte*, ed. B. van de Walle (Cairo, 1975), p. 101.

22. J. Pitts, *A True and Faithful Account of the Religion and Manners of the Mohametans* (Exeter, 1704), p. 110.

23. See G. Poirier, 'French Renaissance travel accounts: Images of sin, visions of the New World', in R. Mendes-Leite and O. De Busscher (eds), *Gay Studies from the French Cultures* (Binghamton, 1993), pp. 215–29.

24. For a global view, see A. Grafton, *New Worlds, Ancient Texts* (New York, 1992). On Medieval exploration, see the excellent study by M. B. Campbell, *The Witness and the Other World* (Ithaca and London, 1988).

25. The Wild Woman, however, appears earlier in European culture than the Wild Man. A first reference dates from the tenth century (Burchard of Worms), while her male counterpart arises as a major protagonist of popular imagination only in the twelfth century. See Cl. Lecouteux, *Les monstres dans la littérature allemande du Moyen Age* (Göttingen, 1982), vol. 1, p. 18.

26. See R. Bartra, *El salvaje en el espejo* (Mexico, 1992); R. Bernheimer, *Wild Men in the Middle Ages* (New York, 1970); P. Mason, *Deconstructing America* (London, 1990), pp. 43–50; T. Husband (ed.), *The Wild Man. Medieval Myth and Symbolism* (New York, 1980); P. Vandenbroeck, *Beeld van de Ander, vertoog over het Zelf* (Antwerp, 1987).

27. P. Mason, *Deconstructing America*, p. 85.

28. E. Magaña and P. Mason, 'Tales of otherness, myths, stars and Plinian men in South America', in E. Magaña and P. Mason (eds), *Myth and the Imaginary in the New World* (Amsterdam-Dordrecht, 1986), pp. 7–40.

29. More subtle analysis can be found in J. Axtell, *The European and the Indian* (New York, 1981); M. Bouyer, *L'Amérique espagnole vue et rêvée* (Paris, 1992); J. Gil, *Mito*

y realidad de los descubrimientos, 3 vols (Madrid, 1992); R. Herren, *La Conquista erótica de las Indias* (Barcelona, 1991); P. Hulme, *Colonial Encounters: Europe and the Native Caribbean* (London and New York, 1986); T. Lemaire, *De indiaan in ons bewustzijn. De ontmoeting van de Oude en de Nieuwe Wereld* (Baarn, 1986); P. Mason, *Deconstructing America*, and the still valid essay by E. O'Gorman, *La invención de America* (Mexico, 1977 (1958)).

30. H. Cortés, *Cartas y documentos* (México, D. F., 1963), p. 25.
31. Anon. [Le Conquistador Anonyme], *Relation de quelques-unes des choses de la Nouvelle-Espagne*, ed. and trans. J. Rose (Montbonnet-St.Martin, 1986), p. 114. I am quoting from the original Italian edition, that figures opposite the editor's French translation.
32. B. Diaz del Castillo, *Historia verdadera de la conquista de la Nueva España*, ed. Miguel León-Portilla (Madrid, 1984), p. 456.
33. P. Cieza de León, *La crónica del Perú*, ed. M. Ballesteros (Madrid, 1984), cap. XLIX, p. 224.
34. The term is taken from C. Bernand and S. Gruzinski, 'La Redécouverte de l'Amérique', *L'homme*, 32, 122/124 (1992), 13–15.
35. P. Cieza de León, *La crónica del Perú*, cap. LII, p. 232.
36. A. de Zárate, *The Discovery and Conquest of Peru*, ed. J. M. Cohen (Harmondsworth, 1968), pp. 33–5.
37. The bones probably originated from an extinct animal species, the mastodon. See S. O. Murray, 'Sodomites in Pre-Inca Cultures on the West Coast of South America', unpublished ms. See also A. Schnapper, 'Persistence des géants', *Annales. E.S.C.*, 41, 1 (January-February 1986), 177–200, on the presence of the 'mythological' mammoth bones in the European curiosity cabinets.
38. G. de la Vega, *Commentários reales* (Lisbon, 1609).
39. J. de Léry, *Histoire d'un Voyage fait en la terre du Brésil en 1557* (Montpellier, 1992 (La Rochelle, 1578)); M. E. de Montaigne, *'Des Cannibales'*, in J. de Léry, *Essais*, ed. A. Micha (Paris, 1969), vol. 1, ch. xxxi, pp. 251–64. The French Calvinist de Léry included a passage about Indian men, who were arguing and called each other *tivira*, a Tupi word which meant a 'man with a broken behind'. See, in this context, J. Beck, 'Montaigne face à l'homosexualité', *Bulletin de la Société des Amis de Montaigne*, 9/10 (1982), 41–50.
40. P. de Magalhães Gandavo, *Tratado da Terra do Brasil* (1576), quoted in J. Trevisan, *Perverts in Paradise* (London, 1986), p. 21.
41. M. da Nóbrega, *Cartas do Brasil e mais escritos (1549–1560)*, quoted in M. Maestri Filho, 'Sodomitas e luxuriosos', unpubl. ms., p. 37.
42. G. Soares de Souza, *Noticia do Brasil*, in *Coleção de Noticias* (Lisbon, 1825), vol. 3, part 1, no. 1, pp. 281–2.
43. P. Correia, quoted by A. Gomes, 'Da homossexualidade ao diformismo sexual entre os indígenas e a questão da moral ameríndia', *Revista do Instituto Histórico e Geográfico de São Paulo*, 52 (1953), 326.
44. A. Brandão, quoted by M. Maestri Filho, 'Sodomitas e luxuriosos', p. 36.
45. P. Mason, *Deconstructing America*, pp. 56–7, 110. See also P. Hulme, 'Polytropic Man: Tropes of Sexuality and Mobility in Early Colonial Discourse', in *Europe and its Others*, vol. 2 (Colchester, 1985), pp. 17–32; L. Montrose, 'The work of gender in the discourse of discovery', *Representations*, 33 (Winter 1991), 1–41.
46. P. Mason, *Deconstructing America*, p. 110.
47. Among the first to apply the Ancient Greek myth of the Amazons to the Americas were Columbus, Vespucci, Carvajal, de Orellana, Raleigh and Thevet, who distinguished African, Scythian and American ones (A. Thevet, *Les Singularités de la France antarctique* (1577–78), ed. F. Lestringant (Paris, 1983), p. 164). De la Condamine,

when exploring the Amazon in 1743, speculated on the past existence of the Amazons in America and interpreted their disappearance as the unfortunate effect of their self-reliance. See P. Mason, *Deconstructing America*, pp. 105, 110–11; E. Irizarry, 'Echos of the Amazon Myth in Medieval Spanish Literature', in B. Miller (ed.), *Women in Hispanic Literature: Icons and Fallen Idols* (Berkeley, 1983), pp. 53–66. Meanwhile, there is evidence that a native Indian belief about an Amazon tribe existed as well. See J. Sued-Badillo, 'El mito indoantillano de las mujeres sin hombres', *Boletín de Estudios Latinoamericanos y del Caribe*, 40 (1986), 15–22; and F. Jara, 'Les monstres dans l'imaginaire des indiens d'Amérique latine', in *Le Monstre*, 4, ed. E. Magaña (Paris, 1988), pp. 49–79.

48. A. Jiménez, 'Imágen y culturas: consideraciones desde la antropologia ante la visión del Indio Americano', in *La imágen del Indio en la Europa Moderna*, ed. Consejo Superior de Investigaciones Científicas (Sevilla, 1990), p. 83.

49. P. Mason, *Deconstructing America*, pp. 56–7 relates this to the text by Aquinas, for whom both practices were susceptible of excess: 'And yet these matters too can apparently be reduced to a kind of lack of control, comparable to the excess of someone who finds pleasure in eating human flesh or in sleeping with men (Et tamen etiam illa videntur reduci ad genus intemperantiae secundum quendam excessum: sicut si aliquis delectetur in comestione carnium humanarum, aut in coitu ... masculorum)', (*Sancti Thomae Aquinatis in Aristotelis librum De anima commentarium*, ed. M. Pirota (Turin, 1925), IIa IIae q. 142, 4, 3, quoted in A. Pagden, *The Fall of Natural Man* (Cambridge and New York, 1982), p. 226). Yet the very existence of Aquinas' text should warn us against 'deconstructing' the sodomy/cannibalism parallel as part of a purposive rhetoric of submission.

50. D. Muñoz Camargo, 'Descripción de la ciudad y provincia de Tlaxcala', in R. de Acuña (ed.), *Relaciones Geográficas del siglo XVI: Tlaxcala* (Mexico, 1984), vol. 1, p. 78.

51. See G. Olivier, 'Conquérants et missionnaires face au "péché abominable" ', *Caravelle*, 55 (1990), 22–3.

52. See S. W. Miles, 'The 16th century Pokom-Maya: A documentary analysis of social structure and archaelogical setting', *Transactions of the American Philosophical Association*, (1957), 763–4.

53. 'El somético paciente es abominable, nefando y detestable, digno de que hagan burla y se rían las gentes, y el hedor y fealdad de su pecado nefando no se puede sufrir, por el asco que da a los hombres; en todos se muestra mujeril o afeminado, en el andar o en el hablar, por todo lo cual merece ser quemado.' B. de Sahagún, *História general de las cosas de la Nueva España*, quoted in A. Cardín, *Guerreros, chamanes y travestís* (Barcelona, 1984), p. 153.

54. European sources remain of utmost importance, however, as pre-Columbian codices were partially destroyed. See D. F. Greenberg, *Construction of Homosexuality*, p. 19 on 'the problems of evidence', where he mentions the destruction of Mayan libraries by Jesuits. The codices that did remain, however, do not offer any indisputable evidence of same-sex behaviour, which leaves the historian with only the archaeological (Mochica ceramics) and the historical-anthropological record to confront with European narratives. See also R. A. Gutiérrez, *When Jezus Came, the Corn Mothers Went Away* (Stanford, 1991); and A. López Austin, *The Human Body and Ideology: Concepts of the Ancient Nahuas*, 2 vols (Salt Lake City, 1988).

55. F. Xavier, letter to colleagues in Goa, Kagoshima, 5 November 1549, quoted in A. Cardín, *Guerreros, chamanes y travestís*, p. 140. On Buddhist perception of male-to-male sexuality, see J. I. Cabezón (ed.), *Buddhism, Sexuality, and Gender* (Albany, 1992).

56. F. Xavier, letter of 29 January 1552, quoted in A. Cardín, *ibid.*

57. See C. R. Boxer, *The Christian Century in Japan, 1549–1650* (Berkeley, 1974 (1951)), pp. 66–7.
58. See J. Spence, *The Memory Palace of Matteo Ricci* (London and Boston, 1985), p. 225.
59. See T. Watanabe and J. Iwata, *La voie des éphèbes. Histoire et histoires des homosexualités au Japon* (Paris, 1987), pp. 22–3.
60. See C. R. Boxer (ed.), *South China in the Sixteenth Century: Being the Narratives of Galeote Pereira, Fr. Gaspar da Cruz, O.P., Fr. Martín de Rada, O.E.S.A. (1550–1575)* (London, 1953), pp. 16–17.
61. J. Spence, *Memory Palace of Matteo Ricci*, pp. 217, 228–9.
62. *Ibid.*, p. 217.
63. On *samurai* sexuality, see T. Watanabe and J. Iwata, *La voie des éphèbes*, pp. 41–66; and P. G. Schalow, 'Male love in early modern Japan: a literary depiction of the "youth" ', in M. B. Duberman *et al.* (eds), *Hidden from History* (New York, 1989), pp. 118–28. On Japanese homosexuality, see also J. C. Bauhain and K. Tokitsu, 'Structures familiales et sexualité au Japon à l'époque moderne', *Cahiers Internationaux de Sociologie*, 76 (1984), 71–90; M. Childs, 'Japan's homosexual heritage', *Gai Saber*, 1 (1977), 41–5; and M. Childs, 'Chigo monogatari: Love stories or Buddhist sermons?', *Monumenta Nipponica*, 35 (1980), 127–51.
64. See B. Hinsch, *Passions of the Cut Sleeve*, Berkeley, 1990; V. Ng, 'Homosexuality and the State in Late Imperial China', in *Hidden from History*, 76–89, and M. M. Anderson, *Hidden Power. The Palace Eunuchs of Imperial China* (Buffalo, 1990). See also D. H. Murray, *Pirates of the South China Coast* (Stanford, 1987); Fang-fu Ruan, *Sex in China* (New York, 1991); Fang-fu Ruan and Yung-mei Tsai, 'Male homosexuality in the traditional Chinese literature', *JHom*, 14, 3/4 (1987), 21–33; J. Spence, *Memory Palace of Matteo Ricci*; R. Van Gulik, *La vie sexuelle dans la Chine ancienne* (Paris, 1977); and Ng Siu-Ming Xiaomingxiong, *Zhongguo tongxingai shilu* (History of Homosexuality in China) (Hong Kong, 1984).
65. See V. Ng, 'Homosexuality and the State', p. 78; and P. G. Schalow, 'Male love in early modern Japan', pp. 124 ff. On the partial persistence of this pre-modern pattern, despite modernization in Japan, see J. Robertson, 'The politics of androgyny in Japan', *American Ethnologist*, 19 (1992), 419–442.
66. For Chinese prints in particular, see R. H. van Gulik, *Erotic Colour Prints of the Ming Period* (Tokyo, 1951), vol. 1, pp. 211–12, 222; vol. 3, plates 4 and 19. For Japanese prints, see T. Watanabe and J. Iwata, *La voie des éphèbes*, plates 1 to 8.
67. See C. R. Boxer, *The Christian Century in Japan*, p. 35.
68. O. van Noort, *Wonderlijcke Voyagie, by de Hollanders ghedaen door de Strate Magalanes* (Utrecht, 1649).
69. B. Varenius, *Descriptio Regni Japoniae* (Amsterdam, 1649).
70. A. Montanus, *Gedenkenwaerdige Gesantschappen der Oost-Indische Maatschappij . . . aan de Kaisaren van Japan* (Amsterdam, 1669) (English edition, *Atlas Jappanensis*, 1670).
71. F. Caron, *A True Description of the Mighty Kingdoms of Japan and Siam*, ed. C. R. Boxer (London, 1935), p. 43. The original, Dutch edition is titled *Rechte Beschrijvinge van het machtigh koninkhrijk Jappan* (The Hague, 1662).
72. A. de Morga, *Sucesos de las Islas Filipinas*, ed. and trans. J. S. Cummins (London, 1972), p. 277.
73. R. Knox, *A Historical Relation of the Island of Ceylon in the East Indies* (London, 1681).
74. B. L. de Argensola, *Conquista de las Islas Malucas al Rey Felipe III* (Madrid, 1992 (1609)); D. F. Navarrete, *Tratados Históricos, Políticos, Ethicos y Religiosos de la Monarchia de China* (Madrid, 1676); O. Dapper, *Asia, of Naukeurige Beschryving van het Rijk des Grooten Mogols* (Amsterdam, 1672); J. Fryer, *A New Account of East-*

India and Persia (London, 1697); A. Hamilton, *A New Account of the East Indies …
from the Year 1688 to 1723*, 2 vols (Edinburgh, 1727); [G. Psalmanazar], *Memoirs of
**** commonly known by the name of George Psalmanazar, Reputed Native of
Formosa* (London, 1714). On this rather obscure figure, see R. A. Day, 'Psalmanazar's
Formosa and the British Reader', in G. S. Rousseau and R. Porter (eds), *Exoticism in
the Enlightenment* (Manchester, 1990), pp. 196 ff.

75.   J. Boswell, *Christianity, Social Tolerance, and Homosexuality*, p. 279, n. 32.

76.   [F. Pyrard de Laval], *The Voyage of François Pyrard de Laval to the East Indies, the
Maldives, the Moluccas and Brazil (1601– 1611)*, ed. and trans. A. Gray and H. C. P.
Bell, vol. 1, pp. 195, 307.

77.   [Francesco Carletti], *Ragionamenti di Francesco Carletti sopra le cose da lui vedute ne'
suoi viaggi* (Florence, 1701) (written around 1606). I have consulted the English
translation, *My Voyage around the World: a 16th Century Florentine Merchant*, trans.
H. Weinstock (London, 1963), pp. 209, 212.

78.   J. Spence, *Memory Palace of Matteo Ricci*, pp. 225–6; D. Lach, *Asia in the Making of
Europe* (Chicago, 1965), vol. 1, pp. 553–4.

79.   C. Fedrici (C. Frederick), *Voyages and Travels (1563–1581)*, in *General History and
Collection of Voyages and Travels*, ed. R. Kerr, vol. 7 (Edinburgh, 1812), pp. 210–11.

80.   J. H. van Linschoten, *The Voyage to the East Indies*, ed. A. C. Burnell and P. A. Tiele
(London, 1885), vol. 1, p. 100, n. 25.

81.   C. E. S. [Coyett et Socius], *'t Verwaerloosde Formosa*, ed. G. C. Molewijk (Leiden,
1991).

82.   On the popularity of this theory, see D. Lasch, *Asia in the Making of Europe* (Chicago
and London, 1965–70), vol. 1, p. 2 and p. 553, n. 298. It was wrongly ascribed to
Galvão by J. Spence, *Memory Palace of Matteo Ricci*, pp. 225–6. In reality, such
devices were an erotic stimulant or a symbol of social status, rather than a tool for
repressing sexual desire. See T. Harrisson, 'The "palang", its history and proto-history
in West-Borneo and the Philippines', *Journal of the Malaysian Branch of the Royal
Asiatic Society*, 37, 2 (1964), 162–174; and D. E. Brown, J. W. Edwards and R. P.
Moore, 'The penis inserts of Southeast Asia: An annotated bibliography with an
overview and comparative perspectives' (Berkeley, 1988). On similar 'Burma bells' or
mien-ling, that were placed inside a women's vagina for heightening the pleasure of
either masturbation or intercourse, see V. L. Bullough, *Sexual Variance*, pp. 298–9.

83.   H. Baudet, *Paradise on Earth. Some Thoughts on European Images of Non-European
Man* (New Haven, 1965), p. 11.

84.   Genesis, 9: 19–28.

85.   W. M. Evans, 'From the land of Canaan to the land of Guinea. The strange adventures
of the sons of Cham', *AHR*, 85 (1980), 15–43.

86.   S. L. Gilman, *Sexuality* (New York, 1989), p. 29.

87.   To demonstrate the historian's neglect, see C. Biondi, 'L'Afrique des philosophes: lieu
mythique, terre d'hommes ou entrepôt de marchandises', in D. Droixhe and P.
Gossiaux (eds), *L'homme des Lumières et la découverte de l'autre* (Brussels, n.d.), pp.
191–2. See also W. B. Cohen, *French Encounter with Africans. White Response to
Blacks, 1530–1880* (Bloomington and London, 1980); Ph. Curtin (ed.), *Africa and the
West. Intellectual Responses to European Culture* (Madison, 1972); U. Bitterli, *Die
Entdeckung des schwarzen Afrikaners* (Zürich, 1965): D. Dabydeen (ed.), *The Black
Presence in English Literature* (Manchester, 1985); C. L. Miller, *Blank Darkness.
Africanist Discourse in French* (Chicago and London, 1986); G. Turbet-Delof,
L'Afrique barbaresque.

88.   See the influential study by W. Jordan, *White over Black: American Attitudes towards
the Negro, 1550–1812* (Chapel Hill, 1968), especially chapter 4: 'Fruits of passion. The
dynamics of interracial sex', pp. 136–76. Focusing on the colonial American context of

master/slave relations in a plantation economy, it is only partially relevant for similar studies on Europe's encounter with blacks. It remains to be seen to what extent the dynamics of 'segregationism' were equally present in a Portuguese, Spanish, or French colonial context. Mostly, homosexuality is studied indirectly, only when it proves inevitable. This is the case with the so-called 'Uganda martyrs' (see chapter five). See, however, H. Standing and M. V. Kisekka, *Sexual Behaviour in Subsaharan Africa* (London: Overseas Development Administration, 1989). Black male (homo-)sexuality is briefly addressed in the following studies also: I. Amadiume, *Male Daughters, Female Husbands, Gender and Sex in an African Society* (London, 1987); D. P. de Pedrals, *La vie sexuelle en Afrique noire* (Paris, 1950); and E. E. Evans-Prichard, 'Sexual inversion among the Azande', *American Anthropology*, 72 (1970), 1428–34.

89. M. Borès, *La beauté de Cham. Mondes juifs, mondes noirs* (Paris, 1992), p. 59.
90. On slave recruitement, see J. Thornton, *Africa and Africans in the Making of the Atlantic World, 1400–1680* (Cambridge, 1992), pp. 98 ff.
91. S. Purchas, *Purchas His Pilgrimes* (London, 1625), vol. 2, p. 1558.
92. J. dos Santos, *History of Eastern Ethiopia*, in J. Pinkerton (ed.), *A General Collection of Voyages and Travels* (London, 1808), vol. 16, p. 172. The book's original, Latin title is *Aethiopia Orientalis*. It was first published in 1558. The Portuguese edition, *Etiópia oriental*, was published in 1609.
93. P. Jarric, *Thesaurus Indicus* (Cologne, 1616), p. 482.
94. E. de Flacourt, *Histoire de la grande isle Madagascar* (Paris, 1658), p. 86.
95. O. Dapper, *Naukeurige Beschrijvinge der Afrikaensche Gewesten* (Amsterdam, 1676 (1668)), p. 617.
96. '[Zij] hout ook vijftigh of zestigh by-zitten, hoewel jonghmans, om den naam quansuis onder de haren niet te hebben, dat ze een vrouwe is: en niet tegenstaende zij zulx wel weten, zoo kleetze deze vijftigh of zestigh jonghmans, de kloekste en fraeiste die te vinden zijn, in vrouwengewaet, volgens haer gewoonte, en gaet zelf in mans kleren, en zeit dat deze mannen vrouwen zijn, en zij vrou een man is, en dez verklede jonghmans hare by-wijven zijn.' See O. Dapper, *Naukeurige Beschrijvinge*, p. 238.
97. 'Há entre o gentio de Angola muito (sic) Sodomia, tendo uns com outros suas imundícias e sujidades vestindo como mulheres. Eles chamam pelo nome da terra: quimbandas, os quais no distrito ou terras onde os há, têm comunicação uns com os outros. E alguns deles são fines feiticeiros para terem tudo mau e todo o mais gentio os respeita ... '. A. de Oliveira Cardonega, *Historia geral das guerras Angolanas* (Lisbon, 1681), p. 86.
98. P. Kolb, *Caput Bonae Spei Hodiernum* (Nürnberg, 1719), p. 362; see also p. 553.
99. Probably the Nquiti were the people, living near the Nkisi river in the mountainous region of Ndembu, Angola/Zaire. See J. Thornton, *Africa and Africans*, pp. xxxi–xxxii.
100. J.-B. Labat, *Relation historique de l'Ethiopie occidentale*, 5 vols (Paris, 1732), vol. 1, pp. 290–1.
101. J.-B. Labat, *Relation historique*, vol. 2, pp. 55–6. Another story about a high priest, named Ganga-Ya-Chibanda, cannot be confirmed as being about a man engaging in sexual relations with men. F. Karsch-Haack (*Das gleichgeschlechtliche Leben der Naturvölker* (Munich, 1911), p. 146) concluded so both because the priest used to dress as a woman and because his name was similar to the 'chibados', a cross-gender role in Angola. To me, his conclusion seems unsound.
102. See J.-B. Labat, *Relation historique*, vol. 2, p. 54, and J.-B. Labat, *Voyage aux isles de l'Amérique, 1693–1705*, 2 vols (The Hague, 1724).
103. J. Katz, *Gay American History* (New York, 1976), pp. 35–6.
104. G. Freyre, *Casa grande e senzala* (Rio de Janeiro, 1989 (1933)), pp. 320–3 *et passim*.
105. See L. Mott, 'Pagode português: a subcultura gay em Portugal nos tempos inquisitoriais', *Ciência e Cultura*, 40, 2 (1988), 129–30. The author describes the case

of a man from Benin, who circulated in Lisbon, dressed in an 'avental de burel cingido e aberto à frente'.

106. L. Mott, 'Escravidão e homossexualidade', in R. Vainfas (ed.), *História e sexualidade no Brasil* (Rio de Janeiro, 1986), pp. 19–40; R. Vainfas, *Trópico dos pecados* (Rio de Janeiro, 1989), pp. 166–7.

107. E. Montejo, *The Autobiography of a Runaway Slave*, ed. M. Barnet (New York, 1973), p. 41.

108. M. B. Karash, *Slave Life in Rio de Janeiro, 1808–1850* (Princeton, 1987), p. 295.

109. C. I. Nero, 'Towards a Black Gay Aesthetic. Signifying in Contemporary Black Gay Literature', in E. Hemphill (ed.), *Brother to Brother. New Writings by Black Gay Men* (Boston, 1991), p. 233.

110. The issue is addressed programmatically in a footnote by P. Drucker, ' "In the tropics there is no sin": Homosexuality and gay/lesbian movements in the third world' (Amsterdam, 1993), p. 29.

111. J. Gorender, *O escravismo colonial* (São Paulo, 1978), pp. 333–46; and K. de Queiros Mattoso, *Ser escravo no Brasil* (São Paulo, 1982), p. 127. Karash indicates that sexual abuse of male as well as female slaves went on until far into the nineteenth century, still as a result of a shortage of women (*Slave Life*, p. 295).

112. See D. Hall, *In Miserable Slavery: Thomas Thistlewood in Jamaica, 1750–86* (Houndsmills, 1989); G. Freyre, *Casa grande e senzala*, p. 321.

113. On the myth of African exclusive heterosexuality, see W. R. Dynes, 'Homosexuality in subsaharan Africa: an unnecessary controversy', *Gay Books Bulletin*, 9 (1983), 20–1.

114. By 'tropicalization', I mean the cognitive scheme, presenting the climatological, social and cultural conditions of the tropical and subtropical regions as determinant of a particular phenomenon, in this instance sexuality.

115. On the impact of Catholic ideology on civil legislation, see M. Goodich, 'Sodomy in medieval secular law', *JHom*, 1, 3 (1976), 295–302. On the legal definitions of sodomy in the New World, see A. D. Wright, *The Counter-Reformation: Catholic Europe and the Non-Christian World* (London, 1982); and A. Lavrin, 'Sexuality in colonial Mexico: A church dilemma', in A. Lavrin (ed.), *Sexuality and Marriage in Colonial Latin America* (Lincoln, Nebraska, 1986), p. 51. See also M. E. Parry and A. J. Cruz (eds), *Cultural Encounters. The Impact of the Inquisition in Spain and the New World* (Berkeley, 1991). For Hispanic America, see C. L. Taylor, 'Mexican gay life in historical perspective', in *Gay Roots*, 28–56; S. Gruzinski, 'Las cenizas del deseo. Homosexuales novohispanos a mediados del siglo XVII', in S. Ortega (ed.), *De la santidad a la perversión* (Mexico, 1986), pp. 225–81; Olivier, 'Conquérants et missionnaires'. For Brazil, see P. Fry, 'Homossexualidade masculina e cultos afro-brasileiros' and 'Da Hierarquia à igualdade. A construção histórica da homossexualidade no Brasil', in P. Fry, *Para Inglês ver* (Rio de Janeiro, 1982), pp. 54–86, 87–115; L. Mott, *Escravidão, homossexualidade e demonologia* (São Paulo, 1988), 19–47; L. Mott, 'Escravidão e homossexualidade', in *Historia e sexualidade no Brasil*, pp. 19–40; L. Mott, *O sexo proibido. Virgens, gays e escravos nas garras da inquisição* (Campinas, n.d.); R. G. Parker, *Bodies, Pleasures and Passions. Sexual Culture in Contemporary Brazil* (Boston, 1991); and R. Vainfas, *Trópico dos pecados*.

116. S. Gruzinski, 'Las cenizas del deseo', p. 268.

117. Gruzinski thus quotes from a *Confessionário en lengua mixe* by father Agustín de Quintana (Puebla, 1733), who admonishes his colleagues to remain silent on the issue of sodomy (S. Gruzinski, 'Confesión, alianza y sexualidad entre los indios de Nueva España', in S. Ortéga (ed.), *El placer de pecar y el afan de normar* (Mexico, D.F., n.d.), p. 204). See also M. Azoulai, *Les péchés du Nouveau Monde* (Paris, 1993).

118. L. Mott, 'Relações raciais entre homossexuais no Brasil Colônia', in L. Mott, *Escravidão*, pp. 32–3; R. Vainfas, *Trópico dos pecados*, p. 164.

119. See, for comparison, the following studies: L. Mott, 'Relações raciais', pp. 29–30; R. Vainfas, *Trópico dos pecados*, pp. 163–5; S. W. Foster, 'Homosexuality and the Inquisition in Brazil, 1591–1592', *Gay Sunshine*, 38/39 (n.d.), 17–18; J. Trevisan, *Perverts in Paradise*, pp. 39–59. Compare, for the Iberian peninsula, W. Monter, *Frontiers of Heresy* (Cambridge and New York, 1989); J. J. Alves Dias, 'Para uma abordagem do sexo proibido em Portugal, no século XVI', in M. H. Carvalho dos Santos (ed.), *Inquisição* (Lisbon, 1989), vol. 1, pp. 151–9; A. Borges Coelho, 'Repressão ideológica e sexual na Inquisição de Evora entre 1533 e 1668. As primeiras gerações de vítimas Cristas-Novas', in *Inquisição*, vol. 1, pp. 423–46.
120. *Denunciações da Bahia*, 1591–92, quoted by Trevisan, *Perverts in Paradise*, p. 55.
121. S. Schwartz, 'Panic in the Indies: the Portuguese threat to the Spanish Empire, 1640–1650', in W. Thomas and B. De Groof (eds), *Rebelión y Resisténcia en el Mundo Hispánico del Siglo XVII* (Leuven, 1992), pp. 212–13.
122. *Ibid.*
123. A. Baião, *A inquisição de Goa* (Lisbon, 1930 and 1945), vol. 1, pp. 43–5; J. C. Boyajian, 'Goa Inquisition: New light on first 100 years', *Purabhilekh-Puratatva*, 4/1 (1986), 1–41; O. H. K. Spate, *The Spanish Lake*, vol. 1: *The Pacific since Magellan* (London, 1979), p. 159. See also A. D. Wright, *Counter-Reformation*, p. 144 on Goa.
124. See J. Spence, *Memory Palace of Matteo Ricci*, p. 220; B. Guy, ' "Ad majorem Societatis gloriam": Jesuit perspectives on Chinese mores in the seventeenth and eighteenth centuries', in *Exoticism in the Enlightenment*, p. 40. Another incident, involving the Jesuit Schall von Bell, has been described by A. Väth, *Johann Adam Schall von Bell, s.J. Missionar in China* (Cologne, 1933).
125. B. Guy, ' "Ad majorem Societatis gloriam" ', p. 76.
126. N. Trigault and M. Ricci, *Histoire de l'expédition chrétienne envoyée en Chine (1582–1610)* (Paris, 1978) (first Latin edition 1615, first French edition, Lyon, 1616); L. Lecomte, *Nouveaux mémoires sur la Chine*, 2 vols (Paris, 1696); J. B. Du Halde, *Description géographique, historique, chronologique et politique de l'Empire de la Chine et de la tartarie chinoise*, 4 vols (Paris, 1735); J. B. Du Halde, *Mémoires concernant l'histoire, les arts, les moeurs, les usages ... des Chinois, par les missionnaires de Pékin*, 16 vols (Paris, 1776–1814); J. B. Grosier, *Description générale de la Chine*, 7 vols (Paris, 1820).
127. See, for example, N. del Techo (Du Toit), *Historia Provinciae Paraquariae Societatis Iesu* (Liège, 1673), lib. 10, c. 9, p. 264.
128. In Nouvelle France, the inquisition was not installed. Few cases of conviction for sodomy are known. See G. Kinsman, *The Regulation of Desire: Sexuality in Canada* (Montreal, 1987), p. 75; and R.-L. Séguin, *La vie libertine en Nouvelle-France au XVIIe siècle* (Montreal, 1972), pp. 346–7. See also D.F. Greenberg, *Construction of Homosexuality*, p. 343.
129. J. D'Emilio and E. B. Freedman, *Intimate Matters. A History of Sexuality in America* (New York, 1988), pp. 15–84; E. Leites, *The Puritan Conscience and Modern Sexuality* (New Haven, 1986), *passim*; D. F. Greenberg, *Construction of Homosexuality*, pp. 343–6; R. F. Oaks, ' "Things fearful to name": Sodomy and buggery in Seventeenth-Century New England', *Journal of Social History*, 12 (1978), 268–81.
130. W. L. Williams, *The Spirit and the Flesh. Sexual Diversity in American Indian Culture* (Boston, 1986), p. 152.
131. A. L. Higginbotham, Jr., *In the Matter of Color* (New York and Oxford, 1978), pp. 281–2; J. Katz, *Gay/Lesbian Almanac. A New Documentary* (New York, 1983), p. 61. See also Ch. I. Nero, 'Towards a Black Gay Aesthetic', p. 234.
132. J. Katz, *ibid.*
133. See R. F. Oaks, 'Perceptions of homosexuality by Justices of Peace in Colonial America', *Sexualaw reporter*, 4 (1978), 33–7.

134. See W. Jordan, *White over Black*; E. D. Genovese, *Roll, Jordan, Roll! The World the Slaves Made* (London, 1975); H. Gutman, *The Black Family in Slavery and Freedom, 1750–1925* (New York, 1976); S. M. Stowe, *Intimacy and Power in the Old South. Ritual in the Lives of the Planters* (Baltimore, 1990); and R. G. Walters, 'The erotic south: Civilization and sexuality in American abolitionism', *American Quarterly*, 25 (1973), 177–201.

135. See, for example, J. L. Quoy-Bodin, 'Autour de deux sociétés libertines sous Louis XIV: L'Ordre de la Félicité et l'Ordre Hermaphrodite', *Revue Historique*, 276 (1986), 57–84.

136. See A. Heriot, *The Castrati in Opera* (London, 1956); and P. Barbier, *Les castrats* (Paris, 1989).

137. See C. Courouve, 'Bardache', in C. Courouve, *Vocabulaire de l'homosexualité masculine*, pp. 59–66; and W. R. Dynes, 'Berdache (originally bardache)', in W. R. Dynes, *Homolexis*, pp. 19–20.

138. On the reports on 'berdaches' by Marquette, Liette, de Charlevoix and others, see J. Katz, *Gay American History*, pp. 423–39; W.L. Williams, *Spirit and the Flesh*, pp. 9–11, 65.

139. B. de Las Casas, *Historia sumaria*, ed. E. O'Gorman (Mexico, 1967), vol. 1, pp. 540–1.

140. A. N. Cabeza de Vaca, *Naufragios y Comentarios*, ed. R. Ferrando (Madrid, 1984), *Naufragios*, XXVI, p. 108.

141. J. Lemoyne de Morgues, 'Indorum Floridam provinciam inhabitantium eicones, primum ibidem ad vivum expressae, addita ad singulas brevi earum declaratione. Nunc vero recens a Theodoro de Bry Leodiense in aes incisae & evulgatae', in M. Bouyer and J.-P. Duviols (eds), *Le Théâtre du Nouveau Monde. Les Grands Voyages de Théodore de Bry* (Paris, 1992), p. 68.

142. 'Les Hermaphrodites sont en grand nombre parmi eux. Ils ont ordinairement plusieurs femmes . . . [et] sont impudiques jusqu'à tomber dans le péché qui est contre nature. Ils ont des garçons, à qui ils donnent l'équipage de filles, par ce qu'ils les emploient à cet abominable usage. Ce[s] garçons ne s'occupent qu'aux ouvrages des femmes, et se meslent ni de la chasse ni de la guerre. Ils sont fort superstitieux . . . '. L. Hennepin, *Nouvelle découverte d'un très grand pays situé dans l'Amérique entre le Nouveau Mexique et la Mer Glaciale* (Utrecht, 1697), pp. 219–20.

143. There were indeed many others, that cannot be discussed in detail here. See not only the inventory in F. Karsch-Haack, *Das gleichgeschlechtliche Leben der Naturvölker*, pp. 314–15, but also W. L. Williams, *Spirit and the Flesh*, ch. 7, pp. 131–51, and J. Katz, *Gay American History*, ibid.

144. See M. Delcourt, *Hermaphrodites* (Paris, 1958).

145. See A. G. Michler, 'Ambiguità e trasmutazione. Discussioni mediche e giuridiche in epoca moderna (secoli XVII e XVIII)', *Memoria*, 24, 3 (1988), 43–60. See also P. Darmon, *Le tribunal de l'impuissance* (Paris, 1979); M. Escamilla, 'A propos d'un dossier inquisitorial des environs de 1590: les étranges amours d'un hermaphrodite', in A. Redondo (ed.), *Amours légitimes, amours illégitimes en Espagne (VI°–XVII° siècles)* (Paris, 1985), pp. 167–82.

146. D. F. Greenberg, *Construction of Homosexuality*, pp. 99–100.

147. J. F. de San Antonio, *The Philippine Chronicles of Fray San Antonio* (Manila, 1977), p. 156.

148. 'Als ze weten dat een man impotent is . . . , verplichten ze hem zich te kleden als vrouw opdat hij met hun groepje zou meelopen. Als hij per toeval weigert, brengen ze hem naar een hoer en ze bevelen hem haar geslachtelijk te benaderen in hun aanwezigheid om te verifiëren of hij impotent is of niet. Als hij het is, grijpen ze hem, castreren hem volledig en nemen hem mee, zelfs als het een heer of een grote van het rijk is. Al die

venten dienen [de mogol] als *Badarnos*.' J. Verberckmoes and E. Stols, *Aziatische omzwervingen. Het leven van Jacques de Coutre, een Brugs diamanthandelaar, 1591–1627* (Berchem, 1988), p. 218.

149. See Verberckmoes and Stols, *ibid.*, p. 254. In the simultaneously published Spanish edition, the word *badarnos*, present in the manuscript, was replaced by *baillarines*, dancers. Such 'transcription' seems to me to be unjustified, as the original word *bardajes* was probably turned into *badarnos* by a mere metathesis. See J. de Coutre, *Andanzas Asiáticas*, ed. E. Stols and B. Teensma (Madrid, 1991), p. 314.

150. See M. J. Rocke, 'Policing homosexuality in 15th century Florence: the Ufficiali di Notte', *Quaderni Storici*, 22, 3 (December 1987), 701–724; G. Ruggiero, *The Boundaries of Eros. Sex Crime and Sexuality in Renaissance Venice* (Oxford, 1985); M. Lever, *Les bûchers de Sodome* (Paris, 1985); J. L. Quoy-Bodin, 'Autour de deux sociétés libertines', M. Rey, 'Parisian homosexuals create a lifestyle, 1700–1750', *Eighteenth-Century Life*, 9 (1985), 179–91; M. E. Perry, *Gender and Disorder*; L. Mott, *Pagode português*; T. van der Meer, *De wesentlijke sonde van sodomie en andere vuyligheeden. Sodomietenvervolgingen in Amsterdam, 1730–1811* (Amsterdam, 1984); A. Bray, *Homosexuality in Renaissance England* (London, 1982); and R. Trumbach, 'London's Sodomites', *Journal of Social History*, 11 (1977), 1–33.

151. The Hippocratic and Galenic theory of the temperaments gradually shifted from a physical interpretation into a model of long-term mental conditions. Its application to the diversity of the human race remained fairly marginal. See V. Nutton, 'Temperaments', in W. F. Bynum *et al.* (eds), *Dictionary of the History of Science* (Princeton, 1981), p. 417.

152. G. Sagard, *Histoire du Canada* (Paris, 1865 (1636)), pp. 377, 380.

153. See B. Lavallé, 'Del Indio al Criollo: evolución y transformación de una imágen colonial', in *La imágen del indio*, p. 331.

154. B. Lavallé, *ibid.*, p. 332.

155. B. Cobo, *História del nuevo mundo*, quoted by B. Lavallé, *ibid.* See also R. Porras Barrenechea, 'El P. Bernabé Cobo, 1582–1657', *História*, 2 (Lima, 1943), 98–104.

156. A. Gerbi, *La disputa del Nuevo Mundo. Historia de una polémica, 1750–1900* (Mexico, D.F., 1982) (Ital. 1955; Span. 1960), p. 15.

157. B. Lavallé, *ibid.* See also E. Esteva Fabregat, *El mestizaje en Iberoamerica* (Madrid, 1988).

158. M. Delon, 'Du goût antiphysique des Américains', *Annales de Bretagne et des pays de l'ouest*, 34, 2 (1977), 320.

159. J.-P. Guicciardi, 'Hermaphrodite et le prolétaire', *Le Dix-huitième siècle*, 12 (1980), 62–4.

160. J. Parsons, *Mechanical and critical enquiry into the nature of hermaphrodites* (London, 1741).

161. A. Paré, *Des monstres et prodiges*, ed. J. Céard (Geneva, 1971), pp. 27, 29–30.

162. J. Bulwer, *Anthropometamorphoses: Man transformed; or, the Artificial Changeling* (London, 1653), p. 380.

163. See T. W. Laqueur, ' "Amor Veneris, vel Dulcedo Appeletur" ', in M. Feher *et al.* (eds), *Fragments for a History of the Human Body*, vol. 3 (New York, 1989), p. 113.

164. Ancillon, *Le traité des eunuques*, ed. D. Fernandez (Paris, 1978 (1707)).

165. D. Fernandez, *Le rapt de Ganymède* (Paris, 1989), p. 30. See also G. S. Rousseau, 'The Pursuit of Homosexuality in the Eighteenth Century: "Utterly Confused Category" and/or Rich Repository?', in Maccubbin, P. R. (ed.) *Unauthorized Sexual Behaviour during the Enlightenment* (Williamsburg, 1985), p. 165, n. 43.

166. See, for example, R. James, *Medicinal Dictionary* (London, 1745). The debate on clitoral hypertrophy gained new urgency in the early twentieth century, when lesbianism was redefined in biomedical terms and ethnographic evidence from Africa

and the Middle East was reinterpreted in this light. E. Donoghue, *Passions between Women* (London, 1993), p. 257 also points at the association between 'cultural otherness' and anatomical evidence of a large clitoris. See also M.-J. Bonnet, *Un choix sans équivoque. Recherches historiques sur les relations amoureuses entre les femmes, XVI°–XX° siècle* (Paris, 1981), pp. 69–80; and T. W. Laqueur, ' "Amor Veneris, vel Dulcedo Appeletur" ', pp. 113–19, 129–30.

167. The term 'amitié particulière' was first used in a text on moral theology of 1690. After Lafitau, it remained unused until 1943, when the French novelist, R. Peyrefitte, used it as a title for one of his books. See C. Courouve, *Vocabulaire de l'homosexualité masculine*, pp. 45–6.

168. J.-F. Lafitau, *Moeurs des sauvages Américains comparées aux moeurs des premiers temps*, ed. E. Hindie Lemay (Paris, 1983), pp. 180–1.

169. One source of Lafitau's knowledge about ritualized homosexuality was R. Beverly's *The History and Present State of Virginia*, originally published in London in 1705. This book contains a description of a ritual abduction of boys by men.

170. 'Ne serait-ce point les mêmes peuples que les Asiatiques adorateurs de Cybèle, ou ces Orientaux dont parle Julius Firmicus, lesquels consacraient, les uns la déesse de Phrygie, les autres à Vénus Uranie, des prêtres qui s'habillaient en femmes, qui affectaient d'avoir un visage efféminé, qui se fardaient, et déguisaient leur véritable sexe sous les habits empruntés de celui qu'ils s'efforçaient de contrefaire?'

171. 'Quoique l'esprit de religion qui leur fait embrasser cet état les fasse regarder comme des hommes extraordinaires, ils sont néanmoins réellement tombés, parmi les Sauvages même, dans ce mépris où étaient anciennement les prêtres de Vénus Uranie et de Cybèle; et soit qu'effectivement ils se soient attiré ce mépris en s'asservissant à des passions honteuses, soit que l'ignorance des Européens sur les causes de leur condition fondât contre eux des soupçons fâcheux, ces soupçons entrèrent si avant dans leur esprit qu'ils s'imaginèrent tout ce qu'on en pouvait penser de plus désavantageux.' J.-F. Lafitau, *Moeurs des sauvages Américains*, pp. 52-3. On Ancient West Asian Cybele cult practices, where initiates severed their genitals and dressed like women in the height of frenzy, see D. F. Greenberg, *Construction of Homosexuality*, p. 98.

172. Lafitau, *ibid.*

173. J.-P. Duviols, 'L'image européenne du 'bon sauvage' américain', in *Les Amériques et l'Europe* (Toulouse, 1985), p. 31.

174. M. Delon, 'The priest, the philosopher, and homosexuality in Enlightenment France', in *Unauthorized Sexual Behaviour*, pp. 126–7.

Chapter two

The Enlightenment, Natural History and the Sodomite (c. 1750 – c. 1815)

> *The 'discovery' of [the] 'new worlds' also gave the Enlightenment a metaphor that could be applied far beyond its immediate geographical meaning. ... Atlases could be collections of maps, but they were also diagrams and illustrations of that other 'terra nondum cognita', the human body.*
>
> – Peter Hulme and Ludmilla Jordanova[1]

The descriptions of both sodomitical practices and cross-gender behaviour, recurrent in a growing number of travel accounts and proto-ethnographic portrayals, provoked questions, within the new intellectual context of the Enlightenment, about whether and, if so, how such phenomena were inter-related. Could they be included in the newly-outlined theory of human nature or did their widespread occurrence amidst 'barbaric' people reveal instead their inherently anomalous character? Had civilization led to the abandonment of both practices or was sodomy a sign instead of decadence, proven by their absence among tribal people unspoilt by civilization – the *bon sauvage* – and demonstrated by the status of sodomy and pederasty in Europe as *vice aristocratique* or *vice du clergé*?

Speculative questions of such nature were further complicated by new dilemmas, springing from scientific innovation. If symptomatic of moral decadence, then how could such an image be reconciled with incipient thought about the biological roots of sexual deviance? Was sex 'circum-stantial' or did it instead reveal a fundamental, biological substratum, that could be inventoried and classified according to indisputable criteria? And, if biology defined sexuality, then how could this be perceived empirically?

Departing from the Enlightenment's rewriting of morality, I will review how the new definitions of human nature altogether altered the terms of debate. Particular attention will be given to how the etiology of same-sex practices was increasingly connected to cross-gender behaviour in a way that lent theoretical significance to the new ethnographic evidence. Emphasis will be laid on how the imperatives of scientific observation were seminal to a tendency to actually pin sodomy down on a cross-gender role, as such a construction was dictated by the new sexual politics of reproductive biology. Age-structured same-sex relations, though equally prominent in many a society, were acknowledged yet remained somewhat irrelevant in view of the newly rising paradigm of Enlightenment body politics.

Proto-ethnography, in this context, did not function exclusively as a repository of empirical information. Its selection of relevant data as well as its descriptive rhetoric conveyed specific meanings that directed the making of scientific theory at the homefront. Both related to one another dialectically and the following survey of evidence will reveal how descriptions of same-sex behaviour and cross-gender roles outside the West both triggered and reflected some paradigmatic changes in European theory about homosexuality. The intellectual map of Enlightenment theory of human sexuality was altogether very complex as the debate on male-to-male sexuality intersected with discourses on gender and, increasingly, 'race', both of which were, in their turn, mutually intertwined by virtue of what Nancy Stepan coined as 'analogous' reasoning. This very dialectic between ethnographic narrative on same-sex behaviour and cross-gender roles on the one hand, and racialist and sexual theory on the other will be a *Leitmotiv* throughout this chapter.

From 'act' to 'minority'

The initial question regarding same-sex behaviour among men was whether it actually belonged to the realm of human nature. To resolve the problem, old and new texts on sodomy among the 'natural' people overseas were read as evidence to prove certain theories held by the authors and commentators of the Enlightenment. One group declared same-sex praxis to be part of a 'natural' sexuality and emphasized its occurrence amidst tribal folk as well as the 'civilized' West. Another group tended to exclude same-sex praxis from the natural order. Advocates of this position followed two lines of argument. Some highlighted tribal societies as a place where same-sex praxis was (believed to be) rare or nonexistent. Others referred to tribal societies as well, if only, however, to indicate how same-sex praxis was part of an initial 'barbarity', yet had been surpassed in order for humanity to reach life according to the laws of nature.

Gradually, a third pattern became visible as more ethnographic descriptions of same-sex relations were disseminated among the European intelligentsia. It was marked by a new emphasis upon the anomalous constitution of men, presumably engaging in sexual relations with other men, and defined this anomaly more and more in cross-gender terms. Rather than presenting the problem of same-sex praxis as an 'act', that was or was not pursued across the world, it previsaged a theory of same-sex praxis as a minority's characteristic, that was more or less visible when compared cross-culturally.

'Natural' sodomy

Among the most influential texts of the former group figured those by Louis-Armand Baron de Lahontan[2] and Louis-Antoine de Bougainville,[3] who 'through their experiences with primitive societies, found that 'natural' sexuality was indeed a free and aggressive sexuality which violated the civilised standards of sexual conduct, and that cultural and moral relativism was a reality [and] not just a philosophical construct'.[4]

Subscribing to the political agenda of moral relativism, Voltaire also stressed the natural character of same-sex practices in the article on *'l'amour socratique'* of his *Dictionnaire philosophique* (1764): 'How is it possible that a vice destructive of the human race is so widely spread, that an infamous act against nature is nevertheless so natural? It seems to be the ultimate degree of deliberate corruption and yet it is an ordinary characteristic of those who have not as yet had the time to be corrupted.'[5] Perhaps more significant than his defence of sodomy, mostly against persecution by the Church, was his claim that the climate played a determinant role. The higher incidence, said Voltaire, of sodomy in warm climates was a proof of how its cause lay outside the reach of the individual.[6]

Jean-Jacques Rousseau, 'curiously enigmatic',[7] was less frank than Voltaire. He seemed to subscribe, at first sight, to the traditional association of Arab culture with sodomitical vice, when relating how he was once subjected, to his great terror, to the advances of an *effroyable Maure*. Yet, in the end, he attached a plea for tolerance to what apparently was 'a common practice around the globe'.[8]

La Douceur, the mysterious author of *De l'Amérique et des Américains*[9] emphasized that pederasty, 'this orthographic error of human Nature (cette faute d'orthographe de la Nature humaine)', was no more or less common among American Indians than it was among the people of the West.[10]

In his influential *Supplément au voyage de Bougainville*, published in 1772, Diderot criticized the Church for having 'attached labels of "vice" and "virtue" to actions that are completely independent of morality'. Stockinger, when quoting Diderot, admits that sodomy is not mentioned explicitly. Yet he argues that it was no doubt included in the overall plea by Diderot for revision of moral norms, as he even defended the Tahitians' incestuous behaviour, then, as today, seen as a far greater taboo than sodomy.[11] Such a conclusion seems only partially justified, as other texts by Diderot contained a clear condemnation of *le goût antiphysique des Américains*.[12] Hélène Clastres has pointed at the contradictions of eighteenth-century casuistics, including Diderot's.[13] Other historians also suggest that the presumed moral radicalism of Diderot ought to be revised.[14] But the fact remains that, if a vice, Diderot nevertheless believed it to be a 'natural' one.

No more radical and uncompromising plea for same-sex praxis can be found than the one by the Marquis D. A. F. de Sade, even though his role has been addressed only marginally by gay and lesbian historians.[15] For de Sade too, sodomy belonged to the realm of human nature, if only because he 'transformed [it] into natural love by redefining nature, both human and nonhuman, as amoral existence'.[16] While highlighting sodomy as at once anomaly and prototype, de Sade justified his point of view with a catalogue of historical and ethnographic precedents. Greeks, Romans, American Indians, Turks, the blacks of Benguela, all supported de Sade's all-encompassing image of human amorality. But sodomy, according to his biographer Jean-Jacques Pauvert, was not singled out as it merely reflected one of nature's choices, and stood amidst other practices that together constituted 'the enigma of the human heart'.[17]

Stockinger claims, somewhat anachronistically, that, while making his case more persuasive at first sight, de Sade can hardly be called 'consistently revolutionary', because he was a misogynist and because he presented homosexual behaviour in a context of scandal and obscenity. Such an interpretation clearly is judgemental, as it applies today's criteria of political correctness to eighteenth-century libertinism. In reality, however, the libertine's rhetoric was impregnated with phallocratic bravado.

This, if you like, 'male chauvinist' attitude was also obvious in the pamphlets, published by the subcultural associations of sodomites in France. Among these figured the *chevaliers de la Manchette*,[18] who published a pamphlet with the epigraph 'Les goûts sont dans la nature / Le meilleur est celui qu'on a.'[19] The *Petits Bougres au Manège* stressed, among other arguments, that sodomy was common in the Middle East: 'All the people of the Levant have the burning desire for sperm in the anus, even though their seraglios enclose jewels of grace and beauty (Tous les peuples du levant ont la fureur de foutre en cul, quoique leurs sérails renferment des prodiges de grâce et de beauté).' More so, it was claimed to be almost ubiquitous throughout the world and sexual education was tied to an outspokenly misogynist pragmatism:

Most of the ancient and modern people have a strong desire for sodomy, though in our society it is less taste than necessity that leads us to it . . . . Beautiful women are rare in Paris, stupid asses very numerous, and venereal diseases proliferate even more . . . . If, by chance, one meets a beautiful woman . . . it most certainly is a prostitute and thus fear for syphilis poisons all the pleasure that one may experience during sex. None of these inconveniences are present among men: narrow entry, hard and white buttocks, unlimited pleasure, everything invites one to seek satisfaction.[20]

Sodomy here was presented, apologetically, as an alternative for sexual relations with women and prostitutes, who were believed to be carriers of sexually transmitted disease. It corresponded to a widespread conviction that one could prevent and even be cured from syphilis by sleeping with young virgins or boys.[21] Though no sources explicitly mention this, it may well be that knowledge about similar beliefs outside the western world comforted libertines in their acquiescence.

Another exponent of *libertinage*, that was homosocial and anticlerical at once, was to be found in the elitist revival of paganism and, more particularly, phallic cults. This paralleled other, simultaneous emanations of neo-classicist scholarship, yet its peculiar focus on sexuality contrasted heavily with the idealism of neoplatonic studies of Greek and Roman art and literature. Especially the writings of Hamann, Winckelmann, Ramdohr, and Beckford, and, soon, Byron were impregnated with a desire to revitalize Greek homoeroticism. Yet this was often stripped of any physicality and seen, instead, as a spiritual alternative to carnal sodomy.[22]

Though apparently irrelevant, this body of literature should be included within the scope of our research. Actually, it was seminal to a debate that would persist throughout the nineteenth century and addressed the presumed difference between Greek 'male love' and the pederastic practices in Asia, Africa and America. The heirs of neoplatonism would insist on maintaining a crucial divide between both, whereas others would discard such distinctions as inaccurate and hypocritical.

Anterior to the latter position were some eighteenth-century representatives of neo-paganism. The obvious source for revitalizing the worship of Priapus was ancient Greece and Rome. Its main instigator was the Englishman Sir William Hamilton, who had founded the Society of Dilettanti and wrote an 'Account of the Remains of the Worship of Priapus lately existing at Isernia, in the Kingdom of Naples'. It was published by Richard Payne Knight as a point of departure to his own extensive study, titled *Discourse on the Worship of Priapus, and its Connexion with the Mystic Theology of the Ancients* (1786–87).[23] Knight's interest in phallic worship was inspired by an intention to retrieve 'natural' spontaneity from centuries of Christian repression. To consolidate his plea for the revival of a classical body politic, he compared the latter with that of the recently discovered people of Tahiti in his *Analytical Enquiry into the Principles of Taste* (1801):

It has been observed by travellers that the attitudes and gestures of savages, particularly those of high rank among them, are extremely dignified and graceful; which arises from their being unperverted and unrestrained, and therefore expressing naturally and emphatically the sentiments of the mind . . . . In the age of the arts in Greece, civilisation had just arrived to that state, in which the manners of men are polished, but yet natural; and consequently their attitudes and gestures expressive and emphatical without ever being coarse or violent.[24]

As a fine example of 'homotextuality', this passage clearly seeks to ascribe a birthright to a masculine sensuality and to extract homoeroticism from the secular rhetoric of vice. The juxtaposition, in fact, of 'unperverted' and 'unrestrained', is not without meaning as it conveyed a hidden message about the natural character of any form of sexual desire.

Less subtle and at times pornographic were the underground publications of Pierre François Hugues, better known as Baron d'Hancarville. His *Monuments de la vie privée des douze Césars* and *Monuments du Culte Secrèt des Dames Romaines*, published around 1770,[25] were composed mostly of erotic drawings, that were to offend Christian sensibilities. More relevant, however, is his book *Recherches sur l'esprit et les progrès des arts en Grèce*, published in London in 1785, that had extended its scope beyond Greek and Roman Antiquity. It could not have been written earlier, says his biographer, Haskell, 'for it took into account ... the very recent intellectual discovery that was on the verge of transforming the consciousness of Europe: first hand knowledge of the religions and literature of India and the Far East'.[26] The Indian historian Partha Mitter has shown how Europe's interest in his country in the 1780s sprang partially from a new tendency to interpret ancient religion in terms of sexual symbolism. India, says Mitter, allowed for understanding how fertility rites were a common denominator of all religions and necessarily against the grain of Christianity. Its mythology also inspired new speculations on the hermaphrodite nature of mankind.[27]

'Un-natural' sodomy

If not the libertines' sexual radicalism, then the pleas for tolerance by Voltaire, Rousseau, Diderot – and I may add Beccaria[28] – certainly influenced the French *Code pénal* of 1791, from which the crime of sodomy was banned. Yet the decriminalization of male same-sex behaviour in France and the countries that, deliberately or not, followed its example, hardly justifies an image of a thoroughgoing liberalization of European sexual mores. In Prussia, the death penalty for sodomy was eliminated in 1794 and the Napoleonic Code was imposed, briefly, from 1810 till 1815. In England, Jeremy Bentham, upholding the 'greatest pleasure principle' as a guideline of utilitarianism, pleaded for the decriminalization of 'paederasty'.[29] He insisted that this would do no harm to society and supported his argument by saying that the low status of women in the Arab world was the outcome of male jealousy, not, as many presumably believed, of widespread sodomitical practices among the men. He also emphasized how the acceptance of same-sex praxis in the Pacific world by no means induced a neglect of women.[30] But, as in Holland, 'sodomites' were prosecuted with unprecedented fervour around 1780. The English moral climate became more severe and eventually triggered the foundation in 1802 of the Society for the Suppression of Vice.[31]

The legal debate on sodomy and the decriminalization in some countries did not altogether result in emancipation. Legal innovation, in reality, only turned matters of sexuality from public into private ones. This in no way excluded negative judgement about sodomy in particular, as the latter often remained stigmatized as an 'unnatural' form of human behaviour. In fact the tyranny of moral condemnation was gradually replaced by one of biological orthodoxy. Yet the 'scientific' demonstration of the unnatural essence of sodomy was itself nurtured by a more general, intuitive notion that was shared by the travellers, missionaries, rationalist and pre-Romanticist scholars alike.

The observations by some travellers of alternative attitudes towards same-sex praxis hardly seemed an incentive to change their sense of moral self-complacency. Texts by them contain only disapproving descriptions of 'animal-like', 'immoral' or 'savage' debauch – a sadly homophobic theme that is hardly relevant to the purpose of this book. The stigmatization of sodomy as 'unnatural' by missionaries most likely was inspired by age-old canonic tradition, and the pressure to speak about it only when necessary generally makes their descriptions hard to evaluate.[32] Some artificially upheld the claim, put forward by de Las Casas and others in the sixteenth century, that same-sex praxis did not occur at all among savage people 'who lived close to nature'.[33] Other documents are more straightforward and explicit. Same-sex praxis, according to Ludovici Muratori, was not tolerated within the compounds of the *reducciones* and a man's hair-do revealed if he was Christianized or not. It was the custom for men to wear long hair, which upset the Jesuits eager to maintain a clear divide between women and men.[34]

Systematic attempts were made, within the reductions, to eradicate same-sex practices among Indian men. When caught, one could be imprisoned for three months or sent away. One ought to be aware of men dressing like women, and clothes should cover the legs of men and women, but not too well, so that disguise of one's sex is impossible. But measures had to be taken against same-sex relations between male (and female) Indians and the Jesuit fathers themselves. Therefore an ordinance was proclaimed by father Augustín de Arragona, proclaiming that gestures of tenderness ought to be controlled.[35]

Rationalism, in its turn, did not lift the stigma from sodomy either, as is revealed in an early scholarly attempt to redefine universal (in this case, North American) reality by Lorenzo Boturini Benaduci. His *Idea de una nueva Historia General de la América Septentrional* (1746) already previsaged the Enlightenment belief that sodomy was ultimately a *perversa costumbre*.[36] Montesquieu, though pleading for decriminalization, also considered same-sex practices as an anomaly against nature and even upheld the age-old, biblical description *contre nature*. It resulted largely from unfortunate social circumstances, such as the nudity of adolescents in the ancient Greek *gymnasia*, polygamy in Asia, or the European school system, that separated boys from girls.[37] Equally negative was the most influential *Encyclopédie*.[38] 'Unnatural' sex was sometimes ascribed to the exigencies of the climate, as with Perrenot[39]or Jacobs,[40] who both pointed to the effect of the Mediterranean. But the animosity of the *Philosophes* towards the clergy and the aristocracy more often gave rise to explanations of sodomy as a *vice aristocratique* or a *vice du clergé*, that is: as decadent and contrary to nature.

Von Herder, among the forerunners of Romanticism, accepted fundamental differences between the people of the world, yet saw them all as jointly on their way to a higher level of humanity. Sodomy, in this perspective, was seen as part of an original, 'barbarous' innocence that characterized Asians, Americans and the ancient Greeks alike, yet that ought to be surpassed by moral virtue in order for humanity to reach its higher goal.[41]

A similar denunciation of sodomy as unnatural and an impediment to human progress was shared by Edward Gibbon. His work *The Decline and Fall of the Roman Empire* (1776–88) is particularly relevant, since it explained the collapse of the Roman empire as partially induced by 'the degenerate Romans, polluted with the mean vices of wealth and slavery'.[42]Gibbon's emphasis upon the pernicious effects of sodomy on state matters was inspired by his disapproval of penal law reform on the European continent. To solidify his argument, he compared Roman decay with similar processes in China, India, pre-Columbian America. He unaccountably omitted the Islamic countries and Japan, but confronted all with Subsaharan Africa, that he believed and hoped to be 'exempt from this moral pestilence'.[43]

The berdache's theoretical appeal

Both the advocates of the presumed 'naturalness' of same-sex practices and their opponents conceived male-to-male sexual relations as a particular form of behaviour in the first place and sought to validate their point of view with ethnographic evidence. In essence, their approach was a moralistic one.

But, underneath a traditional ethnography of nature's moral boundaries, another paradigm became visible as the Enlightenment reached its apogee. It reveals, in fact, how European discourse about same-sex praxis actually was co-defined by 'evidence' from overseas and marked by an increasingly outspoken focus on the cross-gender manifestations of same-sex praxis in particular. Numerous travel narratives no longer presented 'sodomy' as a behavioural pattern, that potentially every one might adopt more or less incidentally, and that was considered good or bad. Instead, they portrayed those engaging in sodomy as members of a more or less clearly visible minority. In such reports, the rhetoric about 'immoral impulses' was now replaced by a nascent, reifying image of a consistently and permanently 'vicious' personality, most commonly seen as having a simultaneously effeminate and passive nature.

Antecedents of this narrative trope, as I described in chapter one, influenced the debate about eunuchs and hermaphrodites. 'Seventeenth- and eighteenth-century dissertations', says the historian Rousseau, were 'permeated with discussions about the physiological characteristics of eunuchs'.[44] They became emblematic for a new kind of 'sodomite', as they were often believed to assume a passive role, like the women they were supervising within the compounds of the seraglio. The fact that eunuchs were forced to tolerate male penetration did not prevent some authors from speculating about a proclivity to same-sex relations that was 'natural' to the eunuchs themselves.

Yet hermaphrodites, rather than the emasculated *castrati*, became the privileged personification of an anomalous sexuality. Since the seventeenth century, European hermaphrodites had been cast as 'sinners *born* to commit crimes' (my italics), their crime being the one against nature. Confusion about the 'essence' of hermaphrodites grew as they became a favourite topic for conversation. In 1744 the English *Gentleman's Magazine* ran a series of 'Observations on Hermaphrodites'. Speculation abounded as to how hermaphrodites developed during the mother's pregnancy or at birth. The results of anatomical studies of animals were compared to human beings with undefined genitalia. Rousseau emphasizes in this context how no one was certain if hermaphrodites were simply sodomites, that is, whether they were physiologically predisposed to commit buggery or just participating in 'a more general type of sin only marginally associated with sodomy'.[45]

To understand fully what Rousseau means by this, we ought to return to the sources of the debate. I have described earlier how the cross-gender behaviour of the berdaches of the New World had stimulated speculation in Europe on the very nature of hermaphroditism. Berdaches indeed showed both masculine and feminine traits, but these did not coincide with the Classical and Medieval image of a simultaneous presence of male (*penis*, *testes*) and female (*mammae*) genitalia. Their femininity was implied, most of all, by their long hair, their clothing and their social and, often, sexual roles.

The following survey of data taken from texts about different areas, will show to what extent such ethnographic information possibly played a substantial role in the debate on hermaphrodites and, along with it, in the changing conceptualization of sexuality and sexual identity. I will explain, in particular, how the disproportionately greater weight of evidence from America and Asia where cross-gender roles were most visible, may have counted for the growing popularity within Europe of the new construction of an 'effeminate sodomite'.

America

The initial relation of 'explorer/explored' was replaced by the far less ephemeral one of colonialism and cultural patriarchy. Social reality and intercultural communication were complicated by miscegenation, if less so in the newly independent United States of America after 1776, as well as by the rise of a new (Creole) elite. The New World became a platform also for experiment, religiously, socially, politically, and sexually. Often, sexual experiment sprang merely from the exigencies of a 'frontier' existence both on land and at sea.[46]

In Europe, the New Worlds were to be integrated within already existing or newly defined views of world order and humanity. Sexual variety too, while gazed at with fascination or disgust, was gradually placed within the new theory of human nature, that became a guideline for the moral judgements of the Enlightenment's *Philosophes*.

Gradually, writers started wondering at the very nature of hermaphrodites in particular and their Early Modern representation as 'ambisexual', two-sexed beings soon lost ground. Cornelis de Pauw, when describing the 'hermaphrodites' of Florida, claimed that 'almost all hermaphrodites are basically girls, whose sexual organs exceed ordinary size and are over-developed (presques tous les hermaphrodites ne sont que des filles, en qui les organes du sexe, en excédants les bornes ordinaires, se sont trop dével-oppés)'.[47] The historian Guicciardi emphasizes how, thus, 'the insertion of hermaphroditism within the realm of feminine nature allowed for annihila-tion of its irreducible character, which, if not, would have threatened radical difference (insertion de l'hermaphrodisme dans la nature féminine permet d'annuler ce qu'aurait de pire la différence radicale: son caractère irréduct-ible)'.[48] Irreducible, certainly, but not really in the sense outlined by de Pauw. Nor was the character of hermaphrodites irreducible in the sense ascribed to it by the Danish scholar, Jens Kraft, who claimed that they were really men, dressed like women, just like their colleagues in Scythian and Assyrian culture.[49] Or, for that matter, by Christian Gottlob Heyne, an armchair scholar who also identified cross-gender roles in America as essentially men in travesty, and then compared them equally to the Scythians.[50]

Reports by Egede, Cranz, Steller, Falkner, Dalrymple, and Palou about effeminate men, who assumed a passive sexual role, confirmed the proximity between hermaphroditism and sodomy.[51] Joseph Billings, when describing sodomitical practices among the Arctic population of the Aljut, emphasized how the passive partners dressed like girls.[52] The question, however, of whether these hermaphrodites showed a male or female genital build had disappeared. What made them hermaphrodites was the fact that they took a female role both in social life and while having sex.

At this point, hermaphrodites and sodomites became interchangeable. The Early Modern idea that men engaging in same-sex behaviour while assuming a cross-gender role must have female genitalia had been dropped and was replaced by a new one, that no longer claimed the genitalia themselves to be relevant but rather the use that was made of them. The term 'hermaphrodites', as a result, became less current and was replaced by 'sodomites'. Such men, though possessing male genitalia, were seen as 'feminine' because they used their genitals in ways that revealed a presumably female orientation. They were thus anomalous individuals, as their sexual life contradicted the order of biology. Such a portrayal, seen from a current anthropological perspective, was accurate insofar as it disconnected the explanation of cross-gender behaviour from an anatomy of genitalia, yet it leaped ahead of evidence by connecting it erroneously to speculations about their presumed 'sodomite' identity. Generally this was not justified, as reconstructions of variant types of berdache roles and identities have indicated that the link between social and sexual transgression did not necessarily coincide.[53]

Not every single observer shared the newly rising theory that same-sex praxis sprang from a biological constitution that essentially contradicted one's sex. Some, in fact, explained the phenomenon of berdaches in more traditional terms. Perrin du Lac attributed the cross-gender behaviour of the berdaches to a propensity to immorality.[54] The British Major Long adopted the indigenous version that they were pushed into their role by the female spirit of the moon.[55] In Southey's *History of Brazil* (1810–19),[56] a reference can be found to Francisco Alvez do Prado, who described men dressing like women among the Guaycurú Indians of the Mato Grosso in 1795. He suggested, like the Guaycurú themselves, that these were somehow impotent, 'just like *cunidas* or bastard animals'.[57] Such explanations gradually became subordinate, however, to a biological etiology that became predominant also in discourse about the Pacific and Asia.

Indian subcontinent and South East Asia

Western Orientalist scholars, studying Indian literature, generally remained silent on non-conformist sexuality. However, the *Mahabharata* and the *Ramayana* both contain detailed descriptions of such.[58] Historical information about the Indian subcontinent and South-East Asia also reveals how in these areas same-sex practices occurred as either age- or gender-structured. Officially, Hinduism was relatively unfavourable towards same-sex practices and tolerated them only when the passive role was assumed by *hijras*.[59]

Same-sex practices seem to have remained common, from before European colonization or control, notwithstanding increasing western influence or regional differences. They were less widespread in Hindu cities than in regions dominated by Islam. The Dutch admiral Johan Splinter Stavorinus confirmed this with reports on both male and female same-sex practices, along with bestiality, in Moghul Bengal:

The sin of Sodom is not only in universal practice among them, but extends to a bestial communication with brutes, and in particular with sheep. ... I do not believe that there is any country upon the face of the globe, where lascivious intemperance, and every kind of unbridled lewdness, is so much indulged in, as in the lower provinces of the empire of Indostan. ... [This] extends likewise to the Europeans, who settle, or trade there.[60]

Stavorinus' portrayal of same-sex praxis in India in no way suggests that such was the exclusive domain of a minority, nor that it was natural to the Indians. Europeans, when arriving in India, presumably adopted the habit easily.

Father Jean Antoine Dubois similarly reported that pederasty and male prostitution flourished in Hindu and Muslim areas of the Indian subcontinent alike. When expressing his astonishment at the numerous male transvestite prostitutes, a Brahmin answered him that there was 'no accounting for tastes'.[61] First published in English in 1816, then in French in 1825, his report contained a frank narrative of Christianization's failure in India and was hard to find, as a result, in libraries across Europe. But it was widely read.[62]

European descriptions of same-sex praxis in the Maldives, Sri Lanka, the Malay Peninsula, Thailand, Indonesia and the Philippines were marked by uncertainty about how sexual boundaries were drawn by the indigenous population itself. William Marsden's *History of Sumatra* (1783) simply denied the existence of same-sex practices on this island of the Dutch East Indies.[63] But the current representations of an endemic, Oriental sodomy was upheld by the missionary John Haensel, as he expressed his amazement at the *insouciance* towards male-to-male sexual relations of the people of both Kedan (Northwest Malaysia) and the Nicobar Islands in 1795.[64] Earlier, in 1756, Charles De Brosse reiterated the story of Thomas Candish, annotated by François Prettie, that male infibulation was to prevent men from having sex among themselves on the Sulu Islands, now part of the Philippines.[65] The text, despite its erratic diagnostics, was indicative of a persistent belief that the Malayan race was in no way exempt from Oriental lasciviousness.

As relatively little anthropological research was done, it is difficult for the modern historian to judge the value of European testimonies. Generally, public attitudes in these areas seem to have been quite benevolent towards sexual relations among men, even though these were marked by social inequality and a significant age difference between both partners. Transvestism was also constitutional to sexual relations among men. Linguistically, the passive role was distinguished, whereas no real term existed for the active insertee.[66]

The prominence of cross-gender roles both on the Indian subcontinent and in South-East Asia did not go unnoticed by European observers, even when the mutual relation of sodomy and cross-gender behaviour, clearly visible in discourse about American Indians, is less prominent in observations about

South-East Asia. This may be partially explained by the widespread occurrence here of age-structured same-sex practices, that did not necessarily imply the adoption of a feminine role.

Nevertheless, a report of hermaphrodites was written by Joinville, who, when describing the training of Hindu novices in Kandy, Ceylon, mentioned that 'hermaphrodites' were sought after. He omitted to clarify, alas, if by this a cross-gender role was meant rather than actual ambisexuality. Instead of investigating the matter, he related it to certain castes, originating from sexual intercourse among genuinely ambisexual beings.[67] Navarrete's earlier references to cross-gender roles among the Macassarese in Celebes were confirmed by Thomas Raffles. This author of a *History of Java* also inventoried cross-gender roles on the islands of Java (*málawáding, kawi, bandu*), Bali (*banchi*) and among the Lampong of southeast Sumatra (*bláding'an*).[68]

China

Descriptions of Chinese same-sex praxis were rather minimal in the Jesuit reports about Christianization by Du Halde, Lecomte and Grosier. Both de Pauw and Toreen claimed that this could hardly be justified and suggested that it was inspired primarily by strategical considerations.[69] The missionary Parrenin, when questioned on the issue by Dortous de Mairan, admitted that sodomy did indeed occur in China, 'if less frequently than elsewhere in Asia'.[70]

Non-clerical authors had been more straightforward in their descriptions. De la Barbinais, among them, ascribed same-sex praxis among Chinese men to a lack of women: 'Due to the lack of women, these miserables seek other objects to satisfy their brutality. Their exterior look hides a black soul, prone to all sorts of vice (Au deffaut des femmes ces scélérats recouvrent à d'autres objets pour assouvir leur brutalité. Leur extérieur cache une âme noire, abandonée à toutes sortes de vices).'[71] But it was considered acceptable, so he reported, as it was frequently depicted in 'picture books'. The widespread practice of sodomy, moreover, did not seem to undermine the Chinese people's fertility, as this was perceived as extraordinarily high.[72] This speculation, though only marginal to the whole of de la Barbinais' text, may well have had an effect as evidence supporting the growing belief that 'lower' races, while prone to sexual vice, were nevertheless reproducing at a faster rate than the 'higher' races, that was also claimed to be applicable to American population.

Apart from the lack of women, presented by de la Barbinais as a major cause of sexual relations among men, other factors too were indicated. De Pauw ascribed the 'sensuality', including sodomy, of the Chinese to their consumption of aphrodisiacs and opium.[73] Barrow, who described sexual relations between the mandarins and their servant boys, believed the wide-spread practice of sodomy to result from lenient religious and moral prescriptions.[74] Others focused on the role of the theatre as a privileged platform for contacts between men and boy-actors, who assumed female roles. Sonnerat reported how male actors imitated a female way of walking.[75] Aeneas Anderson claimed that the female roles were performed by eunuchs[76]– a claim repeated by Henry Ellis in 1817.[77]

Caught within the by then secular trope of Oriental sexuality, discourse about Chinese same-sex praxis remained imbued with a sense of immorality. New, when compared with Early Modern texts, was an increasing emphasis upon 'decadence' and, with it, on 'breeding grounds' like Buddhist convents, the theatre and houses of male prostitution. This way, responsibility was reallocated from the inhabitants' individual souls to their collective status as a different race. At the same time, the combination of same-sex practices and cross-gender roles, as in the theatre and male prostitution, remained far from unnoticed by western observers, who felt compelled to emphasize the 'effeminate' outlook of the boys, who took the passive role during sex.

Japan

Japan's reputation as a haven for sodomy was also hardly challenged during the eighteenth century. Old narratives of age-related same-sex relations within the compounds of Buddhist convents and of male prostitution were reprinted in synoptic studies about Japan, in encyclopedic inventories or in proto-ethnographic surveys of behaviour across the world.[78] The Jesuit father Lejeune expressed his despair at the Japanese reluctance to give up 'animal lust'. While admitting that it springs from nature, he nevertheless insisted that it ought to be nipped in the bud.[79] Von Zimmerman singled out Japan as the country most addicted to 'Asian' sin, thus reiterating the connection that had been made for centuries between sodomy and the Orient.[80]

Virtually no reports are known from the era between 1750 and 1800, as Japan had become inaccessible again after the failed efforts of European missionaries to convert the country to Christianity. This in itself may well have supported clerical writers in their claim that sodomy abounded in Japan. Advocates of sexual enlightenment, on the other hand, may have felt little incentive in changing the image of Japanese sexuality, as it enhanced such a powerful critique of western morality. In reality, same-sex practices were tied to very particular patriarchal relations and virtually always implied that one partner would be a youngster, who would assume the passive role during sex (*nanshoku*). It remained common, not only within the context of Buddhist education or military training, but also among the urban middle-class of Tokugawa Japan (1603–1868).[81]

The Southern Pacific region

The colonization from 1788 onwards of New South Wales followed the exploration of *Terra Australis* by Tasman (1642–59), Roggeveen (1721–2), de Bougainville (1766–8) and James Cook (1768–71; 1772–5; 1776–80). The incorporation of most New World territories into the 'modern world-system' allowed for the archipelagos of Micronesia, Melanesia and Polynesia to become an ultimate *topos* of imagination about the *bon sauvage*, as most islands were subjected to colonial rule only in the nineteenth century.[82] Tahiti was soon turned into an emblem of political enlightenment and sexual freedom. Its quintessential representation as a newly found Arcadia can be found in Diderot's *Supplément*.[83]

The original impartiality, if such existed,[84] was soon set aside by what Bernard Smith has coined 'empirical naturalism'. This abolished the ideal-izing rhetoric of its precedent 'classical naturalism' and made primitive man 'as one creature among others subject to natural laws, at once the flower and the victim of his environment'.[85] In a modest form, Tahitian people were seen as mankind's children.[86] But a less benevolent primitivism also became noticeable as pictorial representations of indigenous people, who originally had embodied classical aesthetical ideals, increasingly emphasized their ugliness. Their sexual freedom was now seen as primaeval promiscuity. Only a minor disparity existed between the late eighteenth-century naturalists and more religiously inspired authors, who took offence at the presumably 'debauched and pagan' genital chants or *mele m'ai* and *hula* dances – both rituals that merely consolidated social adherence and identity.

Evidently, the widespread visibility of same-sex practices both among women and among men was seen as an obstacle to the artificially upheld *nouvelle Cythère*. They were to be banned from paradise along with other 'vices', even though environmental explanations were put forward by some to safeguard the Polynesian people from being called personally responsible. Johann Reinhold Forster, commenting on his son George Forster's travel notes, claimed the climate to be the source of Polynesian sexual indul-gence.[87] And so did Cowper in a poem written in 1783:

> Ev'n the favour'd isles,
> So lately found, although the constant sun,
> Cheer all their seasons with a grateful smile,
> Can boast but little virtue; and, inert,
> Through plenty, lose in morals what they gain
> In manners – victims of luxurious ease.[88]

Moralism gained, however, and Tahitian exoticism soon became emblematic within a more generalized condemnation of the depravity of man. The French maritime surgeon Roblet witnessed how male-to-male relations occurred on the Marquesas Islands – merely an indication for his chronicler,

Etienne Marchand, of how low Polynesian morality had sunk.[89] Disapproval of same-sex practices was part also of the policy of the Missionary Society of London, that was established on Tahiti in 1795. A recurrent focus of attention was the *mahū*, a cross-gender role in traditional Polynesian society,[90] that was first reported by Captain William Bligh.[91] The missionary James Wilson criticized how *mahūs*

chose this vile way of life when young. Putting on the dress of a woman, they follow the same employments, are under the same prohibitions with respect to food, etc. and seek the courtship of men as women do, nay are more jealous of the men who cohabit with them, and always refuse to sleep with women.[92]

He described how they were in no way marginalized, but highly esteemed even by the chiefs, who took them as women. Their privileged position, however, did not prevent Wilson from explaining the phenomenon of 'male brides' as a solution for poor men, who were unable to pay a dowry, consisting of pigs or, soon, European goods.[93] Equally judgemental were Turnbull,[94]Ellis[95] and Löhr, who denounced the *mahūs* along with other practices like abortion and infanticide.[96]

Meanwhile, reports were available also on male-to-male sexual behaviour, that was not gender-structured. James Cook was confronted with coteries of men, accompanying local kings on Hawaii. They were called *aikāne*, translatable as 'man-fucking men' and they in no way trespassed gender boundaries.[97] Similar claims were made by Lisiansky and Dulaure.[98] Marion too related how Maori men in northern New Zealand engaged in sexual acts 'that shock nature, even in their relations with women (qui choquent la nature, même dans l'usage de leurs femmes)',[99] that is, anal intercourse both with women and men, yet did not report any cross-gender roles.

Perhaps careless observation or, as Roy Porter suggests, 'normalisation'[100] caused them to disregard cross-gender roles, as these were quite common among Polynesian people. Among most tribes, *fa'afafine* or boys raised as girls were a common phenomenon. The Maori, people of Polynesian origin, who had sailed to Aotearoa, now know as New Zealand, during the Great Migration of the fourteenth century, did not know *fa'afafine*, but transvestites were part of their tradition.[101]

However, deliberate anathematization of cross-gender roles was altogether exceptional. When surveying the whole of ethnographic reportage on the Pacific, Japan, China, South-East Asia and America, moreover, one easily notices how indigenous same-sex praxis was more often described in relation to cross-gender roles than not. By the end of the eighteenth century, ethnographic narrative was dominated by the image of 'effeminate' sodomites, who presumably monopolized and signified sexual depravity. Their active partners gradually disappeared from the western gaze. This was different from before, when travel narratives tended to focus more on the sodomitical acts of both the passive and active participants.

Africa

The African inland remained largely *terra incognita*, which led Gibbon to believe that sodomy did not occur. Exploration proved hazardous and often unsuccessful. The African Society, founded in 1788, financed a futile attempt by Daniel Houghton to reach Tombouctou (1790–1). Mungo Park described his exploration of the Niger in *Travels in the Interior District of Africa* (Edinburgh, 1799), yet did not mention anything about same-sex behaviour or cross-gender roles. The French explorer Degrandpré reported the frequent use in the Congo basin of the derogatory word *kinkololo*, 'ce qui signifie perdrix'. He himself explained its meaning as someone who had seduced a king's concubine.[102] Perhaps Karsch-Haack's claim that it was a nickname for a male person who engaged in sex with other men was justified, as Aristotle had perceived that male partridges easily mounted one another.[103] It went unnoticed by Degrandpré, however, and may have reinforced beliefs that same-sex practice was indeed uncommon in Subsaharan Africa.

But nothing compels one to believe that Gibbon's optimism – in his own eyes, that is – reflected more than the fact that as yet very little of the African interior had been disclosed. Testimonies about same-sex practices were, as a result, all but nonexistent. I mention merely a brief reference by Robert Norris, who saw 'castrates' during his journey through Dahomey in 1772.[104] Browne claimed that same-sex praxis was rare in Sudan.[105] But Africa remained a 'dark' continent and these few scanty descriptions hardly allow for conclusive evidence.

The Levant

Less inconclusive, though largely reiterating the tenacious bias of earlier texts, were the new descriptions of same-sex praxis in the Arab world. Travel accounts by Poiret,[106] Melling,[107] and Pouqueville[108]hardly deviated from the age-old pattern of horror and amazement at the presumably ubiquitous indulgence of Muslim men in 'this revolting passion'.[109] Richard Burton mentioned a French officer Jaubert, who wrote to general Bruix during the French expedition into Egypt from 1798 to 1799 and complained that 'the Arabs and Mamelukes treated some of our prisoners like Socrates treated Alcibiades. Either one submitted, or one died (les Arabes et les mamelouks ont traité quelques uns des nos prisonniers comme Socrate traitait, dit-on, Alcibiade. Il fallait périr ou y passer).'[110]Around the same time, the French officer Charles Nicolas Sonnini de Manoncourt declared pederasty to be the 'delight of the Egyptians' of his time, but distinguished the latter's bisexual praxis from a more exclusive sodomy in Europe itself: 'Opposite to the effect, that it produces in cooler climates, being that it is exclusive, it goes together here with an inclination for women at the same time ([Au] contraire de l'effet qu'elle produit dans les climats moins chauds, celui d'être exclusive, elle s'y allie avec l'inclination pour les femmes).'[111] Relevant here is not so much the author's claim that those engaging in sodomy in Egypt also maintained sexual relations with women. Such a view in fact corresponded to a traditional assumption by Europeans and Muslims alike that anyone might potentially commit an act of sodomy.[112] More striking, in fact, is Sonnini's suggestion that such would not (or would no longer?) be the case in Europe itself. In a remarkable way, it reflected changes that became visible at this time that I will discuss below. It did not, however, challenge the secular image of Arab sodomy as indiscriminate sexual lust.

An identical image of Muslim people inclining heavily to sodomy found admission, if only incidentally, in historical and philological scholarship. Most publications remained silent on matters of sexuality. Louis de Chénier's *Recherches historiques sur les Maures* described the sexuality of sultan Abdallah V, who ruled from 1729 until 1757, as well as sexual relations among the (male) patrons of the *hammans* – 'case' studies, in the author's eye, of an endemic propensity to sexual vice.[113] Jacob Bartholdy's study on Greece accredited the Ottoman cultural influence, rather than the ancient 'pederastic' tradition, for the presence of same-sex practices.[114] His position was justified as the Ottomans ruled the country since 1453. The unproblematic character of Bartholdy's explanation, however, reveals how powerful the association of sodomy with Islam remained throughout the Age of Enlightenment. No need was felt by Bartholdy to even explore how same-sex practices may have spread equally among the Greek Orthodox monastic clergy, that maintained its freedom and even received great political authority.[115]

The *Alf Layla Wa-Layla* remained only partially translated by, among others, Antoine Galland (1701; 1704–17), while scholars went on searching for the missing parts of the original manuscript.[116] The majority of passages describing boy love were as yet inaccessible for a Western audience. But descriptions of boy love were incorporated in studies of other literary sources by John Hindley[117] and Heinrich Friedrich von Diez.[118]

Very little, however, indicates that discourse on sexual variety in the Arab world was different from before. Perhaps the heritage of previous centuries weighed too heavily upon Enlightenment observers, who felt few incentives to alter their descriptive vocabulary. It seems to me, however, that the repetitiousness of discourse on Islam sexuality also sprang from the relative invisibility of cross-gender roles outside the realm of male prostitution. Later on, descriptions of such would become more prominent as a reflection, as will be demonstrated, of the increasing weight of a gender-defined understanding of homosexuality. Until then, however, texts about same-sex praxis in the Arab world remained exempt from associations with cross-gender roles and perpetuated an age-old discursive trope about endemic sodomitical vice.

The Enlightenment discourse on same-sex praxis remained altogether ambivalent. Pleading for its tolerance through reform of penal law, the philosophers nevertheless excluded it from the realm of nature. It remained a vice, particularly common, so it was claimed by the rising bourgeoisie, among the clergy and aristocracy and at odds with the new ideal of family life. Along with masturbation, it violated the rules of what has been coined by Barker-Benfield as the 'spermatic economy'[119] – a provocative and, as yet, hypothetical construct, but a powerful image of how sexuality was increasingly regulated within the margins of utility rather than pleasure.

Underneath the debate on the moral aspects of sexuality, cognitively more significant discussions took place about the etiology itself of same-sex practices. I have reviewed how ethnographic evidence reflected the debate on the (un-)naturalness of same-sex practices among men. While no consensus existed throughout the Enlightenment, a common belief had nevertheless grown that the issue to be addressed was an environmental and a biological one.

Not everyone shared the deterministic paradigm of the new sciences of life. Some, like the English-born German physician Falconer, advanced more historical explanations as Lafitau had done before.[120] But, to most other writers, the issue of sexuality seemed to transcend historical circumstance. In this light, anomalous phenomena such as eunuchs, hermaphrodites, and sodomites were seen in an entirely different light. I have pointed out how ethnographic reports increasingly emphasized same-sex praxis in relation to cross-gender roles. Especially the role of the American berdache and its equivalents in South-East Asia and the Pacific proved instrumental to the success of the new paradigm. In a different way, male transvestite roles in China and Japan also supported European speculation on the 'feminine' nature of those engaging in (passive) sexual relations with men. The actual or presumed coincidence of cross-gender roles with same-sex praxis made the former instrumental to new sexual theory in Europe that locked sodomy inexorably into the corset of femininity. Passivity, more particularly, as located in the receptive use of the anus, became quintessential to the 'sodomite' identity – a different idea, altogether, from previous notions of sodomy, which included the active partner as well as the passive one, men as well as women.

At the homefront

The closer link, made within numerous ethnographic accounts, between same-sex praxis and cross-gender roles, was not only the outcome of empirical observation. In fact, such observation parallelled new, more embracing innovations of Enlightenment intellectual thought. Some occurred in the margin of colonialism or crystallized into new theories of the human race. Others were intimately intertwined with changing relations between the sexes and, secondly, with the rise of sodomite subcultures in Europe itself. Together they constituted a dialectic of intellectual change and innovation, that would radically alter the parameters of the geography of perversion.

The gender revolution and sodomite subcultures

To a considerable degree, the changing representations, within Europe, of same-sex relations among non-western people, were reinforced by social and intellectual changes in the urban centres of Europe itself. The subcultures namely of libertine sexuality, that had originated in some cities since as early as the twelfth century, changed significantly as the boundaries of sexual orthodoxy were redefined.

Before the change, these subterranean networks consisted of men who engaged in more or less unconventional sexual practices, either with female prostitutes, with adolescent boys or with other men. Only a small minority among them engaged in both passive and active roles. At an early stage of historical research, these microcosms of sexual experimentation were seen as precedents of today's urban gay communities, especially because its members were generally described in sources as 'sodomites'.[121] Such an interpretation has now proved to be inaccurate and anachronistic.

Randolph Trumbach himself has revised his earlier interpretation of the historical evidence and now emphasizes that its members were not merely ancestors of modern gay-identified men.[122] Nor, he adds, may the change, that occurred since approximately 1700, please some advocates of Gay Liberation, who aim at upholding an image of respectability and are therefore reluctant to recognize aspects of the gay past that do not correspond to their agenda.[123]

Targeted here is the increasing prominence within the sodomite subcultures after 1700 of the effeminate male. This was new, compared to before, when assuming an active role during intercourse prevented one from being labeled as effeminate. From now on, 'any sexual desire by one male for another leads to categorization as an effeminate sodomite'. New also was the increasing stigmatization of a passive sexual role, performed by adolescents, which had not substantially undermined the boy's gender status before. 'The seduction', Trumbach continues, 'of adolescents by effeminate sodomites, whatever the role played in the sexual act, therefore becomes very dangerous to both the boy and the sodomite.'[124]

At the root of these changes was a reorganization of gender identity, that substituted a new pattern of individual identity for the preceding one. In the latter, Trumbach explains, 'the debauchee or libertine who denied the relegation of sexuality to marriage had been able to find, especially in cities, women and boys with whom he might indifferently, if sometimes dangerously, enact his desires.'[125] The modern pattern, on the other hand, was different as 'most men conceived first of all that they were male, because they felt attraction to women, and to women alone. Gender differences were presumed therefore to be founded on an irradicable difference of experience: men did not know what it was like to desire men, and women did not desire women, though, in the minds of men, and perhaps women too, the latter was less so. In this culture, the sodomite became an individual interested in his own gender and inveterately effeminate and passive.'[126]

Trumbach's explanation of this cognitive change, though as yet far too little corroborated by empirical research, is as powerful as it is complex. The new role of the effeminate sodomite, says Trumbach, was the indirect outcome of a general shift in Europe towards a more egalitarian organization of both family and social life. It was characterized by an increasingly stronger call for the abolition of slavery, for democracy and for a higher regard of the rights of women and children, and contrasted with a traditional patriarchal morality that allowed for male domination over women, children, slaves and servants alike.

Family life in particular was increasingly ruled by a new code of domesticity, that was accompanied by what Lawrence Stone called 'affective individualism' and 'companionate marriage',[127] but that simultaneously prescribed well-defined gender roles in order to smoothen newly rising anxieties about sexual equality. The view that the genders were 'equal, but separate' was supported by a new belief in male and female incommensurability.

Within this new perspective, same-sex relations, that were previously considered to be a sin, even though pursued by some as part of a libertinist appeal, became 'unnatural' for almost everyone. Those few who did not feel intimidated by the newly defined gender ideology, upheld their subcultural existence, but felt compelled to assume an effeminate role. Adolescents, who had been an easy target in traditional, patriarchal society were no longer available as they too would suffer a loss of gender status once they were to surrender to the advances of a sodomite.[128]

Both social change and intellectual innovation had thus deeply altered the outlook of sodomite subcultures in the West by the mid-eighteenth century. The word 'sodomite' was not only exclusively reserved for men engaging in sexual relations with men, but compromised at once by expectations of effeminacy and, often though not always, a passive role during sexual intercourse. In France, the cognitive shift was accompanied by a conceptual one as 'sodomites' was exchanged for *pédérastes*, a word that already existed but which became intimately linked with homosexually active men from approximately 1740.[129] In England, the birth of the 'queen' was preceded by libertine characters, such as the 'rake', who, in his liking of women as well as boys, personified the traditional libertine, and the 'fop', who, though effeminate, courted women. By 1680, when venereal disease spread widely in London, so-called 'beaus' had prefered virgin girls and especially boys, as these were believed to be an efficient prophylactic. Their indiscriminate libido still reflected an Early Modern libertinism, yet they became entangled in the new mood of times when they were arrested for sodomy and their effeminate dress-code was associated with same-sex relations by the public. 'He-whores' or 'mollies', men who often behaved effeminately and adopted both active and passive roles during intercourse, followed around 1700. By 1750 'men who had sex with men had usually conformed to the new role of the effeminate sodomite'.[130] Similar changes away from an indiscriminate, Early Modern libertinism into modern sexual roles have been uncovered from often fragmentary evidence in France[131] and Holland,[132] whereas the traditional pattern persisted alongside a modern one in the Mediterranean countries.[133]

Trumbach evaluates the significance of the effeminate sodomite for relations between the sexes by comparing his role to cross-gender roles such as the North American berdache, the Polynesian *mahū*, and the *xanith* in Oman.[134] Whereas these serve rather as a bridge between both genders in a context of low role differentiation, the effeminate sodomite seemed to guarantee a barrier where sexual equality grew steadily. His very effeminacy, in fact, ensured that a radical separation between male and female experience remained. '[The] molly's outcast status was the demonstration of what awaited a man who tried to cross the boundary between sexual desire in the two legitimated genders.'[135]

Whereas this may well be true, it is not entirely clear if the transformation of the sodomite subculture and of the gender revolution that it reflected, was most clearly visible among the middle- and upper-class, educated elites. According to R. Norton, same-sex praxis among the lower classes changed likewise from a pattern of incidental, 'unnamed' homosexual encounters to one of subcultural 'molly houses', where the working classes played an even more dominant role.[136]

But the lower classes were probably unaware of intellectual life and of the development of sciences. New scientific representations of the human body were influential amidst the middle and upper classes, however, as they reflected the changing relations between men and women, between marriage and libertine sexualities. Thomas Laqueur claims that 'the context for the articulation of two incommensurable sexes was ... neither a theory of knowledge nor advances in scientific knowledge', but, instead, the outcome of politics.[137] But innovation was not entirely brought about by demands from society. Factors that were inherent to an Enlightenment zeal for classification also played a role. The new biological theory, accordingly, of male and female difference, as well as of its anomalies, was equally inspired by an empiricist conviction that their essence could be located in the body itself. The 'making of sex', moreover, occurred simultaneously with the first, systematic attempts to define and classify human diversity according to the principles of race. New definitions, finally, of sexual and of cultural difference did not develop entirely autonomously from one another but gradually converged by means of a logic that was, in essence, fictitious since it was rooted in 'analogy'.

'L'homme-machine', or the physiology of difference

Scientific innovation in the Age of Enlightenment was, of course, strongly stimulated by the impressive amount of new data reaching Europe through travel accounts and colonial experience. Interpreting the often arbitrarily gathered information required new expeditions, that were often financed by the newly founded royal societies or academies of science and were set up to map systematically the physical landscape and flora and fauna of the entire world.[138]

At home, the richness of data was classified by collectors and scientists, among whom Linnaeus and Buffon are only the best-known, or included in the *Encyclopédie* of Diderot and d'Alembert. The power of nature as an explanatory paradigm was significant for the new, enlightened spirit and offered an alternative to earlier world views, that were built upon ideas of divine providence and creation.[139]

Human diversity, now an object of the systematic study of anthropology,[140] was subjected to classifications that, though not always mutually compatible, shared a belief that nature ought to be the guideline for taxonomy. It is a commonplace by now to point out not only how people across the world were catalogued by nascent scientific theories of 'race', but also how male and female difference was explained as the outcome of 'sex'. Only recently, however, have historians become aware of the significance of their simultaneity, largely because they were to fill the needs of European society both internally and in its colonies overseas. According to Laqueur,

The notion that either by demonstrating the separate creation of various races (polygenesis) or by simply documenting difference, biology could account for differential status in the face of 'natural equality', developed at the same time and in response to the same sorts of pressures as scientific sex.'[141]

Within the family, as we have seen, egalitarianism called for a counter-rhetoric of sexual incommensurability. The 'natural equality' to which Laqueur refers, embodies a persistent, universalist ideal, that received a new impulse from early reactions against the slave trade and slavery.[142] In this new context, sexual and racial discourse were hardly one another's mirror image, yet they mutually shared assumptions about the 'natural' foundation of difference and – this is of utmost importance – defined criteria for distinction, that envisaged a protean 'analogous' rationality.

The new, biological theory of male and female difference replaced the anterior, isomorphic model, that represented the female genitalia as 'underdeveloped', 'exaggerated', or 'inverted', yet essentially similar to the male ones.[143] Testicles and ovaries, that were denoted with a single term before,

were now separated linguistically. Female organs, that had not been distinguished earlier, were now named distinctly. Other parts of the human
body too, such as the skeleton and the nervous system, were presented as
different for men and women, but most emphasis was laid upon the reproductive organs as a new foundation for gender identity. The age-old theory of
orgasm as a precondition for conception was replaced by a more mechanical
physiology, that envisaged an image of female passionlessness.[144]

The novelty of eighteenth-century theory about feminine identity remains
undecided. Some claim that a different female biology was recognized
throughout the Old Regime alongside other notions of the uniqueness of the
female body. Yet such continuities should not disguise the innovative impact
of the Enlightenment's emphasis upon the genital constitution of male and
female identity.[145]

Within this context, both anatomical and physiological differences were
presented by authors such as Barles, Brunet, Daubenton, de Graaf, Gautier-
Dagoty, Haller and Palfyn as proof of the insurmountable difference
between the sexes and the origin of separate gender roles. Michel Delon has
pointed out how the new theory, at first sight, was not different from its
antecedents in its implication of a gender hierarchy that was disadvantageous to women.[146] Nor did it replace the old theories fully at once, as shown
by eighteenth-century republications of influential texts such as *Aristotle's
Masterpiece* (late seventeenth century) and Nicolas Venette's *Tableau de
l'amour considéré dans l'état du mariage* (1687). Someone like Diderot
adhered to the old and the new theories simultaneously.[147] In fact, no
consensus was reached about how to define biology's relevant indices, and
alternative accounts proliferated. Menstruation, for example, was seen by
some as a contingent pathology of civilization, whereas others emphasized
the impact of the uterus over a woman's life and hence of the natural origin
of her gender role. While a majority believed that black women displayed a
greater sexual libido, some instead claimed that their coarse nervous system
or dry mucous mebranes made them insensitive. But, in the end, bodily
constitution became the major explanatory paradigm and the 'distinct sexual
anatomy was adduced to support or deny all manner of claims in a variety of
specific social, economic, political, cultural or erotic contexts'.[148]

The latter especially should draw our attention, as it addresses the biological construction of sexuality. Desire, from now on, was aligned with
reproductive biology. Heterosexuality was natural – hence the new slogan
'opposites attract' – and its aberrations were not. Here too, disagreement
was perpetuated about the symptomatology of sexual deviance, causing
speculation on the morphology of both body and genitalia and on their
physiological functioning. The narratives, by then available, on same-sex
praxis across the world were read alternately as evidence of its 'universal' or
'local' character, but the micropolitics of alternative accounts hardly disguised a growing acceptance of a biological etiology. Enlightenment theory

of sexual desire did not, however, draw from the cross-cultural record fully autonomously, as if the latter simply served as an ethnographic repository. It also intersected in a more interactive way with new theories about cultural difference, that were increasingly centred upon the concept of 'race'.

In essence, the Enlightenment theory of the human race was a compromise between a new, scientific initiative to 'classify' and a traditional, Christian awareness of the threat, imposed upon the West, by the heterogeneity of universal population. This explains why 'racial' difference, while quintessential to the new rationale of biology, was conceived initially as pertinent to the human species' lineage. This way, the biblical doctrine of monogeny could be upheld, whereas racial difference was interpreted as the outcome of environmental circumstances.

Buffon introduced an element of change in the earlier, Linnaean classification by depicting human 'degeneration' as the outcome of Adam and Eve's expulsion into inferior environments. Thus mankind diversified due to climatological and dietary conditions, epidemics, and miscegenation, and this *ad infinitum*. 'Degeneration', in Buffon's *Histoire naturelle* and, more explicitly the works of Blumenbach, comprised 'the ... modifications that arise as one generation succeeds another [and] as an explication of variation within a species as opposed to separate creation'.[149]

The discontinuity with traditional representations of cultural difference, however, was implied by the weight accorded to biological distinctions and, accordingly, by the 'racial' classification of mankind. Of the anatomic characteristics that were selected as parameters of racial difference, the skin colour and texture, the facial features and the size of the skull were considered to be most relevant. The latter soon became a favourite criterion for racialist classification and preceded nineteenth-century craniometry, but it was applied on male skulls only. When comparing women interracially, emphasis was laid, quite significantly, on the skeleton and the pelvic region of the body, as these revealed best woman's destiny to give birth.

The novelty of Enlightenment racial taxonomy was laid out in the correlation of anatomical and psychological characteristics. It was conceived as a reciprocal relation, whereby a race's physical profile was seen as both revelatory *and* causal of its internal, emotional *Affekthaushalt* (N. Elias). Its epistemological structure was, in fact, tautological. This coincidence of diagnostics and symptomatology can hardly be underestimated, as it set the tune for scientific thought to come. The taxonomy of the body as both source and outcome of behavioural patterns would remain an essential part of the epistemological twilight zone that informed racial theory up to the twentieth century.

Enlightenment theory itself was transitional, as it mediated between a fairly familiar concept of 'environmentalism', initiated during the previous century, and a 'neurological' one, that presented the nervous system as a harbour of racial difference and that would become quintessential to the nineteenth-century science of human variety. Not only racial or cultural variety, moreover, but virtually every manifestation of human diversity could be subjected to the 'new semiotics of the nerve': 'The nerves were genderised and sexualised as crucial differences of male and female (such as hypochondriasis and hysteria), caucasian and black, oriental and moham-medan, heterosexual and hermaphroditical, were attributed to this or that nervous strength or defect.'[150]

The actual Enlightenment paradigm, as yet, emphasized the body's visible anatomic characteristics, which sprang from its materialist premises. When applied to humanity, these implied that behaviour could be explained as an essentially physiological process. It was a connection, meanwhile, that reduced the analysis not only of racial, but also of class, personality, and gender differences to a single, universally applicable theorem.

For de La Mettrie, who presented the image of *l'homme-machine*, human-ity was no more than an inventory of physiological effects. Maupertuis went so far as to quantify and measure the phenomena apprehended in conscious-ness.[151] Others, like d'Holbach and Helvétius in France, Hartley and Priestley in England, did not share the extreme mechanistic anthropology of de La Mettrie and Maupertuis, but they did subscribe to the empiricist paradigm of a physiology of the senses.[152]

Racial differentiation, in particular, was seen as the outcome of a sensorial dialectic between one's bodily constitution and environmental factors, at least for those who declared themselves 'monogenists'. These, including Buffon, Blumenbach and John Hunter, claimed that all men shared a common ancestry with Adam and Eve, and that the various races had in fact deviated from the original human stock through environmental pressures, such as the climate, food and lifestyle. Liberals most of them, they were opposed to slavery, contrary to the 'polygenists', who claimed racial charac-teristics to be innate. Monogenists opposed such fatalism and ascribed an equal potential for intellectual and moral achievement to all.[153]

It is one of the Enlightenment's 'shadows', no doubt, that the egalitarian-ism of monogenists nevertheless contributed, just like the polygenists, to a reification of hierarchic difference. 'Even [they] suffered from ethnocen-trism', claims Londa Schiebinger, 'insofar as European physiognomy was taken as the primordial norm.'[154] This gave rise not only to an idealization after European examples, in both literature and painting, of indigenous people,[155] but also, less favourably, to the representation of the physical outlook of real Africans or Afro-Americans, Indians, Arabs and others as unhappy 'derivates' from the original, presumably white Edenic race. Such was different, certainly, from later, evolutionary theory, that represented the white race as the furthest developed and removed from the original, barbaric race, but it is obvious that the taxonomy of physical differences ultimately facilitated a positioning on an hierarchic scale.

Naturally, the polygenists' point of view did this in an even more out-spoken way and their intellectual position was often translated politically into a defence of slavery.[156] Most influential was Samuel Thomas von Soemmering, whose book *Ueber die körperliche Verschiedenheit des Mohren vom Europäer* (1784) would inspire racialist theory about blacks until well into the nineteenth century.[157] Though personally opposed to slavery, he did uphold the belief that racial features were innate. While speculating on the black man's flat nose, for example, he claimed it to be an inheritable trait, as opposed to the deformation of the pubic bone of young, European ladies, that was brought about by the unnatural use of the corset or to the widening of the kneecap after too much kneeling.

The particularities of the poly- versus monogeny debate, however, must not obfuscate the common characteristics of both, as they shared the assumption that anatomical and physiological characteristics could be read as meaningful indices of difference. The races' divergent patterns of behaviour, as a result, were read as the reflection of their physical constitution, just as the different gender roles were ascribed to the incommensurable anatomy and physiology of women and men.

Sexualizing race

It has become common currency, in both academia and politics, to stress how European cultural ideology is marked by the way discourses on sex, gender, race, ethnicity and class were – and, at times, still are – intertwined. They were mutually connected and jointly constituted a set of what is called 'intersecting rhetorics'. It is a powerful concept, that I gladly use, even if not without criticism, for it is too often represented as a conscious male, white, heterosexual strategy to victimize women, people of colour, and homosexuals alike. The intertwined nature of both sexual and racial theories, accordingly, is seen primarily as a timeless characteristic, whose modalities remain unchanged and which is equally sharply defined all the time.

Such a static deconstructive model is inadequate for two reasons. First of all, it underestimates the relative autonomy of scientific thought, that is: of the logic inherent to the subsequent models of explanation, that are put forward by scientists. Secondly, it erratically subscribes to what it wants to dismantle, being the reification of ethnic and cultural identity as 'race' and of gender identity through 'sex'. Historically, theoretical paradigms have alternated as they kept redefining both cultural and gender identities, leading eventually to the very refutation of any analogy between them.

Nevertheless, my critical reflection hardly challenges the fact that 'analogous' reasoning became an essential part of Enlightenment and post-Enlightenment ideology. It was partly the outcome of politics, partly the result of an obstinate search for a single vocabulary, a centralizing principle, that would explain any variety of mankind. In the wake of eighteenth-century scientific innovation, this was claimed to reside in nature and great authority was ascribed, as a result, to anatomy and physiology. Such a focus was congruous with empiricism and complied with a tendency to explain life in mechanistic terms. Just as the human body was represented as a 'machine', so its sexual, social and racial variety was compared to a set of analogous mechanics.[158]

Nancy Stepan, in her seminal article 'Race and gender: The role of analogy in science', admits that analogies were, in fact, 'products of long-standing, long-familiar, culturally endorsed metaphors'.[159] Thus, Aristotle had compared women to slaves for their 'natural' inferiority. Blacks had been associated since the Middle Ages with baseness, sin, the devil, and ugliness, while whites were identified with virtue, purity, holiness, and beauty. Such comparisons were continued in the Age of Enlightenment, when blacks were considered childish, savage, bestial, lecherous and stupid. Madmen were compared to blacks, and so were the labouring poor.[160]

The novelty of Enlightenment analogy was implied by the predominance of texts that presented racial difference in sexual terms. Racial otherness was read from physical and behavioural aspects, that could be ascribed to either the male or the female realm. In the nineteenth century, new indices would nurture analogy. Some, as I will describe in the following chapters, altered the terms of comparison between race and gender. Others temporarily made comparison between racial inferiority and gender characteristics less relevant. The Enlightenment debate on other races' natural status, however, was very clearly marked by an ascription of sexual qualities.

This was shown perhaps most prominently in the ascription of 'feminine' characteristics to the people of America, Asia and the Pacific, while Subsaharan Africans and Arabs were most commonly accredited with a rather exaggerated and 'uncivilized masculinity'. The physical profile of Asians was seen as 'effeminate' since the early days of European expansion. Stereotypical representations of soft-skinned, passive Asians have remained common ever since. Such was illustrated, for example, by an anecdote from the life of the Governor-General of India from 1798 till 1805, Richard, Marquis Wellesley. He was a devoted patron of brothels in both London and the Empire, yet faced a problem once when a cut-throat associate of one of his whores threatened to publicize that his son was an effeminate 'Asiatic debauchee'.[161]

Less consensus seemed to exist among European intellectuals on whether American people could be equally described as 'of an effeminate' nature. It was not just an academic issue. Speculation on America's human stock was really part of a more embracing public debate on the failures and fortunes of colonization – far more so, in fact, than with Japan, China, South-East Asia or even the recently discovered *terra Australis*, whose significance was either commercial or ideological.

Debate on America gradually shifted from moral to biological terms, mostly as a result of the thesis by Buffon, that both flora and fauna in the New World were less developed than on the European continent. Less, also, than in Africa, where great animals did exist in abundance. But American mankind too proved more feeble, in the eyes of Buffon, than its European counterpart:

So there is something in the combination of elements and other physical causes, that limits the development of living nature in this new world . . . . The savage's genitals are weak and small; he has no hair, nor a beard, nor does he show any passion for his female counterpart.[162]

Buffon reiterated the already existing theory, that the hairless body of Indian men revealed their lack of virility. But now, their physical outlook had become more than a mere coincidence as it was presented by Buffon as the immediate effect of climatological circumstance and passed on genetically. It revealed their coldness and sexual frigidity and corresponded with the prominence of amphibians, reptiles and insects in America.

The metaphoric relation between a 'deficient' sexuality and a fauna that is seen as 'of a lower scale', is obvious and seems to confirm Londa Schiebinger's recently developed thesis that Enlightenment zoological taxonomy reflected an agenda of sexual politics.[163] In reality, we are facing a peculiar moment of analogous thinking, as sexual qualifications are ascribed to classes of animals while these animals are presented, in a reverse way, as 'revealing' of their human equivalent's sexuality. The underlying tautology is revealed by what Gerbi called Buffon's 'erotico-hydraulic theory'[164] of American nature, that describes its inferiority as a vicious circle between man and his physical environment:

It is principally because there were few men in America and because most of these men, living the lives of animals, left the land uncultivated and neglected it, that it remained cold and incapable of producing active principles, of developing the germs of bigger quadrupeds, who actually need all the warmth and activity that the sun can give to the loving earth in order to grow and multiply.[165]

Thus, a new impulse was given to a geographical theory of perversion by the mere fact of the distribution of animal species across the world.

Buffon's theory, next, that the American climate defined its people's sexuality, fueled controversy. Many writers subscribed to his image of the Indian man's deficient sexuality and explained it similarly by referring to environmental factors. Among them were Voltaire, who confirmed 'qu'on n'y trouve un seul peuple qui ait de la barbe',[166] and Father Raynal, who distinguished the degenerating climate of Cartagena and the salubrious one in Chile,[167] yet eventually generalized on the American man's weakness as well:

Men are weaker there, less courageous; without beard and hairless; degraded on all levels of virility, weakly endowed with lively and powerful sentiment, with this delicate love that is the source of all passions .... Their lack of interest in the weaker [feminine] sex, to whom nature has given the source of reproduction, suggests an imperfection in the organs, a kind of infancy among the people of America like that among individuals of our continent who have not reached the age of puberty. It is a radical vice in the other hemisphere, the novelty of which is shown by this kind of impotence.[168]

The most extreme position against the Indians, as is known, was taken by Cornelis de Pauw, even when his descriptions of the Egyptians, the Chinese, the Africans and even the Greeks were impregnated with an equally derogatory tone. De Pauw, whose copious detailing about aberrant sexual behaviour was seen by Gerbi as 'Freudian',[169] claimed that 'the whole of the human species is doubtlessly weakened and degenerated on the new continent (la totalité de l'espèce humaine est indubitablement affaiblie et dégénérée au nouveau continent)'.[170] Even Peruvians, the most 'civilized' of all in the eyes of de Pauw, soon lost their reproductive capacities: 'It is the character of their degeneration just as with eunuchs (C'est le caractère de leur dégénération comme dans les Eunuques).'[171] According to de Pauw, physical circumstances lay at the root of degeneration as they debilitated the fauna as well. Many American animals had lost their tail. Dogs stopped barking. And the import of camels was doomed to fail as 'the cold distorted their organs for reproduction (le froid dérangea leurs organes destinés à la reproduction)'.[172] The Scottish Presbyterian William Robertson reiterated de Pauw's negative judgement about the Peruvians, whose 'feeble spirits, relaxed in lifeless inaction, seem[ed] hardly capable of any bold or manly exertion'.[173]

Moreau de Saint-Méry also upheld an environmentalist explanation when he extended the sexual deficiency of the Indians to the colonizers of European origin. Women, so he claimed, lost their virginity early, primarily as a result of masturbation, and often they engaged in sexual relations with one another. And then, 'man too is affected by this climate, that deprives him from his energy and condemns him to indolence (l'homme aussi reçoit de ce climat une impression qui le prive d'une partie de son énergie, et qui le dispose à l'indolence)'.[174] Lord Kames, finally, confirmed that Indians lacked active strength, were hairless and 'feeble in their organs of reproduction'.[175]

Buffon's environmentalism was opposed by just as many authors of the Enlightenment, but only a few refuted the claim that America's indigenous population was sexually deficient. David Hume interpreted human difference as the outcome mostly of divergent economic conditions.[176] The botanist Filippo Mazzei refuted Buffonian determinism and claimed that 'difference sprouts from the moral, not from the physical (la différence vient du moral, non du physique)'.[177] But his work was not very influential, perhaps, one may say, because it went so much against the grain of contemporary discourse itself.

At about the same time, another botanist, Luigi Castiglioni, pleaded for recognition of the moral superiority of the Indian men and claimed that they were neither frigid nor *luxurioso*, the familiar catch-all term for centuries for indulgence in sexual vice. To support his argument, Castiglioni extensively described the custom of 'bundling', that originated from Indian people and was copied later by European settlers in America. Known since the 1950s as 'heavy petting', this practice was described by Castiglioni as a form of premarital lovemaking, where both partners would 'spend the night together and even sleep in the same bed ... being allowed anything that did not potentially lead to any implications afterwards (passare insieme la notte ed anche di dormire nelle stesso letto ... essendo qualunque cosa permessa, da cui non possano derivare conseguenze)'.[178] Yet, while focusing on this practice in particular, he actually confirmed rather than rejected the thesis about the Indian men's sexual lassitude.

Antoine Joseph Pernety, while rejecting the negativism of de Pauw, subscribed to de Las Casas' accusation of the Spaniards for having decimated the indigenous population. He claimed that this, rather than sexual indifference, lay at the root of the scarce population density. He admitted that perhaps Indian men are a bit less 'passionate' – *ab assuetis non fit passio* - but this was largely because they were used to seeing their women walk around virtually undressed. Not so the European men, who witnessed the indigenous women's behaviour and who were extremely aroused by it. Pernety emphasized that such a different attitude in no way makes them less virile, nor does their weaker, physical constitution make them less intelligent. If this were the case, so he argued, then we ought to see women too as 'une espèce abrutie stupide'. And, finally, if aberrant sexual behaviour does occur, then it is given by their own 'débauche outrée', and hardly different from the occasional deviant practices of European settlers.[179]

Gradually, political circumstances lent a peculiar urgency to this debate when America threatened to become independent from its motherland. At the eve of American independence and only a few decades before most Latin American colonies would emancipate themselves from Portugal and Spain, consciousness grew in Europe of its alienation from the Creole elites across the Atlantic. Perhaps this explained why negative qualities, traditionally ascribed to Indians, were now extrapolated to the settlers as evidence of the 'white man's tropicalization'. They were soon opposed by the polemic writings of Franklin, Paine, Hamilton, Crèvecoeur, Jefferson, Molina, Carli, Velasco, Jolís, Peramás and others who stood up as spokesmen for the ingenuity of the race of the New World.

Whereas America was seen largely as an economic asset, the Pacific world initially served as a topos of political, social and sexual imagination. Europe's vision of Pacific people was dominated by a classical naturalism, which evidently led to idealized representations of either its physical profile or its behaviour. I have indicated earlier how Richard Payne Knight eagerly compared the Tahitians to the ancient Greeks. The writings of Banks and Hawkesworth as well as engravings by Bérenger, Buchan and Parkinson equally perceived the Polynesians as embodying classical ideals.

Soon enough, however, this was to end and a more negative stereotyping became current. Christian-inspired authors too gave up their deistically motivated idealism and increasingly 'spread the belief that the native people of the Pacific in their natural state were depraved and ignoble'.[180] At first, the myth of paradise proved obstinate. Commentators felt compelled to somehow separate the good aspects of Pacific society from its bad sides. Pessimism gained ground, however, as Julien Crozet, after witnessing how his captain Marion du Fresne was butchered by Maoris in 1772, declared the 'children of nature' to be as savage as wild animals. After Cook's tragic ending in 1780, *ad hoc* attempts to safeguard one's European audience from disenchantment were given up altogether. Free love, that had first enchanted westerners, was now denounced as barbarous promiscuity and condemned along with other indigenous practices such as infanticide, the *hula* dances and *tupapa'u*, comparable to Haitian 'zombies'.[181] Along with the condemnation of premarital and extramarital sexual relations between men and women, polygamy and occasionally polyandry, the ubiquity of male-to-male sexual relations was disapproved of as well. Indigenous laxity itself was seen as a symptom of moral depravity, of a lack of consideration for the laws of nature. Men were said to lack masculine pride, women to be aggressive and independent. *Mahūs* were depicted as icons of sexual lasciviousness. The Romantics' obstinate belief that the Pacific world was a sexual paradise, which emphasized the Polynesians' soft nature and amiability, indirectly consolidated the western perception of the male population of Polynesia as naive, sensual and complacent – all qualities that were said to belong to the feminine realm.[182]

In contrast with the ascription of feminine characteristics to the men of Asia, America and the Pacific were representations of the men of Subsaharan Africa and the Arab world. The Ethiopian's facial expression was seen as symptomatic of an unbridled sexual appetite, that struck men and women alike. Some claimed that it lent African women a particularly 'manly' outlook. Hot climatological circumstances presumably led to an increased state of sexual arousal – a theory that was supported by a belief that sexuality could be explained in materialistic, i.e. physiological terms.[183] In a strange way, it reflected a late eighteenth-century conviction that warm, tight underwear overirritated a boy's genitalia and lured him into masturbation.[184] It was also the reverse side of explanations of the American Indian's frigidity due to the climate's austerity.

Today, it is easy to see how environmentalist theory was doomed to fail, due merely to the fact that all races were spread across geographical areas that showed great climatological variety. But the model's inner inconsistencies did not make it altogether unconvincing to contemporaries, who eagerly made *ad hoc* adjustments when necessary. Thus the persistence of an 'African' behavioural pattern among the black slave populations of America was explained by the slaves' predominant location in the tropical and subtropical maritime zones both in the Caribbean and on the American continent.

Often, no effort was made to seek empirical consistency, as is shown in western observations of the Arab world. Here too, the climate was said to trigger sexual vice both among women, who were easily depicted as sexually aggressive despite evidence of their subject status, and among men, whose 'priapism' showed little self-containment. It made the Arab world into a man's world, though Arab masculinity was seen rather as an exaggerated kind and in sharp contrast with the disciplined manhood of Europeans.[185] The harem, that embodied much of western imagination about the Orient, became a signifier of male, Oriental despotism.[186] But in parts of Central Asia sexual indulgence could hardly be ascribed to the climate, as the winters were often harsh and cold. Such anomalies were resolved by alternative explanations, some of which are already familiar, such as the one about Muslim lasciviousness. Altogether, climate, religion, regional variety and *couleur locale* were subjected to the exigencies of a more general reification of Oriental identity. This was 'stripping man of specific cultural characteristics and eccentricities while, simultaneously, dressing, masquerading him in the trappings, in the clothes of difference'.[187]

Eventually, stereotypical representation of 'the Orient' would incorporate divergent, even mutually contradictory images. The Middle East and Northern Africa, part of the Orientalist imagination on historical and religious grounds,[188] embodied an image of male aggression, warfare and expansion; the Far East, instead, was pictured as the realm of feminine passivity, commerce and compromise. As such, both the Far and Near East were *topoi* of western imagination, each adorned with different sexual qualities alongside other stereotypes of economic or political tenor.

Regional differences should not obfuscate how the very ascription of sexual qualities itself was instrumental to Europe's coming to grips with cultural Otherness in general, independent of the actual content of such ascriptions. Cultural variety, crystallized through biological concepts of sex and race, not only was thus given a certain rationality, but allowed for justification of colonial exploitation as well.

This is clearly illustrated by the proto-racist oeuvre of Cristoph Meiners, who acknowledged 'racial' variety, yet reduced its significance to a mere dichotomy between the 'beautiful, white' and the 'ugly, dark' people of the world.[189] Both are distinguished by physical and mental characteristics that are seen as the outcome of physical circumstances and cultural habits. Bodily strength, for example, is the outcome of climate, diet and local customs. Hot baths, opium and even laziness, all 'common among the darker races' are thus said by Meiners to have a debilitating effect. The *ad hoc* balancing of geographical and cultural factors is even more obvious in Meiners' sweeping generalization about physical beauty, a romantic variable at that:

Only white people deserve to be called beautiful, whereas the dark one is rightfully called ugly. A main cause of beauty is the climate, whose effects may well be weakened by unfavourable physical and moral factors, but cannot be made fully undone where it is most advantageous.[190]

Most relevant here is how Meiners' dichotomy attached gender connotations to racial classification, and this in a way that reinforced the definition of male and female gender itself. Initially, this was brought about by the author's claim that the 'ugly' people have no beard. A familiar theme, surely, but here it functioned not only as a sign of the dark people's femininity but also, reversely, as a proof of the ingenuity of gender divisions in the West itself. The reciprocity of Meiners' logic is revealed when he relates femininity to inferior qualities, thus justifying male and white domination at once:

In the end, black and ugly people are distinct from the white and beautiful ones due to a sad lack of virtues or to several dreadful anomalies . . . They also combine a more than female cowardice and fear of visible danger and death with an unintelligible quietism.[191]

The significance of Meiners' qualifications can hardly be underestimated despite, or perhaps just because of, their vague descriptions and *ad hoc* character. These in fact allowed for bridging the difficulties that were implied by the comparison of racial and sexual difference as emanations of one singular logic. Conceptual unclarity also allowed for evaluating the dark races' sexuality as pathological, because at odds with expectations about a self-contained, yet vigourous masculinity. *Kränkliche Reissbarkeit* was revealed by 'Shamelessness or . . . an unreasonable inclination for physical love, or also the greatest coldness and a related disdain for the female sex (Schamlosigkeit entweder . . . unmässigster Hang zur sinnlichen Liebe, oder auch die grösste Kälte, und daher entstehende Verachtung des weiblichen Geschlechts).'[192] A remarkable phrase, so full of rationalizations of apparently contradictory evidence, that was to fit within the mould of the author's scheme of analogy! The simultaneous emphasis on sexual lasciviousness and indifference towards the female sex may indeed be hard to understand for today's reader. But it can only be adequately explained as a rhetorical trope that combined femininity, male priapism and racial inferiority in a singular scheme. Logical consistency was thus subjected to the imperatives of ideology.

Sodomites and semiotics

Parallels with the regional accents in portrayals, reviewed at the beginning of this chapter, of same-sex praxis across the world now become visible. But both narrative structures evidently did not simply develop side by side.

Reports about gender-structured same-sex practices in America, Asia and the Pacific were instrumental to their stereotyping as 'feminine' races and they presented cross-gender roles as a metonymy of the lack of virility in entire races. Racial 'femininity', in turn, was seen as a fertile soil for the development of anomalous sexuality and a metaphor of sexual deviance in Europe itself. Similarly, the absence of cross-gender roles in the Arab world was read as a sign of masculinity, if admittedly an 'uncontrolled' one, due to the evidence of widespread sodomy. And the notion of an unbridled Arab lasciviousness was instrumental to the representation of male same-sex relations as 'endemic', rather than as peculiar to a single minority.

I emphasize, however, that the scheme above is archetypal. Images of effeminacy and gender-structured same-sex practices can also be traced, if only marginally, in occasional decriptions of cross-dressing adolescent boys in the Arab world, while discourse on the Pacific, Asia and America was in no way fully exempt from narratives of male sexual aggression or 'endemic' sodomy. Occasionally, they would reinforce one another and jointly support images of the New World as a place

where the sexes, the species approach one another and mingle so that both human sexes lose their distinctive characteristics. Some men produce milk in their breasts, some women stop menstruating or witness an unusual growth of their clitoris as if it were a penis. There are hermaphrodites everywhere and homosexual practices flourish.[193]

Such an amalgamation of vices, though no doubt powerful at the time, is barely interesting to today's historian. But frequently texts are made up of more well-defined narrative patterns, that, when closely read, clearly suggest preconceived theories. Such descriptions of non-conformist practices are not merely expressions of amazement or contempt: their vocabulary, syntax and pragmatics reveal much about the authors' cognitive assessment of information.

One narrative pattern, retrievable despite the discourse's often inarticulate character, was already becoming visible from the early eighteenth century, and gained far greater transparency as the Enlightenment redefined the study of human nature. The traditional model of an 'endemic' sodomitical practice, though persistent in texts about the Arab world, gave way to one of a 'sodomite' minority. A minority, moreover, that was 'recognizable' as its profile trespassed the boundaries of gender as well as sexuality.

The significance of this narrative shift cannot be detached from changes in the sexual landscape in Europe itself, for it reflected not only how so-called 'sodomites' profiled themselves in the urban centres of most European countries, but also how many among them adopted a cross-gender role. It seems improbable, in my judgement, that ethnographic reports have triggered such alterations of sodomy in Enlightenment Europe. The changing conceptualization of male and female gender, itself an answer to the shifting balance of power between men and women, was overall more decisive, but the intertwined character of the discourses on race, gender and sexual anomaly shows that the ethnographic record may well have functioned as a signifier of substantial importance.

Both the new sodomites and those who did not share but opposed their appetites, equally may have recognized a confirmation of their position in stories about sex life outside Europe. Moralists and scientists may have read these as proof of the universally deviant character of sexual relations among men, while interpreting indigenous tolerance as a sign of racial inferiority. Sodomites, on the contrary, may have felt not only that the wide acceptance of such relations in cultures overseas offered a powerful argument against repression, but also that those engaging in it were essentially different from others because 'of an inverted biological constitution'.

Probably such a claim cannot be stretched beyond the circles of the middle- and upper-class elite. Homosexually active men of lower social status may well have subscribed to the new model of 'sodomite' identity also, but they most likely gained only very little access to information about same-sex praxis overseas. Their embracing of a modern sense of sodomite identity did not, however, prevent analogies between inferior races and the lower classes from becoming common currency, especially in the nineteenth century. The presumably 'uncontrolled', instinctive character of lower class homosexuality would be easily compared with the sodomitical practices of Arabs and Africans, as these too reflected a kind of polymorph perversity. By then, however, it was certain that lower class men who maintained sexual relations with other men were about to adopt new definitions of one's sexual self and that the representation of their sexuality by the intelligentsia was patronizing at the least.

Biology provided a language of universality, that not only could be applied to all races and both sexes, but also related one to another by virtue of analogy. This phenomenon is intensely studied by historians of the social and cultural construction of womanhood and 'racial' identities. Yet a question that remained largely unaddressed, was if and how such a cognitive scheme was also reflected in the Enlightenment's new definition of the 'problem' of male same-sex praxis in general and of male same-sex praxis outside the West in particular. Above, I have aimed at doing so and conclude that this was indeed the case. The very analogy, in particular, between the presumed indices of 'femininity' and of racial 'inferiority', *along with* new narratives about same-sex practices outside the West were conducive to new theoretical speculation on the presumably feminine *essence* of sodomites. In one respect, this sprang from the increasing number of reports about same-sex practices that were closely linked with cross-gender roles. Their higher frequency among some 'races' claimed to be inferior thus reinforced a theory about the essentially anomalous nature of sodomites, while simultaneously justifying these populations' lower position in the hierarchy of civilization. In another respect, the analogy was brought about by evidence of the commonality of same-sex practices among the African, Asian, Pacific and American people, all frequently said to be 'effeminate'. Read through the looking-glass of the new, biological paradigm, the numerous testimonies of widespread male same-sex praxis revealed the 'feminine' nature of people of the New World, and the recurrent combination, in ethnographic narratives, of same-sex praxis and cross-gender behaviour turned the latter at once into a *hyperbole* and a *metonymy* of its peoples' anomalous sexualities.

Notes

1. P. Hulme and L. Jordanova, 'Introduction', in P. Hulme and L. Jordanova (eds), *The Enlightenment and Its Shadows* (London, 1990), p. 5.
2. L.-A. Baron de Lahontan, *Nouveaux voyages de Mr. Le Baron de Lahontan dans l'Amérique septentrionale* (The Hague, 1703; 1715 2nd ed.).
3. L.-A. de Bougainville, *Voyage autour du monde*, ed. P. Deslandres (Paris, 1924 (1771)), pp. 84, 149.
4. J. Stockinger, 'Homosexuality and the French Enlightenment', in G. Stambolian and E. Marks (eds), *Homosexualities in French Literature. Cultural Contexts/Critical Texts* (Ithaca and London, 1979), p. 171.
5. 'Comment s'est-il pu faire qu'un Vice destructeur du genre humain s'il était général, qu'un attentat infâme contre la nature, soit pourtant si naturel? Il paraît être le dernier degré de la corruption réfléchie, et cependant il est le partage ordinaire de ceux qui n'ont pas eu encore le temps d'être corrompus.' F. M. A. Voltaire, *Dictionnaire philosophique*, ed. R. Pomeau (Paris, 1964 (1764)), pp. 35–7.
6. See Alain, 'Voltaire, fut-il un infâme?', *Arcadie*, 3 (March 1954), 27–34.
7. J. Stockinger, 'Homosexuality and the French Enlightenment', in *Homosexualities in French Literature*, p. 167. See also J. Schwartz, *The Sexual Politics of J. J. Rousseau* (Chicago and London, 1984).
8. J.-J. Rousseau, *Les confessions* (Paris, 1963 (1770)), pp. 113–15.
9. The full title is *De l'Amérique et des Américains, ou Observations curieuses du philosophes La Douceur, qui a parcouru cet Hémisphère pendant la dernière guerre, en faisant le noble métier de tuer des hommes sans les manger*, and was first published in Berlin in 1771. On the uncertainty about the author, Zacharia De' Pazzi de Bonneville (?), see A. Gerbi, *La disputa del Nuevo Mundo. Historia de una polémica, 1750–1900* (Mexico, D.F., 1982 (It. 1955; Sp. 1960)), pp. 129–30.
10. La Douceur, *De l'Amérique et des Américains*, p. 40.
11. D. Diderot, *Oeuvres philosophiques*, ed. P. Vernière, Paris, 1964, quoted in J. Stockinger, 'Homosexuality and the French Enlightenment', p. 166.
12. D. Diderot, 'Fragments échappés, in *Oeuvres complètes*, ed. J. Assézat and M. Tourneux, vol. 10, p. 86; D. Diderot, 'Histoire des Deux Indes', in *Oeuvres complètes*, vol. 15, p. 467.
13. H. Clastres, 'Sauvages et civilisés au XVIIIe siècle', in P. Châtelet (ed.), *Histoire des idéologies* (Paris, 1978), vol. 3, p. 221.
14. B. Papin, *Sens et Fonction de l'Utopie tahitienne dans l'oeuvre politique de Diderot (Studies on Voltaire and the Eighteenth Century*, 251 (1988)); M. Cardy, *Diderot et la sexualité, (Studies on Voltaire and the Eighteenth Century*, 264 (1989)), 866–7.
15. For a critical review, see G. Hekma, 'Rewriting the history of Sade', *JHS*, 1, 1 (July 1990), 131–6.
16. J. Stockinger, 'Homosexuality and the French Enlightenment', p. 182.

17. J.-J. Pauvert, *Sade vivant*, vol.1: *Une innocence sauvage, 1740–1777* (Paris, 1986), p. 380.

18. The description 'chevaliers de la manchette' is in fact used first by Rousseau, who targeted the members of the sodomite 'ordre de la manchette'. See C. Courouve, *Vocabulaire de l'homosexualité masculine* (Paris, 1985), pp. 156–8.

19. *Les Enfants de Sodome* (Paris, 1790), frontispiece. The complete text was published by P. Hahn in *Gai Pied Hebdo*, 23 (February 1981), 18–20. The author, according to Courouve, *Vocabulaire de l'homosexualité masculine*, p. 157, is the marquis René-Louis d'Argenson, friend of Voltaire.

20. 'La plupart des peuples anciens et modernes ont eu la fureur d'enculer, et que chez nous, c'est moins le goût que la nécessité qui nous y porte . . . . Les belles femmes sont rares à Paris, les grands cons très-nombreux, et les véroles plus nombreuses encore . . . . Si le hasard fait rencontrer une belle femme . . . , c'est à coup sûr, une putain, et alors, la crainte de la vérole empoisonne tout le plaisir qu'on pourrait goûter à la foutre. Aucun de ces inconvéniens ne se présente chez les hommes; passage étroit, fesses dures et blanches, complaisance infinie, tout invite à se satisfaire.' *Les petits bougres au manège* ('Enculons'), L'an II (n.p., 1794), reprint Cahiers Gai-Kitsch-Camp, ed. P. Cardon (Lille, n.d.), p. 17.

21. See A. E. Simpson, 'Vulnerability and the age of female consent', in G. S. Rousseau and R. Porter (eds), *Sexual Underworlds of the Enlightenment* (Chapel Hill, 1988), pp. 195 ff.

22. See G. Hekma, 'Sodomites, Platonic lovers, contrary lovers: The backgrounds of the modern homosexual', in K. Gerard and G. Hekma (eds), The *Pursuit of Sodomy: Male Homosexuality in Renaissance and Enlightenment Europe* (New York, 1989), pp. 435–40; see also D. M. Sweet's chapter on Johann Winckelmann in the same volume, 147–75.

23. G. S. Rousseau, 'The sorrows of Priapus: Anticlericalism, homosocial desire, and Richard Payne Knight', in *Sexual Underworlds*, pp. 101–53.

24. Quoted in B. Smith, *European Vision and the South Pacific* (New Haven and London, 1985), p. 43.

25. On the difficulties in establishing the year of publication of both volumes, see G. S. Rousseau, 'The sorrows of Priapus', p. 113.

26. F. Haskell, 'd'Hancarville: an adventurer and art historian in eighteenth-century Europe', in E. Chaney and N. Ritchie (eds), *Oxford, China, and Italy. Writings in Honour of Sir Harold Acton* (London, 1984), p. 187.

27. P. Mitter, *Much Maligned Monsters: The History of the European Reaction to Indian Art* (Oxford, 1977), pp. 85–96, 98.

28. In his *Dei delitti e delle pene* (1764), Beccaria carefully suggested that laws against sodomy should be repealed because it was, in fact, harmless to society. His Dutch disciple, Abraham Perrenot, did so too in a response to the prosecutions of sodomites in the United Provinces in 1776. See D. F. Greenberg, *The Construction of Homosexuality* (Chicago and London, 1988), p. 351.

29. On Bentham's largely unpublished plea for the decriminalization of pederasty, L. Crompton, *Byron and Greek Love. Homophobia in 19th Century England* (Berkeley, 1985), pp. 20–62, *passim*.

30. *Ibid.*, p. 51.

31. For England, see M. H. Hyde, *The Other Love: An Historical and Contemporary Survey of Homosexuality in Britain* (London, 1970), pp. 91–2; A. D. Harvey, 'Prosecutions for sodomy in England at the beginning of the nineteenth century', *Historical Journal*, 21 (1978), 939–48. For Holland, see T. van der Meer, *De wesentlijke sonde van sodomie en andere vuyligheeden. Sodomietenvervolgingen in Amsterdam, 1730–1811* (Amsterdam, 1984); and the articles by D. J. Noordam, L. J. Boon, and A. H. Huussen, Jr. in *The Pursuit of Sodomy*.

32. Among such descriptions are B. Nusdorfer [aka Don Juan del Campo y Cambroneras], *Schreiben des Jesuiten Bernhard Nusdorfer* (Hamburg, 1768), p. 244; F. X. Veigl, *Gründliche Nachrichten über ... Maynas in Süd-Amerika, bis zum Jahr 1768* (Nürnberg, 1785), pp. 296–7; N. Bossu, *Nouveaux Voyages aux Indes Occidentales* (Amsterdam, 1769), p. 77; and G. H. Loskiel, *Geschichte der Mission der evangelischen Brüder unter den Indianern in Nordamerika* (Barby-Leipzig, 1789), p. 18.

33. See, for example, R. P. Touron, *Histoire générale de l'Amérique* (Paris, 1768–70), vol. 1, p. 220.

34. L. Muratori, *Il cristianismo felice ... nel Paraguai* (Venice, 1743–9), vol. 1, p. 70.

35. B. Ibañez, *El Reyno jesuítico del Paraguay* (1770). I consulted the German translation, titled *Das Reich der Jesuiten in Paraguay* (Frankfurt and Leipzig, 1772), vol. 2, pp. 410–11, 413, 416–17, 420–1, 465–66.

36. L. B. Benaduci, *Idéa de una nueva Historia General de la América Septentrional* (Madrid, 1746), pp. 130–4.

37. Montesquieu, *De l'esprit des lois*, in Montesquieu, *Oeuvres Complètes*, ed. D. Oster (Paris, 1964), pp. 600–1.

38. Article 'Sodomie' in: *Encyclopédie ou dictionnaire raisonné des sciences, des arts et des métiers* (Neuchâtel, 1765), vol. 15, col. 266: 'le crime de ceux qui commettent des impuretés contraires même à l' ordre de la nature'.

39. A. Perrenot, *Bedenkingen over het straffen van zekere schandelijke misdaad* (Amsterdam, 1777), pp. 28–9.

40. F. H. Jacobs, *Schriften* (Leipzig, 1829), vol. 3, pp. 212–54.

41. J. G. von Herder, *Ideen zur Philosophie der Geschichte der Menschheit*, 4 vols (Riga-Leipzig, 1785–92), see esp. vol. 3, book 13, ch. 4, 209–27 on 'Greek eros'.

42. Quoted in M. W. Brownley, 'Gibbon's Artistic and Historical Scope in the *Decline and Fall*', *Journal of the History of Ideas*, 42, 4 (October–December 1981), 641.

43. E. Gibbon, *The Decline and Fall of the Roman Empire*, ed. J. B. Bury (London, 1929), vol. 4, p. 537, note 205.

44. G. S. Rousseau, 'The pursuit of sodomy', p. 140. See also V. L. Bullough, *Sexual Variance*, p. 329.

45. G. S. Rousseau, *Ibid.*, 140–2.

46. For a relatively well documented example of a male-to-male 'frontier' sexual relationship, see G. Solis de Merás (1567), quoted in J. Katz, *Gay American History*, 23–5. A Frenchman maintained a lasting relationship with the son of a *cacique* in sixteenth-century Florida. Though operating as an interpreter for the Spanish, he was killed because he was a 'sodomite' and had warned the Indians not to convert to Catholicism. On pirate (homo-)sexuality, see the (speculative) study by B. R. Burg, *Sodomy and the Pirate Tradition* (New York, 1983). On the 'Brethren of the Coast' at Turtle Island, off the Haitian coast, and composed of Catholics, seeking refuge from Cromwellian England, of Huguenots, political dissenters and soldiers of fortune alike, see Captain L. A. T. Le Golif, *Memoirs of a Buccaneer*, ed. G. Alaux and A. 'tSerstevens (London, 1954).

47. Quoted in J.-P. Guicciardi, 'L'hermaphrodite et le prolétaire', *Le Dix-huitième siècle*, 12 (1980), 60.

48. *Ibid.*

49. I have consulted the German translation, *Die Sitten der Wilden, zur Aufklärung des Ursprungs und Aufnahme der Menschheit*, published in Copenhagen in 1766, pp. 206–8.

50. C. G. Heyne, 'De maribus inter Scytas morbo effeminatis et de Hermaphroditis commentatio recitata in concessu d. XIX Sept. 1778', in *Commentationes Societatis Regiae Scientiarum Gottingensis Historicae et Philologicae Classis* (Göttingen, 1779), vol.1, pp. 28–44.

51.   P. Egede, *Dictionarium Grönlandico-Danico-Latinum* (Copenhagen, 1750), p. 14a; D. Cranz, *Historie von Grönland* (Barby, 1770 (1765)), p. 329; G. W. Steller, *Beschreibung von dem Lande Kamtschatka* (Frankfurt and Leipzig, 1774), pp. 350–1; T. Falkner, *A Description of Patagonia* (Hereford and London, 1774), p. 43; A. Dalrymple, *An Historical Journal of the Expeditions by Sea and Land to the North of California* (London, 1790), *passim*; F. Palou, *Relación histórica de la vida ... del padre Junipero Serra* (Mexico, 1787), p. 57.

52.   [J. Billings], *An account of a geographical and astronomical Expedition to the Northern Parts of Russia* (London, 1802), p. 160.

53.   Anthropological inaccuracy did not prevent the 'unfortunate confusion' (Fitzgerald) between *berdache* and 'homosexual' from becoming a powerful trope in early Gay Liberation literature. The (in-)adequacy of such a view is still debated today. See C. Callender and L. Kochems, 'The North American Berdache', *Current Anthropology*, 24 (1963), 443–70; D. F. Greenberg, 'Why was the Berdache ridiculed?', *JHom*, 11, 3/4 (Summer 1985), 179–90; R. A. Gutiérrez, 'Must we eradicate Indians to find gay roots?', *Out/Look*, (Winter 1989), 61–7; J. Katz, *Gay American History*, ch. 4, pp. 423–503; W. Roscoe, *The Zuni Man-Woman* (Albuquerque, 1991); W. Roscoe, 'How to become a Berdache: Toward a unified analysis of gender diversity', in *Third Sex, Third Gender*, pp. 329–72; H. Whitehead, 'The bow and the burden strap: A new look at institutionalised homosexuality in Native North America', in S. B. Ortner and H. Whitehead (eds), *Sexual Meanings* (Cambridge, 1981), 80–115; W. L. Williams, 'Isthmus Zapotec "Berdaches"', ARGOH Newsletter, 7, 2 (May 1985), 1–6; W. L. Williams, *The Spirit and the Flesh: Sexual Diversity in American Indian Culture* (Boston, 1986).

54.   F.-M. Perrin du Lac, *Voyages dans les deux Louisianes* (Paris, 1805).

55.   J. Long, quoted in W. H. Keating, *Narrative of an Expedition to the Source of St.Peter's River* (Philadelphia, 1824), vol.1, pp. 221–2. See also J. Long, *Voyages and Travels of an Indian Interpreter and Trader* (London, 1791), p. 138.

56.   R. Southey, *History of Brazil* (London, 1810–19), vol. 3, p. 672.

57.   F. Alves do Prado, 'Historia dos Indios Cavalleiros', *Jornal o Patriota*, 3 (Rio de Janeiro, 1814), 23.

58.   See R. Schwab, *The Oriental Renaissance. Europe's Rediscovery of India and the East, 1680–1880* (New York, 1984), pp. 38, 92.

59.   See D. F. Greenberg, *Construction of Homosexuality*, pp. 168–71; and Linganānda, 'India', in *The Encyclopedia of Homosexuality*, pp. 586–93. For an analysis of the still existing *hijra* role, see S. Nanda, 'The Hijras of India: Cultural and individual dimensions of an institutionalised third gender role', *JHom*, 11, 3/4 (1985), 35–54.

60.   J. S. Stavorinus, *Voyages to the East Indies*, trans. S. H. Wilocke (London, 1798), pp. 455–7. The original, Dutch work, titled *Reize van Zeeland over de Kaap van Goede Hoop naar Batavia ... 1768–1771*, was first published in 1771.

61.   J. A. Dubois, *A Description of the Character, Manners, and Customs of the People of India* (London, 1816). I am quoting from a more recent edition, titled *Hindu Manners, Customs and Ceremonies* (Oxford, 1906), p. 312.

62.   See Schwab, *Oriental Renaissance*, p. 45.

63.   W. Marsden, *The History of Sumatra* (London, 1783), p. 223.

64.   J. G. Haensel, *Letters on the Nicobar islands* (London, 1812), p. 16.

65.   C. De Brosse, *Histoire des Navigations aux Terres Australes* (Paris, 1756), 226–7.

66.   For anthropological evidence on the *kathoey*, see P. A. Jackson, *Male Homosexuality in Thailand* (Elmhurst, 1989), p. 20. Also, see N. Miller, *Out in the World* (Harmondsworth, 1992), p. 115; and G. Puterbaugh, 'Thailand', in *Encyclopedia of Homosexuality*, pp. 1288–90. For transvestite roles in traditional Indonesia, see W. Williams, 'Indonesia', in: *Encyclopedia of Homosexuality*, 597–8. For the Philippines,

see F. Witham and R. M. Mathy, *Male Homosexuality in Four Societies* (New York, 1986), esp. pp. 144 ff.

67. Joinville, 'On the religion and manners of the people of Ceylon', *Asiatic Researches* (London), 7 (1807), 424–7, 441.

68. T. S. Raffles, *The History of Java* (London, 1817), vol. 2, p. lxxx.

69. C. de Pauw, *Recherches philosophiques sur les Egyptiens et les Chinois* (Berlin, 1773), vol. 1, pp. 228–9; O. Toreen, *Eine ostindische Reise nach Suratte* (Rostock, 1756), p. 492.

70. See D. de Mairan, *Lettres au P. Parrenin* (Paris, 1770), quoted in F. Karsch-Haack, *Das gleichgeschlechtliche Leben der Kulturvölker* (München, 1906), p. 57.

71. Le Gentil de la Barbinais, *Nouveau voyage autour du monde* (Paris, 1728–9 (1725)), vol. 2, p. 244.

72. *Ibid.*, vol. 2, p. 56.

73. C. de Pauw, *Recherches philosophiques*, vol. 1., pp. 228–9.

74. J. Barrow, *Travels in China* (London, 1804), pp. 150–1.

75. P. Sonnerat, *Voyage aux Indes orientales et à la Chine* (Paris, 1782), p. 109.

76. A. Anderson, *A Narrative of the British Embassy to China* (Basel, 1795), p. 94.

77. H. Ellis, *Journal of the late embassy to China* (London, 1817), p. 419.

78. See R. P. Grasset, *Histoire de l'Eglise du Japon* (Paris, 1715), *passim*; R. P. de Charlevoix, *Histoire de l'établissement, des progrès et de la décadence du Christianisme dans l'empire du Japon* (Rouen, 1715), vol.3, pp. 373–4; E. Kaempfer, *Geschichte und Beschreibung von Japan*, first edited and published by W. Dohm (Lemgo, 1777–9), vol.2, p. 257; S. J. Baumgarten, *Nachrichten von merkwürdigen Büchern* (Halle, 1753), vol. 3, p. 132.

79. [Lejeune], *Observations critiques et philosophiques sur le Japon et les Japonais par l'abbé Lejeune* (Amsterdam, 1780), p. 137.

80. E. A. W. von Zimmerman, *Taschenbuch der Reisen*, 9, 2 (Leipzig, 1810), 227.

81. See T. Watanabe and J. Iwata, *La voie des éphèbes. Histoire et histoires des homosexualités au Japon* (Paris, 1987), pp. 103–13.

82. See especially O. H. Spate, *The Pacific since Magellan*, vol. 3: *Paradise Lost and Found* (Sydney, 1988) for a synthetic view.

83. See E. Vibart, *Tahiti: naissance d'un paradis au siècle des Lumières* (Paris, 1978); and H. Thodes-Arora, 'Der Mythos verfestigt sich – ein "edler Wilder" aus Tahiti in London', in I. Hermann *et al.* (eds), *Exotische Welten, Europäische Phantasien. Mythos Tahiti, Südsee-Traum und Realität* (Stuttgart and Berlin, 1987), pp. 30–41.

84. M. Sahlins, *Islands of History* (Chicago and London, 1985), pp. 1–31, claims that symbolic exchange between the indigenous people and Cook's crew disturbed what was claimed to be Tahitian culture from the first minute. The myth of Tahiti, in his view, was itself compromised by the real-life effects of the western gaze.

85. B. Smith, *Art as Information. Reflections on the Art from Captain Cook's Voyages* (Sydney, 1979), p. 12. See also W. Veit, 'The topoi of the European imagining of the non-European world', *Arcadia*, 18, 1 (1983), 1–21.

86. See D. G. Charlton, *New Images of the Natural in France* (Cambridge, 1984), p. 134.

87. J. R. Forster, *Observations made during a Voyage Round the World* (London, 1778).

88. Quoted in B. Smith, *European Vision and the South Pacific* (New Haven and London, 1985), p. 88. William Cowper (1731–1800), British poet.

89. E. Marchand, *Voyage autour du monde* (Paris, 1798–1800), vol. 1, p. 277, note A.

90. For a study of *mahū* role, both in the past and today, see R. I. Levy, 'The community function of Tahitian male transvestism', *Anthropological Quarterly*, 44 (1971), 12–21.

91. W. Bligh, *A Voyage to the South Seas* (London, 1792), vol. 2, pp. 16–17.

92. J. Wilson, *A Missionary Voyage to the Southern Pacific Ocean* (London, 1799), p. 200.

93. *Ibid.*

94. J. Turnbull, *A Voyage round the World* (London, 1813), pp. 282–3.

95. W. Ellis, *Polynesian Researches* (London, 1830), p. 340.

96. J. A. C. Löhr, *Die Länder und Völker der Erde*, vol. 4: *Amerika und Australien* (Leipzig, 1815), p. 461.

97. For details, see R. Morris, 'Aikāne: Accounts of Hawaiian same-sex relationships in the journal of Captain Cook's third voyage (1776–80)', *JHom*, 18 (1990), 21–54.

98. U. Lisiansky, *A Voyage Round the World* (London, 1814), p. 199; J.-A. Dulaure, *Histoire abrégée de différents cultes* (Paris, 1825), vol. 1, pp. 419–33.

99. Marion, *Voyages autour du monde* (1771), in *Histoire universelle des Voyages*, ed. M. Albert-Montémont (Paris, 1836), vol.4, p. 438.

100. R. Porter, 'The exotic as erotic: Captain Cook at Tahiti', in *Exoticism in the Enlightenment*, p. 138.

101. See J. L. Bouge, 'Un aspect du rôle rituel du "mahū" dans l'ancien Tahiti', *Journal de la Société des Océanistes*, 11 (1955), 147–9. See also N. Miller, *Out in the World*, pp. 300, 305. The absence of indigenous terms for same-sex praxis or for men engaging in it, has made others conclude that not only cross-gender roles but homosexual relations also were unknown in pre-acculturation New Zealand (See L. K. Gluckman, 'Transcultural consideration of homosexuality with special reference to the New Zealand Maori', *Australian and New Zealand Journal of Psychiatry*, 8, 1 (1974), 121–5). Such a thesis, however, was refuted by M. Arboleda and S. O. Murray, 'The dangers of lexical inference with special reference to Maori homosexuality', *JHom*, 12 (1986), 129–34. Also, see S. O. Murray, *Oceanic Homosexualities* (New York, 1992), *passim*.

102. L. Degrandpré, *Voyage à la côte occidentale d'Afrique* (Paris, 1801), vol. 1, pp. 194–5.

103. F. Karsch-Haack, *Das gleichgeschlechtliche Leben der Naturvölker* (New York, 1975 (Berlin, 1911)), p. 147.

104. R. Norris, *Memoirs of the reign of Bossa Ahadee, king of Dahomey* (London, 1789), p. 422.

105. W. G. Browne, *Travels in Africa, Egypt, and Syria, from the Year 1792 to 1798* (London, 1799), pp. 293–5.

106. J. L. M. Poiret, *Voyage en Barbarie* (Paris, 1789), vol. 1, pp. 8–11, 205–6.

107. A. I. Melling, *Voyage pittoresque de Constantinople et des rives du Bospore* (Paris, 1819), p. 113.

108. F. C. H. L. Pouqueville, *Voyage en Morée, à Constantinople en Albanie* (Paris, 1805), vol. 2, pp. 136, 260.

109. F. Pouqueville, quoted in L. Crompton, *Byron and Greek Love*, p. 135.

110. Quoted in Burton, *The Sotadic Zone* (Boston, 1977), p. 50.

111. C. N. Sonnini de Manoncourt, *Voyage dans la haute et basse Egypte* (Paris, 1799), vol. 1, pp. 277–8.

112. An unspoken 'bisexuality' in fact remains current in today's Egypt. See N. Miller, *Out in the World*, pp. 67–92.

113. L. de Chénier, *Recherches historiques sur les Maures* (Paris, 1787), vol. 1, p. 73; vol. 2, pp. 250, 287.

114. J. L. Salomo Bartholdy, *Bruchstücke zur näheren Kenntnis des heutigen Griechenlands* (Berlin, 1805), pp. 372–82.

115. On homosexuality in Modern Greece, see W. A. Percy and J. Taylor, 'Greece, modern', in: *Encyclopedia of Homosexuality*, pp. 501–4.

116. See H. and S. Grotzfeld, 'Die Erzählungen aus Tausendundeiner Nacht. Geschichte und Herkunft', in G. Sievernich and H. Budde (eds), *Europe und der Orient. Lesebuch* (Berlin, 1989), pp. 86–8. See also F. Mannsaeker, 'Elegancy and wildness: Reflections on the East in the eighteenth-century imagination', in *Exoticism in the Enlightenment*, p. 179.

117. J. Hindley, *Introduction to Persian Lyrics or Scattered Poems from the Diwan-I-Hafiz* (London, 1800), pp. 8–9, 33.

118. H. F. von Diez, *Betrachtungen über das Buch des Kabus* (Berlin, 1811), p. 242.

119. G. J. Barker-Benfield, 'The spermatic economy: A nineteenth-century view of sexuality' *Feminist Studies*, 1, 1 (1972), 45–74.

120. W. Falconer, *Remarks upon the Influence of Climate, Situation, Nature of Country, Population, Nature of Food, and Ways of Life, on the Disposition and Temper of Manner, and Behaviour, Intellectual Laws and Religions of Mankind* (London, 1781).

121. Among the early studies, upholding such a theory, see A. Bray, *Homosexuality in Renaissance England* (London, 1982); R. Trumbach, 'London's sodomites: Homosexual behaviour and western culture in the eighteenth century', *Journal of Social History*, 11 (1977), 1–33; D. A. Coward, 'Attitudes to homosexuality in eighteenth–century France', *Journal of European Studies*, 10 (1980), 231–55; M. Daniel, *Libertins du Grand Siècle* (Paris, 1960); Idem, 'A study of homosexuality in France during the reign of Louis XIII and Louis XIV', *Homophile Studies*, 14/15 (1961), 77–93, 125–136; G. Ruggiero, *The Boundaries of Eros. Sex Crime and Sexuality in Renaissance Venice* (Oxford, 1985); and W. Monter, 'La sodomie à l'époque moderne en Suisse romande', *Annales. E.S.C.*, 39 (1974), 1023–33.

122. See the recent articles by R. Trumbach: 'Sodomitical subcultures, sodomitical Roles, and the gender revolution of the eighteenth century: The recent historiography', in *Unauthorised Sexual Behavior*, pp. 115–17; 'Gender and the homosexual role in modern western culture: The 18th and 19th centuries compared', in D. Altman *et al.* (eds), *Homosexuality, which Homosexuality?* (Amsterdam and London, 1989), pp. 149–69; 'The birth of the queen: Sodomy and the emergence of gender equality in modern culture, 1660–1750', in M. B. Duberman *et al.* (eds), *Hidden from History. Reclaiming the Gay and Lesbian Past* (New York, 1989), pp. 129–40. See also R. Norton, *Mother Clap's Molly House. The Gay Subculture in England, 1700–1830* (London, 1992).

123. R. Trumbach, 'Gender and the homosexual role', p. 153.

124. *Ibid.*

125. R. Trumbach, in: *Unauthorized Sexual Behavior*, p. 118.

126. *Ibid.*

127. L. Stone, *The Family, Sex and Marriage in England, 1500–1800* (New York, 1979), pp. 149, 217–18.

128. R. Trumbach, 'Gender and the homosexual role', pp. 154–6.

129. M. Rey, 'Police et sodomie à Paris au XVIII° siècle: du péché au désordre', *Revue d'histoire moderne et contemporaine*, 39 (1982), 124. See also M. Rey, 'Sexual ambiguity and definition of a particular taste: Male relationships from the end of the Middle Ages to the French Revolution', in *Among Men, Among Women* (Amsterdam, 1983), pp. 197–206.

130. R. Trumbach, 'Gender and the homosexual role', p. 158. Also, see R. Trumbach, 'Birth of the queen'.

131. See M. Rey, 'Police et sodomie' and 'Sexual ambiguity'; L. D. Kritzman, *The Rhetoric of Sexuality and the Literature of the French Renaissance* (Cambridge, 1990); C. Courouve, *Les assemblées de la Manchette: documents sur l'amour masculin au XVIII siècle et pendant la Révolution* (Paris, 1988).

132. D. J. Noordam, 'Sodomy in the Dutch Republic, 1600–1725', in *The Pursuit of Sodomy*, pp. 207–28. No studies are available on Germany or Belgium.

133. Very little research has as yet been done besides the studies by R. Carrasco, *Inquisición y represión sexual en Valencia. História de los sodomitas (1565–1785)* (Barcelona, 1985), and L. Mott, 'Pagode português', 120–39. No comprehensive studies on homosexuality in eighteenth-century Italy are available.

134. On today's role of berdaches among Native Americans, see W. Williams, *The Spirit and the Flesh*. On 'mahūs' in Polynesian society, see R. I. Levy, 'The community function'. On Omani 'xanith', see Unni Wikan, 'Man becomes woman. Transsexualism in Oman as a key to gender roles', *Man*, new series, 12, 2 (1972), 304–19; and Unni Wikan, *Behind the Veil in Arabia* (Baltimore, 1982), ch. 9. See, in general, C. Callender and L. M. Kochems, 'Men and not-men: Male gender-mixing statuses and homosexuality', *JHom*, 11, 3/4 (1985), 165–78.

135. R. Trumbach, 'Birth of the queen', p. 140.

136. See R. Norton, *Mother Clap's Molly House*, 11–12.

137. T. Laqueur, *Making Sex. Body and gender from the Greeks to Freud* (Cambridge and London, 1990), p. 152.

138. See, among others, R. Porter, 'The terraqueous globe', in G. S. Rousseau and R. Porter (eds), *The Ferment of Knowledge. Studies in the Historiography of Eighteenth-Century Science* (Cambridge and New York, 1980), pp. 305–13.

139. For more extensive information about the development of so-called 'life sciences' (zoology, botany) in the Enlightenment, see especially R. W. Burckhardt, *The Spirit of System. Lamarck and Evolutionary Biology* (Cambridge and London, 1977); E. Guyénot, *Les sciences de la vie au 17e et 18e siècles* (Paris, 1957); R. Porter, *The Enlightenment* (London, 1990); F. Rigotti, 'Biology and society in the Age of Enlightenment', *Journal of the History of Ideas*, 47, 2 (April–June 1986), 215–33; J. Roger, *Les sciences de la vie dans la pensée française du XVIII° siècle* (Paris, 1963); J. Roger, *Buffon, un philosophe au Jardin du Roi* (Paris, 1989).

140. See, for an excellent synthesis, the still classical work of M. Duchet, *Anthropologie et Histoire au Siècle des Lumières* (Paris, 1977 (1971)).

141. T. Laqueur, *The Making of Sex*, p. 155.

142. On the beginnings of Abolitionism, see R. Blackburn, *The Overthrow of Colonial Slavery, 1776–1848* (London, 1988), pp. 33–66.

143. On Medieval and Renaissance theory of the human sexes, see T. Laqueur, *The Making of Sex*, chapters 2 to 4, pp. 25–148. See also S. L. Gilman, *Sexuality. An Illustrated History* (New York, 1989); and M. W. Ferguson *et al.* (eds), *Rewriting the Renaissance. The Discourses of Sexual Difference in Early Modern Europe* (Chicago and London, 1988).

144. On Enlightenment theory of female identity, see M. Bloch and J. H. Bloch, 'Women and the dialectics of nature in eighteenth-century French thought', in C. P. MacCormack and M. Strathern (eds), *Nature, Culture and Gender* (Cambridge, 1980), pp. 25–41; P. Hoffmann, *La femme dans la pensée des Lumières* (Paris, 1977); L. Jordanova, *Sexual Visions* (New York, 1989); J. Livi, *Vapeurs de femmes* (Paris, 1984); T. Laqueur, 'Orgasm, generation and the politics of reproductive biology', *Representations*, 14 (April 1986), 1–41; S. Tomaselli, 'The Enlightenment debate on women', *History Workshop*, 20 (1985), 101–24.

135. See E. Shorter, *A History of Women's Bodies* (New York, 1982); B. Duden, *Geschichte unter der Haut* (Stuttgart, 1987). See also R. Porter, 'Bodies of thought: Thoughts about the body in eighteenth-century England', in J. H. Pittock and A. Wear (eds), *Interpretation and Cultural History* (London, 1991), p. 97.

146. M. Delon, 'Le prétexte anatomique', *Le Dix-huitième siècle*, 12 (1980), 38.

147. See E. de Fontenay, 'Diderot gynéconome', *Digraphe*, 7 (1976), 29–50.

148. T. Laqueur, 'Orgasm, generation', p. 152.

149. M. Banton, *Racial Theories* (Cambridge, 1987), p. 6.

150. G. S. Rousseau, 'Cultural history in a new key: Towards a semiotics of the nerve', in *Interpretation and Cultural History*, p. 33.

151. See P. Naudin, 'Une arithmétique des plaisirs: esquisse d'une réflexion sur la morale de Maupertuis', *Actes de la Journée Maupertuis* (Paris, 1975), p. 16.

152. See M. Bloch and J. H. Bloch, 'Women and the dialectics of nature', pp. 29–30, 34–5. See also F. Duchesneau, *La physiologie des Lumières* (The Hague, 1982); J. Roger, 'The living world', in *The Ferment of Knowledge*, pp. 253–83; T. Brown, 'From mechanism to vitalism in eighteenth-century English physiology', *Journal of the History of Biology*, 7 (1974), 179–216; and various articles of *Le dix-huitième siècle*, 24 (1992), special issue: 'le matérialisme au siècle des Lumières', ed. O. Bloch and Ch. Porset.

153. L. Schiebinger, 'The anatomy of difference: Race and sex in eighteenth-century science', *Eighteenth-Century Studies*, 23, 4 (Summer 1990), 387–94.

154. L. Schiebinger, 'The anatomy of difference', p. 394.

155. For idealized representations in the eighteenth century of blacks, see H. Honour, *The Image of the Black in Western Art* (Cambridge and London, 1989), vol. 4, part 1, pp. 51 ff. For Native Americans, see Ton Lemaire, *De Indiaan in ons bewustzijn. De ontmoeting van de Oude met de Nieuwe Wereld* (Baarn, 1986). For Pacific people, see B. Smith, *European Vision and the South Pacific*, chapters 1 to 6, pp. 1–189 passim.

156. See P.-P. Gossiaux, 'Anthropologie des Lumières (Culture "naturelle" et racisme rituel)', in D. Droixhe *et al.* (eds), *L'homme des Lumières et la découverte de l'Autre* (Brussels, 1985), pp. 53–9.

157. In 1785, the book was reprinted as *Ueber die körperliche Verschiedenheit des Negers vom Europäer*. Later revisions by the author were never published.

158. C. Glynn Davies, *Conscience as Consciousness: The Idea of Self-Awareness in French Philosophical Writing from Descartes to Diderot* (n.p., 1990), pp. 108–51.

159. N. L. Stepan, 'Race and gender: The role of analogy in science', *Isis*, 77 (1986), 265.

160. *Ibid.*, 265–6.

161. See R. Hyam, *Empire and Sexuality*, p. 42.

162. 'Il y a donc dans la combinaison des éléments et des autres causes physiques quelque chose de contraire à l'agrandissement de la nature vivante dans ce nouveau monde. . . . Le sauvage est foible et petit par les organes de la génération; il n'a ni poil, ni barbe; et nulle ardeur pour sa femelle.' G.-L. Leclerc de Buffon, *Oeuvres complètes*, ed. M. A. Richard (Paris, 1826–8), vol. 15, pp. 443–6.

163. L. Schiebinger, 'Why mammals are called mammals: Gender politics in eighteenth-century natural history', *AHR*, 98, 2 (April 1993), 382–411.

164. A. Gerbi, *La disputa del Nuevo Mundo*, p. 13.

165. 'C'est donc principalement parce qu'il y avoit peu d'hommes en Amérique, et parce que la plupart de ces hommes, menant la vie des animaux, laissoient la nature brute et négligeoient la terre, qu'elle est demeurée froide, impuissante à produire les principes actifs, à développer les germes des plus grands quadrupèdes, auxquels il faut, pour croître et se multiplier, toute la chaleur, toute l'activité que le soleil peut donner à la terre amoureuse.' Buffon, *Oeuvres complètes*, vol. 15, 452–4.

166. F.-M. A. Voltaire, *Essai sur les moeurs et l'esprit des nations* (1756), quoted in A. Gerbi, *La disputa del Nuevo Mundo*, p. 58.

167. G. T. F. Raynal, *Histoire philosophique et politique des établissements et du commerce des Européens dans les Deux Indes*, ed. A. Jay and J. Peuchet (Paris, 1820–1), vol. 4, pp. 79–80, 277.

168. 'Les hommes y sont moins forts, moins courageux; sans barbe et sans poil; dégradés dans toutes les signes de la virilité, faiblement doués de ce sentiment vif et puissant, de cet amour délicieux qui est la source de tous les amours . . . . L'indifférence pour [le] sexe [féminin], auquel la nature a confié le dépôt de la réproduction, suppose une imperfection dans les organes, une sorte d'enfance dans les peuples de l'Amérique comme dans les individus de notre continent qui n'ont pas atteint l'âge de la puberté. C'est un vice radical dans l'autre hémisphère dont la nouveauté se décèle par cette sorte d'impuissance.' *Ibid.*, vol. 9, p. 23.

169. A. Gerbi, *La disputa del Nuevo Mundo*, p. 66.

170. C. de Pauw, *Recherche philosophique*, vol. 1, p. 307.

171. *Ibid.*, vol. 1, pp. 144–5.

172. *Ibid.*, vol. 1, pp. 12–13. De Pauw's sources, according to Gerbi, probably were de Acosta and Garcilaso de la Vega. See Gerbi, *La disputa del Nuevo Mundo*, p. 72, n. 19.

173. W. Robertson, *The History of America* (London, 1777), vol. 2, pp. 324–5.

174. M. L. E. Moreau de Saint-Méry, *Voyage aux Etats Unis de l'Amérique, 1793–1798*, ed. Stewart L. Mims (New Haven, 1913), 352–3.

175. Quoted by A. Gerbi, *La disputa del Nuevo Mundo*, p. 222.

176. D. Hume, 'Of national characters', in *Essays Moral, Political and Literary* (London and Edinburgh, 1904), p. 213.

177. F. Mazzei, *Recherches historiques et politiques sur les Etats Unis de l'Amérique septentrionale* (Paris, 1788), vol. 2, p. 32.

178. L. Castiglioni, *Viaggio negli Stati Uniti dell'America settentrionale* (Milan, 1790), vol. 2, pp. 92–4.

179. A. J. Pernety, *Examen des Recherches philosophiques sur l'Amérique et les Américains* (Berlin, 1771), vol. 1, p. 262; vol. 2, pp. 79, 93, 245.

180. B. Smith, *European Vision*, p. 5.

181. B. Smith, *European Vision*, pp. 86–7, 121–3, 136. See also J. C. Beaglehole, 'Eighteenth-century science and voyages of discovery', *New Zealand Journal of History*, 3 (1969), 107–23; and A. Frost, *The Pacific Ocean – the Eighteenth-Century's 'New World'*, *Studies on Voltaire and the Eighteenth Century*, 152 (1976), 779–882.

182. B. Smith, *European Vision*, pp. 130–2, 143–54.

183. P. D. Curtin, *The Image of Africa. British Ideas and Action, 1780–1850* (Madison, 1964). See also R. A. Austen and W. D. Smith, 'Images of Africa and British slave trade abolition', *African Historical Studies*, 2, 1 (1969), 66–83; G. Turbet-Delof, *L'Afrique barbaresque dans la littérature française aux 16° et 17° siècles* (Geneva, 1973); and W. B. Cohen, *The French Encounter with Africans: White Responses to Blacks, 1550–1880* (Bloomington and London, 1980).

184. P.-G. Boucé, 'Les jeux interdits de l'imaginaire: onanisme et culpabilisation sexuelle au XVIII° siècle', in J. Céard, ed., *La folie et le corps* (Paris, 1985), pp. 223–43. See also J. Stengers and A. Van Neck, *Histoire d'une grande peur: la masturbation* (Brussels, 1984).

185. See E. Said, *Orientalism* (New York, 1978); and M. Delon, 'Un monde d'eunuques', *Europe*, 55 (1977), 79–88.

186. See A. Vartanian, 'Eroticism and politics in the *Lettres Persanes*', *Romantic Review*, 74 (1983), 306–15.

187. S. Rodin Pucci, 'The discrete charms of the exotic: fictions of the harem in eighteenth-century France', in *Exoticism in the Enlightenment*, p. 150.

188. On this matter, see D. Brahimi, *Opinions et regards des Européens sur le Maghreb aux XVIIe et XVIIIe siècles* (Alger, 1978); and A. Thomson, *Barbary and Enlightenment. European Attitudes towards the Maghreb in the Eighteenth Century* (Leiden, 1989).

189. C. Meiners, *Grundriss der Geschichte der Menschheit* (Lemgo, 1793), pp. 58–75.

190. 'Nur der weisse Völkerstamm verdient den Nahmen des Schönen, und der Dunkelfarbige mit Recht den Nahmen des Hässlichen. Eine Hauptursache der Schönheit ist das Klima, dessen Wirkungen zwar durch ungünstige physische und moralische Ursachen geschwächt, aber da, wo es am mächtigsten ist, nie ganz getilgt werden können.' *Ibid.*, p. 89.

191. 'Endlich unterscheiden sich die schwarzen und hässlichen Völker von den weissen und schönen durch eine traurige Leerheit an Tugenden, und durch mehrere fürchterliche Unarten. ... Sie vereinigen ferner mit mehr als *weibischer Feigheit* [my italics], und Furcht von offenbaren herannahenden Gefahren und Tod, eine unbegreifliche Ruhe.' *Ibid.*, pp. 93, 116–17.

192. *Ibid.*

193. 'où les sexes, les espèces se rapprochent, se mélangent [et] les deux sexes humains perdent leurs caractères distinctifs. Certains hommes ont du lait dans les mamelles, certaines femmes voient leurs règles disparaître ou leur clitoris croître démesurément jusqu'à se confondre avec un penis. Les hermaphrodites pullulent . . . et les pratiques homosexuelles abondent.' M. Delon, 'Corps sauvages, corps étranges', *Le dix-huitième siècle*, 9 (1977), 34.

Chapter three

Race, Sex
and the Semiotics of Genitalia
(c. 1810 – c. 1870)

*What is more exciting than the sealed pact ... between racist
biology, political messianism and repressive sexology?*

– Jean-Paul Aron[1]

During the first half of the nineteenth century science was characterized by a
widespread enterprise to submit the speculative constructs of the Enlightenment to empirical verification. Scientists, says Gilman, '[did not accept]
generalisations but ... demanded the examination of specific, detailed case
studies to evolve a "scientific" paradigm'.[2] It has been amply demonstrated
meanwhile that a positivist departure was anything but immune from
ideology. In reality, it rather facilitated the latter's disguise as defined social,
cultural and political options were hidden behind the veil of tables and facts.
The power of the ruling elites over those whom they felt prompted to police
and control prevented the rhetoric of objectivity from being pierced by
criticism.

The claimed 'refinement of method' would not remain without effect in the
debate about same-sex praxis in Europe, nor would it leave unaltered the
terms of comparison with people of another race. The exigencies of empiricism, claims Nancy Stepan, were 'to elevate hitherto unconsciously held
analogies into self-conscious theory, to extend the meanings attached to the
analogies, to expand their range via new observations and comparisons, and
to give them precision through specialised vocabularies and new technolo-
gies'.[3] Internal developments thus led to the further 'naturalization' of
difference, and resulted in a further disguise of the tautological dimension of
analogy.

The intersecting rhetorics of racial and sexual debate became more tangible than before also with regard to the issue of sexual relations among men.
Scientific debate on sodomite or pederastic identity leaned on a rhetoric of
analogy in its own turn. But whereas male/female difference was compared

to racial difference in a way that convinced contemporary scientists, the analogy between the racially different and the sexually deviant seemed less easily verifiable empirically and was almost doomed to fail. In this chapter, I will reconstruct the subsequent attempts to mobilize ethnographic comparison in order to corroborate such an analogy, even when together they proved to be a hazardous and eventually unsuccessful enterprise. The 'semiotics of genitalia' in fact illustrate, somewhat sensationally, how a far too rigorous empiricism was incapable of consolidating the still highly speculative bourgeois 'mythologies' concerning the variety of the human species. Nevertheless, recurrent failures to pin down the 'geography of perversion' in ways that could be empirically shown did not abolish the persistent idea that sexual deviance was unequally spread or qualitatively different across the globe and thus symptomatic of racial inequalities, read: of European superiority. It remained largely intact until around 1860, when a new paradigm, psychopathology, was to revitalize the rhetoric of analogy.

Continuity and change

Colonial hegemony changed as the British abolished slave trade in 1805 and slavery in the British colonies in 1830. France, reluctant after the failed experiment between 1794 and 1802, was pressured to follow the British example in 1848. Spain followed in the 1850s. Officially, slave trade was abolished worldwide in 1851. Slavery, finally, was made illegal in the United States of America after the Civil War (1861–5), in Cuba in 1883, and in Brazil in 1888. The motives behind abolition were in fact complex, and an expression of humanism only to a limited degree. Political circumstances and strategical decisions regarding the declining productivity and profitability of plantation economies proved to be more conducive than compassion. The demands of capitalism and industrialization in fact called for the definition of a new, imperial ideology[4] along with a new regulation of the lives of people within Europe itself. Historically, the 'policing'[5] of social and sexual minorities at home coincided with racialist policies towards the indigenous populations of the colonies.

The Arab world

Initially, the Middle East and northern Africa remained inaccessible to European expansion. The failure in 1802 of Napoleon's military expedition to Egypt was in fact followed by the rule of Mehemed Ali and only the construction of the Suez canal (1859–69) opened the gate to international, soon largely British control in Egypt and the Sudan. Earlier, in 1830, Algiers was occupied by the French.

New political circumstances and colonial policies did not always challenge familiar patterns of description; not, in any case, for the Arab world. For the most part observers simply reiterated the familiar and by then age-old representation of Arab or Muslim immorality, assuming at once that such qualification was a clear enough explanation in itself. John Lewis Burkhardt, whose travel report was published both in English and in German, described how same-sex praxis occurred even in the Beith Allah mosque in Mecca: 'From time to time the holy Kaaba in Mecca ... turns into a theatre of indecent and criminal acts to a degree that can hardly be defined. And these acts do not just remain unpunished, but are pursued in all openness. Often, I was shocked at the spectacle of terrible things, that merely provoked laughter or at the most a slight revulsion among other witnesses.'[6] The missionary Samuel Marinus Zwemer also confirmed that 'unnatural acts were performed in the actual mosk of Mecca itself'.[7]

Ernst Trumpp described how boy love was embraced by the *sufi* religion in particular. The image of Mahbub especially, while an earthly representation of Allah, provided a semi-ritual context for sexual relations with boys in a 'degree that challenges our European taste (unsern europäischen Geschmack anwidernden Grad)'.[8]

Military men were eager to exaggerate the dimensions of same-sex praxis in the Arab world. In his *Terminal Essay*, that will be discussed in chapter seven, Burton included a story about the Dutch consul-general for the Netherlands, M. de Ruyssenaer, who was advised by Sa'id Pasha to try out both active and passive anal sex before judging upon the subject. I have not been able, however, to verify Burton's sources.[9]

A fine example of ascription of vice to the enemy in days of war can be found in a complaint by the Marquis de Boissy, who lamented the wide-spread visibility of *moeurs arabes* among French regiments during the occupation of Algiers in 1830. In his eyes, the African wars had given rise to an *effroyable débordement pédérastique*.[10] Other usually negative descriptions of Arab same-sex praxis can be found in travel reports by Fraser, Morier, Pischon, Pfeifer, Rozet, Saint John, Walsch, and White,[11] or in armchair studies by Clot-Bey, von Osten, Schoelcher, Sprenger, and von Pueckler-Muskau.[12]

Not everyone shared the abhorrence of these authors towards same-sex practices in the Arab world. Some, in fact, were eager to experiment. Well known is Gustave Flaubert's letter to Louis Bouilhet, written from Cairo on 15 January 1850:

As we are talking about berdaches, well this is what I know about them. One admits [to committing] sodomy and talks about it at the table of one's host. Sometimes, one denies it somewhat, upon which everyone reacts and one ends up admitting after all .... It all takes place in the baths. One gets a personal bath (5 francs, including the masseurs, the pipe, the coffee, the linen) and one takes one's boy to one of the rooms. – You know, of course, that all the bathboys are berdaches. Those masseurs ... are usually very sweet young boys.[13]

Shortly afterwards, Flaubert confided that he had indeed had sexual intercourse with a young fellow and that it had made him laugh. He was determined, however, to do it again, as 'for an experience to be complete, it must be repeated'.[14]

The appeal of Arab sexuality to Lord Byron has frequently been claimed, even when the author's ambiguous language obfuscates whether such was brought about by his knowledge of same-sex praxis in the Arab world in particular. Byron, who wrote poems about the East in the years following 1812, surely felt attracted by stories about 'male friendships' in the Muslim world. But reconstructions of the poet's sources inevitably remain speculative.[15] Quite some time ago, Harold Wiener inventoried Byron's sources of information and assumed that only the lyrics, published in Sir William Jones' thirteen-volume anthology, could have provided the poet with evidence of sexual customs in the Arab world.[16] Crompton has pointed out that Jones' books could hardly have provided much explicit information to Byron as his translations were 'thoroughly bowdlerised'.[17] But he adds that Byron may have read other anthologies, such as John Hindley's *Persian Lyrics, or Scattered Poems from the Diwan-i-Hafiz*, published at the turn of the century, which discussed the issue of sodomy more candidly if only in its preface:

To avoid being suspected of disingenuousness, we must here also point out a blemish in our Author, too glaring for disguise, and which, if not explained away, must subject him to the same moral disgrace, which unfortunately attaches itself to some of the first poets, and even to some of the philosophers, of antiquity. Well aware of the dishonour reflected upon VIRGIL and ANACREON, from the names Alexis and Bathyllus, it is not without regret that we find HAFIZ, and indeed all the SUFI poets of this class, continually liable to the opprobrium of similar accusations'.[18]

In the actual translation, Hindley felt reluctant to translate paragraphs that, in his eyes, would offend his readers. Perhaps Byron was more inspired by his own experience when travelling to Albania in 1808. Partly Muslim, partly Christian, Albania was a country where, in the words of Georg von Hahn in 1854, a man 'sings his [lover's] praise in verse, a woman's never'.[19]

In general, Orientalist scholars often preferred to remain silent about same-sex practices in order to promote a high image of Arab culture. As during the Enlightenment, these were only discussed when inevitable. The philologists' position often remained ambiguous, as is illustrated by the Leyden Orientalist, Reinhardt Pieter Dozy. He plainly abstained from translating presumably compromising text fragments that were 'of such a disgusting nature that I cannot include them in a French translation (d'une nature si dégoûtante que je ne puis les faire passer dans une traduction française)'.[20] William MacGuckin Baron de Slane refrained from translating some passages of the work of Ibn Khallikan,[21] and the French Orientalist

Antoine Isaac Silvestre de Sacy retained the Arab language when explicit scenes of boy-love showed up in the manuscripts.[22]

Joseph Hammer-Purgerstall claimed that same-sex practices were unknown in the Arab world initially, but had become common due to the influence of the Persians. The Abbasids were known from an early age onward to indulge in sodomy and had gradually corrupted the Arabs, especially under the reign of the califs Al-Mamoun (813–33). One of his *protégés*, Jahja Ben Akhtam, who held juridical power in Basra, was also known as a fervent devotee of sodomy, and here too the author felt compelled to emphasize that he was of Persian descent. Moral corruption had been most visible, Hammer-Purgerstall continued, within the walls of the harems, where male slaves were sexually abused as much as the women, and where one became disenchanted with heterosexual intercourse and searched for more exciting entertainment – a fine example of scholarly attempts to acquit Arabs from sexual vice.[23]

Vincenz von Rosenzweig did not censor his own translations of passages describing male-to-male eroticism.[24] It was also discussed in Zinkeisen's *Geschichte des Osmanischen Reiches* of 1855,[25] and in some early comparative studies of civil law by Pharaon and Dulau[26] and by Tornau.[27]

As before, same-sex praxis in the Arab world continued to be seen predominantly as a sodomitical act, that many men committed often with younger men or boys, rather than as structured along the dividing line between male and female gender. Exceptions were rare. Alfred Freiherr Von Kremer discussed Islamic law on *muchannisin*, translated by the author as 'hermaphrodites' and seen by him as human beings who had both male and female genitalia.[28] No doubt von Kremer was referring to *mukhannathun*, men or boys who dressed like women and behaved effeminately, and who worked most commonly as male prostitutes. Often their social role included dancing, singing and work as a domestic servant.[29] *Mukhannathun* had actually been persecuted during the caliphate of Sulayman (715–17) and had lost their social prominence as a result. But they never disappeared and continued to live a subcultural existence.[30] Von Kremer evidently had never met or seen any as he held on to an Early Modern model of hermaphroditism. But this may also be interpreted as evidence of how representations of gender-structured same-sex praxis remained unlikely in the discourse on Arab sexuality.

Other travellers did see *mukhannathun*, however. Among them, James Silk Buckingham, who witnessed how in a Hebeb café, near the Euphrates, young boys wore a *keffiah* and female jewellery and sat on the men's lap to seduce them sexually.[31] Edward William Lane's *Account of the Manners and Customs of the Modern Egyptians* (1836) contains a description of male dancers, called *khawals* or *ginks*, who performed at private festivities around weddings, births and circumcision, and who may well have been similar to the *mukhannathun*.[32] Gérard de Nerval also expressed his astonishment as he discovered that two dancing girls, 'very beautiful, with a proud look, Arab eyes brightened by kohl, and full, delicate cheeks (fort belles, à la mine fière, aux yeux arabes avivés par le khôl, aux joues pleines et délicates)', were in fact two boys.[33] Later, Ernest Godard attended a public feast in Cairo and witnessed how boys dressed like girls danced voluptuously in front of a greatly approving male audience. One in fact looked so much like a girl that the author felt compelled to ask about his sex and even verified it himself. The young boy's penis was small, thin and looked gracious, says Godard, who also witnessed another ritual, where a man had strapped an artificial penis around his waist and feigned copulation with another younger man.[34]

The latter spectacle may have been similar to erotic rituals that could be observed until the early twentieth century across the Maghreb.[35] But what is most striking in Godard's testimony is the meaning ascribed by the author to the anatomy of one's genitalia, more precisely to the smallness of the *mukhannath*'s penis. This was significant, in his eyes, for the unmanly biological constitution of the boy and also a sign, historically, of a shifting approach to same-sex praxis in the Arab world.

Indeed, a gradually greater emphasis was laid not only upon the passive partner in sexual relations among men, but also on his presumably deficient sexual anatomy. Physicians in particular brought about this discursive shift, as they redefined Arab immorality in biological terms. Among them were Jacquot,[36] Oppenheim,[37] and Polak.[38] Alphons Bilharz' *Descriptio anatomica organorum genitalium Eunuchi Aethiopis*, published in Berlin in 1859, also reflected a growing attention to the physical anomalies not only of eunuchs, who by then became increasingly rare, but also of all those whose sexual behaviour violated accepted notions of sexual normality. This focus on a presumably anomalous minority was actually quite different from preceding images of 'endemic' sodomy.[39]

Central Asia and the Far East

New ethnographic data also complicated familiar representations of Asian sexuality. Sweeping generalizations about the 'effeminate' Asian race and, at the same time, their propensity to indulge in sodomy made room for more empirical observations of ethnographic circumstance. To an extent this was provoked by the difficulties faced by Europeans on their way to colonial hegemony in India, Malaysia and Indonesia. In the Far East, the United Provinces and Spain maintained their colonial hegemony in Indonesia and the Philippines, while Portugal maintained control over Goa, Macao and East Timor. As yet, France maintained colonial outposts in Chandarnagar (Calcutta), Pondichéry, Yanaon (Yanam), Karikal and Mahé and would only

seek expansion into Indochina after 1862. More impressive was the development of British colonial power. In control of Bengal since 1757 and of
Ceylon since 1796, Britain gained control over Nepal after the Ghurka War
(1814–16) and over most of the Indian subcontinent and Bhutan. Then, in
1858, the East India Company was suspended and India became a colony of
the British crown, run by a viceroy – the era of the Raj. During the 1870s and
1880s, Burma in the East and Beludjistan (present-day Pakistan) in the West
were incorporated in the British empire as well. The Opium War (1840–2)
initiated an era of British – and also French – infiltration in Chinese
territory.

Political and strategic motives were also instrumental for the introduction
of ethnology in Central Asia. A well-known document about same-sex
praxis in Central Asia is Richard Burton's report, of 1845, on male brothels
in Karachi. Then an officer and commissioned by Charles Napier to investigate the matter, Burton wrote a candid report: 'Karachi ... supported no
less than three lupanars or bordels, in which not women but boys and
eunuchs, the former demanding nearly a double price, lay for hire.'[40] Boys
were preferred, so Burton described, to eunuchs, because 'the scrotum of the
unmutilated boy could be used as a kind of bridle for directing the movements of the animal'.[41]

Speaking Sindi and disguised as a local inhabitant, Burton spent many an
hour in these localities to observe, as he maintained, what went on. Napier,
though critical of the report, simply filed it and went about to destroy the
brothels and put down 'the infamous beasts who, dressed as women, plied
their trade in the Meers' time openly'.[42] Only in 1847 was the report sent to
the British authorities in Bombay by Napier's successor, who recommended
that Burton be dismissed from military service.[43]

Whatever the matter, Burton felt prone, as he would remain throughout
his life, to describe in detail how sexual customs often differed greatly from
what was believed 'natural' and 'civilized' in England then. Same-sex praxis
figured in his writings from an early stage, even when he did not, at that time,
intend to publish it. To today's historian, his testimonies are both precious
for their candid style and precarious for their provocative tenor.

Same-sex practices on the Indian subcontinent also were frequently seen as
gender-structured. Victor Jacquemont, while portraying the sexual praxis of
Ranjít Singh, the 'Lion of the Punjab', emphasized the effeminate character
of his male lovers, yet insisted that male-to-male sexuality (*gánd-márá,
gándú*) was not tolerated by the Hindu population itself.[44] Dubois also
reported houses of male prostitution, where the men were dressed like
women.[45] Most probably, these rare descriptions of same-sex behaviour in
India ought to be identified as tied to the still existing cross-gender role of
hijras. These are transvestites or eunuchs, 'who are devotees of the mother
goddess Bahuchara Mata and whose ascribed sacred powers are contingent
upon their asexuality'. But in reality, many are prostitutes.[46] An equally fine

line between exceptional social status and marginal sexuality existed in some regions of South East Asia, even when it was not always tied to prostitution. Historical research may actually reveal if the latter was perhaps partially reinforced by colonial policy against such potentially threatening roles, not only in South East Asia but in India as well.

Malayans hardly committed sodomy, according to Crawfurd, who flirted with the idea that evidence of the contrary was merely a sign of decay. Nor did they have a vocabulary to describe such behaviour, so he claimed in his *History of the Indian Archipelago*.[47] For James Brooke, Malayan sexual morality contrasted with that of China, India and Central Asia. In his diary, he described how some Bugi men in Celebes, now Sulawesi, dressed like women on a permanent basis throughout their lives. He also noted that parents offered their son to one of the *rajahs* of the Wajo kingdom, when they felt that he looked rather delicate. Still, he insisted that, contrary to the practice in Persia, this did not lead to any 'unnatural' acts.[48] Himself one of the 'white' *rajahs* of Sarawak, in North Borneo and now part of Malaysia, James Brooke seemingly showed an extraordinary interest in adolescent boys – which may explain why he was reluctant to admit that sexual relations between the *rajahs* and their 'pageboys' did actually occur.

More numerous were those writers who claimed that same-sex relations were in fact common among the Malayan people both on the Asian continent and in the Indian archipelago. Among them was Von de Wall, who also discussed the effeminate men among the Bugi, on the east coast of Borneo, now Kalimantan. Known as *tjelebei*, their masculine power had remained undeveloped, according to Von de Wall, who explicitly subscribed to the biological definition of gender that was initiated during the Enlightenment. They looked rather weak and had a hoarse voice. 'Though impotent', they felt attracted to younger men, whom they showered with affection. A fairly high number among them were actual hermaphrodites and known among the Bugi as *kedie*.[49]

Franz Junghuhn's study of *Die Battaländer auf Sumatra*, published in 1847, is a highly speculative attempt to weigh indigenous people's morality. The Batak, in his eyes, were 'relatively virtuous', as was demonstrated by severe legislation on adultery. Neither phallic sculptures on their graves, nor widespread and accepted sodomy challenged this, so he claimed.[50] A remarkable rationalization indeed, especially when compared to his assessment of Java's population as lascivious despite the fact that on this island no phallic sculptures were to be found.[51]

In 1846, the Dutchman Hupe claimed that 'unnatural sin' was ubiquitous among the Dajaks of Borneo. He reported first about the *basire*, male priests, who observed religious rituals alongside female *bilangs*. They had healing powers and engaged in sodomy. Some dressed like women and were called *babassirs* – a name erratically translated by Hupe as 'castrate' and 'eunuch'.[52]

Schwaner similarly claimed that *basire* in Pulopetak, Borneo eagerly engaged in passive sexual intercourse. Apart from a present, their partner was expected to pay '30 cents recepis' for one night. During daytime, *basire* were male priests, who operated alongside their female colleagues or *bilians*, and were believed by the population to have healing powers.[53] In Hardeland's *Dayacksch-Deutsches Wörterbuch*, the adjective *basir*, in Pulopetak, means 'infertile'; *babasir* or *basibasir*, 'like a woman, weak, lazy, cowardly'. *Basire* are claimed to dress like women and to engage in sodomitical acts during religious rituals. Some are formally married to men. Among the Kayan, *basir* is said to apply to both women (*basir bawi*) and men (*basir hatua*), both of whom make a living out of 'Sorcery and . . . vice'.[54]

Cross-gender behaviour remained a recurrent theme in European descriptions of same-sex practices in China, Japan, and the Kamchatka peninsula. This was most noticeable in portrayals of the latter territory's population, where von Langsdorff, Choris, Erman and Prince zu Wied perceived cross-structured same-sex relations among the Aleut and the Koryak.[55]

A fair number of testimonies about male-to-male sexual life in China focused on the widespread custom for men to have servant boys or *pages*, who would provide sexual services as well. The habit, so it seemed in the eyes of westerners, was given birthright as it had been elevated into an institution at the imperial court centuries earlier.[56] Even foreigners residing in China were pressured to have them, so claimed Hermann Maron.[57] Equally striking to European observers such as Gützlaff, Morache, and Maron was the widespread evidence of male prostitution in Peking, Shanghai, Hong Kong and 'the Chinese Athens', Canton.[58] Already familiar since Ricci were claims that the theatre was a favourite breeding ground. It was confirmed by, among others, Bonacossi, Morache and Hildebrandt.[59] William Milne stated that female roles were played by either eunuchs or boys.[60] Travesty, as is known, was current in a theatrical context and did not go unnoticed.[61] Its high visibility may in fact have consolidated beliefs that the insertee's role in same-sex relations among men was only congruous with his overall 'feminine' nature. Alas, no single document offers sound proof of this.

Signs are visible, meanwhile, that sodomy continued to be viewed also as a more or less 'endemic' evil, that was spread beyond the confined worlds of pageboys, eunuchs and male prostitutes. Morache emphasized how it was a recurrent theme in Chinese literature.[62] Hildebrandt described what must have been some kind of 'peephole', that was placed at the entrance of the theatre of Macao, and that contained explicit sexual, including homosexual imagery.[63] Delauture d'Escayrac, while speculating on the etiology of same-sex practices across the world, felt that these were typical of cultural decay. China, among other civilizations, was used to prove his point.[64] The French physician Libermann, finally, ascribed Chinese moral leniency to their addiction to opium and set about demonstrating how it 'perverted' one's sexual desire.[65]

Convictions that same-sex praxis was most common across China were consolidated by George Staunton's translation of the *lu* or 'fundamental laws' of the Chinese penal code of 1805. It did not contain any reference to sexual relations among women or men.[66] This conviction was not challenged by Pauthier's translation, published in 1853, of some of the *li* that were more specific and did in fact include regulations against what he translated as *crimes contre nature*. One had to be caught *flagrante delicto*, however, which, as with Arab legislation, was easily interpreted as a sign of leniency.[67]

Discourse on Japanese same-sex praxis largely parallelled texts on China. Maron said it took place easily in the margins of theatre life just as in China[68] – a fact that was confirmed by Gustav Spiess and Richard Andree.[69] Wilhelm Heine reported *weichliche Bonzen*, thereby reiterating the familiar claim by westerners that the Buddhist convents were havens of sodomy.[70] The recurrent connotation of effeminacy was typical of the connection made in these texts between male-to-male sexual praxis and cross-gender behaviour in particular.

Heine's writings are also exemplary, however, of how descriptions of particular surroundings that obviously promoted sexual relations among men or between men and boys, were used to document claims that sodomy was indicative of Japanese overall moral laxity.[71] The Dutch traveller Pompe van Meerdervoort claimed that the people's sex life revealed a shameless, almost naive dwelling upon lustful feelings and had little spiritual bearing.[72] Klemm and Hildebrandt, however, maintained that sexual customs should not blind one to the spiritual dimension of Japanese religion. Their disapproval of these very practices demonstrates their selective desire to achieve a genuine cultural understanding even when immersed in European bias about what constituted 'natural' sexuality.[73] As before, sodomy was read both as a metaphor and metonymy of the Chinese and Japanese peoples' immorality, which reveals the persistence of the age-old European presumption that both the Chinese and Japanese people were an effeminate race.

Yet, the overall image of same-sex praxis in Asia had grown more diversified than the Early Modern one. Sexual life in China and Japan, that had been exemplary of 'Asian' immorality, was seen as distinct from the newly discovered tribal societies of the Indonesian archipelago and the Philippines. The continuing ethnographic exploration, meanwhile, of Central Asia, the Indian subcontinent, the Nicobar and Andaman Islands, Ceylon and Southeast Asia undermined previous generalizations. By 1860, the image of 'Asian' proclivity to sodomy, as it was known before, had been supplemented by narratives about both gender- and age-structured male-to-male relationships, about pageboys and male prostitutes, occasionaly even by claims that sodomy in fact did not occur at all.

Oceania

The Pacific islands remained outside the grip of colonial rule until the 1880s, with the exception of French New Caledonia (since 1853) and the Marianas and the Caroline Islands, that remained Spanish until 1899. Australia, first and foremost seen as a penal colony, gradually became a new home for agricultural settlers as likewise did New Zealand and Tasmania.

New reports on same-sex praxis further undermined the Enlightenment myth that this did not occur in this part of the world. Reports were as yet fairly limited, because most territories of Melanesia, where various forms of ritualized homosexuality existed, remained virtually unexplored. Apart from an ephemeral reference by Victor de Rochas,[74] only a single, explicit testimony is known about same-sex praxis in New Caledonia. Adolphe Bourgarel spent many years on the island and witnessed how social life was often strictly separated into male and female spheres. He described how men would gather in huts and indulge in sexual relations among themselves. Informants, who are impossible to identify, suggested, according to a remarkable 'local' Malthusianism, that this occurred because the land did not allow for overpopulation. Men thus abstained from having sexual relations with women exclusively. Others explained it as a sign of male hatred for women or as the outcome of female prostitution and polygamy, leading to a shortage of women who were available for marriage. The author himself subscribed to the thesis that common men 'loved their own sex' because of the polygamous households of the male elite. Bourgarel's report is hard to evaluate. Probably he merely witnessed a case where same-sex practices occurred as part of a ritual. Both the complexity of Melanesian ethnographic reality and Bourgarel's imprecise data exclude a conclusive answer, however.[75]

On the Australian Aboriginals, a brief indication was given in a book destinated for emigrants to Australia. Its author, Hasskarl, claimed that men were 'not entirely free from unnatural sensuality (nicht ganz frei von unnatürlicher Sinnlichkeit)'.[76]

A few more reports addressed same-sex praxis in Polynesia. Mariner reported that the Tonga Islands were an exception in the South Seas, where same-sex praxis was widely spread.[77] Moerenhout portrayed the Tahitians as people who indulged in any form of sexuality without wondering about its moral dimension. Their partner's sex proved insignificant.[78] Seemann exclaimed that 'all vices of the civilized world (alle Laster der Zivilisierten Welt)' existed there as well.[79] Dumont d'Urville, finally, described 'close friendships' between boys or men, occasionally also between indigenous boys and Europeans, that were of an intimate character in his eyes.[80]

Such descriptions went along with already familiar representations of the Polynesian's putative androgyny, ascribing feminine characteristics to young males, male ones to the girls. The 'instability in gendering', in the words of

Abigail Solomon-Godeau,[81] was also reflected in the nineteenth century by documents that portrayed same-sex praxis as tied to cross-gender roles. The ship's captain Erskine briefly mentioned 'more effeminate Polynesians'.[82] Vincentdon-Dumoulin and Desgraz's compilation about the Marquesas Islands contains an unidentifiable report of cross-dressing men, called *hokis* or *koioas*. They travel from village to village, where they make music, dance and declamate poetry. They rub their skin with a powder extracted from the juice from *papa* roots and coco oil just like women do. According to the authors, they are despised by their folk, yet, if this is true, then it may well have been for reasons that had little to do with the *hokis'* sexuality.[83] The authors' view was at odds, however, with the wider consensus among eyewitnesses that such 'effeminate' minorities were actually respected by the Polynesians. For missionaries, this was one among other reasons for trying to suppress indigenous sexual customs, often in complete disregard of their cultural context. Eventually efforts were bungled, towards the mid-nineteenth century, in the evangelization campaign of the Church Missionary Societies of New Zealand and Melanesia. What might have been an opportunity to rethink a Western understanding of sexual morality was gradually wiped out as the unwanted residue of heathenism.[84]

American Indians

After the American Revolution of 1776, most other American colonies were also emancipated from their respective motherlands. Dessalines declared Haiti independent in 1804. All Spanish colonies, with the exception of Cuba, were emancipated from the motherland between 1810 and 1821, Brazil in 1822. Only France, Britain and Holland were able to maintain colonial hegemony in the Guyanas, the Antilles and the West Indies. Political change did not, however, prevent Europeans from exploring the as-yet largely unmapped inner territories or from organizing ethnographic expeditions among both the peoples in the newly independent countries and those of the few remaining colonies.

As in the eighteenth century, discourse on same-sex practices in America focused primarily on the passive partner, who adopted a cross-gender role. Thus new reports were made known to the European audience especially of North American cross-gender roles. Aside from American ones, I briefly mention those by Richardson about the Cree (*ayekkwew*),[85] by Catlin about the Fox and the Dakota,[86] and by Prince zu Wied-Neuwied about the Fox, the Siksika, the Arikara, the Mandan (*mih-däckä*) and the Crow.[87] The Deputy Postmaster General of British North America, George Heriot reported cross-gender roles among the Illinois, the Sioux and the Iroquois, then compared these to evidence about similar behavioural patterns among the Indians of Florida and Yucatán. He emphasized how such men were both respected as they played a prominent role in ritual, and despised because they engaged in sodomy during daily life.[88] Catlin described and painted the *icoocooa* or berdache dance of the Sioux.[89] When describing the Mandan, he called the men, who dressed like women, 'dandies', 'exquisites' and 'beaus', thus reinforcing a sense of continuity between berdaches among the Mandan and sodomites at home.[90] Duflot de Mofras, finally, reported on *débauchés* among most of the Indian tribes of California.[91]

Less common were descriptions of cross-gender roles in Central and South America. Eduard Pöppig's article on the American Indians in the *Allgemeine Encyklopädie* (1840) suggests indirectly that he too saw passive men in the Andes largely as 'taking the feminine role' throughout.[92] A certain Bardel claimed that *machi* or healer/shamans among the Araucana were frequently dressed as women.[93] Incidental information about same-sex praxis can also be found in some works of Americanist scholarship. Lord Kingsborough's *Antiquities of Mexico* contained a text documenting cross-gender behaviour in what is now the state of Texas.[94] Brasseur de Bourbourg, who edited the *Popol Vuh* and translated it from Quiché into French, described how the Olmecs, when conquering the city of Guatemala, required that the local population offer two young men for the purpose of sodomy. He also speculated about male brothels in the Mexican province of Pánuco[95] and about ritualized homosexuality among Maya populations near the lake Atitlán.[96] Though focusing on the pre-Columbian era, Brasseur de Bourbourg assumed that Maya sexuality at his time still reflected pre-Christian days as he set about to study Maya language. He then indicated that *ixpen* denotated *podicator*[97] whereas *cobol* or *hazacam* meant hermaphrodite. It is not clear what the author meant by this. Perhaps, though no conclusive evidence is as yet available, one word signified a cross-gender role, whereas the other may have referred to actual hermaphroditism. His usage may well reveal how he at least did not see a major difference between either.

But here too, narratives attaching same-sex praxis to gender-structured roles clearly outweighed other descriptions of same-sex praxis. Testimonies such as the one by Isidore Löwenstern, who reiterated a long-familiar image of 'endemic' sodomy, in fact had become quite rare.[98] An alternative script, 'locating' sexual deviance outside the realm of femininity, can be found in *Reise nach Brasilien* (1823–31) by von Spix and von Martius, who emphasized that same-sex praxis could occur within a context of male initiation. Von Martius described how among the Mura, near the present-day city Santarém in the Amazon forest, a yearly ritual took place at which only the men took part. It consisted of mutual flagellation with whips, made of tapir or *manati* skin, and was interpreted by the author as a kind of perverted homoeroticism.[99] Alternatively, same-sex praxis may take place as part of a ritual where the *pajé* or shaman transmitted his healing powers to his younger successor and which required their joint isolation in the woods for a few days.[100]

Von Martius was aware, however, of the widespread habit of men dressing like women and often, though not always, taking a passive role during sexual intercourse. Yet he rejected the idea that these were a separate class of people. In his eyes, such behaviour is merely an extreme sign of the Indian race's *Sittenverderbnis* or moral depravity.[101] His opinion stemmed from a more general speculation on the weak, feminine nature of the Indian race – a familiar idea, as I have described, at least since the late seventeenth century, that was upheld into the nineteenth century by authors such as Wilhelm Ludwig von Eschwege, Eduard Pöppig and, though only partially, Alcide d'Orbigny. Von Eschwege documented his claim by pointing to the 'extraordinarily small size of the penis (ausserordentliche Kleinheit des membris virilis)',[102] whereas Pöppig referred to eyewitness reports by his predecessors.[103] Alcide d'Orbigny classified the Araucana, the Chiquitos and the Guarani among the Indian races with *traits effeminés*, whereas most Peruvian Indians were of the warrior kind.[104]

Fully at odds with the preceding texts, were authors who claimed that sodomy was not to be taken for granted among the Indians. For example the Spaniard Felix de Azara, who denied that same-sex relations were common around the Paraguay.[105] So too Jules Virey: 'One claims that hermaphrodites exist among the Patagonians: I haven't seen any (On a prétendu qu'ils existaient des hermaphrodites chez les Patagons; ce qui ne se voit nulle part).'[106] Still others went so far as to state that sodomy spread across the New World's population only during eras of cultural decay. The theologian Müller ascribed same-sex praxis as visible among American Indians to a preceding culture, that had degenerated and condoned sexual debauchery in the process.[107] Adolf Wuttke, in turn, claimed that *unnatürliche Laster* had spread among the Indians only during the days of European colonization. He stated at the same time that severe legislation against sodomy had existed since pre-Columbian times, yet did not interpret this fact as a sign that same-sex relations were in fact known.[108]

Speculation about the moral qualities of the Indians thus intersected with more 'scientific' attempts to describe and interpret sexual variety. From it resulted a complex picture, especially with regard to same-sex praxis and cross-gender roles, that was composed of both century-old narrative tropes about 'endemic' immorality and new ones that reflected the increasing weight of biological and physical-anthropological theory.

Subsaharan Africans

Subsaharan Africa eventually attracted the interest of European adventurers and numerous new missions (Bowdich, 1819; Denham and Clapperton, 1823–5; Laing, 1825; Clapperton and Lander, 1825–7; Caillé, 1827–8; Niger Expedition, 1841; Cooley, 1845; Krapf and Rebmann, 1848–9; Barth, 1850–5; Erhardt, 1856; Livingstone's Zambezi expedition of 1858–64) were set up to penetrate large parts of the Sahara and West Africa. Arabian slave traders continued their operations from the sultanate of Zanzibar, which led to agreements between the British, the Germans and tribal leaders of East Africa. Southern Africa witnessed the *Grote Trek* (1836–44) as well as the foundation of Oranje Vrijstaat (1842) and Transvaal (1853).

The incipient exploration of the African interior inevitably led to an increasing number of firsthand reports about the sexual behaviour of newly discovered ethnic groups. Yet same-sex practices were reported only incidentally and seemed to confirm the belief of Gibbon *cum suis*, that the African continent was spared from such vice.

Ferdinand Werne confirmed Browne's earlier statement that sodomy did not occur in the Sudan.[109] The Danish father Monrad reacted against earlier, Portuguese claims, probably by dos Santos and Cardonega, that sodomy was current among the Africans. When visiting the Gold Coast, now Ghana, in the early nineteenth century, he only witnessed the indigenous people's disgust at sexual relations among males – which may, however, indicate that it did in fact occur.[110]

Jakob Ludwig Döhne, sent by the Deutsche Gesellschaft der evangelischen Missionen, described male initiation rites, yet asserted that *widernatürliche Unzucht* was virtually unknown to the Amaxosa of Southern Africa. This, so he continued, even though they generally indulged in 'carnal lust'.[111] Another witness claimed that he had seen only one case of 'sodomy' during his twenty-five-year-long stay among the Kaffers. The man was accused and sentenced to pay five units of cattle by the chief.[112] Yet another simultaneous report was given by a certain Brownlee, who said that the fine for sodomy could be as high as ten cows. As with the previous report, it is impossible to find out which of the ethnic denominations – Tswana, Xhosa, Sotha – among the so-called 'Kaffers' were meant.

Among the Temba, David Livingstone briefly described what he called *dandies*, that is, men who wore very decorative clothes and whose shoulders were greasy with all the fat that they smeared in their hair. Yet nothing seemed to indicate, in the author's eyes, that these men actually took a feminine role especially during sex.[113] Alert to dress codes, Livingstone also wondered why some men of the Eastern African Manjanga tribe wore the *pelele*, a ring that is pierced through the upper lip, and worn mostly by women. He dropped the issue once he was told that men too may wear it.[114] Back in Southern Africa, Livingstone claimed that the polygamous households of the elderly chiefs in Matabeleland gave rise to 'immorality' among the younger men.[115]

Other authors, however, repeated the earliest assertions by Dos Santos, Cardonega, Dapper, de Flacourt, Kolb and, eventually, Labat, that 'sodomy' was far from unknown to the African people. Their reports remain hard to interpret, however, as they are often suggestive rather than explicit. But if any conclusion be allowed, it is that more often than not such descriptions were connected with representations of a cross-gender role.

Fleuriot de Langle travelled extensively along the African coast and visited the kingdom of Dahomey, now Benin. In Ouidah he witnessed how the young sons of highly placed families were recruited by the king in order to be raised as *lagredis* or effeminates. They not only policed the king's numerous wives, but also played a significant political role.[116]

Of the Gold Coast's Ashanti people, Thomas Hutchinson reported that highly placed men bought male slaves, who would safeguard their masters' soul and would be killed along with them. These *crabbah* or *ocrah* wore a pearl necklace with a golden pendant and were treated like lovers, according to the author, suggesting that such relations were indeed sexual.[117]

Leguéval de Lacombe, finally, described the *sekatses* among the Betanimene of Madagascar as men who dressed and behaved like women, leading a semi-nomadic existence and enjoying the respect of other people.[118]

Historical evidence admittedly remains 'incidental' and ephemeral. Most authors merely displayed a casual interest in same-sex praxis as seen overseas. Not infrequently, it was discussed only when inevitable in descriptions of religious ritual, court procedure and medical praxis or in studies of art and literature. Yet the overall picture reveals that two major narrative tropes, that had arisen earlier, remained current throughout the first half of the nineteenth century. Sometimes they can be retrieved from beneath many an author's idiosyncratic portrayal of same-sex praxis, as they encountered it on their way. More often, however, they constituted an implicit background to the apparently 'meaningless' phrases of both compilers and eyewitnesses.

The most important trope in the light of future scientific developments, further extended the Enlightenment linking of sexuality with gender and, more specifically, of same-sex praxis with feminine identity. I will describe below not only how this paradigm was held up by nineteenth-century positivism, but also how the search for a more empirically verifiable model, that could be applied to cross-cultural evidence, was eventually revealed to be a methodological *cul-de-sac*.

I will demonstrate how many ethnographic narratives still reiterated an age-old discursive tradition, the trope that represented overseas same-sex practices as a *signifier* of lechery, that was claimed to be endemic, certainly characteristic of the whole people's immorality. The ongoing appeal, in fact, of a moral etiology can be read from an incipient medical and hygienic discourse. Its prophylactic argumentation was supported more by moral considerations than by hard evidence about the 'contaminating' effects of deviant sexuality. The latter, in fact, was still seen largely as an indistinct 'mass', problematic mainly because at odds with the new, bourgeois sense of respectability. It ought to be treated by moral persuasion, so it was claimed by psychiatrists and legal physicians, who increasingly monopolized the public debate on sex.

The moral rhetoric of prophylaxis

Evidence of the moral narrative's long duration can be perceived, remarkably, in psychiatry, where one felt that mental disorder could no longer be adequately explained by the physiological models of the seventeenth and eighteenth centuries. A regime of 'moral treatment' was proposed by Tuke, Pinel and Esquirol, the latter of whom classified sexual pathology as a triad of erotomania, nymphomania and satyriasis – categories that denoted a surplus, rather than a perversion of sexual desire.[119] Even a racialist theoretician such as James Cowley Prichard admitted in an appendix to his *Treatise on Insanity* (1835) that 'there were simply too many instances where overt insanity could not be correlated with structural abnormalities of the brain and nervous system'.[120] His concept of 'moral insanity' lent a new *élan* to the familiar model of sexual deviance as a failure of the will.

After the late-eighteenth- and early-nineteenth-century decriminalization laws, at least on the European continent, same-sex praxis too was subjected to a rhetoric of moral treatment by legal medicine. Capital punishment or prison sentences were abandoned in exchange for a discourse of prophylaxis and moral guidance. Diagnosis, in this context, oscillated between traditional study of the passive partner's anus, mainly to see if anal penetration had occurred, and a newer 'medical' scrutiny of the active partner's genitalia. In the end, however, sodomy was explained as the outcome of social circumstance. Thus the German Johann Valentin Müller, who suggested that a man's choice of sexual relations with men was provoked by social conditions, just as among hunter and warrior tribes in the primitive world.[121] Fournier-Pescay emphasized the demoralizing effect of convents, prisons, and ships.[122] Mende ascribed the origin of sodomitical practice to masturbation.[123]

Ex post facto legal intervention obviously did not single out same-sex praxis as a problem that stood on its own. It was seen as a symptom of immorality, as were female and male prostitution, child abuse, and masturbation. Frequently, it was part of an ongoing *discours antimasturbatoire* as yet another negative effect of self-pollution. Collectively, deviant sexual practices were seen indiscriminately as social disorders, that undermined a new bourgeois organization of public and private life and ought to be submitted accordingly to a policy of prophylaxis.[124] In England, prostitution was somewhat condoned by virtue of a 'double standard' until the 1860s, when subsequent Contagious Diseases Acts were passed and brought about a certain level of control.[125] In France, this was effected by the regime of *réglementation*, developed by Parent-Duchâtelet.[126] Other European countries developed policies that resembled the example of either Great Britain or France.

Less well documented – and as a result less well investigated by historians – are early-nineteenth-century policies against male prostitution, often closely intertwined with police repression of the sodomitical subcultures that were developing in the metropolitan centres of the Old World. In England, sodomy remained illegal and an attempt to abolish the death penalty failed in Parliament in 1841. Only twenty years later, sodomy would be punished with a maximum prison sentence from ten years to life.[127] Legalization in other countries, that adopted the French *Code pénal* of 1791, did not guarantee any tolerance, and hustlers, sodomites and pederasts became targets of a regulatory public discourse of social hygiene.

France exported a prophylactic policy to its colonies, leaving a handful of remarkable documents regarding the presumed etiology of same-sex praxis there. On the one hand, these contained an updated version of Enlightenment environmentalism that explained sodomy as the outcome of climatological circumstance. A physician, Dr Jacquot claimed that sodomy amidst the French army troops in Algeria ought to be ascribed to the heat in the Maghreb.[128] One of his colleagues, Dr Bertulus, expressed his fear for the nations' military defeat since French soldiers in northern Africa seemed less immune against *abougrissement* than the Italian ones.[129]

Yet, environmental explanations were hardly separable from outspoken racialist assumptions about the sexual immorality of the indigenous population. The colonies were subjected to medical surveys like Furnari's *Voyage médical dans l'Afrique septentrionale* (1845), Bertherand's *Médecine et hygiène des Arabes* (1855), and Duchesne's *De la prostitution dans la ville Alger depuis la conquête* (1830, not published until 1853), all studies that aimed at, among other things, the consolidation of social boundaries between the colonizers and the colonized.[130] But the rhetoric of public hygiene within a context of colonial administration hardly disguised moral prejudice as it adopted a vocabulary that sounds familiar. An example is offered by Dr Lallemand's drawing of an imaginary line:

One the one hand, polygamy, harems and seraglios, from which [spring] venereal excesses, barbarious mutilation, revolting sodomy, a population that is small, inactive, indolent, ignorant . . . . On the other hand, monogamy, Christian austerity, a more equal sharing of domestic happiness, increasing freedom, equality, well-being, rapid reproduction, a dense population, that is active, hard working.[131]

Obviously, no room was left for same-sex praxis that would undermine Lallemand's natalist vision of colonial policy. His homophobia was also part of mere disgust at the overall immorality of Oriental men, who traded women like commodities and married them for sexual gratification only;

who abstained from alcohol only because it stimulated their sexual potency. Too much care for their body, hot baths and steam rooms made their bodies look soft. So did polygamy, that made men look *effeminés* like individuals in Europe, who all too eagerly spilled their seed.[132]

French moral concerns were paralleled by British ones as some alarming reports were published about widespread sodomy among European convicts and settlers in Australia. In 1846–7, a British Parliamentary inquiry was undertaken to investigate rumours about sodomy in convict settlements. It proved not only that boys sold their bodies in exchange for tobacco or boots, but that overseers were 'in the game' as well. It was felt that the exclusively male character of these settlements necessarily led to sexual deviance. Yet the inquiry's results also reinforced beliefs that the white man was not immune from a 'tropicalization' or weakening of his sense of morality.[133] Similarly alarming reports reached Europe about same-sex practices committed by colonizers in the Far and Middle East, Subsaharan Africa and the Caribbean. These too represented their behaviour as cases of 'demoralization', strangely mixing climatological explanations with concern about the presumably negative impact of the local population in these areas.[134]

The empiricism of analogy

Aside from the persistence of moral discourse, another trend can be perceived that reduced same-sex praxis to the realm of a distinct minority. The pattern, as indicated, originated during the Enlightenment and was marked by a cognitive distinction between 'sodomites' and the rest of the population. Semantically, the meaning of the word 'sodomy' had shifted from a deliberate, more or less ephemeral act into a more permanent role, that was increasingly connected to a presumably 'feminine' core.

Also during the era under review, a significant number of testimonies focused on cross-gender roles, on transvestism and on male prostitution. Being highly visible, these phenomena at once promoted and confirmed current speculation on the anomalous nature of sodomites – a situation that is demonstrated by the western observers' relative neglect of the active, male partners of *machi*, *basire*, *tsecats*, *crabbah* or *mukhannathun* alike. Testimonies about the latter in particular illustrate how the narrowing of one's focus upon only the passive partner even challenged an age-old obstinate narrative trope about 'endemic' Arab sodomy. Male prostitution in Asia and Africa also most commonly involved boys or young men, who assumed a passive role. It existed alongside female prostitution and often, though not always, implied a cross-dressing code. European witnesses, while only marginally addressing the sexuality of their active patrons, easily represented these passive male prostitutes as 'of a separate class'.

Yet, as nineteenth-century discourse up until the 1860s largely continued an Enlightenment pattern by reinforcing the cognitive axis between 'sodomy' and 'femininity' or 'effeminacy', pressures were felt to corroborate it empirically. At the same time, a new, 'scientific' explanation was due to the unmistakeable evidence that same-sex practices and/or sodomites seemed so prominently present among other races. A conceptual apparatus was needed, that was both empirically sound and universally applicable.

Speculation on the effect of the climate did not altogether disappear, but became less convincing as more ethnographic data became available. Jules Virey, among its critics, claimed that sexual deviance occurred no more frequently in the warm, subtropical and tropical region than in the subarctic and arctic region.[135] In his *History of the British Colonies* (1834–5), Montgomery Martin confirmed that lasciviousness was spread equally among the arctic people of the north.[136] Eduard Pöppig also doubted that climate would be a sufficient explanation of the Indian peoples' sexuality:

One has deduced from the rather weak sexual drive of most of these people that they are physically weaker, even when experience shows that the reproductive drive is far from determined by the climate and related factors alone. The typical character of races is only partially defined by its various forms.[137]

He claimed that a hotter climate did not necessarily lead to sexual deviance and polygamy. These, in fact, occurred also in Canada and Patagonia.

In the end, climatological explanations lost appeal because it proved impossible to demonstrate infallibly that a relationship between sexual morality and climate did exist. An explanatory model was needed that made any relationship more tangible, and sexual anomalies were located within the race's bodily constitution as a result. The inevitable effects of environmental factors, as stated by some Enlightenment writers, were now said to have taken root within the body as anatomical and physiological characteristics that could not be undone for example by migrating to a climatologically more advantageous area.

The shifting emphasis reflected changes that were taking place in biological science. Jean-Baptiste Lamarck's *Philosophie zoologique* of 1809 initiated a theory of the transmutation of organic forms, now known as evolutionary theory, that explained animal variance over time. It triggered a debate on whether the variety of mankind too could be seen as the outcome of evolutionary change within the body itself. The answer to this question had become urgent in the light of European migration overseas, the imminent extinction of some indigenous people, the Abolitionist debate and the growing national consciousness within Europe itself. In essence, the debate occurred between monogenists such as James Cowley Prichard, who proposed the image of a gradual diversification of one original species, and polygenists such as Arthur de Gobineau and Paul Broca, who claimed instead that a variety of types had existed since the beginning of mankind. The latter would win the debate, if only until the coming of Darwinian theory. Even then, however, polygenist assumptions would be integrated in evolutionary theory by stating that diversification had taken place in ancient times and produced a number of racial types that had not changed since.[138]

From the debate emerged a predominantly physical view of race, that explained differences by referring to one's bodily constitution in the first place. Physical anthropologists claimed that racial variance could be directly visualized by pointing out the characteristics of the body, and they went about measuring and classifying brain structure, facial expression, skin texture, proportions of various body parts, and, predictably, genitalia. But the new empiricism was applied to issues other than race, including the scientific study of class and gender identity. An Enlightenment analogous reasoning, moreover, was brought about by the fact that no Archimedean criteria allowed for separating the 'normal' from the 'abnormal' and taxonomists of race, class and sex borrowed heavily from one another to construct hierarchy.

Brain matters

Empiricism did not resolve disagreement as to which variables were relevant. It gave rise instead to a series of theories and paradigms, that were given up soon afterwards in exchange for other, more promising ones. Some left an imprint on the debate about same-sex praxis and, marginally, on scientific explanations of its occurrence among 'primitive' folk. They would all be dropped once proven inconsistent, and left to be disseminated on a more vulgarized level of popular science. They are relevant, however, for they supported the construction of a 'geography of perversion', even when their effect was transitory and, in the end, unsound.

Among the early 'empirical' theories figured Franz Joseph Gall's phrenology, the study of the anatomical characteristics of the human brain. It was a powerful and imaginative theory, that led to the founding of the Société Phrénologique in Paris in 1807, and of the Phrenological Society in London in 1820. On sexual desire, Gall developed a theory that

mankind differs relatively on the level of reproductive drive: among some [people], this drive is virtually nonexistent, among others it is moderate, among yet others it is very strong. Well, observation shows that the brain is developed very poorly among the first, relatively well among the second and very well among the last.[139]

Gall thus studied the brain, that had developed extraordinarily, of a mulatto boy of less than three years. During the boy's life, his penis apparently erected instantly and had drawn the curiosity of many girls, each of whom had abused him sexually. When the boy died around age five, his death was interpreted by Gall as the result of sexual exhaustion.

Lauvergne, subscribing to phrenology as late as 1841, elaborated on sodomites in particular:

[They] have limited intellectual capacity and usually show the *bosse de la merveillosité* [a phrenological term for one part/capacity of the brain, *RB*]. It must be! Aren't their sensual aberrations proof of the outrageousness of their imagination and of a monomaniac phylogeniture? Both phrenological characteristics are typically female.[140]

The author's emphasis upon the feminine nature of pederasts was exemplary of the tightening link, made by western scientists, between same-sex praxis and female gender and prompted the historian, Michael Shortland, to claim that, though studied frequently as a doctrine of mind or as a mere chapter of medical history, phrenology has been hardly evaluated as a contributor to theory about human sexuality.[141] Still, its successes were shortlived, nor did it leave an enduring trace in discourse about same-sex praxis among either whites or men of a different race. It proved useless and irrelevant, perhaps not so much because of its own inherent inadequacy, but because the social reality of sex was far too diverse to be covered by a single model of human qualities localized in the brain.

The location of sex in the brain was not to die an early death with the refutation of Gall's phrenology. The latter's still predominantly materialist profile would soon be dropped in exchange for a more interpretive 'neurological' understanding of sexuality and, especially, sexual deviance. But as yet, theoretical departures that prefigured sexual psychopathology were doomed to remain within the shadows of scientific debate. Until then, some tried to locate sex in ways that were externally visible and that could be physically demonstrated. They declared anatomy, more particularly of the male and female genitalia, to be the foundation of a scientific theory of natural sex and its deviations.

The semiotics of genitalia

The anatomical study of genitalia evidently remained tributary to Enlightenment theory of human sexuality, as it upheld and even corroborated a biological etiology. Sexual deviance, in this context, was either demonstrated or explained by one's anomalous genital constitution. While making its point, it borrowed heavily from racial theory, which in its turn formulated claims about racial hierarchy on the basis of criteria adopted from sexual theory. The tautological epistemology of this 'exchange' thus constituted the core of scientific pseudo-rationality.

This was most easily visible in studies of female sexual anatomy. Even though the present addresses male sexuality, it is necessary, if only briefly, to review their historical significance in order to understand the paradigmatic dimension of its pendant, phalloplethysmography, or the scientific description and measurement of male genitalia.

Historically, the early nineteenth-century debate on female sexual anatomy perpetuated Enlightenment theories of feminine identity, that focused largely on the genitalia. Yet gradually it became dominated by an intention to distinguish the 'normal' from the 'pathological'. This occurred simultaneously with attempts at making racial hierarchy more tangible by means of, in Sander Gilman's words, 'some type of unique and observable physical difference'.[142]

Soon, scientists like Moreau, de Blainville, Virey, Cuvier, Vrolik, Otto, Flower and Murie focused on black women, and on Hottentot women in particular.[143] This was provoked by the eighteenth-century reports of John Barrow and François Le Vaillant about the so-called 'Hottentot apron', a hypertrophy of the labia and nymphae. Though caused by deliberate manipulation among Hottentots, Bushmen, now San, and tribes in Basutoland and Dahomey, it was read by nineteenth-century scientists as an index of the Hottentot female's biological status. From 1810 till her death in 1815, a Hottentot woman, known as Saartje Baartman, also as the 'Hottentot Venus' was exhibited in London and Paris. She drew wide public and scientific attention, not only because of the extraordinary appearance of her genitalia, but also and perhaps foremost because of her protruding buttocks – a phenomenon called steatopygia. Other 'Hottentot Venuses' were displayed in European cities and, together with Saartje Baartman, subjected to autopsy after they had died.[144]

The results were to prove the validity of the polygenetic argument, for 'if [the Hottentot female's] sexual parts could be shown to be inherently different, this would be a sufficient sign that the blacks were a separate (and, needless to say, lower) race, as different from the European as the proverbial orang utan'.[145] The naively positivistic character of these studies can be read from the anatomists' assumption that genital size was congruous with sexual desire, in other words, that greater genitalia demonstrated greater lust. An amusing reflection of this can be found in Felix de Azara's comparison of the American Indian man's small genitalia to the extraordinary size of the labia of their wives. In a very meaningful way, he suggested that the Spanish conquest of the Guarani was facilitated both by the weakness of the men and the women's eagerness to 'copulate' with the enemy.[146] Similarly, Auguste de Saint Hilaire, when travelling in Brazil, stated that Macuani women eagerly sought to have intercourse with black runaway slaves, driven, as he suggested, by the compatibility of their genitalia.[147] Later, racialist evaluations of the labia would extend to the clitoris as well. This, if too big, would lead to lesbianism, according to Hildebrandt in a classical study on gynaecology.[148] Steatopygia next, when seen among European prostitutes, would give rise to speculations about their equally pathological bodily constitution.[149]

The racialist and sexist semiotic of female genitalia was accompanied by a less elaborate one of its male counterparts. When looking closer at other historical evidence, it is clear indeed that only a few anatomical studies were made of male genitalia – a fact that may or may not confirm some feminist claims about the scientific community's predominantly 'masculine gaze'.[150]

Yet, these were meant to corroborate a parallel argument regarding men as had been the case with female anatomy. Perhaps the first systematic attempt to integrate measurements of male genitalia in racialist classification was White's *Account of the Regular Gradation in Man*, published in 1793.[151] Other excursions in this discipline of 'phalloplethysmography'[152] were made by Virey[153] and Kobelt,[154] as well as by travellers who embraced this theory as a heuristic device alongside others for racialist classification. Earlier I mentioned Ludwig von Eschwege's emphasis upon the small member of American Indian men. Von Martius contrasted their modest sexual endowment with the one of blacks, who, in his eyes, seemed to be in *beständigem Turgor*.[155]

A similar logic of the 'unmanliness' of men who were only modestly endowed, underlay claims about the presumed small and fine penis of sodomites. In this context, a single, but influential document is to be found in the previously mentioned study by Mende, who altogether changed the focus of legal medicine. Until then, legal-medical discussions of sodomy had focused on the anus of the passive partner, if only to see if the *act* of anal penetration had taken place. The oldest text, Paolo Zacchia's *Quaestiorum medico-legarum* (1630), thus listed anal infection, widening buttocks, and a softened sphincter (*infundibulum*) as *constuprati pueri signa*, signs of pederasty. Immediately preceding Mende's study and still faithful to this tradition was the *Traité de médecine légale* (1813) by Fodéré.[156] Mende changed perspectives and demonstrated that a sodomite's modestly sized sexual organ made it difficult for him to reach satisfaction through heterosexual intercourse, whereas this was reached easier by penetration in a boy's anus.[157] An identical suggestion was made in Tourdel's article on hermaphroditism in the *Dictionnaire des sciences médicales*.[158]

Within the context of theorizing about the identity of sodomites and pederasts, the project of phalloplethysmography would soon be dropped, however. The lineal relationship between genital size and sexual status, that was postulated by the rhetoric of analogy and that was believed to be valid when applied to women, could not be established with men in an equally convincing way. This is not to say that the semiotics of female genitalia was any less artificial and mythological, of course. Only that the predominantly masculine gaze of anatomists allowed for projection when women were involved, whereas anatomical theory was looked upon more critically when male sexual status was at stake.

A mere quantitative study of male genitalia rapidly refuted itself, especially in the light of racialist presumptions about the superiority of the white race. Ideally, the theory would have worked when comparing the sexual organs of American Indians, Asians and Pacific people only with sexual 'deviates', whose genitalia were unusually small. In reality, however, sodomites were no less well endowed than other men. And then, how could an analogous rhetoric be upheld between sodomites, who were currently depicted as 'effeminate' and African or Arab men, who were currently believed to be virile and extraordinarily well endowed?

These are remote theoretical questions, that cannot even be retrieved from historical evidence. But they were undoubtedly present in the minds of white, male scientists, who felt awkward about explicit discussions of one's own sexuality, especially, it must be added, when this was potentially threatened by the sexual prowess of races claimed to be inferior. The documents' silence easily reminds the historian of a statement by the French politician, Léon Gambetta, that adequately expressed male insecurity: 'Nous en parlons jamais, y pensons toujours.'

Yet, as noted, it was the inner incoherence that probably contributed more to the abandonment of an all too far-reaching empirical semiotic of male genitalia. It would lead a lingering existence, though fragmented and vulgarized, beyond the turn of the century. Traces of it can be found both in *L'amour aux colonies* by the self-proclaimed physician Jacobus X (1893),[159] and in articles such as Schaeffer's 'Beitrag zur Ätiologie der Schwanzbildungen beim Menschen' in as late as 1920.[160] But by then, such speculations were merely nurturing racialist fears and phantasies especially about the black man, who continued to be seen as a threat to the white men's wives.[161] To the debate on sexual deviants, they were no longer relevant.

The effects of anatomy remained altogether unequal. Historically, they revealed both the great appeal of the positivist paradigm and its inner inconsistencies. Never was the demonstration of analogies between race and sexuality interpreted more literally than during the first half of the nineteenth century. Empirical attempts to pin down both racial and sexual difference to body characteristics in fact remained attractive in the twentieth century, only to be dropped in the aftermath of the Holocaust. Yet its limits also became apparent, especially when the project of a 'geography of perversion' was reduced to a mere scrutiny of brain surface or a statistical reading of genitalia. Gradually it became clear that the analogy between racial inferiority and sexual deviance could not be successfully grasped within a simple, transparent theory of clearcut morphological similarities.

Pre-Darwinian evolution theory and sex history

The as yet unsuccessful attempts to unravel the 'bio-logic' of the sexuality of sodomites beyond a vaguely defined femininity did not prevent these from being reflected in writings of a more sociological and historical character. Their authors adopted some of the arguments that were put forward by pre-Darwinian evolution theory and presented a historical narrative, characterized by a linear development from barbarity to civilization, explained at the same time as a process of biological adaptation. Same-sex praxis, in this context, was denounced as infertile, unproductive and thus negative behaviour, that was to be given up in order for humanity to progress.

Gustav Klemm, among such writers, distinguished 'passive' and 'active' races and classified American Indians, not suprisingly, among the first category.[162] He was a liberal democrat, however, who did not see both races as incompatible. To him, both were complementary and humanity would only achieve true culture when both would intermarry.[163] It is not clear if Klemm adopted the term 'race' as an unchanging, biological category or rather as a metaphorical concept. Banton suggests the latter as 'he wrote of humanity as divided in two kinds of races analogous to the division into two sexes'.[164] To me, however, Klemm's work nicely illustrates how racial categories actually 'negotiated' between physical and cultural contents. Banton, in this context, seems to underestimate the power of proclaimed 'analogies' between race and sex in racial theory itself.

A similar mix of biological and historical narrative can be found in Jules Virey's *De la femme* (1826). The author claimed that polygamy gave rise to lesbian relationships and added that both stood in the way of human evolution.[165] Julius Rosenbaum's *Geschichte der Lustseuche im Alterthume* (1839) also merged proto-evolutionary theory with the history of civilization, even when in a reverse way. In his view, pederasty is classified among cults of Venus and Priapus as pathological phenomena that undermined the cultural growth of Ancient Greece.[166]

Altogether critical of the negativism of both prophylactic moralism and biological reification were Charles Fourier and some early nineteenth-century advocates of 'Greek love'. Fourier actually pleaded that sexual relations among people of the same sex ought to be accommodated in the new, anarchist utopia. His plea of 1818, the *Nouveau monde amoureux* remained unpublished, alas, until long after his death and did not influence public debate.[167]

The most reluctant among a small group of early nineteenth-century apologists of Greek love was Zschokke, whose article 'Eros oder über die Liebe', published in 1821, contained a cautious plea for the rehabilitation of erotic relations among men.[168] Zschokke felt that these ought not to become physical, as opposed to the Swiss Heinrich Hössli, who said that such erotic relationships were naturally sensual,[169] or Dulaure, who explained how both homo- and heterosexual sensuality were implied by phallic cults.[170] The disagreement between such writers reflected an ambiguity towards the sexual side of male-to-male relationships, similar to the opposition between Payne Knight and Hamann or de Sade at the time of the Enlightenment. But all writers jointly opposed the advanced biological explanations of male-to-male love that had become so characteristic by then, and aimed at safeguarding their high Platonic ideal from the classificatory zeal of scientists. Implicitly, however, they laid the basis for later discussions about Greek love that would then be opposed to its more lecherous variations in other parts of the world.

Also against all prophylactic rhetoric, though for opposite reasons, was the statement by an outsider like Johann Döllinger, who claimed that same-sex praxis did not disappear as 'civilization' imposed itself upon a nation's people. It seemed, in his eyes, ineradicable.[171] Schopenhauer too drew a picture of ubiquitous pederasty, that could hardly be suppressed. It was the outcome of misguided instinct, according to Schopenhauer, who compared the erratic behaviour of a pederast to the one of a bluebottle, that 'lays its eggs in the flower of the *Arum dranunculus*, rather than in rotting flesh, (as it is) misled by the corpse-like stench of this plant (statt ihre Eier, ihrem Instinkt gemäss, in faulendes Fleisch zu legen, sie in die Blüte des *Arum dranunculus* legt, verleitet durch den kadaverosen Geruch dieser Pflanze)'.[172]

The pessimism of both authors perhaps ought to be seen as a symptom of criticism of the advocates of progress, even when they shared the latters' negative attitude towards male-to-male sex. Without intending to, they in fact anticipated new psychiatric diagnoses of same-sex praxis as a sign of neurasthenia, that is: of civilization's disease – a judgement that turned upside down the claim of some that sodomy was part of an original, barbaric state of mankind. Both points of view would be briefly reconciled by degeneration theory, even when this, as will be described in the following chapter, was only one among the many scientific explanations that proliferated during the second half of the nineteenth and the early twentieth centuries.

Social as well as intellectual concerns about the presumed ubiquity of same-sex praxis outside the 'civilized' West were often no more, really, than a reflection of the age-old denunciation of sodomy as barbaric, immoral and unrespectable. Early nineteenth-century positivism hardly changed this. Instead, it triggered a prophylactic ideology, that was to ban same-sex praxis from the urban centres of the West as well as to prevent indigenous sexual immorality from 'contaminating' western colonial personnel. Only, moral condemnation was phrased far less in religious than in medical terms and consisted mainly of an almost transparent mixture of proto-epidemiological jargon and moral panic.

The growing weight of science was manifest also in an alternative discourse, that represented same-sex praxis as the exclusive behaviour of a distinct minority. This gained ground in view of the increasing prestige of biology and medicine, that corroborated Enlightenment speculations on the 'feminine' nature of sodomites.

The ethnographic record reflected moral discourse as well as scientific initiatives to reify same-sex praxis as bound to a particular minority. It also mirrored new theoretical definitions as resulting from a biological anomaly that was more closely tied to a feminine essence. At this point, narratives of cross-gender roles overseas not only offered a feedback for scientific theory about effeminate sodomites, but also consolidated parallel claims about the presumably 'feminine' character of inferior races by representing cross-gender roles as both metaphorical and metonymical.

Meanwhile, the bourgeois civilizing mission required the upholding of the false rhetoric of analogy, even when it became gradually clear that this could no longer be expressed in a naively empiricist way because of the failure to prove the sodomite's feminine identity through study of the brain or genitalia. Scientists felt compelled to develop a new paradigm that lifted attention from anatomy, yet did not surrender the basic structure of analogy and continued to relate the etiology of male-to-male sexual praxis to a 'core' femininity. Psychopathology, the new explanatory scheme, located sexual deviance within the realm of the mind instead and made cross-cultural comparison not only less direct but also less empirically verifiable. The structure of analogy, as a result, would gain new legitimacy and lend new ideological strength to the 'geography of perversion' as a source of differentiating mythology.

Notes

1. 'Quoi de plus exaltant que le pacte scellé ... entre la biologie racienne, le messianisme politique et la sexologie répressive?' J.-P. Aron, *Le pénis et la démoralisation de l'occident* (Paris, 1978), p. 194.
2. S. L. Gilman, *Difference and Pathology* (Ithaca and London, 1985), p. 83.
3. N. L. Stepan, 'Race and gender: The role of analogy in science', *Isis*, 77 (1986), 266.
4. See, in this context, S. Dreischer, 'The ending of the slave trade and the evolution of European scientific racism', *Social Science History*, 14, 3 (Fall 1990), 15–45.
5. I have borrowed the term from J. Donzelot's influential study, *La police des familles*, Paris, 1977, that analysed very powerfully how the private lives of people were directed by the demands of productivity and respectability. A comparable perspective can be found in most works by Foucault, as in Mosse's study, *Nationalism and Sexuality*.
6. 'Die heilige Kaaba zu Mekka wird ... bisweilen zum Theater unkeuscher und strafwerter Vorgänge in einem Grade, der nicht deutlicher bezeichnet werden kann. Und diese Dinge werden nicht nur ungestraft, sondern fast in aller Oeffentlichkeit getrieben, und öfters überfiel mich Ekel beim Anblick von Abscheulichkeiten, die andern Zuschauern nur ein Lächeln oder höchstens einen leisen Tadel entlockten.' J. L. Burkhardt, *Reisen in Nubien und Arabien* (Jena, 1820), p. 132.
7. Quoted in F. Karsch-Haack, 'Die Rolle der Homoerotik im Arabertum', *JfsZ*, 23 (1923), 154.
8. E. Trumpp, 'Einige Bemerkungen über den Sufismus', *ZdmG*, 16 (1862), 23–9.
9. See the partial reprint of the *Terminal Essay* in R. Burton, *The Sotadic Zone* (Boston, 1977), p. 94.
10. *Ibid.*
11. J. B. Fraser, *Narrative of a Journey into Khorasan* (London, 1825), pp. 566–7; J. Morier, *A Second Journey through Persia* (London, 1818), *passim*; C. N. Pischon, 'Das Sklavenwesen in der Turkei', *ZdmG*, 14 (1860), 243; G. S. F. Pfeifer, *Meine Reise und meine fünfjährige Gefangeschaft in Algier* (Giessen, 1834), *passim*; C. A. Rozet, *Voyage dans la régence d'Alger* (Paris, 1833), vol. 2, pp. 113–14; J. A. Saint John, *Egypt and*

Mohammed Ali, or Travels in the Valley of the Nile (London, 1834), vol. 1, p. 132, vol. 2, pp. 323–4; R. Walsh, *Narrative of a Journey from Constantinople* (London, 1838), p. 86; C. White, *Three Years in Constantinople or Domestic Manners of the Turks* (London, 1845), p. 299.

12. A. B. Clot-Bey, *Aperçus générals sur l'Egypte* (Paris, 1840), vol. 1, p. 336; A. G. P. von Osten, *Denkwürdigkeiten* (Vienna, 1836), vol. 3, pp. 633–4; V. Schoelcher, *L'Egypte en 1845* (Paris, 1846), p. 56; A. Sprenger, *Das Leben und die Lehre des Mohammad* (Berlin, 1831), vol. 3, clxxviii–clxxix; H. L. H. F. von Pueckler-Muskau, *Aus Mehemed Ali's Reich* (Stuttgart, 1844), vol. 2, pp. 303–4.

13. 'Puisque nous parlons de bardaches, voici ce que j'en sais. Ici c'est très bien porté. On avoue la sodomie et on en parle à table d'hôte. Quelquefois on nie un petit peu, tout le monde alors vous engueule et cela finit par s'avouer. ... C'est aux bains que cela se pratique. On retient le bain pour soi (5 fr[ancs], y compris les masseurs, la pipe, le café, le linge) et on enfile son gamin dans une des salles. – Tu sauras du reste que tous les garçons de bain sont bardaches. Les derniers masseurs ... sont ordinairement de jeunes garçons assez gentils.' G. Flaubert, *Correspondance. Vol. 1: (janvier 1830 à avril 1851)*, ed. J. Bruneau (Paris, 1973), p. 572.

14. *Ibid.*, vol. 1, p. 638.

15. See, among others, W. Cable Brown, 'Byron and English interest in the East', *Studies in Philology*, 34 (1937), 55–64; and the rather speculative study by B. Blackstone 'Byron and Islam: The triple eros', *Journal of European Studies*, 4 (1974), 325–62.

16. H. S. L. Wiener, 'Byron and the East: Literary sources of the "Turkish Tales" ', in H. Davis *et al.* (eds), *Nineteenth-Century Studies* (Ithaca, 1940), pp. 89–129. Meant are *The Works of Sir William Jones, with the Life of the Author by Lord Teignmouth* (London, 1807).

17. L. Crompton, *Byron and Greek Love. Homophobia in Nineteenth-Century England* (Berkeley, 1985), p. 115.

18. J. Hindley, *Introduction to Persian Lyrics or Scattered Poems from the Diwan-I-Hafiz* (London, 1800), pp. 8–9.

19. J. G. von Hahn, *Albanesische Studien* (Jena, 1854), p. 166.

20. R. P. A. Dozy, *Historia Abbadidarum* (Leyden, 1846), p. 409, n. 72.

21. W. M. Baron de Slane, *Introduction and Notes to Ibn Khallikan's Biographical Dictionary* (Paris, 1842). See, however, vol. 1, pp. xxxvii, 136, 185, 205; vol. 2, pp. 325, 496.

22. A. I. S. de Sacy, *Chrestomathie arabe* (Paris, 1827), vol. 3, p. 177; A. I. S. de Sacy, *Exposé de la religion des Druses* (Paris, 1838), vol. 2, p. 570.

23. See J. Hammer-Purgstall, *Geschichte der schönen Redekünste in Persien* (Vienna, 1818), vol. 1, p. 150, vol. 3, pp. 230–3, vol. 5, pp. 159–63; J. Hammer-Purgstall, *Geschichte des osmanischen Reiches* (Budapest, 1827), vol. 3, pp. 349 ff. Another discussion by Hammer-Purgstall of Arab boy love can be found in his article 'Auszüge aus Saalebis Buche "Die Stützen des sich Beziehenden und dessen, worauf es sich bezieht" ', *ZdmG*, 9 (1855), 106–31. See also H. Wuttke, 'Über Hammer-Purgstall's Literaturgeschichte der Araber', *ZdmG*, 9 (1855), 169 and 179. For a critical portrayal of his work, see R. Kaiser, 'Josef von Hammer-Purgstall. Sprachknabe, Diplomat, Orientalist', in G. Sievernich and H. Budde (eds), *Europa und der Orient, 800–1900. Lesebuch* (Berlin, 1989), pp. 106–14.

24. V. von Rosenzweig, *Auswahl aus den Diwanen des Dschelaleddin Rumi* (Vienna, 1838), pp. ix–x.

25. J. W. Zinkzeisen, *Geschichte des Osmanischen Reiches in Europa* (Gotha, 1855), vol. 3, p. 57.

26. J. Pharaon and T. Dulau, *Droit musulman* (Paris, 1839), pp. 458–9.

27. N. E. Baron Tornau, *Le droit musulman* (Paris, 1860). I have consulted the German translation *Das islamische Recht*, published in Leipzig in 1885, 234–5.
28. A. F. von Kremer, *Culturgeschichtliche Streifzüge auf dem Gebiet des Islams* (Leipzig, 1873), p. 43.
29. See M. Schild, 'Mukhannath', in *Encyclopedia of Homosexuality*, pp. 849–50.
30. See E. K. Rowson, 'The effeminates of early Medina', *Journal of the American Oriental Society*, 4 (1991), 671–93.
31. J. S. Buckingham, *Travels in Assyria* (Colburn, 1829), pp. 80–95.
32. E. W. Lane, *An Account of the Manners and Customs of the Modern Egyptians* (New York, 1973 (London, 1836)), p. 381.
33. G. de Nerval, *Voyage en Orient* (Paris, 1851), vol. 1, pp. 140–1.
34. E. Godard, *Egypte et Palestine. Observations médicales et scientifiques* (Paris, 1867), pp. 104–6, 111–12.
35. See P. Hahn, 'Islam: le sexe arabe', *GPH*, 76 (2 July 1983), 21–4, including photographs of such an erotic ceremony in Ouargla, Algeria in 1928.
36. F. Jacquot, 'Lettre d'Afrique', *Gazette médicale de Paris*, 3rd series, 18 (1847), 78–9, 93.
37. F. W. Oppenheim, *Ueber den Zustand der Heilkunde und über die Volkskrankheiten in der europäischen und asiatischen Turkei* (Hamburg, 1833), pp. 52, 82–5, 115.
38. J. E. Polak, 'Die Prostitution in Persien', *Wiener medizinische Wochenschrift*, 32 (1861), 516, 627–9.
39. A. Bilharz, *Descriptio anatomica organorum genitalium Eunuchi Aethiopis* (Berlin, 1859).
40. R. Burton, 'Scinde; or, the Unhappy Valley', unpublished manuscript, Huntington Library, San Marino, USA, no page numbering.
41. *Ibid.*
42. Quoted in F. M. Brodie, *The Devil Drives. A Life of Sir Richard Burton* (New York and London, 1967), p. 66.
43. *Ibid.*, p. 69.
44. V. Jacquemont, *Voyage dans l'Inde* (Paris, 1841), pp. 78–9, 93.
45. J. A. Dubois, *Moeurs, institutions et cérémonies du peuple de l'Inde* (Paris, 1825), vol. 1, p. 236.
46. See S. Nanda, *Neither Man, nor Woman. The Hijras of India* (Belmont, 1990), *passim*; and L. W. Preston, 'A right to exist: Eunuchs and the state in nineteenth-century India', *Modern Asian Studies*, 21, 2 (1987), 368–81.
47. J. Crawfurd, *History of the Indian Archipelago* (Edinburgh and London, 1820), vol. 3, p. 139.
48. In R. Mundy, *Narrative of Events in Borneo and Celebes* (London, 1848), vol.1, pp. 61–2, 82–3.
49. C. Von de Wall, 'Vervolg van het extract uit de dagelijksche aanteekeningen van den civielen gezaghebber voor Koetei en de Oostkust van Borneo', *Indisch Archief*, 2, 3 (1850), 462–3.
50. F. Junghuhn, *Die Battaländer auf Sumatra* (Berlin, 1847), vol. 2, p. 140.
51. *Ibid.*, vol. 2, p. 241.
52. C. Hupe, 'Korte Verhandeling over de Godsdienst, zeden, enz. der Dajakkers', *Tijdschrift voor Neêrlands' Indië*, 8, 3 (1846), 145–6.
53. C. A. L. M. Schwaner, *Borneo* (Amsterdam, 1853–4), vol. 1, p. 186.
54. A. Hardeland, *Dajacksch-Deutsches Wörterbuch* (Amsterdam, 1859), pp. 53–4.
55. See G. H. von Langsdorff, *Bemerkungen auf einer Reise um die Welt in den Jahren 1803 bis 1807* (Frankfurt, 1812), vol. 2, pp. 43, 58; L. Choris, *Voyage pittoresque autour du monde* (Paris, 1820–2), p. 8; A. Erman, *Reise um die Erde durch Nord-Asien und die beiden Oceane* (Berlin, 1833–48), vol. 3, p. 250; A. Erman, 'Ethnographische

Wahrnehmungen und Erfahrungen an den Küsten des Bering-Meeres', *ZfE*, 3 (1871), 164; and M. zu Wied-Neuwied, *Reise in das innere Nord-Amerika* (Coblenz, 1839), vol. 2, p. 132.

56. See D. B. de Malpière, *La Chine* (Paris, 1825), vol. 1, no pagination; [C. Gützlaff], *Gützlaff's Geschichte des Chinesischen Reiches* (Stuttgart and Tübingen, 1847), pp. 115–30, 257, 272–5, 323–4; G. Morache, 'Pékin et ses habitants. Etude d'hygiène', *Annales d'hygiène et de médecine légale*, 2nd series, 31 (1868), 130.

57. H. Maron, *Japan und China* (Berlin, 1863), vol. 2, pp. 179–80.

58. C. Gützlaff, *Gützlaff's Geschichte des Chinesischen Reiches*, p. 871; G. Morache, 'Pékin et ses habitants' p. 129; H. Maron, *Japan und China*, vol. 2, pp. 94, 176.

59. A. Bonacossi, *La Chine et les Chinois* (Paris, 1847), p. 276; G. Morache, 'Pékin et ses habitants', p. 130; E. Hildebrandt, *Reise um die Erde* (Berlin, 1867), vol. 2, p. 50.

60. W. C. Milne, *Life in China* (London, 1857), pp. 196–7.

61. See, in this context, C. P. Mackerras, *The Rise of the Peking Opera, 1770–1870* (Oxford, 1972).

62. G. Morache, 'Pékin et ses habitants', p. 130.

63. E. Hildebrandt, *Reise um die Erde*, vol. 2, p. 65.

64. Delauture d'Escayrac, *Le Désert et le Soudan* (Paris, 1853), p. 93.

65. H. Libermann, *Les fumeurs d'opium en Chine. Etude médicale* (Paris, 1862), pp. 48–9, 63, 65.

66. *Ta Tsing Lu Lee, being the Fundamental Laws ... of the Penal Code of China*, ed. and trans. G. T. Staunton (London, 1810).

67. G. Pauthier and M. Bazin, *La Chine Moderne*, vol. 1: G. Pauthier, *Géographie, Organisation politique et administrative de la Chine, Langues, Philosophie* (Paris, 1853), pp. 251, 253–4.

68. H. Maron, *Japan und China*, vol. 1, p. 112.

69. G. Spiess, *Die preussische Expedition nach Ostasien* (Leipzig, 1864), *passim*; R. Andree, *Das Buch der reisen und Entdeckungen Asiens*, vol. 1: *Die Nippon-Fahrer oder das wiedergeschlossene Japan*, 2nd ed. (Leipzig, 1869), pp. 393–5.

70. W. Heine, *Japan und seine Bewohner* (Leipzig, 1860), p. 63.

71. See W. Heine's other work, *Die Expedition in die Seen von China, Japan und Ochotsk* (Leipzig, 1859), vol. 2, pp. 33–4. See also A. Wuttke, *Geschichte des Heidentums* (Breslau, 1852–3), vol. 2, p. 42.

72. J. Pompe van Meerdervoort, *Vijf jaren in Japan, 1857–1863*, Leyden, 1867–1868, vol. 1, 255–261.

73. See G. Klemm, *Allgemeine Culturgeschichte der Menschheit* (Leipzig, 1842–53), vol. 6, p. 511; E. Hildebrandt, *Reise um die Erde*, vol. 2, p. 167.

74. V. de Rochas, *La Nouvelle Calédonie et ses habitants* (Paris, 1862), p. 235.

75. A. Bourgarel, 'Des races de l'Océanie française', *Mémoires de la Société d'Anthropologie de Paris*, 2 (1865), 390.

76. J. K. Hasskarl, *Australien und seine Kolonien Süd-Australien, Australia Felix, etc.* (Elberfeld-Iserlohn, 1849), p. 82.

77. [W. Mariner], *An Account of the Natives of the Tonga Islands, in the South Pacific Ocean* (London, 1817), vol. 2, p. 178.

78. J. A. Moerenhout, *Voyages aux îles du grand Océan* (Paris, 1837), vol. 1, pp. 229–30, vol. 2, pp. 57, 168.

79. B. Seemann, *Reise um die Welt* (Hannover, 1853), vol. 2, p. 60.

80. J. Dumont d'Urville, 'Voyage au Pole Sud et dans l'Océanie', in *Histoire du voyage*, vol. 4 (Paris, 1840), pp. 268, 277–8, 343.

81. A. Solomon-Godeau, 'Going native', *Art in America*, July 1989, p. 124.

82. J. E. Erskine, *Journal of a Cruise among the Islands of the Western Pacific* (London, 1853), p. 280.

83. J. Vincendon-Dumoulin and C. Desgraz, *Iles Marquises ou Nouka-Hiva* (Paris, 1843), pp. 221, 231–2, 264.

84. See N. Gunson, *Messengers of Grace: Evangelical Missionaries in the South Seas, 1797–1860* (Melbourne, 1978), *passim*; and R. Hyam, *Empire and Sexuality. The British Experience* (Manchester and New York, 1990), pp. 102–5.

85. J. Richardson, *Arctic Searching Expedition* (London, 1851), vol. 2, p. 42.

86. G. Catlin, *Letters and Notes on the Manners, Customs, and Condition of the North American Indians* (London, 1841), pp. 96, 111, 112–14, 124–5, 214–15.

87. M. zu Wied-Neuwied, *Reise in das innere Nord-Amerika* (Coblenz, 1839), vol. 1, pp. 133, 401, vol. 2, pp. 132 ff.

88. G. Heriot, *Travels through the Canadas* (London, 1807), pp. 278–9.

89. G. Catlin, *Letters and Notes*, vol. 1, pp. 124–5.

90. *Ibid.*, vol. 1, pp. 96, 111–14.

91. P. Duflot de Mofras, *Exploration du territoire de l'Orégon, des Californiens et de la Mer Vermeille* (Paris, 1844), vol. 2, p. 371.

92. E. Pöppig, 'Indier', in *Allgemeine Encyklopädie der Wissenschaften und der Künste* (Leipzig, 1840), p. 375.

93. Bardel, quoted in Dumont d'Urville, *Voyage au Pole Sud*, vol. 2, p. 276.

94. Morfis, 'History of the Province of Texas', in Lord Kingsborough, *Antiquities of Mexico* (London, 1848), vol. 8, p. 138, note.

95. G. Brasseur de Bourbourg, *Popol Vuh* (Paris, 1861), p. clxix, n. 1.

96. G. Brasseur de Bourbourg, *Histoire des nations civilisées du Mexique et de l'Amérique Centrale* (Paris, 1857–9), vol. 2, pp. 67, 77, 173.

97. 'Paedicatio', 'pedicatio': anal intercourse. The word's etymology is unclear and related alternatively to παιδικος (Greek, 'adolescent') or 'podex' (Latin, 'anus'). See G. Vorberg, *Glossarium eroticum* (Hanau, n.d.), p. 445.

98. See I. Löwenstern, *Le Mexique. Souvenir d'un voyageur* (Paris and Leipzig, 1843), p. 179.

99. J. B. von Spix and K. F. Ph. von Martius, *Reise in Brasilien* (Munich, 1823–31), vol. 3, pp. 1074–5.

100. K. F. P. von Martius, *Das Naturell, die Krankheiten, das Arztthum und die Heilmittel der Urbewohner Brasiliens* (Munich, 1843), pp. 107–14.

101. K. F. P. von Martius, *Von den Rechtszustände unter den Ureinwohner Brasiliens* (Munich, 1832), p. 28; K. F. P. von Martius, *Beiträge zur Ethnographie und Sprachenkunde Amerika's zumal Brasiliens* (Leipzig, 1867), pp. 74–5.

102. W. L. von Eschwege, *Journal von Brasilien* (Weimar, 1818), vol. 1, p. 126.

103. E. Pöppig, 'Indier', p. 375.

104. A. d'Orbigny, *L'homme américain (de l'Amérique méridionale) considéré sous ses rapports physiques et moraux* (Paris, 1839), vol. 1, pp. 250, 338, 385, vol. 2, pp. 5, 125, 265.

105. I have consulted the German translation: F. de Azara, *Reisen in Südamerika, 1781–1801* (Leipzig, 1810), vol. 3, p. 13.

106. J. Virey, *De la femme sous ses rapports physiologiques, morales et littéraires*, 2nd ed. (Brussels, 1826), p. 54, n. 3.

107. J. G. Müller, *Geschichte der Amerikanischen Urreligionen* (Basel, 1855), p. 468.

108. A. Wuttke, *Geschichte des Heidentums* (Breslau, 1852–3), vol. 1, p. 289.

109. F. Werne, *Expedition zur Entdeckung der Quellen des weissen Nils (1840–1)* (Berlin, 1852), pp. 21, 30.

110. H. C. Monrad, *Bidrag til en Skildring af Guinea-Kysten* (Copenhagen, 1822), p. 57. Monrad's book was translated and published in German in 1824.

111. J. L. Döhne, *Das Kafferland und seine Bewohner* (Berlin, 1844), pp. 26, 33–4, 89.

112. The report, dated 1858, is mentioned in Maclean, *A Compendium of kaffir Laws &* *Customs* (Grahamstown, 1906), p. 62.

113. D. Livingstone, *Missionary Travels and Researches in South Africa* (London, 1857), p. 452.

114. D. Livingstone, *Narrative of an Expedition to the Zambesi and Its Tributaries, and of the Discovery of the Lakes Shirwa and Nyassa* (London, 1865), p. 418.

115. D. Livingstone, *Narrative*, p. 284.

116. Fleuriot de Langle, 'Croisières à la côte d'Afrique (1868)', *Le tour du monde*, 31 (1876), 243.

117. T. J. Hutchinson, *Ten Years' Wanderings among the Ethiopians* (London, 1861), pp. 129–30.

118. B.-F. Leguéval de Lacombe, *Voyage à Madagascar et aux îles Comores (1823 à 1830)* (Paris, 1841), vol. 1, pp. 97–8.

119. See H. Beauchesne, *Histoire de la psychopathologie* (Paris, 1986), pp. 46 ff.; M. Galzigna, *La malattia morale. Alle origini della psichiatria moderna* (Venice, 1988), pp. 129 ff.; and G. Hekma, *Homoseksualiteit* (Amsterdam, 1987), p. 53.

120. W. F. Bynum, 'The nervous patient in eighteenth- and nineteenth-century Britain: the psychiatric origins of neurology', in W. F. Bynum, R. Porter and M. Shepherd (eds), *The Anatomy of Madness*, vol. 1 (London and New York, 1985), p. 92.

121. J. V. Müller, *Entwurf der gerichtlichen Arzneywissenschaft* (Frankfurt, 1796), p. 136. For a recent reprint, see J. S. Hohmann, ed., *Der unterdrückte Sexus* (Berlin, 1977), pp. 211–24.

122. Fournier-Pescay, ' Sodomie', in *Dictionnaire des sciences médicales*, vol. 51 (Paris, 1821), pp. 441–8.

123. L. J. L. Mende, *Ausführliches Handbuch der gerichtlichen Medicin*, vol. 4 (Leipzig, 1826), pp. 506–9.

124. On this matter, see the excellent article by R. A. Nye, 'The biomedical origins of urban sociology', *JCH*, 20 (1985), 659–75.

125. See J. Weeks, *Sex, Politics and Society* (London, 1981), pp. 84–6.

126. See A. Corbin, *Les filles de noce* (Paris, 1978).

127. See J. Weeks, *Sex, Politics and Society*, pp. 100–1; and D. F. Greenberg, *The Construction of Homosexuality* (Chicago and London, 1988), p. 354.

128. F. Jacquot, 'Des aberrations de l'appétit génésique', *Gazette médicale de Paris*, 28 July 1849, p. 9.

129. [Dr] Bertulus, 'Considérations sur les causes de la dégéneration physique et morale du peuple dans les grandes villes', *Gazette médicale de Paris* (Paris, 1847), pp. 800–1.

130. See A. Marcovich, 'French colonial medicine and colonial rule: Algeria and Indochina', in R. MacLeod and M. Lewis (eds), *Disease, Medicine, and Empire* (London and New York, 1988), pp. 103–17, as well as the older article by M. D. Grmek, 'Géographie médicale et histoire des civilisations', *Annales. E.S.C.*, 18 (1963), 1082 ff.

131. 'D'un coté, polygamie, harems et sérails: d'où excès vénériens, mutilation barbare, sodomie révoltante, population rare, inactive, indolente, vouée à l'ignorance .... De l'autre côté, monogamie, austérité chrétienne, répartition plus égale du bonheur domestique, augmentation croissante de la liberté, de l'égalité, du bien-être, multiplication rapide, population serrée, active, labourieuse.' [Dr] Lallemand, *Des pertes séminales involontaires* (Paris, 1838), vol. 1, p. 646.

132. *Ibid.*, pp. 647–52.

133. On Australian convict sodomy, see R. Hyam, *Empire and Sexuality*, pp. 100–3. See also R. Hughes, *The Fatal Shore* (London, 1987), pp. 264–72.

134. See R. Hyam, *Empire and Sexuality*, pp. 38–49.

135. J. Virey, *Histoire naturelle du genre humain* (Paris, 1801), vol. 1, p. 289.

136. R. Montgomery Martin, *History of the British Colonies*, vol. 3 (London, 1834), p. 524.

137. 'Aus der geringern Stärke des Geschlechtstriebes der meissten dieser Völker ist ebenfalls grosse Schwächlichkeit gefölgert worden, obgleich die Erfahrung zeigt, dass Zeugungslust keinesweges vom Klima und ähnlichen Einflüssen allein bedingt wird, sondern nach ihren verschiedenen Modificationen [*sic*] einen Teil des typischen Characters bei Racen ausmacht.' E. Pöppig, 'Indier', p. 374.

138. See P. J. Bowler, 'The changing meaning of "evolution" ', *Journal of the History of Ideas*, 36 (1975), 95–114; and G. W. Stocking, 'Race', in W. F. Bynum *et al.* (eds), *Dictionary of the History of Science* (Princeton, 1981), pp. 356–7.

139. 'les hommes diffèrent relativement à l'intensité du penchant à la propagation: chez les uns, ce penchant n'existe presque pas, chez d'autres il se manifeste à un degré modéré, dans quelques-uns il est très impérieux: eh bien! l'observation montre toujours le cervelet peu développé chez les premiers, d'une valeur moyenne chez les seconds et au contraire très prééminent chez les derniers.' F. J. Gall, *Anatomie et physiologie du système nerveux en général et du cerveau en particulier* (Paris, 1818), quoted in Aron, *Le pénis et la démoralisation de l'occident*, p. 258.

140. '[Ils] ont peu de portée intellectuelle et présentent presque généralement la bosse de la merveillosité; cela doit être. Leurs aberrations sensuelles ne sont-elles pas la preuve du dévergondage de leur imagination et d'une phylogéniture monomaniaque? Ces deux caractères phrénologiques sont typiques des femmes.' H. Lauvergne, *Les forçats* (Paris, 1841), p. 296.

141. M. Shortland, 'Courting the cerebellum: Early organological and phrenological views of sexuality', *British Journal of the History of Science*, 20 (1987), 173–4.

142. S. L. Gilman, 'Black bodies, white bodies', *Critical Inquiry*, 12 (1985), 212.

143. The denomination 'Hottentot' is very vague and hardly reflected ethnic reality in Southwestern Africa. Among those who are called Hottentot are the Nama, Namaqua, Chariguriqua, Inqua, and Bergdama. For precise locations and references to the HRA Files, see D.H. Price, *Atlas of World Cultures* (Newbury Park, London and New Delhi, 1990), maps 22 and 24.

144. For bibliographical references of the autopsy reports by De Blainville, Cuvier, Otto, Müller, Flower and Murie, Luschka, Koch and Görtz, see S. L. Gilman, 'Black bodies, white bodies', pp. 216, 240.

145. *Ibid.*, p. 216.

146. F. de Azara, *Reisen in Südamerika*, vol. 2, p. 42.

147. A. de Saint Hilaire, *Voyage dans les provinces de Rio de Janeiro et de Minas Geraes* (Paris, 1830), vol. 2, p. 49.

148. See H. Hildebrandt, 'Die Krankheiten der äusseren weiblichen Genitalien', in T. Billroth, ed., *Handbuch der Frauenkrankheiten* (Stuttgart, 1885–6), vol. 3, 11–12.

149. S. L. Gilman, 'Black bodies, white bodies', pp. 224–37. See also A. Corbin, *Les filles de noce, passim*.

150. See, among others, M. S. H. Hubbard and B. Friend (eds), *Women Look at Biology Looking at Women* (Cambridge, 1979); M. Jacobs *et al.* (eds), *Body/Politics. Women and the Discourses of Science* (London, 1990); R. Hubbard, *The Politics of Women's Biology* (New Brunswick, 1989); and E. Snow, 'Theorising the male gaze: some problems', *Representations*, 25 (Winter 1989), 30–41.

151. C. White, *An Account of the Regular Gradation in Man* (London, 1793).

152. Technically, the term 'penile plethysmography' was first used by the Canadian psychologist Kurt Freud as the name of a volumetric technique to measure male sexual arousal. I use the word more freely as a metaphor to name the scientific and pseudo-scientific theorem of phallometry, reading penis size as an index of sexual and/or racial status. See W. R. Dynes, *Homolexis*, p. 112.

153. Virey, 'Nègre', in *Dictionnaire des sciences médicales*, vol. 35 (Paris, 1819), pp. 398–403.

154. G. L. Kobelt, *Die männlichen und weiblichen Wollust-Organe des Menschen und verschiedene Saugetiere* (Stuttgart, 1844).
155. J. B. von Spix and K. F. P. von Martius, *Reise in Brasilien*, vol. 1, p. 376.
156. See G. Hekma, *Homoseksualiteit*, pp. 50–1.
157. L. J. L. Mende, *Ausführliches Handbuch*, vol. 4, p. 516.
158. G. Tourdel, 'Hermaphrodisme', in *Dictionnaire des sciences médicales*, vol. 13, p. 643.
159. J. X, *L'amour aux colonies* (Paris, 1893), pp. 6, 228–33.
160. *Archiv für Anthropologie*, 20 (1920), 189–302.
161. See, in this context, R. Hyam, *Empire and Sexuality*, pp. 204–5.
162. G. Klemm, *Allgemeine Culturgeschichte*, vol. 2, *passim*.
163. *Ibid.*, vol. 1, pp. 192–204.
164. M. Banton, *Racial Theories*, p. 22.
165. J. Virey, *De la femme* (Paris, 1826), pp. 35–6.
166. J. Rosenbaum, *Geschichte der Lustseuche im Alterthume* (Leipzig, 1971 (Halle, 1839)).
167. F. M. C. Fourier, *Le Nouveau Monde Amoureux*, in F. M. C. Fourier, *Oeuvres complètes* (Paris, 1967), vol. 7, pp. 389–91.
168. H. Zschokke, 'Eros oder über die Liebe', in H. Zschokke, *Ausgewählte Novellen und Dichtungen* (Aarau, 1841), p. 207.
169. H. Hössli, *Eros. Die Männerliebe der Griechen* (St Gallen, 1836).
170. J. A. Dulaure, *Les divinités génératrices ou du culte du phallus chez les Anciens et les Modernes* (Paris, 1825).
171. J. J. I. Döllinger, *Heidenthum und Judenthum* (Regensburg, 1857), p. 685.
172. A. Schopenhauer, *Die Welt als Wille und Vorstellung*, 3rd edition (Leipzig, 1859), vol. 2, p. 618.

Chapter four

'Mapping' Homosexual Vice (c. 1860 – c. 1918)

By mid-century, the idea of degeneracy was beginning to take hold
in fields outside race biology – in medical pathology, psychiatry and
criminology. Fear was growing that degenerations within civilised
peoples threatened civilisation itself. In the study of degeneration,
the racial style of biological analysis was available for more general
use, providing interesting analogies and identities. Racial
stereotypes increasingly became a convenient place for the
projection of new social anxieties and racial degeneration now
became a part of a more general theory of 'morbid anthropology'.

– Nancy Stepan[1]

From around 1860, a new discipline, sexology, emerged from the hotbed of
intellectual innovation in bourgeois Europe. Sexuality became the exclusive
focus of attention of scientists, who felt that its study ought to be detached
from the moral rhetoric of religious authorities. Instead of upholding a single
boundary between virtue and vice, they gradually promoted an image of
'polymorphous desire', some of which was socially acceptable, most of
which was not.[2] Male 'homosexuality', as one among the newly defined
'perversions', would soon attract the attention of many a physician and
psychiatrist.

Historians have amply demonstrated that the alternative discourse of
sexology, constituted largely by physicians who called sex their privileged
domain of professional expertise, was itself not exempt from moralism. In
fact, it potentially consolidated traditional church doctrine on sexual morality by a plea for regulation that was scientific only in its method and
argumentation. Yet, the growing authority of medical rhetoric as opposed to
the directions given by the Church did involve a distinct laicization of the
public debate on sexual matters, that became part of a wider project of social
hygiene and the regulation of class, race and gender alike.

Sexology not only found itself in alliance with medical science, but was
also prompted by the increasingly systematic study of physical and cultural
anthropology. The publication in 1871 of Charles Darwin's Descent of Man[3]
especially provoked questions on the place of sexuality in the evolution of

mankind in particular and, along with it, on the status of sexual behaviour that presumably stood in its way. The complexity of Darwinian and social-Darwinian explanatory schemes, however, made early nineteenth-century positivist schemes redundant and confirmed the definitive failure of a naive semiotics of genitalia, that was ancillary in a still too literal sense to an Enlightenment biology of reproduction. Sexual issues were connected, instead, to a more comprehensive explanation of diachronic evolution, that was passed on from one generation to another phylogenetically. Sexual disorder, within such a view, was soon seen as standing in the way of species development or, conversely, as an atavistic relapse into a less advanced state. Somatic theory, focusing on bodily disorder exclusively, was gradually surpassed by views that relocated sexual anomaly in the human brain. At this point, anthropology met psychiatry and both joined efforts at redefining evolution along the lines of psychological and neurological, rather than anatomical development, and at formulating a comprehensive theory of sexual psychopathology.

The impact of scientific innovation within the field of the newly rising discipline of sexology can also be seen as some authors advocated a policy of sexual reform that addressed the needs and aspirations of sexual minorities. It would be too simple, obviously, to draw a picture of dualism between those who upheld a stigmatizing sexual pathology, as belonging to the ruling 'male chauvinist' bourgeois elite unanimously, and those, who opposed it, as the victims of the bourgeois elite. The dialectic between both groups was far more complex, as will become evident in this and the following chapter.

Initially, I will focus on the cognitive perception and representation of male same-sex behaviour, as these altered in view of evolutionary theory and reflected the 'civilizing mission', unfolded predominantly by the ruling middle and upper class both inwardly at the homefront, and outwardly in the colonies. This relation, subsequently, will be presented as a dialectical one, where ethnographic evidence at once provoked and confirmed theoretical innovation. The rather overwhelming number of documents from the mid-nineteenth century onwards actually suggests that the discursive exchange between ethnological description and sexological theory intensified along-side the increasing impact of science upon the regulation of sexuality both within Europe and in its colonies overseas. Yet, century-old patterns of narration persisted underneath the labyrinth of theoretical innovation, which may explain why the project of a 'geography of perversion' in general and a mapping of 'homosexual vice' in particular remained imbued with ambiguity and contradiction. Often, the scientists' intention to 'clarify' sexual variance across the world by means of a single, comprehensive explanatory scheme was hindered by moral bias, considerations of public policy and resilience of data at the same time. The final result was a highly complex and differentiated conglomerate, a patchwork really, of theoretical departures, some of which were more successful than others, but which collectively illustrated the opacity of Europe's discourse on 'otherness' in a wider sense. Neither the continuity of familiar patterns, nor the opacity of partial and at times contradictory explanations should prevent the historian from trying to identify tangible discursive changes, that reflected altering historical circumstances, both socially and politically, culturally and intellectually.

Outside Europe: imperial anxieties

The issue of homosexuality, alas, was not a clearly delineated one within ethnographic narrative. Its visibility remained rather limited and it surfaced mostly in the margin of themes and problems that were considered more relevant to the functioning and consolidation of colonial authority. In such instances, it was easily ascribed a metaphoric status as a *pars pro toto* index of the general morality – or lack of it – of indigenous people. Such had been the case for centuries and did not alter fundamentally in the heyday of imperialism. Thus the 'problem' of same-sex behaviour was reflective first of all of the more comprehensive European discourse on 'otherness' in general.

Europe's heterogeneous discourse on the Other was dictated both by the factual cultural diversity across the world and by the different outcome and unequal success of colonial and imperial policy. Parts of the Middle East and Northern Africa as well as Subsaharan Africa constituted a new frontier for British and French colonial expansion, the former after the collapse of the Ottoman Empire, the latter as an unknown 'dark continent' that had become accessible in the wake of new expeditions into the interior (Livingstone, 1866–73; Cameroon, 1873–6; Stanley, 1874–7; Savorgnan de Brazza, 1875–9). Further towards the East, the consolidation of French, Dutch and British imperial power on the Indian subcontinent and in South-East Asia went hand in hand with the incorporation of the Pacific Islands into the realm of empire. Germany, until then the major absentee among colonial powers, participated in the adventure of imperialism in the wake of its military victory of 1871. The foundation of the Kolonialverein in 1884 led to German control over Southwest Africa (now Namibia), Cameroon, Togo, and Tanzania, as well as over the Marianas, the Palau Islands, the Marshall Islands, the Caroline Islands, the Bismarck Archipelago, Samoa and the northeastern part of New Guinea, then called Kaiser Wilhelmsland.

Both cultural reality and the unequal successes of military and colonial policy gave rise to a multifaceted ethnography of empire. At times, it consisted of a catch-all rhetoric of exoticism, but more frequently a fascination with ancient Near and Far Eastern civilizations and religions contrasted with proclaimed abhorrence in view of the factual or believed brutality of the

Achehese, the Andamanese, the Aboriginals, or the Ashante. The partition of the African continent by the European nations during the Berlin conference of 1884–5 gave rise to conflict with autochthonous populations – a fact that deeply influenced new departures in ethnographic description away from Christian views of the innocent black soul, that yearned for salvation. The image of African purity was given up as Abolitionist ideology became redundant and Christianization aligned with administrative and punitive policies to turn the African population into a pool of cheap labour. After the abolition of slavery in the Americas and the Caribbean, far-reaching regulation of the social and sexual life was given high priority in the new African colonies as well as being a means of preventing social disorder and maximizing economic gain.

Political rule and economic exploitation required disciplined subjects in other continents as well, and some regionally defined discourses, that addressed the character and nature of particular ethnic groups, were 'invented' on the spot. Thus Bengali men were depicted as 'effeminate' while Afghans carried the burden of being called at once 'aggressive' and 'sodomites'. The Punjab as well as the islands of Borneo had a mystique of ruggedness about them, as opposed to the putatively weak and 'feminine' people in some other parts of Indonesia or in the Philippines. Chinese coolies, mobilized and transported across Asia, Africa and the Americas for the building of traffic infrastructure, were accused of a propensity to sodomy, that could not be sufficiently explained by their living conditions in barracks and devoid of contact with women.

Policies, initiated earlier, were developed further to guarantee the upholding of social boundaries between the local populations and colonizers, as well as to maximize the output of colonial rule. As missionary efforts to 'civilize' the indigenous people often proved inadequate, anxieties arose about the potentially demoralizing effects of local prostitution, concubinage, or higher sexual tolerance among the European population in the colonies themselves.

The problem of the so-called 'tropicalization' of Europeans had actually intensified, not least because of a balance of power that was advantageous for the white, male colonizer, yet he was easily lured into the temptations of indigenous sexual mores. 'One of the causes of exhaustion', a French physician emphasized, 'is the strong sexual need in countries where satisfying it is no sinecure (Une des causes de fatigue est l'acuité du besoin génésique en des pays où le satisfaire est chose malaisée).'[4] The colonial armies in particular seemed prone to 'demoralization' as soldiers were forced to have sexual relations with prostitutes or among themselves. The apparent increase of homosexual contacts within the army or between soldiers and indigenous men alarmed many an observer, who speculated at the same time about the impact of such circumstantial sodomy:

The uprooted easily becomes a sodomite ... [but] real homosexuality is very rare .... Many are sodomites by necessity, but real homosexuals are few in number. The shortage of women or the presence of Arab and black prostitutes, who are dirty, stink and carry diseases pushes the uprooted to prefer sex with ephebes. Their behaviour is incidental and will be dropped when they return to the North.[5]

In Algeria, the French criminologist Armand Corre witnessed how soldiers engaged in a homosexual orgy, while one 'Breton nostalgique' was masturbating as he watched. But he was less optimistic about the future outcome of such events and feared that 'the survivors, crushed by the sad colonial experience, return ... and continue to dislike women or engage in infertile marriages, due to their exhaustion (les survivants, épavés de la triste épreuve coloniale, reviennent ... avec le dégoût de la femme ou, usés, restent, dans le mariage des inféconds).' The threat of *démoralisation*, moreover, manifested itself not only in the minds of undisciplined, impulsive soldiers. It existed as well for colonial officers of higher rank. Thus, 'in the region of Indochina, where the effeminate boy often lives side by side with the mistress, both equally serve the distractions of their master (dans la région indochinoise, où le boy féminisé vit souvent côte à côte avec la maîtresse, tous deux servant indifféremment aux distractions du maître).' An officer, when informed about a compatriot who was expelled to New Caledonia after having abused a minor boy, exclaimed: 'Oh! The poor devil! The poor devil! As if we have to be reprimanded for such minor sins in Cochinchina! (Ah! Le pauvre diable! Le pauvre diable! S'il avait fallu qu'on nous reprît de pareilles peccadilles, en Cochinchine!)'[6]

Neither soldiers, employees, officers, nor administrators were exempt from excursions into vice, whether homo- or heterosexual, and this prompted the colonial administration to prescribe more severe rules of conduct. The very threat, so it seemed, of indigenous sexuality called for a far-reaching regulation, especially towards the end of the nineteenth century, of intimate contacts between the colonizer and the colonized. 'The "embourgeoisement" of imperialism', according to Cooper and Stoler, 'enhanced expectations of hard work, sexual restraint, and racial distancing among the colonial agents, while opening a more intimate domain for condemnation and reform in the lives of the colonized.'[7]

Accordingly guidelines were issued, that were racially and sexually asymmetric and aimed at reinforcing a regime of 'cultural hygiene'. In reality, they also served to safeguard male, white – I add, heterosexual – hegemony.[8] In the same context, prostitution was subjected to social policies of either regulation or suppression. The former was applied in the French, Belgian and Portuguese colonies as well as in Thailand, whereas the British and Dutch empire witnessed a purity campaign to suppress brothels towards the end of the nineteenth century. A first target, as I noted in the previous chapter, had been the boy brothels in Karachi. In the 1870s, feminist pressure intensified and prompted the Colonial Office of Great Britain to act. Eventually an

Advisory Committee on Social Hygiene was installed and international conferences led to the suppression of trade in prostitutes across the world. Soon afterwards, all brothels were suppressed in Ceylon, Malaysia and China. Similar measures were taken by the Dutch in Indonesia.[9]

The perceived urgency of social and sexual regulation did not alter a discursive pattern of reification, however, that reduced the sexuality of indigenous people to something unchangeable and inherent to their racial identity. As such, it merely reiterated the already existing, secular tropes of the imagination and was equally imbued with what Edward Said has called 'synchronic essentialism'.[10] In fact, the rhetoric of regulation, while in contrast, on one hand, with some more exoticist narratives of indigenous civilization and mystery, merely rephrased these in different terms on the other hand. It was not at odds, therefore, with the timeless representations of Primitive or Oriental identity, but reflected, rather, an encounter that was less aesthetical.

The persistence of unchangeable rhetoric is also revealed in documents describing people that are not subjected to European imperial domination. Thus, the people of China and Korea as well as Meiji Japan (1868–1912) remained subjected to an Orientalist gaze despite the country's gradual modernization in a western sense. The Afro-American population too, though freed and theoretically self-reliant, remained the target of exoticist projections not only of European observers, but also of the new, Creole elites. To uphold such distinctions, artificial boundaries were drawn between those who were 'black' and others who were less if not entirely so. The mestizo and mulatto population, aware of their mixed ancestry, yet aspiring to be recognized as part of the upwardly mobile, actually felt compelled to subscribe to the often racialist tenor of cultural discourse in either the Caribbean colonies or the independent, modernizing nations of South and Central America. In Europe, this was reflected by parallel distinctions between the presumed beauty of the mixed-blood people, women especially, and the proclaimed ugliness and inferiority of 'blacks'.

The ongoing or new independence and self-reliance of some areas in the world did not fundamentally challenge the major patterns of western representation, that were largely defined by the historical reality of colonial rule. This, as a matter of fact, required ideological justification as well as cognitive frameworks, that enabled the individual to come to grips with the Otherness of the colonized people. Timeless categories such as 'barbarous', 'pagan', 'decadent' or 'despotic' allowed for disguising the conflict of cultural confrontation and subjugation in the colonial realm, but remained equally valid for descriptions of societies that had successfully resisted subjugation.

Inside Europe: the civilizing mission within

At home, the ruling classes felt compelled to justify their dominant status as traditional social order was undermined by industrialization, urbanization and rising social mobility. The presence of the numerous labouring poor was perceived as a threat to bourgeois hegemony, whereas educated women claimed the right to participate in public life and challenged the power of men. The cities harboured the germs not only of crime and epidemic diseases such as typhus and cholera, but also of venereal infection and immorality. Prostitution flourished with guaranteed recruitment from a proletariat of unemployed females while homosexual subcultures became more visible both on the fringes of society and within the very heart of bourgeois environments.

Such, in the eyes of the ruling elites, indiscriminately somber perceptions of reality called for appropriate strategies to consolidate social hierarchy and to 'regulate' the behaviour of those who potentially threatened it. Comprehensive policies were set up to sanitize the public as well as the private domains.

Presenting the 'civilizing mission' purely as a white, bourgeois, male, and heterosexual initiative, aimed at ethnic, social, and sexual minorities would be highly simplistic, however. Alliances were often made according to the exigencies of well defined issues, and those who took progressive stands at one point might take a conservative or repressive one at another. For example, the educated and sexually independent 'New Women' at once countered male dominance and joined men in Purity Crusades against prostitution and its accompanying 'double moral'. When setting up patronizing programmes of social improvement for working-class women, they proved excellent spokespersons for traditional bourgeois values and obeyed uncritically the unwritten rules of *distinction sociale*.[11]

Men and women also joined efforts to police homosexual men (and lesbian women to a lesser extent). In England, the 1861 Offences Against the Person Act removed the death penalty for buggery, but the Labouchère Amendment to the Criminal Law Amendment Act of 1885 made acts of 'gross indecency' between men punishable by up to two years' hard labour. After 1871, the old paragraph 143 of Prussian penal law was extended to all of Germany as paragraph 175 and reconfirmed same-sex relations among men as a criminal offence.[12] Other countries of the European continent did not have any such restrictive legislations, yet police control was set up to survey the subcultures of pederasts.[13] Stigmatized as asocial beings, homosexuals were identified with the places that they presumably frequented for *l'accrochage*, and subjected to repressive measures of public hygiene: 'As a symbol of anality, positioned near the public toilets, they also take part in the lowness of animal life. As Carlier suggests, the odours of the pederast, an amateur of strong perfumes, show the olfactory proximity between musk and excrement (Symbole de l'analité, installé dans le voisinage des latrines, il[s] participe[nt] [eux] aussi de la fétidité animale. Comme suggère Carlier, les odeurs du pédéraste, amateur des lourds parfums, manifestent la proximité olfactive du musc et de l'excrément).'[14]

The complexity of late-nineteenth-century social policies is yet to be fully clarified by historical research. But the bourgeoisie's representation of 'otherness' was clearly characterized by an ascription of qualities to social, racial or sexual difference, that were unchangeable and 'detached' from historical circumstance. The very outlook of minorities, who were pinned down to timeless essence, thus justified the social and political *status quo* while simultaneously promoting interference in the public and private lives of minorities. At times, such programmes of intervention were inspired by philanthropy. But mostly they were more coercive. Virtually always, however, they were patronizing and imposed from above upon distinct target groups. And, while phrased as ideals of 'national identity' or 'civilization', they most directly supported the confirmed ideology of the ruling bourgeoisie. 'The national stereotype', says Mosse, 'and the middle-class stereotype were identical'.[15]

The parameters of sexual science

While essentially conservative in its upholding of traditional and, frequently, religious beliefs, bourgeois ideology also witnessed the growing weight of science. Familiar moral discourse was exchanged for a rhetoric of social order and public hygiene, lending authority to physicians especially. As sanitary engineers, they profiled and imposed themselves as a newly professionalizing group of decision makers about matters of public and private life.

Evolution versus degeneracy

The growing authority of scientists was partially due to some major innovative theories about human development. On the one hand, a paradigmatic shift took place, in life sciences at first, in social science shortly afterwards, that replaced Christian teleology by one of 'evolution' through time. Almost simultaneously, a new theory of 'degeneration' was built upon Lamarckian theory about the inheritability of acquired characteristics. It 'translated the biblical story of the Fall of Man into secular terms by postulating that many medical, psychiatric, and social problems were due to deterioration of the human body from an initially perfect state, under the impact of an unhealthy environment'.[16] As progeny inherited degenerate traits, morbid deviations from normality increased through time.

Both paradigms not only guided public debate about problems of race and class, but also the now increasingly professional study of gender and sexuality. Theorizing about human sexuality became intertwined once again with the scientific study of social and racial variety as the new paradigm resuscitated the rhetoric of analogy, that had been stranded on the cliffs of raw empiricism. Conceived within the new framework of diachronic biological evolution or degeneration, all three domains were now compared, not as static mirror images of one another, but rather as one another's signifier within the framework of a new teleology of progress.

When applied to the human race as in *The Descent of Man* (1871), Darwinian theory clarified racial hierarchy as the outcome of slow processes of diversification according to the adaptive capabilities of people in different parts of the world. At the same time, it contained a sound apology for colonization by the white, European race, especially when interpreted in a Lamarckian sense. Western intervention would change the environmental conditions in the colonies and accelerate the evolutionary process in people, whose improved adaptive skills would then be transmitted through heredity: 'The peculiar advantage of a more Lamarckian evolutionism was the opening it left for an uplifting philanthropic meliorism. Civilising efforts on behalf of dark-skinned savages could, over time, eliminate savagery from the world ... by modifying their hereditary incapacity'.[17]

Meanwhile, Darwin's theory seemed to explain social difference within a single race as well, just as it offered a theoretical framework for outlining policies of social regulation and public hygiene in Europe itself.[18] Gender disorder was explained as symptomatic of inadequate adaptation,[19] and homosexuality was seen by the American physicians Kiernan and Lydston as a reminder of how the human race evolved from primitive organisms that were essentially hermaphroditical. In Europe itself, a less direct relation was postulated between evolution and homosexuality. Rather than depicting it as a reminder of sexually undifferentiated organisms, one increasingly presented it as an 'atavistic' throwback to an earlier stage of evolution.

Such an approach was symptomatic, moreover, of internal change within Darwinian theory itself. Here, Chamberlin has pointed out how, gradually, an obsessive interest grew in 'abnormal' phenomena, that appeared to be in 'developmental decline'. These challenged scientists 'who were coming to terms with the notion of "descent with modification" that Darwin had popularised and with the theory of "natural selection" that he had affirmed'.[20] At issue was whether such 'degenerative' processes were dictated from within (endogenesis) or from the outside (exo- or epigenesis). The answer to this question, when applied to the human species in particular, easily became ideological, not only because of its moral implications, but also because the choice for either position implied subscription to mutually incompatible social policies. Emphasizing the weight of heredity ('nature') inevitably meant that no remedy to the process of degeneration could be found outside the physical or neurological constitution of the individual. When environmental factors ('nurture') were recognized, however, one could sustain the view that the change of external circumstances potentially led to a stabilization or neutralization of the individual's pathological condition.

The debate persisted as biological evolution was applied to the character of a society and its cultural status. Here too, the controversy between 'environmentalists' and 'hereditarians' divided scientists into two different camps. It was not clear whether social evolution was defined by its institutions or rather by the patterns of belief and action of its individual members. Yet, underneath, an implicit analogy between any cultural psychosis and individual or collective neurosis was recognized. The issue of such rhetoric of 'cultural pathology' was 'whether particular phenomena had proceeded in their development too far, or not far enough, or might even be regressing, and just how "unhealthy" each state could be said to be in relation to the norm'.[21] Darwinian theory, at this point, came very close to degeneration theory.

The publication in 1857 of Bénédicte Auguste Morel's *Traité des dégénérescences physiques, intellectuelles et morales de l'espèce humain* initiated what would soon become an influential theory. It claimed that disadvantageous circumstances led to social problems because of their degenerative effects, that are transmitted hereditarily.[22] Rapidly taking off at first in the France of the *troisième République* (1870–1914), degeneration theory soon spread across Europe and 'gained dominant status as a cultural theory of national decline in the following decades'.[23]

The causes, progression and remedies of degeneration were further developed by authors such as Dallemagne in Belgium, Nordau, Hirsch, Möbius and Arndt in Germany, Lankaster and Talbot in Great Britain, and Lombroso in Italy.[24] Essentially a psychiatric model, degeneration theory represented a major break from early and mid-nineteenth-century anatomical pathology. Its diachronic perspective also implied a rupture with the static scales and registers of craniometry and phrenology. Sexual disorder, until then most commmonly ascribed to anomalous physical or psychic typology, was now described as a gradual process of mental disorientation, due to disadvantageous circumstances and/or hereditary predisposition. Eventually, the degenerative process would make its victim look like an individual of a primitive race. Like mulattoes, juvenile delinquents were depicted as lacking vital energy. The urban poor were 'persistent paupers', whose state reminded one of inferior races. Prostitutes showed arrested development and morbid heredity.[25] Homosexuality, though hardly inheritable in the eyes of biologists and physicians who assumed that homosexuals did not reproduce, was said to be triggered by other degenerate aspects of one's parents' personalities.

Less consensus existed, on the other hand, about whether deviant sexual behaviour merely reflected mankind at a primitive stage, or ought to be understood as a response to circumstances that were historically and socially defined. Regarding homosexuality, this boiled down to the question of whether it pertained to the realm of primitive humanity, or was a product rather of modern western neurosis, a disease of civilization.

The Italian crimonologist Cesare Lombroso depicted pederasty as an atavistic disorder of the mind, that made homosexuals into natural allies of crime.[26] Their sexual praxis revealed a close affinity to inferior races, according to Lombroso who portrayed human evolution as developing away from an original, polymorph perversity that could still be perceived among primitive races across the globe.[27] 'It is obvious', he proclaimed, 'that sodomy flourishes there without a trace of infamy (E v'ha di peggio chè la sodomia pure vi regna senza nota d'infamia).'[28]

Lombroso's linear model was opposed by Ferri[29] and Venturi,[30] who both diagnosed the occurrence of sodomy as a sign of social crisis, a symptom of transition into a new historical era. But within Lombroso's theory, such rephrasings of a familiar Gibbonian theme of decadence were easily absorbed by the understanding of 'degeneration' as a relapse into primitivism.

The founder of the Lyon school of criminology, Alexandre Lacassagne, also opposed Lombroso's linking of a criminal type with primitive man and accounted for crime by reference to the social environment. *Pédérastie*, according to Lacassagne, was no common trait among primitive folk who accordingly could not be described as merely 'atavistic'.[31]

Among his followers, Armand Corre and Charles Letourneau addressed homosexuality more extensively. Corre's survey of criminal behaviour in the French overseas colonies led him to conclude that the situation grew worse with the arrival of the French and that westernization certainly did not enhance a reduction of asocial behaviour among indigenous folk. Homosexuality, among other offenses, did not diminish as the French proved hardly immune themselves.[32] Letourneau in his turn, diagnosed degeneration as the logical outcome of ripened civilization, yet questioned if this implied a regression to an original, primitive state: 'Social organisms, not unlike specific [i.e., biological] organisms, always include pathogenic microbes, waiting merely for a weakening of vital resistance in order to reproduce (Les organismes sociaux, semblables en cela aux organismes spécifiques, renferment toujours des microbes pathogènes, n'attendant, pour germer, qu'un affaiblissement de la résistance vitale).'[33]

Disagreement on the ontology of degeneration did not, however, challenge the theory's seductive power, nor its promises as a guideline for social policy. In a climate of public concern about the health of the national state, degenerate individuals were seen as symptomatic of more comprehensive, negative trends in society and their stigmatization by scientific discourse went along with social-Darwinist measures of social regulation. The individual body was thought to reflect a state's general health and became a metaphor of social order. Deviations from the perfect body, in turn, were read as symbols of social decay. 'Evolution' and its mirror image 'degeneration' thus provided a theoretical context for the biological metaphor of a healthy national organism, that was free of moral weakness and hereditary disease. Demographic growth, within such a perspective, increased as degenerative, asocial minorities were efficiently policed.[34]

The making of the modern homosexual

Both Darwinian and degeneration theory inspired innovative explanations of male-to-male sexual behaviour beyond a mere speculation on the latter's affinity with the primitive. Within the framework of degeneracy or 'atavism', an individual's propensity to sexual relations with a person of his own sex was seen as a personal characteristic, as a permanent pathological *state*. As such, it was different from previous theories, that described sodomy as a vicious or pathological *act*. Among the last representatives, according to Hekma, of such focusing on the act of sodomy, was Kaan, who presented *Päderastie* as an ubiquitous phenomenon that had existed throughout the history of mankind and that sprouted largely from deranged fantasy.[35] For Kaan, 'pederasty' was closely tied to the 'vice' of masturbation, which still positioned him within the tradition of Tissot's *L'onanisme* of 1760.

The paradigmatic turn towards a neurological-deterministic explanation of same-sex behaviour was initiated by Michéa's article on '[les] déviations maladives de l'appétit vénérien' (1849).[36] In it, *philopédie* and *tribadie* (lesbianism) were described as a *passion instinctive*, that was inborn and pathological because of its 'monomaniacal' character. No direct relationship with onanism was claimed. A presumed 'femininity' among *philopèdes* resulted from a rudimentary uterus, that could be detected, according to Michéa, in course of an autopsy – a theory that still reflected eighteenth- and early nineteenth-century reductions of one's sexual identity to the mere anatomy of one's genitalia.

Only after 1857 were new medical explanations of same-sex behaviour given, that aligned at once with evolutionary and degeneration theory. Morel's *Traité des dégénérescences* did not address sexual perversions *per se*, yet it paved the way for explaining them as signs of human degeneration. But uncertainty remained about the physical or psychical characteristics that were revelatory of the degenerate condition of men engaging in same-sex relations. The German professor of juridical medicine in Berlin, Casper, claimed that *Knabenliebe* was most often 'inborn as a kind of hermaphroditism of the mind', yet he was unable to locate any signs of 'degeneracy' besides the smoothness of a pederast's sphincter and his presumed femininity.[37] The very fact that physicians had a problem in recognizing pederasts whereas the pederasts themselves had no major difficulty in recognizing one another led to a controversy between Casper and Tardieu, who went so far as to pretend that a pederast's penis looked like that of a dog as a result of anal penetration.[38] Brouardel, in turn, claimed a funnel-shaped anus to be more revealing along with a non-defined 'femininity'.[39]

The fallacy of an exclusively anatomical diagnostic of the body in order to 'locate' sexual degeneration may well explain the growing authority of a psychiatric etiology from the 1860s onwards. To an extent, this merely reflected the increasing status of psychiatry and psychopathology as these disciplines set out to integrate the empiricism of biology and physiology in their own analysis of the human brain. Their nosology was based on laboratory research on the pathological deviations of the individual brain. Sexual perversions too were classified as the outcome of neurological disorders in the first place.[40]

The first one, however, to locate a same-sex instinct in the brain was Carl Heinrich Ulrichs, who looked forward to social acceptance rather than medical stigmatization of sodomites. He called them *Urninge* and explained their sexual preference as the outcome of a mental condition that came into being during the first thirteen weeks of embryonic development. *Uranismus*, so Ulrichs claimed, was to be seen as a natural state, where a female soul is enclosed in a male body, *anima muliebris in corpore virili inclusa*,[41] and was only one among other less common sexual 'varieties': *Urninginne* (lesbians), *Uranodioninge* (bisexuals), *Uraniaster* ('emergency homosexuality'), *Dionäismus* (feminine-looking heterosexual), and finally, *Weiblinge* and *Männlinge* (respectively the more effeminate and virile varieties of *Urninge* and *Urninginne*).[42]

In the following chapter, I will briefly return to Ulrichs' theory as it was quintessential to the late-nineteenth-century emancipatory movement of homosexual men and women in Europe. But it gave rise also to controversy among physicians and anthropologists and was debated both within and outside Germany. Many in fact adopted Ulrichs' theory, though they did not share his view that *Uranismus* was merely a natural variety. They saw it rather as a deviation that was in essence pathological. Thus the founding father of materialist psychiatry, Griesinger, called *Uranismus* a *Neuropathie*, that was of 'organic' origin.[43] Carl Westphal still doubted if *konträre Sexualempfindung* was to be seen as autonomous or derivative, yet nevertheless acknowledged it as a separate psychopathological disorder.[44]

At odds with his contemporaries' pathological etiology, Carl Maria Benkert proposed the word *Homosexuelle* in 1869. In a way, the new word confirmed the gradual shift from a discourse about the 'act' of sodomy via the so-called 'sodomite' to 'the homosexual'; from a rhetoric of 'vice' to the notion that same-sex behaviour sprang from a permanent condition. Along with *Urning*, 'homosexual' would soon be adopted by men engaging in same-sex relations themselves, and gradually it would gain prominence within the jargon of physicians. Until then, however, it remained just one concept amidst others. Yet they all reflected a new, medical understanding of homosexuality as a permanent condition, as a personality characteristic that dictated one's behaviour beyond his personal will.

Westphal's phrase was upheld by Richard Freiherr von Krafft-Ebing, whose influential study, *Psychopathia sexualis*, first published in 1886, has been reprinted many times since. Von Krafft-Ebing had already classified 'qualitative' and 'quantitative' perversions in his article of 1877, 'Über gewisse Anomalien des Geschlechtstriebes': among the first, impotence, satyriasis and nymphomania; among the latter, cannibalism, necrophilia, passionate murder and, especially, 'contrary sexual desire'. Von Krafft-Ebing distinguished cases of acquired and of inborn homosexuality, yet related both to a hereditary constitution of insanity and neuropathy.

His magnum opus *Psychopathia sexualis* was part of the proliferation of psychiatric studies on 'sexual perversion' after 1880. Among the authors of new inventories and classifications, often brimming with neologisms, were Moreau, Charcot and Magnan, Tarnowsky, Chevalier, Mantegazza, Ball, Binet, Sérieux, Saint-Paul, alias Dr Laupt, and Crocq.[45] Hekma has pointed out how their writings embraced a gradual shift away from sexuality for the purpose of reproduction only and focused increasingly on the 'problems' of eroticism, sexuality and love.[46] Eventually, Albert Moll denied that reproduction was the first and foremost drive to sexuality. In his *Untersuchungen über die Libido sexualis* (1897), Moll distinguished two separate sexual drives: *Kontrektationstrieb* as the pull towards relationships on the one hand, and *Detumeszenztrieb* or the drive to orgasm, leading only incidentally to procreation. Despite his critique of traditional sexual morality, Moll too claimed that heterosexuality ought to be seen as the norm.[47]

The laicization implied by new psychiatric theory did not, however, allow for a less moralistic approach to sexuality. In reality, sin and vice were redefined in terms of perversions that were disapproved of just as much. Different was the psychiatrists' claim that such perversions were pervasive of the individual patient's life. By presenting perversions as deviations of mental constitution, the newly rising *psychopathia sexualis* tended to abolish circumstantial factors altogether and joined similar theories in criminology about the 'inborn criminal'.

No consensus was ever reached, on the other hand, about the explanatory power of constitutional or 'inborn' perversion. Von Krafft-Ebing himself distinguished acquired and inborn homosexuality. From Morel, he borrowed the notion of degeneration. But he claimed that such process did not evolve throughout a timespan of four generations as Morel had said, but as four stages within the single life of an individual. Acquired homosexuality, as a case of degeneration, involved a first stage of attraction to one's own sex, followed by *eviratio* (for women, *efeminatio*). An intermediary phase then lead to a final *metamorphosis sexualis paranoïca*, that made the man feel like a woman, the woman like a man. This stage was compared to non-identifiable ethnographic evidence about cross-dressing men among the Pueblo of North America, whose genitals supposedly shriveled up and who assumed an increasingly female appearance.[48] Constitutional perversion too developed in four stages: *psychische Hermaphrodisie; Homosexuale* or male *Urninge* and female *Urninginne; Effeminatio* or, among women, *Viraginität*; and, at last, *Androgynie* among men and *Gynandrie* among women.[49]

Hardly different from the Enlightenment theory on 'sodomites' was the claim that homosexuality ought to be seen in terms of gender deviance. In the late nineteenth century, such a thesis was inspired by more general fears of the ruling, male elite about both female challenges of the separate spheres and the rising visibility of urban homosexual subcultures. Yet not only were all forms of trespassing gender boundaries, including sexual ones, seen as potentially threatening, but the homosexual's femininity went beyond the level of mere role-playing – which made it different from the eighteenth-century concept of effeminate, passive sodomites.[50] At the same time, it was seen as deeper than mere genital disorder. It surpassed the level of reproductive physiology in that a homosexual's perception of the self was said to be as of a woman, trapped in a man's body. Today, this image fits a transgender personality more than a gay man, but late-nineteenth-century sexology remained permeated by the assumption that an essential link existed between male-to-male sexuality and gender disorder in a wider sense, even when the anatomical diagnosis of earlier periods had been exchanged for a psychiatric one.

Meanwhile, ambiguity about the adequacy of a model of inborn perversion was expressed by authors who emphasized the impact of social factors as well. Moreau, among them, pointed at social misery. The climate too was conducive to increasing lasciviousness, that potentially seduced some into same-sex relations.[51] Ball highlighted the detrimental effects of decadence on individual sexual development.[52] Von Schrenk-Notzing too explained homosexuality as 'acquired'.[53]

Essentially, the theories described above were inspired by appeals for social prophylaxis in a world that had upset traditional morality and unleashed perversity. But on a more complex level too, the model of inborn perversion was countered by embryological theory. Gley adopted the thesis of Charcot and Magnan that homosexuality was in essence a deviation of the brain and suggested that this may have developed as early as during the embryonic stage.[54] Chevalier reiterated the theory of embryonic development as first developed by Ulrichs, and received support from von Krafft-Ebing in his ninth edition of *Psychopathia sexualis*.[55]

Others, like Binet and Max Dessoir, already pointed at childhood sexuality, mostly masturbation, which in their eyes was proof of the sufficiency of constitutional perversion theory, for children could not possibly have learned to masturbate at such an early age. Dessoir accordingly claimed that children had a kind of 'undifferentiated sexual feeling', that would gain direction in response to their social environment.[56] Ironically, such theory threatened to undermine the validity of constitutional perversion theory for now homosexuality or heterosexuality could be seen to develop from a non-differentiated pubescent sexuality.[57] Like the explanations of Gley, Chevalier, the later von Krafft-Ebing and Binet, Dessoir's theory ensued from degeneration theory and leaned more towards Darwinian theory.

In the public field, however, both Darwinian and degeneration theories were acclaimed as equally powerful pleas for prophylaxis of homosexuality, that stood in the way of the reproduction of the human race. Together, they were mobilized to regulate sexual pleasure and propagate a new sexual morality. The presentation of sexual variety as a catalogue of perversions eventually undermined the initial intention of sexology to study sex apart from the call for procreation.

The new inventory of homosexual deviance

Theoretically, the above-described theorizing about 'homosexuality' called for clarification of how this manifested itself outside the 'civilized world'. The evolutionary paradigm, in fact, had provided a theoretical framework, inducing both sexologists and anthropologists to uncover the relationship between sexually deviant practices of other races and the newly defined sexual minorities in Europe itself. Such a project was a logical part of the wider anthropological study of human evolution, that upheld a monogenetic model of growing complexity and control. The scientific study of racial diversity had altogether moved away from a predominantly physical–anatomical study and gradually reoriented itself towards a more ethnological study of the phases of human behavioural development. In France, Paul Broca's morphologie was gradually exchanged for a sociological study of the behavioural patterns of primitive folk,[58] while British and German anthropology witnessed how similar options were taken by Tylor, MacLennan, von Hellwald and others.[59]

Savages, within this new diachronic model, were seen not as inferior offshoots of the human race, but rather as the contemporary, living witnesses of humanity's pristine moral state. Ethnographic observation of living primitive people would thus allow for reconstructing evolutionary processes, that eventually made the white European into the most adapted and developed subspecies of all. He had placed reason above the animistic religion of primitive folk, civilization above anarchy and violence, control above instinct.

Another pattern to be retrieved, according to evolutionist anthropologists, was one from a presumed primitive promiscuity to the sexual morality of the monogamous marriage and the renunciation of all sexual activity except procreative intercourse. The image of a primitive state of general promiscuity, including polygamy, polyandry, and sexual practices that were essentially hedonist, was in fact a hypothetical one, 'a mélange', that is, 'of ethnocentrically evaluated departures from a Victorian cultural norm'.[60] Its reconstruction by anthropologists therefore was not to be detached from the 'civilizing mission' of the European bourgeoisie, directed both to 'uncivilized', sexually deviant groups in Europe and to the indigenous populations in the colonies.

In the eyes of many, homosexuality also figured among the sexual practices that appertained to the primitive state of promiscuity. But it is clear, despite the systematic attempts of some to describe and classify homosexual behaviour across the world, that most anthropologists felt reluctant to dwell upon this controversial theme. The ethnological inventory of same-sex relations outside the West, however, reflected not only moral reticence, but also theoretical disagreement about how the issue of homosexuality ought to be placed within the scheme of evolutionary change.

In general, ethnographic debate on homosexuality remained largely descriptive, even when its vocabulary was increasingly defined by sexological theory. It remained an altogether rather *ad hoc* inventory, a collection of more or less incidental reports about same-sex behaviour and cross-gender roles outside the West. It demonstrates that cognitive confusion resulted not only from the richness of sexual cultures across the globe, but also from the very trappings of both sexological and racialist theory. The etiologies, put forward by each author more or less autonomously, reflected how the presumably simple act of description was defined by practical, theoretical and ideological considerations, and produced a mass of images, that only reluctantly reveal some patterns to the historian.

Central Asia, the Middle East and Northern Africa

Discourse on sexuality in the Arab world remained relatively unchanged and perpetuated timeless schemes and stereotypes despite the changing political reality. Eunuchs kept drawing attention as before, even when their number had declined considerably in real life. Abhorrence from the European side actually accelerated this process and reached a climax by 1890, when the 'white slave trade' was put on the agenda of international conferences. The trade of eunuchs as of women destined to reside in the seraglios, was abolished as a result of it, leaving the remaining ones as witnesses to a barbaric, Arab morality.[61]

As earlier in Claude Ancillon's *Traité des eunuques*, eunuchs were focused upon also in view of the changing conceptualization of sexual identity.

Previous speculations on their 'effeminate' nature or outlook thus gained new relevance when confronted with new theories of 'homosexual' identity. A physician, Demetrius Zambaco Pacha, speculated on the eunuch as feminized, sad, egoistic and childish – qualities that seemed to explain why the eunuch maintained (passive) sexual relations with other men. The author was puzzled, however, at the sight of other, normally shaped men, who did the same. The relation between gender identity and sexual preference or praxis, therefore, was not as tight as he felt compelled to believe at first.[62] Later, Eugen Wilhelm, also known as Numa Praetorius, would blame Zambaco Pacha for trying to reduce the situation of eunuchs, passive pederasts and male prostitutes to a single, identical 'psychoneurosis'. Instead, Wilhelm emphasized that the eunuch's case might be revealing of the negative effects of some eugenic measures that were proposed by racial and sexual hygienists of his time.[63]

Another French physician, traveller and humanist, doctor Paul Desjardin de Régla translated a book on Muslim society and sexuality that was written in Arabic by Omar Haleby Abu Otman. Published first in Paris in 1893 as *Théologie musulmane. El Ktab des lois secrètes de l'amour*, the book not only contained de Régla's translation of the original Arabic manuscript, but also numerous editorial notes.[64] Haleby's passage on eunuchs was in fact at odds with most European texts, as it stressed the very pre-Islamic, Greek and Roman origins of castration. He distinguished three different degrees of emasculation, next, and explained the relation between eunuchs and homosexuality as a matter of seduction, rather than of biological affinity:

Due to his feminine taste and inclination, the complete eunuch has ... developed the evil instinct of pederasty. Finding no single virile impulse in his body, he stopped being a true Muslim and became a soft, kneadable subject, ready to accept any bad proposition. He thus can be compared rightfully to Jews who, as everyone knows, make money with their very own bodies.[65]

Haleby, leaning on the teachings of the Koran rather than on the reality of daily praxis, not only denounced eunuchs but female prostitution as well, for they both provoked masturbation, as well as sexual relations among women and among men: '[All] these shameful and disgusting practices [are] triggered, provoked, awakened and spread by real prostitution to the detriment of population growth and the fertility of women and men ([Toutes] ces pratiques honteuses, épouvantables, que la véritable prostitution traîne à sa suite, qu'elle provoque, vivifie et répand partout, au détriment de l'augmentation des populations et de la fécondité des femmes et des hommes).'[66]

De Régla, though accentuating that 'morality is not one, but varies according to place, country, area, altitude, environment and climate (la morale n'est pas une, mais qu'elle diffère suivant les lieux, les pays, les zones, les altitudes, les milieux et les climats)',[67] did not refute Haleby's simplified thesis on the illegality of sodomy: 'Islam philosophy, being very embracing of anything natural, places the crime of onanism and sexual anomalies, legitimate or illegitimate, behind the one of lying (La philosophie de l'Islam, très large dans tout ce qui est naturel, place après le crime du mensonge ceux de l'onanisme et des dérèglements sensuels, légitimes ou illégitimes.)'[68] But he admitted that it did occur nevertheless, not seldom within a context of prostitution. This, however, had little to do with 'congenital homosexuality'. Not the sex of their partner, but the fact that men and boys, like women, lent (read: prostituted) themselves for passive anal intercourse explained, says de Régla, why same-sex relations were so common alongside male-to-female ones.

Recent studies by Boudhiba, Chebel and others have revealed how same-sex relations in the Arab world could hardly be conceived of as 'homosexual' ones in the modern European sense of the word.[69] In this sense, de Régla's interpretation was, in fact, quite accurate. Yet de Régla's focus on genital compatibility or feasibility itself reflected a particularly European focus on sexual physiology as the foundation of sexual identities. The essential meaning of active role-taking which is respectable, versus passive role-taking which is not, and that defined the boundary of moral approval in the past as well, went unnoticed by de Régla.

Other authors too remained insufficiently aware of this, as of the apparent rupture between official teachings of the Koran and daily sexual practices. Most, either credulous of previous reports or hearsay, or witnesses themselves of an occasional case of sodomy, repeated the claim first made during the Middle Ages, that a close affinity existed between sodomitical practices and Islam.[70] Others deduced this from close study of literary texts that often revelled in the beauty of boys,[71] or from archaeological and historical research.[72] Geiger, eager to uphold the image of Awesta culture as 'of high culture', defensively admitted that same-sex practices did occur, even when hardly as commonly as in today's world of Islam.[73] Felix Oefele, also concerned about the moral status of cultures antecedent to Islam, wondered if the evidence of sexually transmitted diseases in Ancient Egypt was to be explained by widespread 'homosexual excess', as it was, so he presumed, at his time.[74]

Less eager to confirm or speculate upon secular claims were the legal scholars who reviewed Islamic and Ottoman law. Among them were Van den Berg, Hughes, Kohler and Sachau, who each encountered stipulations against the 'sin' of sodomy.[75] But Olegna pointed out that homosexuality did not appear as a 'sin' in Islamic catechisms.[76]

In general, the image of widespread sodomy was disseminated in handbooks about the world of Islam[77] and its countries.[78] Colonial experience also added easily to the ongoing popularity of such a stereotype, especially when sodomy was witnessed on the higher levels of administrative or political rule. Thus the *bey* of Tunis, Mohammed al Sadok, who ruled from 1859 till 1882, was said to maintain a harem full of catamites. One among them, Mustapha

Ibn Ismail, managed to gain great influence and was manipulated accordingly by the French financial overseers to have the bey remove the prime minister, Mustapha Khaznadar. As a reward, Ismail was to take his place.[79]

Such pragmatism from the side of colonial policy makers contrasted heavily with their intervention in the life of common Arabs. These remained subjected to a policy of public hygiene and social regulation that was similar to policies in London, Paris or other cities at the homefront. The policing of same-sex relations stood alongside repression or regulation of female and male prostitution, and shared the criminological rhetoric that had been formulated first in the metropolis. The close affinity between both is revealed yet again by the simultaneous discussion of homosexual relations in texts that addressed prostitution in particular.[80]

Problems arose, however, when defining the responsibilities of the active and the passive partner, as this was addressed quite differently by Arab tradition. The rhetoric of criminal offence also combined with speculations on the pathological nature of men and boys who engaged in sodomy regularly. Certainly, the call for precision of diagnosis and judgement challenged the deeply rooted European beliefs that all Arabs were, essentially, sodomites.

'Like all Oriental people, the Arab (too) is a sodomite (Comme tous les peuples de l'Orient, l'Arabe est sodomiste)', said Kocher, whose study on *La criminalité chez les Arabes* (1884)[81] included statistics on sodomy as a criminal offence. Its casuistics contained detailed descriptions of the incriminating facts:

Obs. VIII. – The examination of the trousers of the accused allows us to demonstrate that Mohammed-ben-Ali is indeed guilty. The anus, in fact, of the young Driss was bleeding and the blood inevitably stained the pederast's penis: it is known, moreover, that Mohammed had let his penis out through a hole in the material without taking off his pants and that he had assaulted his victim this way.[82]

Kocher inventoried all kinds of crimes that were committed both by the indigenous population and by the French in the Northern African colonies. The relatively high number of criminal offences committed by the Europeans was misleading, the author insisted, as the Arabs succeeded better, especially in the countryside, in keeping their activities unknown to the world. Yet it was clear to the author that sodomy in the Arab world was not so much 'congenital' as provoked by polygamy: 'one man, spoilt and unnerved by his abuse of pleasure, tries to awaken his desire by sodomy; others become moral hermaphrodites (l'homme blasé, énervé par l'abus des plaisirs, cherche par la sodomie à réveiller ses désirs, dans d'autres ce sont des hermaphrodites moraux)'.

What, one must ask, did he mean by 'moral hermaphrodites'? Kocher suggested that these were, in fact, a 'dirty race, pushed by laziness and love for money to exploit the perverted instincts of those surrounding them (race immonde que la paresse et l'amour du lucre pousse à exploiter les instincts pervertis de ceux qui les entourent)'. He went on portraying both the *sodomiste passif* and the *pédéraste actif*, who did not display any physical characteristics apart, perhaps, from 'the slightly less visible folds of the anus (les plis de l'anus ... légèrement effacés)'[83] of the passive sodomite. If anything, Kocher's description allowed for defining any Arab man as a potential sodomite and thus conformed to existing preconceptions about the endemic character of sodomy in Northern Africa. Indirectly, it also consolidated European theory about 'congenital' versus 'acquired' homosexuality by deducing from the absence of effeminate, passive boys or men, that no 'real' homosexuals existed in the Arab world.

This was a remarkable view, for some evidence in fact showed that such effeminate boys were still known, albeit in a context of prostitution, in many parts of the Arab world. In the preceding chapter, I cited the testimonies about *mukhannathun*. At the time, similar roles were described by Quedenfeldt, Von der Choven, Stern, Hoche, Feenstra Kuiper, and Schumacher.[84] Letourneau too portrayed how 'in some Arab cities, [unnatural love] gives rise even to a special kind of prostitution, that takes place in bright daylight: little boys, dressed like women, walk openly into cafés and offer themselves to men while sitting on their knees.[85] In 1911, Theo Heerman published an article on pederasty among the Sarts, claiming that it had been imported by the Persians.[86] As a part of the Muslim world, Turkestan upheld the Koran law on *liwatagortchilik* (sodomy among adult men), yet witnessed the widely accepted phenomenon of *bačabozlik* or effeminate boys, who dressed like girls, danced and courted adult men. Similar age-structured same-sex relations, where boys dressed up like girls, apparently existed in Tajikistan and Samarkand. Presumably, it had also spread to Russia. The homosocial organization of social life therefore had to be abolished, according to the author, who drew his information from a Russian source. Recent historical studies have shown that the pattern of men-to-boy eroticism was indeed inherent to social traditions in Central Asia. But Heerman's belief that 'moral contagion' could be prevented by such simple measures was based on a very narrow, or at least very naive, understanding of human sexuality.[87]

Overall, the descriptions of same-sex relations in the Muslim world that were published after approximately 1860, displayed intellectual confusion rather than consistency, and uncertainty about what distinguished 'real' from 'circumstantial' homosexuality. Their common, almost implicit message that only very little 'real, congenital' homosexuality occurred in the Muslim world was most probably provoked by the ongoing weight of

European representations of 'endemic sodomy'. Western intervention, moreover, may well have led to further marginalization, privatization and,
eventually, eclipse of certain practices, involving the prostitution of young,
effeminate boys, and leaving no visible signs of gender-structured sexual
roles, that seemed to conform to medical constructions of 'inversion' or
'congenital homosexuality'. The relative absence of cross-gender roles may
thus explain why western observers felt compelled to minimalize the distribution of 'real' homosexuality in the Muslim realm.

Subsaharan Africans and African Americans

Throughout the nineteenth and early twentieth century, some authors
upheld Gibbon's belief that no same-sex practices occurred in Subsaharan
Africa. For example Herman Soyaux, who questioned the Early Modern
Portuguese reports about sodomy in West and West-Central Africa, stated
that he himself had seen no sign of it.[88] Unbelief about autochthonous same-
sex praxis actually went so far as to suggest that the Portuguese, who had
reported it first, had introduced it on the African continent themselves. This
can be read from a report, dating from 1906, on same-sex practices that
surfaced on the mining compounds of Witwatersrand, South Africa. Though
an indigenous Zulu term existed for the 'boy-brides' or *inkothsane*, who
accompanied miners on their work, the author of the report suggested that its
origin was to be found in the relatively short era of Portuguese influence on
the Cape.[89]

The picture of African reluctance to engage in homosexual relations was
also upheld in a handful of texts about African American societies. Corre,
who admitted that 'colonial neurasthenia' led to an overstimulation of the
senses, denied that pederasty was sought out as a means for relief:

The exceptional moral freedom provokes less crime than our own hypocritical
reticence; it does not, against all odds, lead to this morbid eroticism that triggers
troubling acts in France and the indifference towards *amours irrégulières* tends to
exclude some of its abominable consequences.[90]

Jacobus X, for his part, explained the presumably relative absence of male-
to-male sexual relations in French Guyana as the outcome of easily available
women. He reported only two cases of *copulation contre nature*, one of
which was, significantly, performed by an Arab liquor vendor. His victim,
claiming to be raped, was said to engage in anal intercourse regularly,
according to a speculative Jacobus X, 'as his anus clearly showed an
infundibulum'.[91]

Back in Africa itself, Richard Kandt described black sexuality as 'eine ganz
primitive Heterosexualität' with little romantic feeling or sense of privacy.
Referring to Moll's theory, he claimed that the *Kontrektationstrieb* remained
marginal to a far more dominant *Detumeszenztrieb*. This also explained,
said Kandt, why blacks did not kiss and why the *ars amandi* had remained a

closed book to them. 'Boyish excesses and perversions on a hetero- or homosexual level are remarkably rare and among tribes in the interior only known from hearsay (Knabenhafte Exzesse und Perversitäten auf hetero- oder homosexuellen Gebiet sind verschwindend selten und bei den Stämmen des Inneren kaum vom hörensagen bekannt).'[92] And if they did, then this was to be attributed to foreign influence or to an erroneous understanding of personal hygiene – we can only guess, alas, what the author meant, nor did he further comment how 'foreign influence' was to be understood. But Oetker subscribed to Kandt's belief and declared that, despite the putatively 'public' character of African sexuality, neither masturbation nor homosexuality was known.[93]

Cureau, reluctant also to acknowledge that same-sex practices occurred in Subsaharan Africa, claimed that the *vice solitaire* (masturbation) was triggered by alcohol, nervous tension and European influence, whereas the *nsanga* or *servants d'armes* among the Sandeh ought to be seen as of Turkish origin. These were men who oiled their bodies and dressed like women. They were then called upon for sexual intercourse by men who were without wives.[94] Earlier, another observer, Georg Schweinfurth had only indirectly made clear that these *nsanga* were, in fact, male prostitutes.[95]

The idea of Arab 'import' actually proved most convincing and was also put forward by Roscoe, Corre and Baumann. Roscoe claimed that the 'crime against nature', as it occurred in the Uganda protectorate, was imported by the Arabs. Local people frowned upon it and condemned it. It remained altogether very rare.[96] Corre supported the common European view that the black man is very lascivious. Yet, 'while he indulges in lust, he does hardly pursue any unnatural ways to satisfy his debauche (except in some areas where he has learned from the civilizers) (s'il est grossier dans la salacité, au moins ignore-t-il à peu près complètement (sauf en certains foyers où il a pris leçon des civilisants) les façons antinaturelles d'assaisonner la débauche)'.[97] The *civilisants* supposedly were *Arabes ou arabisants*, the latter phrase laying bare how he perceived 'sodomy' as inherent to Arab identity.[98] Such, claimed Corre, could be seen from the Fulbe (Mali): 'Some vices common among the Moors and the Peul are not policed, despite the precepts of the Koran (Malgré les préceptes du Coran, certains vices, communs chez les Maures et même chez les Peuls, ne sont pas réprimés).'[99] The word *même* actually reveals how the author eagerly upheld an artifically constructed boundary – an 'imaginative geography' (Said) – between Arab people who presumably engaged in sodomy, and black Africans who presumably did not. He further documented his claim about the Arab input by describing male prostitutes in Saint-Louis (Senegal) and Boké (Guinea):

In Saint-Louis I met black men dressed like women and imitating their mannerisms in order, I've been told, to make a living out of prostitution. In Boké, I have seen a *griot* in a foulah prince's residence, whose lascivious dances demonstrated clearly which role he performed within the household of his highness. Pederastic habits do not spring from muslim milieus, moreover. The Wolof expression to designate them is of recent origin and in most African languages there is not even one.[100]

The author's insistence on a general, universally valid image, while discussing divergent ethnic groups in what are now Senegal and Guinea is rather troubling. The statement that no linguistic traces of male-to-male relations or homosexual roles could be found were at best speculative.[101]

Oskar Baumann was most determined about the impact of Arabs on sexual mores on the island of Zanzibar:

Contrary sexuality, both congenital and acquired, is relatively common among the black population of Zanzibar while congenital contrariness is rather rare among the tribes of the African interior. . . . The higher incidence in Zanzibar undoubtedly is due to the influence of Arabs who constitute the main contingent of acquired contraries along with the people from the Comore Islands and Swahili halfbloods.[102]

On the African continent he had witnessed only two cases of *Effeminatio* and 'passive' pederasty. The picture on Zanzibar, however, was very different. In addressing the problem, Baumann upheld the taxonomy of von Krafft-Ebing and Westphal, and distinguished between acquired and congenital homosexuality. The former was induced largely by boredom of the Arabs with heterosexual intercourse. Black slaves were trained to become more effeminate (*kulainishwa*), making them into *aficionados* of the trade themselves. Other Africans, according to Baumann's speculative reconstruction, then started to imitate the Arabs, but, since they could not rely on slaves to satisfy their newly acquired taste, a network of male prostitution developed, composed to some extent of the Arabs' effeminized slaves who were sent away.

Angeborene Conträrsexuale, to Baumann, had always been effeminate:

He seeks sexual satisfaction largely through passive pederasty [*kufira* means to penetrate anally, *kufirwa* means to get penetrated anally] or in acts similar to concubinage. From the outside, the congenitally contrary men cannot be distinguished from the male prostitutes, but the locals do make a clear distinction: professional catamites are despised while the behaviour of congenital contraries is tolerated as amri ya muungu (God's will).[103]

But the actual existence of an indigenous term that is not related to Arab terminology did not make the author believe that same-sex praxis may have been an integral part of the African culture on Zanzibar before the beginning of Arab cultural influence. Still, other terms for 'passive male', like *mkesimune* and *mzebe*, are of defined Swahili origin too and coexisted along with the Arabic word *hanisi*.[104]

Obviously the thesis of Arab import, that also gained support from Schneider[105] and Junod,[106] could not be upheld for areas that were more or less remote from the realm of Arab commerce, slave trade and political influence. As ethnographic and anthropological research on African tribal life proliferated, new data were published about same-sex praxis among numerous tribes of the African interior. It had been observed among the Basonge, the Mayombe, the Bangala, the Waganda, the Atonga, the Bantus, the Basuto, the Ewe, the Zulus and the Oromó.[107] Herman Tönjes reported *omaxenge*, 'passive pederasts' in his eyes, among the Ukuanjama of Ovamboland. Somewhat apologetically, he emphasized that such evidence was not to harshen moral judgement: 'Anyone who once looked into the moral corruption of a metropolis will be rather reluctant to condemn the immorality of a people, immersed in heathenism (Wer einmal in den Sumpf sittlicher Verkommenheit einer Grossstadt geschaut hat, der wird auch ein tief im Heidentum steckendes Volk wegen der bei ihm sich findenden Sittenlosigkeit nicht zu hart verdammen).'[108] No pederasty existed among the Wahehe, said Nigmann, who nevertheless admitted that it was known among other tribes.[109] Jacobus X also questioned if masturbation and homosexuality existed in Subsaharan Africa. *Podicatio* did occur, however, among slaves who were deprived of contact with women. Two freed slaves, baptized by the author as Castor and Pollux, did not stop their sexual relations once they regained freedom.[110] In Cameroon, Hammer explained evidence of same-sex praxis among the Duala, 'teils als Raffinement, teils als Laster'.[111] Among the Kru (Ivory Coast), it occurred primarily because too few women were available. No genuine *dritte Geschlecht* existed as such practices were virtually always transient.[112]

Some, such as Skertchly, Bastian and Barret,[113] confirmed the age-old narratives about Dahomey, while others produced new evidence about same-sex practices within a context of shamanism or initiation rites.[114] Van der Burgt, after listing no fewer than five Urundi words for male-to-male sexuality (*kuswerana nk'imbwa, kunonoka, kwitomba, kuranana inyuma, ku'nyo*) and two for what he called 'hermaphrodites' (*ikihindu, ikimaze*), described how their priests belonged to the latter group. He did question, however, if they actually engaged in sexual acts with men.[115] McCall Theal briefly mentioned 'certain horrible customs' that took place during the initiation rites of the Kaffirs, leaving us to assume whether, by this, he meant mutual masturbation, intracrural or anal intercourse. But from earlier reports we can deduce with great probability that acts of homoerotic tenor were indeed suggested.[116]

Paolo Ambrogetti reported same-sex relations between boys and slave-boys, baptized *diavoletti* by the Italian colonizers, in Eritrea:

relations with 'little devils' are not pursued secretively, but tolerated even by the boys' fathers, especially since such services are always paid extra. At the age of adolescence, when the boy is ready for intercourse with women, he generally stops having relations against nature. But cases are known where some 'little devils', who are attached to their patron, continue such relations till the age of eighteen or twenty.[117]

Hardly ever, Ambrogetti claimed, did such relations spring from 'inclination'; mostly they were the outcome of circumstance: 'I have rarely been able to observe that pederasty was pursued by inclination rather than by opportunity. I only remember one chief, who was 25 years old and married. He nevertheless went on pursuing passive sexual relations with men without pecuniary gain.'[118] He continued by stressing that even the effeminacy of some men must not be falsely interpreted as 'sexual inversion':

I discovered also that there are indigenous men, whose bodily shape or behaviour show feminine characteristics. I even met some who imitated women, especially in the make-up of their faces and in their clothing, but I doubt that they are sexual inverts. They were merely seen as fops and effeminate men.[119]

The author deduced that congenital 'sexual inversion' was actually very rare not only in Eritrea but in all healthy societies, that lived close to nature. If present, then it was a sign of physical degeneration of the individual. The freedom, moreover, of sexual life in Eritrea explained why acquired homosexuality, that was so rampant in Italian colleges, barracks and prisons, was so rare in Eritrea.

Dr Lasnet described the *sekatra* among the Sakalaves (Madagascar):

The sekatra are normally built men, but from early childhood onwards and probably because of their rather delicate and refined appearance they are treated like little girls. Step by step they start seeing themselves as women, adopting their clothing, their character, their habits .... When they fancy a man, they offer him money in order to sleep with him and make him have sex with them either in a cow horn filled with grease and put between their legs or by really penetrating them.[120]

Like Rencurel,[121] Emile Laurent portrayed the *sharimbavy* among the Hova, also at Madagascar. A *sharimbavy*, said the French physician-criminologist, walked 'in the slightly unbalanced way of women, pushing their hips backwards (à la manière un peu déhanchée des femmes, faisant saillir le bassin en arrière)'.[122] He wore a big, white robe (*lamba*) and was entirely shaven. He socialized with women from early childhood onwards, but his genitals were normal and his body showed no signs of physical degeneration. From one case, a *sharimbavy* with gonorrhea, the author concluded, in tune with contemporary beliefs, that he had had sexual intercourse with women.

The author then proceeded to ask what was the nature of a *sharimbavy*'s anomaly. Was he a pederast, a male prostitute, or a real sexual invert? Again, the distinction amply reflected the then current opposition of acquired versus inborn homosexuality. To Laurent, a *sharimbavy* was no pederast as he did

not engage in anal or oral intercourse: 'Actually, the anus was not infundibu-
liform and, while not ascribing too much credit to such an unreliable
symptom, it is nevertheless just to point out its absence. The coitus *ab ore*
does not seem to be part of their customs.'[123] But he was no real invert either,
for he was raised like a woman by a mother who felt that she had already had
too many sons. His anomalous status, according to Laurent, was provoked
more by suggestion than by auto-suggestion, and therefore did not fit into
European sexual taxonomy.[124]

Irle as well as Fritsch visited the Herero and were puzzled at the *omapanga*
or 'male friendships' in the homosocial ambiance of the men's house. These
were hotbeds of male-to-male sex, so they believed, yet this could not be real
homosexuality because the men were married at the same time. Marriage, in
the men's eyes, was a sign that their occasional sexual relations with men
were circumstantial.[125]

The data gathered by numerous eyewitnesses in Steinmetz's comparative
study of indigenous law, only document the absence in most Subsaharan
tribal communities of legal sanctions. This, obviously, did not imply that
same-sex relations were not frowned upon, nor did it reveal if such relations
were common or not. Some of the contributors emphasized that cross-gender
roles did exist, but omitted to comment if and how such roles related to male
homosexuality.[126] Only Nicole dissociated gender-structured behaviour
among the Sara (Chad) from homosexuality, only to provoke a critical
comment of Steinmetz himself, who suggested that the cross-dressing men
may well be 'real "effeminés" '.[127]

Other legal studies proved more successful in locating same-sex relations,
even when they too faced the problem of translating indigenous concepts
into European languages or of fitting the distinctions, made by tribal folk,
into western taxonomies.[128] Such were the hazards of linguistic research
about local terms for so-called 'men/women' and cross-gender roles.[129] The
Swahili word *hanithi*, a derivative of the Arabic *hanisi*, was described both
by Krapf and Madan as indicating 'sexually impotent'. But it may not have
had such a biological connotation at all, as it referred to a socially defined
cross-gender role, that did not imply physiological impotence. It tended to
affirm the marginal role of cross-dressing men rather than explain it through
physical inadequacy. The authors' translation, alas, did just that as it reified
the indigenous, symbolic distinction of 'potent'/'impotent' into one of biological necessity. What to make, next, of as simple a translation of the phrase
asiewesa ku kuéa mke as 'sodomite', or of the clearly syncretic expression,
thambi ya watu wa Sodom as 'sodomy'?[130]

As the nineteenth century proceeded, the Enlightenment image of the 'non-
sodomite' black, promoted by Abolitionists, collapsed. Reports that
same-sex relations were unknown to African tribes grew out of tune with the
growing conviction that these too were often not spared from, using Gibbon's words, this 'moral pestilence'. In 1847, the German physician Pruner

had still upheld that same-sex relations had distinguished the Orient from Subsaharan Africa,[131] but as early as 1863, Winwood Reade drew an altogether different portrait of black Africans. Doing away with the Abolitionist assumptions of before, he represented men as 'effeminate' and with small feet, whereas women were aggressive and overly masculine. Rather than indulging in dance, sexual lasciviousness and abuse, the African black ought to be put at work on plantations and in mines, which would not only make him more virtuous but would also increase his longevity.[132]

Ideas such as Reade's gradually became instrumental to the new 'moral basis',[133] that was to justify the colonization of the Dark Continent during the coming years. At some points, same-sex practices in particular gave rise to initiatives to uproot them. This was perceived as most urgent when political or tribal leaders themselves were involved. Alarmed by the well known images of the Dahomey of West-Africa, British missionaries thus felt compelled to sanction Mwanga, the leader of the Baganda (Ganda, Uganda) from 1884 till 1897. He maintained a 'harem' full of pageboys and resisted Christianization as it became clear that anal intercourse had to be renounced. As gradually more and more boys, who had converted to either Protestantism or Catholicism, refused sexual services to Mwanga and his entourage, a conflict arose. When his favourite pageboy Mwafu resisted as well, Mwanga went into a paroxysm of rage and several boys were killed. It is said that about one hundred boys, later turned into the Martyrs of Buganda, had died.[134]

Yet gender disorder, that was now seen as a characteristic of black African population as well, did not trigger a more comprehensive representation of the sexually passive African male comparable to the Asian and American Indian. The image of black male potency, brought to Europe in the wake of the slave trade and the plantation economies in America and the Caribbean, stood in the way of one-dimensional representations of the black African as weak and effeminate. If anything, the new pathologizing rhetoric on his deviant nature and inadequate physique was to focus on his self-indulgence, his search for pleasure, his 'female' volatility.[135] The location of the black man's 'femininity' within the realm of the psyche obviously facilitated racialist projections of sexual disorder where anatomy did not.

Black male sexuality altogether was represented as a kind of repository for various anomalous behaviours, whether hetero- or homosexual, and directed only by a vague, non-differentiated libidinous drive – 'le sentiment romanesque n'y existe pas'.[136] As such, the symbolic status of black people showed great affinity with that of Jewish people, as a qualitatively and quantitatively deviant sexuality was ascribed to them equally. The presumed lasciviousness of both was depicted as symptomatic of their 'hysteric' nature, whether they were male or female, and their genitalia, though mutually different, were 'read' as signifiers of their pathological state.[137]

American Indians

The sexuality of American Indians was also increasingly seen through the looking-glass of modern sexology. Not that indigenous reports of indigenous 'immorality' were no longer produced. Alfred Russell Wallace's description was typical of an age-old display of incomprehension and disgust:

On the subject of the most prevalent kind of immorality, it is impossible to enter, without mentioning facts too disgusting to be committed to paper. Vices of such a description as at home are never even alluded to, are here the subjects of common conversation, and boasted of as meritorious acts, and no opportunity is lost of putting the vilest construction upon every word or act of a neighbor.[138]

This resembles some of the earliest reports by Portuguese missionaries, first getting acquainted with Indian tribes near the coastal areas of Northeastern Brazil.

But Rudolf Arndt applied a biological rather than an ethical vocabulary, that surely reiterated the Buffonian stereotype of the Indians' presumed asexuality, yet diagnosed it now as a *stigma degenerationis*.[139] The sword of biology cut both ways, moreover, when Paolo Mantegazza positioned the Indians above the African blacks despite the occurrence 'from Alaska to Darien, of youths, dressed like women and living in concubinage with their chiefs and other men'.[140]

The professionalization of physical and cultural anthropology lead to a more defined focus on the relationship between homosexuality and ritual, often, but not always personified and carried out by a tribe's shaman. Such occurred, actually, at a time when such rituals were threatened by white or Creole cultural hegemony, aiming at a redefinition of national civilization after western models. Authors like Latcham, Hutchinson, Preuss, Bancroft and Bastian emphasized the ambiguous sexual status of shamans as being constitutional to their power and status and it may well be that the association of both had consolidated the local authorities' repressive policy. Yet, that is a problem that cannot be addressed here.[141]

The focus on cross-gender roles, intensifying since the sixteenth century, can be read from Preuss's description of the Mexican Huichol. This consisted of men who dressed up like women and participated in temple ceremony while they were 'mounted' by a *yuhuname*, an older man. Referring to pre-Christian phallic cult, said Preuss, it seemed to suggest that passive, male sexuality implied transgression of gender boundaries.[142] Karl von der Steinen first portrayed the central place of *baitó*, the men's house, of the Bororó. Women were not allowed. Same-sex relations putatively occurred, though infrequently, with boys who adopted a female role.[143] The Austrian historian–archaeologist von Tschudi took notice of Inca narratives about hermaphrodites (*wanarpu*), who had worshipped the mythological animal, *chuquichinchay*, at the time of Viracocha Yupanqui. While presenting these hermaphrodites at once as 'passive pederasts',[144] he consolidated the image of gender-structured homosexuality, as did the publications of Lomonaco, Kohler and Stoll.[145]

The systematic neglect by European observers of the active partner in same-sex relations may well reveal how only the passive partner of mostly gender-structured male sexuality was considered eligible for a diagnosis as 'genuinely homosexual'. Whereas the passive partner's sexual status was given ontological status through labels like 'passive pederast' or 'invert', one can only guess, alas, at how the above authors explained the active partner's sexual status.

Japan

Along with China, Japan was depicted persistently as a hotbed of sexual indulgence, obviously including pederasty as one of its most blatant and hard to eradicate vices. Since Francis Xavier, very little had changed, especially as the lack of understanding and tolerance had only led to Japan's renewed state of splendid isolation. Pressure from Europe and the United States of America gradually forced the country to open its gates for foreign influence again, more precisely with the ending of the Tokugawa period in 1868.

The increasing knowledge about Japanese culture and society hardly challenged most Europeans' preconceptions, and pederasty still figured prominently in their xenophobic rhetoric about the Japanese.[146] Translations of literature,[147] along with the reproduction of wood engravings with erotic content, only added to the Old World's indignation at the Japanese people's shameless indulgence in non-conformist sexual practices such as masturbation, cunnilingus and, of course, homosexuality.[148] Generally, an image of unchanged, perennial immorality was upheld, that was the outcome of centuries of moral laxity among Buddhist bonzes[149] and shoguns alike.[150] Such narratives hardly deviated from previous ones, described in the preceding chapters, nor did the recurrent stories about the close affinity between theatre, male cross-dressing actors and male prostitution.[151]

In his study on the Shinto ritual *ohara no kotoba*, Weipert stressed that pederasty did not figure among the sins that were to be washed off – a careful attempt at understanding how the Japanese acceptance of male-to-male sexual relations was in fact embedded in religious and cultural tradition and ought therefore to be evaluated differently.[152]

Some authors, on the other hand, attempted to explain how pederasty had become such a prominent habit among the Japanese. They actually seemed to suggest that such was due to circumstances, rather than to a natural propensity inherent to the Japanese people's identity. Wernich, for example, explained it as the outcome of demographic conditions, that made it impossible for men to marry, as was common, at age seventeen. It gave rise to a high number of hysteric men, who either suffered from involuntary ejaculations, or engaged in homosexual relations.[153]

At the end of the nineteenth century, media hysteria arose about a presumed proliferation of 'sodomy' among Japanese male students in their dormitories, aiming mostly at the perverse effects of a too pronounced separation of social life into a male and a female sphere.[154] Paranoia about the corrupting effect of homosocial arrangements in Japan actually paralleled similar fears especially in continental Europe, where a consensus grew that education was to be made co-educational to avoid pupils' excursions into vice. Populist concerns too nurtured such aspirations, and led some, such as Garrett Droppers, to believe that pederasty 'may have helped to retard the growth of population' in Japan. Droppers' claim is relevant as it implied that homo- and heterosexuality were mutually exclusive and thus reflected the then current sexual taxonomy of the West.[155]

The separate remarks by European observers about homosexuality in Japan stood alongside a western-inspired campaign to promote legal reform in Meiji Japan. This would ensure that sodomy was listed as a criminal offence. It became part of the new penal code of May 1873, even though its enactment did not go without Japanese resistance and called for amendments to the new stipulations on sodomy.[156] The criticism of Europeans remained highly influential upon secular discourse about the 'endemic' character of sodomy in Japan, but it was accompanied by a policy of sexual hygiene, that was to regulate homosexual vice.

China

Much of Europe's insistence that China was sodomy-ridden, first initiated by Matteo Ricci centuries before, remained unchanged. Stereotypes, so it turned out, were accredited by European experience with Chinese migrant workers off the Chinese mainland itself. Schlegel, quoting from previous sources such as Barrow and Hüttner, drew an alarming picture of the province of Fujian, where 'unnatural vice had reached its peak'. It had actually facilitated the victory of the European army during the Opium War (1840–2), but gradually, the keeping of *amasii* or 'houseslaves' for homosexual purposes had spread all over China and had reached Peking:

There English and French troops found entire institutes where boys of 11 or 12 years old were trained for male prostitution. They were dressed like girls and instructed in all forms of female *coquetterie*. Prematurely debauched, they are emasculated at age 14 or 15, unfortunate hermaphrodite creatures, neither men nor women. They are fully castrated when becoming permanent residents of those houses at a later age.[157]

Effeminate boys also frequented barbershops, not, as he quoted from Petronius, to get a haircut or a shave, but rather to meet potential clients for their 'sordid' commerce in sex: 'many actually use these places not in order to get their beard shaven, their hair cut or their beard trimmed, but rather in order to pass the night while venerating – not to phrase it indecently – the boy's

behind lasciviously (Quorum frequenti opera, non in tondenda barba, pilis-
que vellendis modo, aut barba raitanda, sed vero et pygiacis sacris cinaedice,
ne nefarie dicam, de nocte administrandis utebantur).'[158]

Schlegel expressed his fear that, in southern China, sodomy, until then
only pursued by the mandarins, would become endemic as well. His suspicion was justified, so he emphasized, as the Canton Chinese, who worked in
the Dutch colony of Indonesia, proved quite devoted to sodomy. The author
explained this as an answer to the lack of available Chinese women far from
home and pleaded for the employment of captured women in the mines. To
buy and import Chinese women from Canton would be too expensive.
Pragmatically, he suggested that, when compared to both alternatives, the
enforcement of prostitution would be most apt of all: 'One can choose
between pederasty, prostitution, and slave trade – we think that the middle
evil is the minor one (Men heeft de keus tusschen pederastie, prostitutie en
slavenhandel – wij meenen dat het middenste kwaad het geringste is).'[159] The
problem of same-sex practices among Chinese coolies contributed, awk-
wardly enough, to European propaganda against the 'yellow peril' and led,
eventually, to pleas for substituting workers of another ethnic stock for the
corrupting Chinese in as far afield as Cuba[160] and South Africa.[161]

These, along with other narratives of the dissemination of sodomy by the
Chinese,[162] gave rise to speculation on how the Chinese may well have played
a role in the rest of Asia, that could be compared to the Arabs' presumed
spreading of sodomy across the African continent. The northern Chinese,
closely related to Tartars and Mongolians, were considered most dangerous,
while the southern Chinese were initially considered of a more 'manly'
stock.[163] Erwin Baelz actually suggested that this was due to an input of virile,
Malaysian blood[164].

Charles Letourneau, on the other hand, perceived no internal difference:

> The Chinese, according to the numerous witnesses, are very loose; they only know
> sensual love, but refined it and introduced smart techniques that other races don't
> know and that I cannot describe here. One also knows that – and there is a
> connection – sexual aberrations are very common among them.[165]

Matignon, in turn, stressed that *pédérastie* was spread all across China as a
manifestation of 'refined and almost sickly sensuality, characteristic for the
Orientals (sensualité raffinée et quasi maladive qui caractérise les Orientaux)'.[166] This is a meaningful remark, especially because the author added
in footnote that in what is now Cambodia and Vietnam pederasty was
imported by Europeans in the first place. Why then this rhetorical reference
to the imaginary Orient, if not to stress the analogy between the sexual
culture of the Chinese and the pathological character, *quasi maladive*, of
homosexuality? As a member of the Lyons school of criminology, Matignon
further suggested that the Chinese, like pederasts in Europe, walk the thin
line between *raffinement* and decadence, the latter meaning a degenerative

surplus of sensitivity. In China too, said Matignon, men flee from their uncultivated and barbarous wives and seek the company instead of 'young catamites, equipped with enough literary baggage ... in order to let them compete successfully in the bachelor's exam (jeunes pédérés, pourvus ... d'un bagage littéraire suffisant pour leur permettre de participer avec avantage aux concours de baccalauréat)'.[167] These boy prostitutes underwent an intensive training, including gradual dilatation of their anal sphincter and the study of classical Chinese literature,[168] but others were less well trained, nor was their clientele as exigent. They often suffered from syphilis and blennorrhagy, the author continued, thus dismantling the erroneous belief that boys were not able to transmit la vérole.

Though relatively accurate, Matignon's narrative hardly differed from the average document, ascribing a kind of 'endemic' sodomy to the Chinese. Those, such as von Samson-Himmelstjerna, who claimed that male-to-male sexuality was more common around the Mediterranean, were in fact exceptions to the rule.[169] As in texts about same-sex behaviour in Japan, those on China are permeated with suggestions of promiscuity, lasciviousness and sexual abuse. Sodomy's link to prostitution and travesty was closely affirmed, though not omnipresent. In general, the widespread character of same-sex practices remained attributed, as before, to the Chinese and Japanese peoples' failing masculinity.

South East Asia

To a large extent, pre-Enlightenment prejudice about a presumed Asian propensity to sodomy continued to be found between the lines of many an observer's description of South East Asian societies. The Dutch ethnologist Wilken, for example, claimed that male homosexual relations, more so than female ones, abounded among the Balinese, the Dajaks, the Achehese, the Madurese and most of the Philippino tribes.[170] Johan Gerard Riedel depicted virtually all ethnic groups of the Indonesian archipelago as 'neuropathic', implying among other things that they engaged easily in 'unnatural' sex.[171] Ferdinand Blumentritt repeated earlier claims that sodomy had been common on the Philippines before the Spanish arrived and added that very little had changed since.[172] Skeat suggested more of the same by stressing the role in indigenous cults of the male beauty of their gods.[173]

Numerous articles, next, were published on the perforation of the penis, that became less common as western influence grew, yet kept haunting European imagination as a sign of Malayan lewdness and lasciviousness.[174] Bengali men, as previously discussed, were subjected to an indiscriminate portrayal of their presumed effeminacy.[175]

In the French colonies of Cochinchine, Tonkin and Annam, pederasty seemed to flourish in ways that made observers wonder at the moral virtue of the indigenous people. Thus Corre described how despite the extraordinary number of courtesans and the great easiness for men to satisfy their sexual drive, or maybe just because of this, indecent assault and rape are common. Satiation, in fact, leads to exhaustion which itself provokes perversions especially among those individuals who are mentally caught up in erotic stimulation by current habits and the obscene legends of religious myths. . . . In *amour antiphysique*, the spoilt ones try to find new excitement.[176]

Jacobus X was perhaps most graphic when portraying the people of Cambodia and Vietnam:

It would be logical to call the people of Annam monkey-people. They deserve this name in a double sense, since the ape is the one among all animals whose genital organ is the smallest in proportion to his bodily size. The monkey is also the only animal that masturbates voluntarily, something in common with the human race. Well, the Annamite, long civilized, is just as lascivious as the ape.[177]

Veering towards the pornographic, he dwelled upon the reddened and overly sensitive gland of *nays* or *paniers*. These were boys between the age of eight and fifteen and were said to masturbate frantically, thus sinking away in deepest perversion. At age fifteen, the *nay* turned into a *boy* and eagerly pursued his perverse games not infrequently with the European colonial officers and employees: 'The European lies down on a long seat with arm supports or on his bed, while the boy, kneeling or squatting down, kisses his penis, sucks on it and takes the ejaculating semen in his mouth to the very last drop (Que l'Européen soit allongé dans un long fauteuil à bras ou couché sur son lit, le *boy*, agenouillé ou accroupi, inguina osculatur, sugit, emissumque semen in bucca recipit, usque ad ultimam guttam).'

But uncertainty persisted about how pederasty had become so common there: was it inherent to the culture of the Annamites? Or were claims, discussed above, that it had been imported by the Chinese more justified? Jacobus X too, while subject still to Tardieu's diagnosis of genital physiology, claimed that the Annamite's debauched mental state was in fact brought on by the Chinese.[178]

But what about the contribution of Europeans themselves? Matignon had blamed them for practising sodomy shamelessly:

Pederasty is widely pursued by our compatriots in Tonkin . . . . In Hanoi, it is not uncommon to be stopped on the main promenade at night . . . by little boys, who speak French – and what kind of French, dear God! – 'M'r cap'tain! Come with me – me titi really piggy!' is the invitation line. The governors-general are rightfully concerned. Severe police measures were taken, but their efforts were never rewarded with success. The best remedy against these evil habits would be to send as many married agents as possible to Indochina: the level of morality could only increase that way.[179]

Such alarming tendency was criticized by ethnographers who felt that their profession was badly served by all too sweeping generalizations about the South East Asian people's presumed indulgence in sexual vice. Julius Jacobs, among others, distinguished clearly between the widely spread practice of sodomy on Bali, as opposed to Lombok, where it was considered criminal.[180] Most probably, the memory of the painful war against the Achehese explained why Jacobs,[181] like Kruyt[182] and Snouck Hungronje,[183] felt compelled to stress that this people indulged in pederasty. Kruyt described how *sedati* or *sedatti*, boys from nine to twelve, were used as catamites, not only by the chiefs, but also by the men who cultivated the pepper fields. After the season, when most men returned to their wives in far remote villages, these *sedati* would remain at the disposal of the overseers of the plantations themselves.

The *sedati* remained undefined in both Kruyt's and Jacobs's narratives, but they may have been boys who dressed like women, as they functioned largely as substitute wives. Other writers did in fact pay attention to the presence of effeminate boys among other tribes in South East Asia and speculated on how this phenomenon was to be diagnosed in the light of new sexological theory. It was not new to them, of course, as they probably had read the publications of Raffles, Schwaner, Hupe and others. They actually continued the descriptive tradition of their predecessors. Roorda van Eysinga felt at ease with a purely semantic analysis: *bantji*, *pâpaq* or *roebiâ* were local, Malayan terms alongside the Arabic *chontza* for 'hermaphrodite'. A 'sodomite' was known, according to Roorda van Eysinga, as a *djindiq* in Malay, as a *orang pâlat* or *orang lawwath* in Javanese and Javanese-Arabic respectively.[184]

Equally imprecise were brief references to *manangs* by St John Spenser,[185] to *kedi* by Klinkert,[186] to *bissu* by Matthes and the brothers Sarrasin,[187] to *gèksà* by Veth,[188] and finally to *gandrungs* by Van Eck and Van der Tuuk.[189] These were cross-gender roles, that had already been pointed out before, but, alas, none of these authors explicated their sexuality apart from a mere claim of passivity. Nor did other, equally vague reports by Levin, Ling Roth, Breitenstein, and Kéraval.[190]

More instructive, especially in view of this current study, were the texts by Perelaer, Van Brero, Berkusky and Kleiweg de Zwaan. For Perelaer, the social status of *bassirs*, effeminate priests, who were sometimes married to men, was indicative of the widespread presence of same-sex relations among the Dajak. To him, this went so far as to become a potential threat, along with cannibalism, to the growth of the population in Borneo.[191] Perelaer remained undecided as to whether these *bassirs* were genuine 'homosexuals' – a question that would only become urgent after the publication of von Krafft-Ebing's *Psychopathia sexualis*, a work which Perelaer probably had not yet read. For Van Brero, however, this had become a focus of attention as he claimed that these cross-gender roles could not be compared to real homosexuals: 'The change of one's gender must not be confused with contrary sexuality. It is more similar to the imaginary change of gender, that can be seen among lunatics.'[192] Clearly aware of von Krafft-Ebing's dualistic scheme, van Brero compared the 'imagined' *Efeminatio* to similar mental processes occurring with Moroccan *marabouts* or Indian *yogis* and *fakirs*. He felt that it was distinct from the *konträre Sexualempfindung* also, as it was defined by von Westphal, just because it was triggered by the hypnotic character of shamanic rituals. Very different, however, was the case of young boys or *wandu*, whom he saw on the island of Java, and who showed signs of physical effeminacy from early childhood.[193]

H. Berkusky, in turn, stated that not only the sexuality of the *bassirs* but also that of their male partners is to be considered as genuinely 'homosexual':

The presence of such a class of male prostitutes indicates that homosexual inclinations are obviously widely spread among the primitive tribes of Borneo; many men engage in lasting love relationships with a basir. Among the maritime Dajaks in Northern Borneo formal marriages are sealed between such priests and young men. Similar facts also occur in other areas of Indonesia.[194]

One cannot infer if, by 'homosexual', he means the 'congenital' or the 'acquired' kind. The homosocial organization, implying that men and women slept separately in collective sleeping halls, actually promoted homosexuality, said Berkusky, who omitted to explain how this came about. He did point out that homosexual relations may occur outside the pattern of age-structured relations, as opposed to relations in the Arab world that most commonly implied that the passive partner be a younger boy. His emphasis, meanwhile, upon the fact that no inevitable relation existed between homosexuality and cross-gender behaviour would prove to be very accurate, yet was definitely at odds with the predominant beliefs of his time.[195]

A more careful position was taken, finally, by Kleiweg de Zwaan, who claimed homosexuality and masturbation to be rare in South East Asia as men and women were able to marry at an early age. When occurring, it was to be seen mostly as an *Ersatz* solution for adolescent boys. In Central Sumatra, he did witness *anak dwaji*, to be translated literally as 'cow boys' and meaning 'passive boys' rather than what is suggested by the word in an American context. These, so Kleiweg de Zwaan suggested, were to be seen as genuinely homosexually inclined.[196]

In essence, Kleiweg de Zwaan's position was typical of a more general tendency to focus on the passive, effeminate roles exclusively, whereas the same-sex practices of their active partners were diagnosed as merely 'circumstantial'. Such a thesis, though never made explicit in such a clearcut way, not only consolidated the already century-old link between sodomy, now homosexuality, and sexual passivity, but also tightened the knot between homosexual perversion and the transgression of gender boundaries. When these conditions were not fulfilled, observers were reluctant to acknowledge that, in these cases too, same-sex praxis may spring from an inborn drive or propensity.

Australia and the Pacific Islands

Such a reading of ethnographic data – that they not only reflected current, sexological ideas about the nature of homosexuality, but also consolidated these – can also be seen, finally, from documents on the sexual cultures of Australian Aborigines and Pacific people. The past weighed heavily and ethnographic discourse on sexuality in the Pacific world also maintained an image, albeit tarnished, of innocence and hospitality, that authors inherited from their predecessors of the Enlightenment. Jacobus X, for example, accused the British of having infested *la nouvelle Cythère* with puritan vigilance, suggesting indirectly that, if sodomy was present at all, it was largely due to western, corrupting influence.[197] Hagen and Sorge claimed that 'gewisse Laster' were unknown in Kaiser Wilhelmsland[198] and Neumecklenburg.[199] Basil Thomson related that a European had been sent away by the Fijian king Thakombau, because he had engaged in homosexual relations with indigenous men. That such relations were not common among the Fijians was carelessly deduced from the semantic meaning of the term *vavavala valalangi* as 'imported from the white man'.[200]

Yet, evidence of same-sex relations had become substantial as the culture and society of so many different ethnic groups were laid out in new, more or less accurate ethnographic reports. To some extent, the focus was upon cross-gender roles, even when these became less visible due to western pressure and influence. But descriptions of this phenomenon had altered slightly as observers wondered not only what constituted the 'anomalous' status and behaviour of the *fa'afafine* and its equivalents, but also if there was a connection with homosexual perversion, as described in sexological publications at home. How inevitable also was the relation between perversion and effeminacy?

George Pratt, when explaining the word *fa'afafine* in his *Samoan Dictionary* of 1862, presented this role as 'belonging to women', yet seemed to suggest that no immediate connection with same-sex relations was implied.[201] Edward Tregear also portrayed the *tarorirori*-role among the Paumotua largely as a cross-gender role without biological connotation – like Pratt's, a very 'postmodern' position in fact.[202] George Turner stressed the meaning of indigenous beliefs about household gods who incarnated into a male or a female, depending on whether he/she wanted to sleep with a woman or a man. In Samoa, such a god was called Satia.[203] Similarly, Kubary explained the tolerance of cross-gender roles among the Palau as the outcome of their belief in ambisexual household gods and in an original human being, who presumably gave birth to the first woman and the first man, but who was sexless itself.[204]

Von Bülow depicted *fa'afafine* as exponents of biological disorder, however, an 'hermaphrodite' at that, whose physical appearance revealed a 'constitutional anomaly'.[205] James Waterhouse too stressed how 'hermaphrodites' on the Fiji Islands displayed an anomalous sexual build.[206]

Yet, the acquisition of more intimate knowledge about the social life of indigenous tribes provoked a significant shift away from the cross-gender roles that had received most attention until then. Kubary claimed that *outibenet er a ptil*, interpreted by the author as anal intercourse among adult men, was relatively rare but not nonexistent on the Palau Islands. Nor was it illegal, though talking about it in public was taboo: 'Pederasty between adults also, called Outibenet er a ptil, is not unknown, even when this occurs seldom. ... Public discussion [of it] is also frowned upon.'[207] He asked rhetorically if the people of Palau were really that far removed from the civilized world.

Franz Hernsheim reported same-sex relations among adolescent boys, that occurred along with heterosexual ones and were not attached to a particular social role.[208] Adolph Bastian's study on Hawaii inventoried *aikāne* or 'sodomy', first described by James Cook, alongside polygyny, polyandry, abortion and infanticide.[209] In the Kimberley District of Western Australia, Edward Hardman had seen *chookados*, boys above the age of five who became substitute-wives to adult men until they reached the age of ten. When asked about the sexual character of such 'marriages', the interviewees 'repudiate[d] with horror and disgust the idea of sodomy'.[210] Ravenscroft reported age-structured relations between younger boys and older men.[211] Von Hellwald reproduced an unidentified description of *ikoa* or intimate friendships among Nukahuva men on the Marquesas Islands,[212] while Joachim Pfeil quoted from an equally unidentified, English source on mutual masturbation among men in Neumecklenburg:

The natives of New-Pommern occasionally accuse each other of masturbation. In New-Mecklenburg this vice is practised to such an extent that the men are said to be practically independent of their wives. They bring their genitals together wrap a piece of leaf round them, tie it and then put their bodies into a swinging motion till the desired result is obtained.[213]

Dempfwolff claimed that on the Bismarck Islands pederasty was just a children's game,[214] whereas Alfred Haddon 'never heard of any unnatural offenses in the Straits, though sodomy [was] largely practised among the Mowat in Daudi [New Guinea]'.[215] At the same time, Beardmore witnessed a ceremony among the Kiwai and the Mowat, in which a boy leaves his father's house to reside in the men's house, where men copulate anally with him.[216]

The male, homosocial initiation rites of many a tribe in Melanesia and Australia called for special attention. After Foley's testimony on military, male brotherhoods in New Caledonia that were tied to 'pederastic' practices,[217] others too focused on the various forms of ritualized same-sex practices. British residents in Australia paid much attention at first to the *mika*-operation, that took place among some of the Aboriginal tribes. This was a subincision of the initiate's penis, which appliance went along with sexual relations with adult men. The opening then functioned as a kind of orifice for sexual purposes and, often, its owner was said to have a vagina. Speculation grew as to whether such practice was seen by the participants as a substitute solution for vaginal intercourse or rather as an apology for pederastic relations between adolescent boys and adult men.

Purcell claimed that the latter was indeed the case and described how older men were given boys of about five to seven years. These, called *mulla-wongha*, would serve as substitute brides. Purcell's interpretation actually may have been inspired by the practice of swallowing sperm, by then seen in Europe as a 'perverse' sexual activity, that only homosexually inclined men would pursue. His description now was fairly detached and may have led him to acknowledge the symbolic dimension of such practice, were he not informed by contemporary sexual pathology:

> After the third initiation into this remarkable ceremony the youth is made to drink semen that is taken from 6 or as many young clean gins and blacks, as may be in the camp at the bora ground. No gins are admitted to the ceremony other than these. When an old man is dying, they do exactly the same. They hold, that as semen brought them into the world, it should keep them alive and from dying; and when a man dies, they think that the semen germinates and even comes through the earth again and appears in the form of a white man or something else, often a star.[218]

Richard Helms too was somewhat misled by the ritualized emission, either orally or anally, of seminal fluid and explained penis subincision accordingly as a disguise for same-sex intercourse.[219] Hermann Klaatsch confirmed this theory, but explained the occurrence of pederastic acts as the outcome of polygamy. As the elderly men owned more women, some men remained without wives and were forced to seek sexual satisfaction with younger boys.[220] Schmidt supported Klaatsch's theory and considered the *mika*-operation to be aimed directly at the pursuit of pederastic acts.[221] Similar support can be found in Ferdinand von Reitzenstein's text.[222]

A different position was taken by the British anthropologist Matthews who pursued a more comprehensive and comparative study of numerous Australasian tribes. Pederasty, so he discovered, occurred among the Murrumbidgee, the Kamilaroi, the Kurnu, the Darkinung, the Kumbainggeri, the natives of Victoria, the Brabirrawulung, the Yota-Yota, and the Tyattyalla, all ethnic denominations that did not apply the *mika*-operation at all. So why would it have been called upon if pederasty hardly seemed to be a big deal? Same-sex relations did occur mostly, however, within a context of initiation rites and Matthews claimed accordingly that the ubiquity of pederasty among the Aboriginals ought to be seen as a means of deterring growing boys from pursuing it during their adult lives.[223]

Yrnö Hirn, in his study on *The Origins of Art* (1900), supported Matthews' idea:

Knowing the degree of immorality [among] many savage tribes, one may readily understand that the old men in the tribe have resorted [to] these radical means of dissuading the boys from vice. And one feels tempted to apply Mr. Matthews' explanation to similar rites in other tribes than the Kamilaroi. The initiation ceremonies of the Amazulus, for instance, which would in no case be possible in any but extremely degenerate nations, might be explained on the same hypothesis.[224]

Narratives on the *mika*-operation in Australia stood alongside reports of initiation rites in Polynesia, Micronesia and especially Melanesia, where they have remained largely in use until today. It is virtually impossible, however, to discover a pattern in the authors' all too often brief and inadequate descriptions. Hagen's study, already referred to briefly, was perhaps closest to ethnological reality as he connected the occurrence of age-structured sexual relations between men and boys to the ritualized circumcision (*mulung airas*), that took place within the compounds of the 'men's house'.[225] Other testimonies, alas, were either fragmentary, not seldom because of moral reticence, or speculative. The British clergyman James Chalmers witnessed 'sodomy' within the context of male initiation among the Bugilai of New Guinea.[226] So did the German ethnologist Richard Parkinson among the Tolai on New Britain (Bismarck Isles), as he reported how, within the secret society of the Ingriet, the 'abomination' took place between an older man and a young initiate in the culthouse or *balana marawot*. Parkinson stressed that pederasty was not a crime in the eyes of the natives, who merely regarded it 'in an amusing light'.[227] Max Moskowski interpreted the exclusively male rituals as a way for men to get away from female dominance and explained their practising sodomy as a deliberate alternative to the struggle for power between women and men.[228] Otto Finsch ascribed the pederastic praxis of the Ponapé (Caroline Islands) to the people's poorly developed intellect and laziness.[229] Jules Rémy thought simply that the small, constricted housing constituted a hotbed for male-to-male sexual relations between men and boys as well as among men.[230] Stoll blamed poverty and polygamy.[231] Corre did so equally: 'The insufficient number of women leaves the burning desires of the overexcited men unanswered; their needs thus push the man into perversions (pederasty allegedly is common) (La proportion insuffisante des femmes expose malheureusement les ardeurs du mâle, surexcitées, à demeurer sans satisfaction; le besoin entraîne alors l'homme à des perversions (la pédérastie serait commune)).'[232] Jacobus X, finally, subscribed to the theory that same-sex relations in the Pacific region were inspired by necessity and circumstance, rather than by any natural predisposition among its people itself. As opposed to Oriental men, who supposedly displayed a remarkable sexual versatility, Pacific folk engaged in homosexual relations only reluctantly.[233]

When assessing European descriptions of the Pacific Peoples' sexuality, it becomes clear that their narrative has moved away from the initial focus on the cross-gender roles alone. Instead, it dwelled increasingly on the other manifestations of sexual non-conformity, that did not imply transgression of gender boundaries beyond the merely sexual. This very fact, along with an awareness of the temporary, 'transitional' character of same-sex relations, may have encouraged some authors to suggest that 'real' homosexuality was in fact a rarity in the Pacific world as well. For genuine homosexuality would not only imply a display of physical, vestimentary and occupational characteristics that were manifestations of a so-called 'third sex'. It would also mean that such a role was upheld during one's entire life.

At first sight, discourse on Pacific and Aboriginal same-sex practices was at odds with contemporary theory, as it upheld a rhetoric about pederastic *acts* in the first place. But, when looked at more closely, one may perceive how the ethnographic record itself consolidated such a theory and its artificially constructed cognitive divide between 'circumstantial' and 'congenital' homosexuality. At the same time, narratives of the ubiquity of pederastic relations were to emphasize the Primitive and degenerate character of homosexuality. While relatively accurate, when confronted with actual studies on 'ritualized homosexuality' in Melanesia by Herdt, Bleibtreu-Ehrenreich and Schievenhoevel,[234] these documents also contributed to the highly ideological and biased reification of (homo-)sexual identity. The insistence by most observers that 'genuine homosexuality' did not occur actually supported rather than refuted the validity of sexual taxonomies at the home front.

Comparative ethnology and the matrices of homosexuality

The accumulation of new ethnographic data naturally facilitated the development of comparative ethnology. Evidence, organized alongside a vertical axis of ethnic monographs, was now laid out horizontally as well in a more or less specialized form of comparative surveys. Some, like Ratzel, Waitz, or Reclus,[235] were very ambitious in their goal, whereas others focused on separate items like legal systems (Bastian, Post, Kohler, Steinmetz),[236] religion (Frazer, Van Gennep),[237] or psychology (Bastian, Schultze, Letourneau, Wundt).[238] Yet other textbooks aimed at inventorying the position of women (Jaekel, Ploss and Bartels, Friedenthal)[239] or children (Ploss and Benz),[240] and included matters of sexuality. Occasionally, ethnological surveys of initiation rites, male and female social organization or vestimentary codes addressed issues of sexuality as well.[241] Eventually, a handful of ethnological surveys focused specifically on sexual life across the globe (Kohler, Müller, Stoll, Freimark, Berger, Buschan).[242]

None of the surveys above pays systematic attention to same-sex behaviour, however. The authors of two other articles, though promising, remained too eclectic in their choice of material and abstained from developing a more comprehensive theory.[243] An early attempt at including homosexuality in comparative ethnology was made by Friedrich von Hellwald, whose 'cultural history' was strongly defined by considerations of a biological tenor. Within the ever recurring pattern of rise and decline, moral decay was just a natural part of societal development. Influenced by Darwinian theory, von Hellwald drew a universal pattern, going from an original simplicity and innocence to the proliferation of asocial behaviour, including sexual behaviour, that undermined the survival of a society. Ancient Rome, according to von Hellwald, witnessed moral relaxation, which brought about 'vice ... , that we call unnatural, even when (it is) no specific product of civilization either (Laster ... , die wir, obwohl kein spezifisches Erzeugniss der Cultur [sic], unnatürlich nennen)' – a remarkable phrase, that reveals the author's confusion at whether homosexuality belonged to the realm of either nature or culture.[244]

Homosexuality was also said to have characterized the decline of classical Islamic society under Persian influence:

The best and most comprehensive observations about the nameless immorality and cynical lust, combined with measureless oriental luxury also in the higher social circles of Baghdad, can be found in the writings of contemporary poets. As pederasty (spread) in Rome due to Greek influence, so too did Persian influence lead almost simultaneously to a dissemination of pederastic vice among the Arabs, who did not know it before.[245]

Meanwhile, von Hellwald claimed that homosexuality was common also among natural folk. The author's fuzzy etiology – natural or decadent? – in fact reflected ambiguity in a wider sense as well, since Roman decay was not only explained by moral laxity, but also by a presumably increasing share of meso- and brachycephalic people, found later in the ruins of Pompeii. What, one may ask von Hellwald, did define human sexuality after all? Was it culture? Or biology?[246]

Other writers carefully avoided the dilemmas raised by von Hellwald's naturalist theory of history and claimed homosexuality to be part of culture, not infrequently of cultural decadence. The Catholic ethnologist Joseph Müller insisted that 'unnatural acts' were unknown to primitive people. 'The sexual anomaly that forms the base of homosexual inclinations and that leads to male brothels in civilized nations, is far removed from people who live close to nature (Die Triebanomalie, welche den homosexuellen Gepflogenheiten zugrunde liegt und welche schon zu Männerbordellen bei . Kulturnationen führte, ist gleichfalls den der Natur näher stehende Stämmen fernliegend)'.[247] He went so far as to desexualize Greek παιδερασθεια, reducing it to a purely Platonic relationship of friends. It was only later, according to Müller, that it degenerated into something sexual.[248]

Buschan, referring to cultures as divergent as China, Japan, Sumatra, Borneo, Zanzibar, Mexico, Guatemala and Peru, concluded that homosexuality outside Europe was most often an 'acquired taste' and seldom 'inborn'.[249]

To Otto Stoll, homosexuality was basically an 'inborn physical disposition', and such can also be upheld to an extent for societies outside the West:

One can assume a priori that there is always a number of individuals among non-European people, who embody the bad, sterile aberration of the human species from birth. This, in fact, can be demonstrated in Japan and East Africa. Congenital homosexuality probably also exists in other areas.[250]

But ethnographic reports, said Stoll, were to be read cautiously since the authors' notion of what constituted homosexuality may differ from what the interviewees upheld themselves. The latter, so it seemed, only saw anal penetration (Podikation) as 'homosexuality', whereas kissing or mutual masturbation remained within the realm of innocence. Obviously, not the indigenous peoples' definitions were the issue, but rather the incapability of ethnographic language to translate them into western vocabulary.

Stoll himself deduced from ethnographic literature that homosexuality occurred in four different contexts. It first pertained to the world of religious ritual, as was documented both historically by the cult of Cybele, the Roman galli (eunuchs), the effeminates reported by Herrera, de Oviedo, de Landa, de Gomara and Torquemada, and anthropologically by Hammond's report on mujerados. All could be compared to the Lustknaben in Baumann's article on Zanzibar.

Homosexuality could also be provoked by poverty in polygamous societies as in Polynesia, or by demographic disequilibrium as among the Chinese coolies across the world. Thus also was its occurrence to be understood amidst the French-African army, and in Buddhist and Christian convents alike.[251]

Homosexuality, next, was part of Greek culture, that influenced areas as separate as Turkey and Spain. It originated from a mythical belief in the meaning of sperm as Seele, implying the ritualized performance of homosexual acts. Contrary to available evidence, Stoll compared Greek pederasty to pre-Columbian cultures of America, where same-sex relations were most currently gender-structured. While doing so, the author represented the passive partner in both Greek and pre-Columbian culture as identical to the modern Weibling:

From the numerous sources we can at least conclude that a certain number of men with a congenital or an acquired feminine psyche can be found among the

American people also. They assume the passive role during homosexual intercourse, while the active role is performed by the virile individuals of a particular tribe.[252]

The further development of culture eventually would make tolerance of homosexuality unacceptable. Same-sex praxis was thus stigmatized in Europe as well as in late Aztec and Inca society. Whereas it persisted in the coastal region of Veracruz, it was banned by king Nezahualcoyotl of Texcoco as well as by Capac Yupanqui in Peru.[253]

Heinrich Ploss objected to Johann Jakob Bachofen's desexualized image of pederasty. Bachofen's influential study *Das Mutterrecht* (1861) presented pederasty as an idealized kind of love, that was not expressed physically. It offered an alternative to heterosexual, physical intercourse, that aimed at reproduction only,[254] yet virtually turned traditional morality upside down. This provoked criticism by Ploss, who maintained that same-sex relations were basically hedonistic and depraved, lacking spiritual depth. Yet, he admitted too, after reviewing evidence from Persian, Jewish, Northern African, East African, Turkish, Chinese, Pacific and American Indian cultures, that it was not essentially 'primitive' nor necessarily 'decadent'.[255]

Of the sexologists who addressed homosexuality and were reviewed earlier in this chapter, only von Krafft-Ebing included a brief comparative ethnographic approach, even if only in the later editions of his *Psychopathia sexualis*. Referring to Müller's *Sexualleben der Naturvölker*, the author claimed that a sense of shame already altered humanity's sexual life at an early stage and that 'raw anomalies of sexuality can already be called phenomena of degeneration at this early stage (rohe Auswüchse des geschlechtlichen Lebens schon auf dieser Stufe eher als Entartungserscheinungen ... anzusprechen sind)'.[256] Evidence of moral laxity at later stages was to be seen as a sign of a temporary relapse into a more primitive stage. The gradual evolution towards monogamous, heterosexual relationships, strongly promoted by Christianity, according to the Catholic von Krafft-Ebing, could hardly be denied. Such a teleological perspective did not exclude the possibility that moral decay may well lead to a single culture's overall decline. Historically, this was the case with Babylon, Nineveh, Greece, Rome and France at the times of Louis XIV and Louis XV:

Epochs of moral decline in the history of people coincide usually with times of effeminization, frivolity and luxury. ... In such times of national decline many often genuinely monstrous sexual aberrations can be seen, that nevertheless can be reduced partially to the psycho- or at least neuro-pathological state of the population.[257]

Similar symptoms could be observed in the metropolitan centres of contemporary Europe, whereas they were virtually absent among primitive folk. Von Krafft-Ebing's thesis did not prove entirely sound, however, as the presumably urban sexual 'aberrations' occurred among several primitive people as well. In a footnote added to the later editions, this was admitted by reference to Lombroso and Bloch.[258]

Thus, during the period 1860–1918 there emerged an ambiguous image, representing 'homosexual deviance' as both a degenerative syndrome *away from* an original, heterosexual drive, and a regression *into* an original, 'polymorph' sexuality. A Darwinian perspective would permit documenting how modern homosexuality could be retraced to its 'primitive' antecedents. Degeneration theory, on the other hand, was conducive to a nullification of 'genuine' homosexuality in primitive contexts, for this was connected exclusively to modern civilization as a symptom of decadence. The ethnography of male same-sex behaviour accordingly reflected the divergent theories concerning homosexual identity in the West.

Travellers, traders, missionaries, and armchair compilers of ethnographic surveys who were not acquainted with innovative trends in sexual theory, repeated, rather uncritically, the earlier narratives' stereotypes of an unchangeable, static Oriental, Primitive, or in any case 'exotic' reality. Evidence of same-sex relations among men was either seen as symptomatic of indigenous immorality and therefore justifying colonization, or included in a somewhat voyeuristic, exoticist portrayal of *couleur locale*. Few, if any, questions were raised about the more precise outlook, significance or etiology of same-sex relations, as they were merely perceived as typifying the other's 'otherness'.

Structurally, such incidental descriptions consisted of a purely tautological conjunction of sexual and cultural characteristics, leaving little room for a more contextualized anthropological understanding of the meaning of sexuality, such as male-to-male sexual relations within a particular ethnic population. If anything, they represented sexuality as a carrier of 'otherness', a view shared by authors who *were* acquainted with new theories of sexual practices, roles and identities. Many among the latter category were scientifically trained. A large group among them were physicians. Others were criminologists, physical or cultural anthropologists. The use of biological science for a new understanding of humanity's flaws (disease, deviation, crime) explains why these experts of the human body and mind felt called upon to participate in the public debate on matters of sex.

Sharing the diachronic perspective, however, of evolutionary theory, such writers restructured the field of sexual desire, separating socially desirable from unacceptable, criminal and/or pathological sexual practices, and defining the limits of individual responsibility in the light of evolutionary theory. The linear schemes of 'evolution' and 'degeneration' both called for feedback from the anthropological side in the form of ethnographic data and cross-cultural surveys, legitimizing sexual taxonomy and social policy.

But ethnographic data did not allow for sweeping generalizations, and challenged attempts at constructing simplistic geographical maps of 'homosexual vice' that were consistent with evolutionary theory. Not only did same-sex behaviour, in particular, occur unequally among so-called 'primitive' or 'half-civilized' people, but its social and cultural contextualization was too divergent to justify any simple, straightforward etiology. This proved fundamental as ethnographers were unable to align information on same-sex relations among indigenous people with the new, narrowly defined psychopathological definitions of 'congenital homosexuality'.

Seen as being closest to such a description of the modern homosexual were cross-gender roles, especially among American Indians and in South East Asia, but even here, ethnography gave rise to scepticism as such cross-gender roles were often limited to the confines of religious ritual and/or shamanism, which made them look deliberately 'assumed' rather than 'dictated' by virtue of biological constitution. The affinity between cross-gender roles, theatre and male prostitution in China and Japan also compelled observers to question the congenital character of same-sex relations in such contexts. Eventually, these same gender-structured role patterns, that had dominated pre-1860s discourse on non-western same-sex behaviour and had consolidated contemporary theory of 'sodomite' identity, tended to be at odds with what was by then known in the West as 'homosexuality' or 'inversion'.

It is clear from the above, on the other hand, that if 'real' homosexuality was diagnosed externally, it remained linked to a 'feminine core'. The variety of accumulating ethnographic data could not prevent same-sex behaviour outside the West, that was seen as indicatory of 'real homosexuality', from implying a transgression of gender boundaries. Thus the genuinely 'homosexual' character was stressed of berdaches among American Indians, of some cross-gender individuals in Madagascar and Zanzibar, and of the *bassirs* of the Malayan archipelago.

Other forms of same-sex relations, many of which were age-structured (men with boys) were most commonly diagnosed as 'circumstantial' or as symptoms or signs of a people's low morality, rarely as genuine homosexuality. This may be explained by the contemporary assumption that homosexuality was a permanent, pathological state. Ethnographic evidence of the 'transient' character of many such age-structured same-sex relationships, often anteceding heterosexual marriage, thus allowed for interpreting such relations as being prompted by demographic disequilibrium or by cultural habit. The inclusion of same-sex acts mostly between boys and men within a ritualized context of initiation, was also seen as distinct from real homosexuality. Easily denounced as immoral and repugnant, such practices were considered at odds with the new psychopathological construction of modern homosexuality. Occasional boy 'harems' in North, West or East Africa were played down similarly as demonstrations of royal abuse of power and represented as a signifier of primitive despotism.

So, at first sight, theoretical speculations on the 'primitive' dimension of homosexuality seemed to be surpassed by an ethnographic discourse that contradicted such simple analogy. The hypothesis that nineteenth- and early twentieth-century 'morbid anthropology' (Stepan) leaned largely upon a logic of analogy seems invalid when applied to late nineteenth-century discourse on male-to-male sexuality. Evidence of the latter outside the West could not, so it seemed, be aligned with medical and psychiatric data on homosexual perversion in Europe itself. No analogy could be upheld, accordingly, between both. But the ethnographers' insistence on the difference between 'circumstantial' sodomy/pederasty in overseas cultures and genuine 'homosexuality' at home must not distract the historian from recognizing a pattern of analogous reasoning, albeit on a less literal level than the comparison of minorities within and outside the West. This did not result from the internal logic of sexological theory, but rather from the diachronic, evolutionist paradigm that framed discourse on both sexual and cultural difference.

Evolutionism or, as its mirror image, degeneration theory provided a structure that allowed for comparing the 'homosexual' minority in Europe with presumably 'endemic' forms of sexual perversion outside Europe. Thus effeminacy, transvestism, but also promiscuity and sexual violence were suggested as characteristics at once of inferior races and of European homosexuals, even when no strict relationship existed between these traits and same-sex praxis itself. The widespread idea, made popular by the opposition of *Kontrektations-* and *Detumeszenztrieb* by Albert Moll, of primitive 'orgiastic' sexuality as the contrary image to a civilized sexuality that focused on love and procreation, was also reflected in representations of 'homosexual' desire as hedonistic, promiscuous, egocentric. Reinforced, meanwhile, by new ethnographic data about same-sex practices in areas that until then were largely believed to be exempt (Subsaharan Africa, less so the Pacific Islands), one could uphold an image of the ubiquity of sexual deviance among virtually all primitive people, while simultaneously accentuating how its etiology was essentially different from the one applied to European homosexuals. Thus, the 'geography of perversion', that remained solid as the logic of analogy was sustained, allowed for presenting as 'endemic' among less developed cultures, what was identified in a European context as a case of a degenerative pathology. The paucity of documents emphasizing a *formal* similarity between Western homosexuals and sexual roles outside the West, must not obfuscate the historical weight of a coinciding, yet hidden *discursivité*, that stressed the affinity between some 'endemic' characteristics of indigenous sexuality and identity and 'minority' sexuality in the West, *even when their etiologies were formulated in distinctly different ways.*

The ascription of 'congenital' homosexuality to indigenous forms of male-to-male sexual praxis proved improbable. Since all non-western people were considered as occupying an inferior position on the evolutionary scale, same-sex praxis was seen merely as an integral part, an obvious sign of their lower status. But it could not be seen as originating from an innate impulse, shared by virtually every man, as this would have led to the extinction of the race. Presenting indigenous homosexuality as a 'minority trait', on the other hand, would acquit a majority, which went against the imperatives of racialist rhetoric. In the end, same-sex praxis, though not labelled 'genuine homosexuality' was depicted as a characterizing trait of non-western people, whose sexuality was considered distinct from and inferior to the white race's superior sexuality. Racial evolutionism, in other words, impelled ethnographers to present male-to-male sexuality as 'endemic', rather than confined to a minority while at the same time reducing the scope of 'congenital' homosexuality.

The weight of racialist discourse thus proved considerable as the very distinction of 'congenital' versus 'circumstantial' homosexuality itself allowed for simultaneously upholding an etiological model of 'endemic' homosexuality when applied to non-western societies, and a 'minority' model when applied to the West. Representations of the presence of male-to-male sexual praxis among less developed people eventually consolidated the analogical structure of human anthropology in an evolutionary context. More specifically, it sanctified the newly conceptualized medical stigmatization of same-sex praxis at once as a sign of inferior evolutionary status ('endemic sodomy/pederasty') and of 'degenerate', pathological heritage ('homosexuality'). In the end, post-1860s discourse on same-sex behaviour outside the West continued the logic of analogy that had struck roots centuries before, and consolidated it as an integral part of evolutionary human anthropology. Though complex and often most intricate, the new geographical map of homosexual perversion both reflected and corroborated the late nineteenth- and early twentieth-century construction of race, gender and sexual identity as a single project of *civilization*.

Notes

1. N. L. Stepan, 'Biological degeneration: Races and proper places', in J. E. Chamberlin and S. L. Gilman (eds), *Degeneration* (New York, 1985), p. 112.
2. See J.-P. Aron, *Le pénis et la démoralisation de l'occident* (Paris, 1978), p. 62.
3. See the 'Introduction' by T. J. Bonner and R. May in the re-edition of Darwin's *The Descent of Man, and Selection in Relation to Sex* (Princeton, 1981), pp. 5 ff.
4. Dr Dautheville, ' "Le cafard" ou psychose des pays chauds', *Aac*, 26 (1911), 13.
5. 'Le déraciné devient aisément sodomite. [... mais] l'homosexualité vraie est très rare ... Beaucoup sont, par nécessité ... sodomites, mais les homosexuels sont une rareté. Le manque des femmes ou la présence de mégères arabes ou noires, sales, malodorantes, vermineuses, pousse le déraciné à s'adresser aux éphèbes, à les préférer. Ce sont des occasionnels qui reviennent à la normale dès retour dans le Nord.' *Ibid.*, pp. 13–14.
6. A. Corre, *L'ethnographie criminelle d'après les observations et les statistiques judiciaires recueillies dans les colonies françaises* (Paris, 1894), pp. 13–15, 34–5.
7. F. Cooper and A. L. Stoler, 'Tensions of Empire: Colonial control and visions of rule', *American Ethnologist*, 16 (1989), 618.
8. See the pioneering articles by A. L. Stoler, 'Making Empire respectable: the politics of race and sexual morality in 20th-century colonial cultures', *American Ethnologist*, 16

(1989), 651; and R. Hyam, 'Concubinage and the colonial service: The Crewe Circular (1909)', *Journal of Imperial and Commonwealth History*, 14 (1986), 170–86.

9. See R. Hyam, *Empire and Sexuality*, 137–56.

10. E. Said, *Orientalism* (New York, 1978), p. 40.

11. See P. Bourdieu, *La distinction sociale* (Paris, 1979); and J. Weeks, *Sex, Politics and Society* (London, 1981), pp. 19–37.

12. J. Steakley, *The Homosexual Emancipation Movement in Germany* (New York, 1975), p. 21. See also J. C. Fout and H. Oosterhuis (eds), *Male Homosexuals, Lesbians and Homosexuality in Germany: the Kaiserreich through the Third Reich, 1871–1945* (Chicago and London, 1992).

13. See D. F. Greenberg, *The Construction of Homosexuality* (Chicago and London, 1988), p. 353. See also A. Copley, *Sexual Moralities in France, 1780–1980* (London and New York, 1989), p. 135; and G. Hekma, *Homoseksualiteit, een medische reputatie* (Amsterdam, 1987), pp. 80–127.

14. A. Corbin, *Le miasme et la jonquille* (Paris, 1982), p. 172. See also A. Copley, *Sexual Moralities*, pp. 99–107.

15. G. Mosse, *Nationalism and Sexuality* (New York, 1985), p. 16.

16. D. F. Greenberg, *Construction of Homosexuality*, p. 412.

17. G. W. Stocking, Jr., *Victorian Anthropology* (New York and London, 1987), p. 237.

18. Literature on Darwinian theory is prolific. See P. J. Bowler, *Theories of Evolution: a Century of Debate, 1844–1944* (Oxford, 1986); M. Banton, *Racial Theories* (Cambridge, 1987), pp. 68–72; and P. Tort, *La pensée hiérachique et l'évolution* (Paris, 1983), pp. 166–98.

19. L. Birken, 'Darwin and gender', *Social Concept*, 4 (1987), 75–88.

20. J. E. Chamberlin, 'An anatomy of cultural melancholy', *Journal of the History of Ideas*, 42 (1981), 692.

21. *Ibid.*, p. 697.

22. On Morel, see A. Wettley, 'Zur Problemgeschichte der "Dégénérescence" ', *Südhoffs Archiv*, 43 (1959), 193–212. See also J. Borie, *Mythologies de l'hérédité au XIXe siècle* (Paris, 1981); and A. Liégeois, 'Hidden philosophy and theology in Morel's theory of degeneration and nosology', *History of Psychiatry*, 2 (1991), 419–27.

23. R. A. Nye, *Crime, Madness and Politics in Modern France* (Princeton, 1984), p. 131.

24. See F. Bing, 'La théorie de la dégénérescence', in J. Postel and Cl. Quétel (eds), *Nouvelle histoire de la psychiatrie* (Toulouse, 1983), pp. 351–6; and D. Pick, *Faces of Degeneration* (Cambridge and New York, 1989), pp. 1–33.

25. See N. Stepan, 'Biological degeneration', pp. 112–14.

26. C. Lombroso, *L'amore nel suicidio e nel delitto* (Turin, 1881), p. 34.

27. On this matter, see also C. Lombroso, *L'uomo delinquente* (Milan, 1876), pp. 55, 120–34; C. Lombroso and G. Ferrero, *La donna delinquente* (Turin-Rome, 1893), pp. 183–6, 396–429; and C. Lombroso, 'Du paralléllisme entre l'homosexualité et la criminalité innée', *Archivio di psichiatria, scienze penali ed antropologia criminale*, 27 (1906), 378–81.

28. C. Lombroso, ' "Delitti di libidine", *Archivio di psichiatria, antropologia criminale e medicina legale* (1883), p. 172; see also pp. 168–78, 320–49.

29. E. Ferri, 'Intervento al quinto congresso internazionale di antropologia criminale', *Compte rendu de la cinquième session du congrès international d'anthropologie criminelle, Amsterdam, 1901*, pp. 487–9.

30. S. Venturi, 'Le degenerazioni psico-sessuali nella vita degli individui e nella storia della società', *Archivio delle psicopatie sessuali*, 4/5 (1896), 71–6.

31. A. Lacassagne, 'Pédérastie', in *Dictionnaire encyclopédique des sciences médicales*, 2nd series, 22 (Paris, 1886), 239–59.

32. A. Corre, *L'ethnographie criminelle*, pp. 7, 12–13, 330.

33. C. Letourneau, *La psychologie ethnique* (Paris, 1901), p. 26.

34. See G. Mosse, 'Nationalism and respectability: Normal and abnormal sexuality in the nineteenth century', *JCH*, 17 (1982), 228–30.

35. H. Kaan, *Psychopathia sexualis*, Unpubl. diss. (University of Leipzig, 1844), pp. 43, 47–8.

36. C. F. Michéa, 'Des déviations maladives de l'appétit vénérien', *Union médical*, 17 July 1849, pp. 338–9.

37. J. L. Casper, *Practisch handboek der geregtelijke Geneeskunde* (Groningen, 1862), vol. 2, p. 161. The original, German version, *Handbuch der gerichtlichen Medicin* was published in Berlin in 1858.

38. A. Tardieu, *Étude médico-légale sur les attentats aux moeurs* (Paris, 1867 (1857)), pp. 171–262.

39. P. Brouardel, 'Étude critique sur la valeur des signes attribués à la pédérastie', *Annales d'hygiène publique et médicine légale*, 3rd series, 4 (1880), 182 and 188.

40. See C. Lantéri-Laura, *Lecture des perversions* (Paris, 1979); J. Hütter, *Die gesellschaftliche Kontrolle des homosexuellen Begehrens* (Frankfurt, 1992); and C. Wernz, *Sexualität als Krankheit* (Stuttgart, 1993). For France, see R. A. Nye, 'Sex difference and male homosexuality in French medical discourse, 1830–1930', *BHMed*, 63 (1989), 32–51; and A. Copley, *Sexual Moralities*, ch. 6, pp. 135–54. For Germany, see V. L. Bullough, 'The physician and research into human sexual behaviour in nineteenth-century Germany', *BHMed*, 63 (1989), 247–67. For Great Britain, see J. Weeks, *Sex, Politics and Society*, esp. pp. 96–121; and F. Mort, *Dangerous Sexualities* (London and New York, 1987). Also, see G. Hekma, *Homoseksualiteit*, for the Netherlands (and Belgium); G. Dall'Orto, 'Il concetto di degenerazione nel pensiero borghese dell'Ottocento', *Sodoma*, 2 (Summer 1985), 59–74 for Italy. For the Iberian world, see O. Guasch, 'La medicalización del sexo', *Revista ROL de Enfermeria*, 179–80 (July/August 1993), 27–32; and J. Crespo, *A história do corpo* (Lisbon, 1990), pp. 301–34.

41. C. H. Ulrichs, 'Memnon. Die Geschlechtsnatur der mannliebenden Urnings. Eine naturwissenschaftliche Darstellung', p. 7, reprinted in C. H. Ulrichs, *Forschungen über das Rätsel der mannmännlichen Liebe* (New York, 1975).

42. C. H. Ulrichs, 'Memnon'and 'Formatrix. Anthropologische Studien über urnische Liebe', in C. H. Ulrichs, *Forschungen über das Rätsel*, pp. 26–33, 59–62, 84–90.

43. W. Griesinger, 'Vortrag zur Eröffnung der psychiatrischen Klinik zu Berlin', *APN*, 1 (1868/69), 651.

44. Carl F. O. Westphal, 'Die konträre Sexualempfindung', *APN*, 2 (1869), 73–108.

45. P. Moreau, *Des aberrations du sens génésique* (Paris, 1880); J. M. Charcot and V. Magnan, 'Inversion du sens génital', *Archives de neurologie*, 3 (1882), 53–60; 4 (1882), 296–322; J. Chevalier, 'De l'inversion de l'instinct sexuel au point de vue médico-légale', unpubl. thesis (University of Lyon, 1885); J. Chevalier, 'De l'inversion sexuelle au point de vue clinique, anthropologique et médico-légale', *Aac*, 5 (1890), 314–36; 6 (1891), 49–69, 500–19; J. Chevalier, *Une maladie de personnalité. Inversion sexuelle* (Lyon and Paris, 1893); V. M. Tarnowsky, *Die krankhaften Erscheinungen des Geschlechtssinnes: eine forensisch-psychiatrische Studie* (Berlin, 1886); P. Mantegazza, *Gli amori degli uomini* (Milan, 1886); B. Ball, 'La folie érotique', *L'encéphale*, 7 (1887), 188–97, 257–69, 403–15, published separately in Paris in 1888; A. Binet, 'Du fétichisme dans l'amour', *Revue philosophique*, 12, 2 (1887), 143–67, 252–74; and P. Sérieux, 'Recherches cliniques sur les anomalies de l'instinct sexuel', unpubl. thesis (Paris, 1888); Georges Saint-Paul (Dr Laupt), *Tares et poisons. Perversion et perversité sexuelles. Une enquête médicale sur l'inversion* (Paris 1896); J. Crocq, 'La situation sociale de l'uraniste', *Journal de neurologie*, 6 (1901), 591–6; J. Crocq, 'Le troisième sexe', *Progrès médicale*, 10 (1908), 57–64.

46. G. Hekma, *Homoseksualiteit*, p. 66.

47. A. Moll, *Untersuchungen über die Libido sexualis* (Berlin, 1897), p. 4.

48. R. F. von Krafft-Ebing, *Psychopathia sexualis. Mit besonderer Berücksichtigung der konträren Sexualempfindung*, ed. O. Kruntorad (München, 1984), pp. 226–56, esp. 256. This reprint of the fourteenth edition ought to be read carefully, as many additions are based upon literature that was published after the first date of publication in 1886 only.

49. *Ibid.*, pp. 266–96, 297–327.

50. In this context, see R. A. Nye, 'Honor, impotence, and male sexuality in nineteenth-century French medicine', *French Historical Studies*, 16 (1989), 49.

51. P. Moreau, *Des aberrations du sens génésique*, pp. 73–4.

52. B. Ball, *La folie érotique* (Paris, 1888), p. 148.

53. A. Von Schrenk-Notzing, *Die Suggestionstherapie bei den krankhaften Erscheinungen des Geschlechtssinnes, mit besonderer Berücksichtigung der conträren Sexualempfindung* (Stuttgart, 1892), chapter 9.

54. E. Gley, 'Les aberrations de l'instinct sexuel', *Revue philosophique*, 9, 1 (1884), 88–92.

55. See G. Hekma, *Homoseksualiteit*, p. 68.

56. M. Dessoir, 'Zur Psychologie der Vita sexualis', *Allgemeine Zeitschrift für Psychiatrie und psychisch-gerichtliche Medicin*, 50 (1893), 948.

57. *Ibid.*, pp. 969–71.

58. See G. W. Stocking, Jr. (ed.), *Bones, Bodies, Behaviour. Essays on Biological Anthropology* (London, 1990), *passim*; and F. W. Voget, 'Progress, science, history and evolution', *History of Behavioral Sciences*, 3 (1967), 132–55.

59. See G. W. Stocking, Jr., *Victorian Anthropology*, pp. 186–237, 302–4; and W. Conze, 'Evolution und Geschichte', *Historische Zeitschrift*, 242 (1986), 1–30.

60. G. W. Stocking, Jr., *Victorian Anthropology*, p. 202.

61. See, among others, E. Ilex, *Moeurs orientales. Les huis-clos de l'ethnographie* (London, 1878), p. 22; and L. Bey, 'Der Eunuch', *Sexualprobleme*, 7 (1911), 674–80.

62. Demetrius A. Zambaco Pacha, *Les eunuques d'aujourd'hui et ceux de jadis* (Paris, 1911), p. 59.

63. E. Wilhelm, [Untitled], *Sexualprobleme*, 7 (1911), 850–2.

64. Here, I have used the recent reprint, titled *Les lois secrètes de l'amour en Islam* (Paris, 1993).

65. 'Par ses goûts de femme, par ses aptitudes féminines, l'eunuque complet a ... développé le mauvais instinct de la pédérastie. Ne trouvant dans son organisme aucun ressort viril, il a cessé d'être un vrai musulman pour devenir une pâte molle, malléable, prête à subir toutes les mauvaises suggestions. Il est devenu ainsi digne de rivaliser avec les juifs qui, tout le monde le sait, font argent des leurs et de leur propre corps.' O. Haleby Abu Otman, *Théologie musulmane* (Paris, 1893), p. 109.

66. *Ibid.*, pp. 134–5.

67. P. de Régla in O. Haleby Abu Otman, *Ibid.*, p. ix.

68. *Ibid.*, p. xiii.

69. See A. Boudhiba, 'La société maghrébine face à la question sexuelle', *Cahiers internationaux de sociologie*, 76 (1984), 91–110; M. Chebel, *L'esprit de sérail*, 53–71; A. Schmitt and J. Sofer (eds), *Sexuality and Eroticism among Males in Moslim Societies*; and M. Schild, 'De citadel van integriteit'.

70. See, among others, J. A. Comte de Gobineau, *Trois ans en Asie* (Paris, 1859), pp. 176–7; H. K. Eckehardt Helmut, *Meine Wallfahrt nach Mekka* (Leipzig and Stuttgart, n.d.), vol. 1, pp. 139, 298, 308–10; vol. 2, pp. 198–205, 274–5; H. K. Eckehardt Helmut, *Sittenbilder aus Tunis und Algerien* (Leipzig, 1869), pp. 34–5, 39–40, 45, 58–63, 86–93; H. K. Eckehardt Helmut, *Reise nach Südarabien* (Braunschweig, 1873), p. 14; W. G. Palgrave, *Narrative of a Year's Journey through Central and Eastern*

Arabia (London, 1865), vol. 2, pp. 24–5; H. E. O. Rouille Marquis de Boissy, *Les Mémoires du Marquis de Boissy* (Paris, 1870), *passim*; J. Creagh, *Over the Borders of Christendom and Islam* (London, 1876), pp. 162–3; O. Lenz, *Timbuktu* (Leipzig, 1884). vol. 1, pp. 248, 365–7; M. Albrecht, *Russisch Centralasien* (Hamburg, 1896), *passim*; and G. Steindorff, *Durch die Lybische Wüste* (Bielefeld and Leipzig, 1904), p. 111.

71. See W. Bacher, *Nizami's Leben und Werke* (Leipzig, 1871), p. 58; and E. G. Browne, *A Literary History of Persia* (London, 1893), p. 232.

72. No exhaustive list can be included here. See especially C. B. Klunzinger, *Bilder aus Oberägypten* (Stuttgart, 1877), pp. 186–7; G. F. Herzberg, *Geschichte der Byzantiner und des Osmanischen Reiches* (Berlin, 1883), p. 589; C. J. Wills, *Persia as it was* (London, 1886), pp. 61, 76, 96; and F. J. Simonet, *Historia de los Mozarabes de España (Madrid, 1897), p. 592.* See also A. Bebel, *Die Mohammedanisch-Arabische Kulturperiode* (Stuttgart, 1884); and [Anon.], 'Päderastie', in *Brockhaus Konversationslexikon,* 14th ed. (Leipzig, 1894–5), vol. 12, p. 803.

73. W. Geiger, *Ostiranische Kultur im Altertum* (Erlangen, 1882), pp. 341–2.

74. F. Oefele, 'Zum konträren Geschlechtsverkehr in Altägypten', *Monatshefte für praktische Dermatologie,* 19 (1899), 409.

75. L. W. C. Van den Berg, *De beginselen van het Mohammedaansche Recht, volgens de Imma's Aboehanifaten Asj-Sjafe'i* (Batavia and The Hague, 1874), p. 245; T. P. Hughes, *Dictionary of Islam* (London, 1885), pp. 299, 601; J. Kohler, *Über das Islamische Strafrecht* (Stuttgart, 1889), pp. 305, 312; E. Sachau, *Muhammedanisches Recht nach Schafitischer Lehre* (Stuttgart, 1897), pp. 809, 818.

76. R. Olegna, 'Il catechismo turco e l'omosessualità', *Rassegna di studi sessuali,* 2 (1922), 354–6; 3 (1923), 115–18.

77. M. Luttke, *Der Islam und seine Völker* (Gütersloh, 1878).

78. See, among others, D. M. Wallace, *Egypt and the Egyptians* (London, 1863), p. 63; E. Schuyler, *Turkistan* (London, 1876), vol. 1, pp. 132–6; A. Mouliéras, *Le Maroc inconnu. Exploration du Rif* (Paris, 1895), p. 162; and S. G. Wilson, *Persian Life and Customs* (New York, 1899 (Edinburgh, 1896)), p. 229.

79. See H. L. Wesseling, *Verdeel en heers. De deling van Afrika, 1880–1914* (Amsterdam, 1991), p. 40.

80. See C. Houel, *Maroc: mariage, adultère, prostitution: anthologie* (Paris, 1912), esp. pp. 139–42; and P. Remlinger, 'La prostitution en Maroc', *Annales d'hygiène publique,* February 1913, pp. 129–30. Also, see a late document by the female physician Schumacher, 'Prostitution im modernen Ägypten', *Archiv für Menschenkunde,* 1 (1925/26), 61–4.

81. A. Kocher, *De la criminalité chez les Arabes au point de vue de la pratique médico-judiciaire en Algérie* (Paris, 1884), p. 91.

82. 'L'examen du pantalon de l'inculpé contribue à préciser la certitude du fait que l'accusation reproche à Mohammed-ben-Ali. En effet, l'anus du jeune Dris a laissé écouler du sang, ce sang a nécessairement maculé le gland du pédéraste: or, il est acquis à l'instruction que, sans se dépouiller de son pantalon, Mohammed a fait sortir sa verge par le trou existant dans l'étoffe, et que c'est ainsi qu'il a assailli sa victime.' *Ibid.,* p. 99.

83. Ibid., pp. 169–71.

84. H. Quedenfeldt, 'Die Corporationen der Uléd Ssidi Hammed-u-Mûssa und der Ormâ im südlichen Marokko', *ZfE,* 21 (1899), 572–82; H. Von der Choven, 'Über sexuelle Perversionen im Orient', *Obozrénié psichiatrii,* 5 (1900), 229–34 (I have not been able to consult this article. The information was retrieved indirectly from a review in the *JfsZ,* 5 (1903), 681); B. Stern, *Medizin, Aberglaube und Geschlechtsleben in der Türkei* (Berlin, 1903), pp. 561–5; J. Hoche, *Moeurs d'exception. Le vice mortel* (Paris, 1903),

passim; E. T. Feenstra Kuiper, *Jeugdige zondaars te Constantinopel*, ed. W. Ogrinc (Utrecht, 1978 (Amsterdam, 1905)), *passim*; Schumacher, 'Prostitution im modernen Ägypten' on 'walads'.

85. 'dans certaines villes arabes, [l'amour contre nature] donne même lieu à une prostitution spéciale, qui s'étale au grand jour: puisque des petits garçons, parés comme des femmes, vont ouvertement dans les cafés s'offrir aux hommes et s'asseoir sur leurs genoux'. C. Letourneau, *La psychologie ethnique*, p. 318.

86. T. Heerman, 'Die Päderastie bei den Sarten', *Sexualprobleme*, 7 (1911), 400–8.

87. See, on this matter, I. Baldauf, *Die Knabenliebe in Mittelasien: Bačabozlik* (Berlin, 1988); C. M. Naim, 'The theme of homosexual (pederastic) love in pre-modern Urdu poetry', in M. Umar Memon (ed.), *Studies in the Urdu Gazal and Prose Fiction* (Madison, 1979), pp. 120–42; and T. Rahman, 'Boy love in the Urdu Ghazal', *Paidika*, 2, 1 (Summer 1989), 10–27.

88. H. Soyaux, *Aus West-Afrika. 1873–1876. Erlebnisse und Beobachtungen* (Leipzig, 1879), vol. 2, p. 59.

89. See T. Dunbar Moodie, 'Migrancy and male sexuality on the South African gold mines', in M. B. Duberman *et al.* (eds), *Hidden from History*, pp. 411–25.

90. 'La liberté excessive des moeurs engendre moins de crimes que, chez nous, la retenue hypocrite; en dépit des apparences, elle n'aboutit pas à cet érotisme morbide qui, en France, donne lieu à des manifestations si troublantes, et l'indifférence qu'on témoigne vis-à-vis des *amours irrégulières* [my italics] en écarte d'ordinaire certaines conséquences abominables.' A. Corre, *L'ethnographie criminelle*, pp. 448–9.

91. J. X, *L'amour aux colonies* (Paris, 1893), 155–156.

92. R. Kandt, *Caput Nili*, Berlin, 1905, 150.

93. K. Oetker, *Die Negerseele und die Deutschen in Afrika*, München, 1907, 27–30.

94. A. Cureau, 'Essai sur la psychologie des races nègres de l'Afrique Tropicale', *Revue générale des sciences pures et appliquées*, 15 (1904), 638–652; 679–95.

95. G. Schweinfurth, 'Tagebuch einer Reise zu den Niam-Niam und Monbattu 1870', *Zeitschrift der Gesellschaft für Erdkunde zu Berlin*, 7 (1872), 385–475, esp. 237–338.

96. J. Roscoe, 'A cow tribe of Enkole in the Uganda protectorate', *JRAI*, 37 (1907), 93–118.

97. A. Corre, *L'ethnographie criminelle*, p. 79.

98. Idem, *O.c.*, 79–80.

99. Idem, *O.c.*, 68–69.

100. 'J'ai rencontré à Saint-Louis des noirs, parés à la manière des femmes et en affectant les allures, qu'on m'a dit faire métier de leur prostitution. A Boké, j'ai vu auprès d'un prince foulah, un griot, dont les danses lascives traduisaient bien le rôle plus intime qu'il devait remplir en la maison de l'altesse. Les habitudes de pédérastie ne sortent pas des milieux musulmans. Dans le langage wolof, l'expression pour les désigner serait de date récente, et elle n'existerait pas dans la plupart des idiomes africains.' *Ibid.*, 80, note 1.

101. See about homosexuality in Senegal, M.X. Diouf, 'Goor-jigeen', *GPH*, 521 (March 21, 1991), 16–18. Also, see C. Allen Johnson, 'Male Homosexuality in Africa', unpubl. thesis, Columbia University, New York, 1991, *passim*, and M. Cressole – F. Huguier, *Sur les traces de l'Afrique fantôme*, Paris, 1990, esp. 20–21. The book reiterates the path of Michel Leiris' expedition of the 1930s and criticizes the latter's unjustified silence about some aspects of African sexuality.

102. 'Conträre Sexual-Erscheinungen bei der Negerbevölkerung *Zanzibars* sind sowohl als angeborene, wie als erworbene ziemlich häufig, während bei den Stämmen Inner-Africas angeborene Contrarietät wohl nur in seltenen Fällen vorkommt .... Die grössere Häufigkeit in Zanzibar ist zweifellos dem Einfluss der Araber zuzuschreiben, die zusammen mit Komorensern und wohlhabenderen Swahili-Mischlingen auch das Hauptcontingent zu den Erworben-Conträren stellen.'

103. 'Geschlechtliche Befriedigung sucht er hauptsächlich in passiver Päderastie (*kufira* = päderastiren, *kufirwa* = päderastirt werden) und in beischlafähnlichen Handlungen. Im Äusseren sind die angeboren conträren Männer von den männlichen Prostituirten nicht zu unterscheiden, doch machen die Eingeborenen zwischen ihnen einen scharfen Unterschied: die berufsmässigen Lust-Knaben werden verachtet, während man das Verhalten der Angeboren-conträren als amri ya muungu (Wille Gottes) duldet.'

104. O. Baumann, 'Conträre Sexualerscheinungen bei der Negerbevölkerung Zanzibars', *ZfE*, 31 (1899), 668–669.

105. W. Schneider, *Die Naturvölker*, Paderborn-Münster, 1885–86, vol. 1, 295–296.

106. H.A. Junod, *The Life of a South African Tribe*, Neuchâtel, 1912, vol. 1, 492–495.

107. C. Van Overbergh, *Les Basonge (Etat Ind. du Congo). Sociologie descriptive*, Brussels, 1908, vol. 3, 76; 254; Idem – E. De Jonghe, *Les Mayombe (Etat Ind. du Congo). Sociologie descriptive*, Brussels, 1907, 114; 281; Combier, *Missions en Chine et au Congo*, Brussels, 1890–91, vol. 1, 413–414; J.H. Weeks, 'Anthropological Notes on the Bangala of the Upper Congo River', *JRAI*, 39 (1909), 97–136; 416– 459, esp. 448–449 on mutual masturbation and sodomy; R.W. Felkin, 'Notes on the Waganda Tribe of Central Africa', *Proceedings of the Royal Society of Edinburgh*, 13 (1884), 699–770; H.H. Johnston, *British Central Africa*, London, 1897, 472–3; 490, note 1; H. Brincker, 'Charakter, Sitten und Gebräuche speciell der Bantu Deutsch-Südwestafrikas', *Mittheilungen des Seminars für Orientalische Sprachen an der K. Friedrich-Wilhelms-Universität zu Berlin, Abteilung 3: Afrikanische Studien*, 3 (1900), 66–92; H. Grützer, 'Die Gebräuche der Basuto', *Verhandlungen der Berliner Gesellschaft für Anthropologie, Ethnologie und Urgeschichte*, (1877), 78; A.B. Ellis, *The Ewe-speaking Peoples of Slave Coast of West Africa*, S.l., 1890, 183 and 290; E.G. Carbutt, 'Some Minor Superstitions and Customs of the Zulus', *Folklore Journal*, 2 (1880), 12–13; P. Paulitschke, *Ethnographie Nordost-Afrikas. Die materielle Kultur der Danâkil, Galla und Somâl*, Berlin, 1893, 172.

108. H. Tönjes, *Ovamboland, Land, Leute, Mission*, Berlin, 1911, 155.

109. E. Nigmann, *Die Wahehe*, Berlin, 1908, 50.

110. J. X, *L'amour aux colonies* (Paris, 1893), pp. 155, 258.

111. W. Hammer, 'Liebesleben und -Leiden in Westmittel-Afrika, besonders in Kamerun', *Geschlecht*, 4 (1909), 193–201.

112. *Ibid.*, p. 199.

113. J. A. Skertchly, *Dahomey as it is* (London, 1874), *passim*; A. Bastian, *Der Mensch in der Geschichte* (Leipzig, 1860), vol. 3, p. 305; P. Barret, *L'Afrique occidentale* (Paris, 1888), vol. 1, p. 166.

114. M. Delafosse, *Haut-Sénégal Niger, Soudan française* (Paris, 1912).

115. J. M. M. Van der Burgt, *Un grand peuple de l'Afrique Equatorial* (Bois-le-Duc, 1903–4), vol. 1, pp. 93, 462, 500; vol. 2, pp. 107, 118.

116. G. McCall Theal, *History of the Boers in South Africa* (London, 1887), p. 17.

117. 'I rapporti con diavoletti non sono affatto misteriosi e sono tollerati anche dai padri dei ragazzi tanto più che questo supplemento di servizio viene sempre retribuito a parte. Arrivato all'età in cui il ragazzo si è fatto giovane e adatto per la donna, allora generalmente cessa dall'avere rapporti contro natura. Però si verificano casi in cui allcuni diavoletti affezionati ai loro padroni proseguono in quei rapporti anche fino all'età di diciotto o venti anni.' P. Ambrogetti, *La vita sessuale nell'Eritrea* (Rome, 1900), p. 16.

118. 'Raramente ho potuto constatare che la pederastia fosse practicata per inclinazione piuttosto che per opportunità. Ricordo solo un montàz (caporale degl'Indigeni), il quale aveva 25 anni ed era ammogliato; non ostante perseguira ad essere pederasta passivo senza lucro.' *Ibid.*

119. 'Ho cercato anche che esistessero indigeni i quali nelle forme del corpo o nel modo di comportarsi, presentassero caratteri femminili, e ne ho trovati alcuni i quali, specialmente nell'acconciatura della testa en nel vestirsi, imitavano le donne; ma non mi risulta che costoso fossero invertiti sessuali, erano invece ritenuti bellimbusti e uomini effeminati.' *Ibid.*

120. 'Les sekatra sont des hommes normalement constitués; mais, dès leur jeune âge, probablement à cause de leur aspect plus délicat ou plus chétif, on les a traités comme des fillettes, et peu à peu ils se sont considerés comme de véritables femmes, en prenant le costume, le caractère et toutes les habitudes. ... Quand un homme leur plaît, ils lui donnent de l'argent pour coucher avec lui et le font coïter dans une corne de boeuf remplie de graisse qu'ils se placent entre les jambes ou bien ils se font pédérer.' Alexandre Lasnet, 'Notes d'ethnologie et de médecine sur les Sakalaves du Nord-Oest', *Ahmc*, 2 (October–December 1899), 471–97.

121. Dr Rencurel, 'Les Sarimbavy. Perversion sexuelle observée en Émyrne', *Ahmc*, 3, 4 (October–December 1900), 562–8.

122. E. Laurent, 'Les Sharimbavy de Madagascar', *Aac*, 26 (1911), 244.

123. 'L'anus, en effet, chez les sujets examinés, n'était pas infundibuliforme; sans donner grande valeur à ce signe trop infidèle, il convenait cependant d'en remarquer l'absence. Le coït *ab ore* ne paraît pas non plus être dans leurs moeurs.'

124. *Ibid.*, p. 246.

125. See J. Irle, *Die Herero* (Gütersloh, 1906), pp. 56–57; and G. Fritsch, 'Über die Ova-Herero', *Globus*, 28 (1875), 246–7; G. Fritsch, 'Über Omapanga der Hottentotten und über Päderastie der südafrikanischen Eingeborenen', *JfsZ*, 2 (1901), 87–8, 103–5; and G. Fritsch, 'Das angeblich dritte Geschlecht des Menschen', *Archiv für Sexualforschung*, 1 (1916), 197–220.

126. S. R. Steinmetz, *Rechtsverhältnisse von Eingeborenen Völkern in Afrika und Ozeanien* (Berlin, 1903), esp. pp. 14–26, 139–81, 203–17, 218–67, 283–93, 326–45.

127. Nicole, in S. R. Steinmetz, *Rechtsverhältnisse von Eingeborenen Völkern*, 93–138.

128. See P. Rehme, 'Über das Recht der Amaxosa', *ZfvR*, 10 (1892), 32–63; J. Kohler, 'Rechte der deutschen Schutzgebiete', *ZfvR*, 14 (1900), 294–319, 321–94, 409–55; 15 (1901/2), 1–83, 321–36, 337–60; P. Rehme, 'Über das Negerrecht, namentlich in Kamerun', *ZfvR*, 11 (1895), 413–75.

129. H. Goldie, *Dictionary of the Efik Language* (Glasgow, 1862), vol. 2, pp. 235, 318; L. Krapf, *A Dictionary of the Swahili Language* (London, 1882), pp. 68, 95, 333; E. Steele and A. C. Madan (eds), *A Handbook of the Swahili Language as Spoken at Zanzibar* (London, 1885), pp. 274, 283, 382; H. Brincker, *Wörterbuch und kurzgefasste Grammatik des Otji-Hérero* (Leipzig, 1886); C. Sacleux, *Dictionnaire Français-Swahili* (Paris, 1891); A. C. Madan, *English-Swahili Dictionary*, 2nd ed. (Oxford, 1902); A. C. Madan, *Swahili-English Dictionary* (Oxford, 1903), p. 376; J. M. M. Van der Burgt, *Dictionnaire Français-Kirundi* (Bois-le-Duc, 1903); D. Westermann, *Wörterbuch der Ewe-Sprache*, 2 vols (Berlin, 1905–6); C. Velten, *Suaheli-Wörterbuch* (Berlin, 1910).

130. L. Krapf, *A Dictionary of the Swahili Language*, p. 266: 'hanithi: a sexually impotent man; asiewesa ku kúéa mke: sodomite; catamite'; A. C. Madan, *Swahili-English Dictionary*, p. 376: 'thambi ya watu wa Sodom: sodomy'.

131. F. Pruner, *Die Krankheiten des Orients vom Standpunkte des vergleichenden Nosologie betrachtet* (Erlangen, 1847), pp. 66–8.

132. W. Winwood Reade, *Savage Africa* (London, 1863), pp. 546, 548–9, 555, 579.

133. P. Brantlinger, 'Victorians and Africa: The genealogy of the myth of the dark continent', in Henry Louis Gates, Jr. (ed.), *'Race', Writing, and Difference* (Chicago and London, 1986), pp. 185–222.

134. For a more detailed account, see R. Hyam, *Empire and Sexuality*, pp. 186–9. See also J. F. Faupel, *African Holocaust: The Story of the Uganda Martyrs* (London, 1965); and

J. A. Rowe, 'The purge of Christians at Mwanga's court', *Journal of African History*, 5 (1964), 55–71.

135. On this issue, see chapter 7: 'Competing masculinities (III): Black masculinity and the white man's black man', in L. Segal, *Slow Motion. Changing Masculinities, Changing Men* (London, 1990), pp. 168–204.

136. A. B. Ellis in F.-J. Clozel and R. Villamur, *Les coutumes indigènes de la Côte d'Ivoire* (Paris, 1902), pp. 240–3.

137. See also S. L. Gilman, 'Black sexuality and German consciousness', in R. Grimm and J. Hermand (eds), *Blacks and German Culture* (Madison, 1986), pp. 44–7.

138. A. R. Wallace, *A Narrative of Travels on the Amazon and Rio Negro*, 2nd ed. (London, New York and Melbourne, 1889).

139. R. Arndt, *Biologische Studien* (Greifswald, 1895), vol. 2, p. 241.

140. P. Mantegazza, *Gli amori dei uomini* (Milan, 1885–6), vol. 1, p. 147.

141. R. E. Latcham, 'Ethnology of the Araucanos', *JRAI*, 39 (1909), 353; T. J. Hutchinson, 'The Tehuelche Indians of Patagonia', *Transactions of the Ethnological Society of London*, New Series, 7 (1869), 323; K. Th. Preuss, 'Die Religionen der Naturvölker Amerikas 1906–1909', *AfR*, 14 (1911), 236–7; H. H. Bancroft, *The Native Races of the Pacific States of North America*, 5 vols. (London, 1875–6), *passim*; A. Bastian, *Die Culturländer des Alten America* (Berlin, 1878–89), vol. 2, p. 813.

142. K. Th. Preuss, 'Die Religiösen Gesänge und Mythen einiger Stämme der mexikanischen Sierra Madre. Reisebericht', *AfR*, 11 (1908), 369–98.

143. K. von der Steinen, *Unter den Naturvölkern Zentral-Brasiliens* (Berlin, 1894), p. 502.

144. J. J. von Tschudi, *Culturhistorische und sprachliche Beiträge zur kennnis des alten Perús* (Vienna, 1891), pp. 57, 177.

145. A. Lomonaco, 'Sulle razze indigene del Brasile. Studio storico', *Aae*, 19 (1889), 17–92, 187–270, esp. 45–6; J. Kohler, 'Die Rechte der Urvölker Nordamerikas (nördlich von Mexico)', *ZfvR*, 12 (1897), 354–416, esp. 389 and note 329; O. Stoll, *Das Geschlechtsleben in der Völkerpsychologie* (Leipzig, 1908), p. 564.

146. See, for example, W. Heine, *Japan und seine Bewohner* (Leipzig, 1860); E. Fraissinet, *Le Japon*, 2 vols (Paris, 1864); O. Mohnike, 'Die Japaner. Eine ethnographische Monographie', *Natur und Offenbarung*, 18 (1872), 200–21, 251–69, 300–18, 357–75, esp. 269.

147. See, among others, T. Okasaki, *Geschichte der japanischen Nationalliteratur von den ältesten Zeiten bis zur Gegenwart* (Leipzig, 1899), pp. 127, 140.; Nihongi, *Chronicles of Japan from the earliest times to A.D. 697*, trans. W. G. Aston (London, 1896), *passim*.

148. See, among others, W. von Seidlitz, *Geschichte des Japanischen Farbenholzschnitts* (Dresden, 1897), incl. illustrations of male 'actrices'; F. Perzynsky, 'Der Japanische Farbenholzschnitt. Seine Geschichte, seine Einfluss', *Die Kunst*, 13 (n.d.), 102–26.

149. A. Humbert, *Le Japon illustré* (Paris, 1870), vol. 2, p. 276; C. Munzinger, *Japan und die Japaner* (Stuttgart, 1904), p. 104.

150. F. O. Adams, *The History of Japan from the Earliest Period to the Present Time* (London, 1874), vol. 1, p. 70: 'Of the successors of Iyéasu, with the exception of Iyémitsu, there is little to no record. They were mostly fainéants as were their almost hereditary ministers, the róyiu.'

151. See, among others, B. H. Chamberlain, *Things Japanese*, 2nd ed. (London, 1891), pp. 20, 412–17; E. and L. Selenka, *Sonnige Welten*, 2nd ed. (Wiesbaden, 1905), p. 389; E. von Hesse-Wartegg, *China und Japan*, 2nd ed. (Leipzig, 1900), pp. 392, 500.

152. H. Weipert, 'Das Shinto-Gebet der Grossen Reinigung (Ohara no kotoba)', *Mitteilungen der deutschen Gesellschaft für Natur- und Völkerkunde Ostasiens in Tokio*, 58 (1897), 365–75, esp. 374.

153. A. Wernich, 'Über einige Formen nervöser Störungen bei den Japanern', *Mitteilungen der deutschen Gesellschaft für Natur-und Völkerkunde Ostasiens in Tokio*, 10 (1876), 17. Also, see A. Wernich, *Geographisch-medizinische Studien nach den Erlebnissen einer Reise um die Erde* (Berlin, 1878), p. 166.

154. See the articles in the English language press: *Japan Daily Mail*, 2 September 1896; and *Eastern World*, 19 February 1898, 20 and 27 May 1899, reviewed by F. Karsch-Haack, *Das gleichgeschlechtliche Leben der Kulturvölker*, 94–7.

155. G. Droppers, 'The population of Japan in the Tokugawa period', *Transactions of the Asiatic Society of Japan* (Yokohama), 22 (1894), 253–84, esp. 281–2, note 7: 'One other cause which may have helped to retard the growth of population was the practice of pederasty . . . ' etc.

156. See J. H. Longford, 'A summary of the Japanese penal codes', *Transactions of the Asiatic Society of Japan, Yokohama*, 5 (1877), 1–114, esp. p. 88 on sodomy, revised code, sec. 266; G. Michaelis, 'Zur Kenntnis der Geschichte des japanischen Strafrechts', *Mitteilungen der deutschen Gesellschaft für Natur- und Völkerkunde Ostasiens in Tokio*, 38 (1888), 361, 375; and O. Rudorff, 'Tokugawa-Gesetz-Sammlung', *Mitteilungen der deutschen Gesellschaft für Natur- und Völkerkunde Ostasiens in Tokio*, 5 (1889), Supplement, esp. pp. 11–12 and 19.

157. 'Daar vonden de Engelsche en Fransche troepen geheele instituten, waar knapen van 11 tot 12 jaren voor de mannelijke prostitutie werden opgevoed. Als meisjes worden zij daar gekleed, en in alle vrouwelijke coquetteriën onderwezen. Vroegtijdig gedebaucheerd, zijn deze wezens op 14 en 15 jarigen leeftijd ontmand, ongelukkige halfslachtige schepselen, noch man noch vrouw. Worden zij op lateren leeftijd in die gebouwen opgenomen, zoo worden zij eerst totaal geeunuchiseerd.' G. Schlegel, 'Iets over de prostitutie in China', *Verhandelingen van het Bataviaasch genootschap van kunsten en wetenschap*, 32, 3 (1866), 23.

158. *Ibid.*, p. 24.

159. *Ibid.*

160. O. Stoll, *Das Geschlechtsleben*, p. 157; J. J. Matignon, *Superstition, crime et misère en Chine* (Lyons and Paris, 1899), pp. 258–9. The chapter on 'pederasty' was published simultaneously as an article in the *Aac*, 14 (1899), 38–53.

161. See R. Hyam, *Empire and Sexuality*, pp. 99–100 on memorandum on prevalence of unnatural crime among Chinese indentured labourers on the Wirwatersrand, by the superintendant of Foreign Labour (August 1906), and evidence of J. E. Cooke (Chinese interpreter to the Government), etc.

162. See G. Schlegel, 'Thian Ti Hwui. The Hung-League or Heaven-Earth-League', *Verhandelingen van het Bataviaasch Genootschap van Kunsten en Wetenschappen*, 32 (1866), i–xl, 1–253; and O. de Joux, *Die Enterbten des Liebesglückes* (Leipzig, 1893), p. 219.

163. See Schlegel, 'Thian Ti Hwui'; and C. Dallet, *Histoire de l'Eglise de Corée*, 2 vols (Paris, 1874), *passim*; J. H. Gray, *China* (London, 1878), vol. 1, p. 246; E. von Hesse-Wartegg, *China und Japan*, pp. 154, 157–8; E. Baelz, *Die Ostasiaten* (Stuttgart, 1901), pp. 21–2; W. Grube, *Geschichte der chinesischen Literatur* (Leipzig, 1902), pp. 405, 430–1.

164. E. Baelz, *Die Ostasiaten*, p. 22.

165. 'Les Chinois, à en croire de nombreux témoignages, sont fort dissolus; ils ne connaissent guère que l'amour sensuel, mais ils y raffinent et y ont introduit des procédés savants, que les autres races n'ont pas inventés et que je n'ai pas à décrire içi. On sait aussi, et cela est connexe, que les écarts génésiques leurs sont très familiers.' C. Letourneau, *La psychologie ethnique*, p. 249.

166. J. J. Matignon, *Superstition*, pp. 256–7.

167. *Ibid.*, p. 258.

168. *Ibid.*, pp. 264–7; compare G. Carter-Stent, 'Chinese eunuchs', *Journal of the Royal Asiatic Society of Great Britain and Ireland, North China Branch, Shanghai*, New Series, 11 (1877), 143–84.

169. H. von Samson-Himmelstjerna, *Die gelbe Gefahr als Moralproblem* (Berlin, 1902), p. 230.

170. Wilken, 'Het shamanisme bij de volken van den Indischen Archipel', *BTLV*, 5th Series, 2 (1887), 427–97, esp. p. 477; Wilken, 'Plechtigheden en gebruiken bij verlovingen en huwelijken bij de volken van den Indischen Archipel', *BTLV*, 5th Series, 4 (1889), 457.

171. J. G. Riedel, *De sluik- en kroesharige rassen tusschen Selebes en Papua* (The Hague, 1889), pp. 377–8.

172. F. Blumentritt, 'Über die Staaten der philippinischen Eingeborenen in den Zeiten der Conquista', *Mittheilungen der K. K. Geographischen Gesellschaft in Wien*, 28, 2 (1885), 49–82.

173. W. W. Skeat, *Malay Magic* (London, 1900), p. 362.

174. See, among others, N. von Michluko-Maclay, 'Über die künstliche Perforatio Penis bei den Dajaks auf Borneo', *Verhandlungen der Berliner Gesellschaft für Anthropologie, Ethnologie und Urgeschichte* (1876), pp. 23 ff.; A. B. Meyer, 'Über die Perforation des Penis bei den Malayen', *Mittheilungen der Anthropologischen Gesellschaft in Wien*, 7, 9 (1877), 242–4; G. A. Wilken, 'De besnijdenis bij de volken van den Indischen Archipel', *BTLV*, 4th Series, 10, 2 (1885), 165–206; J. G. F. Riedel, 'De Topantunuasu van Centraal Celebes', *BTLV*, 4th Series, 11 (1886), 93.

175. See A. O. Hume, founder of the Indian National Congress, who lamented about frequent masturbation among Bengali men as this presumably led to their effeminization. See L. Wurgraft, *The Imperial Imagination: Magic and Myth in Kipling's India* (Middletown, 1983), p. 50; and M. Sinha, 'Gender and imperialism: Colonial policy and the ideology of moral imperialism in late-nineteenth century Bengal', in M. S. Kimmel (ed.), *Changing Men* (Berkeley, 1987), pp. 217–31.

176. 'malgré le nombre extraordinaire des courtisanes et la grande facilité pour l'homme de satisfaire les exigences de son appétit génésique, peut-être à cause de cela – car la satiété engendre l'épuisement, et celui-ci pousse aux perversions, surtout chez les individus cérébralement maintenus en éréthisme érotique par les habitudes courantes et des légendes obscènes des mythes religieux – les attentats à la pudeur et les viols sont communs. . . . Dans l'*amour antiphysique* [my italics], les blasés cherchent un nouveau piment.' A. Corre, *L'ethnographie criminelle*, pp. 210–11.

177. 'Il sera logique d'appeler les Annamites des *hommes-singes*. Ils méritent cette appellation à double titre, le singe étant de tous les animaux celui dont l'organe génital est le plus petit, proportionellement à la grosseur du corps. Le singe est également le seul des animaux qui se masturbe de propos délibéré, point de contact avec la race humaine. Or, l'Annamite, un vieux civilisé, est aussi lubrique que le singe.'

178. J. X, *L'amour aux colonies*, pp. 17, 58, 68–82.

179. 'La pédérastie est très pratiquée au Tonkin par nos nationaux. . . . A Hanoï, il n'est pas rare d'être raccroché le soir, sur la promenade principale . . . par des petits gamins parlant le français – et quel français, mon Dieu – "M'sieur cap'taine! venir chez moi – moi un titi bien cochon!", c'est la phrase d'invitation. Les gouverneurs généraux s'en sont justement émus, ont fait prendre de sévères mesures de police, mais leurs efforts n'ont jamais été couronnés entièrement de succès. Le meilleur remède à ces fâcheuses habitudes serait d'envoyer le plus possible des agents mariés en Indo-Chine: le niveau moral de la colonie ne pourrait qu'y gagner.' J. J. Matignon, *Superstition*, p. 218.

180. J. Jacobs, *Eenigen tijd onder de Baliërs* (Batavia, 1883), p. 161.

181. J. Jacobs, *Het familie-en kampongleven op Groot-Atjeh* (Leiden, 1894), vol. 1, p. 112; vol. 2, pp. 222–3, 235–7, 328.

182. J. A. Kruyt, *Atjeh en de Atjehers* (Leiden, 1877), p. 63.

183. C. Snouck Hungronje, *De Atjehers* (Batavia and Leiden, 1893), vol. 1, pp. 23, 64; vol. 2, p. 351.

184. P. P. Roorda van Eysinga, *Algemeen Nederduitsch-Maleisch Woordenboek* (The Hague, 1855), pp. 330, 495.

185. St John Spenser, *Life in the Forests of the Far East* (London, 1862), vol. 1, p. 62.

186. H. C. Klinkert, *Supplement op het Maleisch-Nederduitsch Woordenboek van Dr. Pijnappel* (Haarlem and Amsterdam, 1869), p. 189.

187. B. F. Matthes, 'Over de Bissoe's of heidensche priesters en priesteressen der Boeginezen', *Verhandelingen der Koninklijke Akademie van Wetenschappen, Afdeling Letterkunde* (Amsterdam), 7 (1872), 1–50, esp. 1–3; B. F. Matthes, *Boegineesch-Hollandsch Woordenboek* (The Hague, 1874), pp. 975–81; P. and F. Sarrasin, *Reisen in Celebes* (Wiesbaden, n.d.), vol. 2, p. 203.

188. P. J. Veth, *Java* (Haarlem, 1875–84), vol. 1, pp. 481–2; vol. 3, p. 672, note 1.

189. R. Van Eck, 'Schetsen van het eiland Bali', *Tijdschrift voor Nederlandsch-Indië*, New Series, 8, 1 (1879), 50, and 9, 1 (1880), 15; H. N. Van der Tuuk, *Kawi-Balineesch-Nederlandsch Woordenboek* (Batavia, 1897–1901), vol. 3, p. 27.

190. T. H. Levin, *Wild Races of South-Eastern India* (London, 1870), *passim*; H. Ling Roth, *The Natives of Sarawak and British North Borneo* (London, 1896), vol. 1, pp. 270–1; H. Breitenstein, *Einundzwanzig Jahre in Indien* (Leipzig, 1899), vol. 1, p. 226; P. Kéraval, (untitled report), *Archives de neurologie*, 24 (March 1902), 236–7.

191. M. T. H. Perelaer, *Ethnographische beschrijving der Dajaks* (Zaltbommel, 1870), pp. 8–9, 15, 32.

192. 'Die Geschlechtsänderung soll nicht mit der conträren Sexualempfindung identificirt [sic] werden. Sie findet mehr ihre Analogie in dem Wahn der Geschlechtsänderung, welche bei Irren gefunden wird.' P. C. J. Van Brero, 'Einiges über die Geisteskrankheiten der Bevölkerung des malaiischen Archipels', *Allgemeine Zeitschrift für Psychologie und psychisch-gerichtliche Medicin*, 53 (1896), 29.

193. P. C. J. Van Brero, 'Die Nerven- und Geisteskrankheiten in den Tropen', in C. Mense (ed.), *Handbuch der Tropenkrankheiten* (Leipzig, 1905), vol. 1, p. 227.

194. 'Das Vorhandensein einer solchen Klasse männlicher Prostituierten deutet darauf hin, dass unter den primitiven Stämmen Borneos homosexuelle Neigungen ziemlich weit verbreit sind; manche Männer knüpfen dauernde Liebesverhältnisse mit einem basir an, bei den See-Dajak im Norden Borneos werden mitunder sogar förmliche Ehen zwischen einem solchen Priester und einem jungen Manne abgeschlossen. Ähnliches findet sich auch in anderen Gegenden Indonesiens.' H. Berkusky, 'Die sexuelle Moral der primitiven Stämme Indonesiens', *Sexualprobleme*, 8 (1912), 848.

195. *Ibid.*, pp. 854–5. See also H. Berkusky, 'Homosexualität bei den Naturvölkern', *Geschlecht*, 6 (1911), 49–55.

196. J. P. Kleiweg de Zwaan, *De geneeskunde der Menangkabau-Maleiers* (Amsterdam, 1910), pp. 176–7.

197. J. X, *L'amour aux colonies*, pp. 345–6, 384.

198. B. Hagen, *Unter den Papua's* (Wiesbaden, 1899), pp. 234–8.

199. F. Sorge, 'Nissan-Inseln im Bismarck-Archipel', in R. S. Steinmetz (ed.), *Rechtsverhältnisse*, 397–424.

200. B. Thomson, *The Fijians* (London, 1908), p. 68.

201. G. Pratt, *A Samoan Dictionary* (Samoa, 1862), p. 101.

202. E. Tregear, *A Paumotuan Dictionary with Polynesian Comparatives* (Wellington, New Zealand, 1895), p. 77.

203. G. Turner, *Samoa a hundred years ago and long before* (London, 1884), p. 75.

204. J. S. Kubary, 'Die Religion der Pelauer', in A. Bastian (ed.), *Allerlei aus Volks- und Menschenkunde* (Berlin, 1888), p. 56.

205. W. Von Bülow, 'Das Geschlechtsleben der Samoaner', *Anthropophyteia*, 4 (1907), 97–8.

206. J. Waterhouse, *The King and People of Fiji* (London, 1866), p. 345.

207. 'Auch die Päderastie, Outibenet er a ptil, zwischen den Erwachsenen [ist] nicht unbekannt, obwohl die letztere nur vereinzelt vorkommen soll. . . . [Deren] öffentliche Besprechung könnte ohne ein Verletzen des Anstandes nicht geschehen.' J. S. Kubary, 'Die Verbrechen und das Strafverfahren auf den Pelau-Inseln (Mikronesien)', *Original-Mittheilungen aus der Ethnologischen Abtheilung der Königlichen Museen zu Berlin*, 1, 2/3 (1885/6), 84.

208. F. Hernsheim, *Beitrag zur Sprache der Marshall-Inseln* (Leipzig, 1880), p. 40.

209. A. Bastian, *Zur Kenntnis Hawaii's* (Berlin, 1883), p. 25.

210. E. T. Hardman, 'Notes on some habitants and customs of the natives of the Kimberley District, Western Australia', *Proceedings of the Royal Irish Academy*, 3rd Series, 1 (1889–91), 70–5.

211. A. G. B. Ravenscroft, 'Some habits and customs among the Chingalee tribe, Northern Territory, S.A.', *Transactions of the Royal Society of South Australia*, 15, 2 (1892), 121–2.

212. F. von Hellwald, 'Anthropologie und Ethnologie', in G. Jäger (ed.), *Handwörterbuch der Zoologie, Anthropologie und Ethnologie*, vol. 6 (Breslau, 1892), p. 81.

213. G. J. Pfeil, *Studien und Beobachtungen aus der Südsee* (Braunschweig, 1899), p. 74.

214. A. Dempwolff, 'Medicinische Anschauungen der Tami-Insulaner', *ZfE*, 34 (1902), 336.

215. A. C. Haddon, 'The ethnography of the Western Tribe of Torres Straits', *JRAI*, 19 (1890), 315.

216. E. Beardmore, 'The natives of Mowat, Daudi, New Guinea', *JRAI*, 19 (1890), 459–66. On this ceremony, see G. H. Herdt (ed.), *Ritualized Homosexuality in Melanesia* (Berkeley, 1984), pp. 20, 354; and B. M. Knauft, 'The question of ritualized homosexuality among the Kiwai of South New Guinea', *Journal of Pacific History*, 25 (1990), 188–210.

217. Foley, 'Quelques détails et réflexions sur la coutume et les moeurs de la coquette néo-calédonienne', *Bulletin de la société d'anthropologie de Paris*, 3rd Series, 2 (1879), 675–82. Also, see his article 'Sur les habitations et les moeurs des Néo-Calédoniens' in the same issue, 604–6.

218. B. H. Purcell, 'Rites and customs of Australian Aborigines', *ZfE*, 25 (1893), 288.

219. R. Helms, 'Anthropology', *Transactions of the Royal Society of of South Australia, Adelaide*, 16 (1892–96), part 3, 137–332.

220. H. Klaatsch, 'Some notes on scientific travel amongst the black population of tropical Australia', *Australasian Association for the Advancement of Science, Adelaide* (1908), pp. 581–2.

221. W. Schmidt, 'Die soziologische und religiös-ethische Gruppierung der australischen Stämme', *ZfE*, 41 (1909), 373.

222. F. von Reitzenstein, 'Der Kausalzusammenhang zwischen Geschlechtsverkehr und Empfängnis in Glaube und Brauch der Natur- und Kulturvölker', *ZfE*, 41 (1909), 651–2, 683.

223. See R. H. Matthews, 'The Thurrawal language' and 'Some Aboriginal tribes of Western Australia', both in the *Journal and Proceedings of the Royal Society of New South Wales for 1901, Sydney*, 35 (1901), 127–60, 217–22. See also R. H. Matthews, 'Languages of some native tribes of Queensland, New South Wales and Victoria' in the same journal, 36 (1902), 35–190. There are further references to homosexual relations within the context of initiation in articles by R. H. Matthews: 'Languages of the Kamilaroi and other Aboriginal tribes of New South Wales', *JRAI*, 33 (1903), 259–83; 'Das Kumbainggeri', *Mittheilungen der Anthropologischen Gesellschaft in Wien*, 33

(1903), 321–8; 'Language, organisation and initiation ceremonies of the Kogai tribes, Queensland', *ZfE*, 36 (1904), 28–38; and 'Some initiation ceremonies of the Aborigines of Victoria', *ZfE*, 37 (1905), 872–9.

224. Y. Hirn, *The Origins of Art* (London, 1900), pp. 347–8.

225. B. Hagen, *Unter den Papua's*, p. 238.

226. J. Chalmers, 'Notes on the Bugilai, British New-Guinea', *JRAI*, 33 (1903), 109.

227. R. Parkinson, *Dreissig Jahre in der Südsee* (Stuttgart, 1907). I have consulted the English translation by Barry (Port Moresby, n.d.), p. 544.

228. M. Moskowski, 'Die Völkerstamme am Mamberano', *ZfE*, 43 (1911), 339.

229. O. Finsch, 'Ueber die Bewohner von Ponapé (Östl. Karolinen)', *ZfE*, 12 (1880), 320.

230. J. Rémy, *Ka Moolelo Hawaii* (Paris, 1862), pp. xlii–xliii.

231. O. Stoll, *Das Geschlechtsleben*, p. 157.

232. A. Corre, *L'ethnographie criminelle*, p. 404.

233. J. X, *L'amour aux colonies*, pp. 299–301.

234. See G. H. Herdt, *Guardians of the Flute* (New York, 1981); G. H. Herdt (ed.), *Ritualized Homosexuality in Melanesia*; G. Bleibtreu-Ehrenberg, *Mannbarheitsriten* (Berlin, 1980); and W. Schievenhoevel, 'Ritualised adult male/adolescent male sexual behavior in Melanesia', in J. R. Feierman (ed.), *Pedophilia: Biosocial Dimensions* (Berlin, 1990), pp. 349–421.

235. F. Ratzel, *Völkerkunde* (Leipzig and Vienna, 1894) (enlarged, definitive version, 1895); T. Waitz and G. Gerland, *Anthropologie der Naturvölker*, 6 vols (Leipzig, 1859–72); E. Reclus, *Les primitives. Etudes d'ethnologie comparée* (Paris, 1903).

236. A. Bastian, *Rechtsverhältnisse bei verschiedenen Völkern der Erde* (Berlin, 1872), pp. 382–404; A. H. Post, *Bausteine für eine allgemeine Rechtswissenschaft auf vergleichend-ethnologischer Base*, 2 vols (Oldenburg, 1880–1); A. H. Post, *Studien zur Entwicklungs-geschichte des Familienrechts* (Oldenburg and Leipzig, 1890); A. H. Post, *Grundriss der ethnologischen Jurisprudenz*, 2 vols (Oldenburg and Leipzig, 1894–5); J. Kohler, 'Fragebogen zur Erforschung der Rechtsverhältnisse der sogenannten Naturvölker, namentlich in den deutschen Kolonialländern', *ZfvR*, 12 (1897), 427–40; A. Bastian, *Rechtverhältnisse* (Berlin, 1903).

237. J. G. Frazer, *Questions on the Customs, Beliefs and Languages of Savages* (Cambridge, 1907); J. G. Frazer, *The Golden Bough* (Cambridge, 1890); A. Van Gennep, *Religions, moeurs et légendes* (Paris, 1908/9).

238. A. Bastian, *Der Mensch in der Geschichte*; F. Schultze, *Psychologie der Naturvölker* (Leipzig, 1900); Ch. Letourneau, *La psychologie ethnique* (Paris, 1901); W. Wundt, *Völkerpsychologie*, 10 vols (Leipzig, 1900–20).

239. V. Jaekel, *Studien zur vergleichenden Völkerkunde* (Berlin, 1901); H. Ploss and M. Bartels, *Das Weib in der Natur- und Völkerkunde*, 2 vols (Leipzig, 1905); A. Friedenthal, *Das Weib im Leben der Völker*, 2 vols (Berlin, 1910).

240. H. Ploss and B. Benz, *Das Kind in Brauch und Sitte der Völker. Völkerkundige Studien* (Leipzig, 1912).

241. A. Van Gennep, *Les rites de passage* (Paris, 1909); H. Schurtz, *Altersklassen und Männerbunde* (Berlin, 1902); E. Crawley, *The Mystic Rose* (n.p., 1902 (2nd ed. 1927)), pp. ix, xiv; E. Crawley, 'Dress', in *Encyclopaedia of Religion and Ethics*, 5 (1912), 68–71.

242. J. Kohler, *Das sexuelle Leben der Naturvölker* (Augsburg, 1900), pp. 36–40; J. Müller, *Das sexuelle Leben der alten Kulturvölker* (Leipzig, 1902); O. Stoll, *Das Geschlechtsleben*; H. Freimark, *Okkultismus und Sexualität* (Leipzig, 1909); J. M. Berger, *Masochismus, Sadismus und andere Perversitäten aller Zeiten und Völker* (Leipzig, 1914); G. Buschan, 'Das Sexualleben in der Völkerkunde', in I. Bloch, *Handbuch der Sexualwissenschaft* (m.p., n.d.), pp. 299–396.

243. H. Berkusky, 'Geschlechtsleben bei den Naturvölker'; W. Schrickert, 'Zur Anthropologie des gleichgeschlechtlichen Liebe', *Politisch-anthropologische Revue*, 1 (1902), 379–82.

244. F. von Hellwald, *Culturgeschichte in ihrer natürlichen Entwicklung bis zur Gegenwart* (Augsburg, 1875), p. 398.

245. 'Über die namenlose Demoralisation, die mit einem masslosen orientalischen Luxus gepaarte cynische Rohheit, selbst in den höheren Gesellschaftskreise Bagdad's, ruhen die besten, vollgültigsten Zeugnisse in den Werken der gleichzeitigen Dichter. Wie in Rom mit dem griechischen Einflüsse die Päderastie, so verbreitete sich fast gleichzeitig mit dem persischen Einflusse das ursprünglich den Arabern fremde Laster der Knabenliebe zu erschreckender Allgemeinheit.' *Ibid.*

246. *Ibid.*, pp. 456, 508.

247. J. Müller, *Das sexuelle Leben*, p. 48.

248. *Ibid.*, pp. 73–5.

249. G. Buschan, 'Das Sexualleben in der Völkerkunde', pp. 325–7.

250. 'A priori wird anzunehmen sein, dass es auch bei aussereuropäischen Völkern stets eine Anzahl von Individuen gibt, welche die schlechte, sterile Aberration der Spezies auf Grund natürlicher Anlage repräsentieren, und in der Tat ist dieser Nachweis wenigstens für Japan und Ostafrika bereits möglich, für manche andere Gebiete ist eine angeborene Homosexualität wenigstens wahrscheinlich zu machen.' O. Stoll, *Das Geschlechtsleben*, pp. 949–51.

251. *Ibid.*, pp. 957, 958–9.

252. 'Aus all diesen zahlreichen Angaben scheint so viel hervorzugehen, dass auch bei den amerikanischen Völkern eine gewisse Zahl von Männern von originär oder erworben feminiener Psyche vorhanden waren, die ihre Neigungen nach als Passive beim homosexuellen Verkehr dienten, während als Aktive die virilen Individuen der einzelnen Stämme fungierten.' *Ibid.*, p. 965.

253. *Ibid.*, pp. 970–1.

254. J. J. Bachofen, *Das Mutterrecht* (Stuttgart, 1861).

255. H. Ploss and B. Benz, *Das Kind*, pp. 529–31, 815–17.

256. R. F. von Krafft-Ebing, *Psychopathia sexualis*, p. 2.

257. 'Episoden des sittlichen Niedergangs im Leben der Völker falle jeweils zusammen mit Zeiten der Verweichlichung, der Üppigkeit und des Luxus . . . . In solchen Zeiten des staalichen Verfalls traten vielfach geradezu monströse Verirrungen des sexuellen Trieblebens auf, die jedoch zum Teil auf psycho- oder wenigstens neuro-pathologische Zustände in der Bevölkerung sich zurückführen lassen.' *Ibid.*, pp. 6–7.

258. *Ibid.*, p. 7, note 2.

Chapter five

Homosexual Emancipation and the Paradoxes of Universality (c. 1860 – c. 1918)

There were no ready channels to give shape to homosexual lives, and early writings drew on a range of discursive resources to present a public face for same-sex love. The weight of antihomosexual prejudice complicated the task, leading often to indirect morally acceptable characterizations of gay life.

– Barry Adam[1]

In the previous chapter I focused upon the professional discourse of physicians, sexologists, anthropologists and ethnographers, who were not personally involved in the struggle for the emancipation of men engaging in same-sex relations. The paradigmatic medical construction of modern homosexuality admittedly pulled the public debate away from a moral and religious rhetoric of the sodomite's guilt. It was crucial also in the public debate on the decriminalization of male-to-male sexual relations in countries such as Great Britain and Germany. In other European countries, these had been depenalized by or after the example of the French *Code pénal* of 1791, yet a regulative discourse persisted, even when its outlook was shifting from repressive police control to medical patronizing.

But equal, if not greater importance must be accorded to social and intellectual initiatives from within the homosexual subcultures of Europe themselves. In this chapter, I will focus in particular on the 'culture of resistance' that unfolded amidst a self-proclaimed 'homosexual' intelligentsia and whose major advocates were Benkert, Ulrichs, Hirschfeld, Raffalovich, Symonds, and Carpenter. On its margin, other intellectuals, including the later Iwan Bloch, Henry Havelock Ellis, and Edward Westermarck, also subscribed to the political agenda of homosexual emancipation, even when they were not openly homosexual themselves. Participating in a wider movement for social and sexual reform, they all subscribed to the biomedical model, yet, rather than accepting the stigma implied by it, they invoked the natural foundation of sexual identity to recommend a policy of legal, social and cultural emancipation. 'This', says Jeffrey Weeks, '[was] the paradox of the sexological endeavour. It not only sought to regulate through naming; it also provided the springboard for self-definition and individual and collective resistance.'[2]

The question to be answered here is how the politics of affirmation by modern 'homosexuals' and their allies addressed sexual variety outside the West. A reasonable expectation is that their reformulation of the ethnographic record was already distinct because a positive value was ascribed to same-sex praxis and constituted a 'geography of desire', rather than 'perversion'.

But how alternative, really, was the homosexual minority's ethnographic argumentation, aside from a more embracing representation of same-sex practices in societies overseas? Did it challenge the paradigm of evolutionist and related ethnographies, or did it merely ascribe new, more positive meanings to data that otherwise corroborated the rhetoric of perversion and degeneracy? Also, did it discard or reiterate the racialist presumptions that characterized explanations of non-western same-sex practices advanced elsewhere? Did it question the epistemological premises of analogous thinking at all, or did it reproduce them rather uncritically? Finally, if the universality of homosexuality ought to be stressed, then which of its widely variable characteristics across the world were to be included as part of its natural substratum? More concretely, what did the ethnographic record reveal about the 'representational resistance'[3] of the new 'homosexual' intelligentsia?

Medicalization and emancipation of the 'third sex'

Within the urban crucible of European cities, subcultures of homosexual men became more visible as the nineteenth century proceeded. They grew out of the sodomites' networks of the eighteenth and early nineteenth centuries, resurging after epochs of harshened repression in Great Britain and Holland especially. Neither homosexuality's criminal status in Great Britain and Germany, nor the ongoing policing in countries where it had been decriminalized, was sufficient to suppress the sharpening profile of a homosexual community. The very policies of regulation themselves in fact proved instrumental to the intensifying need felt by men engaging in sexual relations with men to create and organize their own, subcultural universe.[4]

In the context of the new, biological construction of gender identity, its members gradually profiled themselves as being at odds with other people not because they deliberately chose to be so, but rather because they experienced their sexuality as having a permanent nature, as a fixed 'role'.[5] The modes of self-identification varied widely between the lower, middle and upper classes, between countryside and city, among those having experienced different moral climates and legal regimes. But the urban clubs and bars especially provided a platform for discrete experimentation and eventually generated a new vocabulary, confirming the new self-assumed homosexual role. Others, who felt less secure, lingered in the twilight zone of male prostitution. The transgressive aspect of having sex with lower class male prostitutes made its homosexual character look more acceptable, analogous, moreover, to the milieu of heterosexual prostitution and its patronage.[6]

The urban homosexual subculture drew the attention of physicians and sexologists, who perceived its self-styled members as congruent with their newly developed theories of perversion. The medical construction of the modern 'homosexual' actually confirmed a new social reality of urban, self-proclaimed men – and gradually women too[7] – who pursued sexual relations or relationships with people of their own sex. 'The medical literature', says George Chauncey, Jr., 'developed in response to challenges to the Victorian sex/gender system and the emergence of sexual subcultures in the cities and it changed in a manner which reflected changes in the actual organisation of sex/gender roles in the society'.[8] The relation between medical theory and the new, modern 'homosexual' was not a simple one, accordingly, and veered from the latter's fierce rejection of the physician's pathological etiology to his acceptance of it as a scientific alibi for his profile of himself having a distinct, inescapable identity. Klaus Müller has demonstrated how the acceptance and interiorization of medical rhetoric alleviated the issue of personal guilt, as anomalous sexuality was seen as the outcome of biological or neurological constitution, rather than of failing morality.[9] That the etiology of homosexuality, along with other 'perversions', was still within the realm of pathology was the price of the ticket for self-affirmation and social tolerance. For many, it also facilitated the difficult psychological process of self-acceptance in a persistently homophobic world that kept denouncing them as sinful, debauched or criminal.

In Germany most prominently, medical theory was embraced by homosexual intellectuals as a powerful instrument in the resistance against legal discrimination stipulated by paragraph 175 of the penal law.[10] Its path was prepared by Carl Heinrich Ulrichs' theory of *Uranismus*[11] and by Karl Marie Benkert, also known as Kertbeny, who pleaded for abolition of the infamous paragraph.

Benkert opposed Ulrichs's theory of *Urninge*, as this connected homosexuality to a 'feminine soul' and explained such by accidental embryological development. The 'riddle' remained unsolved, so he insisted, and it was far from proven that homosexuality was at all tied to feminine gender.[12] So, already, a crucial divide surfaced between a medical model that connected homosexuality to gender disorder and another, that did not. Both, however, shared the assumption that sexuality was rooted biologically. The 'congenital' or inborn character of sexual preference was also emphasized by Magnus Hirschfeld because this made homosexuality incurable. He thus opposed Moll and von Schrenck-Notzing, who had stressed the 'acquired' character of homosexuality and claimed that it could be cured by means of psychotherapy.

Magnus Hirschfeld (1868–1935) was undoubtedly the most reknowned advocate of homosexual emancipation as well as the most obstinate representative of medical argumentation to achieve this goal.[13] A first brief study on male and female homosexuality, *Sappho und Sokrates* (1896), already previsaged his theory that both were the outcome of inborn factors, influenced by the internal secretions of certain glands. The booklet was still influenced by Albert Moll, but it already foreshadowed Ulrichs' theory of the *dritte Geschlecht* or 'third sex'.[14]

In May 1897, Ulrichs founded the Wissenschaftlich-Humanitäres Komitee (Scientific and Humanitarian Committee), that was to gather scientific arguments for a campaign against the legal repression of homosexual men (its motto was *per scientiam ad justitiam*). He then sent out a petition against paragraph 175 that was signed by some five thousand prominent intellectuals and put on the agenda of the Reichstag at once. Parliamentary debate only took place in 1905, however, when it received support by the Social Democrats. But it was defeated in the wake of press scandals about the homosexual entourage of the emperor Wilhelm II.[15]

The polemic character of Hirschfeld's political campaign prompted him to expand and update his scientific database. Anticipating gay and lesbian studies of today, he set out to gather sociological, psychological, historical, anthropological, and legal information about homosexuality and collaborated in due course with Eugen Wilhelm (who also wrote under the name Numa Praetorius), Paul Näcke, and Ferdinand Karsch-Haack, who each subscribed to Hirschfeld's motto that 'no single human behaviour could be alien to humanity'. The results were published in the *Jahrbuch für sexuelle Zwischenstufen*, first issued in 1899. (Volumes 10 to 19 were titled differently as *Vierteljahresberichte des Wissenschaftlich-Humanitären Komitees*.)[16]

After the rejection of the petition in 1905, Hirschfeld joined efforts with Iwan Bloch, pseudonym of Eugen Dühren (1872–1922), who coined the word *Sexualwissenschaft* the next year. The higher standards of scientific rigour made the *Jahrbuch* become of secondary importance next to the *Zeitschrift für Sexualwissenschaft*, initiated in 1908. Historically, the new journal announced the beginning of incorporation with psychoanalysis with an article on 'hysterical fantasy and its relation to bisexuality' by Sigmund Freud himself. It was shortlived, however, and merged after only one year with the more popular journal *Sexualprobleme*. The resulting amalgam was called *Zeitschrift für Sexualwissenschaft und Sexualpolitik*. Despite these failures, Hirschfeld published two voluminous works, *Die Transvestiten* (1910) and *Die Homosexualität des Mannes und des Weibes* (1914), that were to demonstrate the author's scientific integrity.[17] In 1913, he was co-founder with Iwan Bloch and Albert Eulenburg of the Medizinische Gesellschaft für Sexualwissenschaft und Eugenik. It was followed in 1919 by the foundation of the Institut für Sexualwissenschaft, that framed the campaign for homosexual emancipation within a wider programme of sexual and social reform until its destruction by the Nazis in 1933.[18] Hirschfeld, after travelling around the world a second time and setting up a new life in Nice, died in 1935.[19]

Bloch, in his turn, had subscribed initially to the model of acquired perversion in his *Beiträge zur Äthiologie der Psychopathia Sexualis* of 1902-3. In this comprehensive work, he had reacted against the thesis, put forward recurrently by others, that homosexuality, like other perversions, was closely intertwined with the increasingly decadent mentality of *fin-de-siècle* Europe. In reality, it occurred in a more or less equal measure across the globe: 'This general image of sexual anomalies as inherently human, ubiquitous phenomena allows for representing a large part of those, seen as pathological, as really physiological and considerably reduces the terrain of "degeneration".'[20] Social conditions, Bloch maintained, led some to acquire a preference for sexual relations with people of their own sex.

Five years later, however, Bloch aligned with Hirschfeld and called homosexuality an inborn, physiological variety. As such, it was different from the 'pseudo-homosexuality' in ancient Greece as well as the Orient, from 'hermaphroditism' and from 'bisexuality'. Bloch did not subscribe to Hirschfeld's theory of the third sex, however, and stressed that not all homosexuals showed feminine traits, whereas these also occurred occasionally with heterosexuals.[21]

Disagreement was expressed also by the French belletrist and publicist, Marc André Raffalovich (1864-1934), who held that homosexuality was inborn, though he did not share its representation by Ulrichs and Hirschfeld as being linked with femininity.[22] Seeking to present a more favourable account of *uranisme*, this early advocate of homosexual rights called upon medical theory to establish a homosexual role that was masculine-defined. But he felt that sexual encounters must not be actively pursued. Instead, homosexual men should marry like others and remain chaste in body, if not in mind.[23] 'Accordingly, [he] heaped abuse on "effeminate" inverts, arguing that their moral worth was in inverse relation to their degree of effeminacy.'[24] An individual's 'uranian' tendencies ought to be detected at an early stage as well, so that he could be educated to redirect them towards a chaste ideal of love. In France, an equally ambiguous position was taken by Emile Zola (1840-1902), who compared the fate of *inverts* to a hunchback's, who, like the former, had not chosen his condition. Acceptance did not prevent the author, however, from depicting homosexuals as a 'disorganizer of the family'.[25] Only André Gide (1869–1951) positioned himself more radically in his privately published essay Corydon (begun in 1907, published in 1911). Yet, while doing so, he too invested a great effort in separating 'normal homosexuals' from their degenerate, effeminate counterparts.[26]

Like Gide, the Dutch author Arnold Aletrino (1858–1916) had first supported a model of virile homosexuality.[27] But he leaned towards a more Hirschfeldian representation of effeminate homosexuals later on.[28] Their anomalous status, however, must not lead to discrimination, argued Aletrino, who proved more tolerant of effeminate homosexuals than Gide and became one among the first spokesmen of the homosexual movement in the Netherlands.[29] In 1911, he founded the Dutch Scientific and Humanitarian Committee (Nederlandsch Wetenschappelijk Humanitair Komitee) with Schorer (1866–1957) and von Römer (1873–1965), which would guarantee some degree of continuity in the homosexual emancipation movement once its German model was attacked by the Nazis after 1933.[30]

The initiatives of Ulrichs, Benkert, Hirschfeld and Bloch had triggered a protean movement of homosexual emancipation in Great Britain as well, and inspired progressive intellectuals including John Addington Symonds, Henry Havelock Ellis and Edward Carpenter to become advocates of homosexual emancipation especially after the trial of Oscar Wilde in 1895.

As early as 1883, Symonds (1840–1893) published A Problem in Greek Ethics. He was a closeted homosexual[31] and only ten copies were 'privately printed for the Author's use'. It would be followed in 1891 by A Problem in Modern Ethics and by a more comprehensive study on Sexual Inversion, co-written by Havelock Ellis. This was published first in German in Leipzig in 1896.

The fame of Havelock Ellis (1859–1939) grew as a result of new legal actions against the English edition of Sexual Inversion, which stimulated him to further elaborate the theme of homosexuality along with other sexual themes. By then, he had already published another article on the subject in the Italian journal Archivio delle psicopatie sessuali.[32] As 'a representative [of] the new radical/socialist intelligentsia that sprang up in the wake of the socialist revival of the early 1880s',[33] he included a more elaborate version of Sexual Inversion in his Studies in the Psychology of Sex, yet decided again to have this seven-volume work published in its complete form only in New York City as late as 1933.[34]

Edward Carpenter (1844–1929) portrayed himself as a social and sexual reformer with anarchist tendencies. As a prophet of a new kind of 'bisexual' society, he lived together with a working-class man, George Merrill and disseminated his ideas in Love's Coming of Age (1896, enlarged edition, including 'The Intermediate Sex' in 1906), Ioläus: An Anthology of Friendship (1902), and Intermediate Types among Primitive Folk (1914). His 'socialism' was based on moral rather than scientific arguments and imbued with a kind of mystical naturalism. He subsequently formulated a case for homosexuality as part of a sexual millenarian philosophy that depicted both sexes as 'a continuous group'. 'Intermediate types', Carpenter believed, were to be valued as carriers of new, important forces of life.[35]

Common to all three advocates of homosexual emancipation was a shared plea for moral relativism, whereas their etiology of sexual preference was grounded in biology. They emphasized the transience of contemporary Victorian attitudes by comparing them with other cultures both within (ancient Greece) and outside the West. As a 'natural' variety that was inborn, homosexuality could not be seen as a degenerative, morbid disease. Eventually, the efforts of Ellis and Carpenter – Symonds died in 1893 – led to the foundation of the British Society for the Study of Sex Psychology (BSSSP) in 1914. Ideally, it was to parallel similar, investigative initiatives especially in Germany, but it never reached the same dimension and became part of a wider, international movement of sexual reform. The issue of homosexuality gradually became one of secondary importance in the public debate about birth control and eugenics.[36]

The poetics and politics of anthropology

Along with the organization of a political campaign against legal oppression or social intolerance went scientific initiatives, that were to document the case for homosexuality. Tied to such an agenda, these were no less biased than the stigmatization by physicians, moralists and legislators. Their casuistics therefore ought to be read with equal caution. They were very significant, however, for the crystallization of a counter-cultural rhetoric and contain important clues, accordingly, to the historical understanding of the early homosexual politics of resistance. The issue here is an interpretation of the documents not as sources of factual information, but rather as a key to the deconstruction of the emancipatory politics and poetics, or, put differently, of the motives and argumentation, themes and tropes hidden within the textual and contextual structure of these documents themselves.

Hirschfeld's agenda went further than the mere decriminalization of homosexual relations among men. It also called for recognition of the homosexual as a separate identity, a *Zwischenstufe* or 'intermediate, third sex', that is, between women and men. In reality, his model was close to Ulrichs's *Urninge*, even when he acknowledged the latter's pioneering role only reluctantly.[37] The *dritte Geschlecht* was biologically rooted and could not be annulled by psychotherapy or any other treatment, nor could it be successfully repressed.

Initially, Hirschfeld stressed that the third sex combined both male and female traits. A narrow link existed between homosexuality and effeminacy. After the foundation of the Scientific Humanitarian Committee in 1897, he widened his definition of the 'third sex' and included both masculine and effeminate forms of homosexuality. But speculation on the inherently 'feminine' side of homosexual men lingered on and the study of the 'intermediate sex' remained haunted by its cross-gender variety.

Perhaps the problem would have dissolved were it not that Hirschfeld's empirical studies kept focusing predominantly on cross-gender homosexuality. This can be seen in his article 'Ursachen und Wesen des Uranismus' (1903), that contained a photographic juxtaposition of a virile man and a rather feminine-looking *Urning*. In *Berlin's dritte Geschlecht* (1904) too, a picture was drawn of the city's homosexual subculture as deeply marked by cross-gender behaviour and travesty.[38]

In this light, one may ask if and how Hirschfeld's ongoing factual emphasis on the cross-gender variety of homosexuality was reflected in his assessments of ethnographic evidence. Cross-cultural comparison, in fact, was an important component of the *Jahrbücher* and Hirschfeld frequently included ethnographic data from non-western cultures in his books and articles. Yet, a reconstruction of Hirschfeld's own ethnographic discourse remains hazardous because of his predominantly casuistic approach.

Die Homosexualität des Mannes und des Weibes (1914)[39] especially may be called the *Fundgrube* of Hirschfeldian theory. It was based on more than 10,000 case histories of men and women, gathered in Germany, Europe, America, Asia and northern Africa. Many of these case studies were collected by Hirschfeld personally. Some, in fact, dated from his first journey around the world in 1893–4. But he also retrieved information from friends, acquaintances, colleagues, even consulates and embassies across the world. It was the largest and most comprehensive sample ever taken until this very day.

His case studies were organized by a 'psychological questionnaire', allowing him to distinguish between homosexuality, real and pseudo-hermaphroditism, or to construct statistical tables on the distribution of homosexuality in different countries. But references to other ethnographic sources merely function as corroborative material for his central claim that homosexuality was universal and congenital. A disproportionately high number of cases as well as ethnographic cross-references, moreover, pertained to the effeminate or cross-gender form of homosexuality. Regional differences, social, cultural and/or racial conditions were altogether played down to corroborate his model of a universally visible 'third sex'.

Regrettably, Hirschfeld did not keep a diary of his first trip around the world. It might have offered more or different keys to an understanding of his ethnographic discourse. In *Die Weltreise eines Sexualforschers*, published in 1933, he described how his second journey around the world (1930–2) allowed him to collect new, important cross-cultural evidence.[40] Other ethnographic publications or editions of non-western texts were also published during the latter years of his life.[41]

It is important to realize that the rhetoric of universality was not Hirschfeld's invention. Already in 1897, Josef Kohler had presented homosexuality as part of natural folk as well as of civilization in the West:

Not a single people has been wiped out by unnatural vice. ... Sex with persons of the same sex undoubtedly springs from perversities, from an anomalous sexual drive, from a kind of hermaphrodite personality, that usually is not a product of civilization. It occurs among natural folk as well.[42]

Kohler emphasized, moreover, that no historical link existed between increasing evidence of homosexuality and cultural decadence:

It is just as unclear what determines the higher or lower incidence of *Urninge* as so many other problems of folk psychology. It certainly is wrong to believe, as many do, that *Urningthum* is inherent to decadent societies only. Such is contradicted by history.[43]

The presumed cultural stagnation in the Orient was a result, like the widespread pederasty, of the artificial and unbalanced seclusion of women in seraglios. Worldwide very few societies punished homosexuality, said the author, who rejected the current explanation of legal sanctions, when occurring at all, as an incentive to people to abstain from non-procreative sex. Yet, new in Hirschfeld's ethnographic trope of universality was its positive evaluation of homosexuality as a sexual variant, rather than as an anomaly, and, secondly, the notion that it was somehow equally spread across the world.

When looking more closely at today's cross-cultural surveys of homosexual behaviour, it proves that Hirschfeld's model of a 'third sex' was not as accurate and comprehensive as he suggested. Not only was (nor is) homosexuality not always gender-structured, but there were (and are) societies also, where the proliferation of homosexually active men as a separate category of identity, as 'homosexuals', was (and is) absent.

To travellers, ethnographers and anthropologists who felt committed to the cause of homosexual emancipation, often – but not always – because they felt themselves attracted to people of their own sex, this must have been clear as well. Perhaps the power of the biological paradigm, that was shared by sexual pathologists and prominent advocates of homosexual rights alike, was demonstrated by the fact that attempts were made recurrently to fit observations of same-sex behaviour outside the West within a European cognitive framework of homosexual identity. But frequently the latter's narrow definition as an 'intermediate' or 'third' sex was not appropriate for the description and explanation of same-sex behaviour outside the West.

Only a few first hand ethnographic documents are known by authors who were explicitly committed to the representation of homosexuality as a positive, natural variety. These texts are at once exciting and opaque, calling for cautious interpretation not so much because the authors' individual emotions were easily projected onto the people observed – which occurred equally in negativist or homophobic ethnographic narratives – but because the authors' commitment to the cause of homosexual emancipation may have triggered a descriptive mode that was, in the end, inaccurate.

Such was the case of Richard Burton, who, though 'Victorian', held on to a pre-modern notion of sodomy as an act. His environmentalism, on the other hand, recalled Enlightenment theories of sexual morality. It is appropriate to discuss his ethnography of male-to-male sexual behaviour here, as he embodied the transition from a pre-modern into a modern geography of perversion/desire.[44]

Burton, whose wife Isabel burned many of his manuscripts after his death, obviously did not consider marriage to be an obstacle to other sexual pursuits with women, and probably – though no conclusive evidence is known – also with boys or men. The most direct 'confession' is to be found in his early report on boy brothels in Karachi (as discussed in the previous chapter). Indirect biographical information, such as Isabella's act of posthumous censorship, and Burton's semi-voyeuristic erudition in matters of pederasty at least suggest that he felt attracted to men. Passages such as the following from his book on Cameroon may well have made his wife aware of her husband's exceptional empathy for the male:

The male figure here, as all the world over, is notably superior ... to that of the female. The latter is ... meaningless and monotonous. The former far excels it in variety of form and in sinew. In these lands, ... there will be a score of fine male figures to one female, and there she is, as everywhere else, as inferior as is the Venus de Medici to the Apollo Belvedere.[45]

Similar expressions of a homoerotic sensibility can be found in *A Mission to Gelele* (1864)[46] and *Zanzibar* (1872).[47]

Burton's greatest merit consists in his translations of a handful of important texts that described an Oriental *ars amandi*. They were all published by the Kama Shastra Society of London and Benares, a closed circle, counting as its members only Richard Burton and Forster Fitzgerald Arbuthnot,[48] which was sponsored mainly by Richard Monckton Milnes, later Lord Houghton, an eccentric with a leaning towards (heterosexual) sadomasochism whose collection of erotic literature was notorious.[49] Milnes' financial support allowed Burton to publish his own translations of Vatsyayana's *Kama Sutra*, Kalyana Malla's *Ananga Ranga*, both originally in Sanskrit, and of Jâmi's *Behâristân* and Sa'di's *Gulistân*, both Persian texts.[50]

Not all are equally relevant as contributions to the debate on sodomy and homosexuality, nor was his translation of Al Nefzawi's *Al Raud al atir wa nuzhat al Khatir* influential outside the milieu of sexual esoterica. Better known in the West as *The Perfumed Garden*, this was translated twice into French prior to his translating it into English in 1886.[51] Burton's motive to begin a new translation, this time from the Arabic, was not linguistic, but inspired by his intention to include the passages of homosexual content that had been bowdlerized in the previous translations. The manuscript remained unfinished, however, and after Burton's death in 1890, it was destroyed by his wife Isabel.[52]

Burton's translation of the *Alf-Layla Wa-Layla*, however, did become an influential source of reference. His *Arabian Nights* was the first complete translation, based partially on the Arabic text's incomplete Calcutta edition of 1839–42, partially on his own independent translation of the remaining parts.[53] Burton's deliberate and explicit inclusion of the homosexual passages nourished the Orientalist sensibility of many a homosexual reader both in England and on the continent, and was no doubt exemplary for those who not only wanted social acceptance of their homosexuality, but felt like indulging in it avidly.

Their reading of the *Arabian Nights* was perhaps prompted even more by Burton's annotations, providing explicit information on the social and cultural background of the Arabic texts. The Terminal Essay, conluding the tenth volume, is perhaps the best known, if selective, ethnographic synopsis of same-sex practices across the world. In it, the author held that homosexuality was virtually universal, but that a territory could be defined, where it

is popular and endemic, held at the worst to be a mere pecadillo, whilst the races to the North and South of [its] limits ... practise it only sporadically amid the opprobium of their fellows who, as a rule, are physically incapable of performing the operation and look upon it with the liveliest disgust.[54]

This so-called 'Sotadic Zone' was named, somewhat arbitrarily, after the Alexandrian poet Sotades (third century BC) whose apparently innocuous verses became obscene if read backward.[55] It included the Mediterranean world between 30° and 43° northern latitude, then narrowed down eastward, including Asia Minor, Mesopotamia, Chaldaea, Afghanistan, Sind, the Punjab and Kashmir. In Asia 'the belt begins to broaden, enfolding China, Japan and Turkistan' (in that order), then embracing the South Sea Islands and all of the American continent before European colonization.[56]

Burton emphasized moreover that his model was 'geographical and climatic, not racial'[57] but he did flirt with a biological model of homosexual identity, that implied undeniably that male love was at once physical and sexual:

[Within] the Sotadic Zone there is a blending of the masculine and feminine temperaments, a crasis which elsewhere occurs only sporadically. Hence the male *féminisme* whereby the man becomes *patiens* as well as *agens*; and the woman a tribade, a votary of *mascula* Sappho, Queen of Frictrices or Rubbers.[58]

The awkward jargon must not disguise Burton's biological orientation, however, especially as it was reinforced by his implicit subscription to Mantegazza's model of the homosexual's anomalous nervous constitution between the rectum and the genitalia. This model was far-fetched and classified sodomitical desire as 'peripheric', 'luxurious' and 'psychical' according to the degree of nervous dislocation near the anus rather than the penis.[59] Burton himself called the model superficial, yet did not discard its biological premisses. However, rather than ascribing the homosexual's biological difference to embryological development or degenerative processes, he felt that climatological conditions explained sufficiently why men grew prone to male-to-male sexuality: 'Something of the kind is necessary to explain the fact of this pathological love extending over the greater portion of the habitable world, without any apparent connection of race or media, from the polished Greek to the cannibal Tupi of the Brazil.'[60] What is meant by 'media' is not clear.[61] His racialist rhetoric, next, suggests a familiar distinction between the idealistic Greek variety of pederasty and its 'primitive' counterparts. Earlier, Burton had already pointed out that pederasty sometimes had a 'noble sentimental side', referring alternately to Plato and the Sufis.[62] Later, he distinguished the Greek variety also from Etruscan and Roman homosexual 'debauchery'.[63]

His idiosyncratic ethnography of pederasty was often inconsistent and contradicted previously made claims. If homosexuality was not defined racially, then how must we understand his portrayal of the Turkish people as 'a race of born pederasts'?[64] How to reconcile a theory of climatological conditioning with vaguely diffusionist descriptions of the import of homosexuality in Lower Egypt by the Iranians, in Northern Africa by the Romans, of the cult of androgyny in Syria and Palestine by the Egyptians?[65] Or how to align his sweeping model of homosexuality caught between two latitudes with his semi-sociological explanation of a higher rate of homosexuality in cities compared to the countryside? Also, if homosexuality is more prevalent in urban contexts, then how to clarify its presumed ubiquity among rural populations of America? And if climate is indeed a decisive factor, then how could Burton acknowledge, without questioning the ingenuity of his theory, that large areas of the American continent have a moderate and even, at places, hyperborean climate?[66] In its 'second stage', Burton wrote elsewhere, the 'nature-implanted tendency' towards homosexuality may be given sacred meaning within a wider context of animism or other religious cults. This happened in Rome and Egypt, in Mesopotamia as well as in Mexico and Peru. Such portrayal may well make sense, but it was not congruent with the author's self-styled environmentalist theory.[67]

Other inconsistencies would be pointed out by Symonds, as I will indicate later, and Burton may well have anticipated them as he went on gathering data to either corroborate or modify his theory. His new, unfinished translation of Al Nefzawi's work, now destroyed, also was to contain additional notes. Norman Penzer, informed by an intimate acquaintance of Burton himself, indicated that they would include more data on 'anthropological customs, curious vices, and personal experiences connected with Arabia and the Arabs' as well as 'comparisons . . . with those of other Eastern countries, as also with some Western ones, in both classical and modern times, as for example, Babylonia, Egypt, China, and Central America'. Some of the information added to the *Arabian Nights* was to be integrated with the new addenda to *The Perfumed Garden* along with a more theoretical text, relying heavily on Ulrichs.[68]

Burton's translations and commentaries were a mixture of a scientific intention to enlighten and a more polemic taste for provocation. Rana Kabbani remarked that 'he was to out-Nefzawi Nefzawi' and to use the original Arabic text as a pretext for at times sensationalist commentaries on sex.[69] He had been co-founder of the Anthropological Society of London in 1863, later of the Anthropological Institute of Great Britain and Ireland, but his relationship with professional anthropologists soured partly because of his emphasis on sexual themes, easily seen as voyeurism within the Victorian climate of his time.[70] This may well explain why his works resonated more within the subcultural milieu of homosexual aesthetes than among the world of anthropological science. For the aesthetes, the author's vague theoretical views hardly outweighed his attractive theory that elsewhere a different morality reigned.

It is known that the German ethnographer Günther Tessmann felt attracted to men, more particularly to the African men whom he encountered during his ethnographic expedition in Cameroon.[71] While subscribing to the *Kulturkreislehre*,[72] Tessmann's approach was racialist in its biologist assumptions as well as in its hierarchical and rather subjective appreciations of anatomical variety. Thus, the American Indian people were called inferior because of their flat behinds compared to the Apollo of Belvedere or 'an ordinary typical black'.[73] The juxtaposition, moreover, of a Greek icon of male beauty to the male African was not without significance in the light of Tessmann's erotic fascination, and is a fine example of homosexual discourse's 'hidden textuality'.

In Tessmann's major study on the Pangwe or Fang (Cameroon, Equatorial Guinea, Gabon), an apparently contradictory estimate of their sexuality can also be better understood as a reflection of his homosexual inclination. While appreciative at first of their dignity and impartiality in matters of sex, he suddenly became irritated when facing the failing loyalty of his male assistants once they had had intercourse with girls.[74]

But such momentary flashes of subjectivity remained marginal to his intention to offer a scientifically sound portrayal of Fang society and beliefs. Male-to-male sexual behaviour too was usually interpreted within its social and cultural context and not merely as a sign of sexual freedom. While reporting that boy-to-boy and man-to-boy sexual relations were current, he also indicated that the locals frowned upon it, even if rather benevolently.[75]

An example also of the author's detachment is his description of male-to-male anal intercourse, pursued by some under the disguise of *biă'n nkŭ'ma* or, in his words, *Reichtumsmedizin*. The passive partner, and presumed owner of a remedy to gather richness, had another man penetrate him in order to 'transfer' his enriching power upon the active partner. This remarkable subcultural and ethnomedical response to public intolerance leaned on oral tradition, yet, rather than romanticizing such evidence as a sign of local tolerance regarding homosexuality, Tessmann did stress how such a 'treatment' potentially implied lepra for the active partner and anal hemorrhoids for the passive one and was not seen, accordingly, as entirely innocent.[76]

Among the Bafia of Cameroon, more than among the Pangwe, Tessmann discovered far-reaching 'tolerance' of homosexual and heterosexual relations alike, which illustrated the harmony of Bafia body politics: '[Sexual intercourse] is ... the result of a fully natural development, just like the process of growth and decay due to age of the body itself ([Geschlechtsverkehr] ist ... eine Folge der ganz natürlichen einheitlichen Entwicklung, genau wie etwa die aufsteigende und [in Alter] absteigende körperliche Entwicklung überhaupt.)'[77]

The emphasis on the 'natural' dimension of homosexuality is also prominent in another article, focusing exclusively on homosexuality among the Bafia. This people's impartiality, according to Tessmann, to same-sex relations was comparable to the situation in ancient Greece and could be seen, quite significantly, as a kind of *argumentum ex auctoritate* of homosexuality's natural character.[78]

Homosexuality's appearances among the Bafia, however, were manifold and could only be partially defined as 'genuine' homosexuality. The inaccessibility of adolescent girls before marriage especially allowed for male same-sex relations among peers (*lexan* or *Busenfreunde*) or with minor boys, consisting largely of mutual anal intercourse (*jigĕlĕ ketön*). This behavioural pattern, reminding today's reader of the *troca-troca* in Brazil, was as much a confirmation of masculinity (proof of potency) as a temporary excursion into passivity, and had – nor has – little to do, accordingly, with real 'inversion'.[79]

While carefully describing these adolescent forms of pederasty, Tessmann became far less critical when portraying same-sex relations during the stage of *ntu*, when male youths were allowed to have intercourse with women. At this point, social pressure intensified and most young men gave up same-sex relations. Once they had entered fatherhood (*mbang*), same-sex relations were not tolerated at all. But a small minority maintained them and ought to be seen, says the author, as genuine homosexuals. Only, he had not seen any with his own eyes and simply assumed that a percentage as high as in Europe *must* exist among the Bafia as well. In the end, Tessmann's portrayal of a 'natural' homosexual minority turned sour when he pointed out how European influence in the coastal areas of Cameroon had led to a higher number of men with homosexual tendencies.[80] If these were real homosexuals, then how was the effect of western presence to be explained? If they were not, then was this not an indication that, perhaps, social and cultural factors played a role also in the reification of desire?

After the loss of German colonial territory in the aftermath of World War I, Tessmann returned briefly to Lübeck only to depart again for Peru and then Brazil. In Sertanópolis, he edited his African notes and wrote a manuscript on his experience in West Africa.[81] In it, as in the diaries, analysed by Thomas Klockmann, Tessmann reveals himself as having remained very disciplined during his stay in West Africa, even when admittedly at the cost of his psychic equilibrium. He reflected that the 'stimuli in the libidinous sphere of the central (nervous) system caused a great deal of suffering, especially as I became aware while getting older that I never really "lived" according to the demands of my sensual impulses.'[82]

Tessmann altogether rejected some of the then current stereotypes on African sexuality, such as the secular claim about black lasciviousness: 'Sexual intercourse is not deprived of refinement, notwithstanding the greater lasciviousness; tactful communication, loyalty towards prescribed formulas and spiritual depth are not absent (Trotz der grossen Sinnlichkeit ist der Verkehr der Geschlechter nicht ohne feiner Züge; taktvolles Benehmen, genaues Befolgen vorgeschriebener Formen und tiefes seelisches Empfinden fehlen nicht).'[83] His judgement also revealed scepticism towards Richard Kandt's statement that Africans only knew a strong *Detumeszenztrieb* whereas the capacity for love was rather minimal. To Tessmann, African love is just as intense, if less visible from the outside.[84] The author's recognition of African integrity evidently was part of a more general, milder exoticist imagination shared by other Europeans as well. But, whereas often the presumably harmonious sexuality of black Africans was invoked as an explanation for the absence of perversions, it was an incentive for Tessmann rather to integrate homosexual behaviour as part of African impartiality.

The writings of Kurt Falk also reveal how data were used to corroborate the model of innate homosexuality. The latter, moreover, was identified by Falk as of a 'feminine' nature and contrasted with other, more incidental forms of homoeroticism. His first article on homosexual behaviour among the Wawike, the Ovivangella and the Ngine of Angola only touched the surface of the issue.[85] The second, on homosexuality in German Southwest Africa, now Namibia, offered a more explicit inventory of African homosexual roles both within the tribal communities and on the diamond mining compounds, where men were employed in isolation from the female sex. Among the Ovambo, there were *ovashengi*, 'effeminierte Männer, die sich passiv gegen Entgelt zum coitus in anum hingeben'.[86] Falk considered these as *Homoeroten*, a rather misleading term for 'inborn homosexuals', who only secondarily lent themselves to prostitution.

But Falk's narrative becomes problematic in the next phrase: 'Especially the very effeminate men assume deliberately the role of "ovashengi" [since] the virile homosexual looks inconspicuous ([Da] der virile Homosexuelle nicht weiter auffällt, sind es besonders die stark effeminierten Männer, sie sich freiwillig in jene Rolle der "ovashengi" versetzen).'[87] Semantic analysis seemingly implies that the author also recognized a masculine, homosexual role next to the effeminate one, often associated with male prostitution. But from the remaining content of the paragraph one can deduce that he meant to say 'masculine defined men, who engaged in sexual relations with other men', most probably taking an active role during anal intercourse. In this context, Falk's portrait has to be understood as being of boys from ten to twelve years, who were not only employed as kitchen assistants near the mines, but also served as catamites. In fact, they were sent out by the miners' wives to guarantee their husbands' fidelity while away from home.[88]

Falk's narrow, Hirschfeldian concept of homosexual identity is also obvious in his minimalization of particular same-sex relations as 'circumstantial', whereas the sexuality of a shaman among the Ovahimba was diagnosed as genuine inversion. The cross-gender profile attached to shamanism, thus appeared to be instrumental to the distinction of 'real' versus 'incidental' homosexuality. Erotic friendships or *omapanga* among the Herero, though including anal intercourse (*okutunduka vanena*) and mutual masturbation, were discarded by Falk as virtually irrelevant.[89] Similarly, most same-sex relations among other ethnic people were defined as 'circumstantial' when not tied to permanently upheld 'intermediate' roles.

Generally, Falk's portrayal was typical of a tendency among some anthropologists to isolate 'genuine' homosexuality from its more incidental counterparts. The purpose of such a narrative trope was expressed by the author in his critique of the infamous paragraph 175. To consolidate his plea for abolition, it was essential to emphasize that a minority among those men who engaged in sexual relations among themselves did so because they were constituted differently:

Precisely among indigenous people, who are in no way bound by laws, homoeroticism manifests itself very sharply among some individuals. They in no way seduce the others into homoeroticism, as these always return to their wives as soon as possible and seek homosexual contacts only due to a lack of alternatives. ... Anyone who refutes inborn homosexuality should take a look at indigenous people and he will soon change his mind.[90]

The *Jahrbuch für sexuelle Zwischenstufen*, whose editorial board included Hirschfeld, Näcke, Wilhelm, Karsch-Haack among others, played a considerable role in disseminating ethnographic evidence corroborating modern theory of 'homosexual' identity. Many articles provided information that supported Hirschfeld's theory of a universal cross-gender role, but such a narrow definition of the homosexual's profile was often challenged by other cross-cultural information about homosexuality's masculine aura. Sometimes both models were presented simultaneously in a single text, which loosened the connection, postulated by Hirschfeld himself, between homosexual identity and a transgression of gender. The feminine 'third sex' was thus juxtaposed to other manifestations of homosexual desire. Thus the *Jahrbuch*, though basically set up by Hirschfeld himself, was instrumental also to a widening of his rather narrow conceptualization of homosexual identity.

The German-language article by a Japanese writer, Suyewo Jwaya, printed in the journal's fourth volume under the title 'Nan sho'k (die Päderastie in Japan)' illustrates well the point made above. On the one hand, the author subscribed to Hirschfeld's model *sensu stricto*, as he stressed that male actors performing female roles not only behaved effeminately but showed a conspicuously feminine bodily constitution as well. To document his thesis, he included portrait photographs of four actors, whose physical outlook was more or less feminine. But this pattern, most clearly visible in the north, differed considerably from homosexuality in the southern province of Satsuma and on the island Kyushu. Here it was far more common, and yet its profile was very much defined by a cult of masculinity.[91]

If articles such as this reflected an ongoing uncertainty within the intelligentsia concerning the gender profile of a 'genuine homosexual minority', then this was accompanied as well by doubt as to whether the latter model was really universally applicable. It would be historically inaccurate, indeed, to suggest that all eyewitness testimonies by those who subscribed to modern 'homosexual' identity, showed the author's deliberate tendency to 'discover' a genuine, homosexual minority in non-western cultures all the time.

In the same *Jahrbuch*, a German translation was published of an English article by Tytheridge. Nothing, aside from what this text reveals itself, is known about this person. He obviously travelled in the United States of America, in Australia and finally, in 1917–18, in Japan. In each of these countries, he purposively sought homosexual contacts – disguised in his own words as a kind of 'participant observation' – in order to gather knowledge about sexual mores abroad.[92] Tytheridge's narrative contradicted the Hirschfeldian model, for it stressed the absence in Japan of a distinct, organized 'homosexual' minority that defined itself as such towards the outside world:

... homosexuals, even though just as ubiquitous as in other countries, are not organized, nor do they have a sense of community as in Germany etc. Nor do they feel solidarity, neither do they show any of that kind of 'freemasonry' that exists elsewhere.[93]

The occurrence of same-sex behaviour was more accurately described, said the author, as somehow endemic and often triggered by the living conditions in 'homosocial arrangements' (in Hekma's phrase) such as convents, colleges or the army. Apparent signs of a distinct homosexual subculture, such as the availability of books by Oscar Wilde, Edward Carpenter, Henry Havelock

Ellis and Georges Eekhoud's homoerotic novel *Escal-Vigor*,[94] were dismissed by Tytheridge as mere fads of a westernizing elite.

Yet, the inner inconsistencies of ethnographic reportage revealed the strength as much as the weakness of Hirschfeldian discourse. Whereas the narrow model of a cross-gender homosexual role could not be fully sustained cross-culturally, it was ethnographic evidence of such roles *when existing* that nevertheless corroborated theoretical claims by homosexuals to be members of a separate, intermediate sex. And a perverse kind of logic allowed them to postulate that, amidst those engaging in same-sex relations during adolescence, warfare or initiation, a small percentage of 'genuine' homosexuals *had to* exist.

The paucity of first-hand ethnographic narratives by authors whose commitment to the cause of homosexual emancipation as stipulated by Hirschfeld is known, calls for more evidence to support the above interpretation. This can be found in the ethnographic surveys that were written by some of the most prominent advocates of homosexual rights across Europe. For not only new reports by authors who displayed an outspoken empathy for homosexual politics, but the already accumulated literature on the theme that I have reviewed in previous chapters, was used by Bloch, Karsch-Haack, Symonds, Ellis, and Carpenter to document and corroborate the agenda of homosexual emancipation as outlined first by Ulrichs, Hirschfeld and their followers. Others too, both within and outside the newly emerging homosexual intelligentsia, contributed to what I call the subcultural politics of anthropology.

Armchair anthropology and subcultural politics

Among the subscribers to Hirschfeld's theory of homosexuality as an intermediate, 'third sex' that challenged fixed gender roles, the Dutch physician Lucien von Römer was perhaps the most loyal one. By developing a theory of human androgyny, he actually formulated a model of homosexual identity that went even further than Hirschfeld's own qualification of the feminine nature of homosexuality. First documented in his article 'Über die androgynische Idee des Lebens', published in the *Jahrbuch* in 1903,[95] von Römer would further develop his theory in *Het uranisch gezin*. This study was published in 1905, but when he submitted it in a slightly modified version to the medical faculty of the University of Amsterdam, it was refused.[96]

All of his relevant ideas are comprised in the article on the 'androgynous idea'. It contained a theory, at once biological and cultural, of sexual identity as the incorporation of male, female or, with homosexuals, both male and female characteristics. His point of departure was the thesis that absolute love equalled the love for god. As god embodied both male and female, generative and vegetative forces, sexual intercourse aimed at the combination of both as a reflection of god.[97] In this context, von Römer referred to the Indian Mahabharata, to Japanese cosmogony, to the Persian cult of Mithras, finally to Egyptian, Jewish and Scandinavian religion, each time emphasizing the androgynous character of these cultures' deities. He continued by describing how the representation of these androgynous gods in images and sculptures was modelled upon feminine-looking young men, and merged culture and biology by saying 'that these androgynes (to be translated in our language as Uranians) too played the role of androgynous-idea-personification in the Mysteries (dass diese Androgynen (in unserer Sprache durch Uranier zu übersetzen) es auch gewesen sind, welche in den Mysterien die Rolle der Androgynischen-Idee-Personifikation erfüllt haben)'.[98] The eclipse of primitive ritual obscured the historical role of androgynes within religious cults, but they found a new calling in the arts. It explained, according to von Römer, why artists were often 'uranians'.

The remainder of von Römer's elitist *stratégie de résistance* merely rationalized the artistic fascination for the beauty of boys. As opposed to girls, whose passive, nurturing qualities were invisible due to their as yet lacking breasts, and opposed also to women, who embody passivity only, and to men, who were fully masculine, boys revealed both the active, creative side through their genitalia and the passive, receptive side hidden within their still fragile bodies. But such speculations must not disguise how von Römer combined a cultural-philosophical plea for the social recognition of 'androgynes' with a biological theory of 'uranians'. Ethnographic and historical information, in other words, was to serve the author's biological theory of sexual identities.

A similar manipulation can be detected in Hans Freimark's study on African sexuality. At first reacting against the carelessness of many a traveller, the author proceeded to review the literature on, among other issues, same-sex relations in Africa. Theoretically, he subscribed to Hirschfeld's claim that homosexuality was a variation of human nature and rejected degenerative theory.[99] In response to Baumann, he suggested that what looked at first sight like homosexual behaviour pursued by men who were previously heterosexual, may well prove that these men too were really homosexually inclined from the beginning. Similarly, he modified the text by de Flacourt and Lasnet on the *sekats* on the island of Madagascar and claimed that they actually were real homosexuals.[100] He then highlighted the cross-gender roles that had been reported by travellers and ethnographers, as proof of the worldwide ubiquity of *Weiblinge*, i.e., a biologically rooted male cross-gender role.

The unknown author – Hans Freimark? – of an article in *Sexualprobleme*[101] criticized the triple distinction, made by Laurent, between male prostitutes, pederasts and inverts. These were not mutually exclusive, argued the author, who dismissed Laurent's portrayal as an inopportune attempt to exonerate 'natural folk' from 'unnatural crime'.

Paul Näcke upheld the distinction between 'acquired perversion' and 'congenital inversion' largely to distinguish the latter's biological inevitability from the former's logic of immorality. As civilization developed, acquired perversion was increasingly marginalized and rightly so, said Näcke. The ordeal of real 'homosexuals' or *Invertierte*, however, was unjust as they were often amalgamated with perverts whereas they could not be called in any way responsible.

Näcke's cognitive manipulation of data was applied not only to a reinterpretation of the sexual history of humanity, but also to contemporary ethnographic information in order to sustain the Hirschfeldian model of a genuine 'third sex'. For this purpose, he included an eyewitness report of an anonymous informant in his own article on 'homosexuality in the Orient'. Its author, a homosexual military officer, claimed that real inversion was rare. 'Bisexuality', on the contrary, was most common, 'as in Ancient Greece'. Näcke, obviously challenged by this portrayal, dismissed it in the end and stated that the reported bisexual behaviour itself was, often, 'artificial'. Social and religious pressure to marry explained moreover how, among these so-called 'bisexuals,' there were many real homosexuals. Exclusive homosexuals were less visible precisely 'because Orientals often get married very early and bachelors are fewer in number than among us. Islam prescribes coitus, moreover, and homosexual believers have to obey as well so that they pass falsely as bisexuals'.[102]

A similar rationalization can be found in Näcke's articles on homosexuality in Istanbul[103] and Albania.[104] In the latter, he first dismantled the mythical origin of Albanian homosexuality as imported from the Orient either through Ottoman occupation of Albanian territory or as a perverse result of the submission of Albanian slaves to the infamous sexual regime of the Mamelukes. In reality, said Näcke, the Albanian people had already known homosexuality since their migration from Northern Europe in ancient times. But male-to-male sexual behaviour, especially between adult men and adolescent boys, seemed widely spread and was pursued apparently by heterosexual, married men as well. In either case, such relations were sexual indeed and included anal, intracrural and oral intercourse. Näcke accordingly dismissed any idealization of the homosexual's pursuit of pederastic friendship,[105] yet his own upholding of a minority model of homosexual identity embraced a speculation about the difference between heterosexuals engaging in sexual relations with adolescent boys for sexual gratification merely (*Entspannung der Libido*), and real homosexuals, for whom the final goal is more spiritual (*seelische Befriedigung*).[106]

Gustav Jäger's chapter on homosexuality, written to be included in his book *Die Entdeckung der Seele* (Leipzig, 1879), remained unpublished until 1900. In that year, it appeared in Hirschfeld's *Jahrbuch* with an editorial note dismissing some of Jäger's points of view as dated.[107] The article's tenor, however, corresponded with Hirschfeld's theory as it held that homosexuality was in essence an innate variation, that must not be stigmatized or repressed. In fact, it served society well. It prevented overpopulation, and homosexuals, who did not have family duties, were able to concentrate on social tasks more intensely. And it ought to be admitted, against Nietzschean idolatry of the *Übermensch*, that homosexuals were often *gottgesandt* to fulfil assignments of supernatural dimension.[108] Real homosexuals were not to be confused with male prostitutes, moreover, whose motives were merely pecuniary, nor with men who cultivate homosexual relations 'aus Raffinement, aus Blasiertheit'.[109] Only those whose homosexuality was inborn and permanent throughout life justified scientific research, claimed Jäger, who felt defensive about addressing the issue altogether. Ideological bias is revealed next by the inventory of sources demonstrating the universality of homosexuality in both time and space, followed by the uncritical conclusion that '[the] homosexual drive ... must be inborn ([der] Trieb des Homosexualismus ... ein eingeborener sein muss)'.[110]

This quotation reveals how the universality of homosexuality was perceived by Jäger and other advocates of Hirschfeldian theory as an *argumentum a fortiori* that it was 'natural'. Such a rhetorical trope harboured the ambiguity in the mainstream ideology as reconstructed in chapter four. On the one hand, it opposed Darwinian claims that homosexuality was a disadvantageous trait of primitive, promiscuous humanity and symptomatic, when encountered today, of a degenerate neurological constitution. But on the other hand, the cultural politic of anthropology as outlined above shared the presumption of mainstream ideology that sexuality could be grasped adequately as a biological phenomenon – which explains the at first sight illogical conclusion that if homosexuality is universal, it ought to be natural. As such, both medical-pathological and homosexual-emancipatory discourse characterized themselves collectively as heirs to the Enlightenment reification of sexual identity through biology. The significance of ethnographic data, so it proved, was confined within the parameters of this paradigm.

The politics of 'naturalness' are also obvious in the study of Japanese sexuality by the Austrian Friedrich Salomo Krauss.[111] Prior to his discussion of homosexuality, Krauss offered a portrayal of traditional Japanese easygoing attitudes towards nakedness, prostitution and 'phalloctenic' cult[112] – tokens, really, of a typical, rather voyeuristic selectivity in European descriptions of foreign sexuality. But in his introduction, the author subscribed to a biological theory of sexual identities and insisted that numerous commentators had presented homosexuality erroneously as a sign of immorality. He pointed out that he himself was no 'uranian' but declared that he had signed Hirschfeld's petition against paragraph 175 'because homosexuality was a natural phenomenon'.[113]

The actual chapter on *Uranier und Urninden* in Japan contained a reprint of Iwaya's article on *Nan sho'k* as well as another Japanese, anonymous report, that focused on the prevalence of homosexual relations among the *samurai* and Buddhist monks. But these specific cultural settings were fully irrelevant in view of the author's biological premisses. Krauss' own etiology – 'The sexes are not different in value, they are different in kind (Die Geschlechter sind nicht verschieden wertig, sie sind verschieden artig)'[114] – was plainly Hirschfeldian, even when his vocabulary reminded one of Ulrichs as well, and was accompanied by long quotes from the works of his intellectual mentor. Other writers such as Von Römer, Jäger, Wilhelm, and Karch-Haack also were called upon to lend authority to Krauss' representation of Japanese homosexuality as a *Naturphänomen*.

Naturalist assumptions also directed the folklorist enterprise of the journal *Anthropophyteia*, that was edited by Krauss between 1904 and 1913. This journal, subtitled *Jahrbücher für Folkloristische Erhebungen und Forschungen zur Entwicklungsgeschichte der Geschlechtlichen Moral*, was a thesaurus mainly of popular culture and imagination of sexuality. Though the journal exhibited cultural relativism in terms of moral judgement, its theoretical claims concerning the ontology of sexual desire were defined by the bio-medical discourse of its time. The representation of homosexuality too was influenced by Hirschfeld's work in particular and was accompanied at times by expressions of support for his political campaign.[115] Paul Näcke, Alfred Kind and Friedrich Krauss presented Hirschfeldian theory as the right heuristic device.[116] Various articles discussing homosexuality in Pre-Columbian Peru,[117] New Ireland,[118] Ethiopia[119] and Northern Africa[120] also reflected it. Only von Bülow described 'hermaphrodites' on Samoa as 'constitutional anomalies'.[121] Laufer expressed his doubt about Hirschfeld's feminine connotation of the 'third sex', but did subscribe to the latter's claim that a separate, intermediate sex nevertheless could be distinguished.[122]

More *Hineininterpretierung* of old and new ethnographic data can be found in other contributions to Hirschfeld's *Jahrbuch*. An anonymous review, perhaps by Hirschfeld himself, of Lasnet's portrayal of cross-gender roles on Madagascar was typical of the reformulation of the ethnographic record within the Hirschfeldian paradigm:

These Secatra undoubtedly are cases of complete effeminization. The author of this report seems to assume that it is a matter of acquired effeminization; but only those who already have a contrary sexual identity from an early age become real Secatra; the remarkably feminine habits will end up reinforcing their contrary nature and develop it to the fullest.[123]

The *a posteriori* interpretations in the journal were guided by an intention to align the capriciousness of ethnographic narratives with the cognitive framework of Hirschfeldian theory. An etiological discourse explained homosexuality as a variation of nature which implied no pathological connotations. Apart from a few dissident voices, most texts presented male homosexuality's 'intermediate' status as being tied to femininity.

Meanwhile, some more systematic ethnographic surveys were set up by authors in Germany and Great Britain. Their authors shared the political agenda of Hirschfeld and contributed to its widening into a more embracing program of homosexual emancipatory politics that was legitimate everywhere. Yet, none of the comprehensive ethnographic surveys of homosexuality was published in the countries that had decriminalized homosexuality. The works of Bloch, Karsch-Haack, Symonds, Ellis, Carpenter and Westermarck originated from Germany, which retained paragraph 175, and Great Britain, where the Labouchère Amendment was still in force. The illegal status of homosexuality certainly offered a fertile soil for a strategy of resistance, that emphasized the natural character of homosexuality as a major argument for sexual reform, and an anthropological poetic, that emphasized the ubiquity of sexual variance. But the very construction of a synoptic ethnography threatened to undermine the Hirschfeldian scheme as much as it was geared to lending it scientific legitimacy.

Iwan Bloch

A dissident note had already been expressed by Eugen Dühren, alias Iwan Bloch, who explained homosexuality as an acquired trait, facilitated by specific social conditions especially during puberty and adolescence. Seduction played a crucial role and *Suggestionstherapie*, especially when applied at an early stage, could still undo its effects. His *Äthiologie* offered an inventory of such 'acquired perversion' and was gratefully used by the opponents to prove the unsoundness of Hirschfeld's petition against paragraph 175.[124]

Bloch's thesis was promptly criticized by, among others, Wilhelm Schrickert, who pointed out that the effects of seduction were unequal. It seemed that it could only be successful when targeted at an individual who was himself 'equipped' with an innate homosexual drive. The ethnographic evidence, provided ironically by Bloch himself, of the dissemination of homosexuality across the world 'proved' moreover that homosexuality was a quite natural phenomenon.[125]

Later, as Bloch joined Hirschfeld's campaign, he stressed the urgent need for more scientific rigour but subscribed to the model of natural variation. The book witnessing Bloch's theoretical turn, *Das Sexualleben unserer Zeit* (1907), proposed an endocrinological explanation for the development of sexual identity and rejected the author's previous socio-psychological etiology.[126] His new approach also altered the parameters of his ethnographic narrative, as can be read from his new assessment of religion in relation to sex. Religious ritual, depicted in his *Äthiologie* as a favourable circumstance for the spreading of pederasty, was now tied to the biology of sexual instinct in a way that today may reek of obscurantism:

A really objective criterion for the evaluation of the relation between religion and sexual life can only be found when we don't see it as a matter of dogmas and belief, but study it instead from the only acceptable point of view: the anthropological one.[127]

Whereas before sexuality was given legitimacy by religious belief, it was now presented as its own organizing principle and as a constitutional part of humanity, alongside religion, with which it maintained a rather incestuous relationship.[128]

But Bloch still criticized Hirschfeld's identification of homosexuality as an 'intermediate' sex, containing elements of both the male and female. At the same time he upheld a distinction between 'real' and 'pseudo-homosexuality'. The latter included same-sex relations of bisexuals or *Junonen*, circumstantial pederasty in homosocial environments, *überschwengliche Freundschaftsgefühle gewisser Zeitperioden*, the sexual relations with/of physical hermaphrodites, and the *Knabenliebe* of ancient Greece or the Middle East.[129]

Particularly relevant here is Bloch's exclusion of Greek and Middle Eastern pederasty from the realm of homosexuality. It provoked reaction from a more orthodox Hirschfeldian angle, insisting that no qualitative difference existed between modern male homosexuality and male-to-male sexual relations in ancient Greece. Nor was it distinct from such relations in the Orient: 'When all homosexuals would admit their inclination, just as in Ancient times, one would be astonished that so many men ... are homosexual and have homosexual relationships.'[130] This illustrates once again how the claim that real homosexuality also was universal was quintessential to the emancipatory discourse of Hirschfeldian signature. To demonstrate this was the goal also of the German zoologist and publicist, Ferdinand Karsch-Haack.

Ferdinand Karsch-Haack

Karsch-Haack (1853–1936) published one article about homosexuality among animals,[131] yet displayed far greater enthusiasm within the field of ethnography. The resulting surveys no doubt are the most comprehensive of all of those published before the end of World War I. His theoretical position, formulated extensively in his major work *Das gleichgeschlechtliche Leben der Naturvölker* (1911), was an outspoken defense of Hirschfeld's call for recognition of homosexuality's 'natural' roots. Formulated synoptically, the author explained that sexual relations among men

cannot be represented as customs, that developed purely arbitrarily or were forced upon one, not even among people about whom this is repeatedly claimed. [They are] always and everywhere the *naturally determined* state of a greater or smaller percentage of the total population that experiences such an inclination as inevitable. They manifest themselves amidst all groups of any people, but will never disseminate among all of its members, nor will they be confined to one particular, privileged class. [my italics][132]

Sexual variety, in other words, was a natural given to the degree that its percentage distribution was virtually fixed. No geographical area or ethnic population was more prone than another to harbour variant sexualities and it was useless, accordingly, to explain the occurrence of homosexuality in one region as being 'imported' from another.

Diffusionist representations of sexual perversion, migrating across the globe, surfaced frequently in travelogues and ethnographic descriptions alike, and Karsch-Haack had already criticized them in his study on homosexuality in the Far East. The Mongols and the Tartars were assumed to have exported it to the Chinese, who in their turn had infested the Japanese and other people of Asia. The Greeks instructed the Persians, from whom the Turks and Arabs had picked it up. The Arabs subsequently spread it across Subsaharan Africa, but so did the Portuguese. And Greeks and Armenians were both held responsible for importing homosexual vice into Russia, while the French too played an ominous role in South East Asia . . . . The absurdity of such genealogies, argued Karsch-Haack, was demonstrated by posing the question how had the original malefactor come to adopt it himself in the first place.[133]

The author's naturalist position was already obvious in his first lengthy article, 'Uranismus oder Päderastie und Tribadie bei den Naturvölkern', published in the third volume of the *Jahrbuch für sexuelle Zwischenstufen*.[134] But Karsch-Haack dissociated himself from Hirschfeld's rather strict model of a gender-defined 'intermediate sex'. He pointed to what he felt was the predominant position of masculine homosexuals in Europe itself whereas most ethnographic reports focused on *Weiblinge* or effeminate pederasts. Virtually all 'primitive' languages contained words that recognized such gender-crossing roles as part of the people's social universe: '[Virtually] all of their languages contain special, often very meaningful words for the *Weiblinge, Pathici* or *Cynäden* among each tribe ([Fast] jede ihrer Sprachen hat für die Weiblinge, Pathici oder Cinäden, der zugehörigen Völkerstämme ein besonderes, oft überaus bezeichnendes Wort).'[135] The following survey of 'uranists' across the globe indeed embraced numerous 'emic' categories, that tied the latter to a reversal of gender roles.

At this point, attention must be paid to his review, reiterated in his survey of 1911, of the American Indian record especially.[136] The author organized it according to a distinction, presumably made by Louis Hennepin, between 'hermaphrodites', 'effeminate men' and 'masculine-looking men, engaging in sexual relations with either effeminate or equally masculine-looking men'. In chapter one, I have quoted Hennepin's text that served as a basis for Karsch-Haack's taxonomy. But it will be clear to the reader as well that no such categorical distinctions can be deduced from Hennepin's report. What then motivated Karsch-Haack to interpret it as such?

The answer lies in the conclusion to the study of 1911, where the author positioned himself equally against the theory of Ulrichs – and Hirschfeld, if only implicitly – and against the alternative model proposed by Elisár von Kupffer, who criticized Hirschfeldian theory because it incorrectly associated male-to-male love or *Lieblingsminne* with 'effeminacy'.[137] Karsch-Haack shared von Kupffer's point of view in so far as Hirschfeldian theory covered only a part of the homosexual population, not all of it. But he took a stance opposed to von Kupffer as well, not least because the ethnographic record showed that the relation between homosexuality and *Effemination* was close, if not ontologically, then statistically.[138]

This theory explained why Karsch-Haack divided the ethnographic record into three segments, even when, historically speaking, its parameters were falsely deduced from the old text of Hennepin. It revealed some of the author's intellectual bravery, for example when he courageously dismantled the Early Modern narratives about 'hermaphrodites' as a confusion of *psychophysisches Hermaphroditismus* with an anatomical one. If the reported hermaphrodites had indeed been ambisexual beings, then America would have been an Eldorado for anatomists.[139]

But what then did he mean by *psychophysisches Hermaphroditismus*, especially as it seems very much like the *verweibte Männer* or *Effeminierten* of category two? In essence, the distinction was artificial and merely reflected the rather speculative taxonomies of von Krafft-Ebing. No explanation of the word was given, but it was probably close to the primary stage of congenital homosexuality, labelled by von Krafft-Ebing as *psychische Hermaphrodisie*.[140] An evaluation of the evidence surveyed by Karsch-Haack proves that no real difference existed between the first and second categories apart from the tenor of description in the sources reviewed. The result is a simple, dualistic model embracing both masculine- and cross-gender-defined variants of homosexuality, that were both rooted in biology and could be found in different degrees virtually anywhere in the world.

While gathering more ethnographic data, Karsch-Haack further developed his theoretical points of view and reacted against Benedict Friedländer, whose criticism aligned with the claims of his associate von Kupffer and questioned the congenital character of effeminate forms of homosexuality.[141] In *Forschungen über das gleichgeschlechtliche Leben der Ostasiaten*, the author also refuted the central thesis of Iwan Bloch's *Äthiologie*.[142] But he admitted that, aside from congenital homosexuality, there was plenty of evidence that same-sex relations among men were triggered by social circumstances. The outwardly identical behaviour thus required that both 'circumstantial' and 'real' homosexuality be studied at the same time.

It is this categorical distinction *notwithstanding indications that such was often irrelevant to the indigenous peoples themselves* that makes Karsch-

Haack into what Hekma has called an 'essentialist'.[143] It allowed him to separate some culturally circumscribed roles as revealing an underlying homosexual 'constitution' distinct from other forms of homosexual behaviour that were merely 'circumstantial'. Within a Hirschfeldian perspective, this was a powerful argument, but it was weak at the same time as no sound criteria were at hand for diagnosing to which realm the observed behaviour may belong.

The arbitrariness was obvious, for example, in his distinction of the homosexuality of Chinese bonzes, emperors, mandarins and poets alike as congenital, and the milieu of male prostitution (*Buhljungenwesen*) largely catering to a more circumstantial demand for homosexual contact.[144] A similarly intuitive criterion was adopted to rehabilitate same-sex relations among the *samurai* of Japan as genuine, even when the homosocial character of their military bonds might just as legitimately have justified their representation as 'circumstantial': '[That] at times "training" may also play a role is quite probable; yet, one must not call such bonds unnatural merely because of that ([Dass] dabei bisweilen auch "Züchtung" eine Rolle spielt ist wahrscheinlich; doch braucht man deswegen noch nicht von unbedingter widernatürlichkeit solcher Bündnisse zu sprechen).'[145] Clearly, political concerns also played a role. The very combination of biological theory and elitist claims in particular revealed the author's attempt to offer a scientific explanation of homosexuality and boost the confidence of western homosexuals in one move. The presentation of a biologically defined minority of real homosexuals, whose social and cultural status was relatively high, became a central trope in the ethnographic poetics of Karsch-Haack.

Thus, he also rationalized homosexuality in feudal Japan as only partially related to strong marriage regulations. Until the termination of the Tokugawa era in 1868, a rule existed in the southern province of Satsuma that men were not allowed to have sexual intercourse with women until the age of thirty. In other areas, great pressure was imposed upon young men to marry at the early age of seventeen but this did not seem to challenge pederastic practices. Here, Karsch-Haack mentioned Wernich's article on nervous disorders in Japan, suggesting that the increasing social and financial demands of marriage prevented numerous men from marrying at such an early age and encouraged their refuge in pederasty. But such circumstantial homosexuality must not be confused with its congenital counterpart. Social conditions may well explain the widespread character of pederasty, says the author, but not its existence as such.[146]

Similarly, reports about male prostitution in closed houses or in the streets of the port cities Kobe, Nagasaki and Yokohama must not be read as evidence of an exceptionally high degree of real homosexuality, for it was largely circumstantial. As in southern Italy, it was the outcome mostly of foreign demand, greed, lack of opportunities for heterosexual intercourse, and Asian sensuality. In reality, Karsch-Haack thought it too 'low' for inclusion within the realm of congenitality.[147]

Within the pool of men engaging in sexual relations with either men or boys, according to Karsch-Haack, there was only a small nucleus of innate homosexuals, equal in percentage to other parts of the world. As proof of evidence that such a minority had been an integral part of traditional Japanese society, the author subsequently reviewed classical texts such as the *Torikaebaya Monogatari*, the *Shidzu no Odamaki*, the *Mokuzu Monogatarai*, and finally Ihara Saikaku's *Nanshoku Ōkagami* (1687), all including frank descriptions of male homosexuality.[148] At his time, bowdlerized versions of these works were still read at school, just as similarly cleansed editions of classical Greek and Roman texts were used for instruction in Europe itself.

Crucial here is Karsch-Haack's incorporation of Japanese lyrical descriptions of pederastic romances within the realm of genuine homosexuality – a fact made explicit in his evaluation of the *Torikaebaya Monogatari* as 'an anticipation and poetic description of Ulrichs's hypothesis eight centuries later regarding the female soul in a male body (eine Vorahnung und dichterische Ausgestaltung der acht Jahrhunderte späteren Ulrichs'schen Hypothese von der weiblichen Seele im männlichen Körper)'.[149] The education of some boys as girls was an indication for Karsch-Haack that these boys already showed signs of a feminine orientation that was biologically rooted. But Karsch-Haack did recognize a more masculine variant of homosexuality alongside the rather effeminate one, and emphasized it by comparing Saikaku's eulogy of male love to virile icons from classical Greek narratives. He thus consolidated homosexuality's legitimacy in a double fashion.[150]

In fact, homosexuality had been recognized and accepted throughout Japanese history, at least until the 'modernization' of legislation in Meiji Japan. This clearly reflected western influence and accordingly lead to a growing stigmatization of *all* forms of homosexuality. But it could not be eradicated, said Karsch-Haack, who concluded that genuine homosexuality obeyed its own laws fully independent from social circumstance. A comparison of two countries as different as China and Japan proved this clearly since homosexuality remained equally visible in both countries despite their divergent legal policies. Yet, eager to rehabilitate Japanese homosexuality in a time when this country itself had set out to regulate it more thoroughly, Karsch-Haack suggested that the Japanese victory over Russia in 1905 may well be due partially to the persistence of a *samurai* morality.[151] However, if homosexuality were conducive of masculine vigor and combativeness, as Karsch-Haack seemingly implied, then why did China have to give up Dairen, Weihai and parts of Shandong to the Japanese? To rewrite history as an epic of homo-heroism surely proved a hazardous enterprise!

The objective of his study *Das gleichgeschlechtliche Leben der Naturvölker* was primarily to provide an encyclopedic survey of all information on male and female homosexuality among 'natural folk' available at the time. Such an intention must not disguise, however, the fact that this positivistic *status quaestionis* embraced a well defined theory concerning the nature and etiology of homosexuality as well as a political agenda:

Pederasty and Tribadism are ... seen as manifestations of the sexual drive ..., as natural phenomena that occur[red] everywhere and throughout time and that do not deserve to be underestimated, disdainfully avoided, marginalized or, least of all, brutally persecuted by laws opposed to freedom, that may push them undergound at the most.[152]

The natural character of homosexuality alongside heterosexuality was not only proven by its high status in classical Greece – different here from the view of Iwan Bloch – but also by the abundant evidence that it occurred among virtually all primitive people. No necessary relation existed, moreover, between the call for procreation and sex – a fact that was demonstrated also, according to the zoologist, by other forms of procreation among animals as parthenogenesis (*Jungfernzeugung*) and paedogenesis (*Larvenvermehrung*). To call homosexuality unnatural because it was 'nonreproductive' would therefore be wrong.[153]

Karsch-Haack felt that some conceptual clarification was necessary, especially since homosexuality was often incorrectly identified with anal penetration – not each homosexual contact implied it, nor was it a monopoly of homosexuals. Homosexuality or, as Karsch-Haack preferred, *Homoerotik*[154] embraced a far wider range of sexual acts and included mutual masturbation, rubbing ('the Princeton rub', *frottage*), and fellatio alongside *Podikation* (anal intercourse).

Karsch-Haack further differentiated his own theory from the medical-pathological discourse of von Krafft-Ebing, who wrongly stigmatized homosexuality as a neurological disorder.[155] Other etiologies, called somewhat misleadingly 'sociological', were also evaluated and found wanting. Ethnographic and historical information showed clearly, according to the author, that homosexuality was not to be seen as an atavistic remnant of primitive humanity (contrary to Darwinian theory), nor as a symptom of individual degeneration or cultural decadence (contrary to degeneration theory and naturalist historiography). Neither did homosexuality occur more frequently among some races or in some geographical areas, nor was it tied to particular occupations or professional activities. The only certainty to be drawn from the ethnographic record along with other studies on homosexuality, is that this occurred more or less constantly anywhere and anytime.

The somewhat dogmatic trajectory of Karsch-Haack prompted him recurrently to 'edit' ethnographic narratives even more drastically than by 'diagnosing' some forms of homosexual behaviour as merely circumstantial.

Three major flaws, accordingly, can be pointed out in the author's ethnographic narrative.

First, he failed to demonstrate that masculine-profiled homosexual roles were just as common in primitive societies as feminine- or cross-gender defined ones. His intention to do so was nevertheless real, as he modified the common identification of homosexuality with effeminacy and widened the Hirschfeldian definition of a 'third sex'. *Weiblinge* behaved very much like women and felt attracted to adult men especially, acknowledged Karsch-Haack, who leaned heavily on Ulrichs's taxonomy as well. But other *Mannlinge* were plainly masculine and felt attracted to adolescent boys or men.

At first sight, *Mannlinge* seemed predominant among *Kulturvölker*, whereas *Weiblinge* were more prominent in primitive societies. Karsch-Haack himself added a lexicon of one hundred and six different indigenous terms to identify such male cross-gender roles, many of which at the same time denoted shaman or divinatory roles. But he insisted that underneath the surface no real difference was at play. In more developed societies, effeminate men were more repressed and thus less visible, while they were far better tolerated, respected even, amidst many a primitive tribe.[156]

But what about the masculine ones? Their profile may have grown sharper in Europe itself, but why did no equally elaborate vocabulary exist to identify masculine-profiled homosexual roles? This theoretical question was not addressed by Karsch-Haack himself even though he claimed that these were just as present in primitive societies as their feminine- or cross-gender profiled counterparts. Clearly, the anomaly was tied to his intention to demonstrate the natural, biological roots of homosexuality. Admitting that most often no indigenous or 'emic' conceptualization of active, masculine-profiled roles existed may well have threatened to jeopardize his entire theory.

Secondly, Karsch-Haack tended to extrapolate age-structured homosexual relations of men and boys into man-to-man relations in order to uphold the image of an androphile homosexual minority. In a footnote, he thus speculated on the actual age of the boys in Greek παιδερασθεια, extending it, just like its German equivalent *Knabenliebe*, to mutual relations between adult men.[157]

Thirdly, many forms of ritualized homosexuality were interpreted by Karsch-Haack as partially harbouring congenital homosexuality. Whereas he commonly classified homosexual acts performed during initiation rites as circumstantial, he nevertheless claimed that at least a small number among the participants were congenitally homosexual.[158] The passive boys in such contexts were seen, in a strange logic of extrapolation, as indications that a minority among their active, male partners were real homosexuals.[159] Similarly, Karsch-Haack trivialized tribal ritualization of regal power and deduced a genuinely homosexual orientation among some indigenous chiefs merely from the presence of eunuchs or cross-gendered males living within the compounds of their courts.[160]

Karsch-Haack's semantic and cognitive manipulation of the ethnographic record was false in many ways. The adult men who assumed the active role in age-structured same-sex relations were not always exclusively homosexual, nor were they in any way recognized or labelled as such by the indigenous people themselves. The adolescent boys, moreover, who assumed the passive role, usually did not do so deliberately but submitted to it largely because of the unequal balance of power implied by their age itself. Especially when occurring in a context of ritual, it was wrong to obfuscate the social inequality and symbolic drama involved and to present these practices as proof of even minimal congenital homosexuality.

In 1923, Karsch-Haack published yet another survey, this time on homosexuality in the Arab world. As his other publications, this one too reflected the author's intention to fit ethnographic data within the mould of his own naturalist theory of a biologically rooted homosexual minority. This echoed the secular trope presenting homosexuality as an endemic part of Arab identity – 'as a natural state of endemic character ... so natural ... for the Arabs as well (als Naturerzeugnis endemischer Anlage ... so natürlich ... auch für die Araber)' – but in the end, it did not deviate from the author's self-imposed orthodoxy.[161]

Altogether, Karsch-Haack's publications were more useful as repositories of sources than as consistent cross-cultural surveys of homosexuality among primitive folk. They constituted a kind of 'collection' that was to demonstrate the soundness of his theory above anything else, and operated as what James Clifford terms a 'system of authenticity'.[162] In view of today's understanding of sexuality, the project failed not only because it upheld a too stringent cognitive distinction between circumstantial and congenital homosexuality, but also incorrectly categorized some settings of homosexual behaviour within the realm of congenital homosexuality, whereas in reality they were not. At the same time, it failed to acknowledged how indigenous cultures often did not maintain strict boundaries between homosexual and heterosexual identity, and how many strictly speaking homosexual acts really pertained to the realm of a physical bisexuality.

John Addington Symonds

Repressive legislation in Great Britain also called for reaction from its homosexual intelligentsia, especially after the trial of Oscar Wilde in 1895. But already in 1883 John Addington Symonds had published his essay *A Problem in Greek Ethics*. On a rather academic level, he adopted an outsider's view and investigated how the apparently problematic 'sexual inversion' could coexist with the ancient Greek principles of truth and beauty, that inspired modern western civilization. Yet, he ended by stressing the virtue of Greek pederasty and presented this as an apology for more public understanding towards sexual inversion in contemporary British society.

Principally, Symonds subscribed to a theory of universalism – *quod semper ubique* – and offered an inventory of the appearance of sexual inversion appearances across the globe:

It confronts us in the steppes of Asia ..., in the bivouac of Keltish warriors ..., upon the sands of Arabia .... We discern it among the palm-groves of the South Sea Islands, in the card-houses and temple gardens of Japan, under Esquimaux snow-huts, beneath sultry vegetation of Peru, beside the streams of Shiraz and the waters of the Ganges, in the cold clean air of Scandinavian winters. It throbs in our huge cities. The pulse of it can be felt in London, Paris, Berlin, Vienna, no less than in Constantinople, Naples, Teheran, and Moscow. ... It shone with clear radiance in the gymnasium of Hellas.[163]

Anticipating Hirschfeldian theory, the author claimed that sexual inversion was merely a variation of nature, not a deviation, and since 'what is human is alien to no human being', it ought to be the object of systematic study. The invert's attraction to members of his own sex was biologically rooted, even 'instinctive', and 'with this neutral nomenclature the investigator has good reason to be satisfied'.[164]

But, published as early as 1883, Symonds' essay embraced a second line of argumentation that qualified his biological theory of sexual variation and postulated a cultural divide between Hellenic pederasty and its 'primitive' counterparts in other societies. Both were distinct, not only, as was suggested by some classicists, because of the idealized, de-sexualized character of Greek pederasty as opposed to the sexual, even purely genital logic under-lying primitive (read: non-western) same-sex relations among men. Different also was the former's purely masculine outlook in contrast to the gender-defined roles of inversion implied by the latter:

[The] unisexual vices of barbarians follow, not the type of Greek paiderasteia, but that of the Scythian disease or effeminacy, described by Herodotus and Hippocrates as something essentially foreign and non-Hellenic. In all these cases, whether we regard the Scythian impotent effeminates, the North American Bardashes, the Tsecats of Madagascar, ... and so forth – the characteristic point is that effeminate males renounce their sex ... [which] would have been abhorrent to the Doric custom.

The author also denounced pederasty in the 'half-savage nations' of classical Egypt, Tokugawa Japan and Pre-Columbian Mexico and Peru. Its Dorian variant, on the other hand, was superior because it was

elevated ... to the aesthetic standard of Greek ethics. ... We are obliged, in fact, to separate ... the true Hellenic manifestation of the paederastic passion, from the effeminacies, brutalities and gross sensualities which cannot be noticed alike in imperfectly civilized and in luxuriously corrupt communities.

According to Symonds, the development of the Greek variety of pederasty was initiated in Asia Minor, later in Crete, where the population gradually distanced itself from 'Oriental luxury'. Such process was accompanied by more embracing philosophical changes, allowing the Greeks to 'disentangle the spirit from matter and symbolism' and to 'transfuse intellectual and emotional faculties throughout a physical organism'.[165]

Genuine 'Greek love', masculine and invested with a sense of morality, differed also from its variant in classical Rome, that was 'subject to the perturbation of gross instinct'. Such a portrayal reflected a Gibbonian influence and prompted Symonds to further qualify the distinctly moral character of Greek pederasty. The climate obviously was irrelevant, for both northern and southern nations were equally addicted and equally averse to homosexuality. Nor did race or ethnicity offer an adequate explanation. The peculiar etiology of Greek pederasty was to be interpreted, rather, as the outcome of 'social conditions' and 'habits of the mind' that were different from elsewhere.[166]

Influenced by Walt Whitman's poetic ideal of 'comradely love', Symonds believed that homosexuality could be integrated within the social mores of contemporary Europe as well. Its price was the sublimation of male-to-male sexuality into something less physical, rather like Whitman's 'adhesiveness', merely to command respect or at least tolerance from public society. His apology for Greek love accordingly was valid for modern homosexuality as well, if on the condition that it embraced a 'Hellenic' moral ideal.

Meanwhile, new medical and sexological theories prompted Symonds to revise the presentation of his own argumentation. In the essay *A Problem in Modern Ethics* (1891, pirate editions in 1896 and 1901), he upheld the theory of the congenital character of homosexuality while explicitly rejecting all pathological connotations. But his will to humanize attitudes and make homosexuality more acceptable prevented him from formulating a radical critique of the legal and social repression of 'sexual inversion'. It may also explain the author's ongoing hierarchization of noble versus less noble homosexualities.

This surfaced in his critique of Paul Moreau's medical diagnosis of modern homosexuality as a hereditary neuropathy, while its Greek, Persian and Turkish variants were seen as asocial customs – an altogether different etiology for what is essentially an identical phenomenon. In the light of Symonds' own doubts about non-Greek homosexuality, it is remarkable to see how he himself amalgamated Greek, Persian and Turkish homosexuality after the example of Moreau. This may well have been a product of flawed attention, however, and perhaps should not be taken as meaningful. The issue for Symonds was Moreau's simultaneous use of a moral and a medical explanation for behaviour, that was rooted in both cases in biology. That Greek pederasty was still granted an exceptional status can be inferred, in view of his essay of 1883, from his reproach that Moreau took the 'morbid' counterpart of Imperial Rome to be the model. In Symonds's view, this had nothing to do with Greek pederasty, nor, reading between the lines, did Persian or Turkish vice.[167]

In opposition to Tarnowsky, Symonds claimed that congenital homosexuality could not be described in terms of passivity or effeminacy, nor could it be prevented by discipline during youth. He also discarded Tarnowsky's speculation that even long-lasting residence at high altitudes potentially triggered the development of perversion. The latter's belief that this had happened among the Armenians who subsequently exported pederasty to Persia was dismissed by Symonds, who – naively – pointed at the absence of homosexuality in the mountains of Central Europe.[168]

The eclectic use of ethnographic data by sexologists was not countered by a fundamental critique by Symonds of the arbitrariness of such a method. In fact, he also excerpted from the ethnographic record rather opportunistically, not realizing at times that his references potentially undermined his own theory. Thus, he invoked Richard Burton's model of the 'Sotadic Zone' to attack von Krafft-Ebing's hereditary theory[169] as well as to question the pathological connotations of sexological theory in general:

Medical writers abandon the phenomenon in savage races, in classical antiquity, and in the sotadic zone. They strive to isolate it as an abnormal and specifically morbid exception in our civilization. ... But facts tend to show that it is a recurring impulse of humanity, natural to some people, adopted by others, and in the majority of cases incompatible with an otherwise normal and healthy temperament.[170]

Here it should be remarked that not only was Symonds's recognition of acquired homosexuality inconsistent with his dominant idea that homosexuality was a natural variation rooted in instinct, but that his attitude to 'facts' was no less biased than in the works of his intellectual opponents. Symonds himself was aware of the contradiction implied by his own rationalization. How, indeed, was the recognition of geographical variation as a critique of sexual psychopathology to be reconciled with the universalist connotations of his own naturalism? Eventually, he criticized the very work of Richard Burton that he had used against von Krafft-Ebing.

Symonds pointed at some empirical inaccuracies in Burton's work and referred to the repression of homosexuality in contemporary Italy and Greece, as well as to the infamous surrender, exaggerated or not, of French soldiers to sodomy even after they returned from service in Algeria. This indicated that northern people were equally capable of engaging in sodomy. He also objected to Burton's model of homosexual identity. In it, Symonds recognized the influence of Ulrichs and questioned whether Burton's emphasis on the 'crasis' of male and female characteristics was pertinent. Most probably, a certain bisexual predisposition was universal, even when societies across the globe were not equally tolerant of its potential effects.[171] In the end, however, Symonds used ethnographic data to support universalist and regionalist images of homosexuality at the same time.

Remarkable, also, is Symonds's passage on the absence of homosexuality among the people of southern Africa, 'due to their excellent customs of sexual initiation and education at the age of puberty'.[172]Again, it may betray more inspiration by Gibbon as in his portrayal of 'decadent' Roman homosexuality. But it also revealed an inconsistency, for had he not claimed earlier that homosexuality could not be prevented or eradicated since it was congenital? By this, he seemed to suggest that prevention was possible after all or to imply that maybe not all homosexuality was innate. But Symonds did not recognize the problem.

Altogether, his exclusively biological model was problematic. His narrow model of masculine-defined androphilia hardly converged with ethnographic evidence of gender-structured homosexuality. On a theoretical level, this was banned from the realm of genuine homosexuality, but ethnographic data on such cross-gender roles, combined with homosexual behaviour, were used nevertheless to reinforce an image of universally present homosexuality.

Henry Havelock Ellis

Henry Havelock Ellis (1859–1939) finished a manuscript on 'Sexual Inversion' that had been started by Symonds before his death in 1893. It was translated and published in Germany first.[173] The publication in England in 1897 was promptly withdrawn and Symonds's name was removed from the title page of a new edition published the same year. But in the wake of the trial against Oscar Wilde, it drew much legal attention and George Bedborough, secretary of a small sexual reform society called the Legitimation League, was brought to trial for selling 'a certain lewd, wicked, bawdy, scandalous libel', namely Ellis's *Sexual Inversion*. The book itself was judged obscene. But there is no better publicity, then as today, than a court case and the book, distributed underground, soon set the tone for liberal attitudes to homosexuality for generations to come.

A definitive, more elaborate version of *Sexual Inversion* was published as part of Ellis's *Studies in the Psychology of Sex*. Theoretically, it merely reiterated the points of view expressed in the edition of 1897, but additional case histories were included along with new historical and ethnographic evidence.[174] The new ethnographic data, gathered since the publication of 1897, were to support the initial edition's theory presenting 'sexual inversion' as a variation of nature that was congenital. As such, Ellis, who was married to a lesbian woman and was a good friend of Symonds and Carpenter, aligned himself with the politics of sexual reform, even though gently and carefully. 'There was, in his view', says Jeffrey Weeks, 'a need for a reluctant acquiescence in the moral views of society'[175] and tolerance, more than acceptance, was advocated. The historian Paul Robinson has pointed out how Ellis's moderate position can be detected also in his emphasis on a continuity between homosexual and heterosexual identity. He thus postulated a 'latent organic bisexuality' present in any individual and joined in uneasy alliance with Sigmund Freud while highlighting the undifferentiated character of sexual desire during infancy.[176]

Initially, Ellis expressed doubt towards the mostly superficial and inaccurate descriptions by travellers and ethnographers: 'Travellers have spoken vaguely of crimes against nature without defining the precise relationship involved nor inquiring how far any congenital impulse could be distinguished.'[177] And, in another instance:

[There] is abundant evidence to show that homosexual practices exist and have long existed in most parts of the world outside Europe, when subserving no obvious social or moral end. *How far they are associated with congenital inversion is usually very doubtful* [my italics].'[178]

Eventually, Ellis claimed that sufficient ethnographic evidence was available to allow for a universally applicable model of congenital homosexuality. Reports from the Torres Straits Expedition, for example, showed how even among the people untouched by Europeans and 'practically still in the Stone Age' cases of congenital sexual inversion were known. Other proof was given by the *boté* among American Indians,[179] by Oskar Baumann's report on Zanzibar, and by various narratives of *mika* operations and pederasty among the Australian Aboriginals. Future ethnographic descriptions, moreover, would provide more evidence especially as anthropologists were better trained in matters of sexuality and 'crucial points [would] no longer [be] overlooked'.[180]

But what, one may ask, were these 'crucial points', enabling the reader at home to recognize genuine homosexuality? Ellis's phrasing surely reveals that not all same-sex sexual relations could be labelled as such, that some, in other words, belonged to the realm of acquired perversion. But Ellis's model was most comprehensive as it included cross-gender defined roles along with masculine-defined ones, age-structured homosexuality alongside androphilia. The homosexual 'generally passes unperceived', but can be member of a 'secret caste' and assume prominent social roles in religion. Not infrequently, homosexuality goes hand in hand with cross-dressing and cross-gender roles.[181] The age-structured or inter-generational homosexual relations, taking place during initiation rites in Australia and Melanesia, also pertained to the domain of congenital homosexuality.

Ellis may appear less dogmatic than others in his connection of congenital homosexuality to secondary characteristics, yet his empiricism was not transparant nor was it entirely objective. Weeks has rightly pointed out that Ellis's distinction between acquired and congenital homosexuality often relied on purely arbitrary judgements, which makes it difficult to discover

any pattern at all.[182] Ellis remained sceptical, for example, about the congenital character of homosexuality within the context of male bonding among
some warlike tribes, including the Dorians and the Celts, yet eagerly reiterated Foley's portrayal of male brotherhoods in New Caledonia as an
indication of congenital homosexuality. Another discursive anomaly was the
hard to interpret minimalization of homosexuality in China along with the
interpretation of Näcke's data on homosexuality in Constantinople as evidence merely of acquired perversion or bisexuality.[183]

Arbitrariness of judgement as well as racialist presumptions can be detected in Ellis's discussion of ethnographic data about the sexuality of blacks.
Reports by Oscar Baumann and John Weeks indicated, said the author, that
it occurred in Subsaharan Africa, but far less so than among African
Americans in the United States, so he was told by a local unidentified
informant. Ellis's footnote here on the etiology of black homosexual subcultures in American cities is a poignant example of racialist rationalization:
'If inversion is to be regarded as a penalty of "civilization", this is remarkable. Perhaps, however, the Negro, *relatively to his capacity*, is more highly
civilized than we are ... .' This implied that the potential of black evolutionary development was limited. But Ellis went even further and sharpened
his point by attributing the 'civilization' of African Americans to the credit of
white people: 'at any rate [the Negro's] civilisation has been thrust upon him,
and not acquired through the long throes of evolution'.[184] In the end, no
answer is provided by Ellis to the question how congenital homosexuality
could be distinguished from the acquired kind. At different points, racialist
considerations were reflected in the author's judgement, yet his criteria
remained deliberately vague, so that ethnographic evidence could be used in
ways that suited the cause of homosexual politics.

Edward Carpenter

Edward Carpenter (1844–1929) perhaps came closest to a correct understanding of the complex genealogy of homosexual identity as he assessed the
role of social and cultural contextualization more explicitly than anyone else
reviewed above. His almost messianic expectations regarding the active
political role to be played by homosexual men and women in order to change
society in general acknowledged that there was more to biology than just
destiny. Carpenter's vision was at once 'deterministic' and 'utopian' or, as it
is poignantly summarized by Noël Greig,

a midway between the rigid and defensive view of Ulrichs that gays were a small
minority defined firmly by biology, and the view of gay liberation, a century later,
that 'gay shows the way' to a future for humanity free from the tyranny of gender
and the horrors it involves.[185]

Carpenter himself put it as follows:

[It] is possible that the Uranian spirit may lead to something like a general enthusiasm of Humanity, and that the Uranian people may be destined to form the advance guard of that great movement which will one day transform the common life by substituting the bond of personal affection and compassion for the monetary, legal and other external ties which now control and confine society.[186]

The free-will tenor of his messianism must not disguise, however, that it operated within the confines of biology just as did the writings of Hirschfeld, Karsch-Haack, Symonds, or Ellis. Homosexuality, to Carpenter, was congenital and an autonomous product of the development of the human species. His vaguely Lamarckian concept of *exfoliation* allowed him to reconcile the image of a biologically defined minority (homosexual men and women) with the claim that 'the capacity of [the Uranian] kind of attachment also exists – though in a germinal and undeveloped state – in the breast of mankind at large'.[187] Such view surely anticipated a kind of 'homosexual imperialism', characterizing some of the gay revolutionary rhetoric of the 1960s. But it would be wrong to represent it as simply prefiguring the liberationist politics to come, for Carpenter's etiology of homosexual behaviour remained essentially biological.

The ambivalent outline of Carpenter's theory is visible in his own, peculiar *bricolage* of ethnographic data. This not only stressed the universality of an intermediate sex across the globe, but it simultaneously contained elements of a search for a homosexual Utopia. As early as 1890, well in advance of hippies and New Age aficionados alike, he had sailed for India to meet the proverbial wise man or *gñani*. But he may have encountered physical relief alongside the intellectual one, and may have participated in the homosexual exchange brought about by the colonial regime: 'Bombay was very interesting – I managed to pick up acquaintance with sundry native post office and railway clerks and tramway men, and they gave me regular entertainment at the house of one of their number in a back street in the city.'[188] He also witnessed how plantation overseers in Sri Lanka, then Ceylon, maintained sexual liaisons with female and male domestic servants. In Kandy he had met one, 'Ajax', who admitted to have grown fond of his coolies and to be 'quite attached to some'.[189]

Back in England, Carpenter published a handful of studies on homosexuality, including *Intermediate Types among Primitive Folk* in 1914 that is most relevant here. The first part focused largely on effeminate or 'intermediate' homosexual roles related to prophecy and priesthood, and was published initially in the July 1911 issue of the *American Journal of Religious Psychology*. It was translated and published by Hirschfeld's associates in Germany as well.[190] The second part, added in 1914, contained extensive descriptions of Dorian and Japanese *samurai* 'warrior' life and its connection with homosexuality. But the members of such male bonds were hardly effeminate, that is 'intermediate' in the strict sense. The apparent inconsistency of the entire work is admitted by Carpenter himself, even if only in the conclusion, yet he resolved the problem rather sophistically:

If there are men who vary from the normal mantype in the feminine direction – and who may perhaps be termed 'subvirile' – there are also men who vary in the opposite direction, and may be called 'supervirile'. .... These types ... are not between but beyond the normal boundaries.[191]

Before evaluating Carpenter's ethnographic narrative, let us return to its departing line. This was universalist and based on the theory of the congenital roots of homosexuality.[192] But Carpenter's cross-cultural survey of homosexuality went beyond a mere investigation of sexuality and raised questions about the nature of the connection between sexual identity and social and gender roles. This led to an exposition of the affinity between 'Uranian temperament' and prophecy, divination, art and creativity.

Carpenter accredited Reclus, Westermarck, Bastian and Bloch for having touched upon homosexuality's nexus with prophecy and divination in particular, but completed their records with evidence about 'intermediate' priests and prophets in as widely divergent societies as Polynesia, Malaysia, China, Japan, and the African Slave Coast (*kosio*).[193] Historical information was added also on ancient Greek, Hebrew (*kedeshim*) and pre-Columbian American religions (berdaches, *mujerados*), each embracing similar roles. Common to all societies was their shared belief 'that unusual powers of divination and prophecy were to be found in homosexual folk'.[194]

Indigenous beliefs evidently did not reveal whether an actual connection existed between homosexuality and prophecy or, in Carpenter's words, magic and witchcraft – a vocabulary that was still acceptable in his time, but that has been rejected since by cultural anthropologists as Eurocentric and judgemental. Carpenter weighed the view held by Bloch and Bastian that magic power was ascribed to homosexuals because of their anomalous sexuality, yet, eager to discern a more coercive link, Carpenter judged the link to be too tenuous. A theory was advanced also by Karl Pearson,[195] stating that the role of males in witchcraft rituals was initiated at the time of declining matriarchy. Men presumably had taken over the position of female witches and wizards, yet were compelled to dress like women because of lingering matriarchal authority. This theory too was discarded by Carpenter not only as being too speculative, but also because he suspected 'some fundamental causes in human nature itself'.[196]

A clue as to what this may mean is given by Carpenter as he speculated on the presumably prominent role of homosexuals within the field of arts and crafts. But the meaning is bewildering, for it reveals the author's rather uncritical adoption of traditionally defined gender roles:

Some of the Intermediates (though certainly not all) combining the emotionality of the feminine with the practicality of the masculine ... would undoubtedly be greatly superior in ability to the rest of the tribe ... and ... become inventors, teachers, musicians, medicine-men and priests.[197]

At once mystifying and banal, this conjecture crystallized into a psycho-logical speculation on the homosexual's 'cosmic consciousness' or 'double-engine psychic power'.[198] It also combined a theory of congenitality with a somewhat elitist representation of the homosexual's inherent cultural potential – a strategy of affirmation that very much resembled the ethno-graphic narrative of Karsch-Haack.

The inclusion of historical and ethnographic data on the masculine-defined homosexuality among Dorian warriors and Japanese *samurai* compelled Carpenter to expand his initial, narrow definition of homosexual identity as 'in between women and men' in order to embrace masculine-defined variants as well.[199] *Samurai* sexuality also was far from being exclusively homosexual and the accompanying cult of male beauty ought to be seen within a wider framework of an almost obligatory bisexuality. Noël Greig has rightly pointed out that Carpenter's analysis may have been easier had he not adhered to a strictly biological – and I may add dualistic – model of sexual identity.[200] However, since Carpenter shared the paradigm of his time, he could not help but explain the masculine-defined variant as a 'super-virile' expression of intermediate sexuality. As with other early advocates of homosexual emancipation, biological theory was mixed with elitist claims regarding the social and cultural merits of homosexual men (and women).[201] Carpenter too, inspired by some of Gustav Jäger's ideas discussed above, maintained that homosexual love, just as its heterosexual counterpart, was fertile soil for noble human acts. He criticized European misinterpretations of foreign rituals because they wrongly assumed that these were merely dramatizations of 'unadulterated wickedness and licentiousness'. In reality, they were cultural expressions of religious or cosmic beliefs, regardless of whether such rituals included more or less explicit hetero- or homosexual acts. To consolidate his argument, he provided examples from Hebrew, Syrian, Babylonian and Polynesian performances of ritualized heterosexual-ity, then, by way of analogy, of ritualized homosexuality. It is not without significance, here, that he invoked the early eighteenth-century narrative of Lafitau's *Moeurs des sauvages* to stress the virtue of moral relativism. The latter's portrayal, as I described in chapter one, of cross-dressing priests in pre-Columbian America was not all that appreciative, but this was obscured by Carpenter's selective quotation from Lafitau's description elsewhere on the *amitiés particulières* in a more neutral context of daily life.

Such inconsistency, largely inspired by the author's apologetic agenda, did not preclude him from defending homosexual relations in daily life by reference to homosexuality in a ritualized context. This, in fact, was to grant legitimacy to them as a social product somehow derived from cultural and religious belief:

There was a religion of the body, and a belief in the essential sacredness of all its processes, which we somehow have lost – and which we shall not probably socially regain until we once more adopt the free life of the open air and restore the healing and gracious sense of human community and solidarity.[202]

Carpenter's logical error may be pardoned, for identical extrapolations were currently made in ethnographic narratives by authors who did not share or were even opposed to the agenda of homosexual emancipation. All too often, as we have seen, they also depicted forms of ritualized homosexuality as indications of a primitive tribes' biological inclination to pederasty.

Carpenter also stressed, if only in vague, suggestive terms, that homosexuality may well have contributed to human evolution. Such an argument ought to be understood primarily as a counter-argument against mainstream speculations about the negative and degenerative effects of homosexuality on the public order and on the growth and survival of the human race. Against such accusations, it was important to assert that the homosexual's contribution to society should not to be minimized:

[The] foundational occupations of human life – such as fighting, hunting, child-rearing, and agriculture – having been laid down by the normal sex types, it was largely the intermediate types who developed the superstructure. The priest or the medicine-man or shaman was at first the sole representative of this new class, and we have seen that he was almost invariably, in some degree or other, of Uranian temperament.[203]

Rationalizing further on the social legitimacy of homosexuality, he acclaimed its 'super-virile' variety which included generals, organizers and political leaders – a defensive trope, and even a dubious one, to some extent, in the light of Carpenter's own anarchism, that was also an essential part of early endeavours in lesbian and gay history.

Jeffrey Weeks has somewhat disdainfully characterized Carpenter's writings on homosexuality as 'part of a wholesale critique of the values of "civilization"',[204] but they can hardly be underestimated as part of the counter-political discourse of a modern homosexual minority. They were instrumental also to the formulation of an alternative ethnographic narrative. This remained subordinate, however, to the current biological construction of sexual identity and triggered intellectual problems regarding the nature of the link between sexual desire and its manifestation in well defined social, cultural and gender roles. In yet another way, this can be perceived in the work of Westermarck as well.

Edward Westermarck

Edward Westermarck (1862–1939), sociologist and anthropologist of Finnish nationality, visiting professor at the London School of Economics between 1904 and 1930, published *The Origin and Development of Moral Ideas* (1906–8). Earlier he had written a three-volume study of *The History of Human Marriage* (1891), defending the thesis that from an early stage the nuclear family had been crucial to the survival of the human species. Doing so, he went against current evolutionist claims that marriage had developed from a primitive state of promiscuity.[205]

No biographical details about the author are known that reveal a more than scientific commitment to the cause of homosexual emancipation, but his life and career offer no proof of the contrary either. His prolonged activities in Morocco in the 1920s and 1930s may well have been inspired by expectations regarding homosexual opportunity. Although conclusive evidence has not yet been found, I suspect that his personal attraction to men partly motivated his work, and I include it as part of a homosexual cultural politics.[206]

The chapter on 'homosexual love'[207] in *The Origin and Development of Moral Ideas* shared the Hirschfeldian claim concerning its universality and provided a synopsis of its appearances across the world. 'Homosexual practices', the author concluded, 'are due sometimes to instinctive preference, sometimes to external conditions unfavourable to normal intercourse.' Often, male sexual inversion is held to be congenital and is associated by Westermarck with a cross-gender role. Influenced by Hirschfeld, Karsch-Haack and Ellis alike, he first questioned the value of many travellers' reports in order to conjecture subsequently that perhaps acquired homosexuality rested on an inborn predisposition as well:

Our real knowledge of congenital inversion is derived from the voluntary confession of inverts. The large majority of travellers are totally ignorant of the psychological side of the subject, and even to an expert it must very often be impossible to decide whether a certain case of inversion is congenital or acquired. Indeed, acquired inversion itself presupposes an innate disposition which under certain circumstances develops into actual inversion.[208]

The inaccessability of women often contributes to acquired homosexuality, Westermarck said, as did the obligatory celibacy of priests and monks. But it ought to be remembered that 'a profession which imposes abstinence from marriage is likely to attract a comparatively large number of congenital inverts'.[209] Temporary separation of the sexes during war explained why homosexual love was prevalent among 'warlike races' such as the Sikhs, the Afghans, the Dorians and the Normans, as well as among Persian and Moroccan soldiers, Japanese knights (*samurai*) and New Caledonian brotherhoods in arms. While distinguishing 'acquired perversion' from 'innate inversion', Westermarck largely reiterated mainstream discourse, but his commitment to the theory of natural variation is revealed by the way he questioned von Krafft-Ebing's dualistic model and reinterpreted acquired perversion too as essentially rooted in biology.

His Moroccan experience compelled him to rethink evidence of so-called circumstantial homosexuality, for too many among those engaging in it became real inverts in his eyes. He discarded degenerationist explanations that such was due to the fact that marriage, inevitable for homosexually active men as well, guaranteed the inheritance of congenital inversion by one's offspring. If so, then it ought to be equally widespread among all Moroccan tribes of the same stock, whereas in reality it was not. Yet, at this very point, where social conditions seem to play a significant role, Westermarck remains faithful to the biological paradigm. And whereas Ellis had explained acquired homosexuality as 'perverse' and 'anomalous' as opposed to real, congenital inversion, Westermarck merely called it a case of natural variation: 'Of course, [social] influences ... require a favourable organic predisposition to act on, but this predisposition is probably no abnormality at all, only a feature in the ordinary constitution of man.'[210]

Westermarck continued by stressing the often age-structured character of homosexual relations in Muslim countries, which, to him, was similar to the παιδερασθεια in ancient Greece.[211] In both cases, congenital inversion coexisted with the acquired preference especially for adolescent boys. The education system and military training, as in Sparta, were fertile soil for the development of such tastes, but Westermarck insisted that, on this level too, a biological predisposition was at play.

The convergence between congenital and acquired homosexuality, resulting from the author's location of both in biology, clearly demonstrates his intention to set up a single, comprehensive etiology of homosexual behaviour across the world. This intention sprang not solely from his more academic project to reconcile a biological and a sociological understanding of social reality, but reflected his wish to substitute a neutral and value-free model of sexual variation for the pathological connotations residing in the distinction between acquired versus congenital homosexuality.

Despite their idiosyncratic readings at times of ethnographic data, the writers discussed above did share common ground in more than one way. Moreover, their at times comprehensive reformulations of the cross-cultural record were part of a modern movement of 'homosexual' affirmation and reflected some of the most crucial intellectual presumptions upon which its political rhetoric of emancipation was based. Their works were not isolated products. They were carried by the new social and cultural agenda of a self-proclaimed homosexual intelligentsia, who wanted to raise the homosexual's self-esteem and to educate the outside world, through both legal campaigns and scientific research. This first movement of emancipation could be noticed across Europe, but was most visible in Germany and Great Britain, where the legal status of homosexual men was weak and called for assertiveness and combativeness.

Both within and outside Germany, publications by homosexual intellectuals were highly influenced by the innovative emancipatory agenda of

Hirschfeld and the *Jahrbuch*. The new and irreversible cognitive organization of sexual desire into sexual identities, of acts into roles, soon became
quintessential to the social image of men who subsequently called themselves
'homosexual'. Congenitality especially became the cornerstone of one's
defense against the outside world.

Yet the protagonists of homosexual emancipation, including Hirschfeld,
Raffalovich, Symonds, and Carpenter among others, were subject, like
others, to the scientific modes of their time. They all shared a positivistic
belief in the promises and virtues of science – *per scientiam ad justitiam* –
with physicians, jurists and other professional groups coming to the fore in
late nineteenth-century Europe. They subscribed to the paradigmatic authority of biology and medicine, even when the evaluation of homosexuality by
either party was, in the end, different, even irreconcilable. Sexology, as
noted, became a tool for personal affirmation as much as a vehicle for
regulation and control.

Männerfreundschaft, decadence and exile

At the eve of the nineteenth century, intellectual and cultural life witnessed
alternative forms of homosexual affirmation alongside the medical and
emancipatory model of Hirschfeld, Symonds and Carpenter. And, along
with it, ethnographic evidence was selected to construct distinct subcultural
'geographies of desire'.

Especially in Germany, a cult of male bonding or *Männerfreundschaft* was
developed by writers who strongly opposed any representation of homosexuality as a 'third sex'. Pleading for a renewal of Greek παιδερασθεια, when
reading ethnographic data they focused almost exclusively upon age-
structured and/or military bonding, mostly in ancient Greece but also in
Japan.

A strong awareness grew, meanwhile, of *décadence*, perhaps most
intensely but not solely in France. The cultivation of *spleen* and morbidity
(*delectatio morosa*) was characterized by a rhetorical trope, that stood
opposed not only to the social prescriptions of bourgeois society, but also to
the claims to respectability that were formulated by the advocates of sexual
reform who merely aimed at removing the boundary between 'normal' and
'abnormal' behaviour to their own benefit. The 'rhetoric of sickness'[212] was
diametrically opposed also to the plea for male bonding in a natural *Gemein-
schaft*. Transgression, rather than the somewhat nostalgic return to
pre-industrial male *socialité*, was a key concept of the decadent sensibility. It
embraced a deliberate choice of social marginality, of values and lifestyles
from cultures and civilizations that were different from the contemporary
West.[213]

Like pleas for a restoration of virility, this cultivation of decadence
illustrated how late nineteenth-century social politics witnessed a battle not

only '*between* the sexes, but also . . . *within* the sexes, economically, socially and psychologically'.[214] The significance, within this context, of homosexuality and androgyny was considerable, especially as some renowned aficionados of male-to-male love became prominent spokesmen of urban sophistication and decadence. The dramatization of sexual difference that figured so prominently in decadent literature, drawing, painting and photography revealed the intimacy between the pursuit of cultural marginality and a countercultural apology for sexual diversity.[215] The 'reading' of ethnographic narratives from this viewpoint privileged narratives from the Orient as the imaginary 'topos' of projected asocial desire.

Many individuals, finally, exchanged the imaginary travelling of decadent writers for real journeys abroad or chose more or less deliberately to reside in foreign territories. Exile was greatly facilitated by European colonialism, that offered opportunities not only for employment overseas, but also defined formulas of social communication that were more advantageous for the Europeans themselves. Obviously, sexual motives, though rarely made explicit in private correspondence or diaries, played a major role, especially for those whose sexuality was targeted by penal law, police and moral crusaders at home.[216] Often, a sense of alienation towards the orthodoxies of 'homosexual' discourse persuaded the exile to search for a less oppressive environment elsewhere. Escape from the rhetoric of decadence and marginality itself may have provoked a desire for exile, fed by the hope that the new-found habitat would embrace their sexuality in a natural way.

The ethnography of exile revealed divergent sensibilities, ranging between a de-sexualized cult of masculinity and comradeship among colonizers at the frontier, to frank indulgence in age-structured promiscuity across the ethnic boundaries. Its story is told far too briefly by Hama, Marsan, Gourvennec, and Aldrich.[217] They speculate predominantly on the psychological motives of the exiles as escapism to a presumably more tolerant sexual ambiance of 'primitive' or Oriental societies without investigating the cognitive bias of their discursive praxis. The individual experience of the exile is detached from the wider intellectual debates about sexuality in the homeland, as if his position can be satisfactorily explained by personal psychology alone.

The 'nomadic' and implicit character of exile – acts rather than discourse – explain why deliberate exiles are often discarded as 'closet cases' in an increasingly profiled subculture of homosexuality. Hyam is opposed to such 'tendentious desire to extend its roots backward in time in a way that is totally unhistorical'[218] and his criticism ought to be shared by gay and lesbian historians who subscribe to a constructionist model of sexual identity. Exile has indeed been described inaccurately as mere escapism of self-styled 'homosexuals', who fled from legal repression and moral disapproval at home and searched for a more welcoming erotic environment. Hans Mayer, for example, coined the phrase 'Sodom's diaspora',[219] while Jeffrey Meyers recognized in the tropics 'a great temptation to atavism, a universal fascination with the savage and the incomprehensible', shared by homo- and heterosexual travellers alike. But such presentations are too mystifying and, in the end, romantic.[220] I have outlined an alternative approach elsewhere, anticipating a more comprehensive study that cannot be pursued here.[221]

The different geographies of desire reflected not only the idiosyncrasies of small subcultural groups, but also reveal how each 'provincial' strategy of affirmation developed in a dialectical relationship with the predominant model of Hirschfeldian politics. The justification by exiles of their *dépaysement* was characterized by doubt towards or even outright rejection of modern sexological taxonomy and expressed accordingly in alternative representations of male-to-male sexual or emotional relations in the colonies. They favoured settings of homosexual behaviour that were commonly called 'circumstantial' rather than 'congenital'. Among them, male prostitution was one, the bisexual praxis of many indigenous men another. By 'going native' – 'je suis un nègre' (Rimbaud) – or by obeying the dictates of the frontier, one aimed at participating in a less reifying discourse about sexuality. The colonies also provided a way out for pedophiles, whose sexual desire was excluded from the realm of respectable homosexuality.

Hirschfeldian emancipation politics were also echoed in the rhetoric of sickness and decadence. Its indifference to claims for respectability was mirrored by a literary and artistic taste for 'decadent' cultures such as Japan, China, and the Arab world, for the esotericism of the Indian subcontinent, or for the decaying civilizations of Imperial Rome, Egypt, and Persia. Homosexuality's pathological character, disputed by theories of natural variation, was reinforced ironically by the emphasis on the primitiveness or neurasthenia of the Oriental world.

An ideal of natural 'male friendship', on the other hand, was opposed to its reification by Hirschfeld into 'homosexual identity'. The connotation of effeminacy especially was countered by ethnographic narratives about masculine-defined male bonding and, perhaps even more significantly, by a factual omission of the cross-gender forms of male-to-male sexuality, that had been amply documented since the early days of ethnography.

A separate study ought to be pursued ideally, showing how the eclectic use of cross-cultural data clearly reveals a more or less explicit tendency towards social transgression rather than towards the integration of homosexual men as part of modern, respectable society.[222] This surfaces in the assessment of indigenous homosexuality as virtuous or elitist, rather than as genuine or even circumstantial. Regional variance was emphasized, rather than universality. The 'geographies of desire', advanced in each of the competing strategies noted above, were marked by recognition of qualitative differences between various forms of homosexual behaviour in different parts of the world.

In contrast to the prominent iconic status ascribed to the Japanese *samurai* by the advocates of 'male friendship', decadent aesthetes singled out cross-gender roles, especially when tied to a context of ritual, as signifiers of their self-styled androgynous ideals. On the level of imagination, exiles frequently shared ethnographic projections of the *inherently* male-to-male sexual dimension of some indigenous traditions or minorities, even when their pursuit of sexual gratification was defined – and confined – either by indigenous cultural symbolism or by patterns of social communication and exchange in a colonial context.

The obliteration of history that typified both mainstream and Hirschfeldian ethnographic imagination about male-to-male sexuality, surfaces here as well. Again, cross-cultural comparison leaned upon a representation of cultural otherness as timeless and unchangeable. 'Synchronic essentialism' thus allowed for projecting sexual alternatives upon other societies, whereas, in reality, these societies not only defined strict boundaries for male-to-male sexuality just as they did for male-to-female sexuality, but had redefined these, often in the wake of European colonization, or, as for decolonized or independent nations, modernization. Static reduction became most extreme in recurrent amalgamations of sexuality in ancient and/or Early Modern civilizations (Egypt, Babylonia, Persia, Hindu and Moghul India, Tokugawa Japan) with sexuality in the colonies, in the Ottoman empire, or in Meiji Japan. The critique of the reification of desire did not, in the end, challenge the epistemological parameters of European discourse of cultural difference.

From the above reconstruction of a homosexual 'geography of desire', one sees that other issues arose aside from the question whether cross-gender behaviour was or was not an essential trait of the homosexual role. The emphasis on modern homosexuality's congenital character especially was significant, as no clear-cut tool for diagnosis was available to distinguish innate from acquired or circumstantial homosexuality. On this issue, the homosexual ethnographic discourse was a looking-glass in which it can be seen that the self-styled criteria were often not biological, but essentially social and cultural. Strategic considerations about the status of homosexual behaviour as seen in indigenous cultures, rather than 'hard' scientific indicators, were instrumental to its inclusion within or exclusion from the realm of congenital homosexuality. Relevant were those settings of same-sex praxis that were centred in society and invested with social, cultural or even religious significance, or combined with extraordinary professional, military or artistic skills. A prominent place was given to narratives about Japanese *samurai*, shamans, diviners, healers and prophets, to biographies of kings, heros and artists, and to portrayals of same-sex practices in a context of initiation and ritual. Left in the dark, on the other hand, were more marginal settings: warfare, mines, plantations, polygamous societies, male prostitution. In these settings male-to-male sexuality was called 'circumstantial', which is only partly accurate. In such settings genuine homosexuality could not be excluded *a priori*. Nor could the innate character of the more socially centred 'homosexual' settings be labelled as congenital *a priori*. Yet this is what happened. The labelling of the former variants as 'circumstantial' was as tendentious and inaccurate as was the projection of 'genuine' homosexuality upon the more respectable settings of same-sex praxis in the core of indigenous society. The acclamation of homoeroticism in ethnographic portrayals embraced an elitist consciousness, potentially as an antidote against stigmatization by society. Homosexual authors probably felt torn between an agenda of integration with bourgeois respectability and a call for a more radical image of the self.

The homosexual 'geography of desire' was not in itself related to any *political* strategy of affirmation, but was a side-effect rather of the biological reification of desire into identity. Put differently, it was designed according to the *poetic* structure of late nineteenth- and early twentieth-century sexological discourse. Empiricism, which called for the visibility of sexual identities rather than acts, thus directed the homosexual ethnographic gaze as well towards a more exclusive focus upon 'fixed' roles.

It is crucial, however, to realize that the distinction between politics and poetics is an artificial one. In fact, cross-fertilization was instrumental to the efficacy of discourse, including the homosexual 'geography of desire'. The complicity of both can be recognized in the selection of mostly permanent, stable, and visible roles (warriors, shamans, artists, kings) as representatives of 'congenital' homosexuality, while 'circumstantial' homosexuality was found, on the contrary, in conditions that were temporary, transient, invisible: war, seasonal labour, demographic disequilibrium. The projection from sexual roles into social ones was significant, as was the ascription of transient sexuality to transient social conditions. Both tropes of representation reinforced the modern definition of homosexuality as a distinct minority merely by labelling socially visible variants as 'congenital' and socially invisible ones as 'circumstantial' or, at most, 'acquired'. Ethnographic discourse reflected superbly how the reification of desire into identity was the price of the ticket to homosexual affirmation.

The representation of cultural 'otherness' in the homosexual 'geography of desire' resembled mainstream ideology, notwithstanding the positive value ascribed to (particular forms of) homosexual behaviour. Like the 'geography of perversion' deconstructed in the earlier chapters, the alternative reading by the modern homosexual intelligentsia leaned equally on so-called 'partial truths' that were 'committed and incomplete'.[223] In applying the grid of western cognition to non-western cultures and sexualities, it participated in the endeavour of 'white mythology' and, eventually, failed to recognize the radical critique of western vision that these potentially embraced. By now, its 'examples' have become fixed icons of the homosexual imagination, which makes it hard to grasp the artificial criteria for their selection within the homosexual 'geography of desire'.

Notes

1. B. D. Adam, *The Rise of a Gay and Lesbian Movement* (Boston, 1987), pp. 12–13.
2. J. Weeks, 'Questions of identity', in P. Kaplan (ed.), *The Cultural Construction of Sexuality* (London and New York, 1987), p. 38.
3. I derive the term from bell hooks, *Outlaw Culture. Resisting Representations* (London and New York, 1994).
4. On the interaction between public policy and subcultural affirmation, see the still exemplary study by J. Weeks, *Coming Out* (London, 1979 (1977)), esp. chapters 1 and 3. For a European overview, see B. Adam, *The Rise of a Gay and Lesbian Movement*, pp. 10–12; and D. F. Greenberg, *The Construction of Homosexuality* (Chicago and London, 1988).
5. The term 'homosexual role' here is to be understood in the sense given to the word by M. MacIntosh, 'The homosexual role', in K. Plummer (ed.), *The Making of the Modern Homosexual* (London, 1981), pp. 30–49. As such, it is different from Enlightenment definitions of the 'sodomite role', that, as I described in chapter two, was less pervasive in its emphasis upon actual role-taking during sexual intercourse.
6. See J. Weeks, 'Inverts, perverts, and Mary-Annes', in S. J. Licata and R. P. Petersen (eds), *Historical Perspectives on Homosexuality* (New York, 1980/1), pp. 113–34.
7. The birth, in scientific literature, of 'lesbianism' as a separate identity took place only at the turn of the nineteenth into the twentieth century. It was a response largely to an increasingly visible lesbian subculture in the metropolitan centres of Europe, while until then female-to-female sexuality had been addressed, rather reluctantly, as 'tribadism', a term that targeted the act of 'rubbing' (from Greek τριβειν) and was typical for a pre-modern conceptualization, comparable to the Early Modern one of 'sodomy'. See L. Faderman, *Surpassing the Love of Men. Romantic Friendship and Love between Women from the Renaissance to the Present* (London, 1981), pp. 231 ff.
8. G. Chauncey, Jr., 'From sexual inversion to homosexuality', *Salmagundi*, 58/59 (Fall 1982/Winter 1983), 146.
9. K. Müller, *Aber im meinem Herzen sprach eine Stimme so laut* (Berlin, 1991). On the dynamics of cognitive exchange between the -emic discourse of homosexual men and the -etic one of medical scientists, see also M. Maffesoli, 'Homosocialité et identification' and B. Lhomond, 'Un, deux, trois sexes: l'homosexualité comme mélange', both in *Homosexualité & lesbianisme* (Paris and Lille, 1989), pp. 1–10, 11–21.
10. See J. Steakley, *The Homosexual Emancipation Movement in Germany* (New York, 1975), pp. 21 ff., and M. Baumgardt, 'Die Homosexuellen-Bewegung bis zum Ende des Ersten Weltkrieges', in *Eldorado* (Berlin, 1984), pp. 17–27.
11. On Ulrichs' work, see H. Kennedy, *Ulrichs* (Boston, 1988).
12. See M. Herzer, 'Kertbeny and the nameless love', *JHom*, 12 (1985), 3–4.
13. See M. Herzer, *Magnus Hirschfeld* (Frankfurt, 1992), *passim*; and C. Woolf, *Magnus Hirschfeld* (London, 1986), pp. 185–7.
14. Th. Ramien [pseudonym of Magnus Hirschfeld], *Sappho und Sokrates* (Leipzig, 1896), reprinted in *Documents of the Homosexual Rights Movement in Germany, 1836–1927* (New York, 1975).
15. See M. Baumgardt, 'Die Homosexuellen-Bewegung'; J. Steakley, *Homosexual Emancipation Movement*, pp. 21–40; and J. Lauritsen and D. Thorstad, *The Early Homosexual Rights Movement (1864–1935)* (New York, 1974), pp. 6–17.

16. See J. Steakley, *The Writings of Dr. Magnus Hirschfeld. A Bibliography* (Toronto, 1985), p. 5; and M. Dannecker, 'Vorwort', in W. J. Schmidt (ed.), *Jahrbuch für sexuelle Zwischenstufen. Auswahl aus den Jahrgängen 1899–1923* (Frankfurt/Main, 1983), pp. 5–15.

17. See C. Woolf, *Magnus Hirschfeld*, pp. 42–67; and V. L. Bullough, 'The physician and research into human sexual behavior in nineteenth-century Germany', *BHMed*, 63 (1989), 264.

18. See J. S. Hohmann, *Sexualforschung und -aufklärung in der Weimarer Republik* (Berlin, 1985), pp. 15–59.

19. See C. Woolf, *Magnus Hirschfeld*, pp. 380–415.

20. 'Diese generelle Auffassung der sexuellen Anomalien als allgemein menschlichen, ubiquitären Erscheinungen lässt einen grossen Teil derselben, die man bisher als pathologische betrachtet hatte, als physiologische erkennen und schränkt das Gebiet der "Degeneration" bedeutend ein.' I. Bloch, *Beiträge zur Äthiologie der Psychopathia Sexualis* (Dresden, 1902–3), vol. 1, p. xiv.

21. I. Bloch, *Das Sexualleben unserer Zeit in seinen Beziehungen zur modernen Kultur* (Berlin, 1908), pp. 588–607.

22. M. A. Raffalovich, 'Quelques observations sur l'inversion', *Aac*, 9 (1894), 216. Also, see his *Uranisme et Unisexualité* (Lyons and Paris, 1896).

23. P. Cardon, 'A homosexual militant at the beginning of the century: Marc André Raffalovich', *JHom*, 25, 1/2 (1993), 183–92.

24. R. A. Nye, 'Sex difference and male homosexuality in French medical discourse, 1830–1930', *BHMed*, 63 (1989), 46.

25. E. Zola, 'Préface', in G. Saint-Paul, *Tares et poisons. Perversion et perversité sexuelles* (Paris, 1896), pp. 3–4.

26. A. Gide, *Corydon* (Paris, 1924 (1911)), pp. 30–4.

27. A. Aletrino, 'Over uranisme en het laatste werk van Raffalovich', *Psychiatrische en neurologische bladen*, 1 (1897), 351–65, 452–83.

28. A. Aletrino, *Hermaphrodisie en uranisme* (Amsterdam, 1908), pp. 53–8.

29. On Aletrino, see K. Joosse, *Arnold Aletrino* (Amsterdam and Brussels, 1986), ch. 12, pp. 500–48.

30. See R. Tielman, 'Dutch gay emancipation history (1911–1986)', in A. X. van Naersen (ed.), *Gay Life in Dutch Society* (New York, 1987), pp. 9–18.

31. Symonds took a long time coming to grips with his own sexual desire. He was married and found a way out of his emotional impasse when seeking exile in Italy. See H. Hafkamp, 'Een probleem in Victoriaanse ethiek. John Addington Symonds (1840–1893) en Henry Havelock Ellis (1859–1939)', in *Pijlen van naamloze liefde*, pp. 46–8; and P. Grosskurth, *The Woeful Victorian: A Biography of John Addington Symonds* (New York, 1964). Also, see P. Grosskurth, 'Introduction', in *The Memoirs of John Addington Symonds*, ed. P. Grosskurth (New York, 1984), pp. 13–28.

32. H. Ellis, 'Nota sulle facoltà artistiche degli invertiti', *Archivio delle psicopatie sessuali*, 1 (1896), 243–5.

33. J. Weeks, *Coming Out*, p. 57.

34. See J. Weeks, 'Havelock Ellis and the politics of sex reform', in S. Rowbotham and J. Weeks (eds), *Socialism and the New Life* (London, 1977), pp. 141, 183, note 18. For further information on Ellis, see A. Calder-Marshall, *Havelock Ellis* (London, 1959); P. Grosskurth, *Havelock Ellis* (New York, 1980); and P. Robinson, *The Modernisation of Sex* (New York, 1976), pp. 1–41.

35. On Carpenter, see T. Chushichi, *Edward Carpenter, 1844–1929: Prophet of Human Fellowship* (New York and Cambridge, 1980); and N. Greig, 'Introduction', in E. Carpenter, *Selected Writings*, Vol. 1: *Sex*, ed. N. Greig (London, 1984), pp. 9–78.

36. On this process, see J. Weeks, *Sex, Politics and Society*, pp. 180–4.

37. Other influences were Casper, von Krafft-Ebing, and Moll. But, opposite to the latter three, Hirschfeld stressed that the 'third sex' must not be seen as pathological. Ulrichs' influence is indisputable, moreover, as Hirschfeld already used the words 'Urninge' and 'Urninde' in his essay *Sappho und Sokrates*. See C. Woolf, *Magnus Hirschfeld*, pp. 34–6.

38. See M. Hirschfeld, 'Ursachen und Wesen des Uranismus', *JfsZ*, 5 (1903), 1–193; and M. Hirschfeld, *Berlin's dritte Geschlecht* (Grossstadtdokumente, ed. H. Ostwald, vol. 3) (Berlin and Leipzig, 1904). For a more extensive analysis, see G. Grau, 'Hirschfeld Über die Ursachen der Homosexualität – zur Bedeutung seiner ätiologischen Hypothesen', *Mitteilungen der Magnus Hirschfeld Gesellschaft*, 13 (May 1989), 27–30.

39. M. Hirschfeld, *Die Homosexualität des Mannes und des Weibes* (Berlin, 1920 (1914)). I have used the 1984 reprint, published by Walter de Gruyter in Berlin.

40. M. Hirschfeld, *Die Weltreise eines Sexualforschers* (Brugg, 1933).

41. See the items 1930: i, p, r; 1931: y, dd; 1932: e; 1935: d; 1937: b; 1953–55; 1953; 1954 in Steakley's bibliography. These publications, along with his travelogue of the 1930–2 world trip have received far too little attention from historians, perhaps because his ideas about sexuality had become less significant, reminiscences rather of a paradigm gone by.

42. 'Noch kein Volk ist an widernatürlicher Unzucht zu Grunde gegangen. . . . Unzucht mit Personen desselben Geschlechts beruht fast durchaus auf Perversitäten, auf anomaler geschlechtlicher Veranlagung, auf einer Art hermaphroditischen Wesens, das durchaus nicht ein Kulturerzeugnis ist, sondern sich auch schon bei Naturvölkern findet.' J. Kohler, 'Ueber den Begriff der Unzucht mit öffentlichem Ärgerniss', *Archiv für Staatsrecht*, 45 (1897), 175–213 (p. 204 for this reference).

43. 'Welches die Gründe für das mehr oder minder starke Auftreten des Urningwesens sind, ist eben so wenig erklärt, wie so viele andere völkerpsychologische Probleme. Jedenfalls ist es entschieden unrichtig, wenn Viele behaupten, dass nur dekadente Völker in sich ein erhebliches Urningthum bergen. Das widerspricht völlig der Geschichte.' *Ibid.*

44. Studies on Burton's life and writings are, of course, numerous. Apart from the still very useful biography by F. M. Brodie, *The Devil Drives. A Life of Sir Richard Burton* (New York and London, 1967), see also B. Farwell, *A Biography of Sir Richard Francis Burton*, 2nd ed. (Westport, 1975); M. Hastings, *Sir Richard Burton. A Biography* (New York, 1978); and F. McLynn, *Snow upon the Desert: Sir Richard Burton, 1821–1890* (London, 1991).

45. R. Burton, *Abeokuta and the Cameroons Mountains* (London, 1863), vol. 1, pp. 110–11.

46. R. Burton, *A Mission to Gelele, King of Dahome*, 2 vols (London, 1864). See p. 2 of the 1966 edition.

47. R. Burton, *Zanzibar: City, Island, and Coast* (London, 1872), vol. 1, p. 419.

48. For some information on Burton's assistant, see F. M. Brodie, *The Devil Drives*, pp. 293–9.

49. See J. Pope-Hennessy's two-volume biography of *Monckton Miles* (London, 1940, 1951).

50. For details, see F. M. Brodie, *The Devil Drives*, pp. 372–3.

51. See [Al-Nefzawi], *Le jardin parfumé (Al-Raud al-Atir)*, etc., translated from the Arabic by Baron R. (Algiers, 1874) (only 25 copies printed); [Al-Nefzawi], *Le Jardin parfumé du cheikh Nefzaoui. Manuel d'Erotologie Arabe: XVI Siècle*, translated and revised by I. Lisieux (Paris, 1886); and [Al-Nefzawi], *The Perfumed Garden of the Cheikh Nefzaoui* (trans. R. Burton) (London and Benares, 1886).

52. See A. H. Walton, 'Introduction', in: *The Perfumed Garden of the Shaykh Nefzawi*, trans. R. Burton, ed. A. H. Walton (London, 1984 (1963)), p. 21. For a (preliminary)

translation of the remaining passages, including the homosexual ones, see Al Nefzawi, *The Glory of the Perfumed Garden. The Missing Flowers*, trans. H. E. J. (London, 1975).

53. *A Plain and Literal Translation of the Arabian Nights' Entertainments, Now Entitled The Book of The Thousand Nights and a Night. With Introduction Explanatory Notes on the Manners and Customs of Moslem Men and a Terminal Essay upon the History of the Nights*, 10 vols, trans. and ed. R. Burton, (London and Benares: Kama Shastra Society, 1885); and *Supplemental Nights to the Book of a Thousand Nights and a Night. With Notes Anthropological and Explanatory*, 6 vols, trans. and ed. R. Burton (London and Benares: Kama Shastra Society, 1886–8). For a detailed overview of the publication and translation history of the Arabic manuscripts, see H. and S. Grotzfeld, 'Die Erzählungen aus Tausendundeiner Nacht', pp. 86–95.

54. In fact the Terminal Essay as used in most literature on Burton refers to part IV ('Social conditions – pederasty') of the Terminal Essay to vol. 10 only. See *A Plain and Literal Translation*, vol. 10 (1885), pp. 205–54. Here I am using the recent reprint by Longwood Press, titled *The Sotadic Zone* (Boston, 1977), p. 18.

55. See W. R. Dynes, 'Sotadic zone', in W. R. Dynes, *Homolexis* (New York, 1985), p. 135.

56. R. Burton, *The Sotadic Zone*, pp. 16–18.

57. *Ibid.*, p. 18.

58. *Ibid.*, p. 20.

59. See P. Mantegazza, *Gli amori dei uomini. Saggio di una etnologia dell'amore* (Milan, 1885–6).

60. *Ibid.*, p. 21.

61. No explanation is given by Stephen W. Foster either. See his glosses to the Terminal Essay in 'The Annotated Burton', in L. Crew (ed.), *The Gay Academic* (Palm Springs, 1978), pp. 92–101.

62. In Arabic literature on boy-love, Sufi writers indeed occupied a prominent position. See M. Schild, 'De citadel van integriteit', unpubl. thesis (R. U. Utrecht, 1985), pp. 36–69.

63. R. Burton, *Sotadic Zone*, pp. 37 ff.

64. *Ibid.*, p. 62.

65. *Ibid.*, pp. 44, 48–51.

66. *Ibid.*, pp. 76 ff.

67. *Ibid.*, p. 52.

68. N. M. Penzer, *An Annotated Bibliography of Sir Richard Francis Burton* (London, 1923), p. 176. Among the 'new' data was the information taken from the article by G. C. Stent, 'Chinese Eunuchs', *Journal of the Royal Asiatic Society of Great Britain and Ireland. North China Branch, Shanghai*, 11 (1877), 143–84. The *Catalogue of the Library of Sir Richard Burton, M.C.M.G., held by the RAI*, ed. B. J. Kirkpatrick (London, 1978), p. 20, item 205, indicates that this article was indeed known to Burton. In a letter to Henry Stanley, he mentioned another work in process, an 'Anthropology of Men and Women', but no trace of it is left. If it ever existed, it may also have contained relevant evidence of Burton's theoretical views on homosexuality. See F. M. Brodie, *the Devil Drives*, p. 317. The holdings of Burton's library are now at the Huntington Library, San Marino, USA.

69. R. Kabbani, *Europe's Myths of Orient* (Houndsmills, 1986), p. 65.

70. See G. W. Stocking, Jr., *Victorian Anthropology* (New York and London, 1987), pp. 253–4.

71. T. Klockmann, 'Vom Geheimnis menschlicher Gefühle. Günther Tessmanns Pangwe-Monographie im Lichte seiner Lebenserinnerungen sowie neuerer Forschungen', *Wiener Ethnohistorische Blätter*, 29 (1986), 3–20. See also F. W. Kramer, 'Eskapistische und

utopische Motive in der Frühgeschichte der deutschen Ethnologie', in H. Pollig *et al.* (eds), *Exotische Welten, Europäische Phantasien* (Stuttgart, 1987), p. 69.

72. G. Tessmann, 'Die Urkulturen der Menschheit', *ZfE*, 51 (1919), 132–62.
73. G. Tessmann, *Die Indianer Nordost-Perus* (Hamburg, 1930), p. 3.
74. G. Tessman, *Die Pangwe* (Berlin, 1913), vol. 2, pp. 255, 267.
75. *Ibid.*, vol. 2, p. 271.
76. *Ibid.*, vol. 2, pp. 158, 271–4.
77. G. Tessman, *Die Bafia und die Kultur der Mittelkamerun-Bantu* (Stuttgart, 1934), p. 261.
78. G. Tessman, 'Die Homosexualität bei den Negern Kameruns', *JfsZ*, 21 (1921), 124.
79. *Ibid.*, pp. 124–8. Compare P. Fry, 'Sexe et rôles de genre interactifs dans le Brésil contemporain', *Sociétés*, 2, 2 (February 1986), 13–15.
80. G. Tessmann, 'Die Homosexualität', pp. 129, 138.
81. G. Tessman, 'König im weissen Fleck – Erlebnisse eines deutschen Forschers in den Urwäldern Westafrikas' (1940), held at the Völkerkunde-Sammlung of the city of Lübeck, Germany.
82. 'Riss in der Lustsphäre des Zentralsystems, unter dem ich furchtbar gelitten habe, besonders als mir mit beginnendem Alter erst zum Bewusstsein kam, dass ich nie eigentlich richtig "gelebt" hatte, wie meine Sinnlichkeit so gebieterisch gefordert hatte.' G. Tessman, 'Tagebücher', vol. 4, p. 110, quoted in T. Klockmann, 'Vom Geheimnis menschlicher Gefühle', p. 10. The diaries, 12 volumes written between 1930 and his death in 1969, are also kept at the Völkerkunde-Sammlung in Lübeck.
83. G. Tessmann, *Die Pangwe*, vol. 2, p. 255.
84. *Ibid.*, vol. 4, pp. 256, 383–91.
85. K. Falk, 'Gleichgeschlechtliches Leben bei einigen Negerstämmen Angolas', *Archiv für Anthropologie*, New Series, 20 (1923), 42–5.
86. K. Falk, 'Homosexualität bei den Eingeborenen in Südwest-Afrika', *Archiv für Menschenkunde*, 1 (1925/6), 203.
87. *Ibid.*
88. In his article on South Africa, T. Dunbar Moodie has stressed the importance of accurate contextualization and warned for representations of 'mine marriages' as 'of a homosexual nature'. Yet, he also describes how these were somehow rooted in indigenous perceptions of sexual roles and thus not purely circumstantial. See T. Dunbar Moodie *et al.*, 'Migrancy and Male Sexuality on the South African Gold Mines', in M. Duberman *et al.* (eds), *Hidden from History*, pp. 411–425, as well as the chapter on South Africa in N. Miller, *Out in the World. Gay and Lesbian Life from Buenos Aires to Bangkok* (Harmondsworth, 1992), 3–66.
89. Falk, 'Homosexualität bei den Eingeborenen', pp. 205–6.
90. 'Gerade bei den durch keinerlei Gesetze gezwungenen Eingeborenen die Homoerotik sich bei gewissen Individuen gewaltsam Bahn bricht, während die übrigen in keinerlei Weise dadurch zur Homoerotik verleitet werden, sondern immer wieder, sobald sie es nur können, zum Weibe zurückkehren, und sich der Homosexualität nur faute de mieux bedienen. ... Jede Ableugner der angeborenen Homosexualität sollte einmal ohne Vorurteil sich hierüber bei den Eingeborenen zu orientieren suchen, und er würde bald anderer Meinung sein.' *Ibid.*, p. 213.
91. S. Jwaya, 'Nan sho'k (die Päderastie in Japan)', *JfsZ*, 4 (1902), 270–1.
92. A. C. Tytheridge, 'Beobachtungen über Homosexualität in Japan', *JfsZ*, 22 (1922), 23–36.
93. ' ... wenn die Homosexualität hier auch ebenso verbreitet ist wie in anderen Ländern, so besitzen die Homosexuellen doch keine eigene Organisation, sie haben kein Zusammengehörigkeitsgefühl wie in Deutschland usw., keine Solidarität und sehr wenig jener Art "Freimaurerei", die überall sonst existiert.' *Ibid.*, pp. 24–5.

94. This novel by the Belgian writer Georges Eekhoud was published as early as 1898 in the *Mercure de France* (in 1899 as a separate volume) and is revolutionary for its frank portrayal of male homoeroticism. Its author was sued, but acquitted.
95. L. S. A. M. von Römer, 'Über die androgynische Idee des Lebens', *JfsZ*, 5 (1903), 707–921.
96. L. S. A. M. von Römer, *Het uranisch gezin* (Amsterdam, 1905). On von Römer, see G. Hekma, *Homoseksualiteit*, pp. 194–8; and M. van Lieshout, 'Het ongekende leed van een tropendokter. Lucien von Römer (1873–1965)', in *Pijlen van naamloze liefde*, pp. 89–95.
97. *Ibid.*, pp. 715–17.
98. *Ibid.*, pp. 917–18.
99. H. Freimark, *Das Sexualleben der Naturvölker*, vol. 2: *Das Sexualleben der Afrikaner* (Leipzig, 1911), pp. 3, 279–80.
100. *Ibid.*, pp. 273, 276.
101. [Anon.], [Untitled], *Sexualprobleme*, 8 (1912), 142–3.
102. 'weil der Orientale meist früh heiratet, Ledige dort jedenfalls seltener sind, als bei uns, da ausserdem durch den Islam selbst der Coitus direkt vorgeschrieben ist und sich auch die gläubigen Homosexuellen dem fügen müssen und so fälschlicherweise als Bisexuelle gelten'. P. Näcke, 'Die Homosexualität im Oriente', *Archiv für Kriminal-Anthropologie und Kriminalistik*, 16 (1904), 353–5.
103. P. Näcke, 'Die Homosexualität in Konstantinopel', *Archiv für Kriminal-Anthropologie und Kriminalistik*, 26 (1906), 106–8.
104. P. Näcke, 'Über Homosexualität in Albanien', *JfsZ*, 9 (1908), 313–26.
105. P. Näcke, 'Albanien', pp. 329–30.
106. *Ibid.*, p. 336.
107. G. Jäger, 'Ein bisher ungedrucktes Kapitel über Homosexualität aus der "Entdeckung der Seele" ', *JfsZ*, 2 (1900), 53.
108. *Ibid.*, p. 122.
109. *Ibid.*, pp. 80–1.
110. *Ibid.*, pp. 85–6.
111. F. S. Krauss, *Das Geschlechtsleben in Glauben, Sitte, Brauch und Gewohnheitsrecht der Japaner* (Leipzig, 1911, second, revised edition; first edition in 1907). Krauss was trained as a classicist, but developed a noted interest in folklore, especially of Slovenia, Croatia, Bosnia and Serbia. See M. Morad, 'Friedrich Salomo Krauss. Vom Blick in die Volksseele zum Seelengliederer', in J. Clair *et al.*, eds *Wunderblock* (Vienna, 1989), pp. 501–6.
112. From φαλλοσ (penis) and κτεισ (vagina); dualistic cult of male and female generative organs within a context of fertility cult.
113. Krauss, *Das Geschlechtsleben*, 12, 77–8.
114. *Ibid.*, 92.
115. See J. E. Meiners, 'Dr. Magnus Hirschfelds Bestrebungen', *Anthropophyteia*, 4 (1907), 414–16.
116. P. Näcke, 'Sexuelle Umfragen bei halb- und unzivilisierten Völkern', and A. Kind and F. S. Krauss, 'Homosexualität und Volkskunde', both in *Anthropophyteia*, 5 (1907), 193–6 and 197–203.
117. See F. S. Krauss, 'Altperuanische Grabgefässe mit erotischen Gestalten', *Anthropophyteia*, 3 (1906), 420–4; E. H. Brünig, 'Einiges über die Erotik der alten Indianer des Küstengebietes Nordperús', *Anthropophyteia*, 5 (1908), 358–60; and E. H. Brünig, 'Beiträge zum Studium des Geschlechtslebens der Indianer im alten Perú', *Anthropophyteia*, 6 (1909), 101–12, and 7 (1910), 206–11.
118. F. S. Krauss, 'Ein erotischer Alptraum als Holzschnitzwerk aus Neu-Irlan', *Anthropophyteia*, 3 (1906), 408–10.

119. F. J. Bieber, 'Brieflicher Bericht über Erhebungen unter äthiopischen Völkerschaften', *Anthropophyteia* 6 (1909), 402–5; and F. J. Bieber, 'Neue Forschungen über das Geschlechtsleben in Äthiopien', *Anthropophyteia*, 7 (1910), 227–2, and 8 (1911), 184–93.

120. N. Praetorius [i.e., E. Wilhelm], 'Über gleichgeschlechtlichen Verkehr in Algerien und Tunis', *Anthropophyteia*, 7 (1910), 179–88.

121. W. von Bülow, 'Das Geschlechtsleben der Samoaner', *Anthropophyteia*, 4 (1904), 84–99.

122. B. Laufer, 'Ein homosexuelles Bild aus China', *Anthropophyteia*, 6 (1909), 162–6.

123. 'Es handelt sich bei diesen Secatra zweifellos um Fälle völliger Effemination. Der Verfasser des Berichts scheint mehr an erworbene Effemination ... zu denken; doch werden wohl nur diejenigen zich zu Secatra ausbilden, welche schon von Jugend auf eine konträr sexuelle Natur haben; die besonderen weiblichen Gewohnheiten werden dann allerdings diese konträre Anlage noch bestärken und zu vollster Entwicklung bringen.' [Anon.], [Untitled], *JfsZ*, 2 (1900), 387–9.

124. I. Bloch developed his initial theory in *Das Geschlechtsleben in England*, 3 vols (Berlin, 1901–3) and, more elaborately, in his *Äthiologie der Psychopatia Sexualis*, published simultaneously. In *Die Perversen* (Berlin, 1905), Bloch essentially held on to it while claiming that no historical relationship could be demonstrated between epochs of cultural decadence and the occurrence of homosexuality. See J. Steakley, *The Writings of Dr. Magnus Hirschfeld*, pp. 31–5.

125. W. Schrickert, 'Zur Anthropologie der gleichgeschlechtlichen Liebe', *Politisch-anthropologische Revue*, 1 (1902), 379–82. See also [Anon.], [Untitled], *JfsZ*, 5 (1903), 1015–18.

126. W. Schrickert, *Das Sexualleben unserer Zeit in seinen Beziehungen zur modernen Kultur* (Berlin, 1907).

127. 'Eine wirklich objektive Grundlage für die Beurteilung der Beziehungen zwischen Religion und Sexualleben gewinnen wir nur, wenne wir sie nicht als eine Sache des Dogmas und der Konfession auffassen, sondern sie auf diejenige Basis stellen, auf die sie gehören: die anthropologische.'

128. *Ibid.*, p. 105; see also pp. 105–16.

129. *Ibid.*, pp. 593–601.

130. 'Würden, wie im Altertum, alle Homosexuellen sich offen zu ihrer Liebe bekennen dürfen, so würde man erstaunt sein, dass so viele Männer ... und eine grosse Durchschnittsmasse homosexuell sind und homosexuell verkehren.' [Anon.], [Untitled], *JfsZ*, 9 (1908), 484.

131. F. Karsch-Haack, 'Päderastie und Tribadie bei den Tieren auf Grund der Literatur', *JfsZ*, 2 (1900), 126–60.

132. 'nicht als rein willkürlich zur Ausbildung gebrachte oder durch Zwang eingeführte 'Sitte' vorgestellt werden können, auch nicht bei Völkern, für welche das mit der grössten Bestimmtheit behauptet wird, sondern *naturgesetzlich* [my italics] immer und überall die Sonderveranlagung eines mehr oder minder starken Prozentsatzes der Gesamtbevölkerung nach dieser Lieberichtung hin zu notwendigen Bedingung haben, und daher zwar auf alle Teile jeden Volkes sich erstrecken, aber weder jemals über ein ganzes Volk sich ausbreiten können, noch irgendwo auf einen besonders bevorrechten Stand sich einschränken lassen.' F. Karsch-Haack, *Das gleichgeschlechtliche Leben der Naturvölker (Forschungen über gleichgeschlechtliche Liebe, 1. Ethnologische Reihe: Das gleichgeschlechtliche Leben der Völker)* (Munich, 1911), vol. 1, pp. 446–7.

133. F. Karsch-Haack, *Forschungen über gleichgeschlechtliche Liebe*, vol. 1: *Das gleichgeschlechtliche Leben der Kulturvölker, 1: Das gleichgeschlechtliche Leben der Ostasiaten: Chinesen, Japaner, Koreer* (Munich, 1906), p. 56, note 1.

134. F. Karsch-Haack, 'Uranismus oder Päderastie und Tribadie bei den Naturvölkern', *JfsZ*, 3 (1901), 72–181. I have used the re-edition in *Jahrbuch für sexuelle Zwischenstufen. Auswahl*, ed. W. J. Schmidt, pp. 229–296.

135. *Ibid.*, p. 237. The Latin *pathicus* and Greek κιναιδος denominated adolescent boys who, deliberately or not, assumed a passive role during male-to-male sexual relations. See G. Vorberg, *Glossarium eroticum* (Hanau, n.d.), pp. 289, 439–43.

136. F. Karsch-Haack, 'Uranismus', pp. 260–70; and F. Karsch-Haack, *Naturvölker*, pp. 306–20.

137. E. von Kupffer, *Lieblingsminne und Freundesliebe in der Weltliteratur* (Berlin, 1900).

138. F. Karsch-Haack, 'Uranismus', p. 295.

139. *Ibid.*, p. 263.

140. R. F. von Krafft-Ebing, *Psychopathia sexualis*, pp. 267–74.

141. F. Karsch-Haack, *Beruht gleichgeschlechtliche Liebe auf Soziabilität? Eine begründete Zurückweisung. (Kritik an Benedict Friedländer)* (Munich, 1905).

142. F. Karsch-Haack, *Ostasiaten*, pp. vi and 54. The book was the first volume of a never-completed series, that would have included Tibet, India, Burma, Siam, Indochina, along with other cultures of Central Asia and the Near East.

143. See G. Hekma, 'De verre einders van de homoseksuele verlangens', *Homologie*, 8, 6 (November–December 1986), 37–9.

144. F. Karsch-Haack, *Ostasiaten*, pp. 6–12.

145. *Ibid.*, p. 80.

146. *Ibid.*

147. *Ibid.*, pp. 101–2.

148. *Ibid.*, pp. 109–18. For more accurate contextualizations of these texts, see M. H. Childs, 'Chigo Monogatari', *Monumenta Nipponica*, 35, 2 (Summer 1980), 127–51 and P. G. Schalow, 'Introduction', in I. Saikaku, *The Great Mirror of Male Love*, trans. P. G. Schalow (Palo Alto, 1990), pp. 1–46.

149. F. Karsch-Haack, *Ostasiaten*, p. 109.

150. *Ibid.*, p. 115.

151. *Ibid.*, p. 121.

152. 'Päderastie und Tribadie werden als Wirkungen des Geschlechtstriebes ... aufgefasst ... als überall und allezeit vorkommende natürliche Erscheinungen, welche weder Geringschätzung, noch verachtungsvolles Totschweigen, noch gesellschaftliche Ächtung, am wenigsten aber brutale Verfolgung durch ein freiheitsfeindliches Gesetz, das sie doch höchstens ins Dunkel zudrängen vermag, verdienen.' F. Karsch-Haack, *Naturvölker*, p. vii.

153. *Ibid.*, pp. 7–18.

154. I will not use the term *Homo-Erotik* or 'homo-eroticism' as used by Karsch-Haack, however, as it would lead to confusion. Today, the word 'homoeroticism' is used mostly as a mere homosexual equivalent of the usually heterosexually interpreted 'eroticism' and refers more to the sexual *imaginaire* than to its physical realization.

155. *Ibid.*, pp. 45–8.

156. *Ibid.*, pp. 22–6.

157. *Ibid.*, p. 14, note.

158. *Ibid.*, pp. 90 (Aboriginals), 93 (Melanesia), 136 (Subsaharan Africa).

159. *Ibid.*, on Subsaharan Africa: pp. 143, 147–8, 157, 164, 169, 175; on South East Asia: pp. 194, 202, 212; on American Indians: *passim*.

160. *Ibid.*, Subsaharan Africa: pp. 164–7; Polynesia: p. 237.

161. F. Karsch-Haack, 'Die Rolle der Homoerotik im Arabertum', *JfsZ*, 23 (1923), 100–70.

162. J. Clifford, 'Introduction: The pure products go crazy', in J. Clifford, *The Predicament of Culture* (Cambridge, MA, and London, 1988), p. 12.

163. J. A. Symonds, *A Problem in Greek Ethics*, in J. A. Symonds, *Sexual Inversion*, ed. R. Michaels (New York, 1984), pp. 5–6. This edition, including Symonds' later text *A Problem in Modern Ethics* (1891) as well, is a reprint of the joint publication of both essays as *Studies in Sexual Inversion* in 1928.
164. *Ibid.*, p. 6.
165. *Ibid.*, pp. 30–1, 72–3.
166. *Ibid.*, pp. 76–82.
167. *Ibid.*, pp. 120–5.
168. *Ibid.*, pp. 125–8.
169. *Ibid.*, p. 133. See later in this chapter for more details on Burton's model.
170. *Ibid.*, pp. 134.
171. J. A. Symonds, *Sexual Inversion*, pp. 155–6.
172. *Ibid.*
173. H. H. Ellis and J. A. Symonds, *Das konträre Geschlechtsgefühl* (Leipzig, 1896).
174. On the complex genesis of the final text of *Sexual Inversion*, see J. Weeks, *Coming Out*, pp. 60–1. Ethnographic references only reach the year 1913. I used the text in Ellis's *Studies in the Psychology of Sex* (2-volume re-edition, New York, 1936), referred to below as 'Sexual Inversion', *Studies*.
175. S. Rowbotham and J. Weeks, *Socialism and the New Life*, p. 162.
176. P. Robinson, *The Modernisation of Sex*, p. 8.
177. H. Ellis, 'Sexual Inversion', *Studies*, p. 8.
178. *Ibid.*, pp. 13–14.
179. Ellis's source was the American text by A. B. Holder, 'The Bote: Description of a peculiar perversion found among the North American Indians', *New York Medical Journal*, 1 (1889), 623–5. Another source, about so-called *mujerados*, was W. A. Hammond's 'The disease of the Scythians (morbus feminarum) and certain analogous conditions', *American Journal of Neurology and Psychiatry*, 1 (1882), 339–55. About the impact of American studies on Ellis's work, see S. Somerville, 'Scientific racism and the emergence of the homosexual body', *JHS*, 5, 2 (1994), 243–66.
180. H. Ellis, 'Sexual Inversion', *Studies*, pp. 19–21.
181. *Ibid.*, pp. 21–8.
182. J. Weeks, *Coming Out*, p. 62.
183. H. Ellis, 'Sexual Inversion', *Studies*, pp. 9–10, 13.
184. *Ibid.*, p. 19, note 3.
185. N. Greig, 'Introduction', in E. Carpenter, *Selected Writings*, vol. 1: *Sex*, ed. N. Greig (London, 1984), p. 65.
186. E. Carpenter, *The Intermediate Sex*, in *Ibid.*, p. 238.
187. See N. Greig, 'Introduction', p. 65.
188. E. Carpenter in a letter to George Hukin, 16 March 1891, quoted by N. Greig, *Ibid.*, p. 57.
189. E. Carpenter, *From Adam's Peak to Elephanta: Sketches in Ceylon and India* (London, 1910 (1903)), pp. 75–81, also see p. 23.
190. E. Carpenter, 'Über die Beziehungen zwischen Homosexualität und Prophetentum und die Bedeutung der sexuellen Zwischenstufen in frühen Kulturepochen', *Vierteljahrsberichte des wissenschaftlich-humanitären Komitees*, 2 (1911), 289–316, 386–96.
191. E. Carpenter, *Intermediate Types*, pp. 161–2.
192. *Ibid.*, p. 9.
193. Carpenter's source is J. Frazer, *Adonis, Attis and Osiris*, later to be part IV of *The Golden Bough*. Aside from female *kosio*, there were male ones attached to the temples of the python god. Frazer, however, did not infer that these *kosio* were homosexual.
194. *Ibid.*, p. 35.

195. See K. Pearson, *The Chances of Death and Other Studies* (London, 1897), vol. 2, p. 13.

196. E. Carpenter, *Intermediate Types*, p. 54.

197. *Ibid.*, pp. 59–60.

198. *Ibid.*, p. 63.

199. *Ibid.*, pp. 137–60.

200. N. Greig, 'Introduction', p. 306.

201. Discussions of lesbianism are often far less elaborate, partially due to the even scarcer documentary evidence available at the time, but partially also due to a less intensely felt commitment of male authors to the lesbian cause. See, on this matter, J. Weeks, *Coming Out*, pp. 66, 87–95; N. Greig, 'Introduction', p. 37.

202. E. Carpenter, *Intermediate Types.*, pp. 166, 170.

203. *Ibid.*, pp. 171–2.

204. J. Weeks, *Coming Out*, p. 82.

205. E. Westermarck, *The History of Human Marriage* (London, 1891), 3 vols.

206. See the suggestion by Th. Stroup, 'Edward Westermarck: A Reappraisal', *Man*, N. S., 19 (1984), 588. See also *Edward Westermarck: Essays on his Life and Works*, ed. T. Stroup (Helsinki, 1982). More biographical research is necessary, however.

207. E. Westermarck, *The Origin and Development of the Moral Ideas* (London, 1926 (1906–8)), vol. 2, pp. 456–89.

208. *Ibid.*, p. 465.

209. *Ibid.*, p. 467.

210. *Ibid.*, pp. 468–9. Westermarck briefly discussed homosexual behaviour as well in his article 'The Moorish conception of holiness', *Finska Vetenskaps-Societetens Forhandlingar*, 58 (1915–16), 85–97, and in his still valuable study *Ritual and Belief in Morocco* (London, 1926), 2 vols.

211. E. Westermarck, *Origin and Development*, pp. 469–71.

212. I owe this term to B. Spackmann, *Decadent Genealogies: The Rhetoric of Sickness from Baudelaire to d'Annunzio* (Ithaca and London, 1989).

213. It would, of course, lead too far afield to discuss their works in depth, nor can a full portrayal of its context be given here. See, among others, R. Dellamora, *Masculine Desire: The Sexual Politics of Victorian Aestheticism* (Chapel Hill, 1990); J. Fontijn, *Leven in extase* (Amsterdam, 1983); J. Goedegebuure, *Decadentie en literatuur* (Amsterdam, 1987), esp. pp. 106–33; *Journal of Contemporary History*, 17, 1 (1982): special issue: 'Decadence'; J. Pierrot, *L'imaginaire décadent (1880–1900)* (Paris, 1977); W. Rasch, *Die literarische Décadence um 1900* (Munich, 1986); K. Swart, *The Sense of Decadence in Nineteenth-Century France* (The Hague, 1964); and R. Wuthenow, *Muse, Maske, Meduse. Europäisches Ästhetizismus* (Frankfurt, 1978).

214. E. Showalter, *Sexual Anarchy* (Harmondsworth, 1990), p. 9.

215. See A. J. L. Busst, 'The image of the androgyne in the nineteenth century', in I. Fletcher (ed.), *Romantic Mythologies* (London, 1967), pp. 39 ff.; and the rather dated work of M. Praz, *The Romantic Agony* (Oxford, 1988 (Rome, 1930)); and finally B. Dijsktra, 'The androgyne in nineteenth-century art and literature', *Comparative Literature*, 26 (1974), 62–73.

216. Many studies discuss this matter either marginally or directly. See especially B. R. S. Fone, 'The other Eden: Arcadia and the homosexual imagination', *JHom*, 8 (1983), 13–32; and R. Aldrich, *The Seduction of the Mediterranean* (London and New York, 1993). The title of this book is misleading, however, as focus is laid almost exclusively on Greece and Italy. Ideally, Portugal, Spain, Turkey, the Middle East, Egypt and Northern Africa ought to be included in a new, more comprehensive study.

217. A. Hama, 'Les vies cachées des grands aventuriers', *GPH*, 268/269 (4 May 1987), 22–6; H. Marsan, 'Les écrivains de l'exil', *Masques*, 18 (Summer 1983), 69–74; P. Gourvennec, 'Le gai voyage ou les transports amoureux', *GPH*, 428/429 (12 July

1990), 112–17; P. Gourvennec, 'Amours étrangères', *GPH*, 477 (4 July 1991), 78–81; and R. Aldrich, 'Weise und farbige Männer. Reisen, Kolonialismus und Homoseksualität zwischen den Rassen in der Literatur', *Forum*, 7 (1989), 6–24.

218. R. Hyam, *Empire and Sexuality* (Manchester and New York, 1990), p. 8.
219. H. Mayer, *Aussenseiter* (Frankfurt/Main, 1975), p. 181.
220. J. Meyers, *Fiction and the Colonial Experience* (Ipswich, 1973), p. 63.
221. R. Bleys, 'Homosexual exile: The textuality of imaginary paradise, 1800–1980', *Journal of Homosexuality*, 25, 1/2 (1993), 165–82.
222. It would, in fact, remain a fundamental issue within homosexual politics of affirmation until today. On this matter, see M. Pollak, 'Les homosexuels masculins entre le désir de transgression et la quête d'intégration', in M. Guisset *et al.* (eds), *Paroles d'amour* (Paris, 1991), pp. 267–74.
223. See J. Clifford and G. E. Marcus (eds), *Writing Culture* (Berkeley and London, 1986), p. 7.

Conclusion

Strangely, the stranger lives within us: his face is hidden behind our identity, he is the space that ruins our residence, the time during which understanding and sympathy fail ... the stranger starts as soon as I become aware of my difference.

– Julia Kristeva[1]

Today, homosexuality in particular is a controversial issue of contemporary ethnic politics, pregnant with symbolic meaning, and expressed at times in ominous ways. For example, recent Jamaican 'raga' lyrics by Buju Banton and Brand Nubian attach the affirmation of black identity to crude animosity towards homosexuality and contain offensive language against the 'batties' as icons of non-blackness.

Cornel West, commenting upon this in Isaac Julien's documentary film *The Darker Side of Black*, describes how 'black nationalist politics mirror the same kind of patriarchal and homophobic perspective, that was imposed upon blacks at the times of colonization and afterwards, by religion, politics and science'.[2] Julien's own careful suggestion that this may distract attention from harsh economic realities is perhaps too 'Marxist' in the eyes of some, but it seems to be confirmed also by equally rising tides of homophobia in other areas of poverty and distress. In this context, the historian Waldir Freitas Oliveiras has pointed at the growing influence in the Brazilian Northeast of so-called *trios elétricos*, musical bands, that are strongly inspired by the affirmation politics of Rastafarianism and threaten to reduce the cultural authority of traditional Afro-Brazilian *candomblé*.[3] This trend, along with the waning impact of *tropicalismo*, that was reconciliatory on the levels of sexual and 'racial' difference, may indeed be interpreted as an indication of 'cultural resistance' *against* a discourse that is perceived as alienating, *yet embracing* some of its values of patriarchy and morality and contributing to the repression and eclipse of some aspects of indigenous heritage. Popular affirmation of ethnic identity, paradoxically, depends upon a selective amnesia, in this instance forgetting the toleration, if not inclusion of sexual variance by traditional Afro-Brazilian cultural discourse and ritual, an amnesia shared by earlier generations of Third World intellectuals.[4]

The repression of homosexuality in post-colonial discourse on ethnic, cultural and/or national identity, moreover, can be noticed at many levels, from some forms of popular music to official policies defining male-to-male sexuality as 'alien' to one's own culture, and it has gained particular urgency in the wake of decolonization (most countries), modernization (Japan, Central Asian countries, Iraq), communism (China, Cuba, Mozambique), or fundamentalism (Iran).

To some extent, such intolerance may be explained as the expression of a desire to eliminate 'unwanted' indigenous practices at the treshold of ethnic, cultural or national emancipation, and to some extent it is a reaction against some side-effects of colonial sexual exchange between European and indigenous men. But, on a more abstract level, the tropes of homophobia in post-colonial politics also reveal the way in which 'European constructions of sexuality, c.q. homosexuality coincided with the epoch of imperialism and both were mutually intertwined' (K. Mercer). Homophobia constitutes a reply against the way in which non-western sexualities were read, interpreted and represented as a limitless repository of deviance, extravagance, eccentricity and integrated in the European enterprise of cognitive *briccolage* and eclecticism, aiming simultaneously at the marginalization of cultural and sexual minorities.

Yet, the tropes of homophobia nevertheless reflect the ways in which 'structures of location and geographical reference appear[ed] in the cultural languages of literature, history, or ethnography'.[5] Put differently, they remain themselves imbedded, intentionally or not, in a European discourse on male-to-male sexuality, that postulated a meaningful, 'analogous' connection between the *vertical* classification within the West (mainstream versus minority) and the *horizontal* one across the world (cultural, especially 'racial' otherness). But the national emancipationists, while objecting to the very analogies imposed upon them by imperialist rhetoric, do not question its premises and reproduce its signifying connection between sexual and cultural identity at the cost of cultural loss and amnesia. The sexism and homophobia implicit to imperialist rhetoric must be subjected to a new, more radical postcolonial criticism, that combines the analysis of its antecedents' moral and cognitive bias with a more comprehensive 'tropological deconstruction of masculinist universalism',[6] and integrates it within a wider, critical and historical dissection of the modern 'self'.

Significant within this context is the reconstruction of what I have called the discourse of a 'geography of perversion and desire' from the Age of Enlightenment to approximately 1918. While focusing on the 'minority' behaviour of a small group, the discourse itself is relevant to all, whether homosexual, bisexal or heterosexual, western or non-western, merely because of the implied *reification* of desire and the identification of *analogies* and affinities across ethnic, cultural and sexual boundaries. It manifests itself, in other words, as a looking-glass in which the historian can see 'the complex and self-validating interrelationship between attempts to categorize and regulate colonial subjects of imperialism "abroad" and the potentially rebellious, politically seditious subjects of the social underclass [such as homosexuals] "at home" '.[7]

The 'geography of perversion and desire' unravelled itself as a 'polyphonic novel', an 'open-ended, creative dialogue of subcultures, of insiders and outsiders, of diverse factions, [briefly as] a carnavalesque arena of diversity'.[8] Thus, divergent positions were taken by those who approved and those who disapproved of male-to-male sexual relations, which was reflected more clearly as the modernization of sex into sexual identities triggered the development of a clear-cut homosexual cultural politics. The latter itself reflected alternative assessments of one's social and sexual self and accordingly led to divergent representations of the cross-cultural record about male-to-male sexuality across the globe. Different weight was ascribed accordingly to sodomitical acts, to 'circumstantial' or to 'congenital' homosexuality, to imported or endemic sodomy, to gender-structured, masculine-defined or age-structured sexual relations among males. Generally, cross-cultural evidence about cross-gender roles showed a high profile, whereas intergenerational male-to-male sexuality was insufficiently highlighted as distinct from its androphile variant. Another position, within the ethnographic allegory, was taken by masculine-defined male-to-male sexuality and by its 'active' partner in particular. Though quintessential during the Early Modern period as an icon of the 'other's' paganism, lechery or barbarism, it was gradually superseded by an emphasis upon the significance of the 'passive' partner only, and especially cross-gender roles amidst indigenous cultures across the world. Masculine-defined male-to-male sexuality became relevant again only in the wake of 'naturalist' adaptations of a strict Hirschfeldian model of the 'third sex' and, more clearly still, in the minority discourse of *Männerfreundschaft*.

Pluralistic ways of accounting for cross-cultural variety were not only obvious in the subcultural discourse and politics of 'sodomites', adherents of Greek Love, dilettante scholars of phallic cults, 'homosexuals', 'male friends', 'decadents', or practitioners of nomadic sexuality in exile,[9] but also in mainstream moral, scientific and social discourse, where same-sex praxis among males was represented alternately as endemic or imported, as a minority or inherent to the nature of a people, race or creed. Most remarkable is the fact that the very same evidence was used by anthropologists as by spokesmen for the homosexual community, for mainstream and subcultural discourses were more often converging than not.

This suggests that a single logic underlay the cultural politics at both the centre and the margin, and raises doubt about the viability of a purely antagonistic model, which opposes the oppressors and the repressed. Discourse, including the ethnographic one, so it seems, was determined by other factors that cannot be grasped adequately by a victimization model alone.

More fundamental cognitive schemes were at play, that constituted an altogether new conceptualization of sexual desire and were instrumental to the Enlightenment and post-Enlightenment construction of 'sodomite' and 'homosexual' identity. They determined new directions of ethnographic discourse on male-to-male sexuality as something that reached further than a cross-cultural justification or, alternatively, a critique of moral stigmatization, and made transparent an otherwise unintelligible, multifaceted 'geography of perversion and desire'.

The roots of the ethnographic allegory had already been laid out in the Medieval and Early Modern periods, when discourses on the cultural difference of non-western people and on the sexual 'otherness' of sodomy were explicitly linked to one another. During the Enlightenment, 'racialist' classification and reproductive biology aligned to define the link between ethnic and sexual difference in a more coercive way. As an outcome primarily of the 'gender revolution' of the late eighteenth century, representations of other 'races' were characterized by, among other things, speculation on their effeminacy, while the newly 'discovered' cross-gender roles were incorporated as metonymical instances in the new hierarchical taxonomies of cultural diversity.

The biological definition of a modern 'sex/gender system' (in G. Lerner's phrase) was accompanied by a gradual cognitive shift, redirecting the focus of public and subcultural discourse from the 'act' of sodomy to 'sodomite' identity, a complex, intermediary phase, foreshadowing the construction of the modern 'homosexual' identity in the nineteenth and early twentieth centuries. This was reflected, within ethnographic discourse, in a more exclusive attention to cross-gender roles and, dialectically, in the consolidating effect of such cross-cultural information in theoretical claims concerning the femininity and passivity of 'sodomites'. So, whereas narrative structure already connected discourse on cultural and racial inferiority to representations of deviant sexuality, often sodomy, since Early Modern times, it was now further complicated by the new politics of reproductive biology and speculations on the presumably gender-structured 'essence' of sodomy. Etiological explanations of cross-cultural data accordingly shifted from old images of 'endemic' sodomitical acts to new images of biologically constituted 'hermaphrodite', soon 'sodomite' minorities.

From the late nineteenth century onwards, the identity of male sodomites, gradually called 'homosexuals', was detached from a narrowly defined anatomic model and included within the realm of psychopathology. Yet, the Enlightenment threw its shadow across both mainstream and subcultural discourses, that kept the definition of homosexual identity within the paradigmatic straitjacket of biological essentialism, more precisely still, of homosexuality's presumably 'feminine' or 'cross-gender' basis. The etiologies of male-to-male sexuality outside the West remained marked, accordingly, by speculation on the biological roots of its gender characteristics.

This study reveals, however, that an oversimplified image must not be drawn of what some postmodern critics have called 'the Great European text'.[10] This, in fact, was marked by multiplicity and discordance, and the transition from an etiology of 'endemic' same-sex practices to one of biologically defined 'sodomite/homosexual minorities' was unequal and fragmented in divergent, partial tropes. The oldest trope, on Arab/or Muslim sodomy as active and masculine-defined, persisted long after the ones on American Indian, Asian, to a lesser degree Oceanic and Subsaharan African cultures had already exchanged the initial image of endemic sodomy for one of various cross-gender minorities.

European discourse was not marked by a single, linear development, nor was the paradigmatic shift fully complete, not even during the nineteenth century, when evolutionary and degeneration theory introduced a diachronic dynamic into an anthropological discourse that had until then been largely static and taxonomic. Evolutionary theory lent a new, biological rigidity to analogy, comprising the diagnosis of sexual deviance both within and outside the West into a single, linear scheme. 'The phylogenesis', says Donna Haraway, 'of psychopathology of the sexual function was a major concern',[11] that lent particular relevance to cross-cultural comparison. Yet, meanwhile, the racialist signature of evolutionary theories allowed for a joint presentation of male-to-male sexuality as 'endemic' or 'inherent to the inferior races' polymorph perversity' and as 'minority' when occurring in a European context. Sex, in other words, was indicative for a non-western people's identity, whereas it was said to be 'deviant' when Europeans engaged in it.

'Analogous' thinking, also, must not be presented as fully transparent and purposive. It is marked instead by inconsistency. Ethnographic debate on male-to-male sexuality was composed of numerous instances where analogies threatened to fail, yet were 'saved' by new theories. These followed one another and aimed at living up to the requirements of empiricism and objectivity (genital anatomy, phrenology, physical anthropology, then neurology and psychopathology), yet they never fundamentally questioned the legitimacy of comparison by analogy itself. On the contrary, the 'semantic interdependence'[12] of racialist and sexual classification gained power as the flaws of 'surface' empiricism were annulled by less verifiable theories such as neurology and psychopathology. The scientific research paradigm of Enlightenment and post-Enlightenment sexual theory thus persisted, presenting sexuality as a signifier, through analogy, of gender, social and cultural difference.

The fact that biological argumentation and the rhetoric of analogy can be traced not only in mainstream anthropological and medical discourse, but also in 'homosexual' discourse, is additional evidence that it fitted not only the purpose of *marginalization*, but corresponded also to alternative, subcultural needs for *legitimation*. The negativist implications of evolutionary theory, in such a context, had to be turned around into positive ones, and male-to-male sexual praxis anywhere was presented as part of a natural, if minority human drive. The subscription, here, of the homosexual intelligentsia to biological premisses was reflected in its own politics/poetics of ethnography, tracing equivalents of its own own self-styled identity in societies and cultures across the globe. The theoretical weight of such 'universalist' legitimation would seem to be futile at first sight, since most settings of male-to-male sexual relations were discarded as 'circumstantial'. Yet, when looked at more closely, the positive selection of some distinct settings was instrumental to the definition of 'congenital' homosexuality worldwide. No indisputable biological criteria were at hand to distinguish 'congenital' from 'circumstantial' homosexuality, and considerations of a political kind led to the adoption of criteria that were essentially cultural and presented homosexuality to the outside world as extraordinary and, in the end, respectable.

The relationship, meanwhile, between male homosexuality and gender in particular remained problematic, yet seemed inevitable as an issue for both theoretical debate and cross-cultural comparison. This revealed the ongoing impact of the connection between gender and sexuality, initiated during the Enlightenment and reproduced, so it proved, in the countercultural discourse of a 'homosexual' minority as well. The high visibility of cross-gender roles in non-western societies was proof to Ulrichs, Hirschfeld and others that homosexuality ought to be conceived of as a 'third, intermediate sex', whereas the less traceable evidence of masculine-defined homosexuality among non-western people called for a widening of the concept of homosexual identity to some (naturalists) and for a rejection of the Hirschfeldian model to others ('male friendship'). Still another loosely constituted group of individuals read ethnographic evidence largely as an affirmation of the ingenuity of nomadic, unlabelled desire.

The various 'geographies of desire', while demonstrating how the construction of modern homosexuality was marked by plurality and dissidence, nevertheless reflected the paradigmatic power of the modern, biological theory of human sexuality. Its impact on ethnographic assessments of male-to-male sexuality was at once pervasive yet incomplete. Pervasive, as descriptions of sexual praxis were replaced definitively by cross-cultural casuistics of 'minority' sexual identities, and an evaluation of gender characteristics became quintessential to the identification of 'sodomites' or 'homosexuals' across the world. Incomplete, however, because not everyone subscribed to the Enlightenment and post-Enlightenment 'sex/gender system' based on biology.

The preceding study, finally, demonstrates that the connection between cultural/racial 'otherness' and femininity, as retrieved from European discourse in recent historiography and criticism, permeated the ethnographic

narrative on male-to-male sexuality as well. Both its metaphoric and meto-
nymic presentation contributed to what Louis Montrose called 'the
gendering of colonialist discourse',[13] initiated in the early days of European
expansion, and turned it into an even more subtle and intricate signifier of
the culturally 'other's' gender anomaly in the aftermath of the Enlightenment. Yet, a close reading of documents also reveals that the ethnographic
politics of feminization were far from exclusive and competed in numerous
instances with alternative tropes of representation that emphasized the
masculinity, even virility, of non-western people, and reflected fears about
the effeminacy, decadence and deficient combativeness at the core of western
society. Common to either of the above narrative schemes, however, was the
eclipse of history in representations of cultural otherness, which was postulated by the rhetoric of reification and analogy. Applied to European
etiologies of male-to-male sexuality outside the West, this reduced cross-
cultural allegory to static representations of the 'exotic' or the 'pathological'.
Thus the reconstruction of a 'geography of perversion and desire' constitutes
a historical case-study of European racialism at the same time.

Notes

1.   'Etrangement, l'étranger nous habite: il est la face cachée de notre identité, l'espace qui
      ruine notre demeure, le temps où s'abiment l'entente et la sympathie . . . l'étranger
      commence lorsque surgit la conscience de ma différence.' J. Kristeva, *Etrangers à nous-
      mêmes* (Paris, 1988), p. 9.
2.   Interview in *The Darker Side of Black*, documentary film directed by I. Julien, BBC 2
      'Arena', 12 February 1994.
3.   Personal communication.
4.   See P. Fry, 'Homossexualidade masculina e cultos Afro-Brasileiros', in P. Fry, *Para
      Inglês Ver* (Rio de Janeiro, 1982), pp. 54–86.
5.   E. Said, *Culture and Imperialism* (London, 1993), p. 61.
6.   G. C. Spivak, 'Imperialism and sexual difference', *Oxford Literary Review*, special
      issue: 'Sexual Difference' (1986), p. 238.
7.   S. Marshall, 'The contemporary political use of gay history: the Third Reich', in Bad
      Object Choices (ed.), *How Do I Look?*, p. 73.
8.   J. Clifford, *The Predicament of Culture* (Cambridge, MA and London, 1988), p. 46.
9.   The idea of 'plurality' as quintessential to the historical – and I would add, cross-
      cultural – 'bio/mythography' of the gay self is rightly stressed by S. Bravmann in his
      article 'Telling (hi)stories', *Out/Look*, (Spring 1990), p. 74.
10. The term was first used by J.-F. Lyotard, *La condition postmoderne* (Paris, 1979), and
      is found in the works of, among others, E. Said and R. Corbey, whose interpretation of
      European *imaginaire* on Africa is too one-dimensional. See R. Corbey, *Wilheid en
      Beschaving* (Baarn, 1989), esp. pp. 157–66.
11. D. Haraway, *Primate Visions* (New York and London, 1989), p. 23.
12. Term borrowed from A. Sekula, 'The body and the archive', *October*, 39 (Winter
      1986), 10.
13. L. Montrose, 'The work of gender in the discourse of discovery', *Representations*, 33
      (Winter 1991), 2.

Bibliography

Primary sources

Unpublished documents

Burton, Richard, 'Scinde; or, the Unhappy Valley', manuscript, Huntington Library, San Marino, California.

Chevalier, J., 'De l'inversion de l'instinct sexuel au point de vue médico-légale', unpublished thesis (University of Lyons, 1885), Bibliothèque Nationale, Paris.

Sérieux, P., 'Recherches cliniques sur les anomalies de l'instinct sexuel', unpublished thesis (Paris, 1888), Bibliothèque Nationale, Paris.

Published documents

Anon., [Untitled], *JfsZ*, 2 (1900), 387–9.

Anon., [Untitled], *JfsZ*, 5 (1903), 953–5.

Anon., [Untitled], *JfsZ*, 5 (1903), 992–5.

Anon., [Untitled], *JfsZ*, 5 (1903), 1015–18.

Anon., [Untitled], *JfsZ*, 6 (1904), 520–7.

Anon., [Untitled], *JfsZ*, 6 (1904), 561–5.

Anon., [Untitled], *JfsZ*, 9 (1908), 464–91.

Anon., [Untitled], *Sexualprobleme*, 8 (1912), 142–3.

Anon., 'Päderastie', in *Brockhaus Konversationslexikon*, 14th ed., 12 (Leipzig, 1894–95), p. 803.

Anon., 'Sodomie', in *Encyclopédie ou dictionnaire raisonné des sciences, des arts et des métiers* (Neuchâtel, 1765), vol. 15, col. 266.

Anon. [Le Conquistador Anonyme], *Relation de quelques-unes des choses de la Nouvelle-Espagne et de la grande ville de Temistitan Mexico, écrite par un gentilhomme de Fernán Cortes*, ed. and trans. J. Rose (Montbonnet and St Martin, 1986).

Adams, F. O., *The History of Japan from the Earliest Period to the Present Time* (London, 1874).

Albrecht, M., *Russisch Centralasien. Reisebilder aus Transkaspien, Buchara und Turkestan* (Hamburg, 1896).

Aletrino, A., *Hermaphrodisie en uranisme* (Amsterdam, 1908).

Aletrino, A., 'Over uranisme en het laatste werk van Raffalovich', *Psychiatrische en neurologische bladen*, 1 (1897), 351–65, 452–83.

Ambrogetti, P., *La vita sessuale nell'Eritrea* (Rome, 1900).

Ancillon, C., *Le traité des eunuques*, ed. D. Fernandez (Paris, 1978 (1707)).

Anderson, A., *A Narrative of the British Embassy to China* (Basil, 1795).

Andree, R., *Das Buch der Reisen und Entdeckungen Asiens*, vol.1: *Die Nippon-Fahrer oder das wiedergeschlossene Japan* (Leipzig, 1869).

[*Arabian Nights*] *A Plain and Literal Translation of the Arabian Nights' Entertainments, Now Entitled The Book of The Thousand Nights and a Night. With Introduction Explanatory Notes on the Manners and Customs of Moslem Men and a Terminal Essay upon the History of the Nights*, ed. and trans. R. Burton, 10 vols (London and Benares: Kama Shastra Society, 1885); *Supplemental Nights to the Book of a Thousand Nights and a Night. With Notes Anthropological and Explanatory*, ed. and trans. R. Burton, 6 vols (London and Benares: Kama Shastra Society, 1886–8).

Arndt, R., *Biologische Studien* (Greifswald, 1895).

Bacher, W., *Nizami's Leben und Werke* (Leipzig, 1871).

Bachofen, J. J., *Das Mutterrecht. Eine Untersuchung über die Gynaikokratie der alten Welt nach ihrer religiösen und rechtlichen Natur* (Stuttgart, 1861).

Baelz, E., *Die Ostasiaten* (Stuttgart, 1901).

Ball, B., *La folie érotique* (Paris, 1888).

Ball, B., 'La folie érotique', *L'encéphale. Journal des maladies mentales et nerveux*, 7 (1887), 188–97, 257–69, 403–15.

Bancroft, H. H., *The Native Races of the Pacific States of North America*, 5 vols (London, 1875–6).

Barret, P., *L'Afrique occidentale. La nature et l'homme noir* (Paris, 1888).

Barrow, J., *Travels in China* (London, 1804).

Bartholdy, J. L. S., *Bruchstücke zur näheren Kenntnis des heutigen Griechenlands* (Berlin, 1805).

Bastian, A., *Die Culturländer des Alten America*, 3 vols (Berlin, 1878–89).

Bastian, A., *Der Mensch in der Geschichte. Zur Begründung einer psychologischen Weltanschauung*, 3 vols (Leipzig, 1860).

Bastian, A., *Rechtsverhältnisse bei verschiedenen Völkern der Erde. Ein Beitrag zur vergleichende Ethnologie* (Berlin, 1872).

Bastian, A., *Zur Kenntnis Hawaii's. Nachträge und Ergänzungen zu den Inselgruppen Oceaniens* (Berlin, 1883).

Baumann, O., 'Conträre Sexualerscheinungen bei der Negerbevölkerung Zanzibars', *ZfE*, 31 (1899), 668–70.

Baumgarten, S. J., *Nachrichten von merkwürdigen Büchern* (Halle, 1753).

Beardmore, E., 'The Natives of Mowat, Daudi, New Guinea', *JRAI*, 19 (1890), 459–66.

Bebel, A., *Die Mohammedanisch-Arabische Kulturperiode* (Stuttgart, 1884).

Benaduci, L. B., *Idéa de une nueva Historia General de la América Septentrional, fundada sobre material copioso de figuras, symbolos, caractéres, cantares, y geroglíficos, y manuscritos de Autores Indios, ultimamente descubiertos* (Madrid, 1746).

Berger, J. M., *Masochismus, Sadismus und andere Perversitäten aller Zeiten und Völker. Die Perversion: Homosexualität. Kultur- und sittengeschichtlich beleuchtet* (Leipzig, 1914).

Berkusky, H., 'Homosexualität bei den Naturvölkern', *Geschlecht*, 6 (1911), 49–55.

Berkusky, H., 'Die sexuelle Moral der primitiven Stämme Indonesiens', *Sexualprobleme*, 8 (1912), 781–91, 843–58.

Bertulus, [Dr], 'Considérations sur les causes de la dégénération physique et morale du peuple dans les grandes villes', *Gazette médicale de Paris* (Paris, 1847), pp. 800–1.

Beverly, R., *The History and Present State of Virginia* (London, 1705).

Bey, L., 'Der Eunuch', *Sexualprobleme*, 7 (1911), 674–80.

Bieber, F. J., 'Brieflicher Bericht über Erhebungen unter äthiopischen Völkerschaften', *Anthropophyteia*, 6 (1909), 402–5.

Bieber, F. J., 'Neue Forschungen über das Geschlechtsleben in Äthiopien', *Anthropophyteia*, 7 (1910), 227–32; 8 (1911), 184–93.

[Billings, J.], *An account of a geographical and astronomical Expedition to the Northern Parts of Russia, for ascertaining the degrees of latitude and longitude of the mouth of the River Kovima, of the whole coast of the Tshutski, to East Cape, and of the Islands in the Eastern Ocean, stretching to the American coast, performed by command of Her Imperial Majesty Catherine the Second, Empress of all the Russians, by Commodore Joseph Billings in the years 1785 to 1794, the whole narrated from the original papers by Martin Sauer, Secretary of the Expedition* (London, 1802).

Binet, A., 'Du fétichisme dans l'amour', *Revue philosophique*, 12, 2 (1887), 143–67, 252–74.

Bligh, W., *A Voyage to the South Seas*, 2 vols (London, 1792).

Bloch, I., *Beiträge zur Äthiologie der Psychopathia Sexualis*, 2 vols (Dresden, 1902–3).

Bloch, I., *Das Geschlechtsleben in England. Mit besonder Beziehung auf London*, 3 vols (Berlin, 1901–3).

Bloch, I., *Die Perversen* (Berlin, 1905).

Bloch, I., *Das Sexualleben unserer Zeit in seinen Beziehungen zur modernen Kultur* (Berlin, 1908).

Blount, H., *A Voyage into the Levant* (London, 1636).

Blumentritt, F., 'Über die Staaten der philippinischen Eingeborenen in den Zeiten der Conquista', *Mittheilungen der K.K. Geographischen Gesellschaft in Wien*, 28, 2 (1885), 49–82.

Bonacossi, A., *La Chine et les Chinois* (Paris, 1847).

Bossu, N., *Nouveaux Voyages aux Indes Occidentales* (Amsterdam, 1769).

Bourgarel, A., 'Des races de l'Océanie française, de celles de la Nouvelle Calédonie en particulier, part 2: Caractères extérieures, moeurs et coutumes des Néo-Calédoniens', *Mémoires de la Société d'Anthropologie de Paris*, 2 (1865), 376–416.

Boxer, C. R. (ed.), *South China in the Sixteenth Century: Being the Narratives of Galeote Pereira, Fr. Gaspar da Cruz, O.P., Fr. Martín de Rada, O.E.S.A. (1550–1575)* (London, 1953).

Breitenstein, H., *Einundzwanzig Jahre in Indien* (Leipzig, 1899).

Brincker H., 'Charakter, Sitten und Gebräuche speciell der Bantu Deutsch-Südwestafrikas', *Mittheilungen des Seminars für Orientalische Sprachen an der K. Friedrich-Wilhelms-Universität zu Berlin, Abteilung 3: Afrikanische Studien*, 3 (1900), 66–92.

Brincker, H., *Wörterbuch und kurzgefasste Grammatik des Otji-Hérero mit Beifügung verwandter Ausdrücke und Formen des Oshi-N Donga-Otj-Ambo* (Leipzig, 1886).

Brouardel, P., 'Étude critique sur la valeur des signes attribués à la pédérastie', *Annales d'hygiène publique et médicine légale*, 3rd Series, 4 (1880), 182–9.

Browne, E. G., *A Literary History of Persia* (London, 1893).

Browne, W. G., *Travels in Africa, Egypt, and Syria, from the Year 1792 to 1798* (London, 1799).

Brünig, E. H., 'Beiträge zum Studium des Geschlechtslebens der Indianer im alten Perú', *Anthropophyteia*, 6 (1909), 101–12; 7 (1910), 206–11.

Brünig, E. H., 'Einiges über die Erotik der alten Indianer des Küstengebietes Nordperús', *Anthropophyteia*, 5 (1908), 358–60.

Bryk, F., *Neger-Eros* (Berlin and Cologne, 1927).

Buckingham, J. S., *Travels in Assyria* (Colburn, 1829).

Bulwer, J., *Anthropometamorphoses: Man transformed; or, the Artificial Changeling* (London, 1653).

Burkhardt, J. L., *Reisen in Nubien und Arabien* (Jena, 1820).

Burton, R. F., *Abeokuta and the Cameroons Mountains. An Exploration* (London, 1863).

Burton, R. F., *A Mission to Gelele; King of Dahome, With Notices of the So-called 'Amazons', the Grand Customs, the Yearly Customs, the Human Sacrifices, the Present State of the Slave Trade, and the Negro's Place in Nature*, 2 vols (London, 1966 (1864)).

Burton, R. F., *The Sotadic Zone* (Boston, 1977).

Burton, R. F., *Zanzibar: City, Island, and Coast* (London, 1872).

[Busbequius, A. G.], *The Life and Letters of Ogier Ghiselin de Busbecq, seigneur of Bousbecque, Knight, Imperial Ambassador*, ed. C. T. Forster and F. H. B. Daniell (Geneva, 1971 (1881)).

Buschan, G., 'Das Sexualleben in der Völkerkunde', in I. Bloch, *Handbuch der Sexualwissenschaft. Mit besonderen Berücksichtigung der kulturgeschichtlichen Beziehungen* (n.p., 1911), pp. 299–396.

Cabeza de Vaca, A. N., *Naufrágios y Comentarios*, ed. Roberto Ferrando (Madrid, 1984).

Camargo, D. M., 'Descripción de la ciudad y provincia de Tlaxcala', in R. de Acuña (ed.), *Relaciones Geográficas del siglo XVI: Tlaxcala* (Mexico, 1984), vol. 1.

Carbutt, E. G., 'Some minor superstitions and customs of the Zulus', *Folklore Journal*, 2 (1880), 12–13.

Cardonega, A. de Oliveira, *Historia geral das guerras Angolanas* (Lisbon, 1681).

[Carletti, F.], *Ragionamenti di Francesco Carletti sopra le cose da lui vedute ne'suoi viaggi, sì dell'Indie occidentali e orientali come d'altri paesi* (Florence, 1701).

Caron, F., *Rechte Beschrijvinge van het machtigh koninkhrijk Jappan* (The Hague, 1662).

Carpenter, E., *From Adam's Peak to Elephanta: Sketches in Ceylon and India* (London, 1910 (1903)).

Carpenter, E., *Intermediate Types among Primitive Folk. A Study in Social Evolution* (London, 1914).

Carpenter, E., *Selected Writings*, vol. 1: *Sex*, ed. N. Greig (London, 1984).

Carpenter, E., 'Über die Beziehungen zwischen Homosexualität und Prophetentum und die Bedeutung der sexuellen Zwischenstufen in frühen Kulturepochen', *Vierteljahrsberichte des wissenschaftlich-humanitären Komitees*, 2 (1911), 289–316, 386–96.

Carter-Stent, G., 'Chinese eunuchs', *Journal of the Royal Asiatic Society of Great Britain and Ireland, North China Branch, Shanghai*, New Series, 11 (1877), 143–84.

Casper, J. L., *Handbuch der gerichtlichen Medicin*, 2 vols (Berlin, 1858).

[Castiglioni, L.], *Viaggio negli Stati Uniti dell'America settentrionale fatto negli anni 1785, 1786 e 1787 da Luigi Castiglioni con alcune observazioni sui vegetabili più utili di quel paese* (Milan, 1790).

Catlin, G., *Letters and Notes on the Manners, Customs, and Condition of the North American Indians, written during eight Years' Travel amongst the wildest Tribes of Indians in North America, in 1832, 33, 34, 35, 36, 37, 38, and 39* (London, 1841).

Chalmers, J., 'Notes on the Bugilai, British New-Guinea', *JRAI*, 33 (1903), 108–10.

Chamberlain, B. H., *Things Japanese*, 2nd ed. (London, 1891).

Charcot, J. M., and Magnan, V., 'Inversion du sens génital', *Archives de neurologie*, 3 (1882), 53–60; 4 (1882), 296–322.

Chardin, J., *Voyage de Monsieur le Chevalier Chardin en Perse et Autre Lieux de l'Orient* (Amsterdam, 1686).

Chevalier, J., 'De l'inversion sexuelle au point de vue clinique, anthropologique et médico-légale', *Aac*, 5 (1890), 314–36; 6 (1891), 49–69, 500–19.

Chevalier, J., *Une maladie de personnalité. Inversion sexuelle* (Lyons and Paris, 1893).

Choris, L., *Voyage pittoresque autour du monde, avec des portraits de sauvages d'Amérique, d'Asie, d'Afrique, et des Iles du Grand Océan; des paysages, des vues maritimes, et plusieurs objets d'histoire naturelle; accompagné de descriptions de Mammifères et Oiseaux par m. le Baron Cuvier et M.A. de Chamisso, et d'observations sur les crânes humains par M. le docteur Gall* (Paris, 1820–2).

Clavigero, F. J., *Storia antica del Messico, cavata da'migliori storici spagnuoli, e da'manoscritti e dalle pitture antiche degl'Indiani* (Cesena, 1780–1).

Clot-Bey, A. B., *Aperçus générals sur l'Egypte* (Paris, 1840).

Clozel, F.-J., and Villamur, R., *Les coutumes indigènes de la Côte d'Ivoire* (Paris, 1902).

Combier, F., *Missions en Chine et au Congo* (Brussels, 1890–1).

Corre, A., *L'ethnographie criminelle d'après les observations et les statistiques judiciaires receuillies dans les colonies françaises* (Paris, 1894).

Cortés, H., *Cartas y documentos* (Mexico, 1963).

C. E. S. [Coyett et Socius], *'t Verwaerloosde Formosa, of waerachtig verhael, hoedanigh door verwaerloosinge der Nederlanders in Oost-Indien, het Eylant Formosa, van den Chinesen Mandorijn, ende Zeerover Coxinja, overrompelt, vermeestert, ende ontweldight is geworden,* ed. G. C. Molewijk (Leiden, 1991).

Cranz, D., *Historie von Grönland, enthaltend die Beschreibung des Landes und der Einwohner und insbesondere die Geschichte der dortigen Mission der Evangelischen Brüder zu Neu-Herrnhut und Lichtenfels* (Barby, 1770 (1765)).

Crawfurd, J., *History of the Indian Archipelago. Containing an Account of the Manners, Arts, Languages, religions, Institutions, and Commerce of its Inhabitants* (Edinburgh and London, 1820).

Crawley, E., 'Dress', in *Encyclopaedia of Religion and Ethics*, 5 (1912), 68–71.

Crawley, E., *The Mystic Rose* (n.p., 1927 (1902)).

Creagh, J., *Over the Borders of Christendom and Islam* (London, 1876).

Crocq, J., 'La situation sociale de l'uraniste', *Journal de neurologie*, 6 (1901), 591–6.

Crocq, J., 'Le troisième sexe', *Progrès médicale*, 10 (1908), 57–64.

Cureau, A., 'Essai sur la psychologie des races nègres de l'Afrique Tropicale', *Revue générale des sciences pures et appliquées*, 15 (1904), 638–52, 679–95.

Dallet, C., *Histoire de l'Eglise de Corée, précédée d'une introduction sur l'histoire, les institutions, la langue, les moeurs et coutumes coréennes avec carte et planches*, 2 vols (Paris, 1874).

Dalrymple, A., *An Historical Journal of the Expeditions by Sea and Land to the North of California in 1768, 1769, and 1770, when Spanish Establishments were first made at San Diego and Monterey* (London, 1790).

Dapper, O., *Asia, of Naukeurige Beschryving van het Rijk des Grooten Mogols* (Amsterdam, 1672).

Dapper, O., *Naukeurige Beschrijvinge der Afrikaensche Gewesten van Egypten, Barbaryen, Libyen, Biledulgerid, Negrosland, Guinea, Ethiopiën, Abyssinie: Vertoont in de Benamingen, Grenspalen, Steden, Revieren, Gewassen, Dieren, Zeeden, Drachten, Talen, Rijkdommen, Godsdiensten en Heerschappyen. Met Lantkaerten en Afbeeldingen van Steden, Drachten, &c. na 't Leven getekent, en in Kooper gesneden. Getrokken uit verscheyde hedendaegse Lantbeschrijvers en geschriften van bereisde ondersoekers dier Landen* (Amsterdam, 1676 (1668)).

Dapper, O., *Naukeurige Beschryving van Asie: behelsende de gewesten van Mesopotamie, Babylonie, Assyrie, Anatolie of Klein Asie . . . Arabie* (Amsterdam, 1680).

Dautheville, [Dr], ' "Le cafard" ou psychose des pays chauds', *Aac*, 26 (1911), 11–15.

278   Bibliography

de Acosta, J., *Historia natural y moral de las Indias*, ed. E. O'Gorman (Mexico, 1962 (1590)).

de Argensola, B. L., *Conquista de las Islas Malucas al Rey Felipe III* (Biblioteca de Viajeros Hispánicos, 7) (Madrid, 1992 (1609)).

de Azara, F., *Reisen in Südamerika, 1781–1801* (Leipzig, 1810).

de Bougainville, L.-A., *Voyage autour du monde pendant les années 1766, 1767, 1768 et 1769*, ed. P. Deslandres (Paris, 1924 (1771)).

de Bourbourg, G. Brasseur, *Histoire des nations civilisées du Mexique et de l'Amérique Centrale, durant les siècles antérieures à Christophore Colomb, écrite sur des documents originaux et entièrement inédits, puisés aux anciennes archives des indigènes* (Paris, 1857–9).

de Bourbourg, G. Brasseur, *Popol Vuh. Le Livre Sacré et les Mythes de l'Antiquité Américaine, avec les livres héroiques et historiques des Quichés* (Paris, 1861).

De Brosse, C., *Histoire des Navigations aux Terres Australes* (Paris, 1756).

de Buffon, G.-L. Leclerc, *Oeuvres complètes*, ed. M. A. Richard (Paris, 1826–8).

de Charlevoix, R. P., *Histoire de l'établissement, des progrès et de la décadence du Christianisme dans l'empire du Japon* (Rouen, 1715).

de Chénier, L., *Recherches historiques sur les Maures et l'histoire de l'Empire du Maroc*, 3 vols (Paris, 1787).

[de Coutre, J.], *Aziatische omzwervingen. Het leven van Jacques de Coutre, een Brugs diamant-handelaar, 1591–1627*, ed. J. Verberckmoes and E. Stols (Berchem, 1988).

de Flacourt, E., *Histoire de la grand isle Madagascar* (Paris, 1658).

de Gobineau, J. A., *Trois ans en Asie* (Paris, 1859).

Degrandpré, L., *Voyage à la côte occidentale d'Afrique, fait dans les années 1786 et 1787, contenant la description des moeurs, usages, lois, gouvernement et commerce des Etats du Congo, fréquentés par les Européens, et un précis de la traite des Noirs, ainsi qu'elle avait lieu avant la Révolution française, suivi d'un Voyage fait au Cap de Bonne-Espérance, contenant la description militaire de cette colonie* (Paris, 1801).

de Joux, O., *Die Enterbten des Liebesglückes. Ein Beitrag zur Seelenkunde* (Leipzig, 1893).

de la Barbinais, Le Gentil, *Nouveau voyage autour du monde* (Paris, 1728–9 (1725)).

de Lacombe, B.-F. Leguéval, *Voyage à Madagascar et aux îles Comores (1823 à 1830)* (Paris, 1841).

Delafosse, M., *Haut-Sénégal Niger, Soudan française* (Paris, 1912).

de Lahontan, L.-A., *Nouveaux voyages de Mr. le Baron de Lahontan dans l'Amérique septentrionale, qui contiennent une relation des différens peuples qui y habitent* (The Hague, 1703).

de Las Casas, B., *História sumária cuanto a las cualidades, dispusición, cielo y suelo destas tierras, y condiciones naturales, policias, repúblicas, manera de vivir e costumbres de las gentes destas Indias Occidentales y Meridionales, cuyo imperio soberano pertenece a los reyes de Castilla*, ed. E. O'Gorman (Serie de Historiadores y Cronistas de Indias, I) (Mexico, 1967), vol. 1.

de Lauture, S. d'Escayrac, *Le Désert et le Soudan. Etudes sur l'Afrique au nord de l'équateur* (Paris, 1853).

[de Laval, F. P.], *The Voyage of François Pyrard de Laval to the East Indies, the Maldives, the Moluccas and Brazil (1601–1611)*, ed. and trans. A. Gray and H. C. P. Bell (Hakluyt Society, 1888; reprinted in New York, n.d.).

de la Vega, G., *Comentários reales de las Incas*, ed. A. Rosenblat (Buenos Aires, 1943).

del Castillo, B. D., *Historia verdadera de la conquista de la Nueva Espana*, ed. M. León-Portilla (Madrid, 1984 (1605)).

de Leon, P. Cieza, *La crónica del Perú*, ed. M. Ballesteros (Madrid, 1984 (1553)).

de Léry, J., *Histoire d'un Voyage fait en la terre du Brésil en 1557* (Montpellier, 1992 (La Rochelle, 1578)).

della Valle, P., *Viaggi cioè la Turchia, la Persia, e l'Inde* (Rome, 1650).

del Techo, N., *Historia Provinciae Paraquariae Societatis Iesu* (Liège, 1673).

de Malpière, D. B., *La Chine* (Paris, 1825).

de Manoncourt, C. N. Sonnini, *Voyage dans la haute et basse Egypte fait par ordre de l'ancien gouvernement et contenant des observations de tous genres* (Paris, 1799).

de Mofras, P. Duflot, *Exploration du territoire de l'Orégon, des Californiens et de la Mer Vermeille, exécutée pendant les années 1840, 1841 et 1842* (Paris, 1844).

de Montaigne, M. Eyquem, 'Des Cannibales', in *Essais*, ed. A. Micha (Paris, 1969), vol. 1, ch. xxxi, 251–64.

de Morga, A., *Sucesos de las islas Filipinas*, ed. and trans. J. S. Cummins (Works issued by the Hakluyt Society, second series, 140) (London, 1972).

de Morgues, J. Lemoyne, 'Indorum Floridam provinciam inhabitantium eicones, primum ibidem ad vivum expressae, addita ad singulas brevi earum declaratione. Nunc vero recens a Theodoro de Bry Leodiense in aes incisae & evulgatae', in M. Bouyer and J.-P. Duviols (eds), *Le Théâtre du Nouveau Monde. Les Grands Voyages de Théodore de Bry* (Paris, 1992).

Dempwolff, A., 'Medicinische Anschauugen der Tami-Insulaner (nach Mittheilungen des Missionars Balmer)', *ZfE*, 34 (1902), 333–6.

de Nerval, G., *Voyage en Orient* (Paris, 1851).

de Nicolay, N., *Les Navigatiens peregrinatiens et voyages, faicts en la Turquie* (Antwerp, 1576).

de Pauw, C., *Recherche philosophique sur les Américains, ou Mémoires intéressants pour servir à l'histoire de l'espèce humaine* (Berlin, 1768).

de Pauw, C., *Recherches philosophiques sur les Egyptiens et les Chinois* (Berlin, 1773).

de Rochas, V., *La Nouvelle Calédonie et ses habitants. productions, moeurs, cannibalisme* (Paris, 1862).

de Sacy, A. I. S., *Chrestomathie arabe* (Paris, 1827).

de Sacy, A. I. S., *Exposé de la religion des Druses* (Paris, 1838).

de Saint Hilaire, A., *Voyage dans les provinces de Rio de Janeiro et de Minas Geraes* (Paris, 1830).

de Saint-Méry, M. L. E. Moreau, *Voyage aux Etats Unis de l'Amérique, 1793–1798*, ed. S. L. Mims (New Haven, 1913).

de San Antonio, J. F., *The Philippine Chronicles of Fray San Antonio* (Manila, 1977).

de Slane, W. MacGuckin, *Introduction and Notes to Ibn Khallikan's Biographical Dictionary*, 2 vols (Paris, 1842).

de Souza, G. Soares, *Notícia do Brasil. Descripção verdadeira da costa daquelle estado, que pertence à coroa do reino de Portugal, sitio da Bahia de Todos os Santos*, in *Colleção de notícias para a historia e geografia das nações ultramarinas, que vivem nos dominios portugueses, ou lhes sao vizinhas, publicada pela Academia Real das Ciências* (Lisbon, 1825), vol. 3, part 1, no. 1.

Dessoir, M., 'Zur Psychologie der Vita sexualis', *Allgemeine Zeitschrift für Psychiatrie und psychisch-gerichtliche Medicin*, 50 (1893), 941–75.

de Thévenot, J., *Relation d'un Voyage fait au Levant* (Paris, 1664).

de Zárate, A., *The Discovery and Conquest of Peru*, ed. J. M. Cohen (Harmondsworth, 1968 (1555)).

de Zwaan, J. P. Kleiweg, *De geneeskunde der Menangkabau-Maleiers. Ethnologische studie* (Amsterdam, 1910).

Diderot, D., *Oeuvres complètes*, ed. J. Assézat and M. Tourneux (Paris, 1881–97) (vols 10 and 15).

Döhne, J. L., *Das Kafferland und seine Bewohner* (Berlin, 1844).

Döllinger, J. J. I., *Heidenthum und Judenthum. Vorhalle zur Geschichte des Christenthums* (Regensburg, 1857).

d'Orbigny, A., *L'homme américain (de l'Amérique méridionale) considéré sous ses rapports physiques et moraux*, 2 vols (Paris, 1839).

dos Santos, J., *History of Eastern Ethiopia*, in J. Pinkerton (ed.), *A General Collection of the Best and Most Interesting Voyages and Travels in All Parts of the World* (London, 1808), vol. 16.

Dozy, R. P. A., *Historia Abbadidarum* (Leyden, 1846).

Droppers, G., 'The population of Japan in the Tokugawa period', *Transactions of the Asiatic Society of Japan* (Yokohama), 22 (1894), 253–84.

Dubois, J. A., *A Description of the Character, Manners, and Customs of the People of India* (London, 1816).

Dubois, J. A., *Moeurs, institutions et cérémonies du peuple de l'Inde*, 2 vols (Paris, 1825).

Du Halde, J.-B., *Description géographique, historique, chronologique et politique de l'Empire de la Chine et de la tartarie chinoise*, 4 vols (Paris, 1735).

Du Halde, J.-B., *Mémoires concernant l'histoire, les arts, les moeurs, les usages des Chinois, par les missionniares de Pékin*, 16 vols (Paris, 1776–1814).

du Lac, F.-M. Perrin, *Voyages dans les deux Louisianes et chez les Nations sauvages du Missouri, par les Etats Unis, l'Ohio et les provinces qui le bordent, en 1801, 1802 et 1803, avec un aperçu des moeurs, des usages, du caractère et des coutumes religieuses et civiles des peuples de ces diverses contrées* (Paris, 1805).

Dulaure, J.-A., *Les divinités génératrices ou du culte du phallus chez les Anciens et les Modernes* (Paris, 1825).

d'Urville, J. Dumont, 'Voyage au Pole Sud et dans l'Océanie sur les Corvettes L'Astrolabe et La Zelée, exécuté par ordre du roi pendant les années 1837–1840', in *Histoire du voyage* (Paris, 1840).

Egede, P., *Dictionarium Grönlandico-Danico-Latinum, complectens primitiva cum suis derivatis, quibus interjectae sunt voces primariae è Kirondo Angekkutorum* (Copenhagen, 1750).

Ellis, A. B., *The Ewe-speaking Peoples of Slave Coast of West Africa* (n.p., 1890).

Ellis, H., *Journal of the late embassy to China* (London, 1817).

Ellis, H. Havelock, *Studies in the Psychology of Sex*, 2 vols (New York, 1936 (1933).

Ellis, H. Havelock, 'Nota sulle facoltà artistiche degli invertiti', *Archivio delle psicopatie sessuali*, 1 (1896), 243–5.

Ellis, H. Havelock, and Symonds, J. A., *Das konträre Geschlechtsgefühl* (Leipzig, 1896).

Ellis, W., *Polynesian Researches, during a residence of nearly six years in the South Sea Islands, including descriptions of the natural history and scenery of the islands, with remarks on the history, mythology, traditions, government, arts, manners, and customs of the inhabitants* (London, 1830).

Les Enfants de Sodome à l'Assemblée Nationale ou Députation de l'Ordre de la Manchette aux représentants de tous les Ordres Pris dans les soixante districts de Paris et de Versailles y réunis avec figures (Paris, 1790).

Erman, A., 'Ethnographische Wahrnehmungen und Erfahrungen an den Küsten des Bering-Meeres', *ZfE*, 3 (1871), 149–75.

Erman, A., *Reise um die Erde durch Nord-Asien und die beiden Oceane, in den Jahren 1828, 1829 und 1830 ausgeführt. In einer historischen und physikalischen Abtheilung dargestellt und mit einem Atlas begleitet* (Berlin, 1833–48).

Erskine, J. E., *Journal of a Cruise among the Islands of the Western Pacific, including the Feejees and others inhabited by the Polynesian Negro Races in Her Majesty's Ship Havannah* (London, 1853).

Falconer, W., *Remarks upon the Influence of Climate, Situation, Nature of Country, Population, Nature of Food, and Ways of Life, on the Disposition and Temper of Manner, and Behaviour, Intellectual Laws and Religions of Mankind* (London, 1781).

Falk, K., 'Gleichgeschlechtliches Leben bei einigen Negerstämmen Angolas', *Archiv für Anthropologie*, New Series, 20 (1923), 42–5.

Falk, K., 'Homosexualität bei den Eingeborenen in Südwest-Afrika', *Archiv für Menschenkunde*, 1 (1925/26), 202–14.

Falkner, T., *A Description of Patagonia and the adjoining parts of South America, and some particulars relating to the Falkland Islands* (Hereford and London, 1774).

Fedrici, C. (Frederick, C.), *Voyages and Travels (1563–1581)*, in R. Kerr (ed.), *General History and Collection of Voyages and Travels, Arranged in Systematic Order* (Edinburgh, 1812), vol. 7, pp. 142–211.

Felkin, R. W., 'Notes on the Waganda tribe of central Africa', *Proceedings of the Royal Society of Edinburgh*, 13 (1884), 699–770.

Ferri, E., 'Intervento al quinto congresso internazionale di antropologia criminale', *Compte rendu de la cinquième session du congrès international d'anthropologie criminelle* (Amsterdam, 1901), pp. 487–9.

Finsch, O., 'Ueber die Bewohner von Ponapé (Östl. Karolinen). Nach eigenen Beobachtungen und Erkundigungen', *ZfE*, 12 (1880), 301–32.

Flaubert, G., *Correspondance. Vol. 1: (janvier 1830 à avril 1851)*, ed. J. Bruneau (Paris, 1973).

Fleuriot de Langle, A. J. R., 'Croisières à la côte d'Afrique (1868)', *Le tour du monde*, 31 (1876), 241–304.

Foley, A. E., 'Quelques détails et réflexions sur la coutume et les moeurs de la coquette néo-calédonienne', *Bulletin de la société d'anthropologie de Paris*, 3rd Series, 2 (1879), 675–82.

Foley, A. E., 'Sur les habitations et les moeurs des Néo-Calédoniens', *Bulletin de la société d'anthropologie de Paris*, 3rd Series, 2 (1879), 604–6.

Forster, J. R., *Observations made during a Voyage Round the World* (London, 1778).

Fourier, F. M. C., *Le Nouveau Monde Amoureux*, in F. M. C. Fourier, *Oeuvres complètes* (Paris, 1967), vol. 7.

Fournier-Pescay, 'Sodomie', in *Dictionnaire des sciences médicales* (Paris, 1821), vol. 51, pp. 441–8.

Fraissinet, E., *Le Japon; histoire et description, moeurs, coutumes et religion*, 2 vols (Paris, 1864).

Fraser, J. B., *Narrative of a Journey into Khorasan* (London, 1825).

Frazer, J. G., *The Golden Bough. The Roots of Religion and Folklore* (Cambridge, 1890).

Frazer, J. G., *Questions on the Customs, Beliefs and Languages of Savages* (Cambridge, 1907).

Freimark, H., *Okkultismus und Sexualität. Beiträge zur Kulturgeschichte und Psychologie alter und neuer Zeit* (Leipzig, 1909).

Freimark, H., *Das Sexualleben der Naturvölker*, vol. 2: *Das Sexualleben der Afrikaner* (Leipzig, 1911).

Friedenthal, A., *Das Weib im Leben der Völker*, 2 vols (Berlin, 1910).

Fritsch, G., 'Das angeblich dritte Geschlecht des Menschen', *Archiv für Sexualforschung*, 1 (1916), 197–220.

Fritsch, G., 'Über die Ova-Herero', *Globus*, 28 (1875), 246–7.

Fritsch, G., 'Über Omapanga der Hottentotten und über Päderastie der südafrikanischen Eingeborenen', *JfsZ*, 2 (1901), 87–8, 103–5.

Fryer, J., *A New Account of East-India and Persia* (London, 1697).

Gall, F. J., *Anatomie et physiologie du système nerveux en général et du cerveau en particulier* (Paris, 1818).

Geiger, W., *Ostiranische Kultur im Altertum* (Erlangen, 1882).

Gibbon, E., *The Decline and Fall of the Roman Empire*, ed. J. B. Bury (London, 1929 (1776–88)).

Gilij, F. S., *Saggio di storia americana, o sia, Storia naturale, civile e sacra de'regni e delle provincie spagnuole di Terra-ferma nell'America meridionale* (Rome, 1780–4).

Gley, E., 'Les aberrations de l'instinct sexuel', *Revue philosophique*, 9, 1 (1884), 88–92.

Godard, E., *Egypte et Palestine. Observations médicales et scientifiques* (Paris, 1867).

Goldie, H., *Dictionary of the Efik Language* (Glasgow, 1862).

Grasset, R. P., *Histoire de l'Eglise du Japon* (Paris, 1715).

Gray, J. H., *China. A History of the Laws, Manners, and Customs of the People* (London, 1878).

Griesinger, W., 'Vortrag zur Eröffnung der psychiatrischen Klinik zu Berlin', *APN*, 1 (1868/69), 651.

Grosier, J.-B., *Description générale de la Chine*, 7 vols (Paris, 1820).

Grube, W., *Geschichte der chinesischen Literatur* (Leipzig, 1902).

Grützer, H., 'Die Gebräuche der Basuto', *Verhandlungen der Berliner Gesellschaft für Anthropologie, Ethnologie und Urgeschichte* (1877), 76–92.

Guevara, T., *História de la civilización de Araucania* (Santiago de Chile, 1898).

[Gützlaff, C.], *Gützlaff's Geschichte des Chinesischen Reiches von den ältesten Zeiten bis auf den Frieden von Nanking* (Stuttgart and Tübingen, 1847).

Haddon, A. C., 'The ethnography of the western tribe of Torres Straits', *JRAI*, 19 (1890), 297–440.

Haensel, J. G., *Letters on the Nicobar islands, their natural productions, and the manners, customs and superstitions of the Native, with an account of the attempt made by the Church of the United Brethren, to convert them to Christianity* (London, 1812).

Hagen, B., *Unter den Papua's. Beobachtungen und Studien über Land und Leute, Thier- und Pflanzenwelt in Kaiser-Wilhelmsland* (Wiesbaden, 1899).

Haleby Abu Otman, O. [and de Régla, P.], *Les lois secrètes de l'amour en Islam* (Paris, 1993).

Hamilton, A., *A New Account of the East Indies from the Year 1688 to 1723*, 2 vols (Edinburgh, 1727).

Hammer, W., 'Liebesleben und -Leiden in Westmittel-Afrika, besonders in Kamerun', *Geschlecht*, 4 (1909), 193–201.

Hammer-Purgstall, J., 'Auszüge aus Saalebis Buche "Die Stützen des sich Beziehenden und dessen, worauf es sich bezieht" ', *ZdmG*, 9 (1855), 106–31.

Hammer-Purgstall, J., *Geschichte des osmanischen Reiches* (Budapest, 1827).

Hammer-Purgstall, J., *Geschichte der schönen Redekünste in Persien* (Vienna, 1818).

Hammond, W. A., 'The disease of the Scythians (Morbus Feminarum) and certain analogous conditions', *The American Journal of Neurology and Psychiatry*, 1, 3 (August 1882), 339–55.

Hammond, W. A., *Impotence in the Male* (New York, 1887 (1883)).

Hardeland, A., *Dajacksch-Deutsches Wörterbuch* (Amsterdam, 1859).

Hardman, E. T., 'Notes on some habitants and customs of the natives of the Kimberley district, western Australia', *Proceedings of the Royal Irish Academy*, 3rd Series, 1 (1889–91), 70–5.

Hasskarl, J. K., *Australien und seine Kolonien Süd-Australien, Australia Felix, etc., nach mehrjährigen Beobachtungen und Erfahrungen von Wilkinson, Westgarth, Wyld, etc. und den Berichten deutscher Kolonisten. Ein Handbuch für Deutsche Auswanderer* (Elberfeld and Iserlohn, 1849).

Heerman, T., 'Die Päderastie bei den Sarten', *Sexualprobleme*, 7 (1911), 400–8.

Heine, W., *Die Expedition in die Seen von China, Japan und Ochotsk* (Leipzig, 1859).

Heine, W., *Japan und seine Bewohner. Geschichtliche Rückblicke und ethnographische Schilderungen von Land und Leuten* (Leipzig, 1860).

Helms, R., 'Anthropology', *Transactions of the Royal Society of of South Australia, Adelaide*, 16 (1892–96), part 3, 137–332.

Helmut, H. K. E., *Meine Wallfahrt nach Mekka*, 2 vols (Leipzig and Stuttgart, n.d.).

Helmut, H. K. E., *Sittenbilder aus Tunis und Algerien* (Leipzig, 1869).

Helmut, H. K. E., *Reise nach Südarabien* (Braunschweig, 1873).

Hennepin, L., *Nouvelle découverte d'un très grand pays situé dans l'Amérique entre le Nouveau Mexique et la Mer Glaciale* (Utrecht, 1697).

Herbert, T., *A Relation of Some Yeares of Travvels into Africa & Asia the Great, Especially Describing the Famous Empires of Persia and Industant, As also Divers other Kingdoms in the Oriental Indies and I'les Adjacent* (London, 1634).

Heriot, G., *Travels through the Canadas, containing a description of the picturesque scenery of some of the rivers and lakes; with an account of the productions, commerce, and inhabitants of those provinces. To which is subjoined a comparative view of the manners and customs of several of the Indian Nations of North and South America* (London, 1807).

Hernsheim, F., *Beitrag zur Sprache der Marshall-Inseln* (Leipzig, 1880).

Herzberg, G. F., *Geschichte der Byzantiner und des Osmanischen Reiches* (Berlin, 1883).

Heyne, C. G.,'De maribus inter Scytas morbo effeminatis et de Hermaphroditis commentatio recitata in concessu d. XIX Sept. 1778', in *Commentationes Societatis Regiae Scientiarum Gottingensis Historicae et Philologicae Classis* (Göttingen, 1779), vol. 1, pp. 28–44.

Hildebrandt, E., *Reise um die Erde. Nach seinen Tagebüchern und mündlichen Berichten erzählt von E. Kossak* (Berlin, 1867).

Hildebrandt, H., 'Die Krankheiten der äusseren weiblichen Genitalien', in T. Billroth (ed.), *Handbuch der Frauenkrankheiten* (Stuttgart, 1885–6), vol. 3., pp. 5–23.

Hindley, J., *Introduction to Persian Lyrics or Scattered Poems from the Diwan-I-Hafiz* (London, 1800).

Hirn, Y., *The Origins of Art. A Psychological and Sociological Inquiry* (London, 1900).

Hirschfeld, M., *Berlin's dritte Geschlecht* (Grossstadt-dokumente, ed. H. Ostwald, vol. 3) (Berlin and Leipzig, 1904).

Hirschfeld, M., *Die Homosexualität des Mannes und des Weibes* (Handbuch der gesamten Sexualwissenschaft in Einzeldarstellungen, ed. I. Bloch, vol. 3, (Berlin, 1920 (1914)) (Berlin, 1984).

[Hirschfeld, M.], *Sappho und Sokrates, oder wie erklärt sich die Liebe der Männer und Frauen zu Personen des eigenen Geschlechts?* (Leipzig, 1896).

Hirschfeld, M., 'Ursachen und Wesen des Uranismus', *JfsZ*, 5 (1903), 1–193.

Hirschfeld, M., *Die Weltreise eines Sexualforschers* (Bruges, 1933).

Hoche, J., *Moeurs d'exception. Le vice mortel* (Paris, 1903).

Holder, A. B., 'The Bote. Description of a peculiar sexual perversion found among North American Indians', *New York Medical Journal*, 575 (7 December 1889), 623–5.

Hössli, H., *Eros. Die Männerliebe der Griechen. Ihre Beziehungen zur Geschichte, Erziehung, Literatur und Gesetzgebung aller Zeiten. Die Unzuverlässigkeit der äusseren Kennzeichen im Geschlechtsleben des Leibes und der Seele. Oder Forschungen über platonische Liebe, ihre Würdigung und Entwürdigung für Sitten-, Natur- und Völkerkunde* (St Gallen, 1836).

Houel, C., *Maroc: mariage, adultère, prostitution: anthologie* (Paris, 1912).

Hrdlicka, A., *Physiological and medical observations among the Indians of Southwestern United States and Northern Mexico* (Washington, 1908).

Hughes, C. H., 'Postscript to paper on "Erotopathia". An organisation of colored erotopaths', *The Alienist and Neurologist*, 14, 4 (1893), 731–2.

Hughes, T. P., *Dictionary of Islam* (London, 1885).

Hugues, P. F. (Baron d'Hancarville), *Recherches sur l'esprit et les progrès des arts en Grèce, sur leur connexion avec les arts et la religion des plus anciens peuples connus, et sur les monuments antiques de l'Inde, de la Perse, du reste de l'Asie, de l'Europe et de l'Egypte* (London, 1785).

Humbert, A., *Le Japon illustré* (Paris, 1870).

Hume, D., 'Of national characters', in *Essays Moral, Political and Literary* (London and Edinburgh, 1904).

Hungronje, C. Snouck, *De Atjehers*, 2 vols (Batavia and Leiden, 1893).

Hupe, C., 'Korte Verhandeling over de Godsdienst, zeden, enz. der Dajakkers', *Tijdschrift voor Neêrlands' Indië*, 8, 3 (1846), 127–72, 245–80.

Hutchinson, T. J., 'The Tehuelche Indians of Patagonia', *Transactions of the Ethnological Society of London*, New Series, 7 (1869), 313–25.

Hutchinson, T. J., *Ten Years' Wanderings among the Ethiopians with Sketches of the Manners and Customs of the Civilized and Uncivilized Tribes, from Senegal to Gabon* (London, 1861).

Ibañez, B., *Das Reich der Jesuiten in Paraguay*, in J. F. Le Bret, *Magazin zum Gebrauch der Staaten- und Kirchengeschichte, wie auch des geistlichen Staatsrechts catholischer Regenten in Ansehung ihrer Geistlichkeit* (Frankfurt and Leipzig, 1772), vol. 2, pp. 359–539.

Ilex, E., *Moeurs orientales. Les huis-clos de l'ethnographie* (London, 1878).

Irle, J., *Die Herero. Ein Beitrag zur Landes-, Volks- und Missionskunde* (Gütersloh, 1906).

Jacobs, F. H., *Schriften* (Leipzig, 1829).

Jacobs, J., *Eenigen tijd onder de Baliërs. Een reisebeschrijving met aanteekeningen betreffende hygiëne, land- en volkenkunde van de eilanden Bali en Lombok* (Batavia, 1883).

Jacobs, J., *Het familie- en kampongleven op Groot-Atjeh. Een bijdrage tot de ethnographie van Noord-Sumatra*, 2 vols (Leiden, 1894).

Jacquemont, V., *Voyage dans l'Inde* (Paris, 1841).

Jacquot, F., 'Des aberrations de l'appétit génésique', *Gazette médicale de Paris*, 28 July 1849, 7–10.

Jacquot, F., 'Lettre d'Afrique', *Gazette médicale de Paris*, 3rd Series, 18 (1847), 78–9, 93.

Jaekel, V., *Studien zur vergleichenden Völkerkunde. Mit besonderer Berücksichtigung des Frauenlebens* (Berlin, 1901).

Jäger, G., 'Ein bisher ungedrucktes Kapitel über Homosexualität aus der "Entdeckung der Seele" ', *JfsZ*, 2 (1900), 53–125.

Jäger, G. (ed.), *Handwörterbuch der Zoologie, Anthropologie und Ethnologie*, 8 vols (Breslau, 1880–1900).

James, R., *Medicinal Dictionary* (London, 1745).

Jarric, P., *Thesaurus Indicus. Rerum Indicarum Tomus Tertius* (Cologne, 1616).

Johnston, H. H., *British Central Africa. An Attempt to give some account of a portion of the territories under British influence north of the Zambezi* (London, 1897).

Joinville, 'On the religion and manners of the people of Ceylon', *Asiatic Researches, or: Transactions of the Society instituted in Bengal for inquiring into the History and Antiquities, the Arts, Sciences, and Literature of Asia* (London), 7 (1807), 397–444.

Junghuhn, F., *Die Battaländer auf Sumatra* (Berlin, 1847).

Junod, H. A., *The Life of a South African Tribe* (Neuchâtel, 1912).

Jwaya, S., 'Nan sho 'k (die Päderastie in Japan)', *JfsZ*, 4 (1902), 264–71.

Kaan, H., *Psychopathia sexualis* (Leipzig, 1844).

Kaempfer, E., *Geschichte und Beschreibung von Japan* (Lemgo, 1777–9).

Kandt, R., *Caput Nili. Eine empfindsame Reise zu den Quellen des Nils* (Berlin, 1905).

Karsch-Haack, F., *Beruht gleichgeschlechtliche Liebe auf Soziabilität? Eine begründete Zurückweisung. (Kritik an Benedict Friedländer)* (Munich, 1905).

Karsch-Haack, F., *Forschungen über gleichgeschlechtliche Liebe*, vol. 1: *Das gleichgeschlechtliche Leben der Kulturvölker, 1: Das gleichgeschlechtliche Leben der Ostasiaten: Chinesen, Japaner, Koreer* (Munich, 1906).

Karsch-Haack, F., *Das gleichgeschlechtliche Leben der Naturvölker (Forschungen über gleichgeschlechtliche Liebe, 1. Ethnologische Reihe: Das gleichgeschlechtliche Leben der Völker, vol. 1)* (New York, 1975 (Berlin, 1911)).

Karsch-Haack, F., 'Päderastie und Tribadie bei den Tieren auf Grund der Literatur', *JfsZ*, 2 (1900), 126–60.

Karsch-Haack, F., 'Die Rolle der Homoerotik im Arabertum', *JfsZ*, 23 (1923), 100–170.

Karsch-Haack, F., 'Uranismus oder Päderastie und Tribadie bei den Naturvölkern', *Jahrbuch für sexuelle Zwischenstufen. Auswahl aus den Jahrgängen 1899–1923*, ed. W. J. Schmidt (Frankfurt and Paris, 1983), pp. 229–96.

Keating, W. H., *Narrative of an Expedition to the Source of St.Peter's River, Lake Winnepeek, Lake of the Woods, performed in the Year 1823* (Philadelphia, 1824).

Kéraval, P., [Untitled], *Archives de neurologie*, 24 (March 1902), 236–7.

Kiernan, J. G., 'Responsibility in sexual perversion', *The Chicago Medical Recorder* (1892), pp. 385–410.

Kind, A., and Krauss, F. S., 'Homosexualität und Volkskunde', *Anthropophyteia*, 5 (1907), 197–203.

Kingsborough, [Lord], *Antiquities of Mexico. Comprising Fac-Similes of Ancient Mexican Paintings and Hieroglyphics, preserved in the Royal Libraries of Paris, Berlin, and Dresden, in the Imperial Library of Vienna, in the Vatican Library, in the Borgian Museum at Rome, in the Library of the Institute at Bologna, and in the Bodleian Library at Oxford. Together with the Monuments of New Spain by M. Dupaix with their respective Scales of Measurement and Accompanying Descriptions* (London, 1848).

Klaatsch, H., 'Some notes on scientific travel amongst the black population of tropical Australia in 1904, 1905, 1906', *Australasian Association for the Advancement of Science, Adelaide* (1908), pp. 577–92.

Klemm, G., *Allgemeine Culturgeschichte der Menschheit*, 3 vols (Leipzig, 1842–53).

Klinkert, H. C., *Supplement op het Maleisch-Nederduitsch Woordenboek van Dr. Pijnappel* (Haarlem and Amsterdam, 1869).

Klunzinger, C. B., *Bilder aus Oberägypten* (Stuttgart, 1877).

Knight, R. Payne, *Analytical Enquiry into the Principles of Taste* (London, 1801).

Knight, R. Payne, *Discourse on the Worship of Priapus, and its Connexion with the Mystic Theology of the Ancients* (London, 1786–7), in A. Montagu, *Sexual Symbolism: A History of Phallic Worship* (New York, 1957), pp. 1–217.

Knox, R., *A Historical Relation of the Island of Ceylon in the East Indies, together with an Account of the Detaining in Captivity of the Author and divers other Englishmen now living there, and of the Author's Miraculous Escape* (London, 1681).

Kobelt, G. L., *Die männlichen und weiblichen Wollust-Organe des Menschen und verschiedene Saugetiere* (Stuttgart, 1844).

Kocher, A., *De la criminalité chez les Arabes au point de vue de la pratique médico-judiciaire en Algérie* (Paris, 1884).

Kohler, J., 'Fragebogen zur Erforschung der Rechtsverhältnisse der sogenannten Naturvölker, namentlich in den deutschen Kolonialländern', *ZfvR*, 12 (1897), 427–40.

Kohler, J., 'Rechte der deutschen Schutzgebiete', *ZfvR*, 14 (1900), 294–319, 321–94, 409–55; 15 (1901/02), 1–83, 321–36, 337–60.

Kohler, J., 'Die Rechte der Urvölker Nordamerikas (nördlich von Mexico)', *ZfvR*, 12 (1897), 354–413.

Kohler, J., *Das sexuelle Leben der Naturvölker* (Augsburg, 1900).

Kohler, J., Über das Islamische Strafrecht (Stuttgart, 1889).

Kohler, J., 'Über das Negerrecht, namentlich in Kamerun', *ZfvR*, 11 (1895), 413–75.

Kohler, J., 'Ueber den Begriff der Unzucht mit öffentlichem Ärgerniss', *Archiv für Staatsrecht*, 45 (1897), 175–213.

Kolb, P., *Caput Bonae Spei Hodiernum. Das ist: Vollständige Beschreibung des Africanischen Vorgebürges der Guten Hofnung etc., mit dem Undertitel: M. Peter Kolbens Reise an das Capo du Bonne Esperance, oder das Africanische Vorgebürge des Guten Hofnung: nebst einer ausführlichen Beschreibung desselben. In dreyen Theilen abgefasset* (Nürnberg, 1719).

Kraft, J., *Die Sitten der Wilden, zur Aufklärung des Ursprungs und Aufnahme der Menschheit* (Copenhagen, 1766).

Krapf, L., *A Dictionary of the Swahili Language* (London, 1882).

Krauss, F. S., 'Altperuanische Grabgefässe mit erotischen Gestalten', *Anthropophyteia*, 3 (1906), 420–4.

Krauss, F. S., 'Ein erotischer Alptraum als Holzschnitzwerk aus Neu-Irlan', *Anthropophyteia*, 3 (1906), 408–10.

Kraus, F. S., *Das Geschlechtsleben in Glauben, Sitte, Brauch und Gewohnheitsrecht der Japaner* (Leipzig, 1911 (second, revised edition; first edition in 1907)).

Kruyt, J. A., *Atjeh en de Atjehers. Twee jaren Blokkade op Sumatra's Noord-Oost-Kust* (Leiden, 1877).

Kubary, J. S., 'Die Religion der Pelauer', in A. Bastian (ed.), *Allerlei aus Volks- und Menschenkunde* (Berlin, 1888), pp. 1–69.

Kubary, J. S., 'Die Verbrechen und das Strafverfahren auf den Pelau-Inseln (Mikronesien)', *Original-Mittheilungen aus der Ethnologischen Abtheilung der Königlichen Museen zu Berlin*, 1, 2/3 (1885/86), 77–91.

Kuiper, E. T. Feenstra, *Jeugdige zondaars te Constantinopel*, ed. W. Ogrinc (Utrecht, 1978 (Amsterdam, 1905)).

Labat, J.-B., *Relation historique de l'Ethiopie occidentale: Contenant la description des Royaumes de Congo, Angolle & Matamba, traduite de l'Italien du P. Cavazzi & augmentée de plusieurs relations Portugaises des meilleurs Auteurs, avec des Notes, des Cartes géographiques, & un grand nombre de figures en taille-douce* (Paris, 1732).

Lacassagne, A., 'Pédérastie', in *Dictionnaire encyclopédique des sciences médicales*, 2nd Series, 22 (Paris, 1886), 239–59.

La Douceur, [Z. De' Pazzi de Bonneville?], *De l'Amérique et des Américains, ou Observations curieuses du philosophes La Douceur, qui a parcouru cet Hémisphère pendant la dernière guerre, en faisant le noble métier de tuer des hommes sans les manger* (Berlin, 1771).

Lafitau, J.-F., *Moeurs des sauvages Américains comparées aux moeurs des premiers temps*, ed. E. Hindie Lemay (Paris, 1983 (1728)).

Lallemand, [Dr], *Des pertes séminales involontaires* (Paris, 1838).

Lane, E. W., *An Account of the Manners and Customs of the Modern Egyptians* (New York, 1972 (London, 1836)).

Lasnet, A., 'Notes d'ethnologie et de médecine sur les Sakalaves du Nord-Oest', *Ahmc*, 2 (October–December 1899), 471–97.

Latcham, R. E., 'Ethnology of the Araucanos', *JRAI*, 39 (1909), 334–70.

Laufer, B., 'Ein homosexuelles Bild aus China', *Anthropophyteia*, 6 (1909), 162–6.

Laurent, E., 'Les Sharimbavy de Madagascar', *Aac*, 26 (1911), 241–8.

Lauvergne, H., *Les forçats* (Paris, 1841).

Lecomte, L., *Nouveaux mémoires sur la Chine*, 2 vols (Paris, 1696).

Le Golif, L. A. T., *Memoirs of a Buccaneer*, ed. G. Alaux and A. 'tSerstevens (London, 1954).

Lejeune, [Father], *Observations critiques et philosophiques sur le Japon et les Japonais* (Amsterdam, 1780).

Lenz, O., *Timbuktu. Reise durch Marokko, die Sahara und den Sudan, ausgeführt im Auftrage der Afrikanischen Gesellschaft in Deutschland in den Jahren 1879 und 1880* (Leipzig, 1884).

Letourneau, C., *La psychologie ethnique* (Paris, 1901).

Levin, T. H., *Wild Races of South-Eastern India* (London, 1870).

Libermann, H., *Les fumeurs d'opium en Chine. Etude médicale* (Paris, 1862).

Lisiansky, U., *A Voyage Round the World in the Years 1803, 4, 5 & 6* (London, 1814).

Lithgow, W., *The Totall Discourse of the Rare Adventures and Painful Peregrinations* (Glasgow, 1906 (1609–22)).

Livingstone, D., *Missionary Travels and Researches in South Africa* (London, 1857).

Livingstone, D., *Narrative of an Expedition to the Zambesi and its Tributaries, and of the Discovery of the Lakes Shirwa and Nyassa* (London, 1865).

Löhr, J. A. C., *Die Länder und Völker der Erde oder vollständige Beschreibung aller fünf Erdteile unde deren Bewohner*, vol. 4: *Amerika und Australien*, 2nd ed. (Leipzig, 1815).

Lombroso, C., *L'amore nel suicidio e nel delitto* (Turin, 1881).

Lombroso, C., 'Delitti di libidine', *Archivio di psichiatria, antropologia criminale e medicina legale* (1883), pp 168–78, 320–49.

Lombroso, C., 'Du parallellisme entre l'homosexualité et la criminalité innée', *Archivio di psichiatria, scienze penali ed antropologia criminale*, 27 (1906), 378–81.

Lombroso, C., *L'uomo delinquente* (Milan, 1876).

Lombroso, C., and Ferrero, G., *La donna delinquente* (Turin and Rome, 1893).

Lomonaco, A., 'Sulle razze indigene del Brasile. Studio storico', *Aae*, 19 (1889), 17–92, 187–270.

Long, J., *Voyages and Travels of an Indian Interpreter and Trader* (London, 1791).

Longford, J. H., 'A summary of the Japanese penal codes', *Transactions of the Asiatic Society of Japan, Yokohama*, 5 (1877), 1–114.

Loskiel, G. H., *Geschichte der Mission der evangelischen Brüder unter den Indianern in Nordamerika* (Barby and Leipzig, 1789).

Löwenstern, I., *Le Mexique. Souvenir d'un voyageur* (Paris and Leipzig, 1843).

Luttke, M., *Der Islam und seine Völker* (Gütersloh, 1878).

Maclean, *A Compendium of kaffir Laws & Customs, including genealogical tables of Kafir Chiefs and various Tribal Census Returns* (Grahamstown, 1906).

Madan, A. C., *English-Swahili Dictionary*, 2nd ed. (Oxford, 1902).

Madan, A. C., *Swahili-English Dictionary* (Oxford, 1903).

Mantegazza, P., *Gli amori dei uomini. Saggio di una etnologia dell'amore* (Milan, 1885–6).

Marchand, E., *Voyage autour du monde, pendant les années 1790, 1791, et 1792, etc.* (Paris, 1798–1800).

Marcuse, M., 'Geschlechtstrieb und "Liebe" des Urmenschen', *Sexualprobleme*, 5 (1919), 721–40.

[Mariner, W.], *An Account of the Natives of the Tonga Islands, in the South Pacific Ocean. With an original Grammar and Vocabulary of their Language. Compiled and arranged from the extensive communications of Mr. William Mariner, several Years Resident in those Islands by John Martin* (London, 1817).

Marion, *Voyages autour du monde* (1771), in *Histoire universelle des Voyages effectués par mer et par terre dans cinq parties du monde sur les divers points du globe, contenant la description des moeurs, coutumes, gouvernement, cultes, sciences et arts, industrie et commerce, productions naturelles et autres*, ed. M. Albert-Montémont (Paris, 1836), vol. 4, pp. 401–46.

Maron, H., *Japan und China* (Berlin, 1863).

Marsden, W., *The History of Sumatra, containing an account of the government, laws, customs, and manners of the native inhabitants, with a description of the natural productions, and a relation of the ancient political state of that island* (London, 1783).

Martin, R. Montgomery, *History of the British Colonies* (London, 1834).

Matignon, J. J., *Superstition, crime et misère en Chine* (Bibliothèque de Criminologie, 21) (Lyon-Paris, 1899).

Matthes, B. F., *Boegineesch-Hollandsch Woordenboek, met Hollandsch-Boegineesche Woordenlijst, en Verklaring van een tot opheldering bijgevoegden Ethnographischen Atlas* (The Hague, 1874).

Matthes, B. F., 'Over de Bissoe's of heidensche priesters en priesteressen der Boeginezen', *Verhandelingen der Koninklijke Akademie van Wetenschappen, Afdeling Letterkunde* (Amsterdam), 7 (1872), 1–50.

Matthews, R. H., 'Das Kumbainggeri, eine Eingeborenensprache von Neu-Süd-Wales', *Mittheilungen der Anthropologischen Gesellschaft in Wien*, 33 (1903), 321–8.

Matthews, R. H., 'Language, organisation and initiation ceremonies of the Kogai tribes, Queensland', *ZfE*, 36 (1904), 28–38.

Matthews, R. H., 'Languages of some native tribes of Queensland, New South Wales and Victoria', *Journal and Proceedings of the Royal Society of New South Wales for 1901, Sydney*, 36 (1902), 35–190.

Matthews, R. H., 'Languages of the Kamilaroi and other Aboriginal tribes of New South Wales', *JRAI*, 33 (1903), 259–83.

Matthews, R. H., 'Some Aboriginal Tribes of Western Australia', *Journal and Proceedings of the Royal Society of New South Wales for 1901, Sydney*, 35 (1901), 217–22.

Matthews, R. H., 'Some initiation ceremonies of the Aborigines of Victoria', *ZfE*, 37 (1905), 872–9.

Matthews, R. H., 'The Thurrawal Language', *Journal and Proceedings of the Royal Society of New South Wales for 1901*, Sydney, 35 (1901), 127–60.

Mazzei, F., *Recherches historiques et politiques sur les Etats Unis de l'Amérique septentrionale* (Paris, 1788).

Meiners, C., *Grundriss der Geschichte der Menschheit* (Lemgo, 1793).

Meiners, J. E., 'Dr. Magnus Hirschfelds Bestrebungen', *Anthropophyteia*, 4 (1907), 414–16.

Melling, A. I., *Voyage pittoresque de Constantinople et des rives du Bospore* (Paris, 1819).

Mende, L. J. L., *Ausführliches Handbuch der gerichtlichen Medicin* (Leipzig, 1826) (vol 4).

Meyer, A. B., 'Über die Perforation des Penis bei den Malayen', *Mittheilungen der Anthropologischen Gesellschaft in Wien*, 7 (1877), 242–4.

Michaelis, G., 'Zur Kenntnis der Geschichte des japanischen Strafrechts', *Mitteilungen der deutschen Gesellschaft für Natur- und Völkerkunde Ostasiens in Tokio*, 38 (1888), 360–83.

Michéa, C. F., 'Des déviations maladives de l'appétit vénérien', *Union médical*, 17 July 1849, pp. 338–9.

Milne, W. C., *Life in China* (London, 1857).

Moerenhout, J.-A., *Voyages aux îles du grand Océan, contenant des documents nouveaux sur la géographie physique et politique, la langue, la littérature, la religion, les moeurs, les usages et les coutumes de leurs habitans*, 2 vol (Paris, 1837).

Mohnike, O., 'Die Japaner. Eine ethnographische Monographie', *Natur und Offenbarung*, 18 (1872), 200–21, 251–69, 300–18, 357–75.

Moll, A., *Untersuchungen über die Libido sexualis* (Berlin, 1897).

Monrad, H. C., *Bidrag til en Skildring af Guinea-Kysten og dens Indbygere, og til en Beskrivelse over de danske Colonier paa denne Kyst, samlede under mit Ophold i Afrika i Aarene 1805 til 1809* (Copenhagen, 1822).

Montanus, A., *Gedenkwaerdige Gesantschappen der Oost-Indische Maatschappij . . . aan de Kaisaren van Japan* (Amsterdam, 1669).

Montejo, E., *The Autobiography of a Runaway Slave*, ed. M. Barnet (New York, 1973).

Montesquieu, *Oeuvres complètes*, ed. D. Oster (Paris, 1964).

Morache, G., 'Pékin et ses habitants. Etude d'hygiène', *Annales d'hygiène et de médecine légale*, 2nd Series, 31 (1868), 122–31.

Moreau, Paul, *Des aberrations du sens génésique* (Paris, 1880).

Morier, J. J., *A Second Journey through Persia* (London, 1818).

Mouliéras, A., *Le Maroc inconnu. Exploration du Rif* (Paris, 1895).

Mozkowski, M., 'Die Völkerstamme am Mamberano in Holländisch-Neuguinea und auf den vorgelagerten Inseln', *ZfE*, 43 (1911), 315–43.

Müller, J., *Das sexuelle Leben der alten Kulturvölker* (Leipzig, 1902).

Müller, J. G., *Geschichte der Amerikanischen Urreligionen* (Basel, 1855).

Müller, J. V., *Entwurf der gerichtlichen Arzneywissenschaft* (Frankfurt, 1796), in *Der unterdrückte Sexus. Historische Texte und Kommentare zur Homosexualität*, ed. J. S. Hohmann (Berlin, 1977), pp. 211–24.

Mundy, R., *Narrative of Events in Borneo and Celebes, down to the Occupation of Labuan, from the Journals of James Brooke, esq., Rajah of Sarawak, and Governor of Labuan, together with a Narrative of the Operations of H.M.S. Iris* (London, 1848).

Munzinger, C., *Japan und die Japaner* (Stuttgart, 1904).

Muratori, L., *Il cristianismo felice nelle missioni de'Padri della Compagnia di Gesu nel Paraguai* (Venice, 1743–9).

Näcke, P., 'Die Homosexualität im Oriente', *Archiv für Kriminal-Anthropologie und Kriminalistik*, 16 (1904), 353–5.

Näcke, P., 'Die Homosexualität in Konstantinopel', *Archiv für Kriminal-Anthropologie und Kriminalistik*, 26 (1906), 106–8.

Näcke, P., 'Sexuelle Umfragen bei halb- und unzivilisierten Völkern', *Anthropophyteia*, 5 (1907), 193–6.

Näcke, P., 'Über Homosexualität in Albanien', *JfsZ*, 9 (1908), 313–26.

Navarrete, D. Fernandez, *Tratados Históricos, Políticos, Ethicos y Religiosos de la Monarchia de China* (Madrid, 1676).

[Al-Nefzawi], *The Perfumed Garden of the Cheikh Nefzaoui. A Manual of Arabian Erotology (XVI Century): Revised and Corrected Translation.* Cosmopoli: MDCCCLXXXVI: for the Kama Shastra Society of London and Benares, and for private circulation only, trans. R. Burton (London and Benares, 1886).

Nigmann, E., *Die Wahehe* (Berlin, 1908).

Nihongi, *Chronicles of Japan from the earliest times to A.D. 697*, trans. W. G. Aston (London, 1896).

Norris, R., *Memoirs of the reign of Bossa Ahadee, king of Dahomey, an inland country of Guinea* (London, 1789).

Nusdorfer, B. (Don J. del Campo y Cambroneras), *Schreiben des Jesuiten Bernhard Nusdorfer ... wider den portugiesischen Bericht von der Republik der Jesuiten in Paraguay*, in *Neue Nachrichten von den Missionen der Jesuiten in Paraguay und von andern damit verbundenen Vorgängen in der spanischen Monarchie* (Hamburg, 1768).

Oefele, F., 'Zum konträren Geschlechtsverkehr in Altägypten', *Monatshefte für praktische Dermatologie*, 19 (1899), 409–11.

Oetker, K., *Die Negerseele und die Deutschen in Afrika* (München, 1907).

Okasaki, T., *Geschichte der japanischen Nationalliteratur von den ältesten Zeiten bis zur Gegenwart* (Leipzig, 1899).

Olegna, R., 'Il catechismo turco e l'omosessualità', *Rassegna di studi sessuali*, 2 (1922), 354–6; 3 (1923), 115–18.

Oppenheim, F. W., *Ueber den Zustand der Heilkunde und über die Volkskrankheiten in der europäischen und Asiatischen Türkei* (Hamburg, 1833).

Pacha, D. A. Zambaco, *Les eunuques d'aujourd'hui et ceux de jadis* (Paris, 1911).

Palgrave, W. G., *Narrative of a Year's Journey through Central and Eastern Arabia* (London, 1865).

Palou, F., *Relación histórica de la vida y apostólicas tareas del venerable padre Junipero Serra y de las Missiones que fundó en la California Septentrional y nuevos establecimientos de Monterrey* (Mexico, 1787).

Paré, A., *Des monstres et prodiges*, ed. J. Céard (Geneva, 1971 (1573)).

Parkinson, R., *Dreissig Jahre in der Südsee: Land und Leute, Sitten und Gebräuche im Bismarck Archipel und auf den deutschen Salomoninseln* (Stuttgart, 1907).

Parsons, J., *Mechanical and critical enquiry into the nature of hermaphrodites* (London, 1741).

Paulitschke, P., *Ethnographie Nordost-Afrikas. Die materielle Kultur der Danâkil, Galla und Somâl* (Berlin, 1893).

Pauthier, G., and Bazin, M., *La Chine Moderne ou description historique, géographique et littéraire de ce vaste empire d'après des documents Chinois*, vol. 1: G. Pauthier, *Géographie, Organisation politique et administrative de la Chine, Langues, Philosophie* (*L'Univers. Histoire et description de tous les peuples*, vol. 10) (Paris, 1853).

Pearson, K., *The Chances of Death and Other Studies* (London, 1897).

Perelaer, M. T. H., *Ethnographische beschrijving der Dajaks* (Zaltbommel, 1870).

Pernety, A. J., *Examen des Recherches philosophiques sur l'Amérique et les Américains et de la Défense de cet ouvrage*, 2 vols (Berlin, 1771).

Perrenot, A., *Bedenkingen over het straffen van zekere schandelijke misdaad* (Amsterdam, 1777).

Perzynsky, F., 'Der Japanische Farbenholzschnitt. Seine Geschichte, seine Einfluss', *Die Kunst*, 13 (n.d.), 102–26.

Les petits bougres au manège, ou Réponse de M.***. Grand maître des enculeurs, et de ses adhérents, défendeurs, à la requête des fouteuses, des macquerelles et des branleuses, demanderesses ('Enculons', L'an II (1794)), ed. P. Cardon (Lille, n.d.).

Pfeifer, G. S. F., *Meine Reise und meine fünfjahrige Gefangeschaft in Algier* (Giessen, 1834).

Pfeil, J., *Studien und Beobachtungen aus der Südsee* (Braunschweig, 1899).

Pharaon, J., and Dulau, T., *Droit musulman* (Paris, 1839).

Pitts, J., *A True and Faithful Account of the Religion and Manners of the Mohametans* (Exeter, 1704).

Ploss, H., and Bartels, M., *Das Weib in der Natur- und Völkerkunde. Anthropologische Studien*, 2 vols (Leipzig, 1905).

Ploss, H., and Benz, B., *Das Kind in Brauch und Sitte der Völker. Völkerkundige Studien* (Leipzig, 1912).

Poiret, J. L. M., *Voyage en Barbarie* (Paris, 1789).

Polak, J. E., 'Die Prostitution in Persien', *Wiener medizinische Wochenschrift*, 32 (1861), 516, 627–9.

Pöppig, E.,'Indier', in *Allgemeine Encyklopädie der Wissenschaften und der Künste* (Leipzig, 1840), pp. 357–86.

Post, A. H., *Bausteine für eine allgemeine Rechtswissenschaft auf vergleichend-ethnologischer Base*, 2 vols (Oldenburg, 1880–1).

Post, A. H., *Grundriss der ethnologischen Jurisprudenz*, 2 vols (Oldenburg and Leipzig, 1894–5).

Post, A. H., *Studien zur Entwicklungsgeschichte des Familienrechts. Ein Beitrag zu einer allgemeinen vergleichenden Rechtswissenschaft auf ethnologischer Basis* (Oldenburg and Leipzig, 1890).

Pouqueville, F. C. H. L., *Voyage en Morée, à Constantinople, en Albanie pendant les années 1798, 1799, 1800 et 1801* (Paris, 1805).

Pratt, G., *A Samoan Dictionary* (Samoa, 1862).

Preuss, K. T., 'Die Religiösen Gesänge und Mythen einiger Stämme der mexikanischen Sierra Madre. Reisebericht', *AfR*, 11 (1908), 369–98.

Preuss, K. T., 'Die Religionen der Naturvölker Amerikas 1906–1909', *AfR*, 14 (1911), 212–301.

Pruner, F., *Die Krankheiten des Orients vom Standpunkte des vergleichenden Nosologie betrachtet* (Erlangen, 1847).

[Psalmanazar, G.], *Memoirs of **** commonly known by the name of George Psalmanazar, Reputed Native of Formosa* (London, 1714).

Purcell, B. H., 'Rites and customs of Australian Aborigines', *ZfE*, 25 (1893), 286–9.

Purchas, S., *Purchas His Pilgrimes* (London, 1625).

Quedenfeldt, H., 'Die Corporationen der Ulêd Ssidi Hammed-u-Mûssa und der Ormâ im südlichen Marokko', *ZfE*, 21 (1899), 572–82.

Raffalovich, M. A., 'Quelques observations sur l'inversion', *Aac*, 9 (1894), 211–16.

Raffalovich, M. A., *Uranisme et Unisexualité. Etude sur différentes manifestations de l'instinct sexuel* (Lyons and Paris, 1896).

Raffles, T. S., *The History of Java* (London, 1817).

Ratzel, F., *Völkerkunde* (Leipzig and Vienna, 1894; 2nd ed., 1895).

Ravenscroft, A. G. B., 'Some habits and customs among the Chingalee tribe, Northern Territory, S.A.', *Transactions of the Royal Society of South Australia*, 15, 2 (1892), 121–2.

Raynal, G. T. F., *Histoire philosophique et politique des établissements et du commerce des Européens dans les Deux Indes*, ed. A. Jay and J. Peuchet (Paris, 1820–1).

Reade, W. W., *Savage Africa. Being the narrative of a tour in Equatorial, South-Western, and North-Western Africa, with notes on the habits of the gorilla, on the existence of Unicorns and tailed men, on the slave trade, on the origin, character, and capabilities of the Negro, and the future civilization of Western Africa* (London, 1863).

Reclus, E., *Les primitives. Etudes d'ethnologie comparée* (Paris, 1903).

Rehme, P., 'Über das Recht der Amaxosa', *ZfvR*, 10 (1892), 32–63.

Remlinger, P., 'La prostitution en Maroc', *Annales d'hygiène publique*, February 1913, pp. 129–30.

Rémy, J., *Ka Moolelo Hawaii. Histoire de l'archipel Hawaiien (Iles Sandwich). Texte et traduction précédés d'une introduction sur l'état physique, moral et politique du pays* (Paris, 1862).

Rencurel, [Dr], 'Les Sarimbavy. Perversion sexuelle observée en Émyrne', *Ahmc*, 3, 4 (October–December 1900), 562–8.

Richardson, J., *Arctic Searching Expedition: A Journal of a Boat Voyage through Rupert's Land and the Arctic Sea, in search of the Discovery Ships under Command of Sir John Franklin, with an Appendix on the Physical Geography of North America* (London, 1851).

Riedel, J. G., *De sluik- en kroesharige rassen tusschen Selebes en Papua* (The Hague, 1889).

Riedel, J. G., 'De Topantunuasu van Centraal Selebes', *BTLV*, 4th Series, 11 (1886), 75–96.

Robertson, W., *The History of America* (London, 1777).

Roscoe, J., 'A cow tribe of Enkole in the Uganda protectorate', *JRAI*, 37 (1907), 93–118.

Rosenbaum, J., *Geschichte der Lustseuche im Alterthume, nebst ausführlichen Untersuchungen über den Venus- und Phalluskult, Päderastie und andere geschlechtliche Ausschweifungen der Alten* (Leipzig, 1971 (Halle, 1839)).

Roth, H. Ling, *The Natives of Sarawak and British North Borneo* (London, 1896).

Rouille, H. E. O., Marquis de Boissy, *Les Mémoires du Marquis de Boissy* (Paris, 1870).

Rousseau, J.-J., *Les confessions* (Paris, 1963 (1770)).

Rozet, C. A., *Voyage dans la régence d'Alger* (Paris, 1833).

Rudorff, O., 'Tokugawa-Gesetz-Sammlung', *Mitteilungen der deutschen Gesellschaft für Natur- und Völkerkunde Ostasiens in Tokio*, 5 (1889), Supplement.

Sachau, E., *Muhammedanisches Recht nach Schafitischer Lehre* (Stuttgart, 1897).

Sacleux, C., *Dictionnaire Français-Swahili* (Paris, 1891).

Sagard, G., *Histoire du Canada* (Paris, 1865 (1636)).

Saint John, J. A., *Egypt and Mohammed Ali, or Travels in the Valley of the Nile*, 2 vols (London, 1834).

Saint John, S., *Life in the Forests of the Far East* (London, 1862).

Saint-Paul, G. (Dr Laupt), *Tares et poisons. Perversion et perversité sexuelles. Une enquête médicale sur l'inversion* (Paris, 1896).

Sarrasin, P., and Sarrasin, F., *Reisen in Celebes, ausgeführt in den Jahren 1893–1896 und 1902–1903* (Wiesbaden, n.d.).

Schaeffer, O., 'Beitrag zur Aetiologie der Schwanzbildungen beim Menschen', *Archiv für Anthropologie*, 20 (1920), 189–302.

Schidlof, B., *Das Sexualleben der Australier und Ozeanier* (Leipzig, 1908).

Schlegel, G., 'Iets over de prostitutie in China', *Verhandelingen van het Bataviaasch genootschap van kunsten en wetenschap*, 32, 3 (1866), 21–5.

Schlegel, G., 'Thian Ti Hwui. The Hung-League or Heaven-Earth-League. A secret society with the Chinese in China and India', *Verhandelingen van het Bataviaasch Genootschap van Kunsten en Wetenschappen*, 32 (1866), i–xl, 1–253.

Schmidt, W., 'Die soziologische und religiös-ethische Gruppierung der Australischen Stämme', *ZfE*, 41 (1909), 328–77.

Schneider, W., *Die Naturvölker. Missverständnisse, Missdeutungen und Misshandlungen* (Paderborn and Münster, 1885–6).

Schoelcher, V., *L'Egypte en 1845* (Paris, 1846).

Schopenhauer, A., *Die Welt als Wille und Vorstellung*, 3rd ed. (Leipzig, 1859).

Schrickert, W., 'Zur Anthropologie des gleichgeschlechtlichen Liebe', *Politisch-anthropologische Revue*, 1 (1902), 379–82.

Schultze, F., *Psychologie der Naturvölker. Entwicklungspsycho-logische Charakteristik des Naturmenschen in intellektueller, aesthetischer, ethischer und religiöser Beziehung. Eine natürliche Schöpfungsgeschichte menschlichen Vorstellens, Wollens und Glaubens* (Leipzig, 1900).

Schumacher, [Dr], 'Prostitution im modernen Ägypten', *Archiv für Menschenkunde*, 1 (1925/26), 61–4.

Schurtz, H., *Altersklassen und Männnerbunde. Eine Darstellung der Grundformen der Gesellschaft* (Berlin, 1902).

Schuyler, E., *Turkistan* (London, 1876).

Schwaner, C. A. L. M., *Borneo. Beschrijving van het stroomgebied van den Barito en Reisen langs eenige voorname rivieren van het zuid-oostelijk gedeelte van dat Eiland, op last van het Gouvernement van Nederlands Indië gedaan in de Jaren 1843–1847* (Amsterdam, 1853–4).

Schweinfurth, G., 'Tagebuch einer Reise zu den Niam-Niam und Monbattu 1870', *Zeitschrift der Gesellschaft für Erdkunde zu Berlin*, 7 (1872), 385–475.

Seemann, B., *Reise um die Welt und drei Fahrten der Köninchlich Britischen Fregatte Herald nach dem nordlichen Polarmeere zur Aufsuchung Sir John Franklin's in den Jahren 1845–1851* (Hanover, 1853).

Simonet, F. J., *Historia de los Mozarabes de España* (Madrid, 1897).

Skeat, W. W., *Malay Magic, being an Introduction to the Folklore and Popular Religion of the Malay Peninsula* (London, 1900).

Skertchly, J. A., *Dahomey as it is* (London, 1874).

Sonnerat, P., *Voyage aux Indes orientales et à la Chine fait par ordre du roi, depuis 1774 jusqu'en 1781, dans lequel on traite des moeurs, de la religion, des sciences & des arts des Indiens, des Chinois, des Péguins & des Madégasses, suivi d'Observations sur le Cap de Bonne-Espérance, les isles de France et de Bourbon* (Paris, 1782).

Southey, R., *History of Brazil* (London, 1810–19).

Soyaux, H., *Aus West-Afrika. 1873–1876. Erlebnisse und Beobachtungen* (Leipzig, 1879).

Spiess, G., *Die preussische Expedition nach Ostasien* (Leipzig, 1864).

Sprenger, A., *Das Leben und die Lehre des Mohammad* (Berlin, 1831).

Stavorinus, J. S., *Voyages to the East Indies*, trans. S. H. Wilocke (London, 1798).

Steele, E., and Madan, A. C. (eds), *A Handbook of the Swahili Language as Spoken at Zanzibar* (London, 1885).

Steindorff, G., *Durch die Lybische Wüste* (Bielefeld and Leipzig, 1904).

Steinmetz, S. R. (ed.), *Rechtsverhältnisse von Eingeborenen Völkern in Afrika und Ozeanien. Beantwortungen des Fragebogens der Internationalen Vereinigung für vergleichende Rechtswissenschaft und Volkswirtachftslehre zu Berlin* (Berlin, 1903).

Steller, G. W., *Beschreibung von dem Lande Kamtschatka, dessen Einwohner, deren Sitten, Nahmen, Lebensart und verschiedenene Gewohnheiten* (Frankfurt and Leipzig, 1774).

Stern, B., *Medizin, Aberglaube und Geschlechtsleben in der Türkei* (Berlin, 1903).

Stochove, V., *Voyage en Egypte*, ed. B. van de Walle (Cairo, 1975 (1634, 1650)).

Stoll, O., *Das Geschlechtsleben in der Völkerpsychologie* (Leipzig, 1908).

Swift, J., *Gulliver's Travels*, ed. H. Davis (Oxford, 1965 (1726)).

Symonds, J. A., *A Problem in Greek Ethics*, in J. A. Symonds, *Sexual Inversion*, ed. R. Michaels (New York, 1984), pp. 9–97.

Symonds, J. A., *A Problem in Modern Ethics*, in J. A. Symonds, *Sexual Inversion*, ed. R. Michaels (New York, 1984), pp. 101–91.

Tardieu, A., *Étude médico-légale sur les attentats aux moeurs* (Paris, 1867 (1857)).

Tarnowsky, V. M., *Die krankhaften Erscheinungen des Geschlechtssinnes: eine forensisch-psychiatrische Studie* (Berlin, 1886).

Ta Tsing Leu Lee, being the Fundamental Laws and a Selection from the Supplementary Statutes of the Penal Code of China, ed. and trans. G. T. Staunton (London, 1810).

Tessmann, G., *The Bafia und die Kultur der Mittelkamerun-Bantu* (Stuttgart, 1934).

Tessmann, G., 'Die Homosexualität bei den Negern Kameruns', *JfsZ*, 21 (1921), 121–38.

Tessmann, G., *Die Indianer Nordost-Perus. Grundlegende Forschungen für eine systematische Kulturkunde* (Hamburg, 1930).

Tessmann, G., *Die Pangwe. Völkerkundliche Monographie eines west-afrikanischen Neger-stammes*, 2 vols (Berlin, 1913).

Tessmann, G., 'Die Urkulturen der Menschheit', *ZfE*, 51 (1919), 132–62.

Theal, G. McCall, *History of the Boers in South Africa or The wanderings and wars of the emigrant farmers from their leaving the Cape Colony to the acknowledgement of their independence by Great Britain* (London, 1887).

Thevet, A., *Les Singularités de la France antarctique*, ed. F. Lestringant (Paris, 1983 (1577–8)).

Thomson, B., *The Fijians. A Study of the Decay of Custom* (London, 1908).

Tönjes, H., *Ovamboland, Land, Leute, Mission. Mit besonderer Berücksichtigung seines grössten Stammes Oukuanjama* (Berlin, 1911).

Toreen, O., *Eine ostindische Reise nach Suratte, China, etc. von 1750, den 1. April, bis 1752, den 26. Juni. In Briefen an den Herrn Archiater von Linné*, in *Herrn Peter Osbeck's Reise nach Ostindien und China*, translated from Swedish (Rostock, 1756).

Tornau, N. E., *Le droit musulman* (Paris, 1860).

Tourdel, G., 'Hermaphrodisme', in *Dictionnaire des sciences médicales*, vol. 13, p. 643.

Touron, R. P., *Histoire générale de l'Amérique depuis sa découverte, qui comprend l'histoire naturelle, ecclésiastique, militaire, morale & civile des contrées de cette grande partie du monde* (Paris, 1768–70).

Tregear, E., *A Paumotuan Dictionary with Polynesian Comparatives* (Wellington, New Zealand, 1895).

Trigault, N., and Ricci, M., *Histoire de l'expédition chrétienne envoyée en Chine (1582–1610)* (Paris, 1978 (first Latin edition 1615, first French édition Lyons, 1616)).

Trumpp, E., 'Einige Bemerkungen über den Sufismus', *ZdmG*, 16 (1862), 23–9.

Turnbull, J., *A Voyage round the World, in the years 1800, 1801, 1802, 1803, and 1804* (London, 1813).

Turner, G., *Samoa a hundred years ago and long before. Together with notes on the cults and customs of twenty-three other Islands in the Pacific* (London, 1884).

Tytheridge, A. C., 'Beobachtungen über Homosexualität in Japan', *JfsZ*, 22 (1922), 23–36.

Ulrichs, C. H., *Forschungen über das Rätsel der mannmännlichen Liebe* (New York, 1975 (Leipzig, 1864–73)).

Van Brero, P. C. J., 'Einiges über die Geisteskrankheiten der Bevölkerung des malaiischen Archipels. Beiträge zur vergleichenden Rassenpsychopathologie', *Allgemeine Zeitschrift für Psychologie und psychisch-gerichtliche Medicin*, 53 (1896), 25–78.

Van Brero, P. C. J., 'Die Nerven- und Geisteskrankheiten in den Tropen', in C. Mense (ed.), *Handbuch der Tropenkrankheiten* (Leipzig, 1905), vol. 1, pp. 210–35.

Van den Berg, L. W. C., *De beginselen van het Mohammedaansche Recht, volgens de Imma's Aboehanifaten Asj-Sjafe'i* (Batavia and The Hague, 1874).

Van der Burgt, J. M. M., *Dictionnaire Français-Kirundi avec l'initiation succincte de la signification Swahili et Allemagne* (Bois-le-Duc, 1903).

Van der Burgt, J. M. M., *Un grand peuple de l'Afrique Equatoriale. Elements d'une monographie sur l'Urundi et les Warundi*, 2 vols (Bois-le-Duc, 1903–4).

Van der Tuuk, H. N., *Kawi-Balineesch-Nederlandsch Woordenboek* (Batavia, 1897–1901).

Van Eck, R., 'Schetsen van het eiland Bali', *Tijdschrift voor Nederlandsch-Indië*, New Series, 7, 2 (1878), 85–130, 165–213, 325–56, 405–30; 8, 1 (1879), 36–60, 104–34, 286–305, 365–87; 9, 1 (1880), 1–39, 102–32, 195–221, 401–29; 9, 2, 1–18, 81–96.

van Eysinga, P. P. Roorda, *Algemeen Nederduitsch-Maleisch Woordenboek, in het hof-, volksen lage taal, met aanduiding der woorden die uit oostersche en westersche talen ontleend zijn; voorafgegaan van een beschouwing over de Maleijers, hunne geschiedenis, taal en hare verwantschap met Indische en andere talen; verrijkt met aanhalingen uit geschriften en vertalingen van volzinnen, gevolgt door een alphabetisch register van voorname plaatsen en personen* (The Hague, 1855).

Van Gennep, A., *Religions, moeurs et légendes. Essais d'ethnographie et de linguistique* (Paris, 1908–9).

Van Gennep, A., *Les rites de passage. Etude systématique des rites de la porte et du seuil, de l'hospitalité, de l'adoption, de la grossesse et de l'accouchement, de la naissance, de l'enfance, de la puberté, de l'initiation, de l'ordination, du couronnement, des fiançailles et du mariage, des funérailles, des saisons, etc.* (Paris, 1909).

van Linschoten, J. H., *The Voyage to the East Indies, from the English Translation of 1598*, ed. A. C. Burnell and P. A. Tiele (Hakluyt Society Publications, Old Series, 70/71), 2 vols (London, 1885).

van Meerdervoort, J. Pompe, *Vijf jaren in Japan, 1857–1863. Bijdragen tot de kennis van het Japansche keizerrijk en zijn bevolking*, 2 vols (Leyden, 1867–8).

van Noort, O., *Wonderlijcke Voyagie, by de Hollanders ghedaen door de Strate Magalanes, ende voorts den ganthschen kloot des aerdtbodems om, met vier Schepen: onder den Admirael Olivier van Noort, van Utrecht, uytgevaren anno 1598* (Utrecht, 1649).

Van Overbergh, C., *Les Basonge (Etat Ind. du Congo). Sociologie descriptive* (Brussels, 1908).

Van Overbergh, C., and De Jonghe, E., *Les Mayombe (Etat Ind. du Congo). Sociologie descriptive* (Brussels, 1907).

Varenius, B., *Descriptio Regni Japoniae* (Amsterdam, 1649).

Veigl, F. X., *Gründliche Nachrichten über die Verfassung der Landschaft von Mayas in Süd-Amerika, bis zum Jaher 1768*, in C. G. Von Murr, *Reisen einiger Missionarien der Gesellschaft Jesu in Amerika* ... (Nürnberg, 1785), pp. 1–324.

Velten, C., *Suaheli-Wörterbuch* (Berlin, 1910).

Venturi, S., 'Le degenerazioni psico-sessuali nella vita degli individui e nella storia della società', *Archivio delle psicopatie sessuali*, 4/5 (1896), 71–6.

Veth, P. J., *Java, geographisch, ethnologisch, historisch*, 3 vols (Haarlem, 1875–84).

Vincendon-Dumoulin, J., and Desgraz, C., *Iles Marquises ou Nouka-Hiva. Histoire, géographie, moeurs et considerations générales. D'après les relations des navigateurs et les documents recueillis sur les lieux* (Paris, 1843).

Virey, J., *De la femme sous ses rapports physiologiques, morals et littéraires*, 2nd ed. (Brussels, 1826).

Virey, J., *Histoire naturelle du genre humain, ou recherches sur les principaux fondemens physiques et moraux, précédées d'un discours sur la nature des êtres organiques, et sur l'ensemble de leur physiologie. On y a joint une dissertation sur le sauvage de l'Aveyron* (Paris, 1801).

Virey, J.,'Nègre', in *Dictionnaire des sciences médicales* (Paris, 1819), vol. 35, pp. 398–403.

Voltaire, F.-M. Arouet, *Dictionnaire philosophique*, ed. R. Pomeau (1964 (1764)).

Von Bülow, W., 'Das Geschlechtsleben der Samoaner', *Anthropophyteia*, 4 (1907), 84–99.

Von der Choven, H., 'Über sexuelle Perversionen im Orient', *Obozrénié psichiatrii*, 5 (1900), 229–34.

von der Steinen, K., *Unter den Naturvölkern Zentral-Brasiliens. Reiseschilderung und Ergebnisse der zweiten Schingú-Expedition 1887 bis 1888* (Berlin, 1894).

Von de Wall, C., 'Vervolg van het extract uit de dagelijksche aanteekeningen van den civielen gezaghebber voor Koetei en de Oostkust van Borneo', *Indisch Archief. Tijdschrift voor de Indiën*, 2, 3 (1850), 462–3.

von Diez, H. F., *Betrachtungen über das Buch des Kabus* (Berlin, 1811).

von Eschwege, W. L., *Journal von Brasilien, oder vermischte Nachrichten aus Brasilien, auf wissenschaftlichen Reisen gesammelt* (Weimar, 1818).

von Hahn, J. G., *Albanesische Studien* (Jena, 1854).

von Hellwald, F., *Culturgeschichte in ihrer natürlichen Entwicklung bis zur Gegenwart* (Augsburg, 1875).

von Herder, J. G., *Ideen zur Philosophie der Geschichte der Menschheit* (Riga and Leipzig, 1785–92).

von Hesse-Wartegg, E., *China und Japan*, 2nd ed. (Leipzig, 1900).

von Krafft-Ebing, R. F., *Psychopathia sexualis. Mit besonderer Berücksichtigung der konträren Sexualempfindung*, ed. O. Kruntorad (München, 1984).

von Kremer, A. F., *Culturgeschichtliche Streifzüge auf dem Gebiet des Islams* (Leipzig, 1873).

von Kupffer, E., *Lieblingsminne und Freundesliebe in der Weltliteratur. Eine Sammlung mit einer ethisch-politische Einleitung* (Berlin, 1900).

von Langsdorff, G. H., *Bemerkungen auf einer Reise um die Welt in den Jahren 1803 bis 1807* (Frankfurt, 1812).

von Martius, K. F. P., *Beiträge zur Ethnographie und Sprachenkunde Amerika's zumal Brasiliens* (Leipzig, 1867).

von Martius, K. F. P., *Das Naturell, die Krankheiten, das Arztthum und die Heilmittel der Urbewohner Brasiliens* (Munich, 1843).

von Martius, K. F. P., *Von den Rechtszustände unter den Ureinwohner Brasiliens* (Munich, 1832).

von Michluko-Maclay, N., 'Über die künstliche Perforatio Penis bei den Dajaks auf Borneo', *Verhandlungen der Berliner Gesellschaft für Anthropologie, Ethnologie und Urgeschichte* (1876), pp. 23–32.

von Osten, A. Graf Prokesch, *Denkwürdigkeiten* (Vienna, 1836).

von Pueckler-Muskau, H. L. H. Furst, *Aus Mehemed Ali's Reich* (Stuttgart, 1844).

von Reitzenstein, F., 'Der Kausalzusammenhang zwischen Geschlechtsverkehr und Empfängnis in Glaube und Brauch der Natur- und Kulturvölker', *ZfE*, 41 (1909), 644–83.

von Römer, L. S. A. M., *Het uranisch gezin. Wetenschappelijk onderzoek en conclusiën over homosexualiteit. Apologie voor het wissenschaftlich-humanitäre Komitée in Charlottenburg en den schrijver. Naar aanleiding van: Tegen het onnadenkend steunen van een ergerlijke en gevaarlijke propaganda – een waarschuwend woord van jhr.mr. W.F. Rochussen* (Amsterdam, 1905).

von Römer, L. S. A. M., 'Über die androgynische Idee des Lebens', *JfsZ*, 5 (1903), 707–921.

von Rosenzweig, V., *Auswahl aus den Diwanen des Dschelaleddin Rumi* (Vienna, 1838).

von Samson-Himmelstjerna, H., *Die gelbe Gefahr als Moralproblem* (Berlin, 1902).

von Schrenk-Notzing, A., *Die Suggestionstherapie bei den krankhaften Erscheinungen des Geschlechtssinnes, mit besonderer Berücksichtigung der conträren Sexualempfindung* (Stuttgart, 1892).

von Seidlitz, W., *Geschichte des Japanischen Farbenholzschnitts* (Dresden, 1897).

von Spix, J. B., and von Martius, K. F. P., *Reise in Brasilien auf Befehle Sr. Majestät Maximilian Joseph I. Königs von Baiern in den Jahren 1817 bis 1820 gemacht und geschrieben* (Munich, 1823–31).

von Tschudi, J. J., *Culturhistorische und sprachliche Beiträge zur Kenntnis des alten Perús* (Denkschriften des kaiserlichen Akademie der Wissenschaften in Wien, Philosophisch-historische Classe, 39) (Vienna, 1891).

von Zimmerman, E. A. W., *Taschenbuch der Reisen, oder unterhaltende Darstellung der Entdeckungen des 18 Jahrhunderts, in Rücksicht der Länder-, Menschen- und Produkten-kunde, für jede Klasse von Lesern*, 9, 2 (Leipzig, 1810).

Waitz, T., and Gerland, G., *Anthropologie der Naturvölker*, 6 vols (Leipzig, 1859–72).

Wallace, A. R., *A Narrative of Travels on the Amazon and Rio Negro, with an Account of the Native Tribes, and Observations of the Climate, Geology, and Natural History of the Amazon Valley*, 2nd ed. (London, New York, Melbourne, 1889).

Wallace, D. M., *Egypt and the Egyptians* (London, 1863).

Walsh, R., *Narrative of a Journey from Constantinople* (London, 1838).

Waterhouse, J., *The King and People of Fiji: containing a life of Thakombau, with notices of the Fijians, their manners, customs, and superstitions, previous to the great religious reformation in 1854* (London, 1866).

Weeks, J. H., 'Anthropological notes on the Bangala of the Upper Congo River', *JRAI*, 39 (1909), 97–136, 416–59.

Weipert, H., 'Das Shinto-Gebet der Grossen Reinigung (Ohara no kotoba)', *Mitteilungen der deutschen Gesellschaft für Natur- und Völkerkunde Ostasiens in Tokio*, 58 (1897), 365–75.

Werne, F., *Expedition zur Entdeckung der Quellen des weissen Nils (1840–1)* (Berlin, 1852).

Wernich, A., *Geographisch-medizinische Studien nach den Erlebnissen einer Reise um die Erde* (Berlin, 1878).

Wernich, A., 'Über einige Formen nervöser Störungen bei den Japanern', *Mitteilungen der deutschen Gesellschaft für Natur- und Völkerkunde Ostasiens in Tokio*, 10 (1876), 17.

Westermann, D., *Wörterbuch der Ewe-Sprache*, 2 vols (Berlin, 1905–6).

Westermarck, E., *The History of Human Marriage*, 3 vols (London, 1891).

Westermarck, E., 'The Moorish conception of holiness', *Finska Vetenskaps-Societetens Forhandlingar*, 58 (1915–16), 85–9.

Westermarck, E., *The Origin and Development of the Moral Ideas* (London, 1926 (1906–8).

Westermarck, E., *Ritual and Belief in Morocco*, 2 vols (London, 1926).

Westphal, C. F. O., 'Die konträre Sexualempfindung. Symptom eines neuropathischen (psychopathischen) Zustandes', *APN*, 2 (1869), 73–108.

White, C., *An Account of the Regular Gradation in Man* (London, 1793).

White, C., *Three Years in Constantinople or Domestic Manners of the Turks* (London, 1845).

Wilhelm, E., [Untitled], *Sexualprobleme*, 7 (1911), 850–2.

[Wilhelm, E.], 'Über gleichgeschlechtlichen Verkehr in Algerien und Tunis', *Anthropophyteia*, 7 (1910), 179–88.

Wilken, G. A., 'De besnijdenis bij de volken van den Indischen Archipel', *BTLV*, 4th Series, 10, 2 (1885), 165–206.

Wilken, G. A., 'Het shamanisme bij de volken van den Indischen Archipel', *BTLV*, 5th Series, 2 (1887), 427–97.

Wilken, G. A., 'Plechtigheden en gebruiken bij verlovingen en huwelijken bij de volken van den Indischen Archipel', *BTLV*, 5th series, 4 (1889), 380–462.

Wills, C. J., *Persia as it was* (London, 1886).

Wilson, J., *A Missionary Voyage to the Southern Pacific Ocean performed in the years 1796, 97, 98 in the Ship Duff, etc.* (London, 1799).

Wilson, S. G., *Persian Life and Customs* (New York, 1899 (Edinburgh, 1896)).

Wundt, W., *Völkerpsychologie*, 10 vols (Leipzig, 1900–20).

Wuttke, A., *Geschichte des Heidentums in Beziehung auf Religion, Wissen, Kunst, Sittlichkeit und Staatsleben*, 2 vols (Breslau, 1852–3).

Wuttke, H., 'Über Hammer-Purgstall's Literaturgeschichte der Araber', *ZdmG*, 9 (1855), 166–82.

X, J., *L'amour aux colonies. Singularités physiologiques et passionnelles observées durant trente années de séjour dans les Colonies Françaises Cochinchine, Tonkin et Cambodge, Guyane et Martinique, Sénégal et Rivières du Sud, Nouvelle Calédonie, Nouvelles Hébrides et Tahiti* (Paris, 1893).

X, J., *L'ethnologie du sens génital. De l'amour. Etude physiologique de l'amour normale, ses abus, perversions, folies et crimes dans l'espèce humaine* (Paris, 1901 (1898)).

Zinkeisen, J. W., *Geschichte des Osmanischen Reiches in Europa* (Gotha, 1855).

Zschokke, H.,'Eros oder über die Liebe', in H. Zschokke, *Ausgewählte Novellen und Dichtungen* (Aarau, 1841).

zu Wied-Neuwied, M., *Reise in das innere Nord-Amerika in den Jahren 1832 bis 1834* (Coblenz, 1839).

Secondary literature

Adam, B. D., *The Rise of a Gay and Lesbian Movement* (Boston, 1987).

Affergan, F., *Exotisme et altérité. Essai sur les fondements d'une critique de l'anthropologie* (Paris, 1987).

Alain, 'Voltaire, fut-il un infâme?', *Arcadie*, 3 (March 1954), 27–34.

Aldrich, R., *The Seduction of the Mediterranean. Writing, Art and Homosexual Fantasy* (London and New York, 1993).

Aldrich, R., 'Weise und farbige Männer. Reisen, Kolonialismus und Homoseksualität zwischen den Rassen in der Literatur', *Forum. Homosexualität und Literatur*, 7 (1989), 6–24.

Altman, D., *et al.* (eds), *Homosexuality, which Homosexuality? Essays from the International Scientific Conference on Lesbian and Gay Studies* (Amsterdam and London, 1989).

Amadiume, I., *Male Daughters, Female Husbands, Gender and Sex in an African Society* (London, 1987).

L'Amérique vue par l'Europe. Paris, Grand Palais, 17 septembre 1976–3 janvier 1977 (Paris, 1976).

Among Men, Among Women. Sociological and Historical Recognition of Homosocial Arrangements, International Conference, Amsterdam, June 1983 (Amsterdam, 1983).

Anderson, M. M., *Hidden Power. The Palace Eunuchs of Imperial China* (Buffalo, 1990).

Arboleda, M., and Murray, S. O., 'The dangers of lexical inference with special reference to Maori homosexuality', *JHom*, 12 (1986), 129–34.

Ariès, P., and Béjin, A. (eds), 'Sexualités Occidentales' issue of *Communications*, 35 (1982).

Aron, J.-P., *Le pénis et la démoralisation de l'occident* (Paris, 1978).

Austen, R. A., and Smith, W. D., 'Images of Africa and British slave trade abolition: The transition to an imperialist ideology, 1787–1807', *African Historical Studies*, 2, 1 (1969), 66–83.

Austin, A. L., *The Human Body and Ideology: Concepts of the Ancient Nahuas*, 2 vols (Salt Lake City, 1988).

Azoulai, M., *Les péchés du Nouveau Monde. Les manuels pour la confession des Indiens, XVIe–XVIIe siècle* (Paris, 1993).

Baião, A., *A inquisição de Goa* (Lisbon, 1930 and 1945).

Bailey, D., *Homosexuality and the Western Christian Tradition* (London, 1955).

Baldauf, I., *Die Knabenliebe in Mittelasien: Bačabozlik* (Ethnizität und Gesellschaft, Occasional Papers, 17) (Berlin, 1988).

Banton, M., *Racial Theories* (Cambridge, 1987).

Barbedette, G., and Carassou, M., *Paris gay 1925* (Paris, 1981).

Barbier, P., *Les castrats* (Paris, 1989).

Barker-Benfield, G. J., 'The spermatic economy: A nineteenth-century view of sexuality', *Feminist Studies*, 1, 1 (Summer 1972), 45–74.

Bartra, R., *El salvaje en el espejo* (Mexico, 1992).

Baudet, H., *Paradise on Earth. Some Thoughts on European Images of Non-European Man* (New Haven, 1965).

Baudrillard, J., *La transparence du mal. Essai sur les phénomènes extrêmes* (Paris, 1990).

Baumann, H., *Das doppelte Geschlecht. Studien zur Bisexualität in Ritus und Mythos* (Berlin, 1986 (1955)).

Bauserman, R., 'Man-boy sexual relationships in a cross-cultural perspective', *Paidika*, 2, 1 (Summer 1989), 28–40.

Beaglehole, J. C., 'Eighteenth-century science and voyages of discovery', *New Zealand Journal of History*, 3 (1969), 107–23.

Beauchesne, H., *Histoire de la psychopathologie* (Paris, 1986).

Beck, J., 'Montaigne face à l'homosexualité', *Bulletin de la Société des Amis de Montaigne*, 9/10 (1982), 41–50.

Bennassar, B., *L'inquisition espagnole (XVe–XIXe siècle)* (Paris, 1979).

Bernand, C., and Gruzinski, S., 'La Redécouverte de l'Amérique', *L'homme*, 32, 122/124 (April–December 1992), 13–15.

Bernheimer, R., *Wild Men in the Middle Ages. A Study in Art, Sentiment and Demonology* (New York, 1970).

Bhabha, H. (ed.), *Nation and Narration* (New York and London, 1990).

Bhabha, H. K., 'Of mimicry and man: the ambivalence of colonial discourse', *October*, 28 (Spring 1984), 125–33.

Bhabha, H. K.,'The other question: Difference, discrimination and the discourse of colonialism', in Ferguson, R., et al. (eds), *Out There: Marginalization and Contemporary Cultures* (New York and Cambridge, MA, 1990), pp. 71–87.

Bing, F., 'La théorie de la dégénérescence', in J. Postel and Cl. Quétel (eds), *Nouvelle histoire de la psychiatrie* (Toulouse, 1983), pp. 351–6.

Biondi, C., 'L'Afrique des philosophes: lieu mythique, terre d'hommes ou entrepôt de marchandises', in D. Droixhe and P.-P. Gossiaux (eds), *L'homme des Lumières et la découverte de l'autre* (Etudes sur le XVIIIe siècle, hors série, 3) (Brussels, n.d.), pp. 191–7.

Birken, L., 'Darwin and gender', *Social Concept*, 4 (1987), 75–88.

Bitterli, U., *Die Entdeckung des schwarzen Afrikaners* (Zürich, 1965).

Bitterli, U., *Die 'Wilden' und die 'Zivilisierten'. Grundzüge einer Geistes- und Kulturgeschichte der europäisch-überseeischen Begegnung* (Munich, 1976).

Blackburn, R., *The Overthrow of Colonial Slavery, 1776–1848* (London, 1988).

Blackstone, B., 'Byron and Islam: The triple eros', *Journal of European Studies*, 4 (1974), 325–62.

Blackwood, E., 'Breaking the mirror: The construction of lesbianism and the anthropological discourse on homosexuality', *JHom*, 11, 3/4 (Summer 1985), 1–4.

Blanchard, R., and de Candé, R., *Dieux et Divas de l'opéra* (Paris, 1986).

Bleibtreu-Ehrenberg, G., *Mannbarheitsriten: zur institutionellen Päderastie bei Papuas und Melanesiern* (Berlin, 1980).

Bleys, R. C., 'Homosexual exile: The textuality of imaginary paradise, 1800–1980', *JHom*, 25, 1/2 (1993), 165–82.

Bleys, R. C., 'Perversie in het paradijs. Over kolonisatie en homoseksualiteit', *Homologie*, 10 (1988), 4–7.

Bleys, R. C., 'Les réseaux textuels du paradis imaginaire', *Sociétés*, 29 (1990), 65–72.

Bloch, O., and Porset, C. (eds), 'le matérialisme au siècle des Lumières', special issue of *Le dix-huitième siècle*, 24 (1992).

Bonnet, M.-J., *Un choix sans équivoque. Recherches historiques sur les relations amoureuses entre les femmes, XVIe–XXe siècle* (Paris, 1981).

Borès, M., *La beauté de Cham. Mondes juifs, mondes noirs* (Paris, 1992).

Borie, J., *Mythologies de l'hérédité au XIXe siècle* (Paris, 1981).

Boswell, J., *Christianity, Social Tolerance, and Homosexuality. Gay People in Western Europe from the Beginning of the Christian Era to the Fourteenth Century* (Chicago and London, 1980).

Boucé, P.-G., 'Les jeux interdits de l'imaginaire: onanisme et culpabilisation sexuelle au XVIIIe siècle', in J. Céard (ed.), *La folie et le corps* (Paris, 1985), pp. 223–43.

Boucé, P.-G. (ed.), *Sexuality in Eighteenth-Century Britain* (New York and Manchester, 1982).

Boudhiba, A., *La sexualité en Islam* (Paris, 1984 (1975)).

Boudhiba, A., 'La société maghrébine face à la question sexuelle', *Cahiers internationaux de sociologie*, 76 (1984), 91–110.

Bouge, J. L., 'Un aspect du rôle rituel du 'mahū' dans l'ancien Tahiti', *Journal de la Société des Océanistes*, 11 (1955), 147–9.

Bourdieu, P., *La distinction sociale. Critique sociale du jugement* (Paris, 1979).

Bouyer, M., *L'Amérique espagnole vue et rêvée. Les livres de voyages de Colomb à Bougainville, 1492–1767* (Paris, 1992).

Bowler, P. J., 'The changing meaning of "evolution" ', *Journal of the History of Ideas*, 36 (1975), 95–114.

Bowler, P. J., *Theories of Evolution: a Century of Debate, 1844–1944* (Oxford, 1986).

Boxer, C. R., *The Christian Century in Japan, 1549–1650* (Berkeley, 1974 (1951)).

Boyajian, J. C., 'Goa inquisition: New light on first 100 years', *Purabhilekh-Puratatva*, 4/1 (1986), 1–41.

Brahimi, D., *Opinions et regards des Européens sur le Maghreb aux XVIIe et XVIIIe siècles* (Alger, 1978).

Brandon, W., *New Worlds for Old. Reports from the New World and their Effect on the Development of Social thought in Europe, 1500–1800* (Athens, OH and London, 1986).

Bravmann, S., 'Telling (hi)stories: Rethinking the lesbian and gay historical imagination', *Out/ Look*, 8 (Spring 1990), 68–74.

Bravmann, S., 'The lesbian and gay past: It's Greek to whom?', *Gender, Place and Culture*, 1, 2 (1994), 149–67.

Bray, A., *Homosexuality in Renaissance England* (London, 1982).

Brodie, F. M., *The Devil Drives. A Life of Sir Richard Burton* (New York and London, 1967).

Brongersma, E., *Jongensliefde. Seks en erotiek tussen jongens en mannen*, vol. 1: *Partners* (Amsterdam, 1987).

Brown, D. E., and Edwards, J. W., and Moore, R. P., 'The penis inserts of southeast Asia: An annotated bibliography with an overview and comparative perspectives' (Occasional Paper Series, 15) (Berkeley, 1988).

Brown, T., 'From mechanism to vitalism in eighteenth-century English physiology', *Journal of the History of Biology*, 7 (1974), 179–216.

Brown, W. C., 'Byron and English interest in the East', *Studies in Philology*, 34 (1937), 55–64.

Brownley, M. W., 'Gibbon's artistic and historical scope in the *Decline and Fall*', *Journal of the History of Ideas*, 42,4 (October–December 1981), 634–56.

Brundage, J. A., *Law, Sex and Christian Society in Medieval Europe* (Chicago and London, 1987).

Bullough, V. L., 'The physician and research into human sexual behaviour in nineteenth-century Germany', *BHMed*, 63 (1989), 247–267.

Bullough, V. L., *Sexual Variance in Society and History*, Chicago-London, 1976.

Burckhardt, R. W., *The Spirit of System. Lamarck and Evolutionary Biology* (Cambridge and London, 1977).

Burg, B. R., *Sodomy and the Pirate Tradition. English Sea Rovers in the Seventeenth-Century Caribbean* (New York, 1983).

Busst, A. J. L., 'The image of the androgyne in the nineteenth century', in I. Fletcher (ed.), *Romantic Mythologies* (London, 1967), pp. 1–95.

Bynum, W. F., 'The nervous patient in eighteenth- and nineteenth-century Britain: the psychiatric origins of neurology', in Bynum, W. F., *et al.* (eds), *The Anatomy of Madness. Essays in the History of Psychiatry*, vol. 1: *People and Ideas* (London and New York, 1985), pp. 89–102.

Cabezón, J. I. (ed.), *Buddhism, Sexuality, and Gender* (Albany, 1992).

Cahiers Internationaux de Sociologie, 'le sexuel', 76 (1984).

Calder-Marshall, A., *Havelock Ellis* (London, 1959).

Callender, C., and Kochems, L. M., 'Men and not-men: Male gender-mixing statuses and homosexuality', *JHom*, 11, 3/4 (1985), 165–78.

Callender, C., and Kochems, L. M., 'The North American berdache', *Current Anthropology*, 24 (1963), 443–70.

Campbell, M. B., *The Witness and the Other World. Exotic European Travel Writing, 400–1600* (Ithaca and London, 1988).

Cardín, A., *Guerreros, chamanes y travestís. Indícios de homosexualidad entre los exóticos* (Barcelona, 1984).

Cardon, P., 'A homosexual militant at the beginning of the century: Marc André Raffalovich', *JHom*, 25, 1/2 (1993), 183–92.

Cardy, M., *Diderot et la sexualité, Studies on Voltaire and the Eighteenth Century*, 264 (1989), 866–7.

Carrasco, R., *Inquisición y represión sexual en Valencia. História de los sodomitas (1565–1785)* (Barcelona, 1985).

Carvalho dos Santos, M. H. (ed.), *Inquisição. Comunicações apresentadas ao 1º Congreso Luso-brasileiro sobre Inquisição, realizado em Lisboa de 17 a 20 de Fevereiro de 1987* (Lisbon, 1989).

Chamberlin, J. E., 'An anatomy of cultural melancholy', *Journal of the History of Ideas*, 42 (1981), 691–706.

Chamberlin, J. E., and Gilman, S. L. (eds), *Degeneration. The Dark Side of Progress* (New York, 1985).

Charlton, D. G., *New Images of the Natural in France. A Study in European Cultural History, 1750–1800* (Cambridge, 1984).

Chauncey, Jr., G., 'From sexual inversion to homosexuality: Medicine and the changing conceptualization of female deviance', *Salmagundi*, 58/59 (Fall 1982/Winter 1983), 114–46.

Chebel, M., *Le corps dans la tradition au Maghreb* (Paris, 1984).

Chebel, M., *L'esprit de sérail. Perversions et marginalités sexuelles au Maghreb* (Paris, 1988).

Childs, M. H., 'Chigo Monogatari: Love stories or Buddhist sermons', *Monumenta Nipponica*, 35, 2 (Summer 1980), 127–51.

Childs, M. H., 'Japan's homosexual heritage', *Gai Saber*, 1 (1977), 41–5.

Chrisman, L., 'The imperial unconscious? Representations of imperial discourse', *Critical Quarterly*, 32, 2 (1990), 39–58.

Chushichi, T., *Edward Carpenter, 1844–1929: Prophet of Human Fellowship* (New York and Cambridge, 1980).

Clair, J., *et al.* (eds), *Wunderblock. Eine Geschichte der Seele* (Vienna, 1989).

Clarke, C., 'The failure to transform: Homophobia in the black community', in B. Smith (ed.), *Home Girls: A Black Feminist Perspective* (New York, 1983), 197–208.

Clastres, H., 'Sauvages et civilisés au XVIIIe siècle', in P. Châtelet (ed.), *Histoire des idéologies* (Paris, 1978), vol. 3, p. 221.

Clifford, J., *The Predicament of Culture. Twentieth-Century Ethnography, Literature, and Art* (Cambridge, MA and London, 1988).

Clifford, J., and Marcus, G. E. (eds), *Writing Culture. The Poetics and Politics of Ethnography* (Berkeley and London, 1986).

Cohen, W. B., *The French Encounter with Africans: White Responses to Blacks, 1550–1880* (Bloomington and London, 1980).

Cominos, P. T., 'Late Victorian sexual respectability and the social system', *International Review of Social History*, 8 (1963), 18–48, 216–50.

Conze, W., 'Evolution und Geschichte. Die doppelte Verzeitlichung des Menschen', *HZ*, 242 (1986), 1–30.

Cook, B. W., 'The historical denial of lesbianism', *Radical History Review*, 20 (Spring/Summer 1979), 60–5.

Cooper, F, and Stoler, A. L., 'Tensions of empire: colonial control and visions of rule', *American Ethnologist*, 16 (1989), 609–21.

Copley, A., *Sexual Moralities in France, 1780–1980. New Ideas on the Family, Divorce and Homosexuality. An Essay on Moral Change* (London and New York, 1989).

Corbey, R., *Wildheid en beschaving. De Europese verbeelding van Afrika* (Baarn, 1989).

Corbin, A., *Les filles de noce. Misère sexuelle et prostitution, 19e–20e siècles* (Paris, 1978).

Corbin, A., *Le miasme et la jonquille. L'odorat et l'imaginaire social, 18ᵉ–19ᵉ siècles* (Paris, 1982).

Cory, D. W. (ed.), *Homosexuality: A Cross-cultural Approach* (New York, 1956).

Courouve, C., *Les assemblées de la Manchette: documents sur l'amour masculin au XVIII siècle et pendant la Révolution* (Paris, 1988).

Courouve, C., *Vocabulaire de l'homosexualité masculine* (Paris, 1985).

Coward, D. A., 'Attitudes to homosexuality in eighteenth-century France', *Journal of European Studies*, 10 (1980), 231–55.

Crespo, J., *A história do corpo* (Lisbon, 1990).

Cressole, M., and Huguier, F., *Sur les traces de l'Afrique fantôme* (Paris, 1990).

Crompton, L., *Byron and Greek Love. Homophobia in Nineteenth-Century England* (Berkeley, 1985).

Croutier, A. Lytle, *Harem. The World behind the Veil* (New York, 1989).

Curtin, P. (ed.), *Africa and the West. Intellectual Responses to European Culture* (Madison, 1972).

Curtin, P. D., *The Image of Africa. British Ideas and Action, 1780–1850* (Madison, 1964).

Dabydeen, D. (ed.), *The Black Presence in English Literature* (Manchester, 1985).

Dall'Orto, G., 'Il concetto di degenerazione nel pensiero borghese dell'Ottocento', *Sodoma. Rivista omosessuale*, 2 (Summer 1985), 59–74.

Daniel, M., *Libertins du Grand Siècle* (Paris, 1960).

Daniel, M., 'A study of homosexuality in France during the reign of Louis XIII and Louis XIV', *Homophile Studies. One Institute Quarterly*, 14/15 (1961), 77–93, 125–36.

Dannecker, M., 'Towards a theory of homosexuality: Socio-historical perspectives', *JHom*, 9,4 (Summer 1984), 1–8.

Dannecker, M., 'Vorwort', in W. J. Schmidt (ed.), *Jahrbuch für sexuelle Zwischenstufen. Herausgegeben im Namen des wissenschaftlich-humanitäres Comitées von Magnus Hirschfeld. Auswahl aus den Jahrgängen 1899–1923* (Frankfurt/Main, 1983), pp. 5–15.

Darmon, P., *Le tribunal de l'impuissance* (Paris, 1979).

Davies, C. Glynn, *Conscience as Consciousness: The Idea of Self-Awareness in French Philosophical Writing from Descartes to Diderot, Studies on Voltaire and the Eighteenth Century*, 272 (1990), 108–51.

Davis, D. L., and Whitten, R. G., 'The cross-cultural study of human sexuality', *Annual Reviews in Anthropology*, 16 (1987), 69–98.

de Albuequerque, L. *et al.*, *O confronto de olhar. O encontro dos povos na Época das Navegações Portuguesas. Séculos XV e XVI* (Lisbon, 1991).

Debeuckelaere, G., 'Hoe meer zielen, hoe meer vreugde. Homosubkultuur in Antwerpen, 1781', *Homokrant*, (Feb. 1983), 9–12.

de Fontenay, E., 'Diderot gynéconome', *Digraphe*, 7 (1976), 29–50.

Delcourt, M., *Hermaphrodites. Mythes et rites de la bisexualité dans l'antiquité classique* (Paris, 1958).

Dellamora, R., *Masculine Desire: The Sexual Politics of Victorian Aestheticism* (Chapel Hill, 1990).

Delon, M., 'Corps sauvages, corps étranges', *Le dix-huitième siècle*, 9 (1977), 27–38.

Delon, M., 'Du goût antiphysique des Américains', *Annales de Bretagne et des pays de l'ouest*, 34, 2 (1977), 317–30.

Delon, M., 'Un monde d'eunuques', *Europe*, 55 (1977), 79–88.

Delon, M., 'Le prétexte anatomique', *Le Dix-huitième siècle*, 12 (1980), 35–47.

de Martino, G., and Schmitt, A., *Kleine Schriften zu zwischenmännlicher Sexualität und Erotik in der muslimischen Gesellschaft* (Berlin, 1985).

D'Emilio, J., and Freedman, E. B., *Intimate Matters. A History of Sexuality in America* (New York, 1988).

de Pedrals, D. P., *La vie sexuelle en Afrique noire* (Paris, 1950).

Dijkstra, B., 'The androgyne in nineteenth-century art and literature', *Comparative Literature*, 26 (1974), 62–73.

Diouf, M. X., 'Goor-jigeen', *GPH*, 521 (March 21, 1991), 16–18.

Doig, F. Kauffmann, *Sexualverhalten im Alten Peru* (Lima, 1979).

Donoghue, E., *Passions between Women. British Lesbian Culture, 1668–1801* (London, 1993).

Donovan, J. M., [Untitled], *ARGOH Newsletter*, 9, 3 (October 1987), 15–17.

Donzelot, J., *La police des familles* (Paris, 1977).

Douglas, M., *Natural Symbols* (New York, 1973).

Dover, K., *Greek Homosexuality* (Cambridge, 1978).

Dowling, L., *Hellenism and Homosexuality in Victorian Oxford* (Ithaca and London, 1994).

Dreischer, S., 'The ending of the slave trade and the evolution of European scientific racism', *Social Science History*, 14, 3 (Fall 1990), 15–45.

Drucker, P.,' "In the tropics there is no sin": Homosexuality and gay/lesbian movements in the third world', International Institute for Research and Education, Amsterdam, Working Paper 31 (1993).

Duberman, M. B., 'Documents in Hopi Indian sexuality. Imperialism, culture, and resistance', *Radical History Review* (Spring/Summer 1979), 99–130.

Duberman, M. B., *et al.* (eds), *Hidden from History. Reclaiming the Gay and Lesbian Past* (New York, 1989).

Duchesneau, F., *La physiologie des Lumières* (The Hague, 1982).

Duchet, M., *Anthropologie et histoire au siècle des Lumières. Buffon, Voltaire, Rousseau, Helvétius, Diderot* (Paris, 1977 (1971)).

Duden, B., *Geschichte unter der Haut. Ein Eisenacher Arzt und seine Patientinnen um 1730* (Stuttgart, 1987).

Duerr, H. P., *Traumzeit. Ueber die Grenze zwischen Wildnis und Zivilisation* (Frankfurt/Main, 1978).

Dunne, B. W., 'Homosexuality in the Middle East: an agenda for historical research', *Arab Studies Quarterly*, 12, 3/4 (Summer/Fall 1990), 55–82.

Dunton, C., 'Wheyting be dat? The treatment of homosexuality in African literature', *Research in African Literatures*, 20 (1989), 422–48.

Duviols, J.-P.,'L'image européenne du 'bon sauvage' américain', in *Les Amériques et l'Europe. Voyage – émigration – exil. Actes de la 3ième semaine Latino-Américaine, Université de Toulouse-le Mirail, 12–15 mars 1984* (Toulouse, 1985), pp. 27–36.

Dynes, W. R., *Homolexis. A Historical and Cultural Lexicon of Homosexuality*, Gai Saber Monographs, 4 (New York, 1985).

Dynes, W. R., 'Homosexuality in Subsaharan Africa: an unnecessary controversy', *Gay Books Bulletin*, 9 (Spring/Summer 1983), 20–1.

Dynes, W. R. (ed.), *Encyclopedia of Homosexuality*, 2 vols (New York, 1990).

Dynes, W. R.,, and Donaldson, S. (eds), *Studies in Homosexuality*, vol. 2: *Ethnographic Studies of Homosexuality* (New York, 1992–3).

Edelman, L., *Homographesis. Essays on Gay Literature and Cultural Theory* (London and New York, 1994).

Ehrard, J., *L'idée de nature en France dans la première moitié du XVIIIe siècle (Paris, 1963)*.

Eldorado. Homosexuelle Frauen und Männer in Berlin, 1850–1950. Geschichte, Alltag und Kultur (Berlin, 1984).

Elliott, J. H., *The Old World and the New* (Cambridge, 1970).

Escamilla, M. 'À propos d'un dossier inquisitorial des environs de 1590: les étranges amours d'un hermaphrodite', in Redondo, A. (ed.), *Amours légitimes, amours illégitimes en Espagne (VIe–XVIIe siècles)* (Paris, 1985), pp. 167–82.

Escoffier, J., 'Inside the ivory closet: The challenges facing lesbian and gay studies', *OutLook. National Lesbian and Gay Quarterly*, 10 (Fall 1990), 40–8.

Europe and its Others. Proceedings of the Essex Conference on the Sociology of Literature, July 1984, 2 vols (Colchester, 1985).

Evans, A., *Witchcraft and the Gay Counterculture* (Boston, 1978).

Evans, W. M., 'From the land of Canaan to the land of Guinea. The strange adventures of the sons of Cham', *AHR*, 85 (1980), 15–43.

Evans-Prichard, E. E., 'Sexual inversion among the Azande', *American Anthropology*, 72 (1970), 1428–34.

Fabregat, E. Esteva, *El mestizaje en Iberoamérica* (Madrid, 1988).

Faderman, L., *Surpassing the Love of Men. Romantic Friendship and Love between Women from the Renaissance to the Present* (London, 1981).

Fanon, F., *Les damnés de la terre* (Paris, 1961).

Fanon, F., *Peau noire, masques blancs* (Paris, 1952).

Farwell, B., *A Biography of Sir Richard Francis Burton*, 2nd ed. (Westport, 1975).

Faupel, J. F., *African Holocaust: The Story of the Uganda Martyrs* (London, 1965).

Féray, J.-C., 'Une histoire critique du mot "homosexualité" ', *Arcadie*, 325 (January 1981), 11–21; 326 (February 1981), 115–24; 327 (March 1981), 171–81; 328 (April 1981), 246–58.

Ferguson, M. W., *et al.* (eds), *Rewriting the Renaissance. The Discourses of Sexual Difference in Early Modern Europe* (Chicago and London, 1988).

Fernandez, D., *Le rapt de Ganymède* (Paris, 1989).

Filho, M. Maestri, 'Sodomitas e luxuriosos', unpub. MS (n.p., n.d.).

Fitzgerald, T. K., 'A critique of anthropological research on homosexuality', *JHom*, 2, 4 (Summer 1977), 385–97.

Fone, B. R. S., 'The other Eden: Arcadia and the homosexual imagination', *JHom*, 8 (1983), 13–32.

Fontijn, J., *Leven in extase* (Amsterdam, 1983).

Ford, C. S., and Beach, F. A., *Patterns of Sexual Behavior* (New York, 1953).

Foster, S. W.,'The annotated Burton', in Crew, L. (ed.), *The Gay Academic* (Palm Springs, 1978), pp. 92–101.

Foster, S. W., 'Homosexuality and the Inquisition in Brazil, 1591–1592', *Gay Sunshine*, 38/39 (n.d.), 17–18.

Foucault, M., *Histoire de la sexualité*, 3 vols (Paris, 1976–84).

Fout, J. C., 'Sexual politics in Wilhelmine Germany: The male gender crisis, moral purity, and homophobia', *JHS*, 2 (1992), 388–421.

Fout, J. C., and Oosterhuis, H. (eds), *Male Homosexuals, Lesbians, and Homosexuality in Germany: the Kaiserreich through the Third Reich, 1871–1945* (Chicago and London, 1992).

Freedman, E. B., 'Sexuality in nineteenth-century America: Behavior, ideology, and politics', *Reviews in American History* (December 1982), pp. 196–215.

Frost, A., *The Pacific Ocean – the Eighteenth-Century's 'New World'*, *Studies on Voltaire and the Eighteenth Century*, 152 (1976), 779–882.

Fry, P., *Para Inglês ver. Identidade e politica na cultura brasileira* (Rio de Janeiro, 1982).

Fry, P., 'Sexe et rôles de genre interactifs dans le Brésil contemporain', *Sociétés*, 2, 2 (February 1986), 13–15.

Galzigna, M., *La malattia morale. Alle origini della psichiatria moderna* (Venice, 1988).

Garrett, D., 'Other countries: the importance of difference', in Johnson, C. A., *et al.* (eds), *Other Countries. Black Gay Voices* (New York, 1988), pp. 17–28.

Garrett, S., *Gender* (London, 1987).

Gates, Jr., H. L. (ed.), *Black Literature and Literary Theory* (New York, 1984).

Gates, Jr., H. L. (ed.), *'Race', Writing, and Difference* (Chicago and London, 1986).

Gay, P., *The Bourgeois Experience. Victoria to Freud*, 3 vols (New York, 1984–92).

Genovese, E.D., *Roll, Jordan, Roll! The World the Slaves Made* (London, 1975).

Gerard, K., and Hekma, G. (eds), *The Pursuit of Sodomy: Male Homosexuality in Renaissance and Enlightenment Europe* (New York, 1989).

Gerbi, A., *La disputa del Nuevo Mundo. Historia de una polémica, 1750–1900* (Mexico, D.F., 1982 (It. 1955; Sp. 1960)).

Gewecke, F., *Wie die neue Welt in die alte kam* (Stuttgart, 1986).

Gil, J., *Mito y realidad de los descubrimientos*, 3 vols (Madrid, 1992).

Gilman, S. L., 'Black bodies, white bodies: Toward an iconography of female sexuality in late nineteenth-century art, medicine and literature', *Critical Inquiry*, 12 (Autumn 1985), 204–42.

Gilman, S. L.,'Black sexuality and German consciousness', in Grimm, R., and Hermand, J. (eds), *Blacks and German Culture* (Madison, 1986), pp. 35–53.

Gilman, S. L., *Difference and Pathology. Stereotypes of Sexuality, Race, and Madness* (Ithaca and London, 1985).

Gilman, S. L., *Sexuality. An Illustrated History. Representing the Sexual in Medicine and Culture from the Middle Ages to the Age of AIDS* (New York, 1989).

Gilmore, D. D. (ed.), *Honour and Shame and the Unity of the Mediterranean* (Washington, 1987).

Ginzburg, C., *Mythes, emblèmes, traces. Morphologie et histoire* (Paris, 1988).

Gluckman, L. K., 'Transcultural consideration of homosexuality with special reference to the New Zealand Maori', *Australian and New Zealand Journal of Psychiatry*, 8, 1 (1974), 121–5.

Goedegebuure, J., *Decadentie en literatuur* (Amsterdam, 1987).

Goiteen, S.D., 'The sexual mores of the common people', in Al-Sayyid-Marsot, A. L. (ed.), *Society and the Sexes in Medieval Islam* (Mailibu, 1979), pp. 43–62.

Gomes, A. 'De homossexualidade ao diformismo sexual entre os indígenas e a questão da moral ameríndia', *Revista do Instituto Histórico e Geográfico de São Paulo*, 52 (1953), 323–8.

Goodich, M., 'Sodomy in medieval secular law', *JHom*, 1, 3 (1976), 295–302.

Goodich, M., *The Unmentionable Vice: Homosexuality in the Later Medieval Period* (Santa Barbara, 1979).

Gorender, J., *O escravismo colonial* (São Paulo, 1978).

Gossiaux, P.-P., 'Anthropologie des Lumières (Culture "naturelle" et racisme rituel)', in Droixhe, D., *et al.* (eds), *L'homme des Lumières et la découverte de l'Autre* (Brussels, 1985), pp. 53–9.

Gourvennec, P., 'Amours étrangères', *GPH*, 477 (4 July 1991), 78–81.

Gourvennec, P., 'Le gai voyage ou les transports amoureux', *GPH*, 428/429 (12 July 1990), 112–17.

Grafton, A., *New Worlds, Ancient Texts. The Power of Tradition and the Shock of Discovery* (New York, 1992).

Grau, G., 'Hirschfeld Über die Ursachen der Homosexualität – zur Bedeutung seiner ätiologischen Hypothesen', *Mitteilungen der Magnus Hirschfeld Gesellschaft*, 13 (May 1989), 27–30.

Greenberg, D. F., *The Construction of Homosexuality* (Chicago and London, 1988).

Greenberg, D. F., 'Why was the Berdache ridiculed?', *JHom*, 11, 3/4 (Summer 1985), 179–90.

Greenblatt, S., *Marvelous Possessions. The Wonder of the New World* (Chicago and London, 1991).

Greig, N., 'Introduction', in Carpenter, E., *Selected Writings*, vol. 1: *Sex*, ed. N. Greig (London, 1984), pp. 1–77.

Grmek, M. D., 'Géographie médicale et histoire des civilisations', *Annales. E.S.C.*, 18 (1963), 1071–97.

Groppe, H.-H., 'Abenteuer und Eroberung. Was treibt die Männer in die Welt?', in *Männersache. Bilder, Welte, Objekte* (Hamburg, 1987), pp. 58–75.

Grosskurth, P., *Havelock Ellis. A Biography* (New York, 1980).

Grosskurth, P.,'Introduction', in *The Memoirs of John Addington Symonds*, ed. P. Grosskurth (New York, 1984), pp. 13–28.

Grosskurth, P., *The Woeful Victorian: A Biography of John Addington Symonds* (New York, 1964).

Gruzinski, S., 'Las cenizas del deseo. Homosexuales novohispanos a mediados del siglo XVII', in Ortéga, S. (ed.), *De la santidad a la perversión. O de por qué no se cumplía la ley de Dios en la sociedad novohispana* (Mexico, D.F., 1986), pp. 255–82.

Gruzinski, S., 'Confesión, alianza y sexualidad entre los indios de Nueva España. Introducción al estudio de los Confesionarios en lenguas indígenas', in Ortéga, S. (ed.), *El placer de pecar y el afán de normar* (Mexico, D.F., n.d.), pp. 169–215.

Guasch, O., 'La medicalización del sexo', *Revista ROL de Enfermería*, 179–80 (July/August 1993), 27–32.

Guerra, F., *The Pre-Columbian Mind. A Study into the Aberrant Nature of Sexual Drives, Drugs affecting behaviour, and the Attitudes towards Life and Death, with a Survey of Psychotherapy in Pre-Columbian America* (London, 1971).

Guicciardi, J.-P., 'Hermaphrodite et le prolétaire', *Le Dix-huitième siècle*, 12 (1980), 49–77.

Gunson, N., *Messengers of Grace: Evangelical Missionaries in the South Seas, 1797–1860* (Melbourne, 1978).

Gusdorf, G., *Les sciences humaines et la pensée occidentale*, vol. 6: *L'avènement des sciences humaines au siècle des Lumières* (Paris, 1973).

Gutiérrez, R. A., 'Must we eradicate Indians to find gay roots?', *Out/Look*, (Winter 1989), 61–7.

Gutiérrez, R. A., *When Jezus Came, the Corn Mothers Went Away. Marriage, Sexuality, and Power in New Mexico, 1500–1846* (Stanford, 1991).

Gutman, H., *The Black Family in Slavery and Freedom, 1750–1925* (New York, 1976).

Guyénot, E., *Les sciences de la vie au 17e et 18e siècles* (Paris, 1957).

Haeberle, E. J., *The Birth of Sexology. A Brief History in Documents* (Washington, DC, 1983).

Hafkamp, H., and Van Lieshout, M. (eds), *Pijlen van naamloze liefde. Pioniers van de homo-emancipatie* (Amsterdam, 1988).

Hahn, P., 'Islam: le sexe arabe', *GPH*, 76 (2 July 1983), 21–4.

Hall, D., *In Miserable Slavery: Thomas Thistlewood in Jamaica, 1750–86* (Houndsmills, 1989).

Hall, S., 'Reconstruction work', *Ten.8*, 16 (1984), 7–15.

Hall, S. *et al.*, *Culture, Media Language: Working Papers in Cultural Studies 1972–1979* (London, 1980).

Hama, A., 'Les vies cachées des grands aventuriers', *GPH*, 268/269 (4 May 1987), 22–6.

Hankins, T. L., *Science and the Enlightenment* (Cambridge, 1985).

Haraway, D., *Primate Visions. Gender, Race, and Nature in the World of Modern Science* (New York and London, 1989).

Harrisson, T. 'The "palang", its history and proto-history in West-Borneo and the Philippines', *Journal of the Malaysian Branch of the Royal Asiatic Society*, 37, 2 (1964), 162–74.

Harvey, A. D., 'Prosecutions for sodomy in England at the beginning of the nineteenth century', *Historical Journal*, 21 (1978), 939–48.

Haskell, F., 'd'Hancarville: an adventurer and art historian in eighteenth-century Europe', in Chaney, E., and Ritchie, N. (eds), *Oxford, China, and Italy. Writings in Honour of Sir Harold Acton on his Eightieth Birthday* (London, 1984), 177–91.

Hastings, M., *Sir Richard Burton. A Biography* (New York, 1978).

Hekma, G., *Homoseksualiteit, een medische reputatie. De uitdoktering van de homoseksueel in negentiende-eeuws Nederland* (Amsterdam, 1987).

Hekma, G., 'Rewriting the history of Sade', *JHS*, 1, 1 (July 1990), 131–6.

Hekma, G., 'De verre einders van de homoseksuele verlangens. Homoseksualiteit en culturele antropologie', *Homologie*, 8, 6 (November–December 1986), 37–9.

Herdt, G. H., *Guardians of the Flute. Idioms of Masculinity. A Study of Ritualized Homosexual Behavior* (New York, 1981).

Herdt, G. H., 'Representations of homosexuality: An essay on cultural ontology and historical comparison, Part I' and 'Part II', *JHS*, 1, 3 (January 1991), 481–504; 1, 4 (April 1991), 603–22.

Herdt, G. H., *The Sambia. Ritual and Gender in New Guinea* (New York, 1987).

Herdt, G. H. (ed.), *Ritualized Homosexuality in Melanesia* (Berkeley, 1984).

Herdt. G. H. (ed.), *Third Sex, Third Gender. Beyond Sexual Dimorphism in Culture and History* (New York and Cambridge, MA, 1994).

Heriot, A., *The Castrati in Opera* (London, 1956).

Herren, R., *La Conquista erótica de las Indias* (Barcelona, 1991).

Herzer, M., 'Kertbeny and the nameless love', *JHom*, 12 (1985), 3–4.

Herzer, M., *Magnus Hirschfeld. Leben und Werk eines jüdischen, schwulen und sozialistischen Sexologen* (Frankfurt, 1992).

Higginbotham, Jr., A. L., *In the Matter of Color: Race and the American Legal Process: The Colonial Period* (New York and Oxford, 1978).

Hinsch, B., *Passions of the Cut Sleeve. The Male Homosexual Tradition in China* (Berkeley, 1990).

Hoch, P., *White Hero, Black Beast* (New York, 1979).

Hodgen, M. T., *Early Anthropology in the Sixteenth and Seventeenth Centuries* (Philadelphia, 1971 (1964)).

Hoffmann, P., *La femme dans la pensée des Lumières* (Paris, 1977).

Hohmann, J. S., *Sexualforschung und -aufklärung in der Weimarer Republik. Ein Übersicht in Materialien und Dokumenten* (Berlin, 1985).

Homosexualité & lesbianisme: mythes, mémoires, historiographies. Actes du colloque international, Sorbonne, Paris, 1–2 déc. 1989, vol. 1, 1: *Histoire* (Paris and Lille, 1989).

Honour, H., *The New Golden Land. European Images of America from the Discoveries to the Present Time* (New York, 1975).

Honour H., *The Image of the Black in Western Art* (Cambridge and London, 1989).

hooks, b., *Outlaw Culture. Resisting Representations* (London and New York, 1994).

Hoyle, R. L., *Checan. Essay on Erotic Elements in Peruvian Art* (Geneva, 1965).

Hubbard, M. S. H., and Friend, B. (eds), *Women Look at Biology Looking at Women* (Cambridge, 1979).

Hubbard, R., *The Politics of Women's Biology* (New Brunswick, 1989).

Hughes, R., *The Fatal Shore. A History of the Transportation of Convicts to Australia, 1787–1868* (London, 1987).

Hulme, P., and Jordanova, L. (eds), *The Enlightenment and Its Shadows* (London, 1990).

Husband, T. (ed.), *The Wild Man. Medieval Myth and Symbolism* (New York, 1980).

Hütter, J., *Die gesellschaftliche Kontrolle des homosexuellen Begehrens. Medizinische Definitionen und juristische Sanktionen im 19. Jahrhundert* (Frankfurt, 1992).

Hyam, R., 'Concubinage and the Colonial Service. The Crewe Circular (1909)', *Journal of Imperial and Commonwealth History*, 14 (1986), 170–86.

Hyam, R., *Empire and Sexuality. The British Experience* (Manchester and New York, 1990).

Hyde, M. H., *The Other Love: An Historical and Contemporary Survey of Homosexuality in Britain* (London, 1970).

La imágen del Indio en la Europa Moderna, ed. Consejo Superior de Investigaciones Científicas – Fundación Europea de la Ciencia – Escuela de Estudios Híspano-Americanos (Sevilla, 1990).

Irizarry, E., 'Echos of the Amazon myth in medieval Spanish literature', in Miller, B. (ed.), *Women in Hispanic Literature: Icons and Fallen Idols* (Berkeley, 1983), pp. 53–66.

Jackson, P. A., *Male Homosexuality in Thailand. An Interpretation of Contemporary Thai Sources* (Elmhurst, 1989).

Jacobs, M., *et al.* (eds), *Body/Politics. Women and the Discourses of Science* (London, 1990).

Jara, F., 'Les monstres dans l'imaginaire des indiens d'Amérique latine', in *Le Monstre*, 4, ed. E. Magaña (Paris, 1988), pp. 49–79.

Jenkyns, R., *The Victorians and Ancient Greece* (Cambridge, MA, 1980).

Johnson, C. A., 'Male homosexuality in Africa', MA thesis, Columbia University (New York, 1991).

Joosse, K., *Arnold Aletrino. Pessimist met perspectief* (Amsterdam and Brussels, 1986).

Jordan, W., *White over Black: American Attitudes toward the Negro, 1550–1812* (Chapel Hill, 1977 (1968)).

Jordanova, L., *Sexual Visions. Images of Gender in Science and Medicine between the Eighteenth and Twentieth Centuries* (New York, 1989).

Journal of Contemporary History, 'Decadence', 17, 1 (1982).

Kabbani, R., *Europe's Myths of Orient. Devise and Rule* (Houndsmills, 1986).

Kaiser, R., 'Josef von Hammer-Purgstall. Sprachknabe, Diplomat, Orientalist', in Sievernich, G., and Budde H. (eds), *Europa und der Orient, 800–1900. Lesebuch* (Berlin, 1989), pp. 106–14.

Kaplan, P. (ed.), *The Cultural Construction of Sexuality* (London and New York, 1987).

Karash, M. B., *Slave Life in Rio de Janeiro, 1808–1850* (Princeton, 1987).

Katz, J., *Gay American History. Lesbians and Gay Men in the U.S.A.* (New York, 1976).

Katz, J., *Gay/Lesbian Almanac. A New Documentary* (New York, 1983).

Kennedy, H., *Ulrichs: The Life and Works of Karl Heinrich Ulrichs, Pioneer of the Modern Gay Movement* (Boston, 1988).

Kiernan, V. G., *The Lords of Human Kind. Black Man, Yellow Man, and White Man in an Age of Empire* (Boston, 1969).

Kinsman, G., *The Regulation of Desire: Sexuality in Canada* (Montreal, 1987).

Kirkpatrick, B. J. (ed.), *Catalogue of the Library of Sir Richard Burton, M.C.M.G., held by the Royal Anthropological Institute* (London, 1978).

Klockmann, T., 'Vom Geheimnis menschlicher Gefühle. Günther Tessmanns Pangwe-Monographie im Lichte seiner Lebenserinnerungen sowie neuerer Forschungen', *Wiener Ethnohistorische Blätter*, 29 (1986), 3–20.

Knauft, B. M., 'The question of ritualized homosexuality among the Kiwai of South New Guinea', *Journal of Pacific History*, 25 (1990), 188–210.

Koebner, Th. and Pickerodt, G. (eds), *Die andere Welt. Studien zum Exotismus* (Frankfurt, 1987).

Kramer, F. W., 'Eskapistische und utopische Motive in der Frühgeschichte der deutschen Ethnologie', in Pollig, H., *et al.* (eds), *Exotische Welten, Europäische Phantasien* (Stuttgart, 1987).

Kristeva, J., *Etrangers à nous mêmes* (Paris, 1988).

Kritzman, L. D., *The Rhetoric of Sexuality and the Literature of the French Renaissance* (Cambridge, 1990).

LaCapra, D., *Rethinking Intellectual History: Texts, Contexts, Language* (Ithaca and London, 1983).

Lach, D., *Asia in the Making of Europe*, 2 vols (Chicago, 1965).

Lanteri-Laura, C., *Lecture des perversions: histoire de leur appropriation médicale* (Paris, 1979).

Laqueur, T. W., ' "Amor Veneris, vel Dulcedo Appeletur" ', in Feher, M., *et al.* (eds), *Fragments for a History of the Human Body* (New York, 1989), vol. 3, pp. 91–131.

Laqueur, T. W., *Making Sex. Body and gender from the Greeks to Freud* (Cambridge and London, 1990).

Laqueur, T. W., 'Orgasm, generation and the politics of reproductive biology', *Representations*, 14 (April 1986), 1–41.

Lauritsen, J., and Thorstad, D., *The Early Homosexual Rights Movement (1864–1935)* (New York, 1974).

Lavrín, A. (ed.), *Sexuality and Marriage in Colonial Latin America* (Lincoln, Nebraska, 1986).

Lecouteux, C., *Les monstres dans la littérature allemande du Moyen Age* (Göttingen, 1982).

Leites, E., *The Puritan Conscience and Modern Sexuality* (New Haven, 1986).

Lemaire, T., *De Indiaan in ons bewustzijn. De ontmoeting van de Oude met de Nieuwe Wereld* (Baarn, 1986).

Leneman, H., 'Reclaiming Jewish history: Homo-erotic poetry of the Middle Ages', *Changing Men*, Summer/Fall 1987, 22–3.

Lever, M., *Les bûchers de Sodome* (Paris, 1985).

Levy, R. I., 'The community function of Tahitian male transvestism', *Anthropological Quarterly*, 44 (1971), 12–21.

Leyland, W. (ed.), *Gay Roots: Twenty Years of Gay Sunshine. An Anthology of Gay History, Sex, Politics & Culture* (San Francisco, 1991).

Libis, J., *Le mythe de l'androgyne* (Paris, 1980).

Licata, S. J., and Petersen, R. P. (eds), *Historical Perspectives on Homosexuality* (New York, 1981).

Liégeois, A., 'Hidden philosophy and theology in Morel's theory of degeneration and nosology', *History of Psychiatry*, 2 (1991), 419–27.

Livi, J., *Vapeurs de femmes. Esquisse historique de quelques fantasies médicales et philosophiques* (Paris, 1984).

Lyotard, J.-F., *La condition postmoderne* (Paris, 1979).

MacCormack, C. P., and Strathern, M. (eds), *Nature, Culture and Gender* (Cambridge, 1980).

Maccubbin, R. P. (ed.), *Unauthorized Sexual Behaviour during the Enlightenment* (Williamsburg, 1985).

Mackerras, C. P., *The Rise of the Peking Opera, 1770–1870: Social Aspects of the Theatre in Manchu China* (Oxford, 1972).

MacRae, E., *A construição da igualdade. Identidade sexual e politica no Brasil da 'Abertura'* (Campinas, 1990).

Madlener, E., 'Ein kabbalistischer Schauplatz. Die physiognomische Seelenerkundung', in Clair, J., *et al.* (eds), *Seelenblock. Eine Geschichte der modernen Seele* (Vienna, 1989), pp. 159–79.

Magaña, E., and Mason, P., 'Tales of otherness, myths, stars and Plinian men in South America', in Magaña, E., and Mason, P. (eds), *Myth and the Imaginary in the New World*, CEDLA Latin American Studies, 34 (Amsterdam and Dordrecht, 1986), 7–40.

Magnan, J. A. and Walvin, J. (eds), *Manliness and Morality. Middle-Class Masculinity in Britain and America, 1800–1940* (New York, 1987).

Malinowski, B., *Sex and Repression among the Savages* (London, 1927).

Marcovich, A., 'French colonial medicine and colonial rule: Algeria and Indochina', in MacLeod, R., and Lewis, M. (eds), *Disease, medicine, and Empire. Perspectives on Western Medicine and the Experience of European Expansion* (London and New York, 1988), pp. 103–17.

Marsan, H., 'Les écrivains de l'exil', *Masques*, 18 (Summer 1983), 69–74.

Mason, P., *Deconstructing America. Representations of the Other* (London and New York, 1990).

Mass, L., 'Sexual categories, sexual universals. An interview with John Boswell', *Christopher Street*, 13, 6 (1990), 23–40.

Mattoso, K. de Queiros, *Ser escravo no Brasil* (São Paulo, 1982).

May, T. J., and Bonner, R., 'Introduction', in Darwin, Charles, *The Descent of Man, and Selection in Relation to Sex* (Princeton, 1981), pp. 1–7.

Mayer, H., *Aussenseiter* (Frankfurt/Main, 1975).

McLynn, F., *Snow upon the Desert: Sir Richard Burton, 1821–1890* (London, 1991).

Meier, A., *Negro Thought in America, 1880–1915* (Ann Arbor, 1966).

Mercer, K., and Julien, I., 'Race, sexual politics and black masculinity: A dossier', in Chapman, R., and Rutherford, J. (eds), *Male Order. Unwrapping masculinity* (London, 1988), pp. 97–164.

Meyers, J., *Fiction and the Colonial Experience* (Ipswich, 1973).

Michler, A. G., 'Ambiguità e trasmutazione. Discussioni mediche e giuridiche in epoca moderna (secoli XVII e XVIII)', *Memoria. Rivista di storia delle donne*, 24, 3 (1988), 43–60.

Miles, S. W., 'The 16th century Pokom-Maya: A documentary analysis of social structure and archaeological setting', *Transactions of the American Philosophical Association* (1957), 763–4.

Miller, C. L., *Blank Darkness. Africanist Discourse in French* (Chicago and London, 1986).

Miller, N., *Out in the World. Gay and Lesbian Life from Buenos Aires to Bangkok* (Harmondsworth, 1992).

Mitter, P., *Much Maligned Monsters: The History of the European Reaction to Indian Art* (Oxford, 1977).

Monter, W., 'La sodomie à l'époque moderne en Suisse romande', *Annales. E.S.C.*, 39 (1974), 1023–33.

Monter, W., *Frontiers of Heresy. The Spanish Inquisition from the Basque Lands to Sicily* (Cambridge and New York, 1989).

Montrose, L., 'The Work of gender in the discourse of discovery', *Representations*, 33 (Winter 1991), 1–41.

Morris, R., 'Aikāne: Accounts of Hawaiian same-sex relationships in the journal of Captain Cook's third voyage (1776–80)', *JHom*, 18 (1990), 21–54.

Mort, F., *Dangerous Sexualities. Medico-Moral Politics in England since 1830* (London and New York, 1987).

Mosse, G. L., *Towards the Final Solution: A History of European Racism* (New York, 1978).

Mosse, G. L., 'Nationalism and respectability: Normal and abnormal sexuality in the nineteenth century', *JCH*, 17 (1982), 228–30.

Mosse, G. L., *Nationalism and Sexuality. Respectability and Abnormal Sexuality in Modern Europe* (New York, 1985).

Mott, L., 'Escravidão e homossexualidade', in Vainfas, R. (ed.), *História e sexualidade no Brasil* (Rio de Janeiro, 1986), pp. 19–40.

Mott, L., 'Pagode português: a subcultura gay em Portugal nos tempos inquisitoriais', *Ciência e Cultura*, 40 (1988), 120–39.

Mott, L., 'Relações raciais entre homossexuais no Brasil Colônia', in Mott, L., *Escravidão, homossexualidade e demonologia* (São Paulo, 1988), pp. 19–47.

Mott, L., *O sexo proibido. Virgens, gays e escravos nas garras da inquisição* (Campinas, n.d.).

Müller, K., 'Aber im meinem Herzen sprach eine Stimme so laut: Homosexuelle Autobiographien und medizinische Pathographien im neunzehnten Jahrhundert,' *Homosexualität und Literatur*, 4 (Berlin, 1991).

Murphy, M. D., 'Masculinity and selective homophobia: A case from Spain', *ARGOH Newsletter*, 5, 3 (Summer/Fall 1984), 6–12.

Murray, D. H., *Pirates of the South China Coast* (Stanford, 1987).

Murray, S. O., 'The history of anthropology's lavender fringe', *ARGOH Newsletter*, 6, 1 (January 1985), 8–10.

Murray, S. O., *Oceanic Homosexualities*, Garland Gay and Lesbian Studies, ed. W. R. Dynes, 7 (New York, 1992).

Murray, S. O., *Social Theory, Homosexual Realities*, Gai Saber Monographs, 3 (New York, 1984).

Murray, S. O., 'Sodomites in pre-Inca cultures on the west coast of South America', unpublished ms.

Murray, S. O. (ed.), *Cultural Diversity and Homosexualities* (New York, 1987).

Murray, S. O. (ed.), *Male Homosexuality in Central and South America*, Gai Saber Monograph, 5 (San Francisco, 1987).

Naim, C. M.,'The theme of homosexual (pederastic) love in pre-modern Urdu poetry', in Memon, M. Umar (ed.), *Studies in the Urdu Gazal and Prose Fiction* (Madison, 1979), pp. 120–42.

Nanda, S., 'The hijras of India: Cultural and individual dimensions of an institutionalized third gender role', *JHom*, 11, 3/4 (1985), 35–54.

Nanda, S., *Neither Man nor Woman. The Hijras of India* (Belmont, 1990).

Naudin, P., 'Une arithmétique des plaisirs: esquisse d'une réflexion sur la morale de Maupertuis', *Actes de la Journée Maupertuis* (Paris, 1975), pp. 12–34.

Al-Nefzawi, *The Glory of the Perfumed Garden. The Missing Flowers*, trans. H. E. J. (London, 1975).

Nero, C. I.,'Towards a black gay aesthetic. Signifying in contemporary black gay literature', in Hemphill, E. (ed.), *Brother to Brother. New Writings by Black Gay Men* (Boston, 1991), pp. 229–52.

Ng, S.-M. Xiaomingxiong, *Zhongguo tongxingai shilu* (History of Homosexuality in China) (Hong Kong, 1984).

Norton, R., *Mother Clap's Molly House. The Gay Subculture in England, 1700–1830* (London, 1992).

Nye, R. A., 'The biomedical origins of urban sociology', *JCH*, 20 (1985), 659–75.

Nye, R. A., *Crime, Madness and Politics in Modern France. The Medical Concept of National Decline* (Princeton, 1984).

Nye, R. A., 'Honor, impotence, and male sexuality in nineteenth-century French medicine', *French Historical Studies*, 16 (1989), 48–71.

Nye, R. A., 'Sex difference and male homosexuality in French medical discourse, 1830–1930', *BHMed*, 63 (1989), 32–51.

Oaks, R. F., 'Perceptions of homosexuality by justices of peace in Colonial America', *Sexual Law reporter*, 4 (1978), 33–7.

Oaks, R. F., ' "Things fearful to name": Sodomy and buggery in seventeenth-century New England', *Journal of Social History*, 12 (1978), 268–81.

Olivier, G., 'Conquérants et missionnaires face au "péché abominable". Essai sur l'homosexualité en Mésoamérique au moment de la conquête espagnole', *Caravelle*, 55 (1990), 19–51.

Oosterhuis, H., and Kennedy, H. (eds), *Homosexuality and Male Bonding in Pre-Nazi Germany. The Youth Movement, the Gay Movement, and Male Bonding before Hitler's Rise. Original Transcripts from Der Eigene, the First Gay Journal of the World* (New York, 1991).

Opler, M. K., 'Anthropological and cross-cultural aspects of homosexuality', in Marmor, J. (ed.), *Sexual Inversion. The Multiple Roots of Homosexuality* (New York and London, 1965), pp. 108–23.

Ortner, S. B., and Whitehead, H. (eds), *Sexual Meanings. The Cultural Construction of Gender and Sexuality* (Cambridge, 1981).

Padgug, R., 'Sexual matters: on conceptualizing sexuality in history', *Radical History Review*, 20 (1979), 3–23.

Pagden, A., *European Encounters with the New World. From Renaissance to Romanticism* (New Haven, 1993).

Pagden, A., *The Fall of Natural Man. The American Indian and the Origins of Comparative Ethnology* (Cambridge and New York, 1982).

Paglia, C., *Sexual Personae. Art and Decadence from Nefertiti to Emily Dickinson* (New Haven, 1990).

Papin, B., *Sens et Fonction de l'Utopie tahitienne dans l'oeuvre politique de Diderot, Studies on Voltaire and the Eighteenth Century*, S.l. (1988), 251.

Parker, A., *et al.* (eds), *Nationalisms and Sexualities* (New York and London, 1992).

Parker, R., *Bodies, Pleasures and Passions. Sexual Culture in Contemporary Brazil* (Boston, 1991).

Parry, M. E., and Cruz, A. J. (eds), *Cultural Encounters. The Impact of the Inquisition in Spain and the New World* (Berkeley, 1991).

Pauvert, J.-J., *Sade vivant*, vol.1: *Une innocence sauvage, 1740–1777* (Paris, 1986).

Penzer, N. M., *An Annotated Bibliography of Sir Richard Francis Burton* (London, 1923).

Perry, M. B., *Crime and Society in Early Modern Seville* (Hannover, NH, 1980).

Perry, M. B., *Gender and Disorder in Early Modern Seville* (Princeton, 1991).

Pick, D., *Faces of Degeneration. A European Disorder, c. 1848 – c. 1918* (Cambridge and New York, 1989).

Pierrot, J., *L'imaginaire décadent (1880–1900)* (Paris, 1977).

Plummer, K. (ed.), *The Making of the Modern Homosexual* (London, 1981).

Poirier, G., 'French Renaissance travel accounts: Images of sin, visions of the New World', in Mendes-Leite, R., and De Busscher, O. (eds), *Gay Studies from the French Cultures* (Binghamton, 1993), pp. 215–29.

Poliakov, L., *Le mythe aryen* (Paris, 1971).

Pope-Henessey, J., *Monckton Milnes: The Flight of Youth, 1851–1885* (London, 1951).

Pope-Hennessey, J., *Monckton Milnes: The Years of Promise, 1809–1851* (London, 1940).

Porter, D., *Haunted Journeys. Desire and Transgression in European Travel Writing* (Princeton, 1991).

Porter, R., 'Bodies of thought: Thoughts about the body in eighteenth-century England', in Pittock, J. H., and Wear, A. (eds), *Interpretation and Cultural History* (London, 1991), 82–108.

Porter, R., *The Enlightenment* (London, 1990).

Praz, M., *The Romantic Agony* (Oxford, 1988 (Ital. 1930)).

Preston, L. W., 'A right to exist: Eunuchs and the state in nineteenth-century India', *Modern Asian Studies*, 2, 2 (1987), 368–81.

Price, D. H., *Atlas of World Cultures. A Geographical Guide to Ethnographic Literature* (Newbury Park, London and New Delhi, 1990).

'Queer theory. Lesbian and gay sexualities', special issue of *Differences. A Journal of Feminist Cultural Studies*, 3, 2 (Summer 1991).

Quétel, C., *Le Mal de Naples. Histoire de la syphilis* (Paris, 1986).

Quoy-Bodin, J. L., 'Autour de deux sociétés libertines sous Louis XIV: L'Ordre de la Félicité et l'Ordre Hermaphrodite', *Revue Historique*, 276 (1986), 57–84.

Rahman, T., 'Boy love in the Urdu Ghazal', *Paidika*, 2, 1 (Summer 1989), 10–27.

Rasch, W., *Die literarische Décadence um 1900* (Munich, 1986).

Redondo, A. (ed.), *Le problème de l'exclusion en Espagne (XVIᵉ–XVIIᵉ siècles). Idéologie et discours. Colloque international, Sorbonne, 13, 14 et 15 mai 1982* (Paris, 1983).

Rey, M., 'L'art de "raccrocher" au XVIIIe siècle', *Masques*, 24 (Winter 1984/85), 92–9.

Rey, M., 'Parisian homosexuals create a lifestyle, 1700–1750. The police archives', *Eighteenth-Century Life*, 9 (1985), 179–91.

Rey, M., 'Police et sodomie à Paris au XVIIIᵉ siècle: du péché au désordre', *Revue d'histoire moderne et contemporaine*, 39 (January–March 1982), 113–24.

Rigotti, F., 'Biology and society in the age of enlightenment', *Journal of the History of Ideas*, 47, 2 (April–June 1986), 215–33.

Robertson, J., 'The politics of androgyny in Japan. Sexuality and subversion in the theater and beyond', *American Ethnologist*, 19 (1992), 419–42.

Robinson, P., *The Modernization of Sex. Havelock Ellis, Alfred Kinsey, William Masters and Virginia Johnson* (New York, 1976).

Rocke, M. J., 'Policing homosexuality in 15th century Florence: the Ufficiali di Notte', *Quaderni Storici*, 22, 3 (December 1987), 701–24.

Roger, J., *Buffon, un philosophe au Jardin du Roi* (Paris, 1989).

Roger, J., *Les sciences de la vie dans la pensée française du XVIIIᵉ siècle: la génération des animaux de Descartes à l'Encyclopédie* (Paris, 1963).

Roscoe, W., *The Zuni Man-Woman* (Albuquerque, 1991).

Roth, N., ' "Deal gently with the young man": Love of boys in medieval Hebrew poetry of Spain', *Speculum*, 57 (1982), 20–51.

Rousseau, G. S., 'Cultural history in a new key: Towards a semiotics of the nerve', in Pittock, J. H., and Wear, A. (eds), *Interpretation and Cultural History* (London, 1991), 25–81.

Rousseau, G. S., *Perilous Enlightenment: Pre- and Postmodern Discourses. Sexual, Historical* (Manchester, 1991).

Rousseau, G. S., and Porter, R. (eds), *Exoticism in the Enlightenment* (Manchester, 1990).

Rousseau, G. S., and Porter, R. (eds), *The Ferment of Knowledge. Studies in the Historiography of Eighteenth-Century Science* (Cambridge and New York, 1980).

Rousseau, G. S., and Porter, R. (eds), *Sexual Underworlds of the Enlightenment* (Chapel Hill, 1988).

Rowbotham, S., and Weeks, J., *Socialism and the New Life: The Personal and Sexual Politics of Edward Carpenter and Havelock Ellis* (London, 1977).

Rowe, J. A., 'The purge of Christians at Mwanga's court', *Journal of African History*, 5 (1964), 55–71.

Rowse, A. L., *Homosexuals in History: Ambivalence in Society, Literature, and the Arts* (New York and London, 1977).

Rowson, E. K., 'The effeminates of early Medina', *Journal of the American Oriental Society*, 4 (1991), 671–93.

Ruan, F., *Sex in China. Studies in Sexology in Chinese Culture* (New York, 1991).

Ruan, F., and Tsai, Y., 'Male homosexuality in the traditional Chinese literature', *JHom*, 14, 3/4 (1987), 21–33.

Ruggiero, G., *The Boundaries of Eros. Sex Crime and Sexuality in Renaissance Venice* (Oxford, 1985).

Rünzler, D., *Machismo. Die Grenzen der Männlichkeit* (Vienna, Cologne and Graz, 1988).

Sahlins, M., *Islands of History* (Chicago and London, 1985).

Said, E. W., *Beginnings: Intention and Method* (New York, 1975).

Said, E. W., *Culture and Imperialism* (London, 1993).

Said, E. W., *Orientalism* (New York, 1978).

Schalow, P. G., 'Introduction', in Ihara Saikaku, *The Great Mirror of Male Love*, trans. P. G. Schalow (Stanford, 1990), pp. 1–46.

Schiebinger, L., 'The anatomy of difference: Race and sex in eighteenth-century science', *Eighteenth-Century Studies*, 23, 4 (Summer 1990), 387–94.

Schiebinger, L., 'Why mammals are called mammals: Gender politics in eighteenth-century natural history', *AHR*, 98, 2 (April 1993), 382–411.

Schievenhoevel, W., 'Ritualized adult male/adolescent male sexual behavior in Melanesia', in Feierman, J. R. (ed.), *Pedophilia: Biosocial Dimensions* (Berlin, 1990), pp. 349–421.

Schild, M., 'De citadel van integriteit. Een studie naar homoseksueel gedrag in het Midden-Oosten', unpublished thesis (R. U. Utrecht, 1985).

Schild, M., 'The irresistible beauty of boys: Middle Eastern attitudes about boy-love', *Paidika*, 1, 3 (Winter 1988), 37–48.

Schiller, F., *Paul Broca: Founder of French Anthropology, Explorer of the Brain* (Berkeley, 1979).

Schirmann, J., 'The ephebe in medieval Hebrew poetry', *Sefarad*, 15 (1955), 55–68.

Schmitt, A., 'Vorlesung zur mann-männlicher Sexualität: Erotik in der islamischen Gesellschaft', in De Martino, G., and Schmitt, A. (eds), *Kleine Schriften zur zwischenmännlicher Sexualität und Erotik in der muslimischen Gesellschaft* (Berlin, 1985), pp. 1–22.

Schmitt, A., and Sofer, J. (eds), *Homosexuality in Islam* (New York, 1991).

Schmitt, A., and Sofer, J. (eds), *Sexuality and Eroticism among Males in Moslim Societies* (New York, 1991).

Schnapper, A., 'Persistence des géants', *Annales. E.S.C.*, 41, 1 (January–February 1986), 177–200.

Schneider, W., 'Towards the improvement of the human race: The history of eugenics in France', *JMH*, 54 (June 1982), 268–91.

Schwab, R., *The Oriental Renaissance. Europe's Rediscovery of India and the East, 1680–1880* (New York, 1984).

Schwartz, J., *The Sexual Politics of J. J. Rousseau* (Chicago and London, 1984).

Schwartz, S., 'Panic in the Indies: the Portuguese threat to the Spanish Empire, 1640–1650', in Thomas, W., and De Groof, B. (eds), *Rebelión y Resisténcia en el Mundo Hispánico del Siglo XVII. Actas del Coloquio Internacional Lovaina, 20–23 de Noviembre de 1991* (Leuven, 1992), pp. 205–26.

Scott, D., 'Jungle fever? Black gay identity politics, white dick, and the utopian bedroom', *GLQ*, 1, 3 (1994), 299–321.

Sedgwick, E. Kosofsky, *English Literature and Male Homosocial Desire* (New York, 1985).

Sedgwick, E. Kosofsky, *Epistemology of the Closet* (Berkeley, 1990).

Segal, L., *Slow Motion. Changing Masculinities, Changing Men* (London, 1990).

Segalen, V., *Essai sur l'exotisme* (Montpellier, 1978).

Séguin, R.-L., *La vie libertine en Nouvelle-France au XVIIe siècle* (Montreal, 1972).

Sekula, A., 'The body and the archive', *October*, 39 (Winter 1986), 3–64.

Shorter, E., *A History of Women's Bodies* (New York, 1982).

Shortland, M., 'Courting the cerebellum: Early organological and phrenological views of sexuality', *British Journal of the History of Science*, 20 (1987), 173–4.

Showalter, E., *Sexual Anarchy. Gender and Culture at the Fin de Siècle* (Harmondsworth, 1990).

Sievernich, G., and Budde, H. (eds), *Europa und der Orient, 800–1900* (Berlin, 1989).

Sinha, M., 'Gender and imperialism: Colonial policy and the ideology of moral imperialism in late-nineteenth century Bengal', in Kimmel, M. S. (ed.) *Changing Men: New Directions in Research on Men and Masculinity* (Berkeley, 1987), pp. 217–31.

Smith, B., *Art as Information. Reflections on the Art from Captain Cook's Voyages* (Sydney, 1979).

Smith, B., *European Vision and the South Pacific*, 2nd ed. (New Haven and London, 1985).

Smith, P. J., *Representing the Other: 'Race', Text, and Gender in Spanish and Spanish American Narrative* (New York, 1992).

Smyth, C., *Queer Notions* (London, 1992).

Snow, E., 'Theorizing the male gaze: Some problems', *Representations*, 25 (Winter 1989), 30–41.

Solomon-Godeau, A., 'Going native', *Art in America*, July 1989, 119–28.

Somerville, S., 'Scientific racism and the emergence of the homosexual body', *JHS*, 5, 2 (1994), 243–66.

Spackmann, B., *Decadent Genealogies: The Rhetoric of Sickness from Baudelaire to d'Annunzio* (Ithaca and London, 1989).

Spate, O. H., *The Pacific since Magellan*, 3 vols (Canberra and Sydney, 1979–88).

Spector, J. J., *The Aesthetics of Freud. A Study in Psychoanalysis and Art* (New York, 1972).

Spence, J., *The Memory Palace of Matteo Ricci* (London and Boston, 1985).

Spivak, G. C., 'Imperialism and sexual difference', *Oxford Literary Review*, 8 (1986), 225–40.

Sprague, G. A., 'Male homosexuality in western culture: The dilemma of identity and subculture in historical research', *JHom*, 10, 3/4 (Winter 1984), 23–46.

Standing, H., and Kisekka, M. V., *Sexual Behaviour in Subsaharan Africa* (London, 1989).

Steakley, J., *The Homosexual Emancipation Movement in Germany* (New York, 1975).

Steakley, J., *The Writings of Dr. Magnus Hirschfeld. A Bibliography*, Canadian Gay Archives Publication Series, 11 / Schriftenreihe der Magnus-Hirschfeld-Gesellschaft, 2 (Toronto, 1985).

Stein, E. (ed.), *Sexual Orientation and the Social Constructionist Controversy* (New York and London, 1992 (1990)).

Stengers, J., and Van Neck, A., *Histoire d'une grande peur: la masturbation* (Brussels, 1984).

Stepan, N. Leys, 'Race and gender: The role of analogy in science', *Isis*, 77 (1986), 261–77.

Stocking, Jr., G. W., *Observers observed: Essays on Ethnographic Fieldwork* (*History of Anthropology*, vol. 1) (Madison, 1983).

Stocking, Jr., G. W., *Victorian Anthropology* (New York and London, 1987).

Stocking, Jr., G. W. (ed.), *Bones, Bodies, Behaviour. Essays on Biological Anthropology* (London, 1990).

Stockinger, J., 'Homosexuality and the French Enlightenment', in Stambolian, G., and Marks, E. (eds), *Homosexualities in French Literature. Cultural Contexts/Critical Texts* (Ithaca and London, 1979), pp. 161–85.

Stockinger, J., 'Homotextuality: a proposal', in Crew, L. (ed.), *The Gay Academic* (Palm Springs, 1978), pp. 135–51.

Stoler, A. L., 'Making Empire respectable: the politics of race and sexual morality in 20th-century colonial cultures', *American Ethnologist*, 16 (1989), 634–60.

Stoler, A. L., 'Sexual affronts and racial frontiers. European identities and the cultural politics of exclusion in colonial Southeast Asia', *CSSH*, 34 (1992), 514–55.

Stone, L., *The Family, Sex and Marriage in England, 1500–1800* (New York, 1979).

Stone, L., *The Past and the Present Revisited* (London and New York, n.d.).

Stowe, S. M., *Intimacy and Power in the Old South. Ritual in the Lives of the Planters* (Baltimore, 1990).

Stroup, T., 'Edward Westermarck: A reappraisal', *Man*, New Series, 19 (1984), 575–92.

Stroup, T. (ed.), *Edward Westermarck: Essays on his Life and Works*, Acta Philosophiae Fennica, 34 (Helsinki, 1982).

Sued-Badillo, J., 'El mito indoantillano de las mujeres sin hombres', *Boletín de Estudios Latinoamericanos y del Caribe*, 40 (1986), 15–22.

Swart, K., *The Sense of Decadence in Nineteenth-Century France* (The Hague, 1964).

Thodes-Arora, H., 'Der Mythos verfestigt sich – ein "edler Wilder" aus Tahiti in London', in Hermann, I. *et al.* (eds), *Exotische Welten, Europäische Phantasien. Mythos Tahiti, Südsee – Traum und Realität* (Stuttgart and Berlin, 1987), pp. 30–41.

Thomson, A., *Barbary and Enlightenment. European Attitudes towards the Maghreb in the Eighteenth Century* (Leiden, 1989).

Thomson, A., 'From "l'histoire naturelle de l'homme" to the natural history of mankind', in *Transactions of the 6th International Congress on the Enlightenment, Brussels, July 1983* (Oxford, 1983), pp. 121–2.

Thornton, J., *Africa and Africans in the Making of the Atlantic World, 1400–1680* (Cambridge, 1992).

Tielman, R., 'Dutch gay emancipation history (1911–1986)', in van Naersen, A. X. (ed.), *Gay Life in Dutch Society* (New York, 1987), pp. 9–18.

Todorov, T., *Nous et les autres. La réflexion française sur la diversité humaine* (Paris, 1989).

Tomaselli, S., 'The Enlightenment debate on women', *History Workshop*, 20 (1985), 101–24.

Torgovnick, M., *Gone Primitive: Savage Intellectuals, Modern Lives* (Chicago and London, 1990).

Tort, P., *La pensée hiérarchique et l'évolution* (Paris, 1983).

Trevisan, J., *Perverts in Paradise* (London, 1986).

Trumbach, R., 'London's sodomites: Homosexual behaviour and western culture in the eighteenth century', *Journal of Social History*, 11 (1977), 1–33.

Turbet-Delof, G., *L'Afrique barbaresque dans la littérature française aux 16ᵉ et 17ᵉ siècles* (Geneva, 1973).

Vainfas, R., *Trópico dos pecados. Moral, sexualidade e Inquisição no Brasil* (São Paulo, 1989).

Vandenbroeck, P., *Beeld van de Ander, vertoog over het Zelf. Over wilden en narren, boeren en bedelaars* (Antwerp, 1987).

van der Meer, T., *De wesentlijke sonde van sodomie en andere vuyligheeden. Sodomie-tenvervolgingen in Amsterdam, 1730–1811* (Amsterdam, 1984).

van Gulik, R. H., *Erotic Colour Prints of the Ming Period*, 3 vols (Tokyo, 1951).

van Gulik, R. H., *La vie sexuelle dans la Chine ancienne* (Paris, 1977).

Vartanian, A., 'Eroticism and politics in the *Lettres Persanes*', *Romantic Review*, 74 (1983), 306–15.

Väth, A., *Johann Adam Schall von Bell, s. J. Missionar in China. Kaiserlicher Astronom und Ratgeber am Hofe von Peking, 1592–1666. Ein Lebens- und Zeitbild* (Cologne, 1933).

Veit, W., 'The topoi of the European imagining of the non-European world', *Arcadia. Zeitschrift für vergleichende Literaturwissenschaft*, 18, 1 (1983), 1–21.

Vergara, E., 'De rol van de sexualiteit in het Oude Peru', in *Inca-Perú. 3000 jaar geschiedenis* (Brussels, 1990), pp. 400–11.

Vibart, E., *Tahiti: naissance d'un paradis au siècle des Lumières* (Paris, 1978).

Voget, F. W., 'Progress, science, history and evolution', *History of Behavioral Sciences*, 3 (1967), 132–55.

Walkowitz, J., *Prostitution and Victorian Society: Women, Class and the State* (Cambridge, 1980).

Walters, R. G., 'The erotic south: Civilisation and sexuality in American Abolitionism', *American Quarterly*, 25 (1973), 177–201.

Walton, A. Hull, 'Introduction', in *The Perfumed Garden of the Shaykh Nefzawi*, translated by *Sir Richard Burton*, ed. A. Hull Walton (London, 1984 (1963)), pp. 7–58.

Warner, P., *Auchinleck: The Lonely Soldier* (London, 1981).

Watanabe, T., and Iwata, J., *La voie des éphèbes. Histoire et histoires des homosexualités au Japon* (Paris, 1987).

Weeks, J., *Coming Out. Homosexual Politics in Britain from the Nineteenth Century to the Present* (London, 1979 (1977).

Weeks, J., 'Movements of affirmation: Sexual meanings and homosexual identities', *Radical History Review*, 20 (Spring/Summer 1979), 164–80.

Weeks, J., *Sex, Politics and Society. The Regulation of Sexuality since 1800* (London, 1981).

Weeks, J., *Sexuality and Its Discontents. Meaning, Myths & Modern Sexualities* (London, 1985).

Wernz, C., *Sexualität als Krankheit. Der medizinische Diskurs zur Sexualität um 1800*, Beiträge zur Sexualforschung, 67 (Stuttgart, 1993).

Wesseling, H. L., *Verdeel en heers. De deling van Afrika, 1880–1914* (Amsterdam, 1991).

West, C., 'The new cultural politics of difference', *October*, 53 (Summer 1990), 93–109.

Wettley, A., 'Zur Problemgeschichte der "Dégénérescence" ', *Südhoffs Archiv*, 43 (1959), 193–212.

Whitam, F. L., and Mathy, R. M., *Male Homosexuality in Four Societies. Brazil, Guatemala, the Philippines and the United States* (New York, 1986).

White, H. V., *The Content of the Form: Narrative Discourse and Historical Representation* (Cambridge, 1987).

White, H. V., *Metahistory. The Historical Imagination in Nineteenth-Century Europe* (Baltimore and London, 1973).

Wiener, H. S. L., 'Byron and the East: Literary sources of the "Turkish Tales" ', in Davis, H., *et al.* (eds), *Nineteenth-Century Studies* (Ithaca, 1940), pp. 89–129.

Wikan, U., 'Man becomes woman. Transsexualism in Oman as a key to gender roles', *Man*, New Series, 12, 2 (1972), 304–19.

Williams, W. L., 'Isthmus Zapotec "Berdaches" ', *ARGOH Newsletter*, 7, 2 (May 1985), 1–6.

Williams, W. L., *The Spirit and the Flesh. Sexual Diversity in American Indian Culture* (Boston, 1986).

Woolf, C., *Magnus Hirschfeld. A Portrait of a Pioneer in Sexology* (London, 1986).

Wright, A. D., *The Counter-Reformation: Catholic Europe and the Non-Christian World* (London, 1982).

Wurgraft, L., *The Imperial Imagination: Magic and Myth in Kipling's India* (Middletown, 1983).

Wuthenow, R., *Muse, Maske, Meduse. Europäisches Ästhetizismus* (Frankfurt, 1978).

Index